I Have Tried to Tell the Truth
1943–1944

Eric Arthur Blair – better known as George Orwell – was born on 25 June 1903 in Bengal. He was educated at Eton and then served with the Indian Imperial Police in Burma. He lived in Paris for two years, and then returned to England where he worked as a private tutor, schoolteacher and bookshop assistant. He fought on the Republican side in the Spanish Civil War and was wounded in the throat. During the Second World War he served as Talks Producer for the Indian Service of the BBC and then joined *Tribune* as its literary editor. He died in London in January 1950.

Dr. Peter Davison is Professor of English and Media at De Montfort University, Leicester. He has written and edited fifteen books as well as the Facsimile Edition of the Manuscript of *Nineteen Eighty-Four* and the twenty volumes of Orwell's *Complete Works*. From 1992 to 1994 he was President of the Bibliographical Society, whose journal he edited for twelve years. From 1961 Ian Angus was Deputy Librarian and Keeper of the Orwell Archive at University College, London, and from 1975 Librarian of King's College, London. With Sonia Orwell he co-edited the *Collected Essays, Journalism and Letters of George Orwell* (4 vols., 1986). Since early retirement in 1982 he has divided his time equally between assisting in the editing of this edition and growing olives in Italy.

Sheila Davison was a teacher until she retired, for some time teaching the deaf. She checked and proofread all twenty volumes of the complete edition and assisted with the research and indexing.

Down and Out in Paris and London
Burmese Days
A Clergyman's Daughter
Keep the Aspidistra Flying
The Road to Wigan Pier
Homage to Catalonia
Coming Up for Air
Animal Farm
Nineteen Eighty-Four
A Kind of Compulsion (1903–36)
Facing Unpleasant Facts (1937–39)
A Patriot After All (1940–41)
All Propaganda is Lies (1941–42)
Keeping Our Little Corner Clean (1942–43)
Two Wasted Years (1943)
I Have Tried to Tell the Truth (1943–44)
I Belong to the Left (1945)
Smothered Under Journalism (1946)
It is What I Think (1947–48)
Our Job is to Make Life Worth Living (1949–50)

Also by Peter Davison

Books: *Songs of the British Music Hall: A Critical Study; Popular Appeal in English Drama to 1850; Contemporary Drama and the Popular Dramatic Tradition; Hamlet: Text and Performance; Henry V: Masterguide; Othello: The Critical Debate; Orwell: A Literary Life*

Editions: Anonymous: *The Fair Maid of the Exchange* (with Arthur Brown); Shakespeare: *Richard II*; Shakespeare: *The Merchant of Venice*; Shakespeare: *1 Henry IV*; Shakespeare: *2 Henry IV*; Shakespeare: *The First Quarto of King Richard III*; Marston: *The Dutch Courtesan; Facsimile of the Manuscript of Nineteen Eighty-Four*; Sheridan: *A Casebook; The Book Encompassed: Studies in Twentieth-Century Bibliography*

Series: *Theatrum Redivivum* 17 Volumes (with James Binns); *Literary Taste, Culture, and Mass Communication* 14 Volumes (with Edward Shils and Rolf Meyersohn)

Academic Journals: *ALTA: University of Birmingham Review*, 1966–70; *The Library: Transactions of the Bibliographical Society*, 1971–82

Publication of *The Complete Works of George Orwell* is a unique
bibliographic event as well as a major step in Orwell
scholarship. Meticulous textual research by
Dr Peter Davison has revealed that all the current editions
of Orwell have been mutilated to a greater or lesser extent.
This authoritative edition incorporates in Volumes 10-20
all Orwell's known essays, poems, plays, letters, journalism,
broadcasts, and diaries, and also letters by his wife, Eileen,
and members of his family. In addition there are very many of
the letters in newspapers and magazines of readers' reactions
to Orwell's articles and reviews. Where the hands of others
have intervened, Orwell's original intentions have been restored.

I Have Tried to
Tell the Truth

1943-1944

GEORGE ORWELL

Edited by Peter Davison
Assisted by Ian Angus and Sheila Davison

SECKER & WARBURG

LONDON

Revised and updated edition published by Secker & Warburg 2001

2 4 6 8 10 9 7 5 3 1

First published in Great Britain in 1998 by
Secker & Warburg
Random House, 20 Vauxhall Bridge Road,
London SW1V 2SA

Random House Australia (Pty) Limited
20 Alfred Street, Milsons Point, Sydney,
New South Wales 2061, Australia

Random House New Zealand Limited
18 Poland Road, Glenfield,
Auckland 10, New Zealand

Random House South Africa (Pty) Limited
Endulini, 5A Jubilee Road, Parktown 2193, South Africa

The Random House Group Limited Reg. No. 954009
www.randomhouse.co.uk

A CIP catalogue record for this book
is available from the British Library

ISBN 0 436 20552 1

MIX
Paper | Supporting
responsible forestry
FSC® C018179

Typeset in Monophoto Bembo by
Deltatype Limited, Birkenhead, Merseyside

The Random House Group Limited supports The Forest Stewardship
Council® (FSC®), the leading international forest-certification organisation.
Our books carrying the FSC label are printed on FSC®-certified paper.
FSC is the only forest-certification scheme supported by the leading
environmental organisations, including Greenpeace. Our
paper procurement policy can be found at
www.randomhouse.co.uk/environment

Printed and bound in Great Britain by Clays Ltd, St Ives plc

CONTENTS

Titles may be modified and shortened.
Topics discussed in Orwell's column, 'As I Please', are listed in the
Cumulative Index in Volume XX.
Correspondence following Orwell's articles and reviews is not usually listed.

Introduction		xv
Acknowledgements and Provenances		xvii
Editorial Note		xxi
References		xxvii
Chronology, 24 November 1943 to 31 December 1944		xxix
2378.	Orwell at *Tribune*: editorial note	3
2379.	Article: 'Mark Twain—The Licensed Jester', 26 November 1943	5
2380.	Review: E. Allison Peers, *Spain in Eclipse, 1937–1943*; Lawrence Dundas, *Behind the Spanish Mask*, 28 November 1943	8
2381.	Letter to Alex Comfort, 29 November 1943	9
2382.	Letter to T. S. Eliot, 29 November 1943	10
2383.	Letter to Henry Treece, 29 November 1943	10
2384.	Your Questions Answered: Wigan Pier, broadcast 2 December 1943	11
2385.	'As I Please', 1, 3 December 1943	12
2386.	Letter to Leonard Moore, 6 December 1943	17
2387.	Letter to Henry Treece, 7 December 1943	18
2388.	'Life, People and Books', *Manchester Evening News*: editorial note	18
2389.	Review: Arthur Koestler, *Arrival and Departure*; Philip Jordan, *Jordan's Tunis Diary*, 9 December 1943	19
2390.	Letter to Philip Rahv, 9 December 1943	22
2391.	'As I Please', 2, 10 December 1943	23
2392.	Letter to Dwight Macdonald, 11 December 1943	24
2393.	'As I Please', 3, 17 December 1943	25
2394.	Review: *Collected Poems of W. H. Davies*, 19 December 1943	29
2395.	Review: Lancelot Hogben, *Interglossa*; Compton Mackenzie, *Mr. Roosevelt*, 23 December 1943	31
2396.	'As I Please', 4, 24 December 1943	34
2397.	Article: 'Can Socialists be Happy?' by 'John Freeman', 24 December 1943	37
2398.	'As I Please', 5, 31 December 1943	45
2399.	Review: K. C. Chorley, *Armies and the Art of Revolution*, 2 January 1944	51

Contents

2400. Review: Viscount Wavell, *Allenby in Egypt*, 6 January 1944   53
2401. 'As I Please', 6, 7 January 1944   55
2402. F. R. Leavis to Orwell, 8 January 1944   58
2403. Letter to Leonard Moore, 9 January 1944   59
2404. 'As I Please', 7, 14 January 1944   60
2405. 'London Letter', 15 January 1944   64
2406. Review: C. K. Allen, *Democracy and the Individual*; Sir R.
George Stapledon, *Disraeli and the New Age*, 16 January 1944   71
2407. Review: James Burnham, *The Machiavellians*, 20 January 1944   72
2408. John Lehmann to Orwell, 20 January 1944   75
2409. Poem: 'Memories of the Blitz', 21 January 1944   75
2410. 'As I Please', 8, 21 January 1944   76
2411. Letter to Dwight Macdonald, 25 January 1944   79
2412. 'As I Please', 9, 28 January 1944   80
2413. Review: Joshua Trachtenberg, *The Devil and the Jews*; Edmond
Fleg, *Why I Am a Jew*, translated by Victor Gollancz,
30 January 1944   83
2414. Letter to R. S. R. Fitter, 31 January 1944   85
2415. Review: Mark Twain, *Tom Sawyer and Huckleberry Finn*;
Countess of Oxford and Asquith, *Off the Record*, 3 February
1944   86
2416. 'As I Please', 10, 4 February 1944   88
2417. 'As I Please', 11, 11 February 1944   91
2418. Review: Charles Dickens, *Martin Chuzzlewit*, 13 February 1944   95
2419. Review: Jan Fortune and Jean Burton, *Elisabet Ney*,
17 February 1944   97
2420. Letter to R. S. R. Fitter, 17 February 1944   99
2420A. Letter to Daniel George, 17 February 1944   XX, App. 15
2421. Letter to Gleb Struve, 17 February 1944   99
2422. 'As I Please', 12, 18 February 1944   100
2423. Letter to Dwight Macdonald, 21 February 1944   102
2424. 'As I Please', 13, 25 February 1944   103
2425. Review: Alfred Noyes, *The Edge of the Abyss*, 27 February 1944   105
2426. Letter to Rayner Heppenstall, 28 February 1944   107
2426A. Letter to Lydia Jackson, 1 March 1944   108
2427. Letter to C. K. Ogden, 1 March 1944   108
2428. Review: Harry Levin, *James Joyce*, 2 March 1944   109
2429. 'As I Please', 14, 3 March 1944   111
2430. John Davys Beresford to Orwell, 7 March 1944   115
2431. Letter to Roy Fuller, 7 March 1944   116
2432. 'As I Please', 15, 10 March 1944   117
2433. Review: *Other Men's Flowers*, selected and annotated by A. P.
Wavell, 12 March 1944   120
2434. Rejected Review: Harold J. Laski, *Faith, Reason and
Civilisation*, 12 March 1944   122
2435. 'As I Please', 16, 17 March 1944   124
2436. Letter to Leonard Moore, 19 March 1944   126

2437.	Letter to Victor Gollancz, 19 March 1944	127
2438.	Ethel Colquhoun to Orwell, 20 March 1944	128
2439.	Review: Sir William Beach Thomas, *The Way of a Countryman*, 23 March 1944	128
2440.	Letter to Leonard Moore, 23 March 1944	130
2441.	'As I Please', 17, 24 March 1944	131
2442.	Letter to Victor Gollancz, 25 March 1944	134
2443.	Letter to Leonard Moore, 25 March 1944	135
2444.	Review: Derrick Leon, *Tolstoy: His Life and Work*, 26 March 1944	136
2445.	'As I Please', 18, 31 March 1944	137
2446.	Postcard to Leonard Moore, 31 March 1944	141
2446A.	Letter to Lydia Jackson, 3 April 1944	141
2447.	Telegram to Leonard Moore, 5 April 1944	141
2448.	Letter to Leonard Moore, 5 April 1944	142
2449.	Review: Maurice Collis, *She Was a Queen*; Margaret Mead, *Coming of Age in Samoa*, 6 April 1944	143
2450.	'As I Please', 19, 7 April 1944	145
2451.	Review: F. A. Hayek, *The Road to Serfdom*; K. Zilliacus, *The Mirror of the Past*, 9 April 1944	149
2451A.	Letter to Daniel George, 10 April 1944 XX, App. 15	
2452.	'As I Please', 20, 14 April 1944	151
2453.	Letter to Leonard Moore, 15 April 1944	155
2454.	'London Letter', 17 April 1944	156
2455.	Review: Edmund Blunden, *Cricket Country*, 20 April 1944	161
2456.	Letter to W. J. Strachan, 20 April 1944	164
2457.	'As I Please', 21, 21 April 1944	164
2457A.	Letter to Lydia Jackson, 21 April 1944	167
2458.	Review: Hugh Kingsmill, *The Poisoned Crown*, 23 April 1944	167
2459.	Correspondence with Antonia White, 27 April 1944	169
2460.	'As I Please', 22, 28 April 1944	171
2461.	Letter to Philip Rahv, 1 May 1944	174
2462.	'As I Please', 23, 5 May 1944	175
2463.	Review: Alfred Hessenstein, *A Giant in the Age of Steel: The Story of General de Gaulle*, 5 May 1944	177
2464.	Review: *This Changing World*, edited by J. R. M. Brumwell; Julian Huxley, *On Living in a Revolution*; Various Authors, *Reshaping Man's Heritage*, 7 May 1944	179
2465.	Letter to Charles Hamblett, 8 May 1944	181
2466.	Letter to Leonard Moore, 9 May 1944	182
2467.	'As I Please', 24, 12 May 1944	182
2468.	Review: Louis Fischer, *Empire*, 13 May 1944	186
2469.	Letter to W. F. Stirling, Latin American Department, BBC, 16 May 1944	188
2470.	Review: St. John Ervine, *Parnell*, 18 May 1944	188
2470A.	Letter to Arthur Koestler, 18 May 1944: see Vol. XX, p. 314	
2471.	Letter to Noel Willmett, 18 May 1944	190
2472.	William Lynch to *Tribune*, 19 May 1944	192

Contents

2473. 'As I Please', 25, 19 May 1944   193
2474. Review: H. G. Wells, *'42 to '44: A Contemporary Memoir upon
      Human Behaviour During the Crisis of the World Revolution*,
      21 May 1944   197
2475. *The English People*, 22 May 1944: editorial note   199
          England at First Glance   200
          The Moral Outlook of the English People   204
          The Political Outlook of the English People   209
          The English Class System   213
          The English Language   217
          The Future of the English People   221
2475A. Letter to Lydia Jackson, 23 May 1944   228
2476. Letter to Leonard Moore, 24 May 1944   229
2477. Letter to A. S. Umpleby, 25 May 1944   229
2478. 'As I Please', 26, 26 May 1944   230
2479. Letter to The Royal Literary Fund, 26 May 1944   232
2480. Letter to Leonard Moore, 27 May 1944   232
2481. Essay: 'Benefit of Clergy: Some Notes on Salvador Dali',
      1 June 1944   233
2482. Article: 'Are Books Too Dear?', 1 June 1944   241
2483. 'As I Please', 27, 2 June 1944   244
2484. Article: 'Survey of "Civvy Street" ', 4 June 1944   248
2484A. Letter to Lydia Jackson, 5 June 1944   250
2485. Letter to Leonard Moore, 8 June 1944   250
2486. 'As I Please', 28, 9 June 1944   251
2487. Review: Gordon S. Seagrave, *Burma Surgeon*; Horace
      Alexander, *India Since Cripps*, 11 June 1944   253
2488. Letter to Leading Aircraftman C. Hopkins, 14 June 1944   255
2489. Review: William Russell, *Robert Cain*, 15 June 1944   255
2490. 'As I Please', 29, 16 June 1944   258
2491. Letter to [W. F. Stirling, Latin American Department], BBC,
      19 June 1944   261
2492. 'As I Please', 30, 23 June 1944   261
2493. Letter to Mrs Gerry Byrne (Amy Charlesworth), 23 June 1944   265
2494. Letter to Leonard Moore, 24 June 1944   265
2495. Review: L. L. Schucking, *The Sociology of Literary Taste*,
      25 June 1944   266
2495A. Letter to Lydia Jackson, 26 June 1944   268
2495B. 'The World Goes By', 27 June 1944: editorial note   268
2496. Letter to T. S. Eliot, 28 June 1944   269
2497. Broadcast: 'Political Theories and European Literature',
      28/29 June 1944   269
2498. Review: Hilda Martindale, *From One Generation to Another*,
      29 June 1944   269
2499. 'As I Please', 31, 30 June 1944   272
2500. BBC Contract for 'Political Theories and European
      Literature', 6 July 1944   274

2501.	'As I Please', 32, 7 July 1944	275
2502.	Review: *In a Strange Land: Essays by Eric Gill*, 9 July 1944	278
2502A.	Letter to Arthur Koestler, 10 July 1944: see Vol. XX, p. 315	
2503.	Letter to Rayner Heppenstall, 11 July 1944	280
2504.	Review: Martin Johnson, *Art and Scientific Thought*, 13 July 1944	280
2505.	T. S. Eliot to Orwell, 13 July 1944	282
2506.	Orwell's Flat Bombed, 14 July 1944: editorial note	283
2507.	'As I Please', 33, 14 July 1944	284
2508.	John Middleton Murry to Orwell, 11 July 1944	287
2509.	Letter to John Middleton Murry, 14 July 1944	288
2510.	Article: 'The Eight Years of War: Spanish Memories', 16 July 1944	288
2511.	Letter to Rayner Heppenstall, 17 July 1944	290
2512.	Letter to Z. A. Bokhari, 18 July 1944	291
2513.	Letter to Leonard Moore, 18 July 1944	291
2514.	'As I Please', 34, 21 July 1944	292
2515.	Letter to Rayner Heppenstall, 21 July 1944	295
2516.	Letter to John Middleton Murry, 21 July 1944	295
2517.	Review: Jacques Barzun, *Romanticism and the Modern Ego*, 23 July 1944	296
2518.	Letter to Dwight Macdonald, 23 July 1944	298
2519.	'London Letter', 24 July 1944	300
2520.	Letter to Ivor Brown, 24 July 1944	304
2521.	'As I Please', 35, 28 July 1944	304
2522.	Review: *English Diaries of the Nineteenth Century*, edited by James Aitken, 28 July 1944	308
2523.	Article: 'Propaganda and Demotic Speech', Summer 1944	310
2524.	Letter to Rayner Heppenstall, 2 August 1944	316
2525.	Letter to W. J. Strachan, 2 August 1944	316
2526.	'As I Please', 36, 4 August 1944	317
2527.	Letter to John Middleton Murry, 5 August 1944	319
2528.	Review: Hsiao Ch'ien, *The Dragon Beards versus the Blue Prints*, 6 August 1944	321
2528A.	Eileen Blair to Lydia Jackson, [9? August 1944]	323
2529.	Review: Richard Church, *The Porch and The Stronghold*, 10 August 1944	326
2530.	'As I Please', 37, 11 August 1944	328
2531.	Letter to John Middleton Murry, 11 August 1944	332
2532.	Review: On *Branch Street* by Marie Paneth, 13 August 1944	334
2533.	Letter to Leonard Moore, 15 August 1944	335
2534.	'As I Please', 38, 18 August 1944	336
2535.	Review: Denis Saurat, *Milton: Man and Thinker*, 20 August 1944	338
2535A.	Letter to Lydia Jackson, 23 August 1944	340
2536.	Review: Selwyn James, *South of the Congo*, 24 August 1944	340
2537.	'As I Please', 39, 25 August 1944	343

Contents

2538. Essay: 'Raffles and Miss Blandish', 28 August 1944   345
2539. Letter to Leonard Moore, 29 August 1944   358
2540. 'Burma': Interview by G. B. Pittock-Buss, Autumn 1944.   358
2541. 'As I Please', 40 [The Battle of Warsaw], 1 September 1944   362
2542. Review: *Selections from the Works of Gerrard Winstanley*, edited by Leonard Hamilton; Introduction by Christopher Hill, 3 September 1944   376
2543. Letter to T. S. Eliot, 5 September 1944   379
2544. Letter to R. S. R. Fitter, 5 September 1944   380
2545. Letter to Dwight Macdonald, 5 September 1944   381
2546. Article: 'How Long is a Short Story', 7 September 1944   382
2547. 'As I Please', 41, 8 September 1944   385
2548. Essay: 'Arthur Koestler', 11 September 1944   391
2548A. Letter to Lydia Jackson, 11 September 1944   402
2549. 'As I Please', 42, 15 September 1944   402
2550. Letter to Dwight Macdonald, 15 September 1944   405
2551. Review: D. W. Brogan, *The American Problem*, 17 September 1944   406
2552. Article: 'Tobias Smollett: Scotland's Best Novelist', 22 September 1944   408
2553. 'London Letter', October(?) 1944   411
2554. Review: V. R. Pearn, *Burma Background*; O. H. K. Spate, *Burma Setting*; G. Appleton, *Buddhism in Burma*; Ma Mya Sein, *Burma*; Kenneth Hemmingway, *Wings Over Burma*; Charles J. Rolo, *Wingate's Raiders*, 1 October 1944   416
2555. Letter to T. S. Eliot, 3 October 1944   418
2556. Letter to Leonard Moore, 3 October 1944   419
2557. Letter to Stanley Unwin, 3 October 1944   419
2558. Letter to Rayner Heppenstall, 4 October 1944   419
2559. Review: T. S. Eliot, *Four Quartets*, 5 October 1944   420
2560. 'As I Please', 43, 6 October 1944   423
2561. Letter to Daniel George, [9 October 1944]   426
2561A. Letter to Lydia Jackson, 11 October 1944   427
2562. 'As I Please', 44, 13 October 1944   427
2563. Letter to Rayner Heppenstall, 13 October 1944   430
2563A. Letter to Arthur Koestler, 13 October 1944: see Vol. XX, p. 315
2563B. Letter from [Ivor Brown] to Thomas Jones, 14 October 1944 XX, App. 15
2564. Article: 'Home Guard Lessons for the Future', 15 October 1944   431
2565. Review: John Middleton Murry, *Adam and Eve*, 19 October 1944   432
2566. 'As I Please', 45, 20 October 1944   434
2566A. Letter to Lydia Jackson, 23 October 1944   437
2567. Unpublished Review: C. S. Lewis, *Beyond Personality*, Mid-October 1944   437
2568. 'As I Please', 46, 27 October 1944   439

2569. Letter to Mrs. Gerry Byrne (Amy Charlesworth), 28 October
       1944   445
2570. Review: Beverley Nichols, *Verdict on India*, 29 October 1944   446
2571. Letter to Tom Driberg, 30 October 1944   448
2572. Review: Anthony Trollope, *The Warden*; George Eliot, *Silas
       Marner*; Harold Nicolson, *Public Faces*; V. Sackville-West,
       Seducers in Ecuador; Anatole France, *Les Dieux ont Soif*;
       Edmond Vermeil, *Hitler et le Christianisme*, 2 November
       1944   449
2573. 'As I Please', 47, 3 November 1944   451
2574. Letter to Tom Driberg, 4 November 1944   453
2575. Review: Giles Playfair, *Singapore Goes Off the Air*; Sir Richard
       Winstedt, *Britain and Malaya*, 8 November 1944   454
2576. Books and the People: *The Vicar of Wakefield* by Oliver
       Goldsmith, 10 November 1944   456
2577. Review: W. H. Gardner, *Gerard Manley Hopkins*,
       12 November 1944   460
2578. Review: A. L. Rowse, *The English Spirit*; 'Cassius' (Michael
       Foot), *Brendan and Beverley*, 16 November 1944   461
2579. 'As I Please', 48, 17 November 1944   463
2580. Review: J. A. Spender, *Last Essays*; Walter Clay Lowdermilk,
       Palestine, Land of Promise; Reginald Moore, *Selected Writing*,
       23 November 1944   469
2581. 'As I Please', 49, 24 November 1944   471
2582. Review: Herbert J. C. Grierson and J. C. Smith, *A Critical
       History of English Poetry*, 26 November 1944   474
2583. Letter to Gleb Struve, 28 November 1944   475
2584. Review: James Agate, *Noblesse Oblige—Another Letter to
       Another Son*; Jack Lindsay, *Perspective for Poetry*,
       30 November 1944   476
2585. Essay: 'Funny, But Not Vulgar', 1 December 1944   482
2586. 'As I Please', 50, 1 December 1944   487
2587. Letter to Frank Barber, 5 December 1944   490
2588. Letter to Richard C. Elsley, 5 December 1944   492
2589. Review: *Bridge into the Future: Letters of Max Plowman*,
       7 December 1944   492
2590. 'As I Please', 51, 8 December 1944   495
2591. Letter to Frank Barber, 15 December 1944   497
2592. Article: 'Oysters and Brown Stout', 22 December 1944   498
2593. Review: Charles d'Ydewalle, *An Interlude in Spain*, translated
       by Eric Sutton, 24 December 1944   501
2593A. Letter to Daniel George, 28 December 1944   XX, App. 15
2594. Review: Robert Gibbings, *Lovely is the Lee*; Vera T. Mirsky,
       The Cup of Astonishment, 28 December 1944   503
2595. 'As I Please', 52, 29 December 1944   505
2596. Review: Edwin Morgan, *Flower of Evil: A Life of Charles
       Baudelaire*, 31 December 1944   509
INDEX   511

INTRODUCTION to VOLUME XVI

29 November 1943 to 31 December 1944: *I Have Tried to Tell the Truth*

When Orwell left the BBC on 24 November 1943 he threw himself into renewed literary activity with enormous energy. His release from the burdensome duties of broadcasting and his resignation from the Home Guard on medical grounds enabled him to devote himself to writing. He worked as literary editor of *Tribune* (see *2378*), started his 'As I Please' column, wrote reviews and articles regularly for *Tribune, The Observer, Manchester Evening News*, and *Partisan Review*, and occasional (but important) articles, for, among others, *Horizon, Persuasion*, and the New York *Nation*. And he was writing *Animal Farm*. This was also the time when he made a seemingly unimportant visit but one that would colour Orwell's last years. In September 1944 it looks as if he made his first visit to Jura, a year earlier than was thought. When Eileen wrote to her husband on 21 March 1945 (*2638*) it is plain that arrangements for renting and repairing Barnhill were in hand. Orwell had dreamt of 'my island in the Hebrides' as far back as 20 June 1940 (see *639*), perhaps prompted by his reviewing E. L. Grant Wilson's *Priest Island* (*640*). A brief summary of the evidence is given at *2543, n. 1*. Jura would realise some of his dreams, however briefly, and it would be where he would write *Nineteen Eighty-Four*. It would, indeed, be his personal 'golden country.' Less happily, the Orwell's were bombed out on 14 July 1944 and moved for a time into Inez Holden's flat near Baker Street. Early in October 1944 they moved into a flat in Canonbury Square and it was there and at Barnhill that Richard, the baby they adopted in June 1944, grew up.

Orwell served as literary editor of *Tribune* from 29 November 1943 until he went to continental Europe as War Correspondent for *The Observer* and the *Manchester Evening News*, in mid February 1945. He had written for *Tribune* since 29 March 1940 (*603*), but now he became part of its management; he would continue to contribute until 4 April 1947, when his eightieth 'As I Please' appeared. This column is now, in this edition, printed without cuts; fifty-two are included in this volume. Orwell usually discussed three or four topics in each column. He did not give them sub-titles and, for readers' convenience, a list of his topics is given under 'As I Please' in the cumulative index in Volume XX. Aneurin Bevan, the editor of *Tribune*, gave Orwell a free rein and his column ranged very widely and, half-a-century later, can still trouble and entertain. At the time, he often raised the hackles of readers and the rich correspondence that ensued gives an important insight into responses of those on the left in the months before and after the Labour Government of 1945 took office. This is especially apparent following his reference to the Warsaw Uprising (see *2541*, pp. 362–76). Most letters are reprinted, usually in full, immediately after the column to which they refer.

Letters that have come to light very recently (hence the 'A' that follows their item numbers) show Orwell organising contributions and reviews for *Tribune* as part of his work as literary editor. These are to Lydia Jackson (Elisaveta Fen; see pp. 108, 141, 167, 228, 250, 268, 340, 402, 427, and 437), and to Arthur Koestler (to be found in Volume XX, Appendix 14, pp. 314 and 315).

In these thirteen months, in addition to references in 'As I Please', Orwell reviewed 86 books. The reviews of two, Laski's *Faith, Reason, and Civilisation* (*2434*), and C. S. Lewis's *Beyond Personality* (*2567*) were not published. The former was rejected by the *Manchester Evening News* because, he told Dwight Macdonald, of its 'anti-Stalin implications . . . Editors will print nothing anti-Russian,' something Macdonald took up in his journal, *Politics* (see *2518*, especially *n. 1*). It is not known why *The Observer* failed to publish the review of Lewis's book. Both reviews are printed here for the first time. Orwell also ran into censorship difficulties over 'Benefit of Clergy: Some Notes on Salvador Dali' (*2481*). This was intended for the *Saturday Book*. It actually reached the stage of inclusion in the bound book, but, precisely in the manner of the seventeenth-century censor in Spain (the Yorkshireman, William Sankey) who excised *Measure for Measure* from Shakespeare's *Works* with a sharp knife, the publishers, Hutchinson's, had the essay sliced out from the bound book. The text survives because Orwell's copy and one or two other volumes were left uncut. Comically, its title remained in the list of contents.

Among other important essays in this volume are 'Propaganda and Demotic Speech', 'Raffles and Miss Blandish', and those on Twain, Smollett, Thackeray, and *The Vicar of Wakefield*. However, the most intriguing essay is one that has previously neither been accredited to him nor reprinted: 'Can Socialists Be Happy?', written under the pseudonym, John Freeman. Detailed grounds are given for identifying this essay as Orwell's (see *2397*). Orwell's last completed poem, 'Memories of the Blitz,' also appears in this volume (*2409*). Four 'London Letters' were contributed to *Partisan Review* during this period. *The English People* (*2475*), though not published until 1947, is included at the point at which it was completed, 22 May 1944. Although this was one of his books that Orwell did not want reprinted, it still reads well and it is significant that on the second-hand market today the original edition, with its attractive illustrations, is the most costly of all the 126 volumes of the 'Britain in Pictures' series.

At *2479* is one of a number of instances when Orwell went out of his way to help others in need.

A full General Introduction will be found in the preliminaries to Volume X

ACKNOWLEDGEMENTS and PROVENANCES

specific to Volume XVI

The editor wishes to express his gratitude to the following institutions and libraries, their trustees, curators, and staffs for their co-operation and valuable help, for making copies of Orwell material available, and for allowing it to be reproduced: BBC Written Archives Centre, Caversham; Henry W. and Albert Berg Collection, New York Public Library, Astor, Lenox and Tilden Foundations; British Library, Department of Manuscripts (for the Orwell papers, Add. Mss 49384 and 73083); Tom Driberg papers, Christ Church, Oxford; Elisaveta Fen (Lydia Jackson) papers, Leeds Russian Archive, Brotherton Library, University of Leeds; Lilly Library, Indiana University, Bloomington, Indiana; Royal Literary Fund; Harry Ransom Humanities Research Center, University of Texas at Austin; Dwight Macdonald papers, Manuscripts and Archives, Yale University Library; and the Library of University College London for material in the Orwell Archive.

Gratitude is expressed to George Allen & Unwin Ltd, Faber and Faber Ltd and Victor Gollancz Ltd for making their Orwell material available and, in particular, to Corydon Unwin and Livia Gollancz for their help and valuable information.

I am grateful to Rosemary Davidson, Valerie Eliot and Ralph C. Elsley for making their Orwell letters available. I am also deeply indebted to those whose Orwell letters are available because they donated them or presented copies of them to the Orwell Archive. the Hon David Astor (Editor of *The Observer*), Frank Barber, Amy Charlesworth, Alex Comfort, R. S. R. Fitter, Roy Fuller, Dwight Macdonald, Frank Ogden, William Phillips and Philip Rahv (Editors of *Partisan Review*), W. J. Strachan and Gleb Struve. Thanks are due to Brian Alderson for bringing Orwell's letter to A. S. Umpleby to my notice.

I would like to thank the following publications for permission to reproduce material which first appeared in their pages: *The Manchester Evening News*, *The Nation* (New York), *The Observer*, *Partisan Review*, and *Tribune*.

I would like to thank the following for granting me permission to use material whose copyright they own: Peters, Fraser & Dunlop Group Ltd to reprint James Agate's contribution to "Agate and Orwell" in *The Manchester Evening News*; Paul Berry, the Literary Executor of Vera Brittain, to reprint a letter by Vera Brittain to *Tribune*, 23 June 1944, and to quote from an unpublished letter by her to *Tribune*; James B. Burnham, the Literary Executor of James Burnham, to reprint a letter by James Burnham to *Tribune*; Lettice Cooper to quote from her recollections of Eileen and Orwell (item 2528A); Bruce Hunter and David Higham Associates Ltd to quote from a letter by Tom Driberg and from his column in *Reynold's News*; Valerie Eliot to publish a letter by T. S. Eliot to Orwell; William Empson's letter to *Tribune*, 10 November 1944, reproduced with the permission of Curtis Brown Ltd, London, on behalf of the Estate of William Empson. Copyright William Empson, 1944; Polly Bird, the Literary Executor of Douglas Goldring, to reprint two letters by Douglas Goldring to *Tribune*; Celia Goodman to quote from Inez Holden's *Summer Journal*; Robert L. Morris, the Literary Executor of Arthur Koestler, to reprint a letter by Arthur Koestler to *Tribune*; Charles Osborne to quote from a letter by John Lehmann; Michael C. D. Macdonald to quote from Dwight Macdonald's contributions to *Partisan Review* and *Politics*; The Society of Authors, as the literary representative of the Estate of John Middleton Murry, to quote from three letters by John Middleton Murry; Jean Faulks to reprint a letter by Reg Reynolds to *Tribune*; Mary Struve to quote from a letter by Gleb Struve; Julian Symons' letter to *Tribune*, 15 September 1944, reproduced with the permission of Curtis Brown Ltd, London, on behalf of the Estate of Julian Symons. Copyright © Julian Symons 1944; Conrad Voss-Bank to reprint a letter by him to *Tribune*; and the extracts from Antonia White's letter to Orwell are Copyright Antonia White, reproduced by permission of Curtis Brown Ltd, London.

A number of individual acknowledgements are made in foot and headnotes to those who have provided information in books or verbally that I have quoted or referred to.

The editor and publishers have made every effort to trace copyright holders of the material published in this volume, but in some cases this has not proved possible. The publishers therefore wish to apologise to the authors or copyright holders of any material which has been reproduced without permission and due acknowledgement.

PROVENANCES

The locations of letters and documents printed in this volume are indicated against their item numbers in the list given below. Where there are letters or documents at an item which come from more than one source, this is indicated, e.g. 2494 Lilly, VG, OA.

However, letters and documents which are not listed below should be taken as being available for consultation in the Orwell Archive, University College London, either as originals or in the form of copies. Sonia Orwell gave all the Orwell papers then in her possession to the Orwell Archive at its foundation in 1960. Many friends, relations and associates of Orwell have given their Orwell letters or copies of them to the Orwell Archive. There were in Orwell's pamphlet collection that Sonia Orwell gave to the British Museum in 1950 some Orwell papers (now in the British Library, Departments of Manuscripts, Add. Mss. 49384 and 73083) and copies of these, at her request, were given by the Director and Principal Librarian of the British Museum to the Orwell Archive in 1965. For simplicity's sake, the British Library Orwell papers are not indicated as such in the location list, but are regarded as being available for consultation in the form of copies in the Orwell Archive.

KEY TO LOCATIONS

A & U   George Allen & Unwin Ltd

BBC   BBC Written Archives Centre, Caversham

Berg   Henry W. and Albert A. Berg Collection, The New York Public Library, Astor, Lenox and Tilden Foundations

CC   Tom Driberg papers, Christ Church, Oxford

Eliot   Valerie Eliot

Elsley   Ralph C. Elsley

Faber   Faber and Faber Ltd

Leeds   Elisaveta Fen (Lydia Jackson) papers, Leeds Russian Archive, Brotherton Library, University of Leeds

Lilly   Lilly Library, Indiana University, Bloomington, Indiana

OA   Orwell Archive, University College London Library

RLF   Royal Literary Fund

Texas   Harry Ransom Humanities Research Center, University of Texas at Austin

VG   Victor Gollancz Ltd

Yale   Dwight Macdonald papers, Manuscripts and Archives, Yale University Library

2382 Eliot	2448 Lilly	2509 Berg
2383 Texas	2453 Lilly	2511 Texas
2386 Berg	2457A Leeds	2512 BBC
2387 Texas	2466 Lilly	2513 Berg
2392 Yale	2469 BBC	2515 Texas
2403 Lilly	2475A Leeds	2516 Berg
2408 Texas	2476 Lilly	2518 Yale
2411 Yale	2479 RLF	2524 Texas
2423 Yale	2480 Lilly	2527 Berg
2426 Texas	2484A Leeds	2528A Leeds
2426A Leeds	2485 Lilly, VG	2531 Berg
2434 Yale	2491 BBC	2533 Lilly
2436 Lilly	2494 Lilly, VG, OA	2535A Leeds
2437 VG	2495A Leeds	2539 Lilly
2440 Lilly	2495B BBC	2543 Eliot
2442 OA, VG	2496 Faber	2545 Yale
2443 Lilly	2497 BBC	2548A Leeds
2466 Lilly	2500 BBC	2550 Yale
2446A Leeds	2503 Texas	2555 Eliot
2447 Lilly	2508 Berg	2556 Berg

Acknowledgements and Provenances

2557 A & U
2558 Texas
2561A Leeds

2563 Texas
2566A Leeds
2571 CC

2574 CC, OA
2588 Elsley

Editorial Note

THE CONTENTS are, in the main, arranged in chronological order of Orwell's writing. Letters arising from his articles or reviews are usually grouped immediately after that item and Orwell's replies to those letters follow thereon. If there is a long delay between when it is known an article or essay was completed and its publication, it is printed at the date of completion. If items are printed much earlier in the chronological sequence than their date of publication, a cross-reference is given at the date of publication. All entries, whether written by Orwell or anyone else, including lengthy notes and cross-references, are given an item number. Because the printing of the edition has taken place over seven years, some letters came to light after the initial editing and the numbering of items had been completed. These items (or those that had in consequence to be repositioned) are given a letter after the number: e.g., *335A*. Some items included after printing and page-proofing had been completed are given in a final appendix to Volume XX and two (received by the editor in mid January 1997) in the Introduction to Volume XV. Numbers preceding item titles are in roman; when referred to in notes they are italicised.

The provenance of items is given in the preliminaries to each volume. Every item that requires explanation about its source or date, or about textual problems it may pose, is provided with such an explanation. Some articles and broadcasts exist in more than one version. The basis upon which they have been edited is explained and lists of variant readings provided. No Procrustean bed has been devised into which such items must be constrained; individual circumstances have been taken into account and editorial practice explained.

Although this is not what is called a 'diplomatic edition'—that is, one that represents the original precisely even in all its deformities to the point of reproducing a letter set upside down—the fundamental approach in presenting these texts has been to interfere with them as little as possible consistent with the removal of deformities and typographic errors. Orwell took great pains over the writing of his books: the facsimile edition of *Nineteen Eighty-Four*[1] shows that, but in order to meet the demands of broadcasting and publication schedules he often wrote fast and under great pressure. The speed with which he sometimes wrote meant that what he produced was not always what he would have wished to have published had he had time to revise. And, of course, as with any printing, errors can be introduced by those setting the type. It would be easy in places to surmise what Orwell would have done but I have only made changes where there would otherwise have been confusion. Obvious spelling mistakes, which could well be the compositor's or typist's (and the typist might be Orwell), have been corrected silently, but if there is any doubt, a footnote has drawn attention to the problem.

In brief, therefore, I have tried to present what Orwell wrote in his manuscripts and typescripts, not what I thought he should have written; and what he was represented as having written and not what I think should have been typed or printed on his behalf. This is not a 'warts and all' approach because gross errors are amended, significant changes noted, and textual complexities are discussed in preliminary notes. The aim is to bring Orwell, not the editor's version of Orwell, to the fore. Although textual issues are given due weight, an attempt has been made to produce an attractive, readable text.

The setting of this edition has been directly from xeroxes of original letters (if typed), typed copies of manuscript (prepared by one or other of the editors), surviving scripts for broadcasts, and xeroxes of essays, articles, and reviews as originally published (unless a headnote states otherwise). For *The Collected Essays, Journalism and Letters of George Orwell* a 1968 house style was adopted but for this edition, no attempt has been made to impose a late twentieth-century house style on the very different styles used by journals and editors of fifty to eighty years ago. Texts are therefore reproduced in the style given them in the journals from which they are reprinted. To 'correct' might well cause even more confusion as to what was and was not Orwell's: see below regarding paragraphing. Nevertheless, although it is not possible *to know*, one may sometimes hazard a guess at what underlies a printed text. Thus, I believe that most often when 'address' and 'aggression' are printed, Orwell typed or wrote 'adress' (especially until about the outbreak of World War II) and 'agression.' Although American spellings (such as 'Labor') have been retained in articles published in the United States, on very rare occasions, if I could be certain that a form of a word had been printed that Orwell would not have used—such as the American 'accommodations'—I have changed it to the form he would have used: 'accommodation'. Some variations, especially of proper names, have been accepted even if they look incongruous; so, 'Chiang Kai-Shek' as part of a book title but 'Chiang Kai-shek' throughout the text that follows.

Hyphenation presents tricky problems, especially when the first part of a word appears at the end of a line. Examples can be found in the originals of, for example, 'the middle-class,' 'the middle class', and 'the middleclass.' What should one do when a line ends with 'middle-'? Is it 'fore-deck' or 'foredeck'? If 'fore-' appears at the end of a line of the copy being reproduced, should the word be hyphenated or not? *OED* 1991 still hyphenates; Chambers in 1972 spelt it as one word. Where it would help (and it does not include every problem word), the ninth edition of F. Howard Collins, *Authors' & Printers' Dictionary*, Oxford University Press, 1946 (an edition appropriate to the mature Orwell) has been drawn upon. But Collins does not include fore-deck/foredeck. On a number of occasions Orwell's letters, or the text itself, is either obscure or wrong. In order to avoid the irritating repetition of *sic*, a small degree sign has been placed above the line at the doubtful point (°). It is hoped that this will be clear but inconspicuous. It is not usually repeated to mark a repetition of that characteristic in the same item. Orwell was sparing in his use of the question-mark in his letters; his practice has in the main been followed.

Paragraphing presents intractable problems. Orwell tended to write in long paragraphs. Indeed, it is possible to show from the use of many short paragraphs that News Review scripts so written are not by Orwell. The key example is News Review, 30, 11 July 1942 (*1267*), for which there is also external evidence that this is not by Orwell. This has twenty-one paragraphs as compared to eight in the script for the following week. It so happens that we know that Orwell was not at the BBC for two weeks before the 11 July nor on that day: he was on holiday, fishing at Callow End, Worcestershire (and on that day caught a single dace). But though paragraph length is helpful in such instances in identifying Orwell's work, that is not always so. It is of no use when considering his articles published in Paris in 1928–29 nor those he wrote for the *Manchester Evening News*. These tend to have extremely short paragraphs—sometimes paragraphs of only a line or two, splitting the sense illogically. A good example is the series of reviews published on 2 November 1944 (*2572*) where a two-line paragraph about Trollope's *The Small House at Allington* should clearly be part of the preceding four-line paragraph, both relating the books discussed to Barchester; see also *2463, n. 2* and *2608, n. 4*. There is no question but that this is the work of sub-editors. It would often be possible to make a reasonable stab at paragraphing more intelligently, but, as with verbal clarification, the result might be the more confusing as to what really was Orwell's work and what this editor's. It has been thought better to leave the house-styles as they are, even if it is plain that it is not Orwell's style, rather than pass off changes as if the edited concoction represented Orwell's work.

Usually it is fairly certain that titles of essays are Orwell's but it is not always possible to know whether titles of articles are his. Reviews were also frequently given titles. Orwell's own typescript for his review of Harold Laski's *Faith, Reason and Civilisation* (*2309*), which survived because rejected by the *Manchester Evening News*, has neither heading (other than the name of the author and title of the book being reviewed), nor sub-headings. That would seem to be his style. In nearly every case titles of reviews and groups of letters, and cross-heads inserted by sub-editors, have been cut out. Occasionally such a title is kept if it is an aid to clarity but it is never placed within quotation marks. Other than for his BBC broadcasts (where Orwell's authorship is clear unless stated otherwise), titles are placed within single quotation marks if it is fairly certain that they are Orwell's.

Telegrams and cables are printed in small capitals. Quite often articles and reviews have passages in capitals. These look unsightly and, in the main, they have been reduced to small capitals. The exceptions are where the typography makes a point, as in the sound of an explosion: BOOM! Orwell sometimes abbreviated words. He always wrote an ampersand for 'and' and there are various abbreviated forms for such words as 'about'. It is not always plain just what letters make up abbreviations (and this sometimes applies to his signatures) and these have regularly been spelt out with the exception of the ampersand for 'and'. This serves as a reminder that the original is handwritten. Orwell often shortened some words and abbreviations in his own way, e.g., Gov.t, Sup.ts (Superintendents), NB. and N.W (each with a single stop), and ie.; these forms have been retained. In order that the diaries should readily be apparent for what they are, they have been set in sloped roman (rather than italic, long passages of which can be tiring to the eye), with roman for textual variations. Square and half square brackets are used to differentiate sources for the diaries (see, for example, the headnote to War-Time Diary II, *1025*) and for what was written and actually broadcast (see, for example, Orwell's adaptation of Ignazio Silone's *The Fox, 2270*). Particular usages are explained in headnotes to broadcasts etc., and before the first entries of diaries and notebooks.

Orwell usually dated his letters but there are exceptions and sometimes he (and Eileen) give only the day of the week. Where a date has to be guessed it is placed within square brackets and a justification for the dating is given. If Orwell simply signs a letter, the name he used is given without comment. If he signs over a typed version of his name, or initials a copy of a letter, what he signed or initialled is given over the typed version. There has been some slight regularisation of his initialling of letters. If he omitted the final stop after 'E. A. B', no stop is added (and, as here, editorial punctuation *follows* the final quotation mark instead of being inside it). Sometimes Orwell placed the stops midway up the letters: 'E·A·B'; this has been regularised to 'E. A. B'.

Wherever changes are made in a text that can be deemed to be even slightly significant the alteration is either placed within square brackets (for example, an obviously missing word) or the alteration is footnoted. Attention should be drawn to one particular category of change. Orwell had a remarkably good memory. He quoted not only poetry but prose from memory. Mulk Raj Anand has said that, at the BBC, Orwell could, and would, quote lengthy passages from the Book of Common Prayer.[2] As so often with people with this gift, the quotation is not always exact. If what Orwell argues depends precisely upon what he is quoting, the quotation is not corrected if it is inaccurate but a footnote gives the correct reading. If his argument does not depend upon the words actually quoted, the quotation is corrected and a footnote records that.

So far as possible, I have endeavoured to footnote everything that might puzzle a reader at the risk of annoying some readers by seeming to annotate too readily and too frequently what is known to them. I have, therefore, tried to identify all references to people, events, books, and institutions. However, I have not been so presumptuous as to attempt to rewrite the history of this century and, in the main, have relied upon a small number of easily accessible histories. Thus, for the Spanish Civil War I have referred in the main to *The Spanish Civil War* by Hugh Thomas; and for the Second World War, to Winston Churchill's and Liddell Hart's histories. The former has useful and conveniently available documents, and the latter was by a historian with whom Orwell corresponded. They were both his contemporaries and he reviewed the work of both men. These have been checked for factual information from more recent sources, one by Continental historians deliberately chosen as an aid to objectivity in an edition that will have world-wide circulation. It is assumed that readers with a particular interest in World War II will draw on their own knowledge and sources and the annotation is relatively light in providing such background information. Similarly, biographical details are, paradoxically, relatively modest for people as well known as T. S. Eliot and E. M. Forster, but far fuller for those who are significant to Orwell but less well known and about whom information is harder to track down, for example, George(s) Kopp, Joseph Czapski, and Victor Serge. It is tricky judging how often biographical and explicatory information should be reproduced. I have assumed most people will not want more than one volume at a time before them and so have repeated myself (often in shortened form with cross-references to fuller notes) more, perhaps, than is strictly necessary. Whilst I would claim that I have made every attempt not to mislead, it is important that historical and biographical information be checked if a detail is significant to a scholar's argument. History, as Orwell was quick to show, is not a matter of simple, indisputable fact. In annotating I have tried not to be contentious nor to direct the reader unfairly, but annotation cannot be wholly impartial.[3]

Each opening is dated. These dates, though drawn from the printed matter, are not necessarily those of the text reproduced on the page on which a date appears. The dates, known or calculated of letters, articles, broadcasts, diaries, etc., will correspond with the running-head date, but, for example, when correspondence (which may have run on for several weeks) springs from an article and follows directly on that article, the date of the article is continued *within square brackets*. Sometimes an item is printed out of chronological order (the reason for which is always given) and the running-head date will again be set within square brackets. Wherever practicable, the running-head date is that of the first item of the opening; if an opening has no date, the last date of a preceding opening is carried forward. Articles published in journals dated by month are considered for the purpose to be published on the first of the month. Inevitably some dates are more specific than is wholly justified, e.g., that for 'British Cookery' (*2954*). However, it is hoped that if readers always treat dates within square brackets with circumspection, the dates will give a clear indication of 'where they are' in Orwell's life.

Great efforts have been made to ensure the accuracy of these volumes. The three editors and Roberta Leighton (in New York) have read and re-read them a total of six times but it is obvious that errors will, as it used to be put so charmingly in the sixteenth century, have 'escaped in the printing.' I offer one plea for understanding. Much of the copy-preparation and proof-reading has been of type set during and after the war when newsprint was in short supply and mere literary articles would be set in microscopic-sized type. Many of the BBC scripts were blown up from microfilm and extremely difficult to puzzle out. When one proof-reads against xeroxes of dim printing on creased paper, the possibilities for error are increased and the eyes so run with tears that vision is impaired. We hope we have corrected most errors, but we know we shall not have caught them all.

P.D.

A slightly fuller version of this note is printed in the preliminaries to Volume X.

1. *George Orwell, Nineteen Eighty-Four: The Facsimile of the Extant Manuscript*, edited by Peter Davison, London, New York, and Weston, Mass., 1984.
2. Information from W. J. West, 22 July 1994.
3. The problems of presenting acceptable history even for the professional historian are well outlined by Norman Davies in *Europe: A History*, Oxford University Press, Oxford and New York, 1996, 2–7. I am obviously attempting nothing so grand, yet even 'simple' historical explication is not always quite so simple.

REFERENCES

References to Orwell's books are to the editions in Vols I to IX of the *Complete Works* (edited P. Davison, published by Secker & Warburg, 1986–87). The pagination is almost always identical with that in the Penguin Twentieth-Century Classics edition, 1989–90. The volumes are numbered in chronological order and references are by volume number (in roman), page, and, if necessary (after a diagonal) line, so: II. 37/5 means line five of page 37 of *Burmese Days*. Secker editions have Textual Notes and apparatus. Penguin editions have A Note on the Text; these are not identical with the Secker Textual Notes and Penguin editions do not list variants. There is a 32-page introduction to the Secker *Down and Out in Paris and London*. Items in Volumes X to XX are numbered individually; they (and their notes) are referred to by italicised numerals, e.g. *2736* and *2736 n. 3*.

REFERENCE WORKS: These are the principal reference works frequently consulted:

The Oxford English Dictionary, second edition (Compact Version, Oxford 1991): (*OED*).

The Dictionary of National Biography (Oxford 1885–1900, with supplements and *The Twentieth-Century*, 1901–): (*DNB*).

Dictionary of American Biography (New York, 1946, with supplements).

Dictionnaire biographique du mouvement ouvrier français, publié sous la direction de Jean Maitron, 4ᵉ ptie 1914–1939: De la Première à la Seconde Guerre mondiale (t. 16–43, Paris, Les Éditions Ouvrières, 1981–93).

Who's Who; Who Was Who; Who's Who in the Theatre; Who Was Who in Literature 1906–1934 (2 vols., Detroit, 1979); *Who Was Who Among English and European Authors 1931–1949* (3 vols., Detroit 1978); *Contemporary Authors* and its *Cumulative Index* (Detroit, 1993); *Who's Who In Filmland*, edited and compiled by Langford Reed and Hetty Spiers (1928); Roy Busby, *British Music Hall: An Illustrated Who's Who from 1850 to the Present Day* (London and New Hampshire, USA, 1976).

The Feminist Companion to Literature in English, edited by Virginia Blain, Patricia Clements, and Isobel Grundy, Batsford 1990.

The New Cambridge Bibliography of English Literature, edited by George Watson and Ian Willison, 4 vols., Cambridge, 1974–79.

Martin Seymour-Smith, *Guide to Modern World Literature*, 3rd revised edition, Macmillan 1985.

The War Papers, co-ordinating editor, Richard Widdows, 75 Parts, Marshall Cavendish, 1976–78.

The following are referred to by abbreviations:

CEJL: *The Collected Essays, Journalism and Letters of George Orwell*, ed. Sonia Orwell

References

and Ian Angus, 4 volumes, Secker & Warburg 1968; Penguin Books, 1970; references are by volume and page number of the more conveniently available Penguin edition.

Crick: Bernard Crick, *George Orwell: A Life*, 1980; 3rd edition, Penguin Books, Harmondsworth, 1992 edition. References are to the 1992 edition.

Eric & Us: Jacintha Buddicom, *Eric and Us: A Remembrance of George Orwell*, Leslie Frewin, 1974.

Lewis: Peter Lewis, *George Orwell: The Road to 1984*, Heinemann, 1981.

Liddell Hart: B. H. Liddell Hart, *History of the Second World War*, Cassell, 1970; 8th Printing, Pan, 1983.

Orwell Remembered: Audrey Coppard and Bernard Crick, eds., *Orwell Remembered*, Ariel Books, BBC, 1984.

Remembering Orwell: Stephen Wadhams, *Remembering Orwell*, Penguin Books Canada, Markham, Ontario; Penguin Books, Harmondsworth, 1984.

Shelden: Michael Shelden, *Orwell: The Authorised Biography*, Heinemann, London; Harper Collins, New York; 1991. The American pagination differs from that of the English edition; both are given in references, the English first.

Stansky and Abrahams I: Peter Stansky and William Abrahams, *The Unknown Orwell*, Constable 1972; edition referred to here, Granada, St Albans, 1981.

Stansky and Abrahams II: Peter Stansky and William Abrahams, *The Transformation*, Constable 1979; edition referred to here, Granada, St Albans, 1981.

Thomas: Hugh Thomas, *The Spanish Civil War*, 3rd edition; Hamish Hamilton and Penguin Books, Harmondsworth, 1977.

Thompson: John Thompson, *Orwell's London*, Fourth Estate 1984.

West: *Broadcasts*: W. J. West, *Orwell: The War Broadcasts*, Duckworth/BBC 1985.

West: *Commentaries*: W. J. West, *Orwell: The War Commentaries*, Duckworth/BBC, 1985.

Willison: I. R. Willison, 'George Orwell: Some Materials for a Bibliography,' Librarianship Diploma Thesis, University College London, 1953. A copy is held by the Orwell Archive, UCL.

2194 Days of War: *2194 Days of War*, compiled by Cesare Salmaggi and Alfredo Pallavisini, translated by Hugh Young, Arnoldo Mondadori, Milan 1977; rev. edn Galley Press, Leicester 1988.

A Bibliography of works, books, memoirs and essays found helpful in preparing Volumes X to XX of *The Complete Works of George Orwell* will be found in the preliminaries to Volume X.

CHRONOLOGY

In the main, Orwell's publications, except books, are not listed

25 June 1903 Eric Arthur Blair born in Motihari, Bengal, India.

---

23 Nov 1943 Leaves BBC and joins *Tribune* as Literary Editor.
   Leaves Home Guard on medical grounds.
Nov 1943–Feb 1944 Writes *Animal Farm*.
3 December 1943 First of eighty personal columns, 'As I Please', *Tribune*.
9 Dec 1943 Begins reviewing for *The Manchester Evening News*.
May 1944 Finishes *The English People* (published August 1947)
14 May 1944 The Orwells' son, adopted June 1944, born; christened Richard
   Horatio Blair.
28 June 1944 The Orwells' flat bombed; they move to Inez Holden's flat near
   Baker Street, London.
Summer 1944 Visits Jura for the first time.
Early Oct 1944 Moves to Canonbury Square, Islington, London.

---

21 January 1950 Orwell dies of pulmonary tuberculosis, aged 46

THE COMPLETE WORKS OF
GEORGE ORWELL · SIXTEEN

I HAVE TRIED
TO TELL THE TRUTH

2378. Orwell at *Tribune*

29 November 1943—4 April 1947

Orwell's last day at the BBC was Wednesday, 24 November 1943. He started writing letters on *Tribune*'s headed paper on Monday, 29 November, and it seems likely that that was the day he started working for *Tribune* as Literary Editor. He had reviewed for *Tribune* on a couple of dozen occasions from 8 March 1940 until then, and in his preface to the Ukrainian translation of *Animal Farm* he wrote, 'The periodical to which I contribute most regularly is *Tribune*, which represents, generally speaking, the left wing of the Labour Party.'

Tribune was first published on 1 January 1937. Sir Stafford Cripps and George Strauss (both Labour M.P.s) put up most of the capital of about £20,000; William Mellor was appointed editor, with Aneurin Bevan, Cripps, Strauss, Ellen Wilkinson, Harold Laski, and Noel Brailsford on the board controlling the paper. Bevan wrote a weekly column under the pseudonym 'M.P.' and from 1939 to 1945, when he joined the Labour government, he was particularly closely involved in *Tribune*. Raymond Postgate was appointed editor early in 1940 and it was he who greatly improved the standard of the paper and who invited Orwell to review novels for *Tribune*. Bevan, Strauss, and Victor Gollancz formed the editorial board at that time. Bevan and Postgate quarrelled, probably late in 1941, and Bevan became editor on 1 January 1942, with Jon Kimche and Evelyn Anderson as his chief assistants. Kimche had worked with Orwell as an assistant at Booklovers' Corner in 1934–35. When Orwell joined *Tribune*, the letterhead on which he corresponded gave Strauss and Bevan as directors, John Atkins as heading the Editorial Department, and the business and advertising managers as O. Rawson and D. M. Thornton respectively. Atkins, however, was on the point of leaving. He had been assistant editor, 1941–42, and literary editor, 1942–43. An announcement in *Tribune* of 26 November 1943 said he was leaving to join the staff of Mass Observation, having done 'much pioneering work during his successful two years' tenure' and that he would be replaced by Orwell.

One of Orwell's principal contributions to *Tribune* as literary editor was a personal column, 'As I Please,' the first of which was published on 3 December 1943; see *2385*. Raymond Postgate had contributed to a short series under that title in *Controversy* (edited by C. A. Smith) in 1939; Jon Kimche told the editor of this edition in September 1990 that it was he who suggested to Orwell that he use that title for his series. Another earlier use of the title, by a writer whom Orwell noted in a list of those with real or suspected left-wing leanings, was *I Write As I Please*, by Walter Duranty (1935). (Duranty, who died in 1957, was foreign correspondent for the *New York Times*, 1913–39.) Yet another similar title was that for Lord Elton's series of broadcasts, *It Occurs to Me*; those for 1937–38 were published under that title in 1939. Crick suggests that Orwell was probably paid 'only £500 a year' as literary editor of *Tribune* (441). Only two payments from

3

Tribune are noted in Orwell's Payments Book whilst he was literary editor: £5.5.0. for a special article of 2,000 words on 20 December 1943 (see *2397*) and 10s.6d for a poem of thirty-six lines on 17 January 1944 (see *2409*); therefore his salary as literary editor, whatever it was, also covered his writing of 'As I Please.'

Bevan gave Orwell free rein in 'As I Please.' As a result, 'Protests were frequent, both at the frivolous use he made of his column and at his frequent attacks on the Soviet Communist Party.' Bevan defended Orwell, without whose support Orwell 'might not have lasted—even though the circulation manager coolly reported that those who wrote in regularly threatening to cancel their subscriptions were rarely subscribers' (Crick, 445–46).

Orwell's last 'As I Please,' number 80 (and his last contribution to *Tribune*), was published on 4 April 1947, by which time Michael Foot, M.P. (later leader of the Labour Party), was Managing Director of *Tribune* (1945–74). Foot edited *Tribune* 1948–52 and 1955–60. Jon Kimche handled much of Orwell's copy for *Tribune*. This, he informed the editor in September 1990, presented no problems. It was punctual, accurate, to the correct length, and required virtually no sub-editing. Sections of 'As I Please' were often separated by typographical decorations. These were not Orwell's work and they have been omitted here. For a break in the sequence of these contributions between 16 February 1945 and 8 November 1946, see *2622*.

Despite the severe shortage of space owing to wartime paper rationing, *Tribune* published a lively correspondence section and many letters took issue with Orwell. Although he did not edit this section of *Tribune*, Orwell probably had some say in what was selected for publication. A letter from A. Perlmutt of 27 February 1944, expressing disappointment that one of his earlier letters had not appeared (see *2417*), says, 'On enquiry at the Tribune° office I was given to understand that the decision for publishing any letters on this subject rests with your good self.' Perlmutt's informant could, of course, have been someone covering up how the selection process worked. The letters give a vivid picture of those for whom Orwell was writing at an important period in British and Labour Party history. The copyright of these letters rests with *Tribune*, but, when possible, permissions have also been sought from those who wrote these letters. However, few authors can be traced and many cannot be identified from initials alone. The letters are reproduced, often in full, sometimes summarised, by kind permission of *Tribune* as are all Orwell's contributions to *Tribune*. The headings added to letters by sub-editors have been omitted except in a few instances where they might assist readers to differentiate topics.

Orwell frequently wrote letters on the journal's headed paper. This is indicated simply by the word '*Tribune*'; the address (222 Strand, London, WC2) and other details in the heading are omitted. If Orwell typed or wrote *Tribune*'s address, the title of the journal is reproduced as he gave it, in roman, the address being omitted. If his name is typed beneath his signature (as in BBC letters), this, and his signature, are both reproduced; if only his signature appears, that alone is reproduced.

Although no topic sub-headings are given in 'As I Please', and none have been added in this edition, to assist the reader topics have been listed in the cumulative index under 'As I Please'.

2379. 'Mark Twain—The Licensed Jester'

Tribune, 26 November 1943

Mark Twain has crashed the lofty gates of the Everyman Library, but only with *Tom Sawyer* and *Huckleberry Finn*, already fairly well known under the guise of "children's books" (which they are not). His best and most characteristic books, *Roughing It*, *The Innocents at Home*, and even *Life on the Mississippi*, are little remembered in this country, though no doubt in America the patriotism which is everywhere mixed up with literary judgment keeps them alive.

Although Mark Twain produced a surprising variety of books, ranging from a namby-pamby "life" of Joan of Arc, to a pamphlet so obscene that it has never been publicly printed,[1] all that is best in his work centres about the Mississippi river and the wild mining towns of the West. Born in 1835 (he came of a Southern family, a family just rich enough to own one or perhaps two slaves), he had had his youth and early manhood in the golden age of America, the period when the great plains were opened up, when wealth and opportunity seemed limitless, and human beings felt free, indeed *were* free, as they had never been before and may not be again for centuries. *Life on the Mississippi* and the two other books that I have mentioned are a ragbag of anecdotes, scenic descriptions and social history both serious and burlesque, but they have a central theme which could perhaps be put into these words: "This is how human beings behave when they are not frightened of the sack." In writing these books Mark Twain is not consciously writing a hymn to liberty. Primarily he is interested in "character," in the fantastic, almost lunatic variations which human nature is capable of when economic pressure and tradition are both removed from it. The raftsmen, Mississippi pilots, miners and bandits whom he describes are probably not much exaggerated, but they are as different from modern men, and from one another, as the gargoyles of a medieval cathedral. They could develop their strange and sometimes sinister individuality because of the lack of any outside pressure. The State hardly existed, the churches were weak and spoke with many voices, and land was to be had for the taking. If you disliked your job you simply hit the boss in the eye and moved further west; and moreover, money was so plentiful that the smallest coin in circulation was worth a shilling. The American pioneers were not supermen, and they were not especially courageous. Whole towns of hardy goldminers let themselves be terrorised by bandits whom they lacked the public spirit to put down. They were not even free from class distinctions. The desperado who stalked through the streets of the mining settlement, with a Derringer pistol in his waistcoat pocket and twenty corpses to his credit, was dressed in a frock coat and shiny top hat, described himself firmly as a "gentleman" and was meticulous about table-manners. But at least it was not the case that a man's destiny was settled from his birth. The "log cabin to White House" myth was true while the free land lasted. In a way, it was for this that the Paris mob had stormed the Bastille, and when one reads Mark Twain, Bret Harte and Whitman it is hard to feel that their effort was wasted.

However, Mark Twain aimed at being something more than a chronicler of the Mississippi and the gold-rush. In his own day he was famous all over the world as a humorist and comic lecturer. In New York, London, Berlin, Vienna, Melbourne and Calcutta vast audiences rocked with laughter over jokes which have now, almost without exception, ceased to be funny. (It is worth noticing that Mark Twain's lectures were only a success with Anglo-Saxon and German audiences. The relatively grown-up Latin races—whose own humour, he complained, always centred round sex and politics—never cared for them.) But in addition, Mark Twain had some pretensions to being a social critic, even a species of philosopher. He had in him an iconoclastic, even revolutionary vein which he obviously wanted to follow up and yet somehow never did follow up. He might have been a destroyer of humbugs and a prophet of democracy more valuable than Whitman, because healthier and more humorous. Instead he became that dubious thing a "public figure," flattered by passport-officials and entertained by royalty, and his career reflects the deterioration in American life that set in after the Civil War.

Mark Twain has sometimes been compared with his contemporary, Anatole France. This comparison is not so pointless as it may sound. Both men were the spiritual children of Voltaire, both had an ironical, sceptical view of life, and a native pessimism overlaid by gaiety; both knew that the existing social order is a swindle and its cherished beliefs mostly delusions. Both were bigoted atheists and convinced (in Mark Twain's case this was Darwin's doing) of the unbearable cruelty of the universe. But there the resemblance ends. Not only is the Frenchman enormously more learned, more civilised, more alive æsthetically, but he is also more courageous. He does attack the things he disbelieves in; he does not, like Mark Twain, always take refuge behind the amiable mask of the "public figure" and the licensed jester. He is ready to risk the anger of the Church and to take the unpopular side in a controversy—in the Dreyfus case, for example. Mark Twain, except perhaps in one short essay (*What is Man?*) never attacks established beliefs in a way that is likely to get him into trouble. Nor could he ever wean himself from the notion, which is perhaps especially an American notion, that success and virtue are the same thing.

In *Life on the Mississippi* there is a queer little illustration of the central weakness of Mark Twain's character. In the earlier part of this mainly autobiographical book the dates have been altered. Mark Twain describes his adventures as a Mississippi pilot as though he had been a boy of about seventeen at the time, whereas in fact he was a young man of nearly thirty. There is a reason for this. The same part of the book describes his exploits in the Civil War, which were distinctly inglorious. Moreover, Mark Twain started by fighting, if he can be said to have fought, on the Southern side, and then changed his allegiance before the war was over. This kind of behaviour is more excusable in a boy than in a man, whence the adjustment of the dates. It is also clear enough, however, that he changed sides because he saw that the North was going to win; and this tendency to side with the stronger whenever possible, to believe that might *must* be right, is apparent throughout his career. In *Roughing It* there is an interesting account of a bandit named Slade who, among countless other outrages, had committed 28 murders. It is perfectly clear that Mark Twain admires this disgusting scoundrel. Slade was successful; therefore he was admirable. This outlook, no less common to-day, is summed up in the significant American expression "to *make good*."

In the money-grubbing period that followed the Civil War it was hard for anyone of Mark Twain's temperament to refuse to be a success. The old, simple, stump-whittling, tobacco-chewing democracy which Abraham Lincoln typified was perishing: it was now the age of cheap immigrant labour and the growth of Big Business. Mark Twain mildly satirised his contemporaries in *The Gilded Age*, but he also gave himself up to the prevailing fever, and made and lost vast sums of money. He even for a period of years deserted writing for business; and he squandered his time on buffooneries, not merely lecture tours and public banquets, but, for instance, the writing of a book like *A Connecticut Yankee at King Arthur's Court*, which is a deliberate flattery of all that is worst and most vulgar in American life. The man who might have been a kind of rustic Voltaire became the world's leading after-dinner speaker, charming alike for his anecdotes and his power to make business-men feel themselves public benefactors.

It is usual to blame Mark Twain's wife for his failure to write the books he ought to have written, and it is evident that she did tyrannise over him pretty thoroughly. Each morning Mark Twain would show her what he had written the day before, and Mrs. Clemens (Mark Twain's real name was Samuel Clemens) would go over it with the blue pencil, cutting out everything that she thought unsuitable. She seems to have been a drastic blue-penciller even by nineteenth-century standards. There is an account in W. D. Howells's book *My Mark Twain* of the fuss that occurred over a terrible expletive that had crept into *Huckleberry Finn*. Mark Twain appealed to Howells, who admitted that it was "just what Huck would have said," but agreed with Mrs. Clemens that the word could not possibly be printed. The word was "hell." Nevertheless, no writer is really the intellectual slave of his wife. Mrs. Clemens could not have stopped Mark Twain writing any book he really wanted to write. She may have made his surrender to society easier, but the surrender happened because of that flaw in his own nature, his inability to despise success.

Several of Mark Twain's books are bound to survive, because they contain invaluable social history. His life covered the great period of American expansion. When he was a child it was a normal day's outing to go with a picnic lunch and watch the hanging of an Abolitionist, and when he died the aeroplane was ceasing to be a novelty. This period in America produced relatively little literature, and but for Mark Twain our picture of a Mississippi paddle-steamer, or a stage-coach crossing the plains, would be much dimmer than it is. But most people who have studied his work have come away with a feeling that he might have done something more. He gives all the while a strange impression of being about to say something and then funking it, so that *Life on the Mississippi* and the rest of them seem to be haunted by the ghost of a greater and much more coherent book. Significantly, he starts his autobiography by remarking that a man's inner life is indescribable. We do not know what he would have said—it is just possible that the unprocurable pamphlet, "1601," would supply a clue but we may guess that it would have wrecked his reputation and reduced his income to reasonable proportions.

[Fee: £2.2s; 22.11.43]

1. See final sentence of the essay. For a short account of this pamphlet and Twain's writings in a similar vein, see Milton Rugoff, *Prudery and Passion: Sexuality in Victorian America* (1972), 85–90. See also Orwell's letter to Leonard Moore, 2 February 1934 (*191*) for his fruitless offer to write a short biography of Mark Twain.

2380. Review of *Spain in Eclipse, 1937–1943* by E. Allison Peers; *Behind the Spanish Mask* by Lawrence Dundas

The Observer, 28 November 1943

The titles of both of these books are symptomatic of the fact that we know very little of what has been happening in Spain since the end of the Civil War. There have been hunger and pestilence, great numbers of people are in gaol, and the regime has been markedly friendly to the Axis—that is about as far as common knowledge extends. Opinions on anything else are likely to be coloured by the political sympathies of the writer, and one must keep it in mind that Mr. Dundas is vigorously pro-Republic, while Professor Peers should rather be described as mildly and regretfully pro-Franco.

Professor Peers devotes part of his book to the Civil War, but his best chapters are those dealing with the last four years. He considers that the Franco regime for a while enjoyed majority support, that its political persecutions have probably been exaggerated, and that it has not in fact given much solid aid to the Nazis. He does not, however, believe that it will last much longer, and though he himself hopes for some kind of Liberal monarchist regime, he thinks that a swing to the extreme Left is not impossible.

It is noticeable that Professor Peers seems surprised as well as pained that the "non-belligerent" Spanish Government has been so consistently un-friendly to ourselves. He lists the endless provocations, and the inspired campaigns of libel in the Spanish Press, as though these in some way contradicted Franco's earlier record. But, in fact, there was never very much doubt as to where the sympathies of Franco and his more influential followers lay, and the time when it might have been useful to point out that Franco was the friend of our enemies was in 1936. At that time Professor Peers did nothing of the kind. No one would accuse him of falsifying facts, but the tone of the books he was then writing did, there is little doubt, tend to make the Nationalist cause more respectable in British eyes. In so far as books influence events, Professor Peers must be held to have done something towards establishing Franco's regime, and he ought not now to be astonished because Franco has behaved in very much the manner that every supporter of the Republic foretold at the time.[1]

Mr. Dundas's book is written round the speculative but interesting thesis that a quite different kind of rebellion—a Conservative but not Fascist rebellion—had been planned in the beginning, and that events only took the course they did because of Sanjurjo's[2] death and because the Nationalists, having failed in their first coup, had to apply for help to the Germans and Italians, who imposed their own terms. The importance of this is that the regime which has actually been set up is, as Mr. Dundas says, "not Spanish." It is a regime modelled on foreign lines and intolerable from the point of view of an ordinary Spaniard, even an aristocrat; it might therefore turn out to be brittle in a moment of emergency. The book contains some interesting details about Civil War events in Majorca. But Mr. Dundas is surely wrong in suggesting that Franco will fight for the Axis if the Allies invade Europe. Fidelity is not the strong point of the minor dictators.

[Fee: £5.5s; 10.11.43]

1. Also in 1943, under the name of Bruce Truscot, Professor Peers published, *Redbrick University*. This included 'The Nature and Aims of a Modern University,' which proved influential in post-war British university development.
2. General José Sanjurjo Sacanell (1872–1936), a Nationalist (as was Franco), led a coup against the government of the Second Spanish Republic in August 1932. This failed; he was captured, tried, sentenced, then, in 1934, reprieved. He was killed when a plane sent to bring him from Lisbon to Burgos crashed on take-off. Sabotage was suspected, but the cause was more mundane. The plane, a small Puss Moth, was overloaded because Sanjurjo 'insisted on taking with him a heavy suitcase, which contained a full-dress uniform for his use as head of the new Spanish State.' The plane, which had been diverted by the Portuguese authorities to a small outlying airfield, failed to clear the surrounding pine trees. The pilot was injured but thrown clear; Sanjurjo was burned to death '—a victim of conformity rather than sabotage' (Thomas, 254).

2381. To Alex Comfort

29 November 1943   Typewritten

Tribune[1]

Dear Comfort,
I am now Literary Editor of the Tribune. If you have any poems on hand you might send them along. Of course I can't undertake in advance to print anything but would always read anything of yours with interest. (We do pay for poems but nothing enormous as you perhaps know). I should like it very much if you could do another satirical poem.

Yours sincerely
Geo. Orwell

P.S. The subject-matter of a poem isn't as a rule all-important, but we can't undertake to print direct pacifist propaganda.
Did you see our book of Indian broadcasts?[2] It isn't bad for that kind of book.

1. When Orwell writes on *Tribune* headed paper—the title is given in block capitals as THE

TRIBUNE—only the word *Tribune* (in italics) is given here; the address, list of directors and officers, and so on are omitted.

2. *Talking to India*, 18 November 1943; see *2359* and *2360*.

2382. To T. S. Eliot

29 November 1943   Typewritten

Tribune

Dear Eliot,
I have recently become Literary Editor of the Tribune. I know that you are very busy these days, but if you ever do get time we should be greatly honoured if you cared to send us something. We are able to print poems up to about the length of a page (circa 150 lines). Of course you don't get paid anything very grand, but you do get paid something. Or you might possibly care to do an article of some kind some time.

Can you have lunch with me one day next week (ie. week beginning December 6th).[1] I forget which days it is you are in London but Monday and Friday are my best days.

Yours sincerely
Geo. Orwell

1. Eliot replied on 30 November to say that he had heard Orwell had left the BBC but did not know what job he had taken. He would be very glad to have lunch, but was not free until Tuesday, 16 December. Orwell's sentence asking Eliot to lunch lacks a question-mark.

2383. To Henry Treece

29 November 1943   Typewritten

Tribune

Dear Treece,
I am Literary Editor of the Tribune now and am on the look-out for verse. You might care to send us something some time. Of course I can't undertake in advance to print it but would always consider anything of yours with interest. Payment is made for poems though nothing very enormous as you might guess.

Yours sincerely
Geo. Orwell

2384. 'Your Questions Answered': Wigan Pier

Broadcast 2 December 1943

The script in the Orwell Archive for Number 25 of the BBC radio programme
'Your Questions Answered' states that it was broadcast on Thursday, 2
December 1943, from 1830 to 1845 GMT in the General Overseas Service and
repeated on the next day from approximately 1310 to 1315 using disc
SOX23536; this timing is clearly wrong. *London Calling* gives both trans-
missions and the time for the second as 1310–1340. There is no indication in the
Radio Times that the programme was broadcast in the United Kingdom between
28 November and 4 December 1943. The compère was Colin Wills.

WILLS: I am going to try some more of these trick questions on
somebody else in another programme. And now we've got time for just
one more question, asked by Sergeant Salt and Signalman McGrath
serving in India. They say: "How long is the Wigan Pier and what is the
Wigan Pier?" Well, if anybody ought to know, it should be George Orwell
who wrote a book called "The Road to Wigan Pier." And here's what he's
got to say on the subject.

ORWELL: Well, I am afraid I must tell you that Wigan Pier doesn't exist. I
made a journey specially to see it in 1936, and I couldn't find it. It did exist
once, however, and to judge from the photographs it must have been about
twenty feet long.[1]

Wigan is in the middle of the mining areas, and though it's a very pleasant
place in some ways its scenery is not its strong point. The landscape is mostly
slag-heaps, looking like the mountains of the moon, and mud and soot and so
forth. For some reason, though it's not worse than fifty other places, Wigan
has always been picked on as a symbol of the ugliness of the industrial areas.
At one time, on one of the little muddy canals that run round the town, there
used to be a tumble-down wooden jetty; and by way of a joke someone
nicknamed this Wigan Pier. The joke caught on locally, and then the music-
hall comedians get° hold of it, and they are the ones who have succeeded in
keeping Wigan Pier alive as a by-word, long after the place itself had been
demolished.

WILLS: And so Signalman Salt and Sergeant McGrath, if you meant to floor
the experts with a question about Wigan Pier, you'll have to try again with
something else! Now our time's up for this week but we'll be back again on
the air at the same time next week to answer some more of your questions.

1. See the illustration in *George Orwell: The Road to 1984*, by Peter Lewis, 51, and the English
Tourist Board leaflet on Wigan (1988), which advertises a local exhibition, 'The Way We
Were' (c. 1900) in the 'Wigan Pier Heritage Centre,' Wallgate.

2385. 'As I Please,' I

Tribune, 3 December 1943

Scene in a tobacconist's shop. Two American soldiers sprawling across the counter, one of them just sober enough to make unwanted love to the two young women who run the shop, the other at the stage known as "fighting drunk." Enter Orwell in search of matches. The pugnacious one makes an effort and stands upright.

Soldier: "Wharrishay is, perfijious Albion. You heard that? Perfijious Albion. Never trust a Britisher. You can't trust the b——s."

Orwell: "Can't trust them with what?"

Soldier: "Wharrishay is, down with Britain. Down with the British. You wanna do anything 'bout that? Then you can —— well do it." (Sticks his face out like a tomcat on a garden wall.)

Tobacconist: "He'll knock your block off if you don't shut up."

Soldier: "Wharrishay is, down with Britain." (Subsides across the counter again. The tobacconist lifts his head delicately out of the scales.)

This kind of thing is not exceptional. Even if you steer clear of Piccadilly with its seething swarms of drunks and whores, it is difficult to go anywhere in London without having the feeling that Britain is now Occupied Territory. The general consensus of opinion seems to be that the only American soldiers with decent manners are the Negroes. On the other hand the Americans have their own justifiable complaints—in particular, they complain of the children who follow them night and day, cadging sweets.

Does this sort of thing matter? The answer is that it might matter at some moment when Anglo-American relations were in the balance, and when the still powerful forces in this country which want an understanding with Japan were able to show their faces again. At such moments popular prejudice can count for a great deal. Before the war there was no popular anti-American feeling in this country. It all dates from the arrival of the American troops, and it is made vastly worse by the tacit agreement never to discuss it in print.

Seemingly it is our fixed policy in this war not to criticise our allies, nor to answer their criticisms of us. As a result things have happened which are capable of causing the worst kind of trouble sooner or later. An example is the agreement by which American troops in this country are not liable to British courts for offences against British subjects—practically "extra-territorial rights." Not one English person in ten knows of the existence of this agreement; the newspapers barely reported it and refrained from commenting on it. Nor have people been made to realise the extent of anti-British feeling in the United States. Drawing their picture of America from films carefully edited for the British market, they have no notion of the kind of thing that Americans are brought up to believe about us. Suddenly to discover, for instance, that the average American thinks the U.S.A. had more casualties than Britain in the last war comes as a shock, and the kind of shock that can cause a violent quarrel. Even such a fundamental difficulty as the fact that an American soldier's pay is five times that of a British soldier has never been properly ventilated. No sensible person wants to whip up Anglo-

American jealousy. On the contrary, it is just because one does want a good relationship between the two countries that one wants plain speaking. Our official soft-soaping policy does us no good in America, while in this country it allows dangerous resentments to fester just below the surface.

Since 1935, when pamphleteering revived, I have been a steady collector of pamphlets political, religious and what-not.[1] To anyone who happens to come across it and has a shilling to spare I recommend *The 1946 MS.*, by Robin Maugham,[2] published by the War Facts Press. It is a good example of that small but growing school of literature, the non-party Radical school. It purports to describe the establishment in Britain of a Fascist dictatorship, starting in 1944 and headed by a successful general who is (I think) drawn from a living model.[3] I found it interesting because it gives you the average middle-class man's conception of what Fascism would be like, and more important, of the reasons why Fascism might succeed. Its appearance (along with other similar pamphlets I have in my collection) shows how far that average middle-class man has travelled since 1939, when Socialism still meant dividing the money up and what happened in Europe was none of our business.

Who wrote this?

"As we walked over the Drury Lane gratings of the cellars a most foul stench came up, and one in particular that I remember to this day. A man half dressed pushed open a broken window beneath us, just as we passed by, and there issued such a blast of corruption, made up of gases bred by filth, air breathed and rebreathed a hundred times, charged with the odours of unnameable personal uncleanness and disease, that I staggered to the gutter with a qualm which I could scarcely conquer . . . I did not know, till I came in actual contact with them, how far away the classes which lie at the bottom of great cities are from those above them; how completely they are inaccessible to motives which act upon ordinary human beings, and how deeply they are sunk beyond ray of sun or stars, immersed in the selfishness naturally begotten of their incessant struggle for existence and incessant warfare with society. It was an awful thought to me, ever present on those Sundays, and haunting me at other times, that men, women, and children were living in such brutish degradation, and that as they died others would take their place. Our civilisation seemed nothing but a thin film or crust lying over a volcanic pit, and I often wondered whether some day the pit would not break up through it and destroy us all."[4]

You would know, at any rate, that this comes from some nineteenth-century writer. Actually it is from a novel, *Mark Rutherford's Deliverance.* (Mark Rutherford, whose real name was Hale White, wrote this book as a pseudo-autobiography.) Apart from the prose, you could recognise this as coming from the nineteenth century because of that description of the unendurable filth of the slums. The London slums of that day *were* like that, and all honest writers so described them. But even more characteristic is that notion of a whole block of the population being so degraded as to be beyond contact and beyond redemption.

Almost all nineteenth-century English writers are agreed upon this, even Dickens. A large part of the town working class, ruined by industrialism, are simply savages. Revolution is not a thing to be hoped for: it simply means the swamping of civilisation by the sub-human. In this novel (it is one of the best novels in English) Mark Rutherford describes the opening of a sort of mission or settlement near Drury Lane. Its object was "gradually to attract Drury Lane to come and be saved." Needless to say this was a failure. Drury Lane not only did not want to be saved in the religious sense, it didn't even want to be civilised. All that Mark Rutherford and his friend succeeded in doing, all that one could do, indeed, at that time, was to provide a sort of refuge for the few people of the neighbourhood who did not belong to their surroundings. The general masses were outside the pale.

Mark Rutherford was writing of the 'seventies, and in a footnote dated 1884 he remarks that "socialism, nationalisation of the land and other projects" have now made their appearance, and may perhaps give a gleam of hope. Nevertheless, he assumes that the condition of the working class will grow worse and not better as time goes on. It was natural to believe this (even Marx seems to have believed it), because it was hard at that time to foresee the enormous increase in the productivity of labour. Actually, such an improvement in the standard of living has taken place as Mark Rutherford and his contemporaries would have considered quite impossible.

The London slums are still bad enough, but they are nothing to those of the nineteenth century. Gone are the days when a single room used to be inhabited by four families, one in each corner, and when incest and infanticide were taken almost for granted. Above all, gone are the days when it seemed natural to write off a whole stratum of the population as irredeemable savages. The most snobbish Tory alive would not now write of the London working class as Mark Rutherford does. And Mark Rutherford—like Dickens, who shared his attitude—was a Radical! Progress does happen, hard though it may be to believe it, in this age of concentration camps and big beautiful bombs.

[George Orwell will write this column each week.]

From the outset, Orwell's column 'As I Please' attracted letters from many readers, and *Tribune* found space to publish those it considered most interesting. Orwell often took up points made in these letters in a future column. The result is a genuine dialogue. The following letters, which arose from the first 'As I Please,' were published in the issue for 17 December, and Orwell discussed them in his column published in that issue. Thus, 'last week' in the first sentence of the first letter, refers to 3 December, there not having been time to get the letter into print in the intervening week. As in this instance, correspondence arising from Orwell's columns follows immediately after the column to which it refers. If correspondence ran for several weeks, the dates when letters were published are given. Sub-editorial titles to letters are not reprinted. Orwell was not responsible for editing the correspondence section of *Tribune*. The letters are reproduced by kind permission of *Tribune*.

In *Tribune*'s column "As I Please" last week, this anglophile was rather shocked to find that George Orwell is still no closer to knowing the

Americans than before. He is not above citing examples of misbehaviour and inordinate drinking by American soldiers in the pubs to prove his case that Anglo-American relations in England leave much to be desired.

Mr. Orwell mentions "the agreement by which American troops in this country are not liable to British Courts for offences against British subjects." Existence of such "extra-territorial rights" is perfectly true in accordance with international law. But what Mr. Orwell fails to mention to clear up an otherwise erroneous picture is that Americans are subject to drastic disciplinary action by their own military courts for any misdemeanours committed in this country, particularly for discourtesies towards their British Allies in public places, such as pubs and tobacconist shops.

Mr. Orwell obviously has not met those Americans who have mutual interests and pleasant social relations with their English hosts, who, on the credit side of the balance sheet, cannot be ignored. He says that now is the time for plain speaking "because one does want a good relationship between the two countries." I am very glad he remembered to mention this desire otherwise it should have remained a deep, dark secret to most of his readers. Generalising is most often dangerous—certainly in this instance it appears to be—judging two nations of peoples, their capacities for friendship and tolerance, their eagerness to know each other better, by a few irresponsible, obstreperous individuals under the influence of liquor. It is taking advantage of an unpleasant situation to air one's specious knowledge of a subject that needs a more rational analysis than Mr. Orwell has seen fit to give it in his column. One is prompted to ask of Mr. Orwell what critics, not so many years ago, asked of Robert Briffault—Why get so angry?[5]

Richard McLaughlin

About the American soldiers: "The general consensus of opinion seems to be that the only American soldiers with decent manners are the Negroes." I can quarrel with virtually every phrase in that sentence, and I think I will. To begin on a quibble: "general consensus" is a pleonasm. To work up: how did you arrive at this consensus—have you taken a poll, or have you just exchanged glib generalities with your friends over tea? Really getting angry: don't you think that "only" is going a wee bit too far? There are nine other fingers besides that sore thumb. Being objective: isn't it possible that the American set of "decent manners" may differ somewhat from your set? Our boys, in the main, consider a little more heartiness (than most English people show) "decent manners" . . . it's also a quirk of Americans to consider teasing and wise-cracking as an indication of friendliness—and over here it's perhaps too often construed as rudeness. And for a self-incriminating, somewhat irrelevant finale: I'm afraid I must diagnose the decent manners in many Negroes as a projection of their servility—and as such highly lamentable; much more lamentable to me than the bumptiousness of many of the white soldiers. But that is a whole letter in itself.

There are many American soldiers over here—of all kinds, of all trades, of all religions, of all racial backgrounds, of all political shades of opinion, of all temperaments, of all natures. You probably know that *is* America. And they have many justifiable complaints, of which candy-cadging just barely scratches the surface if at all. Some shoot their mouths off about the British and some I have met are violently the other way. I've seen an American soldier get as enraged as anybody I've ever seen when another American made a slighting remark about the British. That a lot of Americans seem obnoxious, which is incontrovertible, is unfortunate. But merely to blame American stupidity, as it seems to me you have done, without suggesting any remedy is even more unfortunate. And to indict the American people by setting up straw-man surmises about American people is worse. Whatever gave you the idea that Americans think more U.S. soldiers were killed during the last war than British? What makes you think Americans don't know their soldiers are by far the best paid in the world? Why, that's one of their great prides. And where did you get the impression that American movies as shown for U.S. consumption are anti-British? Sure, we have comic English butlers, played by willing English actors; but we have infinitely more caricatures of Americans. If there is cutting of American pictures shown here, I'm sure it's because the English might misconstrue something as being anti-British that is not at all anti-British to Americans.

In fine, I accuse you of being guilty of what you accuse the Americans of—first, of attacking with virtually no provocation or objectivity the fine, old American institution of Mark Twain, and then of indicting Americans indiscriminately with insufficient and poorly thought out evidence—indicting them, in fact, for a state of affairs in which they are more accurately the victims.

Harold T. Bers

I cannot speak for London, but I can assure you that Mr. Orwell's "popular anti-American feeling" does not extend to this military centre [Salisbury], where we have probably seen more American soldiers than any other provincial town.

The American authorities are surely not to be blamed for giving their men decent pay; we should give our fighting men equally good payment, not expect others to descend to our own miserable level. Piccadilly at night may be disgusting, but due to our social system there were whores there long before the Americans landed. Drunkenness too was not exactly unknown.

Let us have plain-speaking by all means, but before we criticise Uncle Sam's representatives in this country, let us be perfectly sure that the sons of John Bull are all behaving like perfect little gentlemen in the towns and villages of Italy.

"Unity"

Mr. Orwell's remarks on two drunk U.S. boys in a cigar store—your issue of December 3rd—in my opinion is plainly dirty. It strikes me as "cakes and coffee" lines (penny a line or better).

If the incident did occur the boys would be from tank towns (small towns on the prairie, consisting of half a dozen houses, a grain elevator, and a water tank used by the railway engines), and they would not have words like "perfidious" and "Albion" in their vocabulary.

Such writings as the paragraphs in question can do no good, but plenty of harm. To me they sound prejudiced; cut 'em out, George—help not hinder.

W. T. Grose

How much a situation such as Orwell, rightly and courageously, mentions can be improved it is hard to say; one knows so little of what the "higher-ups" think about these things, and how much they are in touch. The excessive disparity in pay certainly seems to be a blunder which makes it impossible for British and American troops to mix, and one gets the impression that the boys at the top, who find that the mixing-up at the swagger conferences and smart hotels is a very pleasant affair, are apt to assume that the same goes for the soldier on the street and in the pub, and the ordinary civilian. Of course it does not.

G. H. Thomson

1. Orwell's collection of pamphlets was willed to the British Museum. It is held by the British Library in forty-seven boxes (there is no box 22): call number, 1899 ss 1–21, 23–47 plus an index dated by the Library c. 1950 in box 48; see *3733* for partial contents lists. Orwell wrote to Geoffrey Gorer, 22 January 1946 (see *2870*), saying that he was then cataloguing his collection with the secretary he had taken on, probably Siriol Hugh-Jones.
2. Robin Maugham (Robert Cecil Romer Maugham. 2nd Viscount Maugham. 1916–1981). barrister, prose writer, and dramatist, served in the army in World War II until invalided out in 1944. He succeeded his father as Viscount in 1950.
3. Orwell probably had in mind Major-General J. F. C. Fuller. He wrote a pamphlet, *Back to Sanity*, which was published by the British Union of Fascists in the thirties. He was listed by British Intelligence (MI5) as a prospective Gauleiter if the Germans had successfully occupied Britain (although in 1943 Orwell would not have known that). See *1316, n. 1*.
4. The passages will be found on pages 168–69 and 208–9 of the second, corrected, edition of 1888. Orwell has 'until' for 'till' in the first sentence quotation, and 'bottomless' for 'volcano' in the last sentence.
5. From *Reasons for Anger* (1936) by Robert Stephen Briffault (1876–1948), Briffault was a surgeon (he served in France and Gallipoli in the First World War) and author. His books include *The Decline and Fall of the British Empire*, published in New York 1938, and in German and French respectively in Berlin, 1941, and Paris, 1943.

2386. To Leonard Moore

6 December 1943 Typewritten

Tribune

Dear Mr Moore,
Many thanks for the cheque. You will be glad to hear that I *am* writing a book again at last. While with the BBC I hardly had time to set pen to paper, but in

this job with the Tribune I think I can so organise my time as to get 2 spare days a week for my own work. The thing I am doing is quite short,[1] so if nothing intervenes it should be done in 3 or 4 months.

I think sooner or later a book of reprinted critical articles[2] mightn't be a bad idea, but I don't think it's worth reprinting anything shorter than 2000 words. Books made up of short reviews always seem to me to have a hurried scrappy appearance. We must wait till I have 10 or 20 long articles in pickle. I do think however that as "Inside the Whale" was blitzed out of existence[3] the essay on Dickens that was in it should be reprinted some time. The other two essays in the book have been reprinted in periodicals.

Yours sincerely
E. A. Blair

1. It was to be *Animal Farm.*
2. *Critical Essays* (1946) published in the United States as *Dickens, Dali and Others: Studies in Popular Culture* (1946).
3. *Inside the Whale* (1940). In his 'Notes for My Literary Executor,' 1949 (see *3728*), Orwell states that 'it is very difficult to get hold of, as stocks of the book were destroyed in the blitz.'

2387. To Henry Treece

7 December 1943   Typewritten

Tribune

Dear Treece,

Many thanks for sending the poems. I am only keeping one, "Duet For the Times",[1] but will always be interested to see your stuff even if I can't print all of it.

Yours sincerely,
[Signed] Geo. Orwell
George Orwell

This letter was almost certainly typed by a secretary. It is laid out with Treece's address at Barton-on-Humber (to which Orwell had last written to Treece when he was working at the BBC) and 'George Orwell' is typed in capitals below his signature.

1. Published in *Tribune* on 24 December 1943.

2388. 'Life, People and Books'

Manchester Evening News

Between December 1943 and November 1946, Orwell contributed a fortnightly book feature to the *Manchester Evening News* under the general heading 'Life, People and Books.' The reviews were scheduled to be published on Thursdays on the page facing the editorial. Between 8 February and 7 June 1945 and between 25 April and 7 November 1946, Orwell took breaks from this task; Daniel George and Carl Fallas took over from him for the first and second periods respectively. Julian Symons took over book reviewing from 21 November 1946. The average circulation of the *Manchester Evening News* at this time was 250,000.

The reviews were given titles, and the text was broken up by sub-titles and typographical ornaments. The only surviving typescript—for the rejected review of Harold Laski's *Faith, Reason and Civilisation*, 13 March 1944 (see *2434*)—shows no such features, and they have been silently excised here, as they have been for his reviews published in *The Observer*. Titles are retained if the article is of a general nature rather than a review of a named book, but it should not be assumed that the title is Orwell's.

2389. Review of *Arrival and Departure* by Arthur Koestler;
Jordan's Tunis Diary by Philip Jordan

Manchester Evening News, 9 December 1943

For the past dozen years we in England have received our political education chiefly from foreigners. One of the greatest advantages of the dictators in the period of "cold war" was that the mass of English people could not grasp what totalitarianism was like.

The savage warfare of the European political parties, with their coloured shirts and their bewildering names, was dismissed as "not our business"; few people realised that our indifference to the fate of Spaniards, Czechs, Austrians, and what-not meant bombs on ourselves in a few years' time.

But luckily there were voices, mostly the voices of anti-Fascist refugees, crying in the wilderness, and none, except perhaps Silone, cried more effectively than Arthur Koestler. *Spanish Testament* and *Darkness at Noon* did about as much as mere books could do to spread an understanding of revolution and counter-revolution. In *Arrival and Departure* (like *Darkness at Noon* it is written in the form of a novel) Mr. Koestler carries the story further and raises the difficult problem of the revolutionary's own motives and the even more complex question of what this war is about.

It is not a very good novel, because its characters are suggested by its theme instead of the other way about, but as a sort of fable of our own time it is both interesting and valuable. A young man has just escaped from a Nazi-occupied country, which might be Hungary, and made his way to a neutral country, which is evidently Portugal. He is an ex-Communist, he has suffered unspeakable tortures in Fascist gaols, and he is pining to fight for Britain, at that time the only country resisting the Nazis. But he is forced almost at once to make two discoveries.

The first is that the British are not fighting the same war as he is. They are not interested in the struggle against Fascism as such, and they have so little use for himself that it is months before they will even bother to provide him with a passage to England. Moreover, their propaganda is elderly and inept, they have no world picture to set against the Nazi new order. He tears his hair over the follies of the British Council and is jeered at by a young Nazi intellectual to whose arguments he can find no real answer. His second discovery is that his own motives are doubtful in the extreme. He falls in with a psycho-analyst who demonstrates to him that his quarrel with society is a purely personal one, resulting from a trauma in childhood. In struggling against Capitalism he is really struggling against his own father. As the buried childhood memories are skilfully dug out of him he is forced to recognise that this is true. He is simply a neurotic. Then are all revolutionaries no more than neurotics? The young Nazi contributes the penetrating remark that one of the strongest arguments against all the Left-wing movements is the ugliness of their women.

By this time the notion of going to England to fight against Fascism has lost its romantic colours. The young man applies for a passage to still-neutral America. He gets his passage and is actually boarding the ship when something makes him turn back; it is hard to say what—perhaps it is merely the unappetising appearance of the other refugees who are saving their skins in the same way. So he goes to England after all and is promptly sent back to his own country to do sabotage. As he floats towards the earth attached to a parachute he is still uncertain of his own motives. Still, he has chosen England and probable death, and not America and safety, even though in America there is a girl waiting for him.

The moral, if any, is that the struggle is bigger than the individual. One's cause does not cease to be right because one supports it for the wrong reasons. As a novel this book does not succeed. The incidents are altogether too slick, the characters are too "typical," too much all of a piece. But as an allegory it does succeed. It is a story of temptation in almost the traditional form. The young Nazi is the World, the girl in America is the Flesh, the psycho-analyst is the Devil. All that has dropped out of the picture is the Kingdom of Heaven; the martyrdom is now without reward, but it still happens.

The book is also notable for what must be one of the most shocking descriptions of Nazi terrorism that have ever been written. However little one likes horror stories, it is right that such things should be recorded. They really happen, with only a slight change of circumstances they would happen here, and it is lucky for us that a few of the victims have escaped to give us warning.

This hurriedly compiled book (it consists of Mr. Jordan's diaries from June, 1942 to May 1943, supplemented by some of the articles he wrote for the "News Chronicle" at the time) is chiefly interesting because of the contrast between what happened and what Mr. Jordan was allowed to say. All the way through it run two complaints; a minor one, that the Americans are given the credit for everything that the British do, and a major one, that the political side of the North African campaign is being horribly mishandled. Needless to say, none of Mr. Jordan's remarks got through the censorship: indeed, he soon had to stop commenting upon the political situation because he found that his denunciations of the local authorities were so altered as to transform them into praise.

As for the troops, Mr. Jordan cannot praise them highly enough. He says again and again that for good temper, adaptability, and discipline, as well as fighting qualities, British troops are the best in the world. Nor does he find much to criticise in the military conduct of the North African expedition. The first landings were a gamble, but a justifiable gamble, and when the attempt to capture Tunis in the first rush failed, the delay in finishing with Rommel was inevitable.

What infuriates him is the policy of not only doing a deal with Darlan—this, he thinks, may have been necessary as a temporary measure—but keeping the Vichy administration in being, almost unchanged. Under the benevolent eye of Mr. Murphy,[1] frankly pro-Fascist officials kept their jobs, Gaullists continued to be cold-shouldered or persecuted, the Spanish and other anti-Fascist refugees stayed in the concentration camps, and even the anti-Jewish laws made under the Pétain administration were not at first revoked.

It is the greatest pity that these facts could not have been more widely known in Britain and the U.S.A. at the time. Even now our knowledge of what is going on in North Africa is sketchy, and Mr. Jordan helps to fill up a number of gaps.

He saw much of the front-line fighting, he was at the Casablanca conference, and he was in Tunis the day after it fell. It is just possible that this diary has been subsequently touched up in places. As soon as he hears of Darlan's appointment Mr. Jordan remarks that it would be a good thing if some "accident" happened to Darlan when he has served his turn—a remarkable piece of foresight if it was really contemporaneous. However, though the "accident" happened[2] the Darlan policy continued, and Mr. Jordan has done a valuable piece of work in bringing the fact home.

[Fee: £8.8s; 27.11 and 8.12.43 jointly][3]

1. Robert Daniel Murphy (1894–1978), diplomat and author, special representative for the United States in North Africa. Jordan was not alone in expressing unease about the political situation there. King George VI wrote to Churchill on 22 February 1943 that he was not 'at all happy' about the position. He knew the British had to leave the political side of Operation Torch to the Americans, but he asked if there was not something that could be done to strengthen the hands of Harold Macmillan, Minister Resident at Allied Forces Headquarters, and General Harold Alexander, Commander-in-Chief, British and Allied Forces, Western Desert, in order 'to make the two French sides come together.' Churchill (who was ill) replied on the same day to say that although there was much that he would have had done differently, he did not feel seriously disturbed. 'I am sure that Murphy's aim is to uphold Giraud and to procure a quiet, tranquil government for the sixteen million people living in French North Africa. In this way alone would he gain any credit.' Later in the letter he remarked: 'The irruption of de Gaulle or his agents into this field, especially if forcibly introduced by us, would cause nothing but trouble. It is entirely his fault that a good arrangement was not made between the two French factions' (*The Second World War*, II, 656–57; U.S.: *The Hinge of Fate*, 732–33). Giraud was forced to resign his position as Joint-President of the National Liberation Council in November 1943, King George seemed to have a better sense of the position than Churchill.
2. Admiral Jean François Darlan (1881–1942), a leading member of the Vichy government and Vichy's Commander-in-Chief in Africa, sided with the Allies when they invaded North Africa. The Allies, in return, made him High Commissioner for North and West Africa. On

24 December 1942, he was assassinated in Algiers, by Bonnier de la Chappelle, who was executed two days later. The widespread disgust felt at the Allies treating with Darlan was well summed up by *The Spectator*, which asked whether Quislings everywhere could expect to receive 'most-favoured-traitor treatment' (quoted by Sagittarius (Olga Katzin), in *Quiver's Choice*, 1945, 206). For Orwell's review of *Quiver's Choice*, *Tribune*, 7 September 1945, see 2744.

3. This was written as two separate items (as the opening of the second review suggests); see Orwell's Payments Book for 27 November and 8 December 1943, *2831*.

2390. To Philip Rahv

9 December 1943   Typewritten

10a Mortimer Crescent   London   NW 6

Dear Rahv,

Many thanks for your letter. You observe the date of the above. Your letter dated October 15 only reached me this morning. I don't know what to do about these posts. Some people actually say it is now quicker to send a letter by sea. Meanwhile the idea of my doing an extra bit for the December issue is finished. If you are going to become a quarterly and bring out the first number in December, I assume the next number will be in March 1944. That means any copy I send you should reach you by the end of February? So I'll post it about mid-January. I hope this is right, and if this letter gets to you in reasonable time you might be able to confirm this between now and then. It seems impossible to keep anywhere near up to date with these London Letters while the posts are as they are. However, so long as they're dated they have a certain interest as showing what was the state of opinion at the time when written.

You can certainly reprint the *Horizon* article.[1] Connolly won't object, but I'll let him know you are doing it. I don't know how things stand about payment. Better send it to Connolly and then if it is rightfully mine he'll send it on to me.

Dwight Macdonald has written telling me he is starting another review and asking me to contribute.[2] I don't know to what extent he will be in competition with PR, but I am writing telling him that I might do something "cultural" for him but can't do anything "political" while I have this arrangement with PR.

I have left the BBC after two wasted years in it and have become literary editor of the Tribune, a leftwing weekly which you may have seen. It leaves me a little spare time, which the BBC didn't, so I have got another book[3] under weigh which I hope to finish in a few months if nothing intervenes. I'll try to send PR a copy of the book of broadcasts which the Indian Section of the BBC recently published.[4] It might possibly be worth reviewing. In any case it has some interest as a specimen of British propaganda (rather a favourable specimen, however, as we in the Indian Section were regarded as very unimportant and therefore left a fairly free hand).

All the best.

Yours
Geo. Orwell

1. Orwell's review of *Beggar My Neighbour* by Lionel Fielden, *Horizon*, September 1943; see 2257.
2. See headnote to Orwell's letter to Macdonald, 11 December 1943, 2392.
3. *Animal Farm*.
4. *Talking to India*.

2391. 'As I Please,' 2

Tribune, 10 December 1943

The recently-issued special supplement to the *New Republic* entitled *The Negro: His Future in America* is worth a reading, but it raises more problems than it discusses. The facts it reveals about the present treatment of Negroes in the U.S.A. are bad enough in all conscience. In spite of the quite obvious necessities of war, Negroes are still pushed out of skilled jobs, segregated and insulted in the Army, assaulted by white policemen and discriminated against by white magistrates. In a number of the Southern States they are disenfranchised by means of a poll tax. On the other hand, those of them who have votes are so fed up with the present Administration that they are beginning to swing towards the Republican Party—that is, in effect, to give their support to Big Business. But all this is merely a single facet of the world-wide problem of colour. And what the authors of this supplement fail to point out is that that problem simply cannot be solved inside the capitalist system.

One of the big unmentionable facts of politics is the differential standard of living. An English working-man spends on cigarettes about the same sum as an Indian peasant has for his entire income. It is not easy for Socialists to admit this, or at any rate to emphasise it. If you want people to rebel against the existing system, you have got to show them that they are badly off, and it is doubtful tactics to start by telling an Englishman on the dole that in the eyes of an Indian coolie he would be next door to a millionaire. Almost complete silence reigns on this subject, at any rate at the European end, and it contributes to the lack of solidarity between white and coloured workers. Almost without knowing it—and perhaps without wanting to know it—the white worker exploits the coloured worker, and in revenge the coloured worker can be and is used against the white. Franco's Moors in Spain were only doing more dramatically the same thing as is done by half-starved Indians in Bombay mills or Japanese factory-girls sold into semi-slavery by their parents. As things are, Asia and Africa are simply a bottomless reserve of scab labour.

The coloured worker cannot be blamed for feeling no solidarity with his white comrades. The gap between their standard of living and his own is so vast that it makes any differences which may exist in the West seem negligible. In Asiatic eyes the European class struggle is a sham. The Socialist movement has never gained a real foothold in Asia or Africa, or even among the American Negroes: it is everywhere side-tracked by nationalism and race-hatred . Hence the spectacle of thoughtful Negroes getting ready to vote

23

for Dewey,[1] and Indian Congressmen preferring their own capitalists to the British Labour Party. There is no solution until the living-standards of the thousand million people who are not "white" can be forced up to the same level as our own. But as this might mean temporarily *lowering* our own standards the subject is systematically avoided by Left and Right alike.

Is there anything that one can do about this, as an individual? One can at least remember that the colour problem exists. And there is one small precaution which is not much trouble, and which can perhaps do a little to mitigate the horrors of the colour war. That is to avoid using insulting nicknames. It is an astonishing thing that few journalists, even in the Left wing press, bother to find out which names are and which are not resented by members of other races. The word "native," which makes any Asiatic boil with rage, and which has been dropped even by British officials in India these ten years past, is flung about all over the place. "Negro" is habitually printed with a small n, a thing most Negroes resent. One's information about these matters needs to be kept up to date. I have just been carefully going through the proofs of a reprinted book of mine,[2] cutting out the word "Chinaman" wherever it occurred and substituting "Chinese." The book was written less than a dozen years ago, but in the intervening time "Chinaman" has become a deadly insult. Even "Mahomedan" is now beginning to be resented: one should say "Moslem." These things are childish, but then nationalism is childish. And after all we ourselves do not actually like being called "Limeys" or "Britishers."

1. Thomas Edmund Dewey (1902–1971), Governor of New York for three successive terms (1942–54), was Republican Party's Presidential candidate in 1944 and 1948; he lost both elections. He might well have attracted votes 'of thoughtful Negroes' because, as special prosecutor and district attorney, he won seventy-two of seventy-three prosecutions of racketeers involved in organised crime in New York.
2. *Burmese Days*, Penguin Books, published in May 1944. Orwell was alerted to the provision of an initial capital for 'Negro' by Cedric Dover during the proofing of *Talking to India*. Orwell had returned the proofs of *Burmese Days* to Penguin Books on 21 November 1943; see Payments Book, *2831, n. 3*.

2392. To Dwight Macdonald

11 December 1943   Typewritten

Macdonald wrote to Orwell on 22 October 1943 telling him he had resigned from *Partisan Review*. His letter of resignation, with, he said, 'a rather hot reply from my ex-colleagues,' appeared in the July–August issue. He was starting a new journal and asked Orwell whether he had done any writing lately on 'popular culture' (Macdonald gives it quotations marks). He suggested something on British advertising since the war and also asked whether Orwell had ever written anything on the Spanish civil war.

10a Mortimer Crescent   London   NW 6

Dear Macdonald,

Many thanks for your letter dated October 22nd (only just arrived!) I hope your new magazine will be a success. I'd like to write something for it, but I think I can't write anything of a strictly political nature while I have my arrangement with PR. Apart from anything else, my periodical London Letters so to speak use up anything I have to say about the current situation in this country. That article about the Spanish war° that I spoke to you of I did finally write, but I sent it to "New Road 1943", edited by Alex Comfort and Co, who somewhat to my annoyance printed it in a mutilated form.[1] Recently I did a short thing for a French magazine on the English detective story,[2] and it struck me that something interesting could be done on the change in ethical outlook in the crime story during the last 50 years or so. This subject is so vast that one can only attack corners of it, but how would you like an article on Raffles ("The Amateur Cracksman"), comparing him with some modern crime story, eg. something from one of the pulp mags? (I could only do this in a rather sketchy way as one can't buy the pulp mags in this country since the war, but I was a reader of them for years and know their moral atmosphere). Raffles, about contemporary with Sherlock Holmes, was a great favourite in England and I fancy in the USA too, as I remember he is mentioned in the O. Henry stories. And into the essay I could bring some mention of Edgar Wallace, who in my opinion is a significant writer and marks a sort of moral turning-point. Tell me whether you would like this, and if so, how many words about. I dare say I could turn the stuff in fairly soon after hearing from you, but how soon it would get to you I can't say.[3] You see what the posts are like nowadays.

I have left the BBC after wasting 2 years in it, and have become editor[4] of the Tribune, a leftwing weekly I dare say you know. The job leaves me a little spare time, so I am at last getting on with a book again, not having written one for nearly 3 years.

Yours sincerely
Geo. Orwell

1. 'Looking Back on the Spanish War'; the headnote lists the cuts. See *1421*.
2. 'Grandeur et décadence du roman policier anglais,' *Fontaine*, 17 November 1943 (*2357*).
3. Orwell wrote 'Raffles and Miss Blandish,' which appeared in *Horizon*, October 1944; it was reprinted in Macdonald's new journal, *Politics*, the following month with a slightly extended title: 'The Ethics of the Detective story: from Raffles to Miss Blandish.'
4. Literary editor.

2393. 'As I Please,' 3

Tribune, 17 December 1943

So many letters have arrived, attacking me for my remarks about the American soldiers in this country,[1] that I must return to the subject.

Contrary to what most of my correspondents seem to think, I was not trying to make trouble between ourselves and our Allies, nor am I consumed by hatred for the United States. I am much less anti-American than most English people are at this moment. What I say, and what I repeat, is that our policy of not criticising our Allies, and not answering their criticism of us (we don't answer the Russians either, nor even the Chinese) is a mistake, and is likely to defeat its own object in the long run. And so far as Anglo-American relations go, there are three difficulties which badly need dragging into the open and which simply don't get mentioned in the British press.

1. *Anti-American feeling in Britain.*—Before the war, anti-American feeling was a middle-class, and perhaps upper-class thing, resulting from imperialist and business jealousy and disguising itself as dislike of the American accent, etc. The working class, so far from being anti-American, were becoming rapidly Americanised in speech by means of the films and jazz songs. Now, in spite of what my correspondents may say, I can hear few good words for the Americans anywhere. This obviously results from the arrival of the American troops. It has been made worse by the fact that, for various reasons, the Mediterranean campaign had to be represented as an American show while most of the casualties had to be suffered by the British. (See Philip Jordan's remarks in his *Tunis Diary*.[2]) I am not saying that popular English prejudices are always justified: I am saying that they exist.

2. *Anti-British feeling in America.*—We ought to face the fact that large numbers of Americans are brought up to dislike and despise us. There is a large section of the press whose main accent is anti-British, and countless other papers which attack Britain in a more sporadic way. In addition there is a systematic guying of what are supposed to be British habits and manners on the stage and in comic strips and cheap magazines. The typical Englishman is represented as a chinless ass with a title, a monocle and a habit of saying "Haw, haw." This legend is believed in by relatively responsible Americans, for example by the veteran novelist Theodore Dreiser, who remarks in a public speech that "the British are horse-riding aristocratic snobs." (Forty-six million horse-riding snobs!) It is a commonplace on the American stage that the Englishman is almost never allowed to play a favourable role, any more than the Negro is allowed to appear as anything more than a comic. Yet right up to Pearl Harbour the American movie industry had an agreement with the Japanese Government never to present a Japanese character in an unfavourable light!

I am not blaming the Americans for all this. The anti-British press has powerful business forces behind it, besides ancient quarrels in many of which Britain was in the wrong. As for popular anti-British feeling, we partly bring it on ourselves by exporting our worst specimens. But what I do want to emphasise is that these anti-British currents in the U.S.A. are very strong, and that the British press has consistently failed to draw attention to them. There has never been in England anything that one could call an anti-American press: and since the war there has been a steady refusal to answer criticism, and a careful censorship of the radio to cut out anything that the Americans might object to. As a result, many English people don't realise how they are regarded, and get a shock when they find out.

3. *Soldiers' Pay.*—It is now nearly two years since the first American troops reached this country, and I rarely see American and British soldiers together. Quite obviously the major cause of this is the difference of pay. You can't have really close and friendly relations with somebody whose income is five times your own. Financially, the whole American army is in the middle class. In the field this might not matter, but in the training period it makes it almost impossible for British and American soldiers to fraternise. If you don't want friendly relations between the British Army and the American Army, well and good. But if you do, you must either pay the British soldier ten shillings a day or make the American soldier bank the surplus of his pay in America. I don't profess to know which of these alternatives is the right one.

One way of feeling infallible is not to keep a diary. Looking back through the diary I kept in 1940 and 1941 I find that I was usually wrong when it was possible to be wrong. Yet I was not so wrong as the Military Experts. Experts of various schools were telling us in 1939 that the Maginot Line was impregnable, and that the Russo-German pact had put an end to Hitler's eastward expansion; in early 1940 they were telling us that the days of tank warfare were over; in mid 1940 they were telling us that the Germans would invade Britain forthwith; in mid 1941 that the Red Army would fold up in six weeks; in December, 1941, that Japan would collapse after 90 days; in July, 1942, that Egypt was lost—and so on, more or less indefinitely.

Where now are the men who told us those things? Still on the job, drawing fat salaries. Instead of the unsinkable battleship we have the unsinkable Military Expert.

To be politically happy these days you need to have no more memory than an animal. The people who demonstrated most loudly against Mosley's release were the leaders of the defunct People's Convention, which at the time when Mosley was interned was running a "stop the war" campaign barely distinguishable from Mosley's own. And I myself know of a ladies' knitting circle which was formed to knit comforts for the Finns, and which two years later—with no sense of incongruity—finished off various garments that had been left on its hands and sent them to the Russians. Early in 1942 a friend of mine bought some fried fish done up in a piece of newspaper of 1940. On one side was an article proving that the Red Army was no good, and on the other a write-up of that gallant sailor and well-known Anglophile, Admiral Darlan. But my favourite in this line is the *Daily Express* leader which began, a few days after the U.S.S.R. entered the war: "This paper has always worked for good relations between Britain and Soviet Russia."

Books have gone up in price like everything else, but the other day I picked up a copy of Lemprière's *Classical Dictionary*,[3] the *Who's Who* of the ancients, for only sixpence. Opening it at random, I came upon the biography of Laïs, the famous courtesan, daughter of the mistress of Alcibiades:

"She first began to sell her favours at Corinth for 10,000 drachmas, and the immense number of princes, noblemen, philosophers, orators and plebeians who courted her, bear witness to her personal charms . . . Demosthenes visited Corinth for the sake of Laïs, but informed by the courtesan that admittance to her bed was to be bought at the enormous sum of about £200 English money, the orator departed, and observed that he would not buy repentance at so dear a price . . . She ridiculed the austerity of philosophers, and the weakness of those who pretend to have gained a superiority over their passions, by observing that sages and philosophers were not above the rest of mankind, for she found them at her door as often as the rest of the Athenians."

There is more in the same vain. However, it ends on a good moral, for "the other women, jealous of her charms, assassinated her in the temple of Venus about 340 B.C." That was 2,283 years ago. I wonder how many of the present denizens of *Who's Who* will seem worth reading about in A.D. 4226?

In *Tribune*, 31 December 1943, D. N. Pritt, Q.C. (1887–1972), who had been expelled from the Labour Party in 1940 as a result of policy disagreements, but who remained an M.P. as an Independent Socialist until 1950, took up Orwell's comment on the leaders of the People's Convention. This was a Communist-inspired body ostensibly set up to fight for public rights, higher wages, better air-raid precautions, and friendship with the USSR. (Pritt was to become president or joint president of societies for cultural relations and friendship with the USSR, Romania, and Bulgaria and was awarded the Lenin Peace Prize in 1954.) According to some observers, the Convention's purpose was to agitate against the war effort. In July 1941, after the Soviet Union entered the war opposed to Hitler, the Convention immediately demanded a second front.

I read in your issue of the 17th the story that:

"The people who demonstrated most loudly against Mosley's release were the leaders of the defunct People's Convention, which at the time when Mosley was interned was running a 'stop the war' campaign barely distinguishable from Mosley's own."

Let me correct some of the inaccuracies in this. Firstly, the People's Convention never ran a "stop the war" campaign, nor any campaign which could possibly be so described. The suggestion that it did so has occasionally been put forward by some of the worst elements of our various political groupings, but on every occasion, when challenged, they have failed to produce any evidence, because there is none.

Secondly, the People's Convention was not running any campaign of any kind when Mosley was interned, because it did not then exist. Mosely was interned in May, 1940, and the People's Convention was not born until two months later.

D. N. Pritt

The "People's Convention" may not have come formally into being till after Mosley's internment, but the people responsible for it had been running a "Stop the War" campaign since the autumn of 1939. See, for instance, Palme Dutt's pamphlet, "Why This War?", many similar publications, and Mr. D. N. Pritt's own book, "Choose Your Future," which purports to review the European situation without using the word "Nazi." As to "failing to produce any evidence" of defeatist activities by the People's Convention, a whole book, "The Betrayal of the Left," was published by Gollancz, exposing the anti-war campaign of the People's Convention, and was not challenged on any point of fact by the latter's supporters. In any case, the promptitude with which the People's Convention was buried when the U.S.S.R. came into the war[4] is sufficient to stamp it for what it was—an activity objectively useful to the Axis. Some of us have longer memories than Mr. Pritt seems to imagine.

George Orwell

1. See 'As I Please,' 1, 3 December 1943, *2385*.
2. Reviewed by Orwell, 9 December 1943; *see 2389*. Philip Jordan was a well-known war-time correspondent for the *News Chronicle*.
3. John Lemprière (d. 1824) produced his *Bibliotheca Classica* in 1788. It was revised many times and became known by the title given it here.
4. That is, *against* Hitler, not as his ally as in September 1939.

2394. Review of *Collected Poems of W. H. Davies*

The Observer, 19 December 1943

Seen in bulk, W. H. Davies's work gives a somewhat different impression from that given by the handful of poems that have found their way into so many anthologies. So far as manner goes, indeed, almost any of his poems is representative. His great fault is lack of variation—a quality that one might, perhaps, call wateriness, since it gives one the feeling of drinking draught after draught of spring water, wonderfully pure and refreshing, but somehow turning one's mind in the direction of whisky after the first pint or two. On the other hand—and it is here that the anthologies have probably misrepresented him—his subject-matter is remarkably variegated. Not only did his years of vagabondage in common lodging-houses supply a large part of It, but he shows a distinct tinge of morbidity. Behind the lambs and the wildflowers there is an almost Baudelairean background of harlots, drunkenness, and corpses, and in poems like "The Rat" and "Down Underground" he does not flinch from the most horrible subjects that any writer could deal with. Yet his manner never varies, or barely varies: the clouds in the April sky and the dead girl rotting in her grave are spoken of in almost the same tone of voice.

One thing that emerges from this collection of over six hundred poems is the perfection of Davies's taste. If he lacks vitality, at least he has a sort of natural good breeding. None of his poems is perfect, there is not one in which one cannot find an unnecessary word or an annoyingly bad rhyme, and yet nothing is vulgar either. More than this, however empty he may seem, there is nothing that one can put one's finger on and say that it is silly. Like Blake, he appears to avoid silliness by not being afraid of it; and perhaps (like Blake again) this appearance is partly deceptive, and he is less artless than he seems. Davies's best qualities, as well as some of his faults, can be seen in the justly celebrated poem, "The Two Children":—

"Ah, little boy! I see
      You have a wooden spade.
Into this sand you dig
      So deep—for what?" I said.
"There's more rich gold," said he,
      "Down under where I stand,
Than twenty elephants
      Could move across the land."

"Ah, little girl with wool!—
      What are you making now?"
"Some stockings for a bird,
      To keep his legs from snow."
And there those children are,
      So happy, small, and proud:
The boy that digs his grave.
The girl that knits her shroud.

How near this comes to folly and sentimentality! But the point is that it doesn't get there. Whether Davies is being deliberately cunning it would be hard to say. The almost namby-pamby language in which the poem starts may or may not be intended to give force to the two magnificent lines at the end. But at any rate, whether it is consciously or not, Davies always does avoid the silliness and vulgarity which so often seem to be in wait for him.

On the blurb of this book Sir John Squire is quoted as preferring Davies to "the fashionable poets of to-day" (at the time of writing this probably meant Mr. T. S. Eliot) and Mr. Basil de Selincourt as seeing in Davies an upholder of "our English tradition." Davies has had much praise of this kind, and has been used as a stick to beat many another contemporary, basically because he does not force anyone to think. Not to be made to think—and therefore, if possible, to prevent literature from developing—is often the aim of the academic critic. But Davies is not, as Sir John Squire and Mr. de Selincourt seem to claim, the restorer of an ancient tradition. Indeed, if there is one thing that he is not, it is traditional. He belongs in no line of descent; he does not derive from his immediate predecessors, and he has had no influence on his successors. According to his own account, he was brought up by a pious grandmother whose only books were "Paradise Lost," "The Pilgrim's Progress," Young's "Night Thoughts," and (presumably) the Bible. He read Shelley, Marlowe, and Shakespeare on the sly, as another boy might read Sexton Blake. At the age of thirty-four, when still living in a common lodging-house and never having seen even the fringes of the literary world, he began to write poems. He gives the impression of having imitated chiefly the poets of the seventeenth century; there are frequent echoes, though probably no plagiarisms. Having completed his first batch of poems. Davies attempted to sell them from door to door at threepence a copy—needless to say, without success.

Sir Osbert Sitwell contributes a pleasant and informative introduction. It is interesting to learn that when Davies was a child his grandmother once warned him, between blows, that if he did not turn over a new leaf he would end by being no better than his cousin who had "brought disgrace upon the family." This cousin was Sir Henry Irving.[1] These poems are well edited and excellent value for the money. With its agreeable cover, good print, and—by current standards—very good paper, the book would make an attractive as well as a cheap Christmas present.

[Fee: £7.7s; 13.12.43]

1. Sir Henry Irving (John Henry Brodribb, 1838–1905), the outstanding Shakespearean actor of his time, was famed for his spectacular productions, especially at the Lyceum Theatre, London, which he managed for twenty-four years. He was the first actor to be knighted (1895).

2395. Review of *Interglossa* by Lancelot Hogben, *Mr. Roosevelt* by Compton Mackenzie

Manchester Evening News, 23 December 1943

Professor Hogben gives his interesting little book the sub-title: "A draft of an auxiliary language for a democratic world order, being an attempt to apply semantic* principles to language design," and the word "draft" needs emphasising.

Interglossa is a new language—Professor Hogben's own invention. But he is not trying to force it ready-made upon the world. He presents it merely as "the agenda for discussion"—a basis upon which a satisfactory international language might be constructed when the war is over.

He thinks, perhaps rightly, that if a universal second language is finally adopted by the whole world it will have to be worked out by an international team of experts.

Hitherto what has usually happened is that someone invents a new language, someone else says "I can improve on that," and so the process continued until the manufactured languages, if they were used, would create a worse babel than the natural ones.

There have, it seems, been over 300 artificial languages already, and five or six of them (apart from Basic English) are still more or less in the field.

Interglossa is a purely "isolating" language like Chinese. Its words have no inflexions whatever, meaning is indicated by sentence-order and by a small number of "empty" words that show the tense, etcetera.

The advantages of this are, of course, great. A language without inflexions is easier to learn, especially for the hundreds of millions of Asiatics who speak uninflected languages.[1]

It is also easily taught to beginners by means of pictures. A few samples are given in this book. Thus, a picture of a black house with two red men inside it

---

* Semantics is a branch of philosophy concerned with the study of the changes in the meaning of words in the way of specialisation or generalisation [Orwell's note].

is labelled "bi erythro homini in melano domi," while a picture of a red house with two black trees in front of it is labelled "bi melano dendra antero erythro domi." One could hardly use this method with a European language, except perhaps English, which is itself very little inflected.

The vocabulary of Interglossa is based on Latin and Greek—Greek perhaps predominates slightly. The reason is that as far as possible Professor Hogben has made use of words which are internationally current already, mostly scientific and technical words.

Almost the whole educated world already knows the meaning of such roots as photo, phono, ptero, graph, geo, micro, and the like, and the words in Interglossa are based on them whenever they are available. Any educated European, and probably most educated Indians or Japanese, would know at a glance that the Interglossa word "hydro" had something to do with water.

The vocabulary has been worked out with an eye chiefly to word-economy. According to Professor Hogben, it is possible to make do with 750 words, a smaller minimum than is needed for Basic.[2]

Anyone with a good memory could probably master this in a few weeks, and anyone who has learned Latin and Greek could guess his way through many Interglossa sentences at sight.

Now, having set forth some of the advantages of Interglossa, why is it that I don't believe in a future for this language, as I don't, of course.

To begin with, it is difficult to believe in any artificial language, even if one could be agreed upon, making headway against tongues already spoken by hundreds of millions of people.

Professor Hogben's chief foe, of course, is Basic. Basic may be slightly harder to learn than Interglossa, but the only real argument against it is the suspicion, which is bound to arise in many people's minds, that it is an instrument of Anglo-American imperialism.

To offset this there is the enormous advantage of being put in touch, straight off, with two or three hundred million people. Moreover, anyone who chooses to proceed from Basic to standard English has access to a world-wide press and the literature of hundreds of years.

So also with several of the great natural languages. An artificial language has none of these advantages. Years of translation work are needed before it can possess even a technical literature of its own.

My other criticism, perhaps, ought not to be made without learning Interglossa first, but I will take a chance and make it. It is, that I doubt very much whether Professor Hogben is the right person to make up languages, except perhaps for strictly technical purposes.

He writes English so as to suggest that he has no more feeling for language than a deaf person has for music. Two specimen sentences from his introduction will be enough:

"The conclusion is dubious if we give due weight to what has been a powerful motive militating against Peano's radical attitude to superfluous flexions of the type characteristic of Aryan languages."
And again:
"We cannot play ducks and drakes with a native battery of idiom which

prescribes such egregious collocations of vocables as the Basic 'put up with' for 'tolerate' or 'put at a loss' for 'bewilder.'"

People who do that kind of thing to their own language are not likely to be trustworthy creators of new ones.

International languages are not, of course, devised for literary purposes, but if they are to be used as a weapon against the nationalism which Professor Hogben rightly fears they cannot be a merely technical and scientific jargon either. They must be capable of expressing fairly subtle meanings with the maximum of clarity, but in that case they must be devised by someone who really cares about clarity and would, for instance, bother to find out the meaning of the word "egregious."

Still, this is a stimulating book, even an important book. Even if Interglossa is never adopted or even used as the basis for some other language, anything which draws attention to the urgent need for some universal medium of communication, and to the sinister way in which several living languages are being used for imperialist purposes, is to be welcomed.

An 8,000-word English-Interglossa dictionary will follow this preliminary volume.[3]

President Roosevelt, who is even now not too well-known to the British public, deserved a better book than Mr. Mackenzie has given us. It appears to have been written in a hurry, and in spite of much piling up of detail at the beginning (the fact is that Mr. Roosevelt's early years, like those of most well-connected people, were very uneventful), it would not give the average British reader any intelligible picture of the American political scene.

American politics are mysterious from the point of view of an outsider, and Mr. Mackenzie does not do much to lighten the mystery. He is also too much inclined to hero-worship. President Roosevelt is a great man and a good friend to Britain, but just for that reason the British people, who have so much to gain from his continuance in power, deserve a more critical picture of him.

You would only with difficulty gather from this book that Mr. Roosevelt has any of the faults of an ordinary mortal, and you might not even gather that powerful and sinister forces are piling up against him. The best thing in the book is the illustrations, largely photographs, which are interesting, and are perhaps numerous enough to justify the price.

[Fee: £8.8.0; 20.12.43]

On 5 January 1944, the *Manchester Evening News* published the following letter from E. R.:

I read with interest George Orwell's review of Professor Hogben's book, "Interglossa," which deals with the newly invented international language of that name, and I welcomed the article as drawing the attention of readers once again to the all important question of an international tongue.

I would like, however, to point out what appeared to me to be a misstatement. Orwell said, "Professor Hogben's chief foe, of course, is Basic." Rather would I suggest that the chief foe is Esperanto.

I have never met anyone who could speak Basic, and believe there are very few such people. Neither has Basic ever been tried at an international conference.

Esperanto, though, can be found all over the world. Large international Esperanto congresses have been held with complete success. This language has stood the test of over 50 years' usage by people of all nations, and before the war it could be heard over as many as 48 European broadcasting stations.

1. Reviews and articles in the *Manchester Evening News* and the *Evening Standard* sometimes suffer from excessive fragmentation. There can be many more short paragraphs than is customary in Orwell's writing. Presumably the copy editors thought their readers could manage only a small gobbet of information at one time. Compare the even shorter paragraphs of Orwell's Paris articles of 1928–29 (see *81*) and see the headnote to BBC News Review 30 (*1267*). No attempt has been made to reparagraph these articles; to do so would introduce even more uncertainties.
2. The original here and thrice later lacks an initial capital for 'Basic'; this is more probably a copy-editor's change rather than Orwell's, for he was familiar with Hogben's work.
3. See 'As I Please,' 9, 28 January 1944, *2412*.

2396. 'As I Please,' 4

Tribune, 24 December 1943

Reading Michael Roberts's book on T. E. Hulme, I was reminded once again of the dangerous mistake that the Socialist movement makes in ignoring what one might call the neo-reactionary school of writers. There is a considerable number of these writers: they are intellectually distinguished, they are influential in a quiet way, and their criticisms of the Left are much more damaging than anything that issues from the Individualist League or Conservative Central Office.

T. E. Hulme was killed in the last war and left little completed work behind him, but the ideas that he had roughly formulated had great influence, especially on the numerous writers who were grouped round the *Criterion* in the 'twenties and 'thirties. Wyndham Lewis, T. S. Eliot, Aldous Huxley, Malcolm Muggeridge, Evelyn Waugh and Graham Greene all probably owe something to him. But more important than the extent of his personal influence is the general intellectual movement to which he belonged, a movement which could fairly be described as the revival of pessimism. Perhaps its best-known living exponent is Marshal Pétain. But the new pessimism has queerer affiliations than that. It links up not only with Catholicism, Conservatism and Fascism, but also with pacifism (California brand especially) and Anarchism. It is worth noting that T. E. Hulme, the upper middle class English Conservative in a bowler hat, was an admirer and to some extent a follower of the Anarcho-Syndicalist, Georges Sorel.[1]

The thing that is common to all these people, whether it is Petain mournfully preaching "the discipline of defeat," or Sorel denouncing liberalism, or Berdyaev shaking his head over the Russian Revolution, or "Beachcomber" delivering side-kicks at Beveridge in the *Express*, or Huxley advocating non-resistance behind the guns of the American Fleet, is their refusal to believe that human society can be fundamentally improved. Man is non-perfectible, merely political changes can effect nothing, progress is an illusion. The connection between this belief and political reaction is, of course, obvious. Other-worldliness is the best alibi a rich man can have. "Men cannot be made better by act of Parliament; therefore I may as well go on drawing my dividends." No one puts it quite so coarsely as that, but the thought of all these people is along those lines: even of those who, like Michael Roberts and Hulme himself, admit that a little, just a *little*, improvement in earthly society may be thinkable.

The danger of ignoring the neo-pessimists lies in the fact that up to a point they are right. So long as one thinks in short periods it is wise not to be hopeful about the future. Plans for human betterment do normally come unstuck, and the pessimist has many more opportunities of saying "I told you so" than the optimist. By and large the prophets of doom have been righter than those who imagined that a real step forward would be achieved by universal education, female suffrage, the League of Nations, or what-not.

The real answer is to dissociate Socialism from Utopianism. Nearly all neo-pessimist apologetics consists in putting up a man of straw and knocking him down again. The man of straw is called Human Perfectibility. Socialists are accused of believing that society can be—and indeed, after the establishment of Socialism, will be—completely perfect; also that progress is *inevitable*. Debunking such beliefs is money for jam, of course.

The answer, which ought to be uttered more loudly than it usually is, is that Socialism is not perfectionist, perhaps not even hedonistic. Socialists don't claim to be able to make the world perfect. they claim to be able to make it better. And any thinking Socialist will concede to the Catholic that when economic injustice has been righted, the fundamental problem of man's place in the universe will still remain. But what the Socialist does claim is that that problem cannot be dealt with while the average human being's preoccupations are necessarily economic. It is all summed up in Marx's saying that after Socialism has arrived, human history can begin. Meanwhile the neo-pessimists are there, well entrenched in the press of every country in the world, and they have more influence and make more converts among the young than we sometimes care to admit.

From Philip Jordan's *Tunis Diary*:[2]—
"We discussed the future of Germany; and John [Strachey] said to an American present, 'You surely don't want a Carthaginian peace, do you?' Our American friend with great slowness but solemnity said, 'I don't recollect we've had ever much trouble from the Carthaginians since.' Which delighted me."

It doesn't delight me. One answer to the American might have been, "No, but we've had a lot of trouble from the Romans." But there is more to it than that. What the people who talk about a Carthaginian peace[3] don't realise is that in our day such things are simply not practicable. Having defeated your enemy you have to choose (unless you want another war within a generation) between exterminating him and treating him generously. Conceivably the first alternative is desirable, but it isn't possible. It is quite true that Carthage was utterly destroyed, its buildings levelled to the ground, its inhabitants put to the sword. Such things were happening all the time in antiquity. But the populations involved were tiny. I wonder if that American knew how many people were found within the walls of Carthage when it was finally sacked? According to the nearest authority I can lay hands on, five thousand! What is the best way of killing off 70 million Germans? Rat poison? We might keep this in mind when "Make Germany pay" becomes a battle-cry again.

Attacking me in the *Weekly Review* for attacking Douglas Reed,[4] Mr. A. K. Chesterton remarks: " 'My country—right or wrong.' is a maxim which apparently has no place in Mr. Orwell's philosophy." He also states that "all of us believe that whatever her condition Britain must win this war, or for that matter any other war in which she is engaged."

The operative phrase is *any other war*. There are plenty of us who would defend our own country, under no matter what government, if it seemed that we were in danger of actual invasion and conquest. But "any war" is a different matter. How about the Boer War, for instance? There is a neat little bit of historical irony here. Mr. A. K. Chesterton is the nephew of G. K. Chesterton, who courageously opposed the Boer War, and once remarked that "My country, right or wrong," was on the same moral level as "My mother, drunk or sober."

When you have been watching bureaucrats at play, it is some consolation to reflect that the same kind of thing is probably happening in Germany. In general one can't test this, but sometimes the wireless gives a clue. A little while back I was listening to Berlin broadcasting in English, and the speaker spent some minutes in talking about the Indian Nationalists—with whom, of course, the Nazis profess the keenest sympathy. I was interested to notice that all the Indian names were grossly mispronounced, worse even than would be done by the B.B.C. Ras Behari Bose, for instance, was rendered as Rash Beery Bose. Yet the various Indians who also broadcast from Berlin must daily go in and out of the same building as the renegade Englishman who mispronounces their names. So much for German efficiency and also, of course, for Nazi interest in Indian Nationalism.

On 14 January 1944, *Tribune* printed a letter taking up Orwell's lumping Aldous Huxley with Pétain, from Conrad Voss-Bark (1913–2000), on the editorial staff of the *Western Daily Press*, 1943–47, of the *Times* from 1947, and Foreign Correspondent of the BBC for many years.

I refuse to believe that Orwell has understood Huxley and I am afraid of people who gibe at something or somebody they fail to docket in the neat compartments of their politically-tuned minds.

Aldous Huxley simply can't be lumped together with Pétain or the opponents of Beveridge in any satisfactory classification. Orwell says it is "their refusal to believe that human society can be fundamentally improved" which is common to both Huxley and Pétain.˙ I don't know about Pétain. Maybe Orwell is right there. But if Orwell would read *Ends and Means* very carefully he will find that the whole content of that remarkable book is a recipe for reform with the express purpose of improving human society in every way. Nor have Huxley's views changed since the publication. He still believes, I understand, that his own recipe for reform still holds good. Nor is it "un-Socialist." In many ways it is good Socialism.

I understand very well that Huxley's recipes are discredited in Orwell's eyes because they are inherently pacifist as well, and I can understand Orwell disliking that these days; but that does not excuse—(or does it?)—a complete misrepresentation of Huxley and what he stands for. There are no direct charges. Huxley is just lumped in with Pétain and "Beachcomber" and Berdyaev and Uncle Tom Cobbley° and all. George—please keep off these vast and untrue generalisations and red herrings (not to mention the romantic nonsense that "after Socialism has arrived human history can begin"). Otherwise your readers will be driven to believe that even a logical "neo-pessimism" is preferable to an illogical argument.

1. Georges Sorel (1847–1922), French philosopher, was an advocate of Direct Action—radical industrial action outside the parliamentary or constitutional framework. He supported syndicalism, not anarchism. T. E. Hulme translated Sorel's *Réflexions sur la violence* (1906) as *Reflections on Violence* (New York, 1914; London, 1916); see James Joll, *The Anarchists* (2nd ed., 1980, 192–95).
2. Reviewed by Orwell, 9 December 1943, *2389*.
3. A Carthaginian peace is one that is extremely harsh on the defeated party, leading to total destruction.
4. Orwell reviewed Reed's *Lest we Regret* on 7 November 1943, see *2347*, and *2347, n. 1* for a summary of Chesterton's position.

2397. 'Can Socialists be Happy?' by 'John Freeman'

Tribune, 24 December 1943

Orwell's Payments Book records at 20 December 1943 £5.5.0 for a special article of 2,000 words for *Tribune*. This has not been traced under Orwell's name, but it seems certain this must be a slightly longer article, 'Can Socialists be Happy?', attributed to a John Freeman. It was certainly not written by the John Freeman, then on active service, who was later a Labour M.P., 1945–55, editor of *The New Statesman* and British Ambassador in Washington, 1969–71. Mr. Freeman confirmed to the editor, on 26 July 1990, that he was not the author. The name 'Freeman' might be expected to appeal to Orwell as a pseudonym.

The article has many social, political, and literary links with Orwell; some, such as the relation of Lenin to Dickens, is particularly associated with Orwell. Lenin's being read *The Christmas Carol* on his deathbed appears in the second paragraph of Orwell's essay 'Charles Dickens' (written in 1939, published in 1940; see *597*) and again at the opening of his introduction (written in October or

November 1945, published in 1946) to Jack London's *Love of Life and Other Stories* (see *2781*). The article relates strongly to the 'As I Please' published in the same issue of *Tribune* (see *2396*), not only in the matter of Utopianism and Socialism but also in its references to Catholicism and 'pacifism (California brand especially).' Orwell had reviewed *Brave New World* in *Tribune*, 12 July 1940 (see *655*) and Viscount Samuel's *An Unknown Land* in *The Listener*, 24 December 1942 (see *1768*). He had devised a special Christmas edition of the BBC's 'Voice,' No. 6, 29 December 1942 (suggesting that he was not averse to marking Christmas), and in that programme included 'London Snow' by Robert Bridges and T. S. Eliot's 'The Journey of the Magi' (see *1778*). Among Orwell's reading were *A Modern Utopia*, *Gulliver's Travels*, *Portrait of the Artist as a Young Man*, *News from Nowhere*, and the less familiar *La Pucelle* by Voltaire. He mentions *La Pucelle* in 'Funny, But Not Vulgar,' written December 1944, published 28 July 1945 (see *2585*). The reference to a lack of vitality in the last line of the first section echoes the second paragraph of his review of W. H. Davies's *Collected Poems*, 19 December 1943 (see *2394*). The reference to Gerald Heard also supports Orwell's authorship. Heard is mentioned at the end of Orwell's review of Fielden's *Beggar My Neighbour*, *Horizon*, September 1943 (see *2257*) and Orwell later referred to him in his review in the *Manchester Evening News*, 2 August 1945 (see *2713*).

There can be little doubt that 'John Freeman' was another of Eric Blair's pen names. Jon Kimche, who was an assistant editor of *Tribune* at that time, was certain this article was by Orwell, although he did not in 1990 recall the circumstances of its publication.

The reason Orwell chose to write as 'John Freeman' is less clear. It may be that *Tribune* did not wish its literary editor to be seen to be associated with the political section of the journal. Possibly it was a device whereby he could be paid a fee for a special contribution; he was not usually paid for 'literary contributions' (see *2378*), although he was paid 10s.6d for his poem 'Memories of the Blitz' about this time; it was printed 21 January 1944 (see *2409*). He may have wished to see how far *Tribune* would let him go, though he was given plenty of scope in 'As I Please.' Was the pseudonym, with so many internal references, just a tease? Or did he simply think that Christmas as an occasion of positive happiness (rather than that happiness which is no more than the absence of pain) was worth celebrating?

The article was prominently trailed in *Tribune* (perhaps showing a touch of Orwell's mischievous side). Its title was printed in bold letters above the masthead on the first page, and the feature 'What's Happening' concludes with this explanatory note:

"Tribune" Christmas
Our readers will detect in this issue something of the spirit of the season, and particularly John Freeman's article will make a change from the hurly-burly of controversy. However, this is a temporary concession on *Tribune's* part and not a conversion from our past. Next week, we shall resume our traditional role and enter the third year of the new *Tribune* with all our guns blazing. Meanwhile, we wish our readers, who have greatly increased in number, a cheerful Christmas and the right sort of success in the New Year.

No other article by 'John Freeman' which can be attributed to Orwell has been traced. This seems to be a special and unusual instance.

The thought of Christmas raises almost automatically the thought of Charles Dickens, and for two very good reasons. To begin with, Dickens is one of the few English writers who have actually written about Christmas. Christmas is the most popular of English festivals, and yet it has produced astonishingly little literature. There are the carols, mostly medieval in origin; there is a tiny handful of poems by Robert Bridges, T. S. Eliot, and some others, and there is Dickens; but there is very little else. Secondly, Dickens is remarkable, indeed almost unique, among modern writers in being able to give a convincing picture of *happiness*.

Dickens dealt successfully with Christmas twice—in a well-known chapter of *The Pickwick Papers* and in *The Christmas Carol*. The latter story was read to Lenin on his deathbed and, according to his wife, he found its "bourgeois sentimentality" completely intolerable. Now in a sense Lenin was right; but if he had been in better health he would perhaps have noticed that the story has some interesting sociological implications. To begin with, however thick Dickens may lay on the paint, however disgusting the "pathos" of Tiny Tim may be, the Cratchit family do give the impression of enjoying themselves. They sound happy as, for instance, the citizens of William Morris's *News From Nowhere* don't sound happy. Moreover—and Dickens's understanding of this is one of the secrets of his power—their happiness derives mainly from contrast. They are in high spirits because for once in a way they have enough to eat. The wolf is at the door, but he is wagging his tail. The steam of the Christmas pudding drifts across a background of pawnshops and sweated labour, and in a double sense the ghost of Scrooge stands beside the dinner table. Bob Cratchit even wants to drink Scrooge's health, which Mrs. Cratchit rightly refuses. The Cratchits are able to enjoy their Christmas precisely because Christmas only comes once a year. Their happiness is convincing just because it is described as incomplete.

All efforts to describe *permanent* happiness, on the other hand, have been failures, from earliest history onwards. Utopias (incidentally the coined word Utopia doesn't mean "a good place," it means merely "a non-existent place") have been common in the literature of the past three or four hundred years, but the "favourable" ones are invariably unappetising, and usually lacking in vitality as well.

By far the best known modern Utopias are those of H. G. Wells. Wells's vision of the future, implicit all through his early work and partly set forth in *Anticipations* and *A Modern Utopia*, is most fully expressed in two books written in the early 'twenties, *The Dream* and *Men Like Gods*. Here you have a picture of the world as Wells would like to see it—or thinks he would like to see it. It is a world whose keynotes are enlightened hedonism and scientific curiosity. All the evils and miseries that we now suffer from have vanished. Ignorance, war, poverty, dirt, disease, frustration, hunger, fear, overwork, superstition—all vanished. So expressed, it is impossible to deny that that is the kind of world we all hope for. We all want to abolish the things that Wells wants to abolish. But is there anyone who actually wants to live in a Wellsian Utopia? On the contrary, *not* to live in a world like that, *not* to wake up in a hygienic garden suburb infested by naked schoolmarms, has actually become a conscious political motive. A book like *Brave New World* is an expression of the actual fear that modern man feels of the rationalised hedonistic society which it is within his power to create. A Catholic writer said recently that Utopias are now technically feasible and that in consequence *how to avoid Utopia* had become a serious problem. With the Fascist movement in front of our eyes we cannot write this off as a merely silly remark. For one of the sources of the Fascist movement is the desire to avoid a too-rational and too-comfortable world.

All "favourable" Utopias seem to be alike in postulating perfection while being unable to suggest happiness. *News From Nowhere* is a sort of goody-goody version of the Wellsian Utopia. Everyone is kindly and reasonable, all the upholstery comes from Liberty's, but the impression left behind is of a sort of watery melancholy. Lord Samuel's recent effort in the same direction, *An Unknown Country*, is even more dismal. The inhabitants of Bensalem (the word is borrowed from Francis Bacon) give the impression of looking on life as simply an evil to be got through with as little fuss as possible. All that their wisdom has brought them is permanent low spirits. But it is more impressive that Jonathan Swift, one of the greatest imaginative writers who have ever lived, is no more successful in constructing a "favourable" Utopia than the others.

The earlier parts of *Gulliver's Travels* are probably the most devastating attack on human society that has ever been written. Every word of them is relevant to-day; in places they contain quite detailed prophecies of the political horrors of our own time. Where Swift fails, however, is in trying to describe a race of beings whom he *does* admire. In the last part, in contrast with the disgusting Yahoos, we are shown the noble Houyhnhnms, a race of intelligent horses who are free from human failings. Now these horses, for all their high character and unfailing common sense, are remarkably dreary creatures. Like the inhabitants of various other Utopias, they are chiefly concerned with avoiding fuss. They live uneventful, subdued, "reasonable" lives, free not only from quarrels, disorder or insecurity of any kind, but also from "passion," including physical love. They choose their mates on eugenic principles, avoid excesses of affection, and appear somewhat glad to die when their time comes. In the earlier parts of the book Swift has shown where man's folly and scoundrelism lead him: but take away the folly and the scoundrelism, and all you are left with, apparently, is a tepid sort of existence, hardly worth leading.

Attempts at describing a definitely other-worldly happiness have been no more successful. Heaven is as great a flop as Utopia—though Hell,[1] it is worth noting, occupies a respectable place in literature, and has often been described most minutely and convincingly.

It is a commonplace that the Christian Heaven, as usually portrayed, would attract nobody. Almost all Christian writers dealing with Heaven either say frankly that it is indescribable or conjure up a vague picture of gold, precious stones, and the endless singing of hymns. This has, it is true, inspired some of the best poems in the world:

Thy walls are of chalcedony,
Thy bulwarks diamonds square,
Thy gates are of right orient pearl
Exceeding rich and rare!

Or:

Holy, holy, holy, all the saints adore Thee,
Casting down their golden crowns about the glassy sea,
Cherubim and seraphim falling down before Thee,
That wast, and art, and evermore shalt be!

But what it could not do was to describe a place or condition in which the ordinary human being actively wanted to be. Many a revivalist minister, many a Jesuit priest (see, for instance, the terrific sermon in James Joyce's *Portrait of the Artist*) has frightened his congregation almost out of their skins with his word-pictures of Hell. But as soon as it comes to Heaven, there is a prompt falling-back on words like "ecstasy" and "bliss," with little attempt to say what they consist in. Perhaps the most vital bit of writing on this subject is the famous passage in which Tertullian explains that one of the chief joys of Heaven is watching the tortures of the damned.

The various pagan versions of Paradise are little better, if at all. One has the feeling that it is always twilight in the Elysian fields. Olympus, where the gods lived, with their nectar and ambrosia, and their nymphs and Hebes, the "immortal tarts" as D. H. Lawrence called them, might be a bit more homelike than the Christian Heaven, but you would not want to spend a long time there. As for the Moslem Paradise, with its seventy-seven houris per man, all presumably clamouring for attention at the same moment, it is just a nightmare. Nor are the Spiritualists, though constantly assuring us that "all is bright and beautiful," able to describe any next-world activity which a thinking person would find endurable, let alone attractive.

It is the same with attempted descriptions of perfect happiness which are neither Utopian nor other-worldly, but merely sensual. They always give an impression of emptiness or vulgarity, or both. At the beginning of *La Pucelle* Voltaire describes the life of Charles IX with his mistress, Agnes Sorel. They were "always happy," he says. And what did their happiness consist in? Apparently in an endless round of feasting, drinking, hunting and love-making. Who would not sicken of such an existence after a few weeks? Rabelais describes the fortunate spirits who have a good time in the next world to console them for having had a bad time in this one. They sing a song which can be roughly translated: "To leap, to dance, to play tricks, to drink the wine both white and red, and to do nothing all day long except count gold crowns"—how boring it sounds, after all! The emptiness of the whole notion of an everlasting "good time" is shown up in Breughel's picture "The Land of the Sluggard," where the three great lumps of fat lie asleep, head to head, with the boiled eggs and roast legs of pork coming up to be eaten of their own accord.

It would seem that human beings are not able to describe, nor perhaps to imagine, happiness except in terms of contrast. That is why the conception of Heaven or Utopia varies from age to age. In pre-industrial society Heaven was described as a place of endless rest, and as being paved with gold, because the experience of the average human being was overwork and poverty. The houris of the Moslem Paradise reflected a polygamous society where most of the women disappeared into the harems of the rich. But these pictures of "eternal bliss" always failed because as soon as the bliss became eternal (eternity being thought of as endless time), the contrast ceased to operate. Some of the conventions which have become embedded in our literature first arose from physical conditions which have now ceased to exist. The cult of spring is an example. In the Middle Ages spring did not primarily mean swallows and wild flowers. It meant green vegetables, milk and fresh meat after several months of living on salt pork in smoky windowless huts. The spring songs were gay—

> Do nothing but eat and make good cheer,
> And thank Heaven for the merry year
> When flesh is cheap and females dear,
> And lusty lads roam here and there,
> So merrily,
> And ever among so merrily!

because there was something to be gay about. The winter was over, that was the great thing. Christmas itself, a pre-Christian festival, probably started because there had to be an occasional outburst of overeating and drinking to make a break in the unbearable northern winter.

The inability of mankind to imagine happiness except in the form of *relief*, either from effort or pain, presents Socialists with a serious problem. Dickens can describe a poverty-stricken family tucking into a roast goose, and can make them appear happy; on the other hand, the inhabitants of perfect universes seem to have no spontaneous gaiety and are usually somewhat repulsive into the bargain. But clearly we are not aiming at the kind of world Dickens described, nor, probably, at any world he was capable of imagining. The Socialist objective is not a society where everything comes right in the end, because kind old gentlemen give away turkeys. What are we aiming at, if not a society in which "charity" would be unnecessary? We want a world where Scrooge, with his dividends, and Tiny Tim, with his tuberculous leg, would both be unthinkable. But does that mean that we are aiming at some painless, effortless Utopia?

At the risk of saying something which the editors of *Tribune* may not endorse, I suggest that the real objective of Socialism is not happiness. Happiness hitherto has been a by-product, and for all we know it may always remain so. The real objective of Socialism is human brotherhood. This is widely felt to be the case, though it is not usually said, or not said loudly enough. Men use up their lives in heart-breaking political struggles, or get themselves killed in civil wars, or tortured in the secret prisons of the Gestapo, not in order to establish some central-heated, air-conditioned, strip-lighted Paradise, but because they want a world in which human beings love one another instead of swindling and murdering one another. And they want that world as a first step. Where they go from there is not so certain, and the attempt to foresee it in detail merely confuses the issue.

Socialist thought has to deal in prediction, but only in broad terms. One often has to aim at objectives which one can only very dimly see. At this moment, for instance, the world is at war and wants peace. Yet the world has no experience of peace, and never has had, unless the Noble Savage once existed. The world wants something which it is dimly aware could exist, but which it cannot accurately define. This Christmas day, thousands of men will be bleeding to death in the Russian snows, or drowning in icy waters, or blowing one another to pieces with hand grenades on swampy islands of the Pacific; homeless children will be scrabbling for food among the wreckage of German cities. To make that kind of thing impossible is a good objective. But to say in detail what a peaceful world would be like is a different matter, and to attempt to do so is apt to lead to the horrors so enthusiastically presented by Gerald Heard.[2]

Nearly all creators of Utopia have resembled the man who has toothache, and therefore thinks that happiness consists in not having toothache. They wanted to produce a perfect society by an endless continuation of something that had only been valuable because it was temporary. The wiser course would be to say that there are certain lines along which humanity must move, the grand strategy is mapped out, but detailed prophecy is not our business. Whoever tries to imagine perfection simply reveals his own emptiness. This is the case even with a great writer like Swift, who can flay a bishop or a politician so neatly, but who, when he tries to create a superman, merely leaves one with the impression—the very last he can have intended—that the stinking Yahoos had in them more possibility of development than the enlightened Houyhnhnms.

Orwell's article, though not published under a name readers would recognise, nevertheless attracted two correspondents. Their letters were printed in *Tribune* for 7 January 1944.

Meditations like John Freeman's article on Utopias need not be regarded as a mere Christmastime indulgence. Just as amidst the urgent problems of war we feel the need for planning the peace, so we may give some thought, even now, to the question of what politics will consist of when to-day's burning demand for "food, work and homes" is as completely solved and forgotten as prehistoric man's struggle with the beasts. Is that time so remote? President Roosevelt and the Hot Springs experts (not to mention Socialists) agree that want can be abolished in this generation. I believe that this will happen, and that a great increase in creative energy will follow. This can be used only in scientific or artistic work, both of which, fortunately, are as endless as the universe itself. What gives Mr. Freeman the idea that such activities are too rational or too comfortable to be attractive?

Surely the biographies of artists, scientists and inventors show that although most of them were comfortably off in a material sense (contrary to a popular delusion), they found in their work mystery and surprise, sudden inspirations, danger, despair and ecstasy! Of humanity up to now the future historian may well say

> Chill penury repressed their noble rage,
> And froze the genial current of the soul.[3]

The removal of the dull, brutalising influences of poverty and war will be the beginning, not the end, of real adventures, such as the building of magnificent cities, landscape gardening on a national scale, the exploration and control of atoms and of human personality. It is not too soon now to give large-scale communal backing to science and art, and to study how to reconcile this with freedom for the individual practitioner.

J. Cryer

Under the heading "Tribune Christmas" you opine that John Freeman's article, "Can Socialists be Happy?" will make a seasonable change from "the hurley-burley of controversy." I imagine this letter will not be the only evidence that for once you have erred in your judgment. John Freeman's main conclusion is that "The real objective of Socialism is not happiness." In view of the context, how is it possible that we can be expected to take this lying down?

If we Socialists are not out for happiness, what *are* we after? Un-happiness? Not exactly, according to Mr. Freeman. What we want, he thinks, is not happiness but—human brotherhood. The implication of which seems to be there's no happiness in human brotherhood. But, of course, he doesn't really mean that. I venture to suggest that the trouble with Mr. Freeman is that, although he is repelled by the static quality of the chromium-plated Utopias and rolled-gold heavens of various prophets and visionaries, he has yet taken their word for it that what they depict is— happiness, and finding it about as attractive as a case of stuffed birds of Paradise, concludes, so much the worse for happiness. But the point is, surely, that in so far as these writers have failed to make their visions attractive they have failed to convey the impression of happiness; something, admittedly, very difficult to do, but that is not to say that happiness itself is undesirable. How can it be, seeing that it is simply an agreeable state of mind—the state of mind of anyone who is, as we say, enjoying life? Surely Socialists, like other men, do want to enjoy life. Surely "human brotherhood" is one of the essential conditions for the enjoyment of life. "*Not* happiness, *but* human brotherhood"—what an extraordinary antithesis!

One thing we *do* know about happiness is that it comes not merely as a *contrast* to unhappiness, but through creation and development, adventure and interest. It is, of course, not an aim in itself at all, but an emotional state of varying degrees of intensity, that we can't help seeking in the very act of striving to realise our desires, whatever they may be. It does seem important that Socialists should get this straight, because if they imply that Socialism has little or nothing to do with happiness they are going to make potential Socialists muddled and discouraged and miserable, instead of hopeful that they can help to build a world of happier men—an aim which to anyone who cares about human brotherhood must surely appear a thoroughly desirable one.

Ian Freed

1. The original has 'Wells.' The error may be the compositor's (though 'Hells' would be more likely to give rise to 'Wells'), but it is probable that this was Orwell's mistake—a Freudian slip, perhaps.
2. Henry Fitz Gerald Heard (1889–1971), author, broadcaster, and lecturer. Among his many books were *The Ascent of Humanity* (1929), for which he was awarded a British Academy grant; *The Social Substance of Religion* (1931); *This Surprising World* (1932) and *Science in the Making* (1935), both titles of broadcast series, 1930–34 and 1934 respectively; *The Source of Civilisation* (1935); *The Creed of Christ* (1940); and *The Riddle of the Flying Saucers* (1950). Orwell may be referring to Heard's *Pain, Sex and Time* (1939), which concluded with 'an explanation of how Yoga could help Western men to reach peace within their inner selves' (Robert Graves and Alan Hodge, *The Long Week-End: A Social History of Great Britain 1918–1939* (1940).) Heard taught at U.S. universities in 1946, 1951–52, and 1955–56. See also *2713, n. 2*.
3. Thomas Gray, 'Elegy Written in a Country Churchyard,' stanza 13.

2398. 'As I Please,' 5

Tribune, 31 December 1943

Reading the discussions of "war guilt" which reverberate in the correspondence columns of the newspapers, I note the surprise with which many people seem to discover that war is not crime. Hitler, it appears, has not done anything actionable. He has not raped anybody, nor carried off any pieces of loot with his own hands, nor personally flogged any prisoners, buried any wounded men alive, thrown any babies into the air and spitted them on his bayonet, dipped any nuns in petrol and touched them off with church tapers—in fact he has not done any of the things which enemy nationals are usually credited with doing in war time. He has merely precipitated a world war which will perhaps have cost twenty million lives before it ends. And there is nothing illegal in that. How could there be, when legality implies authority and there *is* no authority with the power to transcend national frontiers?

At the recent trials in Kharkov[1] some attempt was made to fix on Hitler, Himmler and the rest the responsibility for their subordinates' crimes, but that the mere fact that this had to be done shows that Hitler's guilt is not self-evident. His crime, it is implied, was not to build up an army for the purpose of aggressive war, but to instruct that army to torture its prisoners. So far as it goes, the distinction between an atrocity and an act of war is valid. An atrocity means an act of terrorism which has no genuine military purpose. One must accept such distinctions if one accepts war at all, which in practice everyone does. Nevertheless, a world in which it is wrong to murder an individual civilian and right to drop a thousand tons of high explosive on a residential area does sometimes make me wonder whether this earth of ours is not a looney-bin made use of by some other planet.

As the 53 bus[2] carries me to and fro I never, at any rate when it is light enough to see, pass the little church of St. John, just across the road from Lord's, without a pang. It is a Regency church, one of the very few of the period, and when you pass that way it is well worth going inside to have a look at its friendly interior and read the resounding epitaphs of the East India Nabobs who lie buried there. But its façade, one of the most charming in London, has been utterly ruined by a hideous war memorial which stands in front of it. That seems to be a fixed rule in London—whenever you do by some chance have a decent vista, block it up with the ugliest statue you can find. And, unfortunately, we have never been sufficiently short of bronze for these things to be melted down.

If you climb to the top of the hill in Greenwich Park, you can have the mild thrill of standing exactly on longitude 0, and you can also examine the ugliest building in the world, Greenwich Observatory. Then look down the hill towards the Thames. Spread out below you are Wren's masterpiece, Greenwich Hospital (now the Naval College) and another exquisite classical building known as the Queen's House. The architects responsible for that shapeless sprawling muddle at the top of the hill had those other two buildings under their eyes while every brick was laid.

As Mr. Osbert Sitwell remarked at the time of the "Baedeker raids"[3]— how simple-minded of the Germans to imagine that we British could be cowed by the destruction of our ancient monuments! As though any havoc of the German bombs could possibly equal the things we have done ourselves!

I see that Mr. Bernard Shaw, among others, wants to rewrite the second verse of the National Anthem. Mr. Shaw's version retains references to God and the King, but is vaguely internationalist in sentiment. This seems to me ridiculous. Not to have a national anthem would be logical. But if you do have one, its function must necessarily be to point out that we are Good and our enemies are Bad. Besides, Mr Shaw wants to cut out the only worthwhile lines the anthem contains. All the brass instruments and big drums in the world cannot turn "God Save the King" into a good tune,[4] but on the very rare occasions when it is sung in full it does spring to life in the two lines—
> Confound their politics,
> Frustrate their knavish tricks!

And, in fact, I had always imagined that the second verse is habitually left out because of a vague suspicion on the part of the Tories that these lines refer to themselves.

Just about two years ago, as we filed past the menu board in the canteen, I said to the next person in the queue: "A year from now you'll see 'Rat Soup' on that board, and in 1943 it will be 'Mock Rat Soup.'" Events have proved me wrong (the war at sea has turned out better than was then foreseeable), but, once again, I can claim to have been less wrong than the full-time prophets. Turning up my copy of Old Moore's Almanac for 1943, I find that the Germans sued for peace and were granted an armistice in June, and Japan surrendered in September. November finds us enjoying "the blessings of peace and the complete removal of lighting conditions,"[5] while "a reduction in taxation is highly appreciated." It is like this all the way through.

Old Moore repeats this performance every year, without ever losing its popularity. Nor is it hard to see why. Its psychological approach is indicated by the advert. on the cover: "Cosmo, famous Mystic, predicts VICTORY, PEACE, RECONSTRUCTION." As long as Cosmo predicts that kind of thing he is safe for a hearing.

Another ninepenny acquisition: "Chronological Tablets, exhibiting every Remarkable Occurrence from the Creation of the World down to the Present Time." Printed by J. D. Dewick, Aldersgate Street, in the year 1801.

With some interest I looked up the date of the creation of the world, and found it was in 4004 B.C., and "is supposed to have taken place in the autumn." Later in the book it is given more exactly as September, 4004.[6]

At the end there are a number of blank sheets in which the reader can carry on the chronicle for himself. Whoever possessed this book did not carry it very far, but one of the last entries is: "Tuesday 4 May. Peace proclaimed here. General Illumination." That was the Peace of Amiens.[7] This might warn us not to be too previous with our own illuminations when the armistice comes.

1. On 15 December 1943 the Russians tried three Germans and a Ukrainian, whom they accused of the mass killing of Soviet civilians and the use of gas–extermination vans. The men were publicly hanged on 19 December. This was the first war crimes trial.
2. Until, and for some time after, the end of World War II, the 53, 53A, and 153 buses followed the general route north of the Thames now taken by the 159 (and at one time the 59 and 59A). Thus Orwell would take a 53 from Trafalgar Square (into which The Strand runs, where he worked at *Tribune*'s offices) along Abbey Road in St John's Wood, and alight near Alexandra Road. In those days that route passed St John's Church, near Lord's Cricket Ground; it has in recent years been diverted down Lisson Grove. The 53 now goes north to Camden Town.
3. Baedeker raids, named after the Baedeker Guide Books, were reprisals for raids by the RAF, especially those on Lübeck, Cologne, and Mainz in mid-1942. Cathedral cities such as Canterbury, York, and Exeter were chosen as the Luftwaffe's targets. These cities were all of far greater touristic than military significance.
4. Whatever one's views about the words and sentiments of 'God Save the King' (or Queen), the tune has much to recommend it, as musicians from Beethoven to Ives have vividly demonstrated. As his choice of music for his broadcasts indicates, Orwell did not have a particularly subtle ear for music.
5. Possibly 'restrictions' was intended.
6. The year 4004 B.C. was calculated by a learned, if mistaken, Biblical scholar, James Ussher (1581–1656), Archbishop of Armagh, 1625. His chronology of Biblical events was printed in the margins of some editions of the Bible.
7. The Peace of Amiens, 27 March 1802, brought a temporary cessation in the Napoleonic Wars, 1800–15. Hostilities were resumed in 1803.

2399. Review of *Armies and the Art of Revolution* by K. C. Chorley

The Observer, 2 January 1944

In the last resort, society, as we know it, rests upon force, and moreover we live in an age in which naked physical power tends more and more to grow in importance as against financial power. The structure and political outlook of armies, navies, and air forces is therefore a subject of the most vital importance, whether one looks at it from a revolutionary or a reactionary point of view. As Captain Liddell Hart says in his foreword to this book, the relation of the armed forces to society has not received as much study as it might. Mrs. Chorley's book, though it has some gaps in it, is a stimulating introduction.

Two important facts emerge from every revolution or civil war that she examines. The first is that in the modern world a popular insurrection cannot succeed against a regular army which is really exerting its strength. In every case that seems to contradict this there has either been foreign intervention, or sympathy with the rebels on the part of the armed forces, or else some hidden factor which may not be strictly military but which is part of the strategic situation. A good example is the Irish Civil War, which Mrs. Chorley examines at some length. The hidden factor here was English (and American) public opinion. The strategy of the Irish nationalists was not to engage in real warfare, in which they must have been defeated, but to make it morally impossible for the British to strike back at them. They used guerrilla tactics (assassinations, sudden attacks on unarmed soldiers by men dressed as civilians, etc.) which could only have been countered by a policy of brutal reprisals. The British were unequal to this, not probably from any excess of humanity but because English opinion was largely sympathetic to the Irish and world opinion could not be disregarded. Similar guerrilla tactics have made little impression on the Japanese, who exclude foreigners from their dominions and do not have a Nonconformist conscience to contend with. Since the invention of the machine-gun, straightforward rebellions have always failed, unless they are either made by the armed forces, or the armed forces are disintegrating as a result of defeat in foreign war.

The second point brought out by Mrs. Chorley is that for political purposes "the army" nearly always means the officers. Except when they have been defeated, or at the end of a long war, the lower ranks tend to be politically apathetic, especially in long-service professional armies. The officers, on the other hand, better educated, more conscious, and more

51

homogeneous socially, tend to regard themselves not as the servants of the State but of a particular political party. Instances of governments being blackmailed into this or that action because "the army," meaning the officers, threatened mutiny are innumerable. Mrs. Chorley concludes that an army whose officers are drawn from the higher ranks of society can never be trusted to support a "left" government.

This raises the very difficult question of how it is possible, if at all, for an army to be democratised. Any government, and especially a "left" government, must have officers who are politically reliable, but the trouble is that they must also be militarily efficient. As an example of an army which is genuinely democratic in structure, and which could not possibly make a reactionary *coup d'etat*, Mrs. Chorley points to the Swiss army. This army, however, is unlikely ever to have to go to war, and its structure is conditioned by that fact. Britain, for instance, or the U.S.S.R., could not possibly make do with a citizens' militia in which even an officer served only 400 days in his whole lifetime. And the prolonged training and rigid discipline needed in modern mechanised forces are probably anti-democratic in tendency. Mrs. Chorley's remarks on the French and Russian revolutions and the Spanish civil war show how even in revolutionary armies the tendency is always away from egalitarianism. An army can only be kept democratic by means of soldiers' committees and political delegates, and both of these are a bar to efficiency.

Mrs. Chorley suggests that the important thing, from the point of view of a democratic government, is to make sure that the corps of officers is not drawn from reactionary strata of the population. This may be so, but it may also be that a professional officer's social origin is almost irrelevant to his political outlook. Modern military methods, and the discipline they demand, may be producing an "officer type" whose outlook will be much the same whether he is the son of a duke or of a factory worker. It is here that the chief omission in Mrs. Chorley's book makes itself felt—namely, that after saying a good deal about the Red Army during the revolution and the civil war, she says little or nothing about its subsequent development.

There are some other omissions. It seems a pity—though perhaps it would have needed another book—to exclude all mention of South America, which must have provided at least one test-tube demonstration of every conceivable revolutionary situation. But this is a valuable book, and, though admittedly written from a "left" angle, about as objective as is possible in these days.

[Fee: £7.7.0; 27.12.43]

2400. Review of *Allenby in Egypt* by Field-Marshal Viscount Wavell

Manchester Evening News, 6 January 1944

Lord Wavell's own career has paralleled Allenby's closely enough to make anything that he says on the subject worthy of special attention. Like Allenby he was sent to the Middle East to win a brilliant victory at a moment when the war was still going disastrously in the West, and again like Allenby he has relinquished his military command to take up an important and thankless job of civilian administration.

He is not, of course, using Allenby as a mouthpiece for his own opinions, but from his comments on the Egyptian situation and the final settlement that was made we can probably get some idea of the policy that he himself would like to put into operation in India.

Lord Wavell's main thesis, as in the other book which he published three years ago,[1] is that Allenby's services have never had due recognition.

Allenby had many gifts, but they did not include personal charm or a flair for publicity, and the great victory that he won in Palestine has been largely overshadowed in the public mind by the picturesque exploits of Colonel Lawrence. Lord Wavell insists that Allenby has also been robbed of the credit for finally effecting a comparatively decent settlement in Egypt.

And whatever the objective merits of Allenby's administration, it can certainly be admitted that he served the interests, as he saw them, of both Britain and Egypt, and cared nothing for what happened to his own reputation in the process.

Like all Imperial administrators in troubled periods Allenby was simultaneously denounced as a hidebound reactionary and a weak-kneed Liberal. To the Egyptian Nationalists he was the symbol of foreign oppression: to the British community in Egypt he appeared to be encouraging the Egyptians to revolt by a policy of ill-judged leniency.

British home opinion was ignorant of the Egyptian situation and British politicians alternated between snubbing the Egyptians and promising them impossibilities.

The story of Allenby's six years in Egypt is the story of a many-sided struggle between King Fuad, Allenby himself, the Wafdists, the British Foreign Office, the British business community in Egypt, and various others, conducted in an atmosphere of intrigue and punctuated by assassinations.

The Egyptian situation was exceptionally complicated. The Sudan since the beginning of the century, and Egypt since much earlier, had been in an ill-defined way under British control.

When Turkey came into the war it had been necessary to make what amounted to an annexation of Egypt, which was still theoretically part of the Turkish dominions, and a protectorate was set up, which lasted until the declaration of Egyptian independence in 1922.

Between 1914 and 1922 the country was governed by martial law.

Meanwhile, a vigorous Egyptian Nationalist movement had grown up, and it was a complicating factor that this was essentially a movement of the Egyptian masses. The old ruling class, and the higher officials, had been Turks. The new politicians who were now appearing represented the aspirations of the Egyptian people, but had no experience of administration and not much taste for responsibility.

Lord Wavell makes it clear that Allenby saw from the start the necessity of declaring Egypt independent, and that if he had had his way he would have done it promptly and made the Nationalist politicians into friends instead of enemies.

The British Government was not, however, ready at first for the necessary concessions, and started off with the grave mistake of arresting and deporting the popular Wafdist leader, Saad Zaghlul, who was later to be Egypt's Prime Minister.

The underlying facts were that the Egyptian desire for self-government was real and could not be ignored, that a weak country like Egypt could not be fully independent, and that Britain could not be expected to relax all hold on Egypt while the Suez Canal remained important to her.

Some arrangement by which Egypt should be self-governing but should allow Britain the necessary military and commercial facilities was obviously possible, and was what Allenby aimed at. But it was not fully achieved till many years later, because negotiations had started off on the wrong foot. The Nationalists had been driven into a violently anti-British attitude, popular anger against the British occupation was easily aroused, and the Liberal politicians could get themselves no following.

In 1922 Egypt was declared an independent State (Lord Wavell insists that this was essentially Allenby's doing), but this made the administration of the country no easier.

Any Egyptian politician who wished to retain his popularity was forced to make demands for the withdrawal of the British troops and the complete cession of the Sudan—which Britain was obviously not going to fulfil—and a long series of murders enraged the British community and made them clamour in and out of season for a "firm hand."

Things were further complicated by the intrigues of the King, who aimed at making himself into an autocrat and by the unwisdom of British politicians, notably Ramsay MacDonald, who floated through the country in 1921 making extravagant promises which—to the surprise of the Egyptians— he failed to keep when he was in office.

However, the 1922 declaration was a real step forward, and three years later the position was somewhat regularised owing, ironically enough, to yet another murder. Sir Lee Stack, the Governor-General of the Sudan, was assassinated towards the end of 1924 by some Nationalist students, and this crime gave Allenby the opportunity to act firmly and put Anglo-Egyptian relations on a surer if not more friendly basis.

Zaghlul's Government resigned and politicians less hostile to Britain came into power. Allenby resigned his post in the following year owing to his disagreements with the British Cabinet.

It is impossible to feel sure, even now, that Allenby was as great a man as Lord Wavell claims him to have been. He was certainly, as Lord Wavell sometimes seems to admit, not a very interesting man in spite of his varied and sometimes unexpected gifts, for in addition to being a brilliant soldier he was a lover of birds and flowers, wrote admirable English, and read Greek with facility.

His greatest qualities, as Lord Wavell points out, were not mental but moral. He would not accept an unworkable policy in order to keep his job, and he was indifferent to what was said about him. In his own even more embarrassing position as Viceroy of India Lord Wavell might certainly have chosen worse models than Allenby.

[Fee: £8.8.0; 4.1.44]

1. *Allenby—A Study in Greatness.*

2401. 'As I Please,' 6

Tribune, 7 January 1944

Looking through the photographs in the New Year Honours List, I am struck (as usual) by the quite exceptional ugliness and vulgarity of the faces displayed there. It seems to be almost the rule that the kind of person who earns the right to call himself Lord Percy de Falcontowers should look at best like an overfed publican and at worst like a tax-collector with a duodenal ulcer. But our country is not alone in this. Anyone who is a good hand with scissors and paste could compile an excellent book entitled *Our Rulers,* and consisting simply of published photographs of the great ones of the earth. The idea first occurred to me when I saw in *Picture Post* some "stills" of Beaverbrook delivering a speech and looking more like a monkey on a stick than you would think possible for anyone who was not doing it on purpose.

When you had got together your collection of fuehrers, actual and would-be, you would notice that several qualities recur throughout the list. To begin with, they are all old. In spite of the lip-service that is paid everywhere to youth, there is no such thing as a person in a truly commanding position who is less than fifty years old. Secondly, they are nearly all undersized. A dictator taller than five feet six inches is a very great rarity. And, thirdly, there is this almost general and sometimes quite fantastic ugliness. The collection would contain photographs of Streicher bursting a blood vessel, Japanese war lords impersonating baboons, Mussolini with his scrubby dewlap, the chinless de Gaulle, the stumpy short-armed Churchill, Gandhi with his long sly nose and huge bat's ears, Tojo displaying thirty-two teeth with gold in every one of them. And opposite each, to make a contrast, there would be a photograph of an ordinary human being from the country concerned. Opposite Hitler a young sailor from a German submarine, opposite Tojo a Japanese peasant of the old type—and so on.

But to come back to the Honours List. When you remember that nearly the whole of the rest of the world has dropped it, it does seem strange to see this flummery still continuing in England, a country in which the very notion of aristocracy perished hundreds of years ago. The race-difference on which aristocratic rule is usually founded had disappeared from England by the end of the Middle Ages, and the concept of "blue blood" as something valuable in itself, and independent of money, was vanishing in the age of Elizabeth. Since then we have been a plutocracy plain and simple. Yet we still make spasmodic efforts to dress ourselves in the colours of medieval feudalism.

Think of the Heralds' Office solemnly faking pedigrees and inventing coats of arms with mermaids and unicorns couchant, regardant and what-not, for company directors in bowler hat and striped trousers! What I like best is the careful grading by which honours are always dished out in direct proportion to the amount of mischief done—baronies for Big Business, baronetcies for fashionable surgeons, knighthoods for tame professors. But do these people imagine that by calling themselves lords, knights and so forth they somehow come to have something in common with the medieval aristocracy? Does Sir Walter Citrine, say, feel himself to be rather the same kind of person as Childe Roland (Childe Citrine to the dark tower came!), or is Lord Nuffield under the impression that we shall mistake him for a crusader in chain armour?

However, this honours-list business has one severely practical aspect, and that is that a title is a first-rate alias. Mr. X can practically cancel his past by turning himself into Lord Y. Some of the ministerial appointments that have been made during this war would hardly have been possible without some such disguise. As Tom Paine put it: "These people change their names so often that it is as hard to know them as it is to know thieves."

I write this to the tune of an electric drill. They are drilling holes in the walls of a surface shelter, removing bricks at regular intervals. Why? Because the shelter is in danger of falling down and it is necessary to give it a cement facing.

It seems doubtful whether these surface shelters were ever of much use. They would give protection against splinters and blast, but not more than the walls of an ordinary house, and the only time I saw a bomb drop anywhere near one it sliced it off the ground as neatly as if it had been done with a knife. The real point is, however, that at the time when these shelters were built it was known that they would fall down in a year or two. Innumerable people pointed this out. But nothing happened; the slovenly building continued, and somebody scooped the contract. Sure enough, a year or two later, the prophets were justified. The mortar began to fall out of the walls, and it became necessary to case the shelters in cement. Once again somebody—perhaps it was the same somebody—scooped the contract.

I do not know whether, in any part of the country, these shelters are actually used in air raids. In my part of London there has never been any question of using them; in fact, they are kept permanently locked lest they should be used for "improper purposes." There is one thing, however, that they might conceivably be useful for, and that is as block-houses in street fighting. And on the whole they have been built in the poorer streets. It would amuse me if when the time came the higher-ups were unable to crush the populace because they had thoughtlessly provided them with thousands of machine-gun nests beforehand.

On page eighteen of this number there will be found an advertisement of the *Tribune* Short Story Competition.[1] We hope for a large number of entries, and we hope that directly and indirectly the competition may help a little towards the rehabilitation of the short story in this country.

Few people would claim that the short story has been a successful art form in England during the past twenty years. American and Irish stories are perhaps a little better, but not much. One could explain the decline of the short story on sociological grounds, but such explanations are not altogether satisfactory, because, if true, they ought to apply equally to kindred forms of literature. Contemporary novels, for instance, are on average nowhere near so bad as contemporary short stories. There must also be technical causes, and I think I can suggest two of them.

The first is something that we cannot remedy in *Tribune*—the difficulty over length. Almost certainly the short story has suffered from the dwindled size of modern magazines. Nearly all the great English short stories of the past—and the same is true of many French stories, though perhaps less true of the Russians—would be far too long for publication in any ordinary modern periodical. But I think it is also true that the short story has suffered unnecessarily from the disappearance of the Victorian "plot." About the beginning of this century the convention of the "surprise in the last chapter" fell out of fashion, and it was not sufficiently noticed that the eventless, non-dramatic kind of story is more effective when it is long than when it is short. A short story has to be a *story*. It cannot, to the same extent as the novel, depend upon "atmosphere" and character-interest, because there is not enough space to build them up. A short story which does not convey any anecdote, any dramatic change, almost invariably ends on a note of weakness and pointlessness. What innumerable stories I have read which have kept me thinking almost up to the last line—"Surely these preliminaries are leading to something? Surely something is going to happen?"—and then the invariable petering-out, to which the writer sometimes tries to give an air of profundity by means of a row of dots. I cannot help feeling that many short-story writers are inhibited by the notion that a "plot" is hopelessly old-fashioned and therefore inadmissible.[2]

I do not suggest that this is the only thing that is wrong with the contemporary short story. But after much reading of short stories this is the impression left upon my own mind, and I offer it as a hint which may be useful to intending contributors.

1. The advertisement (which appeared on page 19) for 'Tribune Short Story Competition' offered a first prize of £25, a second prize of £10, and a third of £5. Stories should 'preferably not exceed 1,500 words' and 'must in no case exceed 1,800 words.' They were to be submitted by 31 March 1944. The advertisement was repeated on 18 and 25 February 1944. The first-prize story was 'The Belt' by David Morgan, published in *Tribune* on 12 May 1944; the second-

prize story, 'Repentence' by Inez Gibson, was published the following week; and the third, 'The Answer' by Anne Dalton, appeared on 26 May 1944.

2. On 14 January 1944, an advertisement in *Tribune* by the British Institute of Fiction-writing Science, Ltd., Regent House, Regent Street, London, W.1., headed 'What *Is* a Plot?,' quoted the final sentence of this paragraph and suggested, in reply to Orwell, 'that lack of plot is due not to any inhibition on the part of writers but to lack of knowledge as to what a "plot" *is*.' 'Who has ever defined a plot?' the advertisement asked, and went on to claim that Martin Walter, Controller of the Institute, had solved this problem, and those who aspired to enter *Tribune*'s competition or to produce stories 'for any existing market,' could obtain Mr. Walter's 'Formula and his Scientific System of Fiction-writing' by sending one guinea to the Institute. Orwell referred to Martin Walter's advertisements in 'As I Please,' 51, *Tribune*, 8 December 1944; see *2590*.

2402. F. R. Leavis to Orwell

8 January 1944

Orwell wrote to F. R. Leavis (1895–1978), Fellow of Downing College and one of the editors of *Scrutiny* (see *194, n. 1*), at the end of 1943 or early in 1944. His letter has not been traced, but Leavis's reply has survived. From this it seems that Orwell had asked Leavis to write for *Tribune* and also asked whether he could recommend any young writers. Leavis refers to an article Orwell had proposed for *Scrutiny* and says he can only be non-committal about it because, owing to the severe shortage of paper, there was little room for other than planned or commissioned work. What the article was is not known; it might possibly have been the English version of the article for *Fontaine* on the English detective story (which Orwell mentions in his letter to Leonard Moore, 9 January 1944; see *2403*). Leavis says he is much too busy with academic duties, *Scrutiny*, washing-up, chopping wood, and taking the children to and from school, to get on with his own books, never mind contributing to *Tribune*. He suggests that, of 'young talent coming on,' R. C. Churchill (1916–1986) might be available and would be glad of the fees offered. Leavis also comments on Ivor Jacobs, though whether he was prompted to do so by Orwell or not is unclear. In conclusion he tells Orwell that the Downing Literary Society had several times considered inviting him to address its members, but since there are 'only priests & a few crocks; reading English,' the Society was hardly functioning.

R. C. Churchill was invited to write for *Tribune*, but no letter to him from Orwell has been traced. An article by Churchill, the first of many he contributed to *Tribune*, 'Gerard Hopkins—A Christian Socialist,' was published on 9 June 1944. It attracted correspondence in which the article was described as 'a stamping ground for the opinions of [Christopher] Fry, Shaw, Leavis, but Gerard Manley Hopkins is quite gone from such a sterile promontory' (7 July 1944). See also *2887*.

2403. To Leonard Moore
9 January 1944   Typewritten

10a Mortimer Crescent
London   NW 6

Dear Mr Moore,
Thanks for your letter. I think there might be the basis for a book of reprinted critical pieces when I have done one or two more which at present are only projected.[1] I don't think it is worth reprinting anything which has already been in print twice, but the other possible ones are:

Charles Dickens.	(about 12,000?)
Wells, Hitler and the World State.	(about 2000).
Rudyard Kipling.	(about 4000).
W. B. Yeats.	(about 2000).
Gandhi in Mayfair.	(about 3000).

The last 4 are all in "Horizon". In addition, when I can get the books for it, I am going to do for an American magazine an essay on "Raffles", probably about 3–4000. I also did one of about 2000 on Sherlock Holmes for the Free French magazine "Fontaine".[2] This I think could be put in but could do with some expansion. I would also like to put in an "imaginary conversation" I did on the wireless with Jonathan Swift, and perhaps the substance of another talk I did on Gerrard° Manley Hopkins, if I can get hold of the script of the latter. In all this might make a book of about 30,000 words or more.

I can't see to this now because I am overwhelmed with work. I am getting on with my book and unless I get ill or something hope to finish it by the end of March.[3] After that I have contracted to do one for the "Britain in Pictures" series, but that shouldn't take long.[4]

This thing I am doing now will be very short, about 20,000 to 25,000 words. It is a fairy story but also a political allegory, and I think we may have some difficulties about finding a publisher. It won't be any use trying it on Gollancz nor probably Warburg, but it might be worth dropping a hint elsewhere that I have a book coming along. I suppose you know which publishers have paper and which haven't?

Yours sincerely
Eric Blair

1. The collection was published in England by Secker & Warburg on 14 February 1946 as *Critical Essays*, and in the United States by Reynal & Hitchcock, New York, on 29 April 1946 as *Dickens, Dali & Others: Studies in Popular Culture*. Of the essays mentioned, 'Gandhi in Mayfair' and those on Sherlock Holmes, Swift, and Hopkins are not included; not mentioned here, but included are 'Boys' Weeklies,' 'The Art of Donald McGill,' and those on Dali, Koestler, and P. G. Wodehouse.
2. See *2357*.
3. *Animal Farm*.
4. *The English People*.

2404. 'As I Please,' 7

Tribune, 14 January 1944

The old custom of binding up magazines and periodicals in book form seems to have gone out almost entirely, which is a pity, for a year's issue of even a very stupid magazine is more readable after a lapse of time than the majority of books. I do not believe I ever had a better bargain than the dozen volumes of the *Quarterly Review*, starting in 1809, which I once picked up for two shillings at a farmhouse auction; but a good sixpennyworth was a year's issue of the *Cornhill* when either Trollope or Thackeray, I forget which, was editing it, and another good buy was some odd volumes of the *Gentleman's Magazine* of the mid-sixties, at threepence each. I have also had some happy half-hours with Chambers's *Papers for the People*, which flourished in the 'fifties, the *Boy's Own Paper* in the days of the Boer War, the *Strand* in its great Sherlock Holmes days, and—a book I unfortunately only saw and didn't buy—a bound volume of the *Athenæum* in the early 'twenties, when Middleton Murry was editing it, and T. S. Eliot, E. M. Forster and various others were making their first impact on the big public. I do not know why no one bothers to do this nowadays, for to get a year's issue of a magazine bound costs less than buying a novel, and you can even do the job yourself if you have a spare evening and the right materials.

The great fascination of these old magazines is the completeness with which they "date." Absorbed in the affairs of the moment, they tell one about political fashions and tendencies which are hardly mentioned in the more general history books. It is interesting, for instance, to study in contemporary magazines the war scare of the early 'sixties, when it was assumed on all sides that Britain was about to be invaded, the Volunteers were formed, amateur strategists published maps showing the routes by which the French armies would converge on London, and peaceful citizens cowered in ditches while the bullets of the Rifle Clubs (the then equivalent of the Home Guard) ricochetted in all directions.

The mistake that nearly all British observers made at that time was not to notice that Germany was dangerous. The sole danger was supposed to come from France, which had shot its bolt as a military power and had in any case no reason for quarrelling with Britain. And I believe that casual readers in the future, dipping into our newspapers and magazines, will note a similar aberration in the turning-away from democracy and frank admiration for totalitarianism which overtook the British intelligentsia about 1940. Recently, turning up a back number of *Horizon*, I came upon a long article on James Burnham's *Managerial Revolution*, in which Burnham's main thesis was accepted almost without examination.[1] It represented, many people would have claimed, the most intelligent forecast of our time. And yet—founded as it really was on a belief in the invincibility of the German army—events have already blown it to pieces.

Shortly, Burnham's thesis is this. *Laissez-faire* capitalism is finished and Socialism, at any rate in the present period of history, is impossible. What is now happening is the appearance of a new ruling class, named by Burnham the "managers." These are represented in Germany and the U.S.S.R. by the Nazis and Bolsheviks, and in the U.S.A. by the business executives. This new ruling class expropriates the capitalists, crushes the working-class movements and sets up a totalitarian society governed by the concept of efficiency. Britain is decadent and is bound to be rapidly conquered by Germany. After the conquest of Britain will come the attack on the U.S.S.R., and Russia's "military weakness" will cause her to "fall apart to east and west." You are then left with three great super-States, Germany, Japan and the U.S.A., which divide the world between them, make ceaseless war upon one another, and keep the working class in permanent subjection.

Now, there is a great deal in what Burnham says. The fact that collectivism is not inherently democratic, that you do not do away with class rule by formally abolishing private property, is becoming clearer all the time. The tendency of the world to split up into several great power blocks is also clear enough, and the fact that each of these would probably be invincible has sinister possibilities. But the test of a political theory is its power to foretell the future, and Burnham's predictions were falsified almost as soon as made. Britain was not conquered, Russia turned out not to be militarily weak, and—a much more fundamental error—Germany did attack Russia while the war against Britain was still in progress. Burnham had declared this to be impossible, on the ground that the German and Russian régimes were essentially the same and would not quarrel until the struggle against old-style capitalism was finished.

Obviously these mistakes were partly due to wish-thinking. Hating both Britain and the U.S.S.R., Burnham (and many American intellectuals of similar outlook) wanted to see both these countries conquered, and was also unable to admit that there *was* an essential difference between Russia and Germany. But the basic error of this school of thought is its contempt for the common man. A totalitarian society, it is felt, *must* be stronger than a democratic one: the expert's opinion *must* be worth more than the ordinary man's. The German army had won the first battles: therefore it must win the last one. The great strength of democracy, its power of criticism, was ignored.

It would be absurd to claim that either Britain or the U.S.A. are true democracies, but in both countries public opinion can influence policy, and while making many minor mistakes it probably avoids the biggest ones. If the German common people had had any say in the conduct of the war it is very unlikely, for instance, that they would have attacked Russia while Britain was still in the field, and still more unlikely that they would have wantonly declared war on America six months later. It takes an expert to make mistakes as big as that. When one sees how the Nazi régime has succeeded in smashing itself to pieces within a dozen years it is difficult to believe in the survival value of totalitarianism. But I would not deny that the "managerial" class *might* get control of our society, and that if they did they would lead us into some hellish places before they destroyed themselves. Where Burnham and his fellow-thinkers are wrong is in trying to spread the idea that totalitarianism is *unavoidable*, and that we must therefore do nothing to oppose it.

James Burnham, writing from New York, took issue with Orwell in *Tribune*, 24 March 1944; Orwell's reply was printed with it; see below. See also Orwell's review of *The Machiavellians*, 20 January 1944, *2407*; 'Second Thoughts on James Burnham,' May 1946, *2989*, and 'Burnham's View of the Contemporary World Struggle,' 29 March 1947, *3204*.

In your issue of January 14th, which I have just now seen, Mr. George Orwell comments at some length on my book, *The Managerial Revolution*—and comments also, for some strange reason, on me, of whom he knows nothing. Mr. Orwell, perhaps because he has not read my book, makes a number of mis-statements of fact on matters of some consequence, and I am therefore compelled to try to correct at least the more gross of these.

The greater part of the views which Mr. Orwell attributes to me I have not stated in *The Managerial Revolution*, or anywhere else, for the very simple reason that I do not believe them and have never believed them. I have never held a belief "in the invincibility of the German army." I never wrote that Britain "is bound to be rapidly conquered by Germany." I did not predict that Germany, Japan and the U.S.A. would be the three great super-states of the future, but, rather, a very different thing, that the Germany, Japan and U.S.A. of 1940 were "nuclear stages" in the historical process of the development of those super-states which nearly everyone now sees to be taking form out of this terrible war and its probable aftermath. Though I believed (and still believe) that there are important weaknesses in the Russian regime, and though I did not expect war to come so soon between Germany and Russia, I did not speak of Russia's "military weakness" (though Mr. Orwell puts the phrase between quotation marks), and I specifically predicted a Russo-German war. Nor have I ever stated that "totalitarianism is *unavoidable*." I have stated, and I do believe, that totalitarianism is, in all major nations, *probable*. Does Mr. Orwell understand the difference between these two judgments? Does he not grasp the fact that only through absolute clarity about the probability of totalitarianism, and about the direction of its advance (so carefully obscured by the totalitarians themselves), will we be able, precisely, to have a chance to overcome or avoid it?

To explain these non-existent views, and others which he reports correctly, Mr. Orwell suddenly turns from my book to me. "Hating both Britain and the U.S.S.R., Burnham . . . wanted to see both those countries conquered. . . ." This, really, is a little excessive. These personal psychological matters are, of course, irrelevant, but since Mr. Orwell has, from somewhere, dragged them in, let me note for his information: I hate no one, and if I hated, I should not squander so personal an emotion on that modern deified abstraction of ours, the "nation." So far as Britain goes, I am linked to her by blood, by culture, and by extended direct acquaintance; and I rate her political achievements more highly than those of any other nation. I have no such close relation to the U.S.S.R., and, consequently, no very strong feelings about them, taken as a whole, one way or another; I try, merely, to understand them. About the Stalinist regime in the U.S.S.R., however, I have, not feelings, but a convinced opinion: the opinion, namely, that, from the point of view of human well-being and of those human ideals of freedom, truth, love and beauty which for me constitute the justification of human existence, this regime is the worst so far known in history. But even accepting this judgment, I would not for a moment "want" the U.S.S.R. to be "conquered"—a conqueror, alas, would not bring those ideals with his armies.

May I add, finally, that I readily admit a number of deficiencies and errors in *The Managerial Revolution*, some of which have been made clear by the events of the past few years and others by criticism which the book has received. I am at present writing for English publication an article wherein I hope to introduce necessary corrections in my earlier estimate of the outlook for Britain in that "managerial society" which, in spite of the denunciations directed against those who talk about it, continues to develop, more rapidly than ever, on a world-scale around us.

James Burnham

George Orwell writes:
Two points here seem to be of importance:—

1. *The inevitability of totalitarianism.* Mr Burnham states over and over again that Socialism is almost certainly impossible, that democracy in the sense of self-government is impossible, that there must always be an oligarchy and that this oligarchy must inevitably rule by force and fraud. "The primary object, in practice, of all rulers, is to serve their own interest. . . . There are no exceptions. No theory, no promises, no morality, no amount of good will, no religion will restrain power." If democracy is impossible and all rulers are as described, what prospect can there be except totalitarianism? It is true that for a couple of chapters at the end of *The Machiavellians* Mr. Burnham hedges from this position, but these chapters are obviously a product of his personal quarrel with the Roosevelt administration and can easily be shown to be incompatible with the rest of the book.

2. *The Russo-German war.* Mr. Burnham now tries to water down his previous statement into "I did not expect war to come so soon between Russia and Germany." Actually he stated ex-cathedra that it *could* not come till after Britain had been defeated, and the fact that it did so invalidates his whole theory. Here are his own words:

"First had to come the death-blow that assured the toppling of the capitalist world order, which meant above all the destruction of the foundations of the British Empire (the keystone of the capitalist world order). This is the basic explanation of the Nazi-Soviet Pact, which is not intelligible on other grounds. The future conflict between Germany and Russia will be a managerial conflict proper; prior to the great world-managerial battles, the end of the capitalist order must be assured. The belief that Nazism is 'decadent capitalism' (which is besides *prima facie* implausible in that not Nazi Germany but France and England have displayed all the characteristics which have distinguished decadent cultures in past historical transitions) makes it impossible to explain reasonably the Nazi-Soviet Pact. From this belief followed the always-expected war between Germany and Russia, not the actual war to the death between Germany and the British Empire. The war between Russia and Germany is one of the managerial wars of the future."

If this does not mean that Britain is bound to be defeated, and that only *after* the defeat of Britain will Germany attack Russia, it means nothing at all. As to the coming war between Germany and the U.S.S.R.: "the Russian weaknesses indicate that Russia will not be able to endure, that it will crack apart, and fall towards east and west."

As we have seen, Britain was *not* conquered, Germany did attack Russia while Britain was still in the field, and the U.S.S.R. is "cracking apart" in a rather curious fashion. In view of all this I can well understand that Mr. Burnham may want to "correct" some of his earlier estimates. But don't let him therefore claim that they have been justified. We could all be true prophets if we were allowed to alter our prophesies after the event.

1. 'The Twentieth Century Revolution' by Dennis Routh, a sixteen-page review of Burnham's *The Managerial Revolution* and E. H. Carr's *The Conditions of Peace, Horizon*, September 1942. James Burnham (1905–1987) was a professor of philosophy at New York University, 1932–54. His book *The Managerial Revolution* was published in 1941; a revised edition in 1972. *The Machiavellians* (1943), *The Struggle for the World* (1947), *The Coming Defeat of Communism* (1950), *Suicide of the West* (1964), and *The War We Are In* (1967) were among his many publications. He was educated at Princeton University and Balliol College, Oxford, and was co-editor, with Philip E. Wheelwright of *The Symposium*, 1930–33. From 1933 to about 1939 he was associated with the Trotskyist, Fourth Internationalist group, and, for a time, edited its journal, *The New International*. Following disagreement with Trotsky, he broke with Trotskyism and pursued what his obituary in *The Times* (4 August 1987) described as a 'career of political prophecy and right-wing exaltation which brought him fame.' He was a founder editor with William F. Buckley, Jr., of *The National Review* in 1955 and was associated with the journal until his death.

2405. London Letter, 15 January 1944

Partisan Review, Spring 1944

I suppose by the time this is printed the Second Front will have opened. It is generally assumed that this will happen within the next few months, that the German part of the war will end this year; and that there will be a general election turning on domestic issues soon afterward. Meanwhile not much is happening politically. It has occurred to me that it might be useful if I gave you some background stuff about two contestants in the British political scene, Parliament and the Monarchy, which I have rather taken for granted in previous letters. But first of all something about current developments, in so far as there are any.

The Government's whole policy, internal and external, continues to move more and more openly to the right, while public feeling continues to swing leftward as strongly, I should say, in a more disillusioned way, as it did in 1940. Fed-upness and disbelief in sunshine promises are general, and show themselves in sudden outbursts of indignation like the row that occurred over

Mosley's release from internment. On the face of it this was a bad symptom amounting as it did to a popular protest against habeas corpus (incidentally there was far more clamor against Mosley's release than there had been in favor of locking him up in the beginning), and it is also true that most of the public demonstrations were stage-managed by Communists anxious to live down their own anti-war activities. But there was a great deal of genuine feeling, especially among working people, always on the ground that "they've only let him out because he's a rich man." Since 1940 we have suffered a long series of Thermidors, and people grasp the general drift, but only through events that influence their own lives. There is no authoritative voice on the left to tell them that things like the AMG[1] policy in Italy, or the jailing of the Indian Congress leaders, also matter. By-elections show a big turnover of votes against the Government, and in some cases a big rise in the percentage of the electorate voting. Since I wrote to you last, the Government has only lost one election (out of about half a dozen), but might have lost others if the opposition vote had not been split. There is a new crop of "Independent" candidates, whose policy is usually of a kind to split the opposition rather than the Government vote. Some people think that these "independents" are financed by the Conservative Party.

My own fear is that the moment the war is over the Conservatives will conduct a whirlwind campaign, present themselves as "the party that won the war," bring forward hundreds of handsome young RAF officers as candidates, promise everything under the sun, and then chuck it all down the drain as soon as they are back in office. However, more experienced observers than I think that they couldn't bring this off, the people have grown too wise to be fooled again, and the Government can only win the general election by keeping on the Coalition. Theoretically, this puts the Labor Party in the strong position of being able to extort a high price for their support, or else to fight the election on their own with a good chance of winning. In practice the existing Labor leaders, who are terrified of power, will certainly keep on the Coalition and demand very little in return, unless very strongly prodded from below: in which case we shall get a Parliament similar to the present one but with a stronger opposition. There have been a few tentative moves towards some kind of Popular Front, but they don't get far in the face of official Labor disapproval and the hostility of the minor left parties towards one another. The only organized opposition is still Common Wealth, which has made a little headway (they have won another by-election), but is suffering from mysterious internal dissensions. Control of it seems to have partly passed out of Acland's hands into those of a rather sinister business man[2] who is helping to finance it and is thought by some to have entered the party with the object of neutralizing it. Since Acland no leading figure has appeared on the Left except for Beveridge, who has won a kind of popular renown and probably has political ambitions. Though a professor rather than a politician, he is just conceivable as a popular leader— a lively, attractive little man, rather like Cripps in his willingness to talk to anybody, but much more genial. Nor has anyone worth bothering about appeared on the other side. The group of Disraelian "Young Tories," apart from having no definite policy, are a wretched crew, with not one really talented person among them.

Pro-Russian sentiment is still strong but is cooling off in my opinion. The Kharkov trials dismayed a lot of people. Even the distinctly doubtful public-opinion polls conducted by the Russophile *News-Chronicle* show that the mass of the people don't want reprisals or a vindictive peace, though they do want Germany disarmed. If they grasped what was happening I can imagine them turning anti-Russian quite rapidly if there were any question of forced labor or mass trials of war criminals; or even as the result of heavy casualties when the Second Front opens. Relations between the American troops and the locals are better, I think, though one could not call them good. There is much jealousy between American white and colored troops. The press shuts down on this subject to such an extent that when a rape or something like that happens, one can only discover by private inquiry whether the American involved is white or colored. Discussion of inter-allied relations is still avoided in the press and utterly taboo on the air. The best example of this is the BBC celebrating the 25th anniversary of the Red Army without mentioning Trotsky, but American susceptibilities are studied even more carefully than Russian. We are still not broadcasting in Russian—this at the request of the Russians themselves—though we are broadcasting in nearly 50 other languages.

Well, now a word or two about our ancient institutions.

PARLIAMENT

When I was working with the BBC I sometimes had to go and listen to a debate in the Commons.[3] The last time I had been there was about ten years previously, and I was very much struck by the deterioration that seemed to have taken place. The whole thing now has a mangy, forgotten look. Even the ushers' shirt fronts are grimy. And it is noticeable now that, except from the places they sit in (the opposition always sits on the Speaker's left), you can't tell one party from another. It is just a collection of mediocre-looking men in dingy, dark suits, nearly all speaking in the same accent and all laughing at the same jokes. I may say, however, that they don't look such a set of crooks as the French Deputies used to look. The most striking thing of all is the lack of attendance. It would be very rare indeed for 400 members out of the 640 to turn up. The House of Lords, where they are now sitting, only has seating accommodation for about 250, and the old House of Commons (it was blitzed) cannot have been much larger. I attended the big debate on India after Cripps came back. At the start there were a little over 200 members present, which rapidly shrank to about 45. It seems to be the custom to clear out, presumably to the bar, as soon as any important speech begins, but the House fills up again when there are questions or anything else that promises a bit of fun. There is a marked family atmosphere. Everyone shouts with laughter over jokes and allusions which are unintelligible to anyone not an MP, nicknames are used freely, violent political opponents pal up over drinks. Nearly any member of long standing is corrupted by this kind of thing sooner or later. Maxton,[4] the ILP MP, twenty years ago an inflammatory orator whom the ruling classes hated like poison, is now the pet of the House, and Gallacher,[5] the Communist MP, is going the same road. Each time I have been in the House recently I have found myself thinking the same thought— that the Roman Senate still existed under the later Empire.

I don't need [to] indicate to you the various features of capitalism that make democracy unworkable. But apart from these, and apart from the dwindling prestige of representative institutions, there are special reasons why it is difficult for able men to find their way into Parliament. To begin with, the out-of-date electoral system grossly favors the Conservative Party. The rural areas, where, on the whole, people vote as the landlords tell them to, are so much over-represented, and the industrial areas so much under-represented that the Conservatives consistently win a far higher proportion of seats than their share in the total vote entitles them to. Secondly, the electorate seldom have a chance to vote for anyone except the nominees of the party machines. In the Conservative Party safe seats are peddled round to men rich enough to "keep up" the seat (contributions to local charities, etc.), and no doubt to pay an agreed sum into the party funds as well. Labor Party candidates are selected for their political docility, and a proportion of the Labor MP's are always elderly trade-union officials who have been allotted a seat as a kind of pension. Naturally, these men are even more slavishly obedient to the party machine than the Tories. To any MP who shows signs of independent thought the same threat is always applied—"We won't support you at the next election." In practice a candidate cannot win an election against the opposition of his own party machine, unless the inhabitants of that locality have some special reason for admiring him personally. But the party system has destroyed the territorial basis of politics. Few MP's have any connection with their constituency, even to the extent of living there: many have never seen it till they go down to fight their first election. At this moment Parliament is more than usually unrepresentative because, owing to the war, literally millions of people are disenfranchised. There has been no register of voters since 1939, which means that no one under 25, and no one who has changed his place of residence, now has a vote; for practical purposes the men in the forces are disenfranchised as well. On the whole, the people who have lost their votes are those who would vote against the Government. It is fair to add that in the general mechanics of an election in England there is no dirty work—no intimidation, no miscounting of votes or direct bribery, and the ballot is genuinely secret.

The feeling that Parliament has lost its importance is very widespread. The electorate are conscious of having no control over their MP's; the MP's are conscious that it is not they who are directing affairs. All major decisions, whether to go to war, whether to open a second front, and where, which power to go into alliance with, and so forth, are taken by an Inner Cabinet which acts first and announces the fait accompli afterwards. Theoretically, Parliament has the power to overthrow the Government if it wishes, but the party machines can usually prevent this. The average MP, or even a minor member of the Government, has no more information about what is going on than any reader of the *Times*. There is an extra hurdle for any progressive policy in the House of Lords, which has supposedly been shorn of its powers but still has the power of obstruction. In all, only two or three bills thrown out by the Lords have ever been forced through by the Commons. Seeing all this, people of every political color simply lose interest in Parliament, which they refer to as "the talking shop." One cannot judge from wartime, but for years before the war the percentage of the electorate voting had been going down. Sixty percent was considered a high vote. In the big towns many people do not know the name of their MP or which constituency they live in. A social survey at a recent election showed that many adults now don't know the first facts about British electoral procedures—e.g., don't know that the ballot is secret.

Nevertheless, I myself feel that Parliament has justified its existence during the war, and I even think that its prestige has risen slightly in the last two or three years. While losing most of its original powers it has retained its power of criticism, and it is the only remaining place in which one is free, theoretically as well as practically, to utter literally any opinion. Except for sheer personal abuse (and even that has to be something fairly extreme), any remark made in Parliament is privileged. The Government has, of course, devices for dodging awkward questions, but can't dodge all of them. However, the importance of Parliamentary criticism is not so much its direct effect on the Government as its effect on public opinion. For what is said in Parliament cannot go altogether unreported. The newspapers, even the *Times*, and the BBC probably do tend to play down the speeches of opposition members, but cannot do so very grossly because of the existence of Hansard, which publishes the Parliamentary debates verbatim. The effective circulation of Hansard is small (2 or 3 thousand), but so long as it is available to anyone who wants it, a lot of things that the Government would like to suppress get across to the public. This critical function of Parliament is all the more noticeable because intellectually this must be one of the worst Parliaments we have ever had. Outside the Government, I do not think there can be thirty able men in the House, but that small handful have managed to give every subject from dive bombers to 18B[6] an airing. As a legislative body Parliament has become relatively unimportant, and it has even less control over the executive than over the Government. But it still functions as a kind of uncensored supplement to the radio—which, after all, is something worth preserving.

THE MONARCHY

Nothing is harder than to be sure whether royalist sentiment is still a reality in England. All that is said on either side is colored by wish-thinking. My own opinion is that royalism, i.e., popular royalism, was a strong factor in English life up to the death of George V, who had been there so long that he was accepted as "the" King (as Victoria had been "the" Queen), a sort of father figure and projection of the English domestic virtues. The 1935 Silver Jubilee, at any rate in the south of England, was a pathetic outburst of popular affection, genuinely spontaneous. The authorities were taken by surprise and the celebrations were prolonged for an extra week while the poor old man, patched up after pneumonia, and in fact dying, was hauled to and fro through slum streets where the people had hung out flags of their own accord and chalked "Long Live the King. Down with the Landlord" across the roadway.

I think, however, that the abdication of Edward VIII must have dealt royalism a blow from which it may not recover. The row over the abdication, which was very violent while it lasted, cut across existing political divisions, as can be seen from the fact that Edward's loudest champions were Churchill, Mosley and H. G. Wells; but broadly speaking, the rich were anti-Edward and the working classes were sympathetic to him. He had promised the unemployed miners that he would do something on their behalf, which was an offense in the eyes of the rich; on the other hand, the miners and other unemployed probably felt that he had let them down by abdicating for the sake of a woman. Some continental observers believed that Edward had been got rid of because of his association with leading Nazis and were rather impressed by this exhibition of Cromwellism. But the net effect of the whole business was probably to weaken the feeling of royal sanctity which had been so carefully built up from 1880 onwards. It brought home to people the personal powerlessness of the King, and it showed that the much-advertised royalist sentiment of the upper classes was humbug. At the least I should say it would need another long reign, and a monarch with some kind of charm, to put the royal family back where it was in George V's day.

The function of the King in promoting stability and acting as a sort of keystone in a non-democratic society is, of course, obvious. But he also has, or can have, the function of acting as an escape-valve for dangerous emotions. A French journalist said to me once that the monarchy was one of the things that have saved Britain from fascism. What he meant was that modern people can't, apparently, get along without drums, flags and loyalty parades, and that it is better that they should tie their leader-worship onto some figure who has no real power. In a dictatorship the power and the glory belong to the same person. In England the real power belongs to un-prepossessing men in bowler hats: the creature who rides in a gilded coach behind soldiers in steel breastplates is really a waxwork. It is at any rate possible that while this division of function exists a Hitler or a Stalin cannot come to power. On the whole the European countries which have most successfully avoided fascism have been constitutional monarchies. The conditions seemingly are that the royal family shall be long-established and taken for granted, shall understand its own position and shall not produce strong characters with political ambitions. These have been fulfilled in Britain, the Low Countries and Scandinavia, but not in, say, Spain or Rumania. If you point these facts out to the average left-winger he gets very angry, but only because he has not examined the nature of his own feelings toward Stalin. I do not defend the institution of monarchy in an absolute sense, but I think that in an age like our own it may have an innoculating effect, and certainly it does far less harm than the existence of our so-called aristocracy. I have often advocated that a Labor government, i.e., one that meant business, would abolish titles while retaining the royal family. But such a move would only have meaning if royal sentiment exists, and so far as I can judge it is much weakened. I am told that the royal visits to war factories are looked on as time-wasting ballyhoo. Nor did the news that the King had caused a black line to be painted round all the baths in Buckingham Palace do much to popularize the five-inch bath.

Well, no more news. I am afraid I have written rather a lot already. It is a foul winter, not at all cold, but with endless fogs, almost like the famous "London fogs" of my childhood. The blackout seems to get less and not more tolerable as the war goes on. Food is much as usual, but wine has almost vanished and whisky can only be bought by the nip, unless you have influential pals. There are air-raid alarms almost every night, but hardly any bombs. There is much talk about the rocket guns[7] with which the Germans are supposedly going to bombard London. A little while before the talk was of a four-hundred ton bomb which was to be made in the form of an enormous glider and towed across by fleets of German airplanes. Rumors of this kind have followed one another since the beginning of the war, and are always firmly believed in by numbers of people, evidently fulfilling some obscure pscyhological need.

Yours ever,
George Orwell

[Fee: £3.10.0; 15.1.44]

1. Allied Military Government.
2. Sir Richard Acland (1906–1990) became a Liberal M.P. in 1935; he announced his conversion to Socialism in 1939 and founded, in 1942, a new political party, Common Wealth, of which he became president. He was defeated as a Common Wealth candidate in 1945, then joined the Labour Party and entered Parliament at a by-election in 1947, representing Gravesend until 1955. From 1959 to 1974 he was a senior lecturer at St Luke's College of Education, Exeter. In 1944 he gave his estates in Devon and Somerset to the nation, because ownership of large estates was a heavy burden on his conscience (*SEAC News*, South East Asia Command, No. 352, 26 December 1944). The standpoint taken by Common Wealth was Utopian Socialism. It supported the war effort but, with the anti-war Independent Labour Party, formed the only organised Socialist opposition to the political truce and the Churchill government. Acland was one of the most brilliant and effective orators in the country and could fill a large provincial hall despite the blackout. Common Wealth was largely financed and organised by a businessman, Alan P. Good (1906–1953), who mystified many of his colleagues. As he explained himself, he was not a Socialist but believed that Acland's doctrines were good for industrial relations. However, he certainly made no discernible attempt to influence the party's policies, and confined himself to organising and providing its finances. For Orwell's profile of Acland in *The Observer*, 23 May 1943, see *2095*.
3. Presumably in connexion with the programme 'The Debate Continues.'
4. James Maxton (1885–1946), Independent Labour M.P., 1922–46; Chairman of the Independent Labour Party (ILP), 1926–31, 1934–39.
5. William Gallacher (1881–1965), Communist M.P., 1935–50, was the sole representative of his party in Parliament, 1935–45, but was then joined by Phil Piratin (who also lost his seat in 1950). Gallacher was Chairman of the Clyde Workers' Committee during World War I and a member of the Communist International from 1920.
6. Regulation 18b, under the Emergency Powers (Defence) Act, enabled aliens to be imprisoned on grounds that they might give aid and comfort to the enemy; see *2467, n. 1*.
7. The rumours were to be proved true. V-1 rockets were launched on London on the night of 13–14 June 1944, a week after D-Day. The first V-2 was launched against Paris on 6 September 1944 and on London on 8 September.

**2406. Review of *Democracy and the Individual* by C. K. Allen;
Disraeli and the New Age by Sir R. George Stapledon**

The Observer, 16 January 1944

Marxism may possibly be a mistaken theory, but it is a useful instrument for testing other systems of thought, rather like one of those long-handled hammers with which they tap the wheels of locomotives. Tap! Is this wheel cracked? Tap! Is this writer a bourgeois? A crude question, ignoring much, based on the principle of *cui bono* and assuming in advance that you know what is meant by *bono*: and yet it is surprising how often a pretentious book will seem suddenly hollow if you apply to it the simple question: Does this writer, or does he not, take account of the economic basis of society?

By this test both these books—the one by an old-fashioned Liberal, the other by an old-style Tory repainted and brought up to date—fail, or partly fail. Mr. Allen's able and quite extensive inquiry into the working of democracy gives one all the time a feeling of unreality, because he never seems ready to admit that economic inequality makes democracy impossible. It is not of much value to discuss methods of making Parliaments more representative, or private citizens more public-spirited, or laws more just, or liberty more secure, unless one starts by asking where the real seat of power lies. If the economic structure of any society is unjust, its laws and its political system will necessarily perpetuate that injustice. No tinkering with juridical forms, nor even that panacea, "education," will ever make much difference.

Though dismayed by certain features in our society, Mr. Allen seems to assume that Britain is a democracy. He is partly right, but he persistently underrates the power of money and privilege. It is staggering for instance to be told—and told immediately after an admission that rich men can and do buy up all the best lawyers—that we are all more or less equal before the law. On the other hand, Mr. Allen is quite right in emphasising the relative *decency* of British society, the lack of official corruption, the absence of a gendarmerie, the tolerance of minorities, the freedom of speech and—in theory—the Press. If democracy means popular rule, it is absurd to call Britain democratic. It is a plutocracy haunted by the ghost of a caste system. But if democracy means a society in which you can safely go into the nearest pub and utter your true opinion of the Government, then Britain is democratic. In any country two things are of fundamental importance, its economic structure and its history. Mr. Allen at any rate does not ignore the second when he is dealing with Britain. But if he would take a leaf out of Marx's book, he might come to feel that such questions as the plural vote or the exact limits of individual liberty are hardly of first-rate importance while five per cent. of the population own everything that matters.

In a way, Sir George Stapledon's incoherent book—it is not so much a book on Disraeli as a commentary on modern life with texts from Disraeli as starting-points—shows a better grasp of the nature of society than Mr. Allen's. His agricultural bias gives him something real to cling to, and he knows, more or less, what kind of world he wants to live in, and is aware that the spirit matters more than the forms. But he, too, seems to think it possible to effect a social change without any radical economic change. He wants a simpler, less hedonistic, more agricultural society, than our own, a society with the emphasis on duty and loyalty rather than on "rights" and the cash nexus. Much of what he says, especially when he speaks of a favourite subject, the decay of English agriculture, is acute and stimulating. But he nowhere makes it clear how drastically, if at all, he would be willing to redistribute property. He does not even make clear, while mentioning agriculture on almost every page, what are his feelings about the private ownership of land. And though he rightly deplores the way in which the English people have deserted the soil, when it comes to showing *why* they have deserted the soil he can only give superficial reasons.

Disraeli's name is much in the air at this moment, because of a widespread recognition that hedonism and the profit motive will not keep society healthy. Disraeli had a sense of *noblesse oblige*. He did not think in terms of "enlightened self-interest" and devil take the hindmost. But he did think in terms of hereditary privilege, and was able to combine this with very enlightened views on many subjects because, as a foreigner, he had an unjustified admiration for the British aristocracy. The society he wished for was a kind of moralised feudalism, a society neither plutocratic nor equalitarian. Herein lies his attraction for the neo-Tories, who are aware that laisser-faire capitalism is finished, but are frightened of the real alternatives. They want more charity, but not more justice—a redistribution of income, for instance, but not a redistribution of property. In other words, they want a better world with the same people at the top. But unfortunately the world is what it is just because those people are at the top, and it is sad to see anyone as sympathetic as Sir George Stapledon chasing an *ignis fatuus*.

[Fee: £7.7.0; 14.1.44]

2407. Review of *The Machiavellians* by James Burnham

Manchester Evening News, 20 January 1944

It is notorious that certain sins, crimes, and vices would lack attraction if they were not forbidden. Mr. Gandhi has described the shuddering joy with which, as a child, he sneaked down to some secret haunt in the bazaar and ate a plate of beef, and our grandfathers derived acute pleasure from drinking champagne out of the satin slippers of actresses.

So also with political theories. Any theory which is obviously dishonest and immoral ("realistic" is the favourite word at this moment) will find adherents who accept it just for that reason. Whether the theory works, whether it attains the result aimed at will hardly be questioned. The mere fact that it throws ordinary decency overboard will be accepted as proof of its grown-upness and consequently of its efficacy.

Mr. Burnham, whose managerial revolution won a large if rather short-lived renown by telling American business-men what they wanted to hear, has now set forth the political doctrine which he derives from Machiavelli and Machiavelli's modern followers, Mosca, Pareto, Michels,[1] and—though it is doubtful whether he really belongs in this school—Georges Sorel.[2]

The world-picture which Mr. Burnham has built up from the teachings of these writers is something like this:

Progress is largely an illusion, Democracy is impossible, though useful as a myth to deceive the masses.

Society is inevitably ruled by oligarchies who hold their position by means of force and fraud, and whose sole objective is power and still more power for themselves. No revolution means more than a change of rulers.

Man, as a political animal, is moved solely by selfish motives, except so far as he is under the influence of myths.

Conscious, planned action for the good of the community is impossible, since each group is simply trying to secure its own advantage.

Politics is, and can be, nothing except a struggle for power. Human equality, human fraternity are empty phrases.

All moral codes, all "idealistic" conceptions of politics, all visions of a better society in the future are simply lies, conscious or unconscious, covering the naked struggle for power.

Having set forth this thesis Mr. Burnham contradicts it to some extent by adding that various checks on the exercise of power are desirable, in particular, freedom of speech. He also, following Pareto, points out that a ruling caste decays if it is not renewed from time to time by able recruits from the masses.

In one place he even finds himself admitting that the Anglo-Saxon version of democracy has some survival value, and that the Germans might have avoided some of their strategic mistakes if they had not crushed internal opposition.

However, the sudden outburst in favour of freedom of speech, which occupies a chapter or two, is probably only a part of Mr. Burnham's quarrel with the Roosevelt Administration. He ends by looking forward to the emergence of a new ruling class, who will rule "scientifically" by the conscious use of force and fraud, but who will to some small extent serve the common good because they will recognise that it is to their own interest to do so.

Now, when one examines a political theory of this kind, the first thing one notices is that it is no more scientific than the idealistic creeds it professes to debunk. The premise from which Mr. Burnham starts out is that a relatively decent society, a society, for instance, in which everyone has enough to eat and wars are a thing of the past, is impossible. He puts this forward as an axiom.

Why is such a thing impossible? How is it "scientific" to make this quite arbitrary assumption?

The argument implied all the way through the book is that a peaceful and prosperous society cannot exist in the future because it has never existed in the past. By the same argument one could have proved the impossibility of aeroplanes in 1900, while only a few centuries earlier one could have "proved" that civilisation is impossible except on a basis of chattel slavery.

The fact is that much of Machiavelli's teaching has been invalidated by the rise of modern technology.

When Machiavelli wrote, human equality was, if not impossible, certainly undesirable. In the general poverty of the world a privileged class was needed to keep the arts of civilisation alive. In the modern world, where there is no material reason why every human being should not enjoy a fairly high standard of living, this need disappears.

Human equality is technically possible whatever the psychological difficulties may be, and of course the philosophies of Pareto, Mr. Burnham, and the rest are simply efforts to avoid this unwelcome fact.

The scientific approach to Machiavelli's teachings would have to find out what statesmen had modelled themselves upon Machiavelli, and how successful they had been. Mr. Burnham hardly makes this test. He does remark, as an illustration of Machiavelli's prestige, that Thomas Cromwell, Henry VIII's Chancellor, always carried a copy of "The Prince" in his pocket. He does not add that Cromwell ended on the block.

In our own day, Mussolini, the conscious pupil of Machiavelli and Pareto, does not seem to have made a very brilliant success of things. And the Nazi regime, based on essentially Machiavellian principles, is being smashed to pieces by the forces which its own lack of scruple conjured up.

It would seem that the theory that there is no such thing as a "good" motive in politics, that nothing counts except force and fraud, has a hole in it somewhere, and that the Machiavellian system fails even by its own test of material success.

In the managerial revolution[3] Mr. Burnham foretold that Britain would be swiftly conquered, that Germany would not attack Russia till the war with Britain was over, and that Russia would then be torn to pieces. These prophecies, obviously based on wish-thinking, were falsified almost as soon as made.

In the present book he has wisely refrained from foretelling anything so concrete, but assumes the same air of omniscience. It is doubtful whether he and the many others like him have done more than turn a copybook maxim on its head.

"Dishonesty is the best policy" is the sum of their wisdom. The fact that this shallow piece of naughtiness can—just because it sounds "realistic" and grown-up—be accepted without any examination does not speak well for the Anglo-American intelligentsia.

[Fee: £8.8.0; 19.1.44]

1. Gaetano Mosca (1858–1941), Italian jurist, Vilfredo Pareto (1848–1923), Italian economist and sociologist, and Robert Michels (1876–1936), German sociologist and economist, were all concerned with defining the nature and functions of political élites. Perhaps the most important work emanating from these theorists was Pareto's *Trattato di sociologia generale* (1916), translated as *Mind and Society* (1935). Italian Fascism drew on Pareto's theories.
2. For Georges Sorel, see *2396, n. 1.*
3. Presumably The Managerial Revolution (see *2404*) is intended.

2408. John Lehmann to Orwell

20 January 1944

On 20 January 1944, John Lehmann, editor of *Penguin New Writing*, which had reprinted 'Shooting an Elephant' in its first number, October 1940, the essay having first appeared in Lehmann's *New Writing*, No. 2, 1936, wrote to ask Orwell whether he had anything else on the lines of that essay which he could offer to *Penguin New Writing* or *New Writing & Daylight*. Lehmann had also published Orwell's essay 'Marrakech' in *New Writing*, Christmas 1939, and 'My Country Right or Left' in *Folios of New Writing*, Autumn, 1940. No reply to this letter has been traced, and Orwell did not contribute to either of these collections. It is curious that the essay 'How the Poor Die' was not then published. It must have been available and with discussions then being conducted on the setting up of a Welfare State it would have been timely. Whether or not Orwell offered it is not known. The essay eventually appeared in *Now*, November 1946; see *3103* for some account of its pre-publication history.

2409. 'Memories of the Blitz'

Tribune, 21 January 1944

> Not the pursuit of knowledge,
> Only the chances of war,
> Led me to study the music
> Of the male and the female snore;
>
> That night in the public shelter
> With the seats no pillow could soften,
> Where I fled, driven out of my bed
> By bombs too near and too often.
>
> And oh! the drone of the plane,
> And the answering boom of the gun,
> And the cups of tea in the dawn
> When the flames outdid the sun!
>
> That was so long ago,
> Three years ago or nearly,
> And more has perished than gasmasks;
> I could not tell you clearly
>
> What there can be to regret
> In a time of casual slaughter,
> When windows were empty of glass
> And pavements running with water;

But the guns have changed their tune,
And the sandbags are three years older;
Snow has kissed the flesh
From the bones of the German soldier;

The blimp[1] has a patch on its nose,
The railings have gone to the smelter;[2]
Only the ghost and the cat
Sleep in the Anderson shelter,[3]

For the song the sirens sang
Is sunk to a twice-told story,
And the house where the chartered accountant
Perished in headline glory

Is only a clump of willow-herb
Where I share my sorrow
With the deserted bath-tub
And the bigamous sparrow.

[Fee: 10s.6d; 17.1.44]

1. Barrage balloon, to make dive-bombing impracticable.
2. Metal railings were collected from around parks and gardens to be smelted down to provide raw material for war supplies.
3. A bomb shelter of corrugated iron set into earth, named after the Home Secretary, Sir John Anderson, who authorised its use in November 1938.

2410. 'As I Please,' 8

Tribune, 21 January 1944

The dropping of the Forces programme and the rumours of large-scale commercial broadcasting after the war have once again set people talking about the B.B.C. and its shortcomings. We hope to publish in the not too remote future some articles on various aspects of broadcasting, but I would like to suggest here, just as something to think over, that the B.B.C. is what it is because the public is not radio-conscious. People are vaguely aware that they don't like the B.B.C. programmes, that along with some good stuff a lot of muck is broadcast, that the talks are mostly ballyhoo and that no subject of importance ever gets the honesty of discussion that it would get in even the most reactionary newspaper. But they make no effort to find out, either in general or particular terms, *why* the programmes are bad, or whether foreign programmes are any better, or what is or is not technically possible on the air.

Even quite well-informed people seem completely ignorant of what goes on inside the B.B.C. When I was working in the B.B.C. I was concerned solely with broadcasting English programmes to India. This did not save me from being constantly buttonholed by angry people who asked me whether I could not "do something about" some item on the Home Programme—

which is like blaming a North Sea Coastguard for something that happens in Central Africa. A few months back there was a debate in the House of Commons in which our radio propaganda to America was criticised. Several M.P.s maintained that it was totally ineffective, which it is. But seemingly they knew this only by instinct. Not one of them was in a position to stand up and tell the House how much we spend every year in broadcasting to the U.S.A., and how many listeners this secures us—facts which they could quite easily have found out.

When the B.B.C. is attacked in the press, the attack is usually so ignorant that it is impossible to meet it. Some time ago I wrote to a well-known Irish writer,[1] now living in England, asking him to broadcast. He sent me an indignant refusal, which incidentally revealed that he did not know (a) that there is a Broadcasting Corporation in India, (b) that Indians broadcast every day from London, and (c) that the B.B.C. broadcasts in Oriental languages. If people don't even know that much, of what use are their criticisms of the B.B.C. likely to be? To quite a large extent the B.B.C. is blamed for its virtues while its real faults are ignored. Everyone complains, for instance, about the Kensingtonian accent of B.B.C. news-readers, which has been carefully selected *not* in order to cause annoyance in England, but because it is a "neutral" accent which will be intelligible wherever English is spoken. Yet how many people are aware that millions of public money are squandered in broadcasting to countries where there is virtually no audience? [2]

Here is a little catechism for amateur radio critics.

You say you don't like the present programmes. Have you a clear idea of what kind of programmes you *would* like? If so, what steps have you taken towards securing them?

In your opinion, are the B.B.C. news bulletins truthful? Are they more or less truthful than those of other belligerent countries? Have you checked this by comparison?

Have you any ideas about the possibilities of the radio play, the short story, the feature, the discussion? If so, have you bothered to find out which of your ideas are technically feasible?

Do you think the B.B.C. would benefit by competition? Give your opinion of commercial broadcasting.

Who controls the B.B.C.? Who pays for it? Who directs its policy? How does the censorship work?

What do you know of B.B.C. propaganda to foreign countries, hostile, friendly or neutral? How much does it cost? Is it effective? How would it compare with German propaganda? Add some notes on radio propaganda in general.

I could extend this considerably, but if even a hundred thousand people in England could give definite answers to the above questions it would be a big step forward.

A correspondent reproaches me with being "negative" and "always attacking things." The fact is that we live in a time when causes for rejoicing are not numerous. But I like praising things, when there is anything to praise, and I would like here to write a few lines—they have to be retrospective, unfortunately—in praise of the Woolworth's Rose.

In the good days when nothing in Woolworth's cost over sixpence, one of their best lines was their rose bushes. They were always very young plants, but they came into bloom in their second year, and I don't think I ever had one die on me. Their chief interest was that they were never, or very seldom, what they claimed to be on their labels. One that I bought for a Dorothy Perkins turned out to be a beautiful little white rose with a yellow heart, one of the finest ramblers I have ever seen. A polyantha rose labelled yellow turned out to be deep red. Another, bought for an Albertine, was like an Albertine, but more double, and gave astonishing masses of blossom. These roses had all the interest of a surprise packet, and there was always the chance that you might happen upon a new variety which you would have the right to name John Smithii or something of that kind.

Last summer I passed the cottage where I used to live before the war.[3] The little white rose, no bigger than a boy's catapult when I put it in, had grown into a huge vigorous bush, the Albertine or near-Albertine was smothering half the fence in a cloud of pink blossom. I had planted both of those in 1936. And I thought, "All that for sixpence!" I do not know how long a rose bush lives; I suppose ten years might be an average life. And throughout that time a rambler will be in full bloom for a month or six weeks each year, while a bush rose will be blooming, on and off, for at least four months. All that for sixpence—the price, before the war, of ten Players or a pint and a half of mild, or a week's subscription to the *Daily Mail*, or about twenty minutes of twice-breathed air in the movies!

Orwell's delight in sixpenny roses from Woolworth's brought forth this rebuke, printed on 4 February under the heading 'Sentimentality':

What a pity that the desultory paragraphs of "As I Please" are so uneven in character! After some interesting and instructive remarks on the nature of amateur radio-criticism it would seem that the remaining printing space had been allocated to Godfrey Winn rather than to George Orwell. It is unfortunate that *Tribune*, which has done much, consciously or unconsciously, to nourish a high standard of literary taste among its readers, should publish such a passage, instinct as it is, with bourgeois nostalgia, and in which sentiment gives place to sickly sentimentality. Obviously the meanest rose that blows has hardly "thoughts that lie too deep for tears" for Orwell, who addresses himself to the readers of best sellers and sentimentalised films, rather than to those who appreciate and enjoy good writing. Let him remember that the former type of reading public are singularly few in number amongst regular readers of *Tribune*.

Eileen E. Purber

[George Orwell writes:]
I am interested to learn that being fond of flowers is a sign of "bourgeois nostalgia." If so we are all bourgeois. One of the outstanding characteristics

of the working class of this country is their love of flowers, which not only accounts for the window boxes where nasturtiums try to flourish in the smokiest parts of London, but leads the agricultural labourer to spend his spare hours of daylight in cultivating his garden, sometimes even growing roses to the exclusion of vegetables. Or is "bourgeois" meant to apply to the extravagance of spending sixpence on a rosebush—this in a country where few working men spend less than a shilling a day on cigarettes?

1. Unidentified. It was unlikely to be Shaw, who allowed extracts of his work to be broadcast, or O'Casey, who did a broadcast for Orwell on 5 September 1943 (though no correspondence with him survives from Orwell's time at the BBC).
2. Orwell probably has the BBC service to India in mind. There was one radio to 3,875 people in India compared with 1 to 5.36 in England then, and broadcasts to India had to be made in several languages; see *892*.
3. Orwell's Albertine (or 'near-Albertine') was still flourishing at The Stores, Wallington, Hertfordshire, some fifty years later; see Pam Dajda, 'Careful restoration of Orwell's "awful" cottage,' *Cambridge Weekly News*, 24 November 1988.

2411. To Dwight Macdonald

25 January 1944   Handwritten

[On *Tribune* headed paper]
10a Mortimer Crescent
NW. 6

Dear Macdonald,

I don't know what one can do about these posts. I have just had your letter dated Dec. 24 saying you had not heard from me, although I must have written 2 or 3 months ago.

I told you in that letter (in case it's gone astray) that I was contemplating a thing on "Raffles". I wanted some modern crime story to compare it with & finally fixed on "No Orchids for Miss Blandish", which you've doubtless heard of. This may come out too long for your purposes but anyway I'll send you a copy when done & perhaps you might like to use a piece of it.[1] I don't know when it will be done—anything like this has to be sandwiched in with my regular work, & in addition I am writing a book[2] & under contract to do another.[3] But I will finish the thing some time as I have been much impressed with the importance of "No Orchids for Miss B."

I am going to try the experiment of sending this by ship this time & see if it gets there any sooner. All the best

Yours
Geo. Orwell

1. The essay, 'Raffles and Miss Blandish,' was published in England in *Horizon*, October 1944 (see *2538*) and in the United States in Macdonald's *Politics*, November 1944. *Politics* ran from Vol. 1, No. 1 to Vol. 6, No. 1, February 1944–Winter 1949, despite Macdonald's doubts as to its prospects, expressed in a letter to Orwell, 21 February 1944.
2. *Animal Farm*.
3. *The English People*.

2412. 'As I Please,' 9

Tribune, 28 January 1944

I see that Mr. Suresh Vaidya, an Indian journalist living in England, has been arrested for refusing military service.[1] This is not the first case of its kind, and if it is the last it will probably be because no more Indians of military age are left to be victimised.

Everyone knows without being told them the juridical aspects of Mr. Vaidya's case, and I have no wish to dwell on them. But I would like to draw attention to the commonsense aspect, which the British Government so steadily refuses to consider. Putting aside the seamen who come and go, and the handful of troops who are still here, there might perhaps be two thousand Indians in this country, of all kinds and ages. By applying conscription to them you may raise a few score extra soldiers; and by coercing the minority who "object" you may swell the British prison population by about a dozen. That is the net result from the military point of view.

But unfortunately that isn't all. By behaviour of this kind you antagonise the entire Indian community in Britain—for no Indian, whatever his views, admits that Britain had the right to declare war on India's behalf or has the right to impose compulsory service on Indians. Anything that happens in the Indian community here has prompt repercussions in India, and appreciable effects further afield. One Indian war-resister victimised does us more harm than ten thousand British ones. It seems a high price to pay for the satisfaction the Blimps probably feel at having another "Red" in their clutches. I don't expect the Blimps to see Mr. Vaidya's point of view. But they really might see, after all their experience, that making martyrs does not pay.

A correspondent has sent us a letter in defence of Ezra Pound,[2] the American poet who transferred his allegiance to Mussolini some years before the war and has been a lively propagandist on the Rome radio. The substance of his claim is that (a) Pound did not sell himself simply for money, and (b) that when you get hold of a true poet you can afford to ignore his political opinions.

Now, of course, Pound did not sell himself solely for money. No writer ever does that. Anyone who wanted money before all else would choose some more paying profession. But I think it probable that Pound did sell himself partly for prestige, flattery and a professorship. He had a most venomous hatred for both Britain and the U.S.A., where he felt that his talents had not been fully appreciated, and obviously believed that there was a conspiracy against him throughout the English-speaking countries. Then there were several ignominious episodes in which Pound's phoney erudition was shown up, and which he no doubt found it hard to forgive. By the mid-thirties Pound was singing the praises of "the Boss" (Mussolini) in a number of English papers, including Mosley's quarterly, *British Union* (to which Vidkun Quisling was also a contributor). At the time of the Abyssinian war Pound was vociferously anti-Abyssinian. In 1938 or thereabouts the Italians gave him a chair at one of their universities, and some time after war broke out he took Italian citizenship.

Whether a poet, as such, is to be forgiven his political opinions is a different question. Obviously one mustn't say "X agrees with me: therefore he is a good writer," and for the last ten years honest literary criticism has largely consisted in combating this outlook. Personally I admire several writers (Céline, for instance) who have gone over to the Fascists, and many others whose political outlook I strongly object to. But one has the right to expect ordinary decency even of a poet. I never listened to Pound's broadcasts, but I often read them in the B.B.C. Monitoring Report, and they were intellectually and morally disgusting. Anti-Semitism, for instance, is simply not the doctrine of a grown-up person. People who go in for that kind of thing must take the consequences. But I do agree with our correspondent in hoping that the American authorities do not catch Pound and shoot him, as they have threatened to do. It would establish his reputation so thoroughly that it might be a hundred years before anyone could determine dispassionately whether Pound's much-debated poems are any good or not.

The other night a barmaid informed me that if you pour beer into a damp glass it goes flat much more quickly. She added that to dip your moustache into your beer also turns it flat. I immediately accepted this without further inquiry; in fact, as soon as I got home I clipped my moustache, which I had forgotten to do for some days.

Only later did it strike me that this was probably one of those superstitions which are able to keep alive because they have the air of being scientific truths. In my notebook I have a long list of fallacies which were taught to me in my childhood, in each case not as an old wives' tale but as a scientific fact. I can't give the whole list, but here are a few hardy favourites:—

That a swan can break your leg with a blow of its wing.

That if you cut yourself between the thumb and forefinger you get lockjaw.

That powdered glass is poisonous.

That if you wash your hands in the water eggs have been boiled in (why anyone should do this is a mystery) you will get warts.

That bulls become infuriated at the sight of red.

That sulphur in a dog's drinking water acts as a tonic.[3]

And so on and so forth. Almost everyone carries some or other of these beliefs into adult life. I have met someone of over thirty who still retained the second of the beliefs I have listed above. As for the third, it is so widespread that in India, for instance, people are constantly trying to poison one another with powdered glass, with disappointing results.

I wish now that I had read *Basic English versus the Artificial Languages* before and not after reviewing the interesting little book in which Professor Lancelot Hogben sets forth his own artificial language, Interglossa.[4] For in that case I should have realised how comparatively chivalrous Professor Hogben had been towards the inventors of rival international languages. Controversies on serious subjects are often far from polite. Followers of the Stalinist-Trotskyist controversy will have observed that an unfriendly note tends to creep into it, and when the *Tablet* and the *Church Times* are having a go at one another the blows are not always above the belt. But for sheer dirtiness of fighting the feuds between the inventors of various of the international languages would take a lot of beating.

Tribune may before long print one or more articles on Basic English. If any language is ever adopted as a world-wide "second" language it is immensely unlikely that it will be a manufactured one, and of the existing natural ones English has much the best chance, though not necessarily in the Basic form. Public opinion is beginning to wake up to the need for an international language, though fantastic misconceptions still exist. For example, many people imagine that the advocates of an international language aim at suppressing the natural languages, a thing no one has ever seriously suggested.

At present, in spite of the growing recognition of this need, the world is growing more and not less nationalistic in language. This is partly from conscious policy (about half a dozen of the existing languages are being pushed in an imperialistic way in various parts of the world), and partly owing to the dislocation caused by the war. And the difficulties of trade, travel and intercommunication between scientists, and the time-wasting labour of learning foreign languages, still continue. In my life I have learned seven foreign languages, including two dead ones, and out of those seven I retain only one, and that not brilliantly. This would be quite a normal case. A member of a small nationality, a Dane or a Dutchman, say, has to learn three foreign languages as a matter of course, if he wants to be educated at all. Clearly this position could be bettered, and the one great difficulty is to decide which language is to be adopted as the international one. But there is going to be some ugly scrapping before that is settled, as anyone who has even glanced into this subject knows.

On 4 February, *Tribune* published a rejoinder from Douglas Goldring.[5] Although he thought most of Pound's ideas 'barmy,' he defended him in his predicament and attempted to explain how Pound came to think Mussolini a superman. He concluded:

In his present predicament Ezra has proved a useful scapegoat for recent turncoats. His views on Abyssinia were shared by most English Catholic converts as well as by a considerable number of English Army officers and Foreign Office high-ups. Admiration of Mussolini, as of Franco, was prevalent among our Conservative class, at least until June, 1940. . . .

Ezra, though a romantic and misguided ass, was never a rat; consequently, he failed to leave the sinking ship while the going was good.

George Orwell's comment that Pound "did not sell himself solely for money" looks like an indulgence, on his part, in that favourite public school pastime, "kicking a man when he is down."

1. Suresh Vaidya had informed the Council for the International Recognition of Indian Independence some eighteen months earlier that 'he would take his stand on purely political grounds and would never submit to medical examination.' A campaign was prepared by the

Council on this basis, but he did not take his stand on political grounds alone and he did submit to a medical examination. The Council therefore decided that it 'could not base any *public agitation* on the case presented by Mr. Suresh Vaidya.' This led to bitter dissension among groups supporting a campaign for Indian independence, and, in particular, an attack by Fenner Brockway (see *363, n. 4*) in a letter which, though marked personal to A. N. Bose, Vice-Chairman of the Council, was circulated by Brockway. This resulted in a strong denunciation of his behaviour by Bose. Bose's letter was also circulated, and a copy was sent to Orwell by P. B. Seal, the Council's General Secretary. It is from that letter that the quotations above are taken. Bose also commented on the Indian Section of the BBC:

> I should like at this stage to add a word or two about the Indian section of the B.B.C. It is well known that this section of the B.B.C. was organised for the sole purpose of doing propaganda in India, and stimulating war effort there. Therefore, any person who takes part in its programme° cannot at the same time claim that he is against war effort in India. Two kinds of Indians have taken part in its programme. First, there are those who for financial and other personal reasons have taken part in it. Others have spoken for this section of the B.B.C., because, they do support war effort on wider ideological grounds. It is immaterial for our purpose whether a person gives a straight political talk or not.

This letter was amongst Orwell's papers at his death.

2. Paul Potts (author of *Dante Called You Beatrice*, which includes a moving tribute to Orwell, 'Don Quixote on a Bicycle') wrote in defence of Ezra Pound, who was then facing trial for collaboration with the enemy, in *Tribune*, 28 January 1944. See also, 'A Prize for Ezra Pound', May 1949, *3612*.
3. See material for 'The Quick and the Dead,' *2376*, f1 and f17, and explanatory note, *2375*. The reason that water in which eggs had been boiled might be used for washing was that, when running hot water was less common than it is today, it could be added to cold water to raise its temperature.
4. Orwell reviewed *Interglossa* in the *Manchester Evening News*, 23 December 1943; see *2395*.
5. Douglas Goldring (1887–1960), novelist, critic, and travel writer; Lecturer in English, University College of Commerce, Gothenburg, Sweden, 1925–27. Orwell reviewed his *Facing the Odds* in *Tribune*, 5 July 1940, describing Goldring as 'a Socialist with a love of the past,' (see *650*), and *The Nineteen-Twenties*, 6 January 1946 (see *2843*). Orwell included Goldring in his list of Crypto-Communists and Fellow-Travellers (see *3732*), describing him as 'Probably venal. Shallow person.'

2413. Review of *The Devil and the Jews* by Joshua Trachtenberg; *Why I Am a Jew* by Edmond Fleg, translated by Victor Gollancz

The Observer, 30 January 1944

It is time that Mass Observation or some similar body made a full inquiry into the prevalence of anti-Semitism, delicate though this subject is in the context of the present war. Popular prejudice against Jews is certainly widespread, and may be growing. But it is very important to determine how far this is true anti-Semitism, an essentially magical doctrine, and how far it is mere xenophobia and rationalisation of economic grievances.

Explanations of anti-Semitism generally fall into two schools which might be called the "traditional" and the "economic." Neither is fully satisfying. Left Wing thinkers nearly always accept the second explanation, seeing the Jew as simply a convenient scapegoat whom the rulers of society can make responsible for their own misdeeds. When crops fail or unemployment increases, blame it on the Jews—that is the formula, roughly. The trouble is that it is not clear why the Jews, rather than some other minority group, should always be picked on, why anti-Semitism also flourishes among people who have no strong economic grievance, or why it should be mixed up with irrelevant magical beliefs. But the other theory, which sees anti-Semitism as chiefly a heritage from the Middle Ages, does not cover all the facts either, as these two books show.

Edmond Fleg, in his touching little book – it describes his return to the faith of his forefathers after many years of scepticism—suggests that the Jews are persecuted simply "because they are Jews": that is, because they have clung to their religious and cultural identity in an alien environment. But so have many other small groups all over the world, and it is very doubtful whether modern Europe cares enough for doctrinal questions to want to persecute people merely because they are not Christians.

Mr. Trachtenberg thinks that anti-Semitism is a medieval hangover which the modern world has somehow forgotten to get rid of. With immense wealth of instances and copious illustrations he traces the persecution of the Jews from the early Middle Ages onward. They were lynched, burned, broken on the wheel, expelled from one country after another; they were accused of poisoning, sodomy, communicating with the Devil, practising ritual murder, drinking the blood of children, seducing Christian maidens, emitting a distinctive and disgusting smell, desecrating the Host, riding on broomsticks, giving birth to young pigs—pretty well everything, in fact. Although "infidels" they were also, somewhat illogically, regarded as "heretics," and the worst persecution of the Jews more or less coincides with the period of heresy-hunting—that is, from about the twelfth century onwards. The Reformation did them little good, for they were equally heretics from the Protestant point of view, Martin Luther being an exceptionally bitter anti-Semite.

Mr. Trachtenberg has no difficulty in showing the irrational nature of the medieval attitude towards the Jews. There was no clear basis for it except the charge that the Jews were usurers, and, as he points out, Christian competition invaded this field as soon as moneylending became really profitable. Had he extended his survey to modern times he might have added that contemporary ideas about the Jews are often equally irrational—for instance, the characteristic Fascist belief that the Jew somehow contrives to be a capitalist and a Communist simultaneously, or that the poverty-stricken Jewish working class are all secretly millionaires.

But two things remain unexplained. One is why the persecution of Jews, which is, after all, a pre-Christian thing, ever started. The other is why—if Mr. Trachtenberg's thesis is correct—this particular medieval superstition should have survived when so many others have perished. Very few people now believe in witchcraft, belief in which, according to Mr. Trachtenberg, led to a hundred thousand executions between 1450 and 1550 in Germany alone. Why are so many people still ready to believe that Jews "smell," or that they caused the war, or that they are plotting to conquer the world, or that they are responsible for slumps, revolutions, and venereal disease? The whole subject needs cold-blooded investigation. And the fact that we should probably find that anti-Semitism of various kinds is alarmingly common, and that educated people are not in the least immune from it, ought not to deter us.

[Fee: £7.7.0; 26.1.44]

This review produced a flood of correspondence. One or two letters were appreciative; most were appalling examples of anti-Semitism. One suggestion— that 'A new law making defamation of a race a penal offence'—was eventually passed (Race Relations Act, November 1965), but as a result of attacks on black immigrants. All of this correspondence was redirected by *The Observer* to Orwell, and no letters were published in the newspaper. In fact, *The Observer* published no letters in 1944 until 30 July. See the opening sentence of 'As I Please,' 11, 11 February 1944, *2417*.

2414. To R. S. R. Fitter

31 January 1944   Typewritten

Tribune

Dear Mr. Fitter,[1]
I am very sorry to say that your review for "Harriet Martineau"[2] appears to have gone astray. At any rate I can find no trace of our ever having had it. Whether we or the Post Office are to blame I don't know. Do you think you could manage to do it again? Thanks for the carbon copy of "The Economist".

I wonder whether you would like to review "A Gang of Ten" (a novel for young people) by Erika Mann, which I am sending you? I should say 500 words or thereabouts.

Yours truly,
[Signed] Geo. Orwell
George Orwell, Literary Editor

1. Richard S. R. Fitter (1913–) published *London's Natural History* (1945) and *London's Birds* (1949), followed by several more books on birds. His review of J. C. Nevill's *Harriet Martineau* appeared in *Tribune*, 10 March 1944. The review of *A Gang of Ten* followed on 17 March. On 11 February 1944 his review of *The Economist, 1843–1943: A Centenary Volume* was published.
2. Harriet Martineau (1802–1876), writer and journalist; her early books were on religious topics but she then turned to political economy. Her book on her visit to the United States (*Society in America*, 1837) contains remarks upon slavery. She also wrote novels, a wide variety of other work, from *Two Letters on Cow-Keeping* to guidebooks and *England and Her Soldiers*. Her autobiography (3 volumes, 1877) is still of considerable interest.

2415. Review of *Tom Sawyer and Huckleberry Finn* by Mark Twain; *Off the Record* by the Countess of Oxford and Asquith

Manchester Evening News, 3 February 1944

Everyman Library editors are in error when they describe "Tom Sawyer" and "Huckleberry Finn" as "the best of Mark Twain," but these two books are certainly among the half-dozen that he will be remembered by, and they are of special interest for their picture of the background—and not only the physical background—from which Mark Twain sprang.

All that is best in Mark Twain has some connection either with the Mississippi River or with the Western mining towns. Take him away from that environment—the environment he had known in his youth and early manhood—and he always fumbles, whether he is attempting a travel diary, a novel, or a life of Joan of Arc. In a sense he never grew up, he never made up his mind on the most fundamental questions, and nothing really significant seems to have happened to him when he was much past thirty.

That wonderful boyhood in the 'forties, on the banks of the Mississippi, was a sort of mine that he was still exploiting into old age. It produced, besides the two books named above, "Roughing It," "The Innocents at Home," and, above all, "Life on the Mississippi," which Arnold Bennett described with pardonable exaggeration as "that incomparable masterpiece for which I would exchange the entire works of Thackeray and George Eliot."

"Huckleberry Finn" overlaps with "Life on the Mississippi" somewhat more than does "Tom Sawyer."

Everyone knows its story, in so far as it has a story. A runaway boy, the kind of ragged homeless, vagabond boy who in those days in Western America could not only exist but grow up into a fairly decent human being, is floating down the river on a raft in company with an escaped slave. They have incredible adventures (the best is when they fall in with two rogues who describe themselves as a duke and a king and work various swindles in the riverside towns), but the real hero of the book is the river itself.

Although there is little scenic description (the story is supposedly told in Huckleberry Finn's own words) the vast, warm, muddy, uncontrollable stream, which carries whole villages away in its floods but also makes possible an easy, lounging, hospitable, tobacco-chewing kind of life, seems to dominate every page.

"Huckleberry Finn" is a kind of sequel to "Tom Sawyer," and Tom himself reappears towards the end, bringing with him the less adult atmosphere which characterises the earlier book.

Huck is a pure savage, but in some ways precociously wise, prizing liberty above everything and yet naturally unromantic. Tom is a more typical American boy, with a good home behind him, ignorant enough and yet full of intellectual curiosity, his head stuffed with adventure stories and youthful love affairs.

It was not an accident that for two generations or more the best books dealing with childhood came from America. The real secret of books like "Tom Sawyer" on the one hand and "Helen's Babies" or "Little Women" on the other, was that nineteenth-century America was a very good place in which to be young.

The American boy dreamed of becoming President, or, alternatively, of becoming a pilot on a Mississippi steamboat. He did not have the consciousness of being doomed in advance to a stool in a bank or an insurance office. But above all, the easy, generous life that Mark Twain and the others describe rests on a basis of Puritanism.

Puritan ethics and religious beliefs were still firm. The family was still a powerful institution. Tom Sawyer may run away from home and live a wild life in the woods for a week at a time, but Aunt Polly is always there with her Bible and her doughnuts, and though he regards Sunday school without enthusiasm he is certain that he will be struck by lightning if he fails to say his prayers. He is full of superstitions, learned largely from the negroes, and his education does not go much beyond the three R's and a painfully acquired collection of hymns and Biblical texts. But he has the advantage of never having heard of a movie or a soda fountain.

Of the two books contained in this volume "Tom Sawyer" is probably the better.

It has in it a well-constructed and reasonably credible story, and it is not written in the dialect which makes "Huckleberry Finn" rather tiresome to read for more than a short stretch at a time.

As social history both books are of the greatest value. It would be nice if, at some time, the Everyman Library decided to reprint "Roughing It" and "The Innocents at Home," neither of which is now easy to procure. Meanwhile "Tom Sawyer" is a good introduction to Mark Twain's work, a sort of curtain-raiser for his larger masterpiece, "Life on the Mississippi."

The chief impression left by "Off the Record," a little pendant to Lady Oxford's autobiography, is one of astonishment. How can anyone who has known every Prime Minister from Gladstone onwards have so little to say about them, and how can anyone who has enjoyed every possible educational advantage write so badly?

The book abounds with superlatives—"He was the kindest of men," "A more generous man never lived," "The most brilliant man I have ever known," etc., etc.—so that with two exceptions our leading politicians of the past fifty years appear as a gallery of rather uninteresting angels. The exceptions are Ramsay MacDonald and, of course, Lloyd George.

The best passage in the book describes a visit to No. 10, Downing Street on the night before Chamberlain resigned. But once again a piece of probably valuable information is withheld. Chamberlain told Lady Oxford that "there is only one man that I find hard to forgive."

Who this man was would be worth knowing. Apart from one or two tantalising touches like this the book is very thin stuff, and in some passages incoherently written.

[Fee: £8.8.0; 2.2.44]

2416. 'As I Please,' 10

Tribune, 4 February 1944

When Sir Walter Raleigh was imprisoned in the Tower of London, he occupied himself with writing a history of the world. He had finished the first volume and was at work on the second when there was a scuffle between some workmen beneath the window of his cell, and one of the men was killed. In spite of diligent enquiries, and in spite of the fact that he had actually seen the thing happen, Sir Walter was never able to discover what the quarrel was about: whereupon, so it is said—and if the story is not true it certainly ought to be—he burned what he had written and abandoned his project.[1]

This story has come into my head I do not know how many times during the past ten years, but always with the reflection that Raleigh was probably wrong. Allowing for all the difficulties of research at that date, and the special difficulty of conducting research in prison, he could probably have produced a world history which had some resemblance to the real course of events. Up to a fairly recent date, the major events recorded in the history books probably happened. It is probably true that the battle of Hastings was fought in 1066, that Columbus discovered America, that Henry VIII had six wives, and so on. A certain degree of truthfulness was possible so long as it was admitted that a fact may be true even if you don't like it. Even as late as the last war it was possible for the *Encyclopædia Britannica*, for instance, to compile its articles on the various campaigns partly from German sources. Some of the facts—the casualty figures, for instance—were regarded as neutral and in substance accepted by everybody. No such thing would be possible now. A Nazi and a non-Nazi version of the present war would have no resemblance to one another, and which of them finally gets into the history books will be decided not by evidential methods but on the battlefield.

During the Spanish Civil War I found myself feeling very strongly that a true history of this war never would or could be written. Accurate figures, objective accounts of what was happening, simply did not exist. And if I felt that even in 1937, when the Spanish Government was still in being, and the lies which the various Republican factions were telling about each other and about the enemy were relatively small ones, how does the case stand now? Even if Franco is overthrown, what kind of records will the future historian have to go upon? And if Franco or anyone at all resembling him remains in power, the history of the war will consist quite largely of "facts" which millions of people now living know to be lies. One of these "facts," for instance, is that there was a considerable Russian army in Spain. There exists the most abundant evidence that there was no such army. Yet if Franco remains in power, and if Fascism in general survives, that Russian army will go into the history books and future schoolchildren will believe in it. So for practical purpose the lie will have become truth.

This kind of thing is happening all the time. Out of the millions of instances which must be available, I will choose one which happens to be verifiable. During part of 1941 and 1942, when the Luftwaffe was busy in Russia, the German radio regaled its home audience with stories of devastating air-raids on London. Now, we are aware that those raids did not happen. But what use would our knowledge be if the Germans conquered Britain? For the purposes of a future historian, did those raids happen, or didn't they? The answer is: If Hitler survives, they happened, and if he falls they didn't happen. So with innumerable other events of the past ten or twenty years. Is the Protocols of the Elders of Zion[2] a genuine document? Did Trotsky plot with the Nazis? How many German aeroplanes were shot down in the Battle of Britain? Does Europe welcome the New Order? In no case do you get one answer which is universally accepted because it is true: in each case you get a number of totally incompatible answers, one of which is finally adopted as the result of a physical struggle. History is written by the winners.

In the last analysis our only claim to victory is that if we win the war we shall tell less lies about it than our adversaries. The really frightening thing about totalitarianism is not that it commits "atrocities" but that it attacks the concept of objective truth: it claims to control the past as well as the future. In spite of all the lying and self-righteousness that war encourages, I do not honestly think it can be said that that habit of mind is growing in Britain. Taking one thing with another, I should say that the press is slightly freer than it was before the war. I know out of my own experience that you can print things now which you couldn't print ten years ago. War-resisters have probably been less maltreated in this war than in the last one, and the expression of unpopular opinions in public is certainly safer. There is some hope, therefore, that the liberal habit of mind, which thinks of truth as something outside yourself, something to be discovered, and not as something you can make up as you go along, will survive. But I still don't envy the future historian's job. Is it not a strange commentary on our time that even the casualties in the present war cannot be estimated within several millions?

Announcing that the Board of Trade is about to remove the ban on turned-up trouser-ends, a tailor's advertisement hails this as "a first instalment of the freedom for which we are fighting."

If we were really fighting for turned-up trouser-ends, I should be inclined to be pro-Axis. Turn-ups have no function except to collect dust, and no virtue except that when you clean them out you occasionally find a sixpence there. But beneath that tailor's jubilant cry there lies another thought: that in a little while Germany will be finished, the war will be half over, rationing will be relaxed, and clothes snobbery will be in full swing again. I don't share that hope. The sooner we are able to stop food rationing the better I shall be pleased, but I would like to see clothes rationing[3] continue till the moths have devoured the last dinner jacket and even the undertakers have shed their top hats. I would not mind seeing the whole nation in dyed battledress for five years if by that means one of the main breeding points of snobbery and envy could be eliminated. Clothes rationing was not conceived in a democratic spirit, but all the same it has had a democratising effect. If the poor are not much better dressed, at least the rich are shabbier. And since no real structural change is occurring in our society, the mechanical levelling process that results from sheer scarcity is better than nothing.

A copy of *The Ingoldsby Legends* which someone gave me for Christmas, with illustrations by Cruikshank, set me wondering about the reasons for the decline in English comic draughtsmanship. The decline in comic verse is easier to explain. Barham himself, Hood, Calverley, Thackeray, and other writers of the early and middle nineteenth century, could write good light verse, things in the style of

> Once, a happy child, I carolled
> On green lawns the whole day through,
> Not unpleasingly apparelled
> In a tightish suit of blue,[4]

because on the whole, life—middle-class life—was carefree and one could go from birth to death with a boyish outlook. Except for an occasional thing like Clough's "How pleasant it is to have money," or "The Walrus and the Carpenter," English comic verse of the nineteenth century does not have any ideas in it. But with the draughtsmen it is just the other way about. The attraction of Leech, Cruikshank and a long line of them stretching back to Hogarth is in their intellectual brutality. *Punch* would not print Leech's illustrations to *Handley Cross* if they were new to-day. They are much too brutal: they even make the upper classes look as ugly as the working class! But they are funny, which *Punch* is not. How came it that we lost both our light-heartedness and our cruelty round about 1860? And why is it that now, when class-hatred is as fierce and political passion as near the surface as they were in the time of the Napoleonic wars, cartoonists who can express them are hardly to be found? [5]

1. Sir Walter Raleigh (1552?–1618) was imprisoned in the Tower at the accession to the English throne of James VI of Scotland in 1603. Whilst there he began his *History of the World*, intended for James's son Prince Henry (who, it is claimed, said, 'Only my father would keep such a bird in a cage'). The first volume, to 130 BC, was published in 1614. Raleigh was released in 1616 to lead an expedition to Guiana for gold. Against orders, he attacked the Spanish settlement at St. Thomas and on his return was beheaded at the behest of the Spanish ambassador. Whether or not there is truth in Orwell's anecdote, Raleigh had insufficient time to write much more of his *History* and, in any case, Prince Henry had died, much mourned, in 1612.

2. *The Protocols of the Elders of Zion* was a particularly vicious fraud purporting to show how Judaism should spread throughout the world subverting liberalism and Christian societies. Its origins are expertly described by Nicolas Barker in the British Library's *Fake? The Art of Deception*, edited by Mark Jones (1990, 70–72), from which these notes are extracted. The fraud is based on two works: an attack on the French Third Empire by a lawyer, Maurice Joly, *Dialogue aux enfers entre Montesquieu et Machiavel* (Brussels, 1864), and a virulent anti-Semitic tract by the Serb, Osman Bey, *Die Eroberung der Welt durch die Juden* (Wiesbaden, 1875). The two were (according to Mikhail Lepekhine) written up by Mathieu Golovinski (*Daily Telegraph*, 19.11.99) in the anti-Semitic newspaper *Znamya* (St. Petersburg, 1903). Joly's text was manipulated, and a measure of the work's preposterous nature can be gauged from its proposal that underground railways should join capital cities so that the Elders could quell opposition by using them to blow up the cities should the need arise. This fraudulent work was printed many times in Rusia and after 1917 spread abroad. It was reported in *The Times*, 8 May 1920, but exposed in August 1921. Nevertheless it is still in print, and Barker reports that it was 'printed recently in Los Angeles by a body called the Christian Nationalist Crusade.'

3. Each man, woman, and child was given 66 clothing coupons a year. The number of coupons required varied for each of these categories. Thus an overcoat for a man required 16 coupons; for a woman, 14; for a boy, 7, and for a girl, 11. Shoes required 7, 5, 3, and 3 coupons respectively.

4. In writing about humour in verse Orwell discreetly displays a subtle wit of his own. These lines are taken from R. S. Calverley's ode 'On a Distant Prospect of Making a Fortune,' a prospect Orwell might well have understood until *Animal Farm* proved successful. But the relevance of quoting from this particular example of humorous verse is that Calverley was parodying Thomas Gray's 'Ode on a Distant Prospect of Eton College.' Gray not only wrote of those who 'from the stately brow / Of Windsor's heights the expanse below / Of grove, of lawn, of mead survey' where the schoolboys—'the little victims'—play, but of that 'Poverty . . . That numbs the soul with icy hand, / And slow-consuming Age' that awaited so many. The lines are again quoted in Orwell's essay 'Funny, But Not Vulgar'; see *2585*. The allusion to 'green lawns' may also have an Eton connexion. It may refer to the 'Sixth Form Lawn' upon which only members of that form (of which Orwell became a member) could walk, and play croquet.

5. A letter from H. Jacobs in *Tribune*, 18 February 1944, asked what gave Orwell the privilege of writing such dogmatic nonsense as '*Punch* is not funny' and that we had lost our lightheartedness and cruelty about 1860. As for the lack of appropriate cartoonists, had he not (overlooking Orwell's 'hardly to be found') heard of Low? See 'As I Please,' 12, 18 February 1944, *2422*.

2417. 'As I Please,' 11

Tribune, 11 February 1944

There are two journalistic activities that will always bring you a come-back. One is to attack the Catholics and the other is to defend the Jews. Recently I happened to review some books dealing with the persecution of the Jews in medieval and modern Europe.[1] The review brought me the usual wad of anti-Semitic letters, which left me thinking for the thousandth time that this problem is being evaded even by the people whom it concerns most directly.

The disquieting thing about these letters is that they do not all come from lunatics. I don't greatly mind the person who believes in the Protocols of the Elders of Zion, nor even the discharged army officer who has been shabbily treated by the Government and is infuriated by seeing "aliens" given all the best jobs. But in addition to these types there is the small business or professional man who is firmly convinced that the Jews bring all their troubles upon themselves by underhand business methods and complete lack of public spirit. These people write reasonable, well-balanced letters, disclaim any belief in racialism, and back up everything they say with copious instances. They admit the existence of "good Jews," and usually declare (Hitler says just the same in *Mein Kampf*) that they did not start out with any anti-Jewish feeling but have been forced into it simply by observing how Jews behave.

The weakness of the Left wing attitude towards anti-Semitism is to approach it from a rationalistic angle. Obviously the charges made against Jews are not true. They cannot be true, partly because they cancel out, partly because no one people could have such a monopoly of wickedness. But simply by pointing this out one gets no further. The official Left wing view of anti-Semitism is that it is something "got up" by the ruling classes in order to divert attention away from the real evils of society. The Jews, in fact, are scapegoats. This is no doubt correct, but it is quite useless as an argument.

One does not dispose of a belief by showing that it is irrational. Nor is it any use, in my experience, to talk about the persecution of the Jews in Germany. If a man has the slightest disposition towards anti-Semitism, such things bounce off his consciousness like peas off a steel helmet. The best argument of all, if rational arguments were ever of any use, would be to point out that the alleged crimes of the Jews are only possible because we live in a society which rewards crime. If all Jews are crooks, let us deal with them by so arranging our economic system that crooks cannot prosper. But what good is it to say that kind of thing to the man who believes as an article of faith that Jews dominate the Black Market, push their way to the front of queues and dodge military service?

We could do with a detailed enquiry into the causes of anti-Semitism, and it ought not to be vitiated in advance by the assumption that those causes are wholly economic. However true the "scapegoat" theory may be in general terms, it does not explain why the Jews rather than some [other] minority group are picked on, nor does it make clear what they are a scapegoat *for*. A thing like the Dreyfus Case, for instance, is not easily translated into economic terms. So far as Britain is concerned, the important things to find out are just what charges are made against the Jews, whether anti-Semitism is really on the increase (it may actually have decreased over the past thirty years), and to what extent it is aggravated by the influx of refugees since about 1938.

One not only ought not to assume that the causes of anti-Semitism are economic in a crude, direct way (unemployment, business jealousy, etc.), one also ought not to assume that "sensible" people are immune to it. It flourishes especially among literary men, for instance. Without even getting up from this table to consult a book I can think of passages in Villon, Shakespeare, Smollett, Thackeray, H. G. Wells, Aldous Huxley, T. S. Eliot and many another which would be called anti-Semitic if they had been written since Hitler came to power. Both Belloc and Chesterton flirted, or something more than flirted, with anti-Semitism, and other writers whom it is possible to respect have swallowed it more or less in its Nazi form. Clearly the neurosis lies very deep, and just what it is that people hate when they say that they hate a non-existent entity called "the Jews" is still uncertain. And it is partly the fear of finding out how widespread anti-Semitism is that prevents it from being seriously investigated.

The following lines are quoted in Anthony Trollope's *Autobiography*:—

> "When Payne-Knight's *Taste* was issued on the town
> A few Greek verses in the text set down
> Were torn to pieces, mangled into hash,
> Hurled to the flames as execrable trash;
> In short, were butchered rather than dissected,
> And several false quantities detected;
> Till, when the smoke had risen from the cinders
> It was discovered that—the lines were Pindar's!"

Trollope does not make clear who is the author of these lines, and I should be very glad if any reader could let me know. But I also quote them for their own sake—that is, for the terrible warning to literary critics that they contain—and for the sake of drawing attention to Trollope's *Autobiography*, which is a most fascinating book, although or because it is largely concerned with money.[2]

The dispute that has been going on in *Time and Tide* about Mr. J. F. Horrabin's *Atlas of War Geography*[3] is a reminder that maps are tricky things, to be regarded with the same suspicion as photographs and statistics.

It is an interesting minor manifestation of nationalism that every nation colours itself red on the map. There is also a tendency to make yourself look bigger than you are, which is possible without actual forgery since every projection of the earth as a flat surface distorts some part or other. During the Empire Free Trade "crusade," there was a free distribution to schools of large coloured wall-maps which were made on a new projection and dwarfed the U.S.S.R. while exaggerating the size of India and Africa. Then there are ethnological and political maps, a most rewarding material for propaganda. During the Spanish civil war, maps were pinned up in the Spanish villages which divided the world into Socialist, Democratic and Fascist States. From these you could learn that India was a democracy, while Madagascar and Indo-China (this was the period of the Popular Front Government in France) were labelled "Socialist."

The war has probably done something towards improving our geography. People who five years ago thought the Croats rhymed with goats and drew only a very shadowy distinction between Minsk and Pinsk, could now tell you which sea the Volga flows into and indicate without much searching the whereabouts of Guadalcanal or Buthidaung. Hundreds of thousands, if not millions, of English people can nearly pronounce Dnepropetrovsk. But it takes a war to make map-reading popular. As late as the time of Wavell's Egyptian campaign I met a woman who thought that Italy was joined up with Africa, and in 1938, when I was leaving for Morocco, some of the people in my village—a very rustic village, certainly, but only 50 miles from London—asked whether it would be necessary to cross the sea to get there. If you ask any circle of people (I should particularly like to do this with the members of the House of Commons) to draw a map of Europe from memory, you get some surprising results.[4] Any Government which genuinely cared about education would see to it that a globe map, at present an expensive rarity, was accessible to every schoolchild. Without some notion of which country is next to which, and which is the quickest route from one place to another, and where a ship can be bombed from shore, and where it can't, it is difficult to see what value the average citizen's views on foreign policy can have.

As Orwell probably expected, the original review in *The Observer* (see *n. 1*) and this article brought him a number of letters. Among his papers at his death were ten letters sent to *The Observer* and four sent to *Tribune*. In addition, *Tribune* published three letters: from A. Perlmutt and from H. Pollins on 3 March and from Peter Lambda on 17 March. Perlmutt wrote twice to Orwell, initially on

15 February (the letter that *Tribune* printed) and then on the 27th to express disappointment that his first letter had not yet appeared in print. He was, he wrote, 'a regular and ardent reader of Tribune° since its inception' and he could not recall an occasion 'when the Zionist solution to the Jewish problem' had been given publicity. He asked for his letter to be reconsidered. The delay in publishing his and Pollins's letters (in fact, only two publication dates intervened) was probably no more than a combination of time and shortage of space. Perlmutt offered what was basically a Zionist response; he argued that anti-Semitism would disappear when all Jews had returned to Palestine. Pollins wanted Jews to be treated as normal human beings and asked that a greater effort be made to ensure widespread recognition of what Jews were doing to aid the war effort. He asked how many people in Britain had heard of the fight put up by Jews in the Warsaw Ghetto and how many people imagined that the Jews of Europe had accepted their massacre passively. Lambda argued that there was no such thing as a 'Jewish race' and such a belief was mere superstition. To him, anti-Semitism was a conditioned reflex: 'A part of mankind (the one usually called "Whites") has become conditioned to howl against JEWS whenever there is any grievance.' Contemporary Man, he concluded, realised that mankind was manifold, of various colourings, traits and habits, but all of one species: Homo Sapiens. Of the unpublished letters that Orwell kept, there was one from the thriller writer Sydney Horler.[5] He was at pains to claim, not wholly convincingly, that he did not hate Jews but went on to explain what, in his opinion, were the reasons for such hatred.[6]

1. Joshua Trachtenberg's *The Devil and the Jews* and Edmond Fleg's *Why I Am a Jew*, *The Observer*, 30 January 1944, *2413*.
2. Richard Payne Knight (1750–1824), numismatist, Greek scholar, and mediocre poet, inadvertently set off a literary squabble when he published *An Analytical Enquiry into the Principles of Taste*, in 1805. The alleged incompetence of some Greek verses in it was savagely attacked in the *Edinburgh Review*. It was discovered too late in the printing process that these were by Pindar. Byron, in *English Bards and Scotch Reviewers* (1809), thinking the review was by the historian Henry Hallam (1777–1859), sneered at 'classical Hallam, much renown'd for Greek' because of this error of judgement (line 513). Hallam protested that he was not the reviewer, and in a contemptuous note to the second edition of his poem, Byron said that if Hallam had not reviewed the book he was glad and that if Hallam gave him the reviewer's name he would substitute it provided it was composed of 'two orthodox and musical syllables' in order to fit the verse. Until this day Hallam's name has stood in Byron's poem. Trollope says the lines are from *The Biliad* but gives no author. The editor is indebted to Dr. Martin Davies for tracing the author, and it is hardly surprising that neither Orwell nor his readers knew of him. *The Biliad, or, How to Criticize: A Satire* was written by Terence McMahon Hughes (1812–1849), an Irishman living in Portugal. The first edition has not been traced, but internal evidence suggests that, like the second and third (augmented), it was published in 1846 by the author himself. *The Biliad* might have appealed to Orwell. It was a lively and learned attack on 'the vile and abominable system of illiberal and groundless deprecation of all new authors and their works (a favoured few excepted)' by the 'Tomahawk school of criticism.' His satire was directed at *The Athenaeum* and its editor in 1845, C. W. Dilke ('Bilk' to Hughes), and it concluded with a plea that 'our *litterae*' be made '*humaniores*.' The lines Orwell quotes are on pages 41 and 42 of the second and third editions. For a comparison of Trollope's earnings and Orwell's, see P. Davison, "Orwell: Balancing the Books", *The Library*, VI, 16 (1994), 95.
3. In a very unfavourable reference to his *Atlas of Post-War Problems*, an article in *Time and Tide*, 8 January 1944, accused Horrabin of, among other things, implying that it had been unfortunate to dismember the Austro-Hungarian Empire after 1918 because of the excellence of its system of transport, and added: 'As an indictment of the Treaty of Versailles [Horrabin's] tendentious maps are a free gift to Goebbels.'

4. Among Orwell's collection of pamphlets in the British Library is a group of freehand maps of Europe drawn by schoolchildren aged 13–17; see *3733*, Uncatalogued Box 46.
5. Sydney Horler (1888–1954) began his working life as a journalist but turned with great success to writing thrillers. He published more than 150 books.
6. See Orwell's essay 'Anti-Semitism in Britain,' completed 26 February 1945, *2626*; also, David Walton, 'George Orwell and Antisemitism,' *Patterns of Prejudice*, 16, 1982, 19–34.

2418. Review of *Martin Chuzzlewit* by Charles Dickens

The Observer, 13 February 1944

It is now a hundred years since the final numbers of "MARTIN CHUZZLEWIT" were published[1] and though it came thus early in Dickens's career (it was his fourth novel, if one counts "Pickwick" as a novel), it has more the air of being a pot-boiler than any of his books except the "Sketches." There cannot be many people living who could outline its plot from memory. Whereas books like "Oliver Twist," or "Bleak House," or "Great Expectations," have a central theme which can in some cases be reduced to a single word, the various parts of "Martin Chuzzlewit" have not much more relationship to one another than the sounds produced by a cat walking across the piano. The best characters are "supers."

What do people remember when they think of "Martin Chuzzlewit"? The American interlude, Mrs. Gamp, and Todgers's (especially Bailey). Martin Chuzzlewit himself is a stick, Mark Tapley a tedious paradox on two legs, Pecksniff a partial failure. It is ironical that Dickens should have tried, more or less unsuccessfully, to make Pecksniff into a monumental figure of a hypocrite, and at the same time, almost incidentally, should have painted such a devasting picture of hypocrisy in the American chapters. Dickens's comic genius is dependent on his moral sense. He is funniest when he is discovering new sins. To denounce Pecksniff did not call into play his special powers, because, after all, no one supposes that hypocrisy is desirable. But to see through the pretensions of American democracy, or even, at that date, to see that Mrs. Gamp was a luxury that society might well do without, did need the eye of a Dickens. The book's lack of any real central theme can be seen in its fearful ending. It is as though Dickens were dissolving into lukewarm treacle, and—as so often when he says something that he does not really feel—whole paragraphs of the final chapter will go straight into blank verse:

> Thy life is tranquil, calm, and happy, Tom.
> In the soft strain which ever and again
> Comes stealing back upon the ear, the memory
> Of thine old love may find a voice perhaps;
> But it is a pleasant, softened, whispering memory,
> Like that in which we sometimes hold the dead,
> And does not pain or grieve thee, God be thanked!

Yet the man who could write this stuff could also record the conversations of

Bailey, and could not only create Mrs. Gamp but could throw in, just for good measure, that metaphysical puzzle, Mrs. Harris.

The American chapters are a good example of Dickens's habit of telling small lies in order to emphasise what he regards as a big truth. No doubt many of the things he reports actually happened (other travellers of the time confirm him on some details) but his picture of American society as a whole cannot possibly be true: not only because no community is wholly bad, but because the chaos of real life has been deliberately left out. Every incident, every character, is simply an illustration of Dickens's thesis. Moreover, the strongest charge that he makes against the Americans, that they boast of being democratic while actually living on slave labour, is obviously unfair. It implies that American opinion as a whole acquiesced in slavery, whereas a bloody civil war was to be fought mainly on this issue only twenty years later. But Dickens says these things in order to hit at what he feels to be the real fault of the Americans, their ignorant contempt for Europe and unjustified belief in their own superiority. Perhaps there *were* a few Americans who did not edit libellous newspapers or emit sentences like "the libation of freedom must sometimes be quaffed in blood"; but to lay too much stress upon them would have been to spoil the picture. After all, the business of a caricaturist is to make his point, and these chapters have worn very much better than "American Notes."

The mental atmosphere of the American interlude is one that has since become familiar to us in the books written by British travellers to Soviet Russia. Some of these report that everything is good, others that everything is bad, but nearly all share the same propagandist outlook. A hundred years ago America, "the land of the free," had rather the same place in the European imagination that Soviet Russia has now, and "Martin Chuzzlewit" is the 1844 equivalent of André Gide's *Retour de l'URRS*. But it is a sign of the changing temper of the world that Dickens's attack, so much more violent and unfair than Gide's, could be so quickly forgiven.

"Martin Chuzzlewit" stands somewhere near the turning-point of Dickens's literary development, when he was becoming less of a picaresque writer and more of a novelist. The times were changing with the rise of the new cautious middle class, and Dickens was too much alive not to be affected by the atmosphere he lived in. "Martin Chuzzlewit" is his last completely disorderly book. In spite of its frequent flashes of genius, it is difficult to feel that by following up this vein in himself Dickens could have given us anything to compensate for the loss of "Hard Times" and "Great Expectations."

[Fee: £7.7.0; 9.2.44]

1. This was not a review of a particular edition but a celebration of the hundredth anniversary of the completion of the novel's publication in twenty (as nineteen) parts from January 1843 to July 1844.

2419. Review of *Elisabet Ney* by Jan Fortune and Jean Burton

Manchester Evening News, 17 February 1944

There is some substance in the claim that the life of Elisabet Ney, grand-niece of Napoleon's marshal and the first woman sculptor in Europe, was the most remarkable life of the 19th century. At any rate it had the unusual feature of being, in effect, two separate lives, each of fairly familiar type, but seemingly quite incompatible with one another.

Elisabet Ney was born in the thirties in Western Germany of devout Catholic parents, her father being a carver of church images. When she was hardly more than a child she announced that she, too, intended to become a sculptor, and when her mother tried to put her foot down on this—as it seemed—outrageous notion Elisabet simply took to her bed and refused food until she was grudgingly given leave to begin her studies.

At this date there does not seem anything very startling in the idea of a woman sculptor, but in the mid-19th century it seemed both shocking and ridiculous, because, among other things, it was thought impossible for a woman to study naked models or to attend classes in dissection. Bone and muscle structure was practically a male secret, and even Elisabet, though she did in the end win her way into the "life" classes in Munich and Berlin, kept her subjects draped whenever possible.

By the time she was thirty she was a brilliant success and was kept busily at work making busts of half the celebrities of Europe. But she had had a very hard struggle in the first few years, and in the struggle some peculiar contradictions in her character displayed themselves.

To begin with she was a passionate feminist, despising the male sex from the bottom of her heart and looking on marriage as the final degradation, but at the same time willing to use the grossest flattery towards any man whom she thought capable of helping her. She even won the heart of the misogynist Schopenhauer, and left him wondering whether it is true, after all, that every woman has short legs and a diminutive brain.

Though a feminist and contemptuous of public opinion she was no democrat, and it is even doubtful how far her impulse towards sculpture was genuinely aesthetic. Asked why she was so anxious to go to Berlin and study she answered: "To see the great ones of the earth." And in this in the earlier part of her life she was strikingly successful.

For nearly ten years she was one of the most famous figures in Europe. Bismarck, Garibaldi, Schopenhauer, and Queen Victoria sat for her. Gottfried Keller, the novelist, and Von Humboldt, the famous traveller and naturalist, were her friends. Cosima von Bulow, the mistress of Wagner, was her hated rival.

It was a good time for such a woman to be alive, for in the mid-19th century, although painting and sculpture happened to be at a low ebb, the arts were taken seriously. It was the period of little German Principalities with enlightened monarchs, when whole populations interested themselves in the love affairs of musicians, when a new opera could cause a riot, and a discussion of prose style could end in a duel.

Against this background Elisabet Ney led an extravagant, adventurous life that was rather like a less sordid version of Isadora Duncan's.[1]

But it all ended strangely and abruptly in the late sixties. In 1863 Elisabet had married Edwin Montgomery, a young Scottish biologist. To her dying day she kept this fact secret—for in her eyes marriage was "bourgeois" and disgraceful—and passed everywhere as Montgomery's mistress.

A few years later she was seized with a passionate desire to make a statue of King Ludwig of Bavaria, who was to be deposed and die insane in the mid-eighties. It was no easy business, for Ludwig—already only doubtfully sane—could hardly bear women in his presence.

After two years of intrigue and flattery Elisabet got her wish, and then, when the statue was still unfinished, suddenly fled to America, taking Montgomery with her. She had become pregnant, which was perhaps part of the reason for her flight, but it is clear that there must have been some other reason which the authors of this book have failed to disclose. The Montgomerys bought a large estate in Texas and mismanaged it for the next 30 years, losing enormous sums of money.

Elisabet, in the rude frontier village where they lived, continued to wear the Greek costumes she had always affected, or alternatively wore man's clothes with two revolvers strapped to her belt. She also forced her elder child to wear Greek dress amid the jeers of the village boys and caused him to hate her as few sons can ever have hated their mothers.

The strangest fact of all is that for 20 years she almost abandoned sculpture, and then, an old, white-haired woman, took it up again and won for herself a new reputation. She was commissioned to make statues of all the public men of Texas, and she even made journeys to and fro across the Atlantic, was lionised by a younger generation of artists, and put the finishing touches to her statue of Ludwig of Bavaria.

When she died in 1907 she was known and respected all over America. The citizens of Texas, who had once regarded her as an immoral and eccentric foreigner, now looked on her as one of the leading ornaments of the State—this although it was never known during her lifetime that she was legally married. Her husband died four years after her, leaving behind him a mass of now-forgotten scientific treatises.

The book contains various photographs of Elisabet Ney's work. Some of her statues have the obvious stamp of a bad period and others are difficult to judge from photographs, but a model of her own head and a statue of Lady Macbeth, which is perhaps a self-portrait, at last make it clear why even the busiest men in Europe were ready to give up their time to her.

[Fee: £8.8.0; 4.1.44][2]

1. Isadora Duncan (1878–1927), innovative American dancer who greatly influenced twentieth-century dance. She was killed when accidentally strangled by her scarf.
2. Orwell's Payments Book lists two reviews submitted to the *Manchester Evening News* on 4 January 1944; see *2831*. The first must be Wavell's *Allenby in Egypt*, printed 6 January (see *2400*); the second would seem to be this review.

2420. To R. S. R. Fitter

17 February 1944   Typewritten

Tribune

Dear Mr. Fitter,

I am sorry to make further trouble, but could you just add to this review a line or two about the book itself, i.e. about Nevill's book. What you say about Harriet Martineau is interesting and in a review of this kind it is all right to devote most of the space to exposition, but I think we ought to just mention whether the author has done his work well or badly.

Yours truly,
[Signed] Geo. Orwell
George Orwell,
Literary Editor.

2420A. To Daniel George, 17 February 1944: see Vol. XX,

Appendix 15

2421. To Gleb Struve

17 February 1944   Typewritten

10a Mortimer Crescent
London NW 6

Dear Mr Struve,[1]

Please forgive me for not writing earlier to thank you for the very kind gift of "25 Years of Soviet Russian Literature", with its still more kind inscription. I am afraid I know very little about Russian literature and I hope your book will fill up some of the many gaps in my knowledge. It has already roused my interest in Zamyatin's "We", which I had not heard of before. I am interested in that kind of book, and even keep making notes for one myself that may get written sooner or later.[2] I wonder whether you can tell if there is an adequate translation of Blok? I saw some translated fragments about ten years ago in "Life and Letters", but whether they were any good as a translation I do not know.

I am writing a little squib which might amuse you when it comes out, but it is so not O.K. politically that I don't feel certain in advance that anyone will publish it. Perhaps that gives you a hint of its subject.[3]

Yours sincerely
Geo. Orwell

1. Gleb Struve (1898–1985), born in St. Petersburg, taught at the School of Slavonic and East European Studies, London University, 1932–47, and was Professor of Slavic Languages and Literature, University of California, Berkeley, 1947–65. He was the author of *Soviet Literature 1917–50* and *Russian Literature in Exile*.
2. This is Orwell's first reference to *Nineteen Eighty-Four*.
3. *Animal Farm*.

2422. 'As I Please,' 12

Tribune, 18 February 1944

After the war there is going to be a severe housing shortage in this country, and we shall not overcome it unless we resort to prefabrication. If we stick to our traditional building methods the necessary houses will take decades to produce, and the discomfort and misery that this will lead to, the patching-up of blitzed premises and filthy slums, the rent rackets and overcrowding, are easy to foresee. So are the effects of a housing shortage on our already perilous birthrate. Meanwhile not only prefabrication, but any large, concerted effort at rehousing, has powerful vested interests working against it. The building societies, and the brick and cement trades, are directly involved, and the whole principle of private ownership in land is threatened. How could you rebuild London, for instance, on a sane plan without disregarding private property rights? But the people who traffic in bugs and basements are not going to come out into the open and say clearly what they are fighting for. By far their best card is the Englishman's sentimental but partly justified yearning for a "home of his own." They will play this card over and over again, and it is up to us to counter it before it takes effect.

To begin with, prefabrication does not mean—as people are already beginning to fear that it means—that we shall all be forced to live in ugly, cramped, flimsy and unhomelike chicken houses. The thing that ought to be pointed out in this connection is that existing English houses are for the most part very badly built. They are not built to withstand either heat or cold, they are lacking in cupboards, their water pipes are so placed as to ensure that they will burst every time there is a hard frost, and they have no convenient means of rubbish-disposal. All these problems, which a speculative builder will tell you are insoluble, are easily solved in various other countries. If we tackled our rehousing problem boldly we could get rid of discomforts which have come to be accepted like the weather, but are in fact quite unnecessary. We could get rid of "blind back" houses, basements, geysers, filth-collecting gas stoves, offices where the light of day never penetrates, outdoor w.c.s, uncleanable stone sinks, and other miseries. We could put a bath in every house and install bells that actually ring, plugs that pull at the first attempt, waste-pipes that don't get blocked by a spoonful of tea-leaves. We could even, if we chose, make our rooms relatively easy to clean by streamlining them and making the corners curved instead of rectangular. But all this depends on our being able to build houses rapidly, by mass-production. Failing that, the housing shortage will be so desperate that we shall have to "make do" with every mouse-ridden ruin that remains, and encourage the speculative builder to do his worst as well.

Secondly, the dislike of flats will somehow have to be exorcised. If people are going to live in big towns they must either live in flats or put up with overcrowding: there is no way out of that. A big block of flats, covering only an acre or two of ground, will contain as many people as live in a small country town, and give them as much room-space as they would have in houses. Rebuild London in big blocks of flats, and there could be light and air for everybody, and room for green spaces, allotments, playgrounds. People could live out of the noise of the traffic, children would not grow up in a world of bricks and dustbins, and historic buildings like St. Paul's would be visible again instead of being swamped by seas of yellow brick.

Yet it is notorious that people, especially working-class people, don't like flats. They want a "home of their own." In a sense they are right, for it is true that in most blocks of working-class flats there isn't the privacy and freedom that you can get in a private house. They are not built to be noise-proof, the people who dwell in them are often burdened by nagging restrictions, and they are often quite unnecessarily uncomfortable. The first blocks built definitely as working-class flats did not even have baths. Even now they seldom have lifts, and they usually have stone stairs, which means that one lives in an endless clattering of boots. Much of this arises from the half-conscious conviction, so powerful in this country, that working-class people must not be made too comfortable. Deafening noise and irritating restrictions are not inherent in the nature of flats, and we ought to insist on that. For the feeling that four rooms are "your own" if they are on the ground, and not "your own" if they are in mid-air—and it is especially strong in women with children—is going to be a big obstacle in the way of replanning, even in areas where the Germans have already done the necessary clearance work.

A correspondent reproaches me for wanting to see clothes rationing continue until we are all equally shabby; though she adds that clothes rationing hasn't, in fact, had an equalising effect. I will quote an extract from her letter:—

"I work in a very exclusive shop just off Bond Street . . . When I, shivering in my 25/- utility frock, serve these elegant creatures in sables, fur caps and fur-lined boots, who regard me uncomprehendingly when I say 'Good morning, it's very cold to-day, madam' (very stupid of me—after all, how should they know?), I do not wish to see them deprived of their lovely and warm attire, but rather that such attire was available to me, and for all . . . We should aim not at reducing the present highest standard of living, but at raising any and everything less than the highest. It is a malicious and mean-spirited attitude that wishes to drag Etonians and Harrovians from their fortunate positions of eminence and force them down the mines. Rather, in the present reshuffling of society we should seek to make these places accessible to all."

I answer, first of all, that although clothes rationing obviously bears hardest on those who don't possess large stocks of clothes already, it *has* had a certain equalising effect, because it has made people uneasy about appearing too smart. Certain garments, such as men's evening dress, have practically disappeared; also it is now considered permissible to wear almost any clothes for almost any job. But my original point was that if clothes rationing goes on long enough even wealthy people will have worn out their extra stocks of clothes, and we shall all be somewhere near equal.

But is it not the case that we ought always to aim at levelling "up" and not levelling "down"? I answer that in some cases you can't level "up." You can't give everyone a Rolls Royce car. You can't even give everyone a fur coat, especially in war time. As to the statement that everyone ought to go to Eton or Harrow, it is meaningless. The whole value of those places, from the point of view of the people who go there, is their exclusiveness. And since certain luxuries—high-powered cars, for instance, fur coats, yachts, country houses and what-not—obviously can't be distributed to everybody, then it is better that nobody should have them. The rich lose almost as much by their wealth as the poor lose by their poverty. Doesn't my correspondent bring that out when she speaks of those ignorant rich women who cannot even imagine what a cold morning means to a person without an overcoat?

Another correspondent writes indignantly to know what I mean by saying that *Punch* is not funny.[1] Actually I exaggerated a little. Since 1918 I have seen three jokes in *Punch* that made me laugh. But—as I always tell puzzled foreign visitors who enquire about this—*Punch* is not meant to be funny, it is meant to be reassuring. After all, where do you most frequently see it? In club lounges and in dentists' waiting rooms. In both places it has, and is meant to have, a soothing effect. You know in advance that it will never contain anything new. The jokes you were familiar with in your childhood will still be there, just the same as ever, like a circle of old friends. The nervous curate, the apoplectic colonel, the awkward recruit, the forgetful plumber—there they all are, unchangeable as the Pyramids. Glancing through those familiar pages, the clubman knows that his dividends are all right, the patient knows that the dentist will not really break his jaw. But as to being funny, that is a different matter. Jokes that are funny usually contain that un-English thing, an idea. The *New Yorker*, though it is overrated, is quite often funny. Thus a recent number has a picture of two German soldiers leading a huge ape into the orderly room on a chain. The officer is saying to them angrily, "Can't you spell?" This seems to me funny. But it might take five seconds' thought to see the joke, and as it is an axiom of the middle class—at least the golf-playing, whisky-drinking, *Punch*-reading part of the middle class—that no decent person is capable of thought, jokes of that kind are barred from *Punch*.

1. See 'As I Please', 10, 4 February 1944, *2416*.

2423. To Dwight Macdonald
21 February 1944   Typewritten

Tribune

Dear Macdonald,
We received the prospectus etc. of "Politics", and I have told a certain number of people about it, but I suppose you know we can't take out subscriptions here because of the prohibition against sending money out of the country. The Editor[1] says, could we make some exchange arrangement between "Politics" and TRIBUNE?

I've got ready the stuff for my article but probably can't start writing it for the next few weeks. I am snowed under with work until I finish the book I am doing. Hope all goes well.

Yours,
[Signed] Geo. Orwell
George Orwell

1. Aneurin Bevan.

2424. 'As I Please,' 13

Tribune, 25 February 1944

A short story in the *Home Companion and Family Journal*, entitled "Hullo, Sweetheart," recounts the adventures of a young girl named Lucy Fallows who worked on the switchboard of a long-distance telephone exchange. She had "sacrificed her yearning to be in uniform" in order to take this job, but found it dull and uneventful. "So many silly people seemed to use long-distance just to blather to each other . . . She felt fed up; she felt that she was a servant to selfish people"; and there was "a cloud in her hazel eyes." However, as you will readily guess, Lucy's job soon livened up, and before long she found herself in the middle of thrilling adventures which included the sinking of a U-boat, the capture of a German sabotage crew, and a long motor-ride with a handsome naval officer who had "a crisp voice." Such is life in the Telephone Exchange.

At the end of the story there is a little note:

Any of our young readers themselves interested in the work of the Long Distance Telephone Exchange (such work as Lucy Fallows was doing) should apply to the Staff Controller, L.T.R., London, who will inform them as to the opportunities open.

I do not know whether this is an advertisement likely to have much success. I should doubt whether even girls of the age aimed at would believe that capturing U-boats enters very largely into the lives of telephone operators. But I note with interest the direct correlation between a Government recruiting advertisement and a piece of commercial fiction. Before the war the Admiralty, for instance, used to put its advertisements in the boys' adventure papers, which was a natural place to put them, but stories were not, so far as I know, written to order. Probably they are not definitely commissioned even now. It is more likely that the departments concerned keep their eye on the weekly papers (incidentally I like to think of some stripe-trousered personage in the G.P.O.[1] reading "Hullo, Sweetheart" as part of his official duties) and push in an ad. when any story seems likely to form an attractive bait. But from that to the actual commissioning of stories to be written round the A.T.S.,[2] Women's Land Army,[3] or any other body in need of recruits, is only a short step. One can almost hear the tired, cultured voices from the M.O.I.[4] saying:

"Hullo! Hullo! Is that you, Tony? Oh, hullo. Look here, I've got another script for you, Tony, 'A Ticket to Paradise.' It's bus conductresses this time.

They're not coming in. I believe the trousers don't fit, or something. Well, any way, Peter says make it sexy, but kind of clean—*you* know. Nothing extramarital. We want the stuff in by Tuesday. Fifteen thousand words. You can choose the hero. I rather favour the kind of outdoor man that dogs and kiddies all love him°—*you* know. Or very tall with a sensitive mouth. I don't mind, really. But pile on the sex, Peter says."

Something resembling this already happens with radio features and documentary films, but hitherto there has not been any very direct connection between fiction and propaganda. That half-inch ad. in the *Home Companion* seems to mark another small stage in the process of "co-ordination" that is gradually happening to all the arts.

Looking through Chesterton's introduction to *Hard Times* in the Everyman Edition (incidentally, Chesterton's introductions to Dickens are about the best thing he ever wrote), I note the typically sweeping statement: "There are no new ideas." Chesterton is here claiming that the ideas which animated the French Revolution were not new ones but simply a revival of doctrines which had flourished earlier and then been abandoned. But the claim that "there is nothing new under the sun" is one of the stock arguments of intelligent reactionaries. Catholic apologists, in particular, use it almost automatically. Everything that you can say or think has been said or thought before. Every political theory from Liberalism to Trotskyism can be shown to be a development of some heresy in the early Church. Every system of philosophy springs ultimately from the Greeks. Every scientific theory (if we are to believe the popular Catholic press) was anticipated by Roger Bacon and others in the thirteenth century. Some Hindu thinkers go even further and claim that not merely the scientific theories, but the products of applied science as well, aeroplanes, radio and the whole bag of tricks, were known to the ancient Hindus, who afterwards dropped them as being unworthy of their attention.

It is not very difficult to see that this idea is rooted in the fear of progress. If there is nothing new under the sun, if the past in some shape or another always returns, then the future when it comes will be something familiar. At any rate what will never come—since it has never come before—is that hated, dreaded thing, a world of free and equal human beings. Particularly comforting to reactionary thinkers is the idea of a cyclical universe, in which the same chain of events happens over and over again. In such a universe every seeming advance towards democracy simply means that the coming age of tyranny and privilege is a bit nearer. This belief, obviously superstitious though it is, is widely held nowadays, and is common among Fascists and near-Fascists.

In fact, there *are* new ideas. The idea that an advanced civilisation need not rest on slavery is a relatively new idea, for instance: it is a good deal younger than the Christian religion. But even if Chesterton's dictum were true, it would only be true in the sense that a statue is contained in every block of stone. Ideas may not change, but emphasis shifts constantly. It could be claimed, for example, that the most important part of Marx's theory is contained in the saying: "Where your treasure is, there will your heart be also." But before Marx developed it, what force had that saying had? Who had paid any attention to it? Who had inferred from it—what it certainly implies—that laws, religions and moral codes are all a superstructure built over existing property relations? It was Christ, according to the Gospel, who uttered the text, but it was Marx who brought it to life. And ever since he did so the motives of politicians, priests, judges, moralists and millionaires have been under the deepest suspicion—which, of course, is why they hate him so much.

On 10 March, *Tribune* published this letter, followed by Orwell's *Note*:

The "little note" to which Mr. Orwell refers, at the end of the story "Hello, Sweetheart," in our issue dated February 26th, 1944, was not an advertisement. We received no payment or other consideration from the G.P.O. or any other Government Department for publishing the story or the "little note." The story was written for us by one of our regular contributors in the hope of drawing attention to a most useful form of national service.

   As, therefore, the statements of fact in Mr. Orwell's article are incorrect, I think you will agree that you cannot plead that the comments are fair.

Robert A. Lewis,
Editor, *Home Companion*

[*Note*: I do not think I said the Amalgamated Press received payment from the G.P.O. for publishing the story referred to, but if I seemed to imply this, I am sorry. I would still like to know, however, who was responsible for inserting the "little note," and for its precise wording, with instructions as to where to apply for a job. Surely it is not usual for contributors to do this kind of thing off their own bat?—George Orwell.]

1. General Post Office.
2. Auxiliary Territorial Service: the women's army auxiliary corps.
3. The Land Army was composed of women recruited to work on farms.
4. Ministry of Information, the headquarters of which was Senate House of the University of London—Minitru of *Nineteen Eighty-Four*.

2425. Review of *The Edge of the Abyss* by Alfred Noyes

The Observer, 27 February 1944

Incoherent and, in places, silly though it is, this book raises a real problem and will set its readers thinking, even if their thinking only starts to be useful at about the place where Mr. Noyes leaves off. His thesis is that western civilisation is in danger of actual destruction, and that it has been brought to this pass not by economic maladjustments but by the decay of the belief in absolute good and evil. The rules of behaviour on which any stable society has to rest are dissolving:

> What promise can we trust, what firm agreement can ever be made again, in a world where millions upon millions have been educated to believe that, if it seems in their interest to violate it, no pact or pledge, however solemnly drawn up, need be regarded by "realistic" minds, or "cold statesmanship," as more than a "scrap of paper," even though its violation involve the murder by night of sleeping and innocent millions?

There is much force in this question, which Mr. Noyes repeats over and over again in various forms. In the chaos in which we are living, even the prudential reasons for common decency are being forgotten. Politics, internal or international, are probably no more immoral than they have always been, but what is new is the growing acquiescence of ordinary people in the doctrines of expediency, the callousness of public opinion in the face of the most atrocious crimes and sufferings, and the black-out memory which allows blood-stained murderers to turn into public benefactors overnight if "military necessity" demands it. Quite new, too, is the doubt cast by the various totalitarian systems on the very existence of objective truth, and the consequent large-scale falsification of history. Mr. Noyes is quite right to cry out against all this, and he probably even underemphasises the harm done to ordinary common sense by the cult of "realism," with its inherent tendency to assume that the dishonest course is always the profitable one. The loss of moral standards does, indeed, seem to undermine the sense of probability. Mr. Noyes is also within his rights in saying that the intelligentsia are more infected by totalitarian ideas than the common people, and are partly to blame for the mess we are now in. But his diagnosis of the reasons for this is very shallow, and his suggested remedies are doubtful, even from the point of view of practicability.

To begin with it will not do to suggest, as Mr. Noyes does throughout, that a decent society can only be founded on Christian principles. It amounts to saying that a good life can only be lived on the fringes of the Atlantic. About a quarter of the population of the world is nominally Christian, and the proportion is constantly diminishing. The vast block of Asia is not Christian, and without some unforeseeable miracle it never will be. Are we to say that a decent society cannot be established in Asia? If so, it cannot be established anywhere, and the whole attempt to regenerate society might as well be given up in advance. And Mr. Noyes is probably wrong in imagining that the Christian faith, as it existed in the past, can be restored even in Europe. The real problem of our time is to restore the sense of absolute right and wrong when the belief that it used to rest on—that is, the belief in personal immortality—has been destroyed. This demands faith, which is a different thing from credulity. It seems doubtful whether Mr. Noyes has fully grasped the distinction.

Then there is the question of the amount of blame attaching to "the highbrows" ("our pseudo-intellectuals" is Mr. Noyes's favourite name for them) for the breakdown of moral standards. Mr. Noyes writes on this subject in rather the same strain as the *London Mercury* of twenty years ago. "The highbrows" are gloomy, they are obscene, they attack religion, patriotism, the family, etc., etc. But they are also, it appears, in some way responsible for the rise of Hitler. Now this contradicts the facts. During the crucial years it was precisely the "pseudo-intellectuals" whom Mr. Noyes detests who cried out against the horrors of Fascism, while the Tory and clerical Press did its best to hush them up. Mr. Noyes condemns the policy of appeasement, but what was the attitude of his own Church and its Press on that subject?

On the other hand, the intellectuals whom he *does* approve of are only very doubtfully on the side of the angels. One, of course, is Carlyle, who was one of the founders of the modern worship of power and success, and who applauded the third German war of aggression as vociferously as Pound did the fifth. The other is Kipling. Kipling was not totalitarian, but his moral outlook is equivocal at best. Mr. Noyes remarks at the beginning of his book that one cannot cast out devils with the aid of Beelzebub, but he is also extremely angry because anti-British books can still be published in England and praised in British newspapers. Does it not occur to him that if we stopped doing this kind of thing the main difference between ourselves and our enemies would have disappeared?

[Fee: £7.7.0; 21.2.44]

2426. To Rayner Heppenstall

28 February 1944   Typewritten

Tribune

Dear Rayner,

The Blake book[1] doesn't come out for some weeks, but I have rung up Warburg and earmarked the book to be sent to you when received. We don't seem to have much else in at present. On spec. I am sending you "Poetry Scotland", which I think should be noticed (tho' it's largely the same old gang) and the Collected Rhymes° and Verses of de la Mare. I think he is bloody but I think I once heard you express approval of him.

I hope things aren't too unbearable. It does seem a bit thick having to share a bed, or is the other occupant a girl?

Yours,
[Signed] Geo. Orwell
George Orwell

1. Jacob Bronowski, *A Man Without a Mask*, published in 1943 (revised as *William Blake and the Age of Revolution*, New York, 1965, London, 1972), was reviewed by Heppenstall in *Tribune*, 28 April 1944. He reviewed *Poetry Scotland*, No. 1, 7 April 1944, and Walter de la Mare, *Collected Poems & Verses*, 7 April 1944.

2426A. To Lydia Jackson

1 March 1944   Typewritten

Tribune

Dear Lydia,

I wonder if you would like to review these stories for us (say 600 words)?[1]

Yours,
[Signed] George
George Orwell

[Postscript] Polish Short Stories – Faber & Faber

1. Lydia Jackson wrote under the pen-name Elisaveta Fen and all her reviews and articles published in *Tribune* and referred to in this edition are so signed. See headnote to *534A* for biographical details and a brief account of her and Orwell's relationship. The letter is annotated (not by Orwell) indicating that the book was despatched for review on 27 March. The review was published on 21 April; the publisher was given as Minerva Publishing Co. Ltd.

2427. To C. K. Ogden

1 March 1944   Typewritten

Tribune

Dear Mr. Ogden,[1]

Very many thanks for the booklet. I was aware, of course, that you have much to put up with from the Esperanto people, and that that was why you drew attention to their very unfortunate choice for the verb "to be" or whatever it is. We have had them on to us since mentioning Basic, but I have choked them off. Also the Ido[2] people.

As I told you when I was in the B.B.C. (I have left there now) there was great resistance against doing anything over the air about Basic, at any rate for India. I rather gathered that its chief enemies were the writers of English textbooks, but that all Indians whose English is good are hostile to the idea, for obvious reasons. At any rate it was with great difficulty that I got Miss Lockhart on to the air.[3]

I don't know a great deal about G. M. Young.[4] He is the ordinary silly-clever "intelligent" conservative whose habitual manoeuvre is to deal with any new idea by pointing out that it has been said before. The only time I met him he struck me as ordinarily snobbish, talking about the terrible sacrifices the upper classes had made on account of the war etc. He was also trying to chase our little Indian Section of the B.B.C. for broadcasting "unsound" ideas. I think he was a supporter of appeasement. That's about all I know about him.

Hope to see you some time.

Yours sincerely,
[Signed] Geo. Orwell
George Orwell,
Literary Editor

1. See *1746, n. 1*.
2. An artificial language based on Esperanto, officially Linguo Internaciona di la Delegitaro (Sistema Ido), made public in 1907.
3. See Orwell's letter to Leonora Lockhart, 18 August 1942, *1393*.
4. George Malcolm Young (1882–1959), historian and essayist specialising in Victorian England. His *Charles I and Cromwell* was published in 1935, and he contributed *The Government of Britain* to the Britain in Pictures series in 1941.

2428. Review of *James Joyce* by Harry Levin

Manchester Evening News, 2 March 1944

No one writing in English in our time has excited so much controversy as James Joyce, and even among his declared followers there is a division of opinion. Is *Finnegans Wake* Joyce's masterpiece, or is it simply an elephantine crossword puzzle, product of emotional sterility? On the whole Mr. Levin is a *Finnegans Wake* man. He defends not merely the obscurity but the essential frivolity of Joyce's later work, and though he will not convert anyone who does not like that kind of thing, he can at least show what Joyce was aiming at and what is the connection between *Finnegans Wake* and the relatively intelligible *Ulysses*.

Now that it begins to be possible to see it in perspective the essential process in Joyce's work appears to be the thinning out of a tragic impulse. A novelist is being gradually smothered by a lexicographer. If one compares *Dubliners*, the little book of short stories which Joyce wrote round about 1910 and published in 1914, with *Ulysses*, published in 1922, one notes an enormous increase in virtuosity in the later book, but also a relative lack of feeling.

Dubliners as well as being "slight" is often clumsy, but it is the product of someone who is intensely sorry for the people about him and indignant over their warped, miserable lives. The last story in it, *The Dead*, is one of the most touching stories in English. *Ulysses*, as Mr. Levin rightly says, is conceived primarily in a comic spirit, but even where it ought to be moving it is not. The would-be hero, Stephen Dedalus, whose problems at least seemed real in the earlier book, *Portrait of the Artist*, is by general consent completely intolerable in *Ulysses*, and even Leopold Bloom, sympathetic though he is, somehow does not evoke much pity even when his situation is pitiful.

Ulysses is even now a difficult book unless one has been given certain clues beforehand, and Mr. Levin's chapters on it will be a useful guide to anyone who is reading it for the first time. They help to dispose of the merely surface difficulties, but the one great fault of *Ulysses* remains—that is, that it is impossible to be completely certain what it is aiming at. It may be first and foremost an attempt to portray life as it actually is, or an attempt to denigrate the present by comparing it with the past. Probably the second motive predominates, otherwise it is difficult to see why this tale of Dublin in 1904 should be so laboriously stretched on to the framework of the *Odyssey*.

Every episode in Odysseus's wanderings reappears in some dwindled and ridiculous form. Odysseus himself has shrunk into the out-at-elbow Jewish advertisement canvasser Leopold Bloom, the Cyclops is a dropsical Sinn Feiner, the sirens are two barmaids gossiping while Bloom tucks into liver and bacon, the chaste Penelope has turned into Mollie Bloom, with her twenty-five lovers, and so on.

If Joyce is definitely saying any one thing he appears to be saying, "Just look how we have deteriorated since the Bronze Age!" But some of the incidents are tiresome and unconvincing, and again and again the story is overwhelmed or diverted by mere literary cleverness. It is this that gives the book its fragmentary character and also its chief fascination.

If anything Mr. Levin seems rather to underrate the writing of *Ulysses*. The book is like a scrapheap littered with jewels: wonderful snatches of poetic prose ("waves, the sea-horses, champing, brightwind-bridled, steeds of Manahaan"), brilliant word pictures (for instance, of a butcher's shop: "sheepsnouts bloodypapered snivelling nosejam on sawdust"), parodies of newspaper articles and Irish Bronze Age epics, some of them uproariously funny, and experiments in the rendering of thought-processes, such as the "bronze by gold" chapter, and Bloom's silent soliloquies, which had never before been attempted in English.

But some passages, such as the elephantine conversation about *Hamlet*, are terribly boring, and moreover Joyce, like so many English and Irish novelists, can never resist the temptation to burlesque. Nor can he ever resist turning aside to try a literary experiment: in *Ulysses* even the growling of a dog is irrelevantly turned into a poem. *Ulysses* has every merit except those that a novel ought to have. *The Dead* would still be a good story if it were told in other words, but in *Ulysses* the words are already winning as against the subject-matter.

Clearly *Ulysses* is the more original book and the more interesting to professional writers, but it would not be surprising if in the long run *Dubliners* and *Portrait of the Artist* came to be rated above it.

In *Finnegans Wake*, which starts where *Ulysses* leaves off—*Ulysses* ends with Bloom falling asleep, and the whole of *Finnegans Wake* happens in the dreaming brain of one H. C. Earwicker, a Dublin publican—the words have finally won. There is no emotional interest, and no attempt at any, and the entire book is written in a private language which Joyce has evolved by telescoping together the words of many tongues, living and dead.

Mr. Levin says that what Joyce is doing is to "escape from the nightmare of history," by which he seems to mean that H. C. Earwicker, whose initials also stand for Haveth Childers Everywhere and Here Comes Everybody, represents the entire human race. Just by having so much crammed into him, however, Earwicker loses any individual interest.

Some of Joyce's portmanteau words are expressive as well as ingenious (for instance, "umbroglio" to describe Mr. Chamberlain's foreign policy), but the book as a whole is unreadable unless one regards it as a sort of word-game. Mr. Levin does describe it among other things as a game, and says that digging out the buried meanings is a fascinating job: which may be true, but one has the right to answer that that is not the kind of fascination one looks for in a work of art.

On *Finnegans Wake* one can suspend judgment: in fifteen years it will be either intelligible or forgotten. But now that *Ulysses* is legally purchasable[1] again no one who is interested in contemporary literature should neglect to read it. Mr. Levin's book is an excellent introduction to it, and the fact that he also deals at length with the other books helps to put *Ulysses* in its proper perspective.

[Fee: £8.8.0; 28.2.44]

1. See *2432*.

2429. 'As I Please,' 14

Tribune, 3 March 1944

Some weeks ago a Catholic reader of *Tribune* wrote to protest against a review by Mr. Charles Hamblett. She objected to his remarks about St. Teresa, and about St. Joseph of Copertino, the saint who once flew round a cathedral carrying a bishop on his back. I answered defending Mr. Hamblett, and got a still more indignant letter in return. This letter raises a number of very important points, and at least one of them seems to me to deserve discussion. The relevance of flying saints to the Socialist movement may not at first sight be very clear, but I think I can show that the present nebulous state of Christian doctrine has serious implications which neither Christians nor Socialists have faced.

The substance of my correspondent's letter is that it doesn't matter whether St Teresa and the rest of them flew through the air or not: what matters is that St. Teresa's "vision of the world changed the course of history." I would concede this. Having lived in an Oriental country I have developed a certain indifference to miracles, and I well know that having delusions, or even being an outright lunatic, is quite compatible with what is loosely called genius. William Blake, for instance, was a lunatic in my opinion. Joan of Arc was probably a lunatic. Newton believed in astrology,[1] Strindberg believed in magic. However, the miracles of the saints are a minor matter. It also appears from my correspondent's letter that even the most central doctrines of the Christian religion don't have to be accepted in a literal sense. It doesn't matter, for instance, whether Jesus Christ ever existed. "The figure of Christ (myth, or man, or god, it does not matter) so transcends all the rest that I only wish that everyone would look, before rejecting that version of life." Christ, therefore, may be a myth, or he may have been merely a human being, or the account given of him in the Creeds may be true. So we arrive at this position: *Tribune* must not poke fun at the Christian religion, but the existence of Christ, which innumerable people have been burnt for denying, is a matter of indifference.

Now, is this orthodox Catholic doctrine? My impression is that it is not. I can think of passages in the writings of popular Catholic apologists such as Father Woodlock and Father Ronald Knox in which it is stated in the clearest terms that Christian doctrine means what it appears to mean, and is not to be accepted in some wishy-washy metaphorical sense. Father Knox refers specifically to the idea that it doesn't matter whether Christ actually existed, as a "horrible" idea. But what my correspondent says would be echoed by many Catholic intellectuals. If you talk to a thoughtful Christian, Catholic or Anglican, you often find yourself laughed at for being so ignorant as to suppose that anyone ever took the doctrines of the Church literally. These doctrines have, you are told, a quite other meaning which you are too crude to understand. Immortality of the soul doesn't mean that you, John Smith, will remain conscious after you are dead. Resurrection of the body doesn't mean that John Smith's body will actually be resurrected—and so on and so on. Thus the Catholic intellectual is able, for controversial purposes, to play a sort of handy-pandy game, repeating the articles of the Creed in exactly the same terms as his forefathers, while defending himself from the charge of superstition by explaining that he is speaking in parables. Substantially his claim is that though he himself doesn't believe in any very definite way in life after death, there has been no change in Christian belief, since our ancestors didn't really believe in it either. Meanwhile a vitally important fact—that one of the props of Western civilisation has been knocked away—is obscured.

I do not know whether, officially, there has been any alteration in Christian doctrine. Father Knox and my correspondent would seem to be in disagreement about this. But what I do know is that belief in survival after death—the individual survival of John Smith, still conscious of himself as John Smith—is enormously less widespread than it was. Even among professing Christians it is probably decaying; other people, as a rule, don't even entertain the possibility that it might be true. But our forefathers, so far as we know, did believe in it. Unless all that they wrote about it was intended to mislead us, they believed it in an exceedingly literal, concrete way. Life on earth, as they saw it, was simply a short period of preparation for an infinitely more important life beyond the grave. But that notion has disappeared, or is disappearing, and the consequences have not really been faced.

Western civilisation, unlike some Oriental civilisations, was founded partly on the belief in individual immortality. If one looks at the Christian religion from the outside, this belief appears far more important than the belief in God. The Western conception of good and evil is very difficult to separate from it. There is little doubt that the modern cult of power-worship is bound up with the modern man's feeling that life here and now is the only life there is. If death ends everything, it becomes much harder to believe that you can be in the right even if you are defeated. Statesmen, nations, theories, causes are judged almost inevitably by the test of material success. Supposing that one can separate the two phenomena, I would say that the decay of the belief in personal immortality has been as important as the rise of machine civilisation. Machine civilisation has terrible possibilities, as you probably reflected the other night when the ack-ack guns started up: but the other thing has terrible possibilities too, and it cannot be said that the Socialist movement has given much thought to them.

I do not want the belief in life after death to return, and in any case it is not likely to return. What I do point out is that its disappearance has left a big hole, and that we ought to take notice of that fact. Reared for thousands of years on the notion that the individual survives, man has got to make a considerable psychological effort to get used to the notion that the individual perishes. He is not likely to salvage civilisation unless he can evolve a system of good and evil which is independent of heaven and hell. Marxism, indeed, does supply this, but it has never really been popularised. Most Socialists are content to point out that once Socialism has been established we shall be happier in a material sense, and to assume that all problems lapse when one's belly is full. But the truth is the opposite: when one's belly is empty, one's only problem is an empty belly. It is when we have got away from drudgery and exploitation that we shall really start wondering about man's destiny and the reason for his existence. One cannot have any worthwhile picture of the future unless one realises how much we have lost by the decay of Christianity. Few Socialists seem to be aware of this. And the Catholic intellectuals who cling to the letter of the Creeds while reading into them meanings they were never meant to have, and who snigger at anyone simple enough to suppose that the Fathers of the Church meant what they said, are simply raising smokescreens to conceal their own disbelief from themselves.

I have very great pleasure in welcoming the reappearance of the *Cornhill Magazine* after its four years' absence. Apart from the articles—there is a good one on Mayakovsky by Maurice Bowra, and another good one by Raymond Mortimer on Brougham and Macaulay—there are some interesting notes by the editor on the earlier history of the *Cornhill*. One fact that these bring out is the size and wealth of the Victorian reading public, and the vast sums earned by literary men in those days. The first number of the *Cornhill* sold 120,000 copies. It paid Trollope £2,000 for a serial—he had demanded £3,000—and commissioned another from George Eliot at £10,000. Except for the tiny few who managed to crash into the film world, these sums would be quite unthinkable nowadays. You would have to be a topnotcher even to get into the £2,000 class. As for £10,000, to get that for a single book you would have to be someone like Edgar Rice Burroughs. A novel nowadays is considered to have done very well if it brings its author £500—a sum which a successful laywer can earn in a single day. The book ramp is not so new as "Beachcomber" and other enemies of the literary race imagine.

Charles Hamblett had reviewed *The Eagle and the Dove* by Victoria Sackville-West in *Tribune* on 4 February 1944. His review was short and uncomplimentary towards what he called 'Roman Catholic hocus-pocus' which Miss Sackville-West discussed with 'objectivity.' He concluded:

The book is crammed with facts about holy freaks who have capered epileptically Godwards. Saint Joseph of Cupertius, for instance, who "at any moment was apt to rise in the air and remain suspended for a long time." This moron, who was so absent-minded that he forgot to eat, was known familiarly as *Bocca aperta*, the gaper.

Perhaps some worthy person is lighting a candle to the air-minded Saint at this moment.

The following week Mary Murphy wrote protesting at 'the extraordinary vulgarity' of this review. She claimed that reviews by critics not of the Catholic faith had written differently of the book: 'It remained for *Tribune* alone to lower itself to such depths of offensiveness and bad taste.' The issue of 24 March printed two letters which took up Orwell's article. The novelist J. H. Symons (1873–1994) argued that Orwell's remarks were 'a very good example of the state of profound ignorance in which the ordinary man flounders, when he begins to discuss the subject of "a belief in life after death." ' The letter from Charles Davey suggested that for Orwell to take Fathers Woodlock and Knox as representatives of the Roman Catholic Church was rather like taking H. G. Wells and Bernard Shaw as representatives of Socialism. However, he congratulated Orwell 'on being one of the first of his generation of intellectuals who has realised that even if you solve the problems concerned with man's daily bread, you can't leave those of man's destiny in doubt, or settle them with easy philosophising that doesn't satisfy men's instinctive feelings.'

It was not only Orwell's own writing that led to vigorous discussion: his work as literary editor was called into question. In the same issue as his 'As I Please,' 14, *Tribune* published this protest (as it was titled).

During the last few months *Tribune* has published in its literary section a number of highly doubtful articles against which we vigorously protest. Among these are certain passages of Arthur Koestler's article "Literary Idolatry," which mixes effective criticism of Aragon and "Silence de la Mer," with historical fallacies so flagrant that they undermine the integrity of the Socialist point of view. Also a stupid note by a very stupid person who signs° Stevie Smith.[2] This note refers to a young poet writing in French, called Feyyaz Fergar. Your critic claims that this poet is a Frenchman, and builds up all the attack on the assumption that he is living in an occupied country. Actually, it transpires that he is a Turk living in London. The absurdity is increased by attributing the sources of this Turk's inspiration to Baudelaire and Hugo, when in reality he is an obvious follower of Paul Eluard—Eluard of the nineteen-thirties. Further, the article by Stephen Spender on Gascoyne's book *Poems*, 1937–42, is given the headline "Surrealism." We do not wish to discuss the merits of Mr. Gascoyne's poems and Mr. Spender himself does not mention Surrealism in his review. He probably appreciates only too well that Mr. Gascoyne's collapse into the erotic-mysticism of Pierre-Jean Jouve has no longer anything in common with the Surrealists. But why, then, should your editorial create this false impression and announce in the contents of No. 371, "Surrealism," by Stephen Spender?

Two of the present signatories, in an attempt to clarify some of the confusion created by recent articles, notes and letters, sent to your paper an article which was refused on the pretext that "enough has been written recently about French poetry." This refusal to admit that mistakes have been made betrays a scandalous indifference to the real trend of progressive thought outside this country and an attitude which can only create a very favourable breeding ground for reaction and the revival of patriotic hysteria.

If *Tribune* is to take a lead between those who pull back and those who are ignorant, it will be necessary to adopt an attitude which is both better informed and more willing to accept the criticism of those who believe in intellectual as well as political integrity.

E. L. T. Mesens,
Editor, *London Bulletin*, former leader
Surrealist Movement in Belgium.
Roland Penrose,
Surrealist Group in England.
Jacques B. Brunius,
Surrealist Movement in France.
Patrick Waldberg
Surrealist Group in the U.S.A.

The Koestler article appeared in *Tribune* on 26 November 1943, a day or two before Orwell assumed office. Stevie Smith's 'Poems from France,' a review of *Gestes à la Mer* by Feyyaz Fergar, an editor of *Dint* (see *2357, n.1*), was in the 21 January 1944 issue; and 'Surrealism,' a review by Stephen Spender of David Gascoyne's *Poems 1937– 1942*, in the 4 February 1944 issue.

Orwell did have his defenders, however. On 5 May 1944, J. B. Allwood wrote to say how pleased he was that *Tribune* refused to accept 'the international aridity of "Marxist" writing, or the cosmopolitan sloppiness of the surrealists.' The editors then concluded correspondence on this topic. Nevertheless, letters of protest about another surrealist topic were published on 18 August 1944.

1. Newton believed in alchemy, not astrology.
2. Stevie Smith (pseudonym of Florence Margaret Smith, 1902–1971), poet and novelist and a friend of Orwell's; see Crick, 422–24 and *1582, n. 1.*

2430. John Davys Beresford to Orwell

7 March 1944

J. D. Beresford (1873–1947), prolific novelist and writer of short stories, acknowledged a gift of £2 from Orwell on behalf of the novelist and essayist, John Cowper Powys (1872–1963), who was then in need of financial help. Beresford told Orwell that Powys's publishers had responded 'in practical ways' that should enable Powys to keep going comfortably for some time. The appeal on Powys's behalf was therefore being suspended, at least for the time being. There would probably be no need to call upon Orwell again for money.

Evidently, when sending his gift. Orwell had told Beresford how much he admired his novel, *A Candidate for Truth*, the second volume of Beresford's Jacob Stahl trilogy and one of his earliest works (1912). Beresford was plainly delighted to have a novel of thirty-two years ago remembered.

2431. To Roy Fuller

7 March 1944   Typewritten

10a Mortimer Crescent
London NW 6

Dear Mr Fuller,[1]

Since receiving your letter I have procured a copy of the Little Reviews Anthology[2] and read your story, "Fletcher". I must say that I myself cannot see anything anti-semitic in it. I imagine that what Cedric Dover[3] meant was that the central character was a Jew and also a not very admirable character, and perhaps that counts as anti-semitism nowadays. I am sorry about this, but you will understand that as Literary Editor I cannot read all the books sent out for review and have to take the reviewers' judgement for granted. Of course if he had made a bald-headed attack on you as an anti-semite I should have checked up on it before printing, but I think he only said "subtly anti-semitic" or words to that effect.[4] I am sorry that you should have had this annoyance. I must add, however, that by my own experience it is almost impossible to mention Jews in print, either favourably or unfavourably, without getting into trouble.

Yours truly
[Signed] Geo. Orwell
George Orwell

1. Roy Fuller (1916–), a solicitor, gave his recreation as 'writing' in his personal details. Several books of his poems had been published by this time: *Poems* (1940), *The Middle of a War* (1942), *A Lost Season* (1944), the latter two reflecting the war, in which he served in the Royal Navy, 1941–45. He contributed to *Tribune*, *The Listener*, and *Poetry* (Chicago). He published volumes of poetry frequently after the war whilst continuing his profession as solicitor to the Woolwich Building Society. He became Professor of Poetry at Oxford in 1968, the year he was awarded the Duff Cooper Memorial Prize. In 1969 he became Vice-President of the Building Societies Association. He replied to Orwell's letter on 14 March, saying that he found it particularly regrettable that it should be *Tribune* that described his story as anti-Semitic. Had any other journal done this, he would have taken a much stronger stand and an apology would long since have been printed. *Tribune* did not print an apology. See *n. 4*.
2. *Little Reviews Anthology* was edited by Denys Val Baker (1917–1984), novelist, short-story writer, and editor. Five numbers appeared, in 1943, 1945, 1946, 1947–48, and 1949. Cedric Dover reviewed Baker's *Little Reviews, 1914–1943* at the same time ('a useful but pedestrian record'), *Tribune*, 18 February 1944. Orwell's review of three of T. S. Eliot's *Four Quartets*, which had first appeared in *Poetry (London)*, October–November 1942, was included in the *Anthology*. For Dover, see *633, n. 1* and *926, n. 1*.
3. Cedric Dover had collaborated with Orwell at the BBC and it was he who had suggested to Orwell that it was racialist to print 'Negro' without a capital 'N' in *Talking to India*. See also 'As I Please,' 2, 10 December 1943, *2391*.
4. Dover had written: 'Roy Fuller's "Fletcher" is subtle and subtly anti-Semitic: a good example, in fact, of the growing anti-Semitism of which Alec° Comfort complains'—a reference to Alex 'Comfort's biting analysis of the "Social Conventions of the Anglo-American Film,"' which Dover had just mentioned. It is very difficult to understand how the story can be regarded as anti-Semitic. The only reference to Fletcher direct or indirect as Jewish is the statement, 'Fletcher, a middle-aged bachelor of Jewish ancestry and intellectual tastes. . . .' He is shown as sensitive and alone. There is loud knocking at his door, and three men enter, 'quietly enough but with an air of violence and savagery. They held, as they walked, their

arms away from their bodies like apes'; they are booted and in uniform. They question him, hit him, and carelessly drop a first edition of Shelley's poems on the floor. When they have gone, Fletcher goes for a walk and comes across the body of a girl who has been raped and killed. Her dead, 'brilliant eyes' meet his—and that is all. Fuller's story is entirely from the point of view of those who attack the vulnerable, whether they be Jewish or women. Whether or not Comfort was correct in saying 'I do not know whether the increasing anti-semitism of films here and in America—paralleled very closely in the novel—is significant,' the words cannot justifiably be related to Fuller's story.

2432. 'As I Please,' 15

Tribune, 10 March 1944

Reading as nearly as possible simultaneously Mr. Derrick Leon's *Life* of Tolstoy, Miss Gladys Storey's book on Dickens, Harry Levin's book on James Joyce, and the autobiography (not yet published in this country) of Salvador Dali, the surrealist painter,[1] I was struck even more forcibly than usual by the advantage that an artist derives from being born into a relatively healthy society.

When I first read *War and Peace* I must have been twenty, an age at which one is not intimidated by long novels, and my sole quarrel with his book (three stout volumes—the length of perhaps four modern novels) was that it did not go on long enough. It seemed to me that Nicholas and Natacha Rostov, Peter Besukhov, Denisov and all the rest of them, were people about whom one would gladly go on reading for ever. The fact is that the minor Russian aristocracy of that date, with their boldness and simplicity, their countrified pleasures, their stormy love affairs and enormous families, were very charming people. Such a society could not possibly be called just or progressive. It was founded on serfdom, a fact that made Tolstoy uneasy even in his boyhood, and even the "enlightened" aristocrat would have found it difficult to think of the peasant as the same species of animal as himself. Tolstoy himself did not give up beating his servants till he was well on into adult life.

The landowner exercised a sort of *droit du seigneur* over the peasants on his estate. Tolstoy had at least one bastard, and his morganatic half-brother was the family coachman. And yet one cannot feel for these simple-minded, prolific Russians the same contempt as one feels for the sophisticated cosmopolitan scum who gave Dali his livelihood. Their saving grace is that they are rustics, they have never heard of benzedrine or gilded toenails, and though Tolstoy was later to repent of the sins of his youth more vociferously than most people, he must have known that he drew his strength—his creative power as well as the strength of his vast muscles—from that rude, healthy background where one shot woodcocks on the marshes and girls thought themselves lucky if they went to three dances in a year.

One of the big gaps in Dickens is that he writes nothing, even in a burlesque spirit, about country life. Of agriculture he does not even pretend to know anything. There are some farcical descriptions of shooting in the

Pickwick Papers, but Dickens, as a middle-class radical, would be incapable of describing such amusements sympathetically. He sees field-sports as primarily an exercise in snobbishness, which they already were in the England of that date. The enclosures, industrialism, the vast differentiation of wealth, and the cult of the pheasant and the red deer, had all combined to drive the mass of the English people off the land and make the hunting instinct, which is probably almost universal in human beings, seem merely a fetish of the aristocracy. Perhaps the best thing in *War and Peace* is the description of the wolf hunt. In the end it is the peasant's dog that outstrips those of the nobles and gets the wolf; and afterwards Natacha finds it quite natural to dance in the peasant's hut.

To see such scenes in England you would have had to go back a hundred or two hundred years, to a time when difference in status did not mean any very great difference in habits. Dickens's England was already dominated by the "Trespassers will be Prosecuted" board. When one thinks of the accepted Left Wing attitude towards hunting, shooting and the like, it is queer to reflect that Lenin, Stalin and Trotsky were all of them keen sportsmen in their day. But then they belonged to a large empty country where there was no necessary connection between sport and snobbishness, and the divorce between country and town was never complete. The society which almost any modern novelist has as his material is very much meaner, less comely and less carefree than Tolstoy's, and to grasp this has been one of the signs of talent.[2] Joyce would have been falsifying the facts if he had made the people in *Dubliners* less disgusting than they are. But the natural advantage lay with Tolstoy: for, other things being equal, who would not rather write about Peter and Natacha than about furtive seductions in boarding-houses or drunken Catholic business-men celebrating a "retreat"?

In his book on Joyce Mr. Harry Levin gives a few biographical details, but is unable to tell us much about Joyce's last year of life. All we know is that when the Nazis entered France he escaped over the border into Switzerland, to die about a year later in his old home in Zurich. Even the whereabouts of Joyce's children is not, it seems, known for certain.

The academic critics could not resist the opportunity to kick Joyce's corpse. The *Times* gave him a mean, cagey little obituary, and then—though the *Times* has never lacked space for letters about batting averages or the first cuckoo—refused to print the letter of protest that T. S. Eliot wrote. This was in accordance with the grand old English tradition that the dead must always be flattered unless they happen to be artists. Let a politician die, and his worst enemies will stand up on the floor of the House and utter pious lies in his honour, but a writer or artist must be sniffed at, at least if he is any good. The entire British press united to insult D. H. Lawrence ("pornographer" was the usual description) as soon as he was dead. But the snooty obituaries were merely what Joyce would have expected. The collapse of France, and the need to flee from the Gestapo like a common political suspect, were a different matter, and when the war is over it will be very interesting to find out what Joyce thought about it.

Joyce was a conscious exile from Anglo-Irish philistinism. Ireland would have none of him, England and America barely tolerated him. His books were refused publication, destroyed when in type by timid publishers, banned when they came out, pirated with the tacit connivance of the authorities, and, in any case, largely ignored until the publication of *Ulysses*. He had a genuine grievance, and was extremely conscious of it. But it was also his aim to be a "pure" artist, "above the battle" and indifferent to politics. He had written *Ulysses* in Switzerland, with an Austrian passport and a British pension, during the 1914–18 war, to which he paid as nearly as possible no attention. But the present war, as Joyce found out, is not of a kind to be ignored, and I think it must have left him reflecting that a political choice *is* necessary and that even stupidity is better than totalitarianism.

One thing that Hitler and his friends have demonstrated is what a relatively good time the intellectual has had during the past hundred years. After all, how does the persecution of Joyce, Lawrence, Whitman, Baudelaire, even Oscar Wilde, compare with the kind of thing that has been happening to Liberal intellectuals all over Europe since Hitler came to power? Joyce left Ireland in disgust: he did not have to run for his life, as he did when the panzers rolled into Paris. The British Government duly banned *Ulysses* when it appeared, but it took the ban off 15 years later, and what is probably more important, it helped Joyce to stay alive while the book was written. And thereafter, thanks to the generosity of an anonymous admirer,[3] Joyce was able to live a civilized life in Paris for nearly twenty years, working away at *Finnegans Wake* and surrounded by a circle of disciples, while industrious teams of experts translated *Ulysses* not only into various European languages but even into Japanese. Between 1900 and 1920 he had known hunger and neglect: but take it for all in all, his life would appear a pretty good one if one were viewing it from inside a German concentration camp.

What would the Nazis have done with Joyce if they could have laid hands on him? We don't know. They might even have made efforts to win him over and add him to their bag of "converted" literary men. But he must have seen that they had not only broken up the society that he was used to, but were the deadly enemies of everything that he valued. The battle which he had wanted to be "above" did, after all, concern him fairly directly, and I like to think that before the end he brought himself to utter some non-neutral comment on Hitler—and coming from Joyce it might be quite a stinger—which is lying in Zurich and will be accessible after the war.

1. *The Secret Life of Salvador Dali*, Dial Press, New York, 1942.
2. In a letter published by *Tribune* on 24 March 1944, N. and J. A. Turnbull considered that Orwell gave a 'very misleading picture of Tolstoy,' particularly with regard to 'hunting and similar barbarities which Mr. Orwell seems to regard as desirable.' They also took exception to his statement that 'the hunting instinct is probably universal in human beings.' There was, they wrote, a connection between 'such savage survivals and the bloodstained condition of the earth today—a connection which Tolstoy did not fail to appreciate.' For Orwell's review of Leon's biography, see *2444*.
3. Orwell probably had in mind the New York lawyer and patron of the arts John Quinn, who, until his death in August 1924, supported Joyce in various ways, although Joyce 'did not consider Quinn especially generous' (Richard Ellmann, *James Joyce*, New York, 1959, 494; see

also 427, 504, 570, 602). Quinn defended the *Little Magazine*, without a fee, against the charge of obscenity when it printed part of the Nausicaa episode of *Ulysses* in 1920 (Ellmann, 517–19).

2433. Review of *Other Men's Flowers*, selected and annotated by A. P. Wavell

The Observer, 12 March 1944

Most of the poems in Lord Wavell's anthology are probably to be found in other anthologies, but that is nothing to complain about at a time when libraries are bombed or shut for the duration and almost any book is liable to be out of print. Picking almost at random among the two hundred or more poems that the book contains, here are some of the things that one comes upon:

> "High Tide on the Coast of Lincolnshire" (Jean Ingelow), "The Mary Gloster" (Rudyard Kipling), "I've been in Debt, in Love, and in Drink" (Alexander Brome), the Rubaiyat of Omar Khayyam, "I have a Rendezvous with Death" (Alan Seeger), "The Owl and the Pussy-Cat" (Edward Lear), "Auguries of Innocence" (Blake), "Bishop Blougram's Apology" (Browning), "She was Poor but She was Honest" (Anon.), "The Hound of Heaven" (Francis Thompson), "To his Coy Mistress" (Marvell), "How we Beat the Favourite" (Adam Lindsay Gordon), "An Irish Airman Foresees his Fate" (W. B. Yeats), "Cynara" (Ernest Dowson), "Dream-Pedlary" (Thomas Lovell Beddoes).

Even to put one's hand on all of these one would have to be better provided with books than most people are nowadays, and Lord Wavell's choice ranges more widely than this list indicates. But it is, he says, "a purely personal anthology," consisting of "the poems I could repeat, entire or in great part." Like many other people, he likes to repeat verse to himself when driving a car or riding a horse (but not when walking, he adds), and he admits a preference for verse that can be declaimed. This perhaps accounts for his having included in his collection some distinctly "phoney" battle-pieces by G. K. Chesterton. Quoting a poem written about London during the blitz, Lord Wavell adds this footnote:

> I read these verses in an Egyptian newspaper while flying from Cairo to Barce in Cyrenaica at the beginning of April, 1941, to try to deal with Rommel's counter-attack. I was uncomfortable in body—for the bomber was cramped and draughty—and in mind, for I knew I had been caught with insufficient strength to meet a heavy counter-attack; reading this poem and committing it to memory did something to relieve my discomforts of body and mind.

It so happens that the poem in question is a very bad one,[1] but these lines could only have been written by a true lover of poetry. It is a peculiarity of poetry that it always makes its strongest impact at odd and unsuitable moments (when one is dodging the traffic in Oxford Circus, for instance), and though we have not all got Lord Wavell's prodigious memory, no one can ever be truly said to "care about" a poem unless he has made at least an effort to learn it by heart.

To review an anthology is inevitably to find fault, and some serious charges can be made against this one. One could forgive Lord Wavell for allowing too much space to Browning and Kipling, but in too many cases he has represented a poet by only one poem and then chosen the wrong one. For instance, if Suckling is to appear only once it was a pity to put in the hackneyed "Why so pale and wan, fond lover?" and not the less-known and immensely superior "Ballad upon a Wedding." Or again, with only one piece from the "Ingoldsby Legends," why pick on "The Lay of St. Cuthbert" instead of, say, "The Lay of St. Dunstan" or "Bloudie Jacke of Shrewsberrie"? Thackeray is represented by "The Chronicle of the Drum" and "The King of Brentford": "The Ballad of the Bouillabaisse" would have been better. Gerard Manley Hopkins, who is none too accessible and needs all the reprinting he can get, is only represented by four rather colourless lines. It was also a pity to quote only a tiny fragment of Hilaire Belloc's brilliant early poem, "The Modern Traveller," which is now seemingly almost unprocurable.

One could extend this list of complaints—though, of course, such complaints add up in the end to the statement that the only perfect anthology is the one you have compiled for yourself. At least there will be something in this book to please everyone who cares for poetry at all, and though some readers may squirm when they come across "Lepanto" or Newbolt's "Drake's Drum" (why not the comparatively sympathetic "Vitai Lampada" if Newbolt was to appear at all?), still, they must admire the catholic taste which can find enjoyment in this kind of thing along with Shakespeare's Sonnets, "Sir Patrick Spens" and "La Belle Dame Sans Merci."

Lord Wavell has arranged his chosen pieces according to their subject matter and added notes which, he says, were demanded by the publisher and should not be taken too seriously. They are, nevertheless, well worth reading, especially his remarks on war poetry. He has little enjoyment in any modern verse—anything subsequent to 1919, that is—but with unusual humility admits he may be wrong. When a poem lacks a title he gives it one himself, sometimes with happy results. It was a neat touch to reprint the passage from "Henry IV" in which Hotspur complains of the "popinjay" who came to claim the prisoners and head it "The Staff Officer." This is not a perfect anthology, but it is quite good enough to make one feel a certain regret that the man who compiled it should be wasting his talents on the most thankless job in the world.[2]

[Fee: £5.5.0; 9.3.44]

1. 'London under Bombardment' by Greta Briggs. It begins: 'I, who am known as London, have faced stern times before, / Having fought and ruled and traded for a thousand years and more. . . .'

2. Field-Marshal Lord Wavell (1883–1950, 1st Earl Wavell) commanded British forces in North Africa, 1939 to July 1941, when he was transferred to the Far East. He was appointed Viceroy of India in June 1943—the 'most thankless job in the world.' See also *712, n. 1.*

2434. Rejected Review of *Faith, Reason and Civilisation* by Harold J. Laski[1]

For *Manchester Evening News*; submitted 13 March 1944   Typescript

It is about a year since Professor Laski produced his *Reflections on the Revolution of Our Time*, a larger and more elaborate book than the present one, but dealing with approximately the same subject. At that time there were unmistakable signs of uneasiness in Professor Laski's mind. There were even passages in his book which called up irresistably° the picture of a child swallowing castor oil. Now, however, Professor Laski has found out the right method of dealing with castor oil. Squirt a little lemon and brandy on top of it, hold your nose, shut your eyes, gulp the stuff down, follow it up immediately with a lump of chocolate, and really the experience becomes almost bearable.

What is this castor oil with which Professor Laski used once to have difficulties? It is the authoritarian element in Russian Socialism: more broadly, it is the extreme danger of using dictatorship as a road to democracy. Professor Laski is a Socialist, but he is also a democrat and a believer in freedom of thought. He is justly concerned about the danger of world-wide counter-revolution, and he is aware that the USSR is the real dynamo of the Socialist movement in this country and everywhere else. Therefore the USSR must be safeguarded at all costs. But this, as he sees it, means shutting one's eyes to purges, liquidations, the dictatorship of a minority, suppression of criticism and so forth. It is a painful problem, and in his last book he talked about it and about.[2] Now, however, he has found the answer to it in an analogy—a false analogy as it happens, but evidently a comforting one for the time being.

It is, that the USSR in the modern world corresponds to the Christian Church in the period of the break-up of the Roman Empire. It is the repository of the new doctrines which can both save civilisation and make a fresh advance possible. Just as the early Christians saved the crumbling world of the ancients by giving a new meaning to life, so "the Russian idea" can revivify Western society and take the place of the religious beliefs which (Professor Laski thinks) have outlived their usefulness.

Throughout, Professor Laski uses "the Russian idea" and "Socialism" interchangeably. The Russian regime is assumed not to have altered substantially since 1917: it aims at the establishment of human brotherhood and equality just as singlemindedly as the early Church aimed at the establishment of the Kingdom of God. And it is easy to see how useful this analogy is in reconciling Professor Laski to the principle of totalitarianism. After all, anything can be forgiven to fanatics! Heresy-hunting, persecution, mental dishonesty—they were all common enough among the early Christians, who were nevertheless the founders of our civilisation. And though there were thoughtful pagans who objected to the crudity and superstition of the Christians, at bottom they were only seeking to defend their own privileges. Similarly, those in our own day who object to dictatorship are, at bottom, merely defenders of laissez-faire capitalism.

Look a little more closely at this analogy, and you can see that it is false in every particular. To begin with, Christian doctrine was formed at a time when the Church had no power. The early Christians were a hunted sect, largely consisting of slaves: the Russian government rules over a sixth of the earth. Secondly, in spite of heresies and controversies, Christian doctrine was relatively stable. Communist doctrine changes so often and so drastically that to continue believing in it is almost incompatible with mental integrity. Professor Laski ignores both of these differences. He assumes, as though it were not in dispute, that Stalin's aims are identical with Lenin's, and that the whole trend of development within the USSR has been in the direction of more democracy, more liberty and more social equality. Here and there he admits, usually in a parenthesis, that certain features of the Soviet regime are open to criticism, but always defends them on "tu quoque" lines—that is, by pointing out that similar abuses exist in Britain or the U.S.A.

Now, the problem that Professor Laski came near to meeting in his last book, but completely evades in this one, is a problem that does not necessarily involve the USSR at all, except perhaps for purposes of illustration. It is simply this: that if you set up a dictatorship, you have no way of ensuring that the dictator will do what he has promised to do. Any non-democratic version of Socialism necessarily puts all power into the hands of a small clique, and that clique has as much interest in clinging to its privileges as the capitalist class in Britain or America, or any other oligarchy. Despotism based on power instead of money is the inherent danger of Socialism, and it is vitally necessary that it should be foreseen in advance. Instead of warning his readers against it, Professor Laski has chosen to assume that it does not exist.

Why? At bottom, no doubt, because he knows that capitalism is still very strong, that after the war it is capable of making a temporary come-back, with disastrous results, and he fears that it may be demoralising to point out that Socialism also has its dangers. Therefore, don't criticise the USSR, don't insist on the all-importance of freedom of speech, don't mention doubtful subjects like the[3] GPU and the "Soviet millionaires"; because if you speak of such things there is danger that the average man will think you are defending capitalism. That, probably, is how Professor Laski's thoughts run. And certainly the dilemma is a painful one. To work all your life for Socialism, to see at last a state definitely describable as Socialist arise and triumphantly hold its own amid a hostile world, and then to have to admit that it too has its failings—that needs courage. But we expect courage of Professor Laski, and he would write a better book if he would occasionally take the risk of giving ammunition to the reactionaries.

1. Orwell's Payments Book notes for 13 March 1944 that a review for the *Manchester Evening*

News had been rejected and no payment was made; see *2831*. A typescript has survived, because Orwell, having seen a review of the same book in *Politics*, thought it might amuse the editor, Dwight Macdonald, and sent him a copy; see 23 July 1944, *2518*. Orwell thought the review had been rejected because of its 'anti-Stalin implications.' For Macdonald's response, see *2518*, *n. 1*. Orwell's typescript has no title, other than that of the author and the book reviewed, and no subheadings. This must mean that titles and sub-headings of *Manchester Evening News* (and *Observer*) printings of his work were introduced by sub-editors.

2. Compare 'On a huge hill, / Cragged, and steep, Truth stands, and hee that will / Reach her, about must, and about must goe,' Donne, 'Satyr 3,' lines 79–81; and Orwell's later use of the phrase in his review of D. W. Brogan's *The American Problem*, 17 September 1944, *2551*, with other examples, *n. 2*.

3. the] *Orwell typed* to

2435. 'As I Please,' 16

Tribune, 17 March 1944

With no power to put my decrees into operation, but with as much authority as most of the exile "governments" now sheltering in various parts of the world, I pronounce sentence of death on the following words and expressions:—

Achilles heel, jackboot, hydra-headed, ride roughshod over, stab in the back, petty-bourgeois, stinking corpse, liquidate, iron heel, blood-stained oppressor, cynical betrayal, lackey, flunkey, mad dog, jackal, hyena, blood bath.

No doubt this list will have to be added to from time to time, but it will do to go on with. It contains a fair selection of the dead metaphors and ill-translated foreign phrases which have been current in Marxist literature for years past.

There are, of course, many other perversions of the English language besides this one. There is official English, or Stripetrouser, the language of White Papers, Parliamentary debates (in their more decorous moments) and B.B.C. news bulletins. There are the scientists and the economists, with their instinctive preference for words like "contraindicate" and "deregionalisation." There is American slang, which for all its attractiveness probably tends to impoverish the language in the long run. And there is the general slovenliness of modern English speech with its decadent vowel sounds (throughout the London area you have to use sign language to distinguish between "threepence" and "three-half-pence") and its tendency to make verbs and nouns interchangeable. But here I am concerned only with one kind of bad English, Marxist English, or Pamphletese, which can be studied in the *Daily Worker*, the *Labour Monthly*, *Plebs*, the *New Leader*, and similar papers.

Many of the expressions used in political literature are simply euphemisms or rhetorical tricks. "Liquidate," for instance (or "eliminate"), is a polite word for "to kill," while "realism" normally means "dishonesty." But Marxist phraseology is peculiar in that it consists largely of translations. Its characteristic vocabulary comes ultimately from German or Russian phrases which have been adopted in one country after another with no attempt to find suitable equivalents. Here, for instance, is a piece of Marxist writing—it happens to be an address delivered to the Allied armies by the citizens of Pantelleria:—

The citizens of Pantelleria "pay grateful homage to the Anglo-American forces for the promptness with which they have liberated them from the evil yoke of a megalomaniac and satanic regime which, not content with having sucked like a monstrous octopus the best energies of true Italians for twenty years, is now reducing Italy to a mass of ruins and misery for one motive only—the insane personal profit of its chiefs, who, under an ill-concealed mask of hollow, so-called patriotism, hide the basest passions, and, plotting together with the German pirates, hatch the lowest egoism and blackest treatment while all the time, with revolting cynicism, they tread on the blood of thousands of Italians."

This filthy stew of words is presumably a translation from the Italian, but the point is that one would not recognize it as such. It might be a translation from any other European language, or it might come straight out of the *Daily Worker*; so truly international is this style of writing. Its characteristic is the endless use of ready-made metaphors. In the same spirit, when Italian submarines were sinking the ships that took arms to Republican Spain, the *Daily Worker* urged the British Admiralty to "sweep the mad dogs from the seas." Clearly, people capable of using such phrases have ceased to remember that words have meanings.

A Russian friend tells me that the Russian language is richer than English in terms of abuse, so that Russian invective cannot always be accurately translated. Thus when Molotov referred to the Germans as "cannibals," he was perhaps using some word which sounded natural in Russian, but to which "cannibal" was only a rough approximation. But our local Communists have taken over, from the defunct *Inprecorr*[1] and similar sources, a whole series of these crudely-translated phrases, and from force of habit have come to think of them as actual English expressions. The Communist vocabulary of abuse (applied to Fascists or Socialists according to the "line" of the moment) includes such terms as hyena, corpse, lackey, pirate, hangman, bloodsucker, mad dog, criminal, assassin. Whether at first, second or third hand, these are all translations, and by no means the kind of word that an English person naturally uses to express disapproval. And language of this kind is used with an astonishing indifference as to its meaning. Ask a journalist what a jackboot is, and you will find that he does not know. Yet he goes on talking about jackboots. Or what is meant by "to ride roughshod"? Very few people know that either. For that matter, in my experience, very few Socialists know the meaning of the word "proletariat."

You can see a good example of Marxist language at its worst in the words "lackey" and "flunkey." Pre-revolutionary Russia was still a feudal country in which hordes of idle menservants were part of the social set-up; in that context "lackey," as a word of abuse, had a meaning. In England, the social landscape is quite different. Except at public functions, the last time I saw a footman in livery was in 1921. And, in fact, in ordinary speech, the word "flunkey" has been obsolete since the 'nineties, and the word "lackey" for about a century. Yet they and other equally inappropriate words are dug up for pamphleteering purposes. The result is a style of writing that bears the same relation to writing real English as doing a jigsaw puzzle bears to painting a picture. It is just a question of fitting together a number of ready-made pieces. Just talk about hydra-headed jackboots riding roughshod over bloodstained hyenas, and you are all right. For confirmation of which, see almost any pamphlet issued by the Communist Party—or by any other political party, for that matter.

1. The spelling is *Inprecor* in *Homage to Catalonia*; see Appendix II, 221 and 228–35. *Inprecor's* title varied. It was published from Vienna and Berlin in the 1920s as *Internationale Press, Korrespondenz*, and French and Swiss versions were issued. Its frequency was at least weekly, but there was some irregularity in its publication. As *International Press Correspondence* it was published in an English edition in London at least from Vol. 13, No. 11 to Vol. 18, No. 32, 29 September 1927–1 February 1929, and 9 March 1933 to 25 June 1938. Thereafter, from Vol. 18, No. 33 to Vol. 33, No. 50, 2 July 1938 to 19 December 1953, it was published as *World News & Views*. It was a Communist news-sheet opposed to the POUM when Orwell was in Barcelona.

2436. To Leonard Moore

19 March 1944   Typewritten

10a Mortimer Crescent
London NW 6

Dear Mr Moore,

I have finished my book[1] and will be sending you the MS in a few days' time. It is being typed now. I make it about 30,000 words. To avoid wasting time I think we ought to decide in advance what to do about showing it to Gollancz. According to our contract he has the first refusal of my fiction books, and this would come under the heading of fiction, as it is a sort of fairy story, really a fable with a political meaning. I think, however, Gollancz wouldn't publish it, as it is strongly anti-Stalin in tendency. Nor is it any use wasting time on Warburg, who probably wouldn't touch anything of this tendency and to my knowledge is very short of paper. I suggest therefore that we ought to tell Gollancz but let him know that the book is not likely to suit him, and say that we will only send it along if he very definitely wants to see it. I am going to write to him in this sense now. The point is that if Gollancz and his readers get hold of it, even if they end by not taking it, they will probably hang onto the MS for weeks. So I will write to him, and then he will know about it before you get the MS.

As to what publisher to approach, I think Nicholson and Watson might be the best.[2] I told one of their men I had a book coming along and he seemed anxious to get hold of it. Or else Hutchinson, where I have a contact in Robert Neumann. Or anyone else who (a) has got some paper and (b) isn't in the arms of Stalin. The latter is important. This book is murder from the

Communist point of view, though no names are mentioned. Provided we can get over these difficulties I fancy the book should find a publisher, judging by the stuff they do print nowadays.

I am going to send two copies. I think we might have a try at an American publication as well. About a year ago the Dial Press wrote asking me to send them the next book I did, and I think they might like this one.[3]

I am contracted now to do a Britain in Pictures book, which I suppose will take me 6–8 weeks. After that I am arranging to do two longish literary essays, one on "No Orchids for Miss Blandish", and one on Salvador Dali, for two magazines. When I have done those two we shall have enough stuff for the book of reprinted essays.

Yours sincerely
Eric Blair

1. *Animal Farm*.
2. At the top of this letter to Moore someone has written the names of two more publishers: Eyre & Spottiswoode and Hollis & Carter.
3. In *Partisan Review*, 63 (1996), William Phillips claimed he was the first person in America to read *Animal Farm*; he then recommended it to the Dial Press (182–3). See also *2443, 2446*, and *2461*.

2437. To Victor Gollancz

19 March 1944   Typewritten

10a Mortimer Crescent
London NW 6

Dear Mr Gollancz,
I have just finished a book[1] and the typing will be completed in a few days. You have the first refusal of my fiction books, and I think this comes under the heading of fiction. It is a little fairy story, about 30,000 words, with a political meaning. But I must tell you that it is—I think—completely unacceptable politically from your point of view (it is anti-Stalin). I don't know whether in that case you will want to see it. If you do, of course I will send it along, but the point is that I am not anxious, naturally, for the MS to be hanging about too long. If you think that you would like to have a look at it, in spite of its not being politically O.K., could you let either me or my agent (Christy & Moore) know? Moore will have the MS. Otherwise, could you let me know that you *don't* want to see it, so that I can take it elsewhere without wasting time?

Yours sincerely
[Signed] Eric Blair
Eric Blair

1. *Animal Farm*.

2438. Ethel Colquhoun to Orwell

20 March 1944

Orwell rejected a poem called 'The Signalman' that Ethel Colquhoun had sent to *Tribune*. Instead of sending it back simply with a rejection slip, he had written a personal note of explanation. In thanking him for that, Ethel Colquhoun said she assumed that that implied he would like to know what the poem meant, though she felt it was not particularly abstruse. Having explained it, she remarked that she had submitted it to give him a chance 'of publishing a *poem*,' for *Tribune*'s 'poetic level is rather low.'

2439. Review of *The Way of a Countryman* by Sir William Beach Thomas

Manchester Evening News, 23 March 1944

It is uncertain whether the general public would think of Sir William Beach Thomas primarily as a war correspondent or as a naturalist,[1] but he is in no doubt about the matter himself. The world, as he sees it, really centres round the English village, and round the trees and hedges of that village rather than the houses and the people.

In a long life he has travelled to every corner of the earth and met everyone from George Meredith to Marshal Pétain, and from Frank Harris to Theodore Roosevelt, but a glimpse of a bittern in the East Anglian marshes, a grizzly in the Canadian rockies, a twelve-pound trout in New Zealand, means more to him than any merely human celebrity.

Even the Battle of the Somme is chiefly memorable to him because, amid the tremendous roar of the opening bombardment, he saw a grey shrike for the first time.

This book is, in some sort, an autobiography, but it is only fair to give prospective readers the warning, "If you don't like 'nature books' keep away."

Sir William's memories begin some time in the early seventies in a little village in the Shires, where his father was rector, and "four species of animal provided the bulk of our amusements . . . ponies, dogs, rabbits and foxes."

Later, he was to break records for the quarter-mile at Shrewsbury and Oxford, spend busy week-ends with Lord Northcliffe, and "cover" the Ruhr during the lamentable days of the French occupation, but none of it is so vivid to him as the memory of that village childhood.

"What a number of 'necessities of life' we did without. We had no bicycles, of course, no motor-cars, no telephones, no wireless, no gramophone, no preserved fruit—except some repulsive dried apples—no tomatoes, no bananas, no keyless watches, and few games . . . We journeyed to the nearest town, nine miles away, by pony, whose feet churned up inches of white dust."

And, needless to say, Sir William preferred it like that, including the absence of games, for though a born athlete he rightly objects to the "tyranny" of games, which was just beginning to become operative in his boyhood.

Sir William describes himself throughout as a "countryman," but for his purposes "the country" means sport, bird-watching, and botanising rather than agriculture, and his book raises certain doubts about the whole of this class of literature.

There is no question that a love of what is loosely called "nature"—a kingfisher flashing down a stream, a bullfinch's mossy nest, the caddis-flies in the ditch—is very widespread in England, cutting across age-groups and even class-distinctions, and attaining in some people an almost mystical intensity.

Whether it is a healthy symptom is another matter. It arises partly from the small size, equable climate, and varied scenery of England, but it is also probably bound up with the decay of English agriculture. Real rustics are not conscious of being picturesque, they do not construct bird sanctuaries, they are uninterested in any plant or animal that does not affect them directly.

In many languages all the smaller birds are called by the same name. Even in England a genuine farm labourer usually thinks that a frog and a toad are the same thing, and nearly always believes that all snakes are poisonous and that they sting with their tongues.[2]

The fact is that those who really have to deal with nature have no cause to be in love with it. On the East Anglian coast the older cottages for the fishermen are built with their backs to the sea. The sea is simply an enemy from the fisherman's point of view.

Sir William's comparatively sentimental attitude towards the land is shown by the fact that he regrets the war-time destruction of the rabbit. Probably he would also regret the extermination of that even deadlier enemy of agriculture, the pheasant.

"Nature" books are a growth of the past two hundred years. The first and probably still the best of them is Gilbert White's "Natural History of Selborne."

Sir William couples with this Izaak Walton's "Compleat Angler," written a century earlier, but Walton's more limited and utilitarian book does not seem quite to belong in this category.

The most characteristic "nature writers" of all are W. H. Hudson, and Richard Jefferies. One may guess that it is on Jefferies that Sir William Beach Thomas has modelled himself. But Jefferies, for all his charm and his detailed observation, is curiously inhuman. His daydream expressed in a whole book was of an England from which the human beings had vanished and only the wild creatures remained.

The same outlook is implied in W. H. Hudson, whose only successful novel, "Green Mansions," has a heroine who is half human and half bird. Hudson also wrote a whole rapturous essay on the spectacle of a field ruined by dandelions.

Nature-worship carried to this length is inherently anti-social. The more normal attitude is expressed by Crabbe, a true countryman, who wrote at least one diatribe against wild-flowers, which in his eyes were simply weeds.[3] Needless to say, Sir William does not much approve of Crabbe.

Sir William started his journalist career at about the same time as Shaw, Barrie, Max Beerbohm, and J. L. Garvin. That was in the bustling days when Northcliffe had just started the "Daily Mail," and the journalistic reminiscences are probably the best thing in this book.

The war of 1914–18 is hardly mentioned, though it is interesting to learn that for the first year or two the whole British Press was only allowed to send five correspondents to the front, and these were as far as possible prevented from seeing anything.

The book ends with a plea for the preservation and revival of rural England, with which everyone can agree even while suspecting that Sir William's ideal picture of rural England might contain too many rabbits and not enough tractors.

[Fee: £8.8.0; 22.3.44]

1. William Beach Thomas (1868–1957; Kt., 1920), journalist and author, wrote on country matters from about 1898 until shortly before he died. He was a prolific author, and *The Way of a Countryman* was his second volume of autobiography, *Traveller in News* (1925) being the first. He proved an outstanding war correspondent in France for the *Daily Mail* (for which he had written a column on country life) and published *With the British on the Somme* in 1917. In 1918 he was sent to the United States and met, among others, President Woodrow Wilson, Theodore Roosevelt, and Henry Ford.
2. R. V. Walton accused Orwell of lacking a knowledge of nature in a letter to the *Manchester Evening News*, 29 March 1944. To state that farm labourers confused frogs and toads and thought all snakes poisonous and that they stung with their tongues 'proves beyond doubt that Mr Orwell's natural history field is very limited.' He also disagreed that the pheasant was a deadlier enemy to agriculture than the rabbit and pointed out that the pheasant more than made up for the small amount of seed it ate by the large number of insects it consumed.
3. Orwell may have had in mind George Crabbe's condemnation of thistles, poppies, blue bugloss, slimy mallow, and 'clasping tares,' 'Rank weeds, that every art and care defy, / Reign o'er the land, and rob the blighted rye.' Crabbe asks of the impoverished peasant, 'Can poets soothe you' with 'tinsel trappings of poetic pride . . . when you pine for bread?' *The Village* (1783), from I, 48–76.

2440. To Leonard Moore

23 March 1944   Typewritten

10a Mortimer Crescent
London NW6

Dear Mr Moore,

Thanks for your letter. I sent off two copies of the MS of the book yesterday and hope they reached you safely. I haven't heard from Gollancz and I dare say he will write direct to you.

We must *on no account* take this book to either Eyre & Spottiswoode or Hollis & Carter. They are both Catholic publishers and Hollis, in particular, has published some most poisonous stuff since he set up in business. It would

do me permanent harm to be published by either of these. I don't know what
the objections to Hutchinson's and N. & W.[1] are, but perhaps you could let
me know. I should think Cape is another possibility. Or Fabers. I have a
contact in Faber's and a slight one at Cape's.[2] But let me know whom you are
going to take it to. I should like it settled as early as possible.

Yours sincerely
Eric Blair

1. Nicholson & Watson.
2. T.S. Eliot at Faber & Faber and Miss C. V. Wedgwood at Cape (see *2453*). Daniel George
   (who reviewed novels for *Tribune*) was chief reader at Cape (see *2561, n. 2*); see also Crick,
   454–58.

2441. 'As I Please,' 17

Tribune, 24 March 1944

Of all the unanswered questions of our time, perhaps the most important is:
"What is Fascism?"

One of the social survey organisations in America recently asked this
question of a hundred different people, and got answers ranging from "pure
democracy" to "pure diabolism." In this country if you ask the average
thinking person to define Fascism, he usually answers by pointing to the
German and Italian regimes. But this is very unsatisfactory, because even the
major Fascist states differ from one another a good deal in structure and
ideology.

It is not easy, for instance, to fit Germany and Japan into the same
framework, and it is even harder with some of the small states which are
describable as Fascist. It is usually assumed, for instance, that Fascism is
inherently warlike, that it thrives in an atmosphere of war hysteria and can
only solve its economic problems by means of war-preparation or foreign
conquests. But clearly this is not true of, say, Portugal or the various South
American dictatorships. Or again, anti-Semitism is supposed to be one of the
distinguishing marks of Fascism; but some Fascist movements are not anti-
Semitic. Learned controversies, reverberating for years on end in American
magazines, have not even been able to determine whether or not Fascism is a
form of Capitalism. But still, when we apply the term "Fascism" to
Germany or Japan or Mussolini's Italy, we know broadly what we mean. It is
in internal politics that this word has lost the last vestige of meaning. For if
you examine the Press you will find that there is almost no set of people—
certainly no political party or organised body of any kind—which has not
been denounced as Fascist during the past ten years.

Here I am not speaking of the verbal use of the term "Fascist." I am
speaking of what I have seen in print. I have seen the words "Fascist in
sympathy," or "of Fascist tendency," or just plain "Fascist," applied in all
seriousness to the following bodies of people:

Conservatives: All Conservatives, appeasers or anti-appeasers, are held to be subjectively pro-Fascist. British rule in India and the Colonies is held to be indistinguishable from Nazism. Organisations of what one might call a patriotic and traditional type are labelled crypto-Fascist or "Fascist-minded." Examples are the Boy Scouts, the Metropolitan Police, M.I.5,[1] the British Legion. Key phrase: "The public schools are breeding-grounds of Fascism."

Socialists: Defenders of old-style capitalism (example, Sir Ernest Benn)[2] maintain that Socialism and Fascism are the same thing. Some Catholic journalists maintain that Socialists have been the principal collaborators in the Nazi-occupied countries. The same accusation is made from a different angle by the Communist Party during its ultra-Left phases. In the period 1930–5 the *Daily Worker* habitually referred to the Labour Party as the Labour Fascists. This is echoed by other Left extremists such as Anarchists. Some Indian Nationalists consider the British trade unions to be Fascist organisations.

Communists: A considerable school of thought (examples, Rauschning, Peter Drucker, James Burnham, F. A. Voigt)[3] refuses to recognise a difference between the Nazi and Soviet regimes, and holds that all Fascists and Communists are aiming at approximately the same thing and are even to some extent the same people. Leaders in the *Times* (pre-war) have referred to the U.S.S.R. as a "Fascist country." Again from a different angle this is echoed by Anarchists and Trotskyists.

Trotskyists: Communists charge the Trotskyists proper, i.e., Trotsky's own organisation, with being a crypto-Fascist organisation in Nazi pay. This was widely believed on the Left during the Popular Front period. In their ultra-Right phases the Communists tend to apply the same accusation to all fractions[4] to the Left of themselves, e.g., Common Wealth or the I.L.P.

Catholics: Outside its own ranks, the Catholic Church is almost universally regarded as pro-Fascist, both objectively and subjectively.

War-resisters: Pacifists and others who are anti-war are frequently accused not only of making things easier for the Axis, but of becoming tinged with pro-Fascist feeling.

Supporters of the war: War-resisters usually base their case on the claim that British Imperialism is worse than Nazism, and tend to apply the term "Fascist" to anyone who wishes for a military victory. The supporters of the People's Convention came near to claiming that willingness to resist a Nazi invasion was a sign of Fascist sympathies. The Home Guard was denounced as a Fascist organisation as soon as it appeared. In addition, the whole of the Left tends to equate militarism with Fascism. Politically conscious private soldiers nearly always refer to their officers as "Fascist-minded" or "natural Fascists." Battle schools, spit and polish, saluting of officers are all considered conducive to Fascism. Before the war, joining the Territorials was regarded as a sign of Fascist tendencies. Conscription and a professional army are both denounced as Fascist phenomena.

Nationalists: Nationalism is universally regarded as inherently Fascist, but this is held only to apply to such national movements as the speaker happens to disapprove of. Arab nationalism, Polish nationalism, Finnish nationalism, the Indian Congress Party, the Muslim League, Zionism, and the I.R.A. are all described as Fascist—but not by the same people.

It will be seen that, as used, the word "Fascism" is almost entirely meaningless. In conversation, of course, it is used even more wildly than in print. I have heard it applied to farmers, shopkeepers, Social Credit, corporal punishment, foxhunting, bullfighting, the 1922 Committee, the 1941 Committee, Kipling, Gandhi, Chiang Kai-Shek, homosexuality, Priestley's broadcasts, Youth Hostels, astrology, women, dogs and I do not know what else.

Yet underneath all this mess there does lie a kind of buried meaning. To begin with, it is clear that there are very great differences, some of them easy to point out and not easy to explain away, between the regimes called Fascist and those called democratic. Secondly, if "Fascist" means "in sympathy with Hitler," some of the accusations I have listed above are obviously very much more justified than others. Thirdly, even the people who recklessly fling the word "Fascist" in every direction attach at any rate an emotional significance to it. By "Fascism" they mean, roughly speaking, something cruel, unscrupulous, arrogant, obscurantist, anti-liberal and anti-working-class. Except for the relatively small number of Fascist sympathisers, almost any English person would accept "bully" as a synonym for "Fascist." That is about as near to a definition as this much-abused word has come.

But Fascism is also a political and economic system. Why, then, cannot we have a clear and generally accepted definition of it? Alas! we shall not get one—not yet, anyway. To say why would take too long, but basically it is because it is impossible to define Fascism satisfactorily without making admissions which neither the Fascists themselves, nor the Conservatives, nor Socialists of any colour, are willing to make. All one can do for the moment is to use the word with a certain amount of circumspection and not, as is usually done, degrade it to the level of a swearword.

Richard Pugh, Jnr , writing in *Tribune*, 7 April 1944, attempted to pin down the real meaning of Fascism by relating it to the economic system introduced by Mussolini into Italy and then, by way of some historical and contemporary allusions, to the use of the word 'to describe any such system, regime or things, whether they be Right or Left, Tory or Communist, totalitarian or "democratic", where the principle of "Might is Right" prevails.' However, Pugh's clarification was found by J. P. N., in *Tribune* for 21 April 1944, to be so 'delightfully vague' as to include 'almost every known institution.' To Socialists, he said, Fascism was a collective name for that system which developed when Liberal (capitalist) democracy has been replaced by monopoly capitalism and 'the workers are agitating against existing conditions.' He went on to say that it was designed

to overcome the contradictions of capitalism by organising production for maximum output; by promoting the fusion of banks and trusts with the State, which openly reflects the domination of a small but powerful ruling class intent on imperialist expansion by war.

The Liberal methods of deception and conciliation of the workers—by then inadequate to curb the class struggle—are replaced by suppression of the workers' organisations and democratic rights and by openly terrorist methods against the militant labour vanguard using a party recruited from the discontented petit-bourgeoisie. Political expression and opposition (e.g., Parliament) are strictly curtailed; State regulation of wages and labour conditions by a Labour Front is substituted for the strike weapon. These measures are obscured by extensive demagogic propaganda preaching nationalism, chauvinism and anti-Marxism.

Fascism does not imply *any* form of violence or reaction—British India and Tsarist Russia are not Fascist States; though it first developed in Italy, Fascism may occur in any capitalist State. While Fascism is totalitarian, so is Socialism in that production is under centralised control.

Mr. Pugh would do well to adopt a precise definition of Fascism: he may then be less unlikely to recognise its advent in Britain when the time comes.

1. Military Intelligence [Section] 5: the British internal security service answerable for many years only to the Prime Minister through the Home Secretary. M16, the Secret Intelligence Service, operated outside the United Kingdom and was answerable to the Foreign Secretary.
2. Sir Ernest Benn (1875–1954), publisher; see *913, n. 3*.
3. Hermann Rauschning (1887–1982) was described by Orwell in 'Wells, Hitler and the World State' (see *837*) as among the best authors of the 'political book.' Orwell equated him in this respect with Trotsky, Silone, Borkenau, and Koestler among others. William Steinhoff, in *George Orwell and the Origins of 1984* (1975), arguing that 'Orwell understood totalitarianism,' states that the long dialogue between O'Brien and Winston Smith in *Nineteen Eighty-Four* 'demonstrates Orwell's awareness that implicit in totalitarianism is a desire for expansion—physical, intellectual, spiritual—that, as Rauschning said, recognizes no limits' (208); Steinhoff lists Rauschning's *The Revolution of Nihilism* (London and New York, 1939) in his bibliography. Rauschning also published (in several language versions), *Hitler Speaks: A Series of Political Conversations with Adolf Hitler on His Real Aims* (1939) and *The Conservative Revolution* (New York, 1941). From 1948 until his death he lived as a farmer in Oregon. For Peter Drucker, see *2668, n. 2*; for James Burnham, *2404, n. 1*; and for F. A. Voigt, *513, n. 1* and *604, n. 4*.
4. 'factions' may be intended. Compare *737, n. 11*.

2442. To Victor Gollancz

25 March 1944

Victor Gollancz replied to Orwell's letter of 19 March 1944 (see *2437*) on the 23rd. He said that he would certainly like to see Orwell's manuscript of *Animal Farm*. He professed not to understand what 'anti-Stalin' meant and, far from being the 'Stalinist stooge' that he thought Orwell took him to be, he had been banned from the Soviet Embassy for three years as an 'anti-Stalinist.' (See Sheila Hodges, *Gollancz: The Story of a Publishing House, 1928–1978*, 109; Crick, 453.) Orwell wrote to Gollancz on 25 March; the following extract is all that survives of this letter.

Thank you for your letter. I have written to Moore telling him to send the MS along. I should be much obliged if you could make your decision fairly quickly, so that if you don't want it I can take it elsewhere with as little delay as possible. I still don't think it likely that it is the kind of thing you would print. Naturally I am not criticising the Soviet regime from the Right, but in my experience the other kind of criticism gets one into even worse trouble.

2443. To Leonard Moore

25 March 1944   Typewritten

10a Mortimer Crescent
London NW 6

Dear Mr Moore,
Thank you for your letter. I have just heard from Gollancz that he *does* want to see the MS, so could you let him have it? I still don't think it likely that he will publish it, however. If you have read it by this time you will have seen what the allegory is. Could you impress on him not to keep it too long if he doesn't want it?

I should think it would be all right to go straight ahead about an American edition, wouldn't it? I wonder whether the Dial Press people have any representatives over here? If there are difficulties, I dare say I could do something via my friends on the "Partisan Review", who are probably in touch with a good many publishers and have once or twice asked me if I have any books going.

Failing Gollancz we must decide on whom else to approach. I knew of course that Hatry[1] is behind N. and W., but does that matter if one got the money in advance? From what I hear they are being very generous. As to Hutchinsons, Robert Neumann is arranging for them some business about publishing books for Europe after the war, and approached me some time back to know if I had something suitable. But he also said they are on the look-out for authors for their ordinary lists. Anand the Indian novelist has just left Cape's for Hutchinsons, and he tells me he gets four times the advance Cape used to give him.

You might just ask Gollancz what his idea would be about the projected book of essays, which would have to include either one or two out of "Inside the Whale", so that the book would consist of about 8 essays and be about 40,000 words long.

Let me know what you are doing about the book.
                                        Yours sincerely
                                        Eric Blair

On 28 March 1944 Gollancz wrote to Orwell, saying he was glad Orwell was sending him the manuscript. He did understand that Orwell was criticising the Soviet regime from the Left, and again pointed out that he was banned by the Soviet Embassy and that he was 'regarded by the Communists here as a far worse enemy than you are.' In the same letter, he said he would like to see Orwell's book of essays and that he had no objection to the Dickens essay being reprinted in it.

1. Clarence Hatry (1888–1965) is mentioned by Orwell in his London Letter to *Partisan Review*, Summer 1946 (probably written early in May; see *2990*): 'Hatry, the financial wizard, who went into the book trade after he came out of prison' was said to be behind a new kind of 'streamlined, high-powered, slickly got-up, semi-intellectual magazine' then beginning to appear. Hatry, company promoter, financier, and (in the 1920s) a millionaire, was deeply involved in the collapse through fraudulent dealing of Austin Friars Trust Ltd in 1929. He was sentenced to fourteen years' penal servitude but released in 1938 because of assistance he had given in clearing up the financial difficulties that arose from the collapse of the Trust. There were those who felt he had been harshly treated. His pamphlet *The "Hatry Case": Eight Current Misconceptions* was published in 1938; it listed the names of many distinguished supporters. In 1939 he published *Light out of Darkness*, subtitled 'Or the redistribution of populations as a solution of the world's economic problems.'

2444. Review of *Tolstoy: His Life and Work* by Derrick Leon

The Observer, 26 March 1944

Tolstoy's adult life—it starts with a brilliant, worldly, rather dissolute young aristocrat and ends with a tormented old man who had renounced every thing, or come as near renouncing it as his family would let him—is dramatic enough, but finally it is less interesting than his work, and the most valuable part of Mr. Leon's biography is the careful exposition that he gives of each of Tolstoy's books in turn, showing just how it is related to Tolstoy's spiritual development.

Tolstoy's creed, gradually developed over a period of about fifty years, could be described as Christian Anarchism. All material aims, all violence, all revolutions, in the last analysis all laws and governments, are evil: there is no happiness except in self-abnegation: man has no rights, only duties, being on earth solely to do the will of God. All this is derived from his reading of the Gospels, but before his beliefs were fully formulated he had adopted two doctrines which are only doubtfully Christian. One is a strict determinism. A man's actions, Tolstoy holds, are all predetermined, his sole freedom consisting in the knowledge of necessity. The other is a conviction of the essential misery of earthly life, and the wickedness of physical pleasures, which goes far beyond anything the churches have ever countenanced.

Mr. Leon writes as a disciple, and he does not seriously answer, though he does mention, the charge many people have made—that Tolstoy's later work is largely the projection of his own egoism. In stretching self-abnegation to mean practically a refusal of the process of life—in saying, for instance, that marriage is of its nature "misery and slavery"—it is doubtful whether he is saying much more than that he is unhappy himself and would like to make others unhappy as well. Tolstoy was, of course, extremely conscious of the dangers of egoism, indeed his life was in some sense a continuous struggle against it, but he does not seem to have seen that the form it took in himself was not a desire for money or success, but simply a taste for intellectual bullying: his essay on Shakespeare is an outstanding example of this.

Nevertheless his life-story is inspiring as well as tragic, and we should still feel him to be a remarkable man even if he had written nothing except his pamphlets. Directly, his influence on the life of our time has not been very great, because he abjured all the methods by which anything can actually be achieved. But indirectly, through individuals, it must have been enormous. No one can read Tolstoy and come away with quite the same feeling about war, violence, success, government, and "great" men—though, somewhat ironically, the special thing that he has to say is said most effectively in the novels of his middle period, "Anna Karenina" and "War and Peace," which he afterwards came to look on as almost reprehensible.

It is a pity that throughout his narrative Mr. Leon shows such an implacable hostility for the wretched Countess Tolstoy, for by assuming that in every disagreement the Countess must have been in the wrong he avoids discussion of one of the most difficult problems of a writer's life—the conflict between the literary and the private personality, or, to put it differently, between love of humanity and ordinary decency. Otherwise this is an outstanding book, and though one cannot advise people to buy books costing twenty-five shillings, at least everyone who can borrow a copy should read it.

[Fee: £5.5.0; 20.3.44]

2445. 'As I Please,' 18

Tribune, 31 March 1944

The other day I attended a Press conference at which a newly arrived Frenchman, who was described as an "eminent jurist"—he could not give his name or other specifications because of his family in France—set forth the French point of view on the recent execution of Pucheu. I was surprised to note that he was distinctly on the defensive, and seemed to think that the shooting of Pucheu was a deed that would want a good deal of justification in British and American eyes. His main point was that Pucheu was not shot for political reasons, but for the ordinary crime of "collaborating with the enemy," which has always been punishable by death under French law.

An American correspondent asked the question: "Would collaborating with the enemy be equally a crime in the case of some petty official—an inspector of police, for example?" "Absolutely the same," answered the Frenchman. As he had just come from France he was presumably voicing French opinion, but one can assume that in practice only the most active collaborators will be put to death. Any really big-scale massacre, if it really happened, would be quite largely the punishment of the guilty by the guilty. For there is much evidence that large sections of the French population were more or less pro-German in 1940 and only changed their minds when they found out what the Germans were like.

I do not want people like Pucheu to escape, but a few very obscure quislings, including one or two Arabs, have been shot as well, and this whole business of taking vengeance on traitors and captured enemies raises questions which are strategic as well as moral. The point is that if we shoot too many of the small rats now we may have no stomach for dealing with the big ones when the time comes. It is difficult to believe that the Fascist regimes can be thoroughly crushed without the killing of the responsible individuals, to the number of some hundreds or even thousands in each country. But it could well happen that all the truly guilty people will escape in the end, simply because public opinion has been sickened beforehand by hypocritical trials and cold-blooded executions.

In effect this was what happened in the last war. Who that was alive in those years does not remember the maniacal hatred of the Kaiser that was fostered in this country? Like Hitler in this war, he was supposed to be the cause of all our ills. No one doubted that he would be executed as soon as caught and the only question was what method would be adopted. Magazine articles were written in which the rival merits of boiling in oil, drawing and quartering and breaking on the wheel were carefully examined. The Royal Academy exhibitions were full of allegorical pictures of incredible vulgarity, showing the Kaiser being thrown into Hell. And what came of it in the end? The Kaiser retired to Holland and (though he had been "dying of cancer" in 1915) lived another twenty-two years, one of the richest men in Europe.

So also with all the other "war criminals." After all the threats and promises that had been made, no war criminals were tried: to be exact, a dozen people or so were put on trial, given sentences of imprisonment and soon released. And though, of course, the failure to crush the German military caste was due to the conscious policy of the Allied leaders, who were terrified of revolution in Germany, the revulsion of feeling in ordinary people helped to make it possible. They did not want revenge when it was in their power. The Belgian atrocities, Miss Cavell,[1] the U-boat captains who had sunk passenger ships without warning and machine-gunned the survivors— somehow it was all forgotten. Ten million innocent men had been killed and no one wanted to follow it up by killing a few thousand guilty ones.

Whether we do or don't shoot the Fascists and quislings who happen to fall into our hands is probably not very important in itself. What is important is that revenge and "punishment" should have no part in our policy or even in our day-dreams. Up to date, one of the mitigating features of this war is that in this country there has been very little hatred. There has been none of the nonsensical racialism that there was last time—no pretence that all Germans have faces like pigs, for instance. Even the word "Hun" has not really popularised itself. The Germans in this country, mostly refugees, have not been well treated, but they have not been meanly persecuted as they were last time. In the last war it would have been very unsafe, for instance, to speak German in a London street. Wretched little German bakers and hairdressers had their shops sacked by the mob. German music fell out of favour, even the breed of dachshunds almost disappeared because no one wanted to have a "German dog." And the weak British attitude in the early period of German rearmament had a direct connection with those follies of the war years.

Hatred is an impossible basis for policy, and curiously enough it can lead to over-softness as well as to over-toughness. In the war of 1914–18 the British people were whipped up into a hideous frenzy of hatred, they were fed on preposterous lies about crucified Belgian babies and German factories where corpses were made into margarine and then as soon as the war stopped they suffered the natural revulsion, which was all the stronger because the troops came home, as British troops usually do, with a warm admiration for the enemy. The result was an exaggerated pro-German reaction which set in about 1920 and lasted till Hitler was well in the saddle. Throughout those years all "enlightened" opinion (see any number of the *Daily Herald* before 1929, for instance) held it as an article of faith that Germany bore no responsibility for the war. Treitschke,[2] Bernhardi,[3] the Pan-Germans, the "Nordic" myth, the open boasts about "Der Tag"[4] which the Germans had been making from 1900 onwards—all this went for nothing. The Versailles Treaty was the greatest infamy the world had ever seen: few people had even heard of Brest-Litovsk.[5] All this was the price of that four years' orgy of lying and hatred.

Anyone who tried to awaken public opinion during the years of Fascist aggression from 1933 onwards knows what the after-effects of that hate-propaganda were like. "Atrocities"[6] had come to be looked on as synonymous with "lies." But the stories about the German concentration camps were atrocity stories: therefore they were lies—so reasoned the average man. The left-wingers who tried to make the public see that Fascism was an unspeakable horror were fighting against their own propaganda of the past fifteen years.

That is why—though I would not save creatures like Pucheu[7] even if I could—I am not happy when I see trials of "war criminals," especially when they are very petty criminals and when witnesses are allowed to make inflammatory political speeches. Still less am I happy to see the Left associating itself with schemes to partition Germany, enrol millions of Germans in forced labour gangs and impose reparations which will make the Versailles reparations look like a bus fare. All these vindictive daydreams, like those of 1914–18, will simply make it harder to have a realistic post-war policy. If you think *now* in terms of "making Germany pay," you will quite likely find yourself praising Hitler in 1950. Results are what matter, and one of the results we want from this war is to be quite sure that Germany will not make war again. Whether this is best achieved by ruthlessness or generosity I am not certain: but I am quite certain that either of these will be more difficult if we allow ourselves to be influenced by hatred.

1. Nurse Edith Cavell (1865–1915), executed by the Germans in Brussels for assisting Allied soldiers to escape from occupied Belgium. A Belgian, Philippe Baucq, who had acted as a guide, was also shot. Her execution was regarded as particularly shameful. A statue to her memory, inscribed with her last words, 'Patriotism is not enough,' stands in St Martin's Place, London, WC2.
2. Heinrich Gotthard von Treitschke (1834–1896; spelt 'Tretschke' in 'As I Please'), German historian and writer on political science, advocated German power politics and believed in the total authority of the state unfettered by a parliament (though he was a member of the Reichstag, 1871–84). He was a prolific writer, though he did not live to complete his major work, a history of Germany. Bernhardi (see *n. 3*) wrote that, though Treitschke followed a 'decidedly national tendency,' he defended him from the charge that he aspired to world

dominion [for Germany]. 'By his inspired and inspiring writing, as well as through the living word of his lectures, Treitschke undoubtedly contributed to the promotion of German consciousness of herself and the fostering of the longing for increased political power; but that he dreamt any dream of German world dominion is a pure invention . . .' (*The New Bernhardi*, 1915, 42–43). Despite—indeed, because of—the war, a collection of his essays, *Germany, France, Russia and Islam*, was published in England in 1915. These included 'What we demand of France' (1870, just before the outbreak of the Franco-Prussian War). Adolf Hausrath's study, in an English translation, *Treitschke: His Doctrine of German Destiny and of International Relations*, was published in 1914.

3. Friedrich von Bernhardi (1849–1930), General of Cavalry from 1901; Acting Commanding-General, Posen, 1915; author of several influential books, especially *Deutschland und der nächste Krieg* (1912) (translated by A. M. Powles as *Germany and the Next War*, many editions), a direct outcome of the Agadir crisis in Morocco, 1911. This he believed would lead to war with France, Russia, and Britain because Germany's 'natural development' was threatened. He served on the Eastern Front until 1917 and in 1920 published *Vom Kriege der Zukunft* (*The War of the Future in the Light of the Lessons of the World War*, translated by F. A. Holt, 1920). He also wrote several books on army organisation, tactics, and the deployment of cavalry. Orwell may have come across his writing through the translations mentioned or *The New Bernhardi*, *"World Power or Downfall*," which was published in English in 1915 (with 'An Answer'), and was the outcome of articles published in the *New York American* and the (London) *Times*. Among other things he pressed the claim for imperial and world power for Germany (especially because Britain had an empire and did not hesitate, in his words, to subjugate and exploit it, 55) and he made much of the way his phrase 'Weltmacht oder Niedergang' had been mistranslated as 'World Dominion or Death' (instead of 'World Power or Decline,' 41). He regarded war as a biological necessity and is credited with the expression 'Might is Right' (12). War, he wrote, 'is a necessity in the life of nations—notwithstanding that it carries in its train unspeakable misery; notwithstanding that it often allows the lower instincts of the human being to assert themselves; for, on the other hand, all the noble characteristics of human nature, most noble of all the unselfish devotion to an ideal, the spirit of self-sacrifice in the service of that ideal, are in war exhibited' (23). Peter Buitenhuis quotes Gerhard Ritter as saying that although Bernhardi was 'cited on countless occasions as proof that the German General Staff was systematically fostering war' he was an outsider and not in the General Staff's good graces. The Chief of the General Staff, Helmuth von Moltke, described Bernhardi as 'a perfect dreamer' (*The Great War of Words: Literature as Propaganda 1914–18 and After*, 1989, 31–32).

4. "Der Tag" is in quotation marks because, in all probability, it refers to the use of these words as an after-dinner toast to the day when Germany would achieve what Bernhardi called 'Weltmacht'—'World Power' in his own translation (for, as he wrote, 'I never thought of world dominion by Germany,' *The New Bernhardi*, 41). James Barrie (creator of Peter Pan) wrote a propaganda play called *Der Tag* in 1914. Peter Buitenhuis describes it as almost as great a fiasco as Barrie's recent lecture tour of the United States (*The Great War of Words*, 111). It opened at the London Coliseum, 21 December 1914, and was published in New York in 1914 and 1919.

5. The Treaty of Versailles imposed harsh penalties on Germany and demanded formidable reparations. In the Manifesto 'If War Comes, We Shall Resist,' *The New Leader*, 30 September 1938 (see *489A*), which Orwell signed, it was stated: 'The danger of war arises from the injustices of the Treaties which concluded the last war and the imperialist economic rivalries which they embodied.' Here, however, Orwell points to the harsh treatment the Germans meted out to Russia in the Treaty of Brest-Litovsk, March 1918. The Soviets were forced to recognise the independence of Poland, Estonia, Latvia, Lithuania, Georgia, and the Ukraine; allow German occupation of Belorussia; cede territories to Turkey (Germany's ally); and were required to pay a heavy indemnity. Trotsky was the chief Soviet negotiator. The treaty was nullified with the cessation of hostilities on the Western Front.

6. It may be no more than coincidence, but Orwell's placing of 'Atrocities' within quotation marks, as he usually did for titles of books, could be significant. What he says—that most atrocity stories (and many of the worst ones, such as shooting babies from cannon) were lies— was well-enough understood when he wrote this article. However, on the back cover of *The*

New Bernhardi (see *n. 2* above) were advertisements for several books, ranging from *Is the Kaiser Insane?* to *Our Regiments and Their Glorious Deeds*; the sixth and last was *Official Book of the German Atrocities*, told by Victims and Eye-Witnesses, being 'The complete verbatim Report of the Belgian, French, and Russian Commissions of Enquiry. Published by Authority.'

7. Pierre Pucheu, formerly Vichy Minister of the Interior, fled to North Africa and was shot on the orders of General de Gaulle. Further trials followed; General Blanc was condemned to death and Colonel Magnin sentenced to solitary confinement for twenty years.

2446. To Leonard Moore

   31 March 1944   Handwritten postcard

Friday
I have wired the Dial Press to know whether they want to see the MS. We should get the answer within a week.

Eric Blair

2446A. To Lydia Jackson

   3 April 1944   Typewritten

Tribune

Dear Lydia,
Many thanks for the article which I'll be glad to use (after an interval of some weeks probably).[1]

Yours,
[Signed] George
George Orwell

1. Presumably 'A Soviet Patriot: A Sketch of Serghei Dikovsky,' published in *Tribune*, 28 April 1944, signed by Elisaveta Fen. This, and all later letters sent from *Tribune*, though having the salutation, 'Dear Lydia,' were formally addressed to her by her pen-name, Elisaveta Fen.

2447. To Leonard Moore

   5 April 1944

PLEASE SEND ANIMAL FARM TO DIAL PRESS AT ONCE   BETTER SEND TO[P] COPY = BLAIR

2448. To Leonard Moore

5 April 1944[1]   Typewritten

10a Mortimer Crescent
London NW 6

Dear Mr Moore,

You will have had my wire. The Dial Press wired back "send at once". I don't know which is the quickest way of sending—I suppose air mail is safest but they are all slow nowadays. I thought it best to send the top copy because American standards of typing are probably better than ours are nowadays.

Gollancz wrote to say he can't publish the book,[2] as I knew he would. I have contacted my friend at Nicholson and Watson's to see what terms they will offer (they have another copy of the book and will let me know next week). I cannot see what harm it would do to go to them for one book. The only harm they could do me would be to go bankrupt while still owing me money, and one could avoid that by getting a good wad in advance. Whatever their position may be financially they are quite respectable intellectually. For instance it is they who issue "Poetry, London". They have also published the Ministry of Food's cookery books with success. Of course maybe they will say they don't want the book either, but if they do want it I think it would be stupid not to close with them, given good terms. (Naturally it would not be wise to promise them future books, but my contract with Gollancz protects me from that). If you read the book you will have seen what the allegory is, and you must realise we shall have great difficulty in getting this book published in England though it may be easier in the USA. Naturally I want it in print, and if all else fails I shall take it to one or other of the little highbrow presses I know of. If the Dial people decide they don't want it I don't know which other American publisher to try, but I am going to write to my friends of the Partisan Review for advice. There are a lot of highbrow publishers there, but I don't know which of them are politically OK from the point of view of this book. I suppose in the event of the Dial people accepting it will be all right to publish simultaneously or perhaps even first in the USA? It wouldn't really affect sales here because there is almost no interchange of books now.

I have got started on the Britain in Pictures book, which I suppose I shall finish some time in May, after which I can get down to the various literary essays I am projecting.

Yours sincerely
Eric Blair

1. '5' and '6' have been typed one on top of the other, but the letter is marked as having been received and answered by Moore on 6 April.
2. On 3 April 1944, Gollancz wrote to Leonard Moore to thank him for *Animal Farm*, which, he said, he would read at the earliest possible moment. That he did. He returned the manuscript to Moore on the next day, with a copy of a note he had sent to Orwell. He told Moore that although he was highly critical of many aspects of Soviet policy, he could not publish a general attack such as that in *Animal Farm*—'as Blair anticipated.' The note to Orwell simply said, 'You were right and I was wrong. I am so sorry. I have returned the manuscript to Moore'

(Crick, 454). Gollancz was not alone in finding *Animal Farm* inopportune. Crick summarises the book's publication history of the book (452–62).

2449. Review of *She Was a Queen* by Maurice Collis; *Coming of Age in Samoa* by Margaret Mead

Manchester Evening News, 6 April 1944

Burma is an ill-documented subject, and even those who know something of its modern history have only dim ideas of what went on there before 1884, when the British entered Mandalay and Thibaw, the last King of Burma, was deported to India with a selection of his 500 wives.

Mr. Collis's narrative deals with the late thirteenth century, the period in which all Burma down to the delta of the Irrawaddy was over-run by the Tartars.

At that date the capital of Burma was at Pagan, whose imposing ruins are still in existence, if the bombings of the last year or two have spared them. About the year 1260 there was born on a mountain-side in Upper Burma a peasant girl, name *Ma Saw*, for whom a brilliant future was prophesied when a Hamadryad cobra was seen performing a sort of dance about her cradle.

This was justified, for Ma Saw became the wife of two successive kings, and during the reign of the second one, who was not much better than half-witted, she was the virtual ruler of the kingdom. Until the irruption of the Tartars the society that Mr. Collis is describing follows the immemorial Asiatic pattern. Life, beneath friendly skies, is one long round of singing, dancing, concubinage, murders, civil war, hunting and religious observances.

In spite of the fact that any king who died a natural death was exceptionally lucky, it was a fairly highly-cultured society. Buddhism was gaining ground against Animism; poetry was held in high esteem; the court had good contacts with India and China; it contained slave girls from as far afield as Persia. It had even heard vague rumours of the barbarians of the Far West. But unfortunately the great Tartar chieftain, Kublai Khan, cast his eyes upon Burma, and the Pagan Dynasty was doomed.

Incidentally, one of the envoys whom Kublai sent to Burma as a preliminary to his invasion was no less a person than Marco Polo.

Except for Chang Hsien Ch'Ung, a Chinese who had fled to Burma from another Tartar invasion, Ma Saw was the only intelligent person at the court, and if she had had a free hand she might conceivably have saved the kingdom from destruction.

As it was, the foolish king sent his army to fight in the open field, where it was defeated as so many other armies had been by the hordes of Tartar horsemen.

The chief military secret of the Tartars was a bow (the "composite" bow) which was made of buffalo horn and greatly outranged any other weapon then in existence. Their archers shot the Burmese elephants full of arrows until the great beasts, mad with pain, stampeded and broke up the rest of the Burmese army.

Pagan was sacked and the king and all his court fled down the Irrawaddy with the maids of honour, the concubines, the royal treasure, the year's rice crop, the sacred white elephant and as many slaves as there was room for, all packed into barges. In Lower Burma they were safe, for the Tartar cavalry could not penetrate the swamps, just as at the other end of the world they had been defeated by the forests of Germany.

The King, however, had hardly arrived when he was poisoned by one of his sons, who intended to usurp the kingdom and play the part of a quisling towards the Tartars. Ma Saw, having had enough of palace life, married Chang Hsien Ch'Ung, and then put off her costly robes and went back to the village where she had been born.

This story is substantially true, or so Mr. Collis believes. Although expanded into novel form, it is derived from the Glass Palace Chronicle, a history of Burma compiled by order of the Burmese King Bagyidaw in 1829.

It probably gives an adequate picture of Burma as it was throughout the whole period between the Middle Ages and the British occupation. Even the 13th century costumes, as described by Marco Polo, were similar to the modern ones, and when King Hibaw came to the throne about 1800 he celebrated his accession by putting his brothers to death, a deed which would fit straight into Mr. Collis's story.

This book contains some interesting illustrations, including what is believed to be a contemporary portrait of Kublai Khan.

It is a far cry from Burma to Samoa, though curiously enough one or two customs—for instance that of tattooing all males from the waist to the knees—were till recently common to both people.

Some time in the nineteen-twenties Miss Mead, who was interested in the psychology of adolescent girls, decided that this problem could be best studied in a primitive community, and went to live for a while in a Samoan village. From the point of view of the average reader the purely psychological part of the book is perhaps less valuable than the sociological information it gives: for Samoa is among other things an exceptionally happy example of colonial development. Both the American Government and the missionaries have gone on the principle of interfering as little as possible with the traditional pattern of life. Only a few obviously evil customs, such as cannibalism and public deflorations have been put down.

The Samoans are Christians (Congregationalists—they were converted by the London Missionary Society), but have known how to adapt the Christian religion to their own needs, simply rejecting those doctrines which do not fit in with their inherited outlook.

For example, they do not believe in original sin. Except for matches, cotton cloth, and a few other trifles they have taken very little from machine civilisation, and even the diseases of the civilised world have not played such havoc with them as with some of the Polynesian peoples.

Part of the reason for this is no doubt that the Samoan islands are too poor to be worth exploiting. But still, the Samoans have been very lucky as primitive peoples go, and both the American Government and the missionaries deserve credit for their intelligent attitude.

[Fee: £8.8.0; 5.4.44]

2450. 'As I Please,' 19

Tribune, 7 April 1944

Sometimes, on top of a cupboard or at the bottom of a drawer, you come on a pre-war newspaper, and when you have got over your astonishment at its enormous size, you find yourself marvelling at its almost unbelievable stupidity. It happens that I have just come across a copy of the *Daily Mirror* of January 21st, 1936. One ought not, perhaps, to draw too many inferences from this one specimen, because the *Daily Mirror* was in those days our second silliest daily paper (the *Sketch* led, of course, as it still does[1]), and because this particular number contains the announcement of the death of George V. It is not, therefore, entirely typical. But still, it is worth analysing, as an extreme example of the kind of stuff that was fed to us in the between-war years. If you want to know why your house has been bombed, why your son is in Italy, why the income tax is ten shillings in the pound and the butter ration is only just visible without a microscope, here is part of the reason.

The paper consists of 28 pages. Of these the first 17 are devoted in their entirety to the dead King and the rest of the Royal Family. There is a history of the King's life, articles on his activities as statesman, family man, soldier, sailor, big and small game shot, motorist, broadcaster and what-not, with, of course, photographs innumerable. Except for one advertisement and one or two letters, you would not gather from these first 17 pages that any other topic could possibly interest the *Daily Mirror*'s readers. On page 18 there appears the first item unconnected with royalty. Needless to say this is the comic strip. Pages 18 to 23 inclusive are entirely given up to amusement guides, comic articles, and so forth. On page 24 some news begins to creep in, and you read of a highway robbery, a skating contest, and the forthcoming funeral of Rudyard Kipling. There are also some details about a snake at the Zoo which is refusing its food. Then on page 26 comes the *Daily Mirror*'s sole reference to the real world, with the headline:

BOMBING PLEDGE BY DUCE
NO MORE ATTACKS ON RED CROSS.

Underneath this, to the extent of about half a column, it is explained that il Duce "deplores" the attacks on the Red Cross, which were not committed "wilfully," and it is added that the League of Nations has just turned down Abyssinia's requests for assistance and refused to investigate the charges of Italian atrocities. Turning to more congenial topics the *Daily Mirror* then follows up with a selection of murders, accidental deaths and the secret wedding of Earl Russell. The last page of the paper is headed in huge letters: LONG LIVE KING EDWARD VIII, and contains a short biography and a highly idealised photograph of the man whom the Conservative Party were to sack like a butler a year later.

Among the topics *not* mentioned in this issue of the *Daily Mirror* are the unemployed (two or three millions of them at that date), Hitler, the progress of the Abyssinian war, the disturbed political situation in France, and the trouble already obviously blowing up in Spain. And though this is an extreme instance, nearly all newspapers of those days were more or less like that. No real information about current affairs was allowed into them if it could possibly be kept out. The world—so the readers of the gutter Press were taught—was a cosy place dominated by royalty, crime, beauty-culture, sport, pornography and animals.

No one who makes the necessary comparisons can possibly doubt that our newspapers are far more intelligent than they were five years ago. Partly it is because they are so much smaller. There are only four pages or so to be filled, and the war news necessarily crowds out the rubbish. But there is also a far greater willingness to talk in a grown-up manner, to raise uncomfortable topics, to give the important news the big headlines, than there used to be, and this is bound up with the increased power of the journalist as against the advertiser. The unbearable silliness of English newspapers from about 1900 onward has had two main causes. One is that nearly the whole of the Press is in the hands of a few big capitalists who are interested in the continuance of capitalism and therefore in preventing the public from learning to think: the other is that in peacetime newspapers live off advertisements for consumption goods, building societies, cosmetics and the like, and are therefore interested in maintaining a "sunshine mentality" which will induce people to spend money. Optimism is good for trade, and more trade means more advertisements. Therefore, don't let people know the facts about the political and economic situation; divert their attention to giant pandas, channel swimmers, royal weddings and other soothing topics. The first of these causes still operates, but the other has almost lapsed. It is now so easy to make a newspaper pay, and internal trade has dwindled so greatly, that the advertiser has temporarily lost his grip. At the same time there has been an increase in censorship and official interference, but this is not nearly so crippling and not nearly so conducive to sheer silliness. It is better to be controlled by bureaucrats than by common swindlers. In proof of which, compare the *Evening Standard*, the *Daily Mirror* or even the *Daily Mail* with the things they used to be.

And yet the newspapers have not got back their prestige—on the contrary they have steadily lost prestige as against the wireless—partly because they have not yet lived down their pre-war follies, but partly also because all but a few of them retain their "stunt" make-up and their habit of pretending that there is news when there is no news. Although far more willing than they used to be to raise serious issues, most of the papers remain completely reckless about details of fact. The belief that what is "in the papers" must be true has been gradually evaporating ever since Northcliffe set out to vulgarise journalism, and the war has not yet arrested the process. Many people frankly say that they take in such and such a paper because it is lively, but that they don't believe a word of what it says.

Meanwhile the B.B.C., so far as its news goes, has gained prestige since about 1940. "I heard it on the wireless" is now almost equivalent to "I know it must be true." And throughout most of the world B.B.C. news is looked on as more reliable than that of the other belligerent nations.

How far is this justified? So far as my own experience goes, the B.B.C. is much more truthful, in a negative way, than the majority of newspapers, and has a much more responsible and dignified attitude towards news. It tells less direct lies, makes more effort to avoid mistakes, and—the thing the public probably values—keeps the news in better proportion. But none of this alters the fact that the decline in the prestige of the newspapers as against the radio is a disaster.

Radio is an inherently totalitarian thing, because it can only be operated by the Government or by an enormous corporation, and in the nature of things it cannot give the news anywhere near so exhaustively as a newspaper. In the case of the B.B.C. you have the additional fact that, though it doesn't tell deliberate lies, it simply avoids every awkward question. In even the most stupid or reactionary newspaper every subject can at least be *raised*, if only in the form of a letter. If you had nothing but the wireless to go upon, there would be some surprising gaps in your information. The Press is of its nature a more liberal, more democratic thing, and the Press lords who have dirtied its reputation, and the journalists who have more or less knowingly lent themselves to the process, have a lot to answer for.

Orwell's argument was taken up by Frank Preston, in *Tribune*, 21 April 1944. He refers in his final paragraph to his special interest in wireless; he may therefore have been Frank Preston (b. 1913), assistant editor of *Practical Wireless* (and other periodicals), 1933–40, Technical Books Adviser to Odhams Press, 1937–45; served in the RAF, 1940–45. He wrote:

I hope you will allow me space to comment on what George Orwell had to say on Press Lords and the prestige of newspapers. I am not concerned with defence of Press Lords. When they choose to take up pen they can look after themselves very well. I am concerned with Orwell as one who would be a leader of opinion, and I would like him to lead it according to fact and not according to fiction. It is a common practice of contributors to the literary weeklies to have a tilt at the daily newspapers, yet few of them seem to have any practical acquaintance with "dailies," otherwise they would not fall into so many "howlers," so obvious to the despised daily journalist.

Orwell argues that it is the proprietors who are responsible for the dailies having so many stories about the biggest broad bean or the filmiest silk stocking. This side is left almost exclusively in the hands of the news editor and the night editor. It is a peculiar fact, and one which is almost overlooked, that all the great newspaper proprietors, having made their fortunes, are much more interested in politics than they are in the "silly story" features condemned by Orwell. But politics don't sell newspapers.

I would challenge Orwell or Professor Joad, or Kingsley Martin, who are equally fond of scoffing at the daily Press, to run a "serious" daily paper successfully in London. If I had a million pounds to lend I would lend it [to] any one of them to provide the necessary capital, on condition I could have my million back after they had shown what they could do. Look at the facts of experience. The *Daily Herald* was started as a serious political paper. It failed. When it copied the frivolities of successful rivals it equalled their success. The *Daily Mirror* was founded as a serious paper (for women). It failed. Converted almost overnight into a picture paper, with further pages of trivialities, it was immediately successful. The *Westminster Gazette* was a serious evening paper. It failed. Tried as a semi-serious daily it still failed. It was the public, not any Press Lord, who decided the fate of these three journals. I challenge Orwell to name any exclusively serious London daily that is a financial success. And the hard fact is that if a newspaper is not a commercial success it dies.

I also challenge Orwell's statement that the prestige of the wireless is greater than that of the newspapers among the masses of the public. For some while I have had exceptional opportunities of studying this. If he had heard the yell, "Oh, turn off that 'dope' " as often as I have, from a crowd of intelligent working-men, he would not have risked the assertion. For the first two years or so of the war there was something in this theory, but from the days of the Cairo "spokesman" the prestige of the wireless slumped rapidly, and has continued to fall. Would Orwell suggest that anybody now looks upon the B.B.C. as they did in the days of Sir John Reith?[2] Hardly.

Orwell responded in 'As I Please,' 21, 21 April 1944, *2457*. On 19 May, *Tribune* published a letter from R. J. Walden, which, whilst agreeing with Preston 'that the public did not want serious newspapers,' questioned whether it was the public alone which was responsible for 'this shameless prostitution of British journalism.' He was appalled to think that the mentally-warped people who enjoyed such newspapers could use their vote to direct Britain's future.

1. The *Daily Sketch*, first published on 23 December 1908, ceased independent publication on 1 June 1946 and was incorporated in the *Daily Graphic* (which ceased publication on 3 January 1953).
2. John Reith (1889–1971; baron, Lord Reith of Stonehaven, 1940), was the first general manager of the BBC, 1922, and Director General, 1927–38. He laid down the lines for public-service broadcasting in Britain, and, despite wholesale changes, and considerable disparagement of what he stood for, his influence is still felt. In 1948 the BBC inaugurated a series of lectures bearing his name to mark his achievements.

2451. Review of *The Road to Serfdom* by F. A. Hayek; *The Mirror of the Past* by K. Zilliacus

The Observer, 9 April 1944

Taken together, these two books give grounds for dismay. The first of them is an eloquent defence of *laissez-faire* capitalism, the other is an even more vehement denunciation of it. They cover to some extent the same ground, they frequently quote the same authorities, and they even start out with the same premise, since each of them assumes that Western civilisation depends on the sanctity of the individual. Yet each writer is convinced that the other's policy leads directly to slavery, and the alarming thing is that they may both be right.

Of the two, Professor Hayek's book is perhaps the more valuable, because the views it puts forward are less fashionable at the moment than those of Mr. Zilliacus. Shortly, Professor Hayek's thesis is that Socialism inevitably leads to despotism, and that in Germany the Nazis were able to succeed because the Socialists had already done most of their work for them: especially the intellectual work of weakening the desire for liberty. By bringing the whole of life under the control of the State, Socialism necessarily gives power to an inner ring of bureaucrats, who in almost every case will be men who want power for its own sake and will stick at nothing in order to retain it. Britain, he says, is now going the same road as Germany, with the Left Wing intelligentsia in the van and the Tory Party a good second. The only salvation lies in returning to an unplanned economy, free competition, and emphasis on liberty rather than on security.

In the negative part of Professor Hayek's thesis there is a great deal of truth. It cannot be said too often—at any rate, it is not being said nearly often enough—that collectivism is not inherently democratic, but, on the contrary, gives to a tyrannical minority such powers as the Spanish Inquisitors never dreamed of.

Professor Hayek is also probably right in saying that in this country the intellectuals are more totalitarian-minded than the common people. But he does not see, or will not admit, that a return to "free" competition means for the great mass of people a tyranny probably worse, because more irresponsible, than that of the State. The trouble with competitions is that somebody wins them. Professor Hayek denies that free capitalism necessarily leads to monopoly, but in practice that is where it has led, and since the vast majority of people would far rather have State regimentation than slumps and unemployment, the drift towards collectivism is bound to continue if popular opinion has any say in the matter.

Mr. Zilliacus's able and well-documented attack on imperialism and power politics consists largely of an exposure of the events leading up to the two world wars. Unfortunately the enthusiasm with which he debunks the war of 1914 makes one wonder on what grounds he is supporting this one. After re-telling the sordid story of the secret treaties and commercial rivalries which led up to 1914, he concludes that our declared war aims were lies and that "we declared war on Germany because if she won her war against France and Russia she would become master of all Europe, and strong enough to help herself to British colonies." Why else did we go to war this time? It seems that it was equally wicked to oppose Germany in the decade before 1914 and to appease her in the nineteen-thirties, and that we ought to have made a compromise peace in 1917, whereas it would be treachery to make one now. It was even wicked, in 1915, to agree to Germany being partitioned and Poland being regarded as "an internal affair of Russia": so do the same actions change their moral colour with the passage of time [?].

The thing Mr. Zilliacus leaves out of account is that wars have results, irrespective of the motives of those who precipitate them. No one can question the dirtiness of international politics from 1870 onwards: it does not follow that it would have been a good thing to allow the German army to rule Europe. It is just possible that some rather sordid transactions are going on behind the scenes now, and that current propaganda "against Nazism" (c.f. "against Prussian militarism") will look pretty thin in 1970, but Europe will certainly be a better place if Hitler and his followers are removed from it.

Between them these two books sum up our present predicament. Capitalism leads to dole queues, the scramble for markets, and war. Collectivism leads to concentration camps, leader-worship, and war. There is no way out of this unless a planned economy can be somehow combined with the freedom of the intellect, which can only happen if the concept of right and wrong is restored to politics.

Both of these writers are aware of this, more or less: but since they can show no practicable way of bringing it about the combined effect of their books is a depressing one.

[Fee: £7.7.0; 3.4.44]

On 3 July, George Dickson, OBE, Chairman and Employers' Representative of Medway Towns District Full Employment Council, wrote to Aneurin Bevan, M.P., at *Tribune*, to follow up on an earlier letter he had sent about *The Road to Serfdom* that had not been printed but which Bevan had said was 'helpful.' He sent Bevan a copy of *Jobs for All After the War* by Noel F. Cohen (1944). This reprinted articles that had appeared in the local press. He drew particular attention to the diagram on the back cover which showed how 'the basic pattern for any kind of social group living is also the basic pattern for industrial group living'; that, he argued, was 'the democratic answer to Burnham's Managerial Revolution in theory.' He said his Council had four committees working on the Council's tasks and they would welcome 'contributory thought.' Dickson's letter was evidently passed to Orwell, for it was among his papers.

2451A. To Daniel George, 10 April 1944: see Vol. XX,

Appendix 15

2452. 'As I Please,' 20

Tribune, 14 April 1944

The April issue of *Common Wealth* devotes several paragraphs to the problem of the falling British birthrate. A good deal of what it says is true, but it also lets drop the following remarks:

"The know-alls are quick to point to contraceptives, nutritional errors, infertility, selfishness, economic insecurity, etc., as basic causes of decline. But facts do not support them. In Nazi Germany, where contraceptives are illegal, the Birth Rate has reached a record low ebb, whereas in the Soviet Union, where there are no such restrictions, population is healthily on the up and up . . . Reproduction, as the Peckham experiment has helped to prove, is stimulated in an environment marked by fellowship and co-operation . . . Once meaning and purpose are restored to life, the wheels of production are kept humming, and life is again an adventure instead of just an endurance, we shall hear no more of the baby shortage."

It is not fair to the public to treat all-important subjects in this slapdash way. To begin with, you would gather from the passage quoted above that Hitler lowered the German birthrate. On the contrary, he raised it to levels unheard-of during the Weimar Republic. Before the war it was above replacement level, for the first time in many years. The catastrophic drop in the German birthrate began in 1942, and must have been partly caused by so many German males being away from home. Figures cannot be available yet, but the Russian birthrate must almost certainly have dropped over the same period.

You would also gather that the high Russian birthrate dates from the Revolution. But it was also high in Czarist times. Nor is there any mention of the countries where the birthrate is highest of all, that is, India, China, and (only a little way behind) Japan. Would it be accurate to say, for instance, that a South Indian peasant's life is "an adventure instead of just an endurance"?

The one thing that can be said with almost complete certainty on this subject is that a high birthrate goes with a low standard of living, and vice versa. There are few if any real exceptions to this. Otherwise the question is exceedingly complex. It is, all the same, vitally important to learn as much about it as we can, because there will be a calamitous drop in our own population unless the present trend is reversed within ten or, at most, twenty years. One ought not to assume, as some people do, that this is impossible, for such changes of trend have often happened before. The experts are proving now that our population will be only a few millions by the end of this century, but they were also proving in 1870 that by 1940 it would be 100 millions. To reach replacement level again, our birthrate would not have to take such a sensational upward turn as, for instance, the Turkish birthrate did after Mustapha Kemal took over. But the first necessity is to find out *why* populations rise and fall, and it is just as unscientific to assume that a high birthrate is a by-product of Socialism as to swallow everything that is said on the subject by childless Roman Catholic priests.

When I read of the goings-on in the House of Commons the week before last, I could not help being reminded of a little incident that I witnessed twenty years ago and more.

It was at a village cricket match. The captain of one side was the local squire, who, besides being exeedingly rich, was a vain, childish man to whom the winning of this match seemed extremely important. Those playing on his side were all or nearly all his own tenants.

The squire's side were batting, and he himself was out and was sitting in the pavilion. One of the batsmen accidentally hit his own wicket at about the same moment as the ball entered the wicketkeeper's hand. "That's not out," said the squire promptly, and went on talking to the person beside him. The umpire, however, gave a verdict of "out," and the batsman was half-way back to the pavilion before the squire realised what was happening. Suddenly he caught sight of the returning batsman, and his face turned several shades redder.

"What!" he cried, "he's given him out? Nonsense! Of course he's not out!" And then, standing up, he cupped his hands and shouted to the umpire: "Hi, what did you give that man out for? He wasn't out at all!"

The batsman had halted. The umpire hesitated, then recalled the batsman to the wicket and the game went on.

I was only a boy at the time, and this incident seemed to me about the most shocking thing I had ever seen. Now, so much do we coarsen with the passage of time, my reaction would merely be to inquire whether the umpire was the squire's tenant as well.

Attacking Mr. C. A. Smith[1] and myself in the *Malvern Torch* for various remarks about the Christian religion, Mr. Sidney Dark[2] grows very angry because I have suggested that the belief in personal immortality is decaying. "I would wager," he says, "that if a Gallup poll were taken seventy-five per cent. (of the British population) would confess to a vague belief in survival." Writing elsewhere during the same week, Mr. Dark puts it at eighty-five per cent.

Now, I find it very rare to meet anyone, of whatever background, who admits to believing in personal immortality. Still, I think it quite likely that if you asked everyone the question and put pencil and paper in his hands, a fairly large number (I am not so free with my percentages as Mr. Dark) would admit the possibility that after death there might be "something." The point Mr. Dark has missed is that the belief, such as it is, hasn't the actuality it had for our forefathers. Never, literally never in recent years, have I met anyone who gave me the impression of believing in the next world as firmly as he believed in the existence of, for instance, Australia. Belief in the next world does not influence conduct as it would if it were genuine. With that endless existence beyond death to look forward to, how trivial our lives here would seem! Most Christians profess to believe in Hell. Yet have you ever met a Christian who seemed as afraid of Hell as he was of cancer? Even very devout Christians will make jokes about Hell. They wouldn't make jokes about leprosy, or R.A.F. pilots with their faces burnt away: the subject is too painful. Here there springs into my mind a little triolet by the late G. K. Chesterton:

> It's a pity that Poppa has sold his soul,
> It makes him sizzle at breakfast so.
> The money was useful, but still on the whole
> It's a pity that Poppa has sold his soul
> When he might have held on like the Baron de Coal,
> And not cleared out when the price was low.
> It's a pity that Poppa has sold his soul,
> It makes him sizzle at breakfast so.

Chesterton, a Catholic, would presumably have said that he believed in Hell. If his next-door neighbour had been burnt to death he would not have written a comic poem about it, yet he can make jokes about somebody being fried for millions of years. I say that such belief has no reality. It is a sham currency, like the money in Samuel Butler's Musical Banks.[3]

When anyone enters the *Tribune* office nowadays, the first thing that strikes his eyes is a huge mound of papers from beneath which a nose makes occasional and momentary appearances. This is myself dealing with the entries for the Short Story Competition. The response has been what is usually called generous. The competition closed on March 31st, but we shall not be able to announce the results for several weeks. We hope to be able to publish the winning story in our Book Number of April 28th.

In *Tribune*, 28 April 1944, an anonymous correspondent and G. W. Gower contested the accuracy of Orwell's statistics, and on 26 May, A. M. Currie correctly attributed the triolet.

Population Statistics

Mr Orwell's criticism of *Common Wealth's* paragraphs on the problems of the falling birthrate leaves one serious error uncorrected and introduces a number of new inaccuracies.

(1) The statement made by *Common Wealth* that contraceptives are illegal in Nazi Germany is incorrect. They are not illegal. The only legal change brought by the Nazis that is relevant here is the tightening up of the laws against abortion.

(2) Mr. Orwell's statement that Hitler raised the German birthrate "to levels unheard of during the Weimar Republic" is incorrect. The highest birthrate attained by Nazi Germany was 20.3 in 1939, a figure considerably lower than those of the "Weimar" years 1919–1925. The average of the years 1935–1937, moreover, was practically the same as the average for the years 1920–1928.

(3) The renewed fall in the German birthrate began in 1940, not as stated by Mr. Orwell in 1943. [Orwell had said 1942.]

(4) The Russian birthrate during the inter-war period was considerably higher than that of India or Japan, not lower as Mr. Orwell implies. It

appears also that the birthrate of Soviet Russia was higher than the birthrate of Czarist Russia, although this is not entirely certain.

(5) There are no figures for the birthrate of China.

(6) Mr. Orwell's statement that "the experts are proving now that our population will be only a few millions by the end of this century" is both incorrect and misleading. "Experts," if they are any good, do not make prophecies without stating their assumptions. Dr. Enid Charles has made two estimates: one based on the assumption of stable fertility and mortality rates on the level of 1933: the other on the assumption of a certain further decline in both rates. The first estimate gives for England and Wales, at the end of the century, a population of 28.5 millions; the second, 17.7 millions. Both figures could hardly be called "only a few millions."

(7) I should be interested to learn of the source which enabled Mr. Orwell to state that a "sensational upward turn" in the Turkish birthrate took place after Mustapha Kemal took over. I am not aware of any reliable statistical information being available on this point, and fear that this statement may be derived from some rather extravagantly pro-Kemalist sources.

It is pleasant to find Mr. Orwell pleading for a more scientific attitude in the treatment of important social problems like this one. Many *Tribune* readers will hope, as I do, that Mr. Orwell himself will set an example.

Statistician.

George Orwell rightly says that a high birthrate goes with a low standard of living and vice versa, but what he and Common Wealth fail to point out is the evidence of survival figures.

If he looks up infant mortality figures he will find that, whereas in the higher income groups, infant mortality is only 20 per 1,000, the infant mortality in the lower income groups is 100 per 1,000.

It follows, therefore, that if living conditions were the same in the lower income groups as in the higher, infant mortality would fall to 20 per 1,000 all round, with an enormous increase in the female replacement group, which is, after all, what counts.

G. W. Gower.

[*George Orwell writes:*]

I am sorry that I was too free with dates and figures. But the various errors pointed out by "Statistician" do not alter my main contention, i.e., that there is no very clear connection between a rising population and what might be broadly called "good" government. On the whole, the low-standard nations sometimes, like India and Japan, under definitely despotic rule, multiply fastest. The statement about the Turkish birthrate was from Turkish sources, and may be incorrect, but we would expect the practical abolition of polygamy to have that effect. With all deference to "Statistician," I would regard 18 or even 29 millions as "only a few millions" relative to our present population.[4]

Chesterton

In fairness to Chesterton I feel that I must point out George Orwell's mistake recently in attributing to him a not-so-bright triolet of mine. The verse was written—like most triolets, perhaps—to fill up space in a feature which I used to contribute to *G.K.'s Weekly* under the signature of "Agag."[5] It appeared some time in the late 'twenties. I cannot trace the date at the moment, but if it were of interest the Editor of the paper's successor, *The Weekly Review*, could no doubt do so. So far as I am aware, it has not been reprinted.

And, as I am an agnostic, the lines cannot be cited to support Orwell's opinion, which I am inclined to share, that there appears to be an increasing lack of conviction about the average latter-day Christian's belief in personal immortality.

A. M. Currie.

[*George Orwell writes*]:
I am sorry about this inaccuracy. The poem appeared in *G.K.'s Weekly*, and it resembled Chesterton's own style so closely that I assumed it to be his. At any rate, he had no objection to printing it, which seems to bear out my contention. The title was "A Fryolet" if I remember rightly.

1. C. A. Smith was the editor of *Controversy*, 1936–39, which became *Left Forum* later and then *Left*. He published Orwell's 'Eye-Witness in Barcelona' in August 1937; see *382*.
2. Sidney Dark (1874–1947), editor of the *Church Times*, 1924–41; see *2347, n. 2*.
3. Musical Banks represent churches in Butler's *Erewhon*. Orwell describes them in a broadcast for schools; see *2674*.
4. By the late 1980s, the population of England and Wales was nearly 50,000,000.
5. Presumably after Agag of 1 Samuel 15, 32–3, who approached Samuel 'delicately' (but was nevertheless hewn in pieces by Samuel).

2453. To Leonard Moore

15 April 1944   Typewritten

10a Mortimer Crescent
London NW 6

Dear Mr Moore,
Nicholson & Watson refuse to print "Animal Farm", giving much the same reason as Gollancz, ie. that it is bad taste to attack the head of an allied government in that manner etc.[1] I knew we should have a lot of trouble with this book, at any rate in this country. Meanwhile I have taken the copy I had round to Cape's, as Miss Wedgwood[2] there had often asked me to let them see something, but I wouldn't be surprised if they made the same answer. I think Faber's is *just* possible, and Routledges rather more so if they have the paper. While Cape's have it I'll sound both Eliot and Herbert Read.[3] I saw recently a book published by Eyre and Spottiswoode and I think they must be all right—perhaps, as you say, I was mixing them up with Burns, Oates and

Washburne. Failing all else I will try to get one of the small highbrow presses to do it, in fact I shouldn't wonder if that is the likeliest bet. I know of one which has just started up and has a certain amount of money to dispose of. Naturally I want this book printed because I think what it says wants saying, unfashionable though it is nowadays.

I hope the copy went off to the USA? I suppose you still have one copy, so perhaps you might send it me to show to Read if I can contact him.

How do my copyrights with Gollancz stand? When I have done the necessary stuff I want to compile that book of essays and I am anxious to include the Dickens essay which was printed by Gollancz. I suppose if I fixed up with some other publisher, eg. Cape, to do "Animal Farm" they might ask for my next book, which would be the essays. Have I the right to reprint the Dickens essay, since the book is out of print?

Your sincerely
Eric Blair

1. In a letter to *The Observer*, 23 November 1980, André Deutsch, who was working for Nicholson & Watson in 1944, told how, having been introduced to Orwell in 1943 by George Mikes, he had occasionally been commissioned to write reviews for *Tribune* for a fee of £1. About Whitsun 1944, Orwell let him read the typescript of *Animal Farm*, and he was convinced that Nicholson & Watson would be keen to publish Orwell's book. Unfortunately, though they did not share Gollancz's political reservations, they lectured Orwell on what they perceived to be errors in *Animal Farm*. Orwell was calm but depressed; Deutsch, deeply embarrassed. Deutsch was even then hoping to start publishing in his own right, but though Orwell twice offered him *Animal Farm*, and he would dearly have loved to publish it, he felt himself still a novice and not yet able to start his own firm.
2. Veronica Wedgwood (1910–1989; DBE, 1968), the historian. was then working for Jonathan Cape.
3. T. S. Eliot was working for Faber & Faber, and Herbert Read for Routledge.

2454. London Letter, 17 April 1944

Partisan Review, Summer 1944

Spring is here, a late spring after a mild winter, and there is universal expectation that "It" (I don't have to tell you what "It" is) will begin some time next month. The streets swarm with American troops. In the expensive quarters of the town British soldiers, who are not allowed to spend their leave in London unless they have their homes there, are hardly to be seen. The air raids began to hot up about the beginning of February and there have been one or two biggish ones—nothing like 1940 but still very trying because of the deafening noise of the ack-ack. On the other hand, the scenic effects are terrific. The orange-colored flares dropped by the German planes drift slowly down, making everything almost as light as day, and carmine-colored tracer shells sail up to meet them: and as the flares get lower the shadows on the window pane move slowly upwards. The food situation is as always. I am ashamed to say that only very recently I had my first meal in a British restaurant and was amazed to find that food quite good and very cheap. (These places are run by the public authorities on a non-profit basis.) Various kinds of manufactured goods are now almost unprocurable. It is almost impossible to buy a watch or clock, new or secondhand. A typewriter which before the war would have cost twelve pounds now costs at least thirty pounds secondhand, supposing that you can get hold of one at all. Cars are scarcer than ever on the roads. On the other hand the bourgeoisie are coming more and more out of their holes, as one can see by the advertisements for servants quite in the old style, e.g., this one from the *Times*: "Countess of Shrewsbury requires experienced Head Housemaid of three." There were several years during which one did not see advertisements of that kind. Evening dress (for men) is said to be reappearing though I haven't seen anyone wearing it yet.

There isn't a great deal of political news. Churchill, if one can judge by his voice, is aging a good deal but grows more and more intolerant of opposition. It is assumed on all sides that if anything should happen to Churchill, Eden will automatically become PM. Those who know Eden say he is such a weakling that the right-wing Tories would find it more convenient to keep him in office as a figurehead than to put in a strong man after their own hearts. The Labor Party has sunk a few feet deeper in everyone's estimation after the vote of confidence business—the government were out-voted on a minor issue, Churchill told the Members to take their votes back, and nearly everyone did so. Common Wealth is still making some headway but constantly rumbles with internal dissensions which I can't get the hang of. It came out recently that up to date, three-fifths of its expenses have been paid by Acland (who has now come to the end of his money) and a rather doubtful person named Alan Good, a wealthy business man (light industries) who has been in the party since almost the beginning. The Communists have been taking a slightly more anti-government line and on one occasion have supported an opposition candidate at a by-election.

The big event of the last few months has been the large-scale coal strikes, which are the culmination of a long period during which coal production has been behind schedule and—coming on the eve of the Second Front— obviously indicate very serious grievances. The immediate trouble is over money, but the root cause is the unbearable conditions in the British mines, which naturally seem worse in wartime when unemployment hardly enters into the picture. I don't know a great deal about the technical side of mining, but I have been down a number of mines and I know that the conditions are such that human beings simply will not stand them except under some kind of compulsion. (I described all this years ago in a book called *The Road to Wigan Pier*.) Most of the British mines are very old, and they belong to a multitude of comparatively small owners who often haven't the capital to modernize them even if they wanted to. This means not only that they often lack up-to-date machinery, but that the "travelling" may be almost more exhausting than the work itself. In the older mines it may be more than three miles from the shaft to the coal face (a mile would be a normal distance) and most of the way the galleries will be only four feet high or less. This means that the miner has to do the whole journey bent double, sometimes crawling on all fours for a hundred yards or so, and then on top of this do his day's work, which may have to be done kneeling down if it is a shallow seam. The exertion is so great that men who come back to work after a long go of unemployment sometimes fall by the wayside, unable even to get as far as the coal face. Added to this there are the ghastly hovels that most of the miners have to live in, built in the worst period of the Industrial Revolution, the general lack of pithead baths, the dullness of the mining towns compared with the newer towns that have sprung up round the light industries, and, of course, very poor wages. In peace time,[1] when the dole is the alternative, people will just put up with this, but now every miner is aware that if he could only get out of the mines (which he isn't allowed to, of course) he could be earning twice the money for easy work in some hygienic factory. It has been found impossible to recruit enough miners and for some time past they have had to be conscripted. This is done by ballot, and it is an index of how mining is regarded that to be drawn as a miner (instead of, say, being put in a submarine) is looked on as a disaster. The conscripted youths, who include public-school boys, have been to the fore in the strikes. On top of all the other causes for discontent, it is said that the coal owners, while reading the miners sermons on patriotism, are doing jiggery-pokery by working uneconomic seams, saving up the good seams for after the war when the demand for coal will have dropped again.[2]

Everyone except the interested minority is aware that these conditions can't be cured without nationalization of the mines, and public opinion is entirely ready for this step. Even the left-wing Tories, though not facing up to nationalization, talk of compelling the coal-owners to amalgamate into larger units. It is, in fact, obvious that without centralizing the industry it would be impossible to raise the enormous sums needed to bring the mines up to date. But nationalization would solve the short-term problem as well, for it would give the miners something to look forward to, and in return they would certainly undertake to refrain from striking for the duration of the war. Needless to say there is no sign of any such thing happening. Instead there has been a hue and cry after the Trotskyists, who are alleged to be responsible for the strikes. Trotskyism, which not one English person in a hundred had heard of before the war, actually got the big headlines for several days. In reality the English Trotskyists only number, I believe, about five hundred, and it is unlikely they have a footing among the full-time miners, who are very suspicious of anyone outside their own community.

As this end of the war approaches its climax, the extraordinary contradictions in the attitude of the intelligentsia become more apparent. Even now large numbers of pinks claim to believe that no Second Front is intended, in spite of the vast American armies that have been brought here. But at the same time as they cry out for the Second Front to be opened immediately they protest against the bombing of Germany and Italy, not merely because of the loss of life but because of the material destruction. I have also heard people say almost in the same breath (a) that we must open a Second Front at once, (b) that it is no longer necessary because the Russians can defeat the Germans singlehanded, and (c) that it is bound to be a failure. Simultaneously with the desire to finish the war quickly there is quite frank rejoicing when something goes wrong, e.g., the stalemate in Italy, and a readiness to believe any rumor without examination so long as it is a rumor of disaster. Almost simultaneously, again, people approve the Russian proposals to partition Germany and exact enormous reparations, and tell you what a lot Hitler has done for Europe and how much preferable he is to the British Tories. Again—I notice this every day in the short stories and poems sent in to the *Tribune*—numbers of left-wingers have a definitely schizophrenic attitude towards war and militarism. What one might call the official left-wing view is that war is a meaningless massacre brought about by capitalists, no war can ever lead to any good result, in battle no one has any thought except to run away, and the soldier is a downtrodden slave who hates his officer like poison and looks on the enemy soldier as a comrade. But as soon as the Red Army is involved the whole of this conception is turned upside down. Not only does war become glorious and purposeful, but the soldier becomes a happy warrior who positively enjoys military discipline, loves his officer like a dog, hates the enemy like the Devil (a phrase that occurs frequently in these stories that are sent in to me is "his heart was fired with passionate hatred") and utters edifying political slogans while in the act of slinging a hand grenade. There is further schizophrenia on the subject of atrocities: any atrocity story reported by the Russians is true, anything reported by the British or Americans untrue. Ditto with the Asiatic quislings. Wang Ching-wei is a contemptible traitor, Subhas Chandra Bose a heroic liberator. Emotionally, what the Left intelligentsia wish for is that Germany and Japan should be defeated but that Britain and America should not be victorious. Once the Second Front has started it would not surprise me to see them change their attitude, become defeatist about the whole business and disclaim the demands for a Second Front which they have been making for more than two years.

Russophile feeling is on the surface stronger than ever. It is now next door to impossible to get anything overtly anti-Russian printed. Anti-Russian books do appear, but mostly from Catholic publishing firms and always from a religious or frankly reactionary angle. "Trotskyism," using the word in a wide sense, is even more effectively silenced than in the 1935–39 period. The Stalinists themselves don't seem to have regained their influence in the press, but apart from the general Russophile feeling of the intelligentsia, all the appeasers, e.g., Professor E. H. Carr,[3] have switched their allegiance from Hitler to Stalin. The servility of the so-called intellectuals is astonishing. The *Mission to Moscow* film,[4] which I gather raised something of a storm in the USA, was accepted here with hardly a murmur. It is interesting too that pacifists almost never say anything anti-Russian, though temperamentally they are not always Russophile. Their implied line is that it is wrong for us to defend ourselves by violence, but is all right for the Russians. This is sheer cowardice: they dare not flout prevailing left-wing opinion, which, of course, they are more afraid of than public opinion in the wider sense.

I suspect, however, that Russian and pro-Russian propaganda will in the long run defeat itself simply by being overdone. Lately I have several times been surprised to hear ordinary working-class or middle-class people say,

"Oh, I'm fed up with the Russians! They're too good to live," or words to that effect. One must remember that the USSR means different things to the working-class and the Left intelligentsia. The former are Russophile because they feel Russia to be the working-class country where the common man is in control, whereas the intellectuals are influenced at least partly by power-worship. The affection they feel for the USSR is still vaguely bound up with the idea of the meek inheriting the earth, and the tone of latter-day Soviet propaganda obviously contradicts this. In any case, English people usually react in the end against too-blatant propaganda. A good illustration of this is General Montgomery, idolized a year or two ago and now thoroughly unpopular because over-publicized.*

I don't think I have any more news. You will be interested to hear that several American soldiers have rung me up, introducing themselves as readers of PR. These are still the only contacts I have made with American soldiers. The troops and the public, other than girls, are still very stand-offish. I notice that Negroes do not seem to pick up girls so easily as the whites, though everyone says they like the Negroes better. A little while back a young American soldier had rung up and I asked him to stay the night at our flat. He was quite interested and said it was the first time he had been inside an English home. I said, "How long have you been in this country?" and he said, "two months." He went on to tell me that the previous day a girl had come up to him on the pavement and seized hold of his penis with the words, "Hullo Yank!" Yet he had not seen the interior of an ordinary English home. This makes me sad. Even at their best English people are not very hospitable to strangers, but I would like the Americans to know that the cold welcome they have had in this country is partly due to the fact that the rations are not easy to stretch and that after years of war people are ashamed of the shabby interiors of their houses, while the films have taught them to believe or half-believe that every American lives in a palace with a chromium-plated cocktail bar.

I am going to send two copies of this, one air mail and one sea mail, hoping that the latter may get there a bit sooner. The time that letters take to cross the Atlantic nowadays has made some people wonder whether the air mail travels in balloons.

George Orwell

[Fee: £2.10.0; 17.4.44]

---

* Here is a sample of the kind of story now told about Montgomery. General Eisenhower is having lunch with the King. "How do you get on with Montgomery?" asks the King. "Very well," replies Eisenhower, "except that I have a kind of feeling that he's after my job." "Oh," says the King, "I was afraid he was after mine."[5]

Other similar stories are told of Eisenhower or Montgomery interchangeably. For example: Three doctors who had just died arrived at the gates of Heaven. The first two, a physician and a surgeon, were refused admittance. The third described himself as a psychiatrist. "Come in!" said St. Peter immediately. "We should like your professional advice. God has been behaving in a very peculiar way lately. He thinks He's General Eisenhower (or Montgomery)" [Orwell's footnote].

1. time] times *in original*
2. 'Total British coal output dropped by 12 per cent between 1938 and 1944, while German output rose by 7.2 per cent. Even though nearly a third of German coal miners had been drafted into the forces by 1944 and replaced by foreign workers with barely more than half their productivity, German production per wage-earner per annum at 298.7 metric tons remained significantly more impressive than the 1944 British figure of 252.2 tons. In the Ruhr, and despite Allied bombing, total production dropped by only 1.18 per cent from 1938–9 to 1943–4' (Correlli Barnett, *The Audit of War*, 1986, 60–61).
3. Edward Hallett Carr (1892–1982), political scientist and historian specialising in the history, politics, and literature of the Soviet Union. He wrote *Propaganda in International Politics* (1939), *The Twenty Years' Crisis, 1919–39* (1939; New York, 1964), *Conditions of Peace* (1942), and *What is History?* (1961; New York, 1962). He also wrote biographies of Dostoievsky (1931), Marx (1934), and Bakunin (1937; New York, 1961). He was assistant editor of *The Times*, 1941–46. Despite his awareness of the atrocities perpetrated by Stalin, he remained wedded to the role and outcome of the October Revolution.
4. *Mission to Moscow* (released by Warner Bros., 30 April 1943) was 'the most extreme example of official attempts to create support [for the Soviet Union] by distorting history.' It was one of a number of Hollywood films instigated by the U.S. Government to dispel 'widespread popular distrust of the Soviet Union' (David Culbert, 'Our Awkward Ally', *American History/American Film*, edited by John E. O'Connor and Martin A. Jackson (New York, 1979), 122. Culbert devotes his chapter to an analysis of the 'extreme fabrications' of this 'Frankenstein monster'.)
5. The asterisked paragraph and the first five lines of Orwell's footnote were reprinted, under the heading 'Unexpected Effects of Propaganda,' in the regular feature 'Through the Press,' *War Commentary—for Anarchism*, October 1944. The policy of this periodical was described in the mid-October 1942 issue as being 'against the war because we are opposed to the governments now at war with each other; because the war is caused by conflicting commercial interests and imperial desires; and because the war is not waged in the interests of the common people anywhere, and acts as an obstacle in the way of social transformation by the nationalist and subservient ideas it brings into being.'

2455. Review of *Cricket Country* by Edmund Blunden

Manchester Evening News, 20 April 1944

Cricket arouses strong feelings, both "for" and "against," and during recent years it is the anti-cricket school that has been in the ascendant. Cricket has been labelled the Sport of Blimps. It has been vaguely associated with top hats, school prize days, fox-hunting, and the poems of Sir Henry Newbolt.[1] It has been denounced by Left-wing writers, who imagine erroneously that it is played chiefly by the rich.

On the other hand, its two bitterest enemies of all are "Beachcomber" and "Timothy Shy," who see in it an English institution which they feel it their duty to belittle, along with Wordsworth, William Blake, and Parliamentary government. But there are other reasons besides spite and ignorance for the partial decline in the popularity of cricket, and some of them can be read between the lines of Mr. Blunden's apologia, eloquent though it is.

Mr Blunden is a true cricketer. The test of a true cricketer is that he shall prefer village cricket to "good" cricket. Mr. Blunden's own form, one guesses, is somewhere midway between the village green and the county ground, and he has due reverence for the famous figures of the cricketing world, whose names pepper his pages. He is old enough to have seen Ranjitsinhji play his famous leg glide, and since then he has watched first-class matches regularly enough to have seen every well-known player, English or Australian. But it is obvious that all his friendliest memories are of village cricket: and not even cricket at the country-house level, where white trousers are almost universal and a pad on each leg is *de rigueur*, but the informal village game, where everyone plays in braces, where the blacksmith is liable to be called away in mid-innings on an urgent job, and sometimes, about the time when the light begins to fail, a ball driven for four kills a rabbit on the boundary.

In his love of cricket Mr. Blunden is in good literary company. He could, he says, almost make up an eleven of poets and writers. It would include Byron (who played for Harrow), Keats, Cowper, Trollope, Francis Thompson, Gerard Manley Hopkins, Robert Bridges, and Siegfried Sassoon. Mr. Blunden might have included Blake, one of whose fragments mentions an incident all too common in village cricket, but he is perhaps wrong to number Dickens among the lovers of cricket, for Dickens's only reference to the game (in "Pickwick Papers") shows that he was ignorant of its rules. But the essential thing in this book, as in nearly everything that Mr. Blunden writes, is his nostalgia for the golden age before 1914, when the world was peaceful as it has never since been.

The well-known lines from one of his poems:

> *I have been young and now am not too old,*
> *And I have seen the righteous man forsaken,*
> *His wealth, his honour, and his quality taken:*
> *This is not what we were formerly told*

sound as though they had been written after the dictators had swallowed Europe. Actually, however, they refer to the war of 1914–18, the great turning-point of Mr. Blunden's life. The war shattered the leisurely world he had known, and, as he sadly perceives, cricket has never been quite the same since.

Several things have combined to make it less popular. To begin with, the increasing hurry and urbanisation of life are against a game which needs green fields and abundant spare time. Then there is the generally-admitted dullness of first-class cricket. Like nearly everyone else, Mr. Blunden abhors the kind of game in which 20 successive maiden overs are nothing unusual and a bastman may be in for an hour before he scores his first run. But they are the natural result of too-perfect grass and a too-solemn attitude towards batting averages. Then again cricket has been partly supplanted, at any rate among grown-up people, by golf and lawn tennis. There can be no doubt that this is a disaster for these games are not only far inferior aesthetically to cricket but they do not have the socially binding quality that cricket, at any rate, used to have.

Contrary to what its detractors say, cricket is not an inherently snobbish game, as Mr. Blunden is careful to point out. Since it needs about 25 people to make up a game it necessarily leads to a good deal of social mixing. The inherently snobbish game is golf, which causes whole stretches of country-side to be turned into carefully-guarded class preserves.

But there is another good reason for the decline in the popularity of cricket—a reason Mr. Blunden does not point out, the extent to which it has been thrust down everybody's throat. For a long period cricket was treated as though that were a kind of religious ritual incumbent on every Englishman. Interminable Test matches with their astronomical scores were given large headlines in most newspapers, and every summer tens of thousands of unwilling boys were—and still are—drilled in a game which merely bored them. For cricket has the peculiarity that either you like it or you don't, and either you have a gift for it, or you have not. Unlike most games, it cannot be learned if you have no talent to start with. In the circumstances there was bound to be a large-scale revolt against cricket.

Even by children it is now less played than it was. It was most truly rooted in the national life when it was voluntary and informal—as in the Rugby of Tom Brown's schooldays, or in the village matches on lumpy wickets, which are Mr. Blunden's most cherished memory.

Will cricket survive? Mr. Blunden believes so, in spite of the competition from other interests that it has to face, and we may hope that he is right. It is pleasant to find him, towards the end of his book, still finding time for a game or two during the war, against R.A.F. teams. This book touches on much else besides cricket, for at the bottom of his heart it is perhaps less the game itself than the physical surroundings that appeals to Mr. Blunden. He is the kind of cricketer who when his side is batting is liable to stroll away from the pavilion to have a look at the village church, and perhaps come across a quaint epitaph.

In places this book is a little over-written, because Mr. Blunden is no more able to resist a quotation than some people are to refuse a drink. But it is pleasant reading, and a useful reminder that peace means something more than a temporary stoppage of the guns.

[*Tee. £0.0.0, 19.4.44*]

1. Orwell would have in mind Newbolt's poem 'Vitaï Lampada,' which describes the final moments of a school cricket match: 'There's a breathless hush in the Close to-night— / Ten to make and the match to win . . .'; it includes the line 'Play up! play up! and play the game!' later inscribed on the boundary wall of Lord's Cricket Ground, which advocated an approach to games in sharp contrast to that which now espouses 'the professional foul.' The Close referred to is that at Clifton College, Sir Henry Newbolt's old school.

2456. To W. J. Strachan

20 April 1944   Typewritten

Tribune

Dear Mr. Strachan,[1]

Thank you, I would like to use your poem, but as it is rather long if ° may have to wait over for a few weeks.

Yours truly,
[Signed] Geo. Orwell
George Orwell,
Literary Editor

1. W. J. Strachan (1903–), poet and translator, taught at Bishop's Stortford College, 1924–68, where he was Head of Modern Languages. Collections of his poetry include *Moments of Time* (1947), *The Season's Pause* (1950), and *Poems* (1976). In 1948 he published *Apollinaire to Aragon*, modern French verse in translation. He has also written several books on sculpture. *The Living Curve: Letters to W. J. Strachan 1929–1979*, edited by Christopher Hewett (1938–1983; one of Strachan's pupils), was published in 1984.

2457. 'As I Please,' 21

Tribune, 21 April 1944

In a letter published in this week's *Tribune*,[1] someone attacks me rather violently for saying that the B.B.C. is a better source of news than the daily papers, and is so regarded by the public. I have never, he suggests, heard ordinary working men shouting "Turn that dope off!" when the news bulletin comes on.

On the contrary, I have heard this frequently. Still more frequently I have seen the customers in a pub go straight on with their darts, music and so forth without the slightest slackening of noise when the news bulletin began. But it was not my claim that anyone likes the B.B.C., or thinks it interesting, or grown-up, or democratic, or progressive. I said only that people regard it as a relatively sound source of news. Again and again I have known people, when they see some doubtful item of news, wait to have it confirmed by the radio before they believe it. Social surveys show the same thing—i.e., that as against the radio the prestige of newspapers has declined.

And I repeat what I said before—that in my experience the B.B.C. *is* relatively truthful and, above all, has a responsible attitude towards news and does not disseminate lies simply because they are "newsy." Of course, untrue statements are constantly being broadcast and anyone can tell you of instances. But in most cases this is due to genuine error, and the B.B.C. sins much more by simply avoiding anything controversial than by direct propaganda. And after all—a point not met by our correspondent—its reputation abroad is comparatively high. Ask any refugee from Europe which of the belligerent radios is considered to be the most truthful. So also in Asia. Even in India, where the population are so hostile that they will not listen to British propaganda and will hardly listen to a British entertainment programme, they listen to B.B.C. news because they believe that it approximates to the truth.

Even if the B.B.C. passes on the British official lies, it does make some effort to sift the others. Most of the newspapers, for instance, have continued to publish without any query as to their truthfulness the American claims to have sunk the entire Japanese fleet several times over. The B.B.C., to my knowledge, developed quite early on an attitude of suspicion towards this and certain other unreliable sources. On more than one occasion I have known a newspaper to print a piece of news—and news unfavourable to Britain—on no other authority than the German radio, because it was "newsy" and made a good "par."

If you see something obviously untruthful in a newspaper and ring up to ask "Where did you get that from?" you are usually put off with the formula: "I'm afraid Mr. So-and-So is not in the office." If you persist, you generally find that the story has no basis whatever but that it looked like a good bit of news, so in it went. Except where libel is involved, the average journalist is astonished and even contemptuous if anyone bothers about accuracy with regard to names, dates, figures and other details. And any daily journalist will tell you that one of the most important secrets of his trade is the trick of making it appear that there is news when there is no news.

Towards the end of May, 1940, newspaper posters were prohibited in order to save paper. Several newspapers, however, continued to display posters for some time afterwards. On inquiry it was found that they were using old ones. Such headlines as "Panzer Divisions Hurled Back" or "French Army Standing Firm" could be used over and over again. Then came the period when the paper-sellers supplied their own posters with a slate and a bit of chalk, and in their hands the poster became a comparatively sober and truthful thing. It referred to something that was actually in the paper you were going to buy, and it usually picked out the real news and not some piece of sensational nonsense. The paper-sellers, who frequently did not know which way round a capital "S" goes, had a better idea of what is news, and more sense of responsibility towards the public, than their millionaire employers.

Our correspondent considers that the public and the journalists rather than the proprietors are to blame for the silliness of English newspapers. You could not, he implies, make an intelligent newspaper pay because the public wants tripe. I am not certain whether this is so. For the time being most of the tripe has vanished and newspaper circulations have not declined. But I do agree—and I said so—that the journalists share the blame. In allowing their profession to be degraded they have largely acted with their eyes open, whereas, I suppose, to blame somebody like Northcliffe for making money in the quickest way is like blaming a skunk for stinking.

One mystery about the English language is why, with the biggest vocabulary in existence, it has to be constantly borrowing foreign words and phrases. Where is the sense, for instance, of saying *cul de sac* when you mean blind alley? Other totally unnecessary French phrases are *joie de vivre, amour propre, reculer pour mieux sauter, raison d'être, vis-à-vis, tête-à-tête, au pied de la lettre, esprit de corps.* There are dozens more of them. Other needless borrowings come from Latin (though there is a case for "i.e." and "e.g.," which are useful abbreviations), and since the war we have been much infested by German words, *Gleichschaltung, Lebensraum, Weltanschauung, Wehrmacht, Panzerdivisionen* and others being flung about with great freedom. In nearly every case an English equivalent already exists or could easily be improvised. There is also a tendency to take over American slang phrases without understanding their meaning. For example, the expression "barking up the wrong tree" is fairly widely used, but inquiry shows that most people don't know its origin nor exactly what it means.

Sometimes it is necessary to take over a foreign word, but in that case we should anglicise its pronunciation, as our ancestors used to do. If we really need the word "café" (we got on well enough with "coffee house" for two hundred years), it should either be spelled "caffay" or pronounced "cayfe." "Garage" should be pronounced "garridge." For what point is there in littering our speech with fragments of foreign pronunciation, very tiresome to anyone who does not happen to have learned that particular language?

And why is it that most of us never use a word of English origin if we can find a manufactured Greek one? One sees a good example of this in the rapid disappearance of English flower names. What until twenty years ago was universally called a snapdragon is now called an antirrhinum, a word no one can spell without consulting a dictionary. Forget-me-nots are coming more and more to be called myosotis. Many other names, Red Hot Poker, Mind Your Own Business, Love Lies Bleeding, London Pride, are disappearing in favour of colourless Greek names out of botany textbooks. I had better not continue too long on this subject, because last time I mentioned flowers in this column an indignant lady wrote in to say that flowers are bourgeois. But I don't think it a good augury for the future of the English language that "marigold" should be dropped in favour of "calendula," while the pleasant little Cheddar Pink loses its name and becomes merely Dianthus Cæsius.[2]

1. This letter, from Frank Preston, follows 'As I Please,' 19, 7 April 1944, to which it refers; see *2450*.
2. Orwell clearly had an affection for the Cheddar Pink. They featured in his garden at Barnhill, Jura.

2457A. To Lydia Jackson

    21 April 1944   Typewritten

Tribune

Dear Lydia,

Thanks so much for the review which is very nice.[1]

Yes, we are using the article but it'll have to stand over for a few weeks.[2]

               Yours,

           [Signed] George

           George Orwell.

1. *Polish Short Stories*; see *2426A, n. 1*.
2. Despite the reference to 'a few weeks', 'A Soviet Patriot: A Sketch of Serghei Dikovsky' was published on 28 April; see *2446A*. A compliment note from the Business Manager of *Tribune* dated 28 April 1944 shows that Lydia Jackson was that day sent a fee of £2 12s 6d. This was more likely to be for an article than a review; see Orwell's letter to her of 23 May 1944 regarding payment for reviews (*2475A*).

2458. Review of *The Poisoned Crown* by Hugh Kingsmill

    The Observer, 23 April 1944

Totalitarianism is generally considered to be traceable to the wickedness of a few ambitious individuals, or else is explained away as a last effort to prop up a collapsing economic system. However, there is another school of thought, of which Mr. F. A. Voigt is the best-known exponent, which holds that any attempt to set up a materialistic Utopia must inevitably lead to despotism. Mr. Hugh Kingsmill belongs to this school, and in this brilliant book he illustrates his thesis by four short biographies of Queen Elizabeth, Cromwell, Napoleon and Abraham Lincoln.

As Mr. Kingsmill sees it, all of these illustrate "the barrenness of action and the corrupting effects of power." They are nevertheless not very easy to fit into a single pattern, and of the four of them only Cromwell bears a close resemblance to the dictators of our own day. It is especially difficult to see why Mr. Kingsmill included Elizabeth, who was absorbed from early youth with the problem of remaining alive and on the throne, and who by the standards of her own day was neither bigoted nor cruel. Her unhappy sister Mary, who burned her subjects alive because she loved them so much, would probably have been a better example. Lincoln, on the other hand, does not seem to have been much corrupted by power, and Mr. Kingsmill has to press his case rather hard to show that Lincoln's achievement was valueless.

Nevertheless the section dealing with Lincoln is probably the best thing in the book. Lincoln's one great concession to expediency, Mr. Kingsmill thinks, was his declaration that slavery would be abolished if the Confederate states were defeated. He had not wanted to make this declaration (in its origins the war was only indirectly concerned with the issue of slavery), partly because he saw that the country as a whole was not ready for it and the slaves would not benefit by emancipation, partly because he did not wish to give the war the character of a crusade, with all the self-righteousness and vindictiveness that that implies. He was driven into making the declaration by the necessity of winning the war. By proclaiming slavery to be the issue he cut the moral ground from beneath Britain and France, who might otherwise have intervened on the side of the South. But in doing so he was also surrendering to the extremists among his followers, who were not, as one might expect, high-minded Abolitionists but hard-faced business men determined to break the economic power of the Southern states.

The complete victory won by the North left the business men in control, and the moral atmosphere of the United States deteriorated accordingly. Lincoln had sacrificed everything, including a fragment of his conscience, to winning the war, and the result was a country where there could be no more Lincolns—that at least is Mr. Kingsmill's picture. Incidentally he suggests that the obscure lunatic who murdered Lincoln was employed not by Southerners but by Lincoln's own rivals among the Republicans.

One frequently has the feeling that Mr. Kingsmill is being unfair, not, perhaps, to Lincoln himself, but to his achievement and therefore to the United States. Was it not, after all, a step forward that the slaves should be freed, even though they were merely converted into wage-slaves? And one even has the feeling that he is unfair to Napoleon, who was a crook but may have been a necessary instrument of history. Without Napoleon, or at least somebody like Napoleon, revolutionary France would probably have been crushed round about 1800, and the peasants would not have kept the land. Napoleon, though his motives were totally selfish, did stave off defeat long enough to make it impossible for the *Ancien Régime* to be restored. On the other hand, Mr. Kingsmill's debunking of Cromwell, though probably it is not fair either, is a good antidote to the usual middle-class worship of this prototype of all the modern dictators, who perpetrated massacres which make the German exploits at Lidice look like a schoolgirls' romp.

Mr. Kingsmill's book begins with a chapter entitled "The Genealogy of Hitler." The line of descent is traced from Napoleon and Byron through Dostoievski, Nietzsche, and H. G. Wells to Hitler and Charlie Chaplin. (Chaplin, says Mr. Kingsmill, is the Little Man's version of Byron, Hitler his version of Napoleon.) There are many quarrels, big and small, that one could pick with Mr. Kingsmill. Like all thinkers of his school, he assumes that reformers want to make the world perfect, whereas in general they only want to make it better, and he frequently writes as though progress, even material progress, were of its nature impossible, which implies that we are still in the Stone Age. But this is an outstanding book, and a telling blow at every form of tyranny, not excluding the ones which it is now fashionable to admire.

[Fee: £7.7.0; 17.4.44]

2459. Correspondence with Antonia White

27 April 1944

A long letter—some 3,500 words—from Antonia White[1] to Orwell, dated 27 April 1944, survives and is the only extant element of a correspondence between them arising from Orwell's 'As I Please' of 14 April, in which he wrote that he found it very rare to meet anyone of whatever background who believed in personal immortality; see 2452. It is possible from Antonia White's letter to recover some idea of what Orwell and she were discussing, and it is just possible that there was a little more to Orwell's questioning than a simple delight in arguing over this controversy. The implications of Orwell's points of view (as represented by Antonia White's summaries) go beyond belief or otherwise in an after-life and indicate that he had political and social implications in mind. The extracts below are *not* intended to summarise Antonia White's letter, but only to indicate the matters Orwell was raising. They are numbered here for convenience; they are not the numbers in Antonia White's letter (of which there are only three; she appears to have given up numbering). As she twice points out, she is writing as a Roman Catholic and with reference to the Roman Catholic Church.

1 Thank you very much for your letter which was very far from 'Incoherent' and extremely interesting. It raises so many points that I despair of even attempting to answer them and wish that I could call in some more competent Catholic to do so. . . .

2 As to 'ordinary' people not retaining even any vestige in the belief in personal immortality, I don't see how one can be sure of that, except by a universal head or heart count. Again it's hard to define 'ordinary'. . . .

3 I am much puzzled by the Catholic who laughed at you for saying that survival was an obligatory belief. I think she must have misunderstood her Dominican. All Catholic doctrine and tradition is firm on this point. . . .

4 As to unbelievers 'repenting' or not on their deathbeds, there is a traditional Catholic belief—*not* an article of faith, but held by such authorities as St. Thomas Aquinas, that there is a moment, even so late that consciousness may seem to be extinct, when the soul has a true apprehension of God and makes its final acceptance or rejection. . . .

5 If, as you say, extinction is taken for granted (and certainly my own experience bears out yours as regards friends of mine, other than Catholics, who have died during the last ten years) it does 'mark a very great departure from the outlook of our ancestors!' I also agree with you that people didn't necessarily behave better because they believed in hell. One has only to look at the Middle Ages. Yet then, as you so truly say, they had a 'religious attitude' however monstrously they behaved. And it is probably true today that the average 'atheist' behaves as well as, if not considerably better than, the average 'believer'. I suspect that you are almost certainly right in connecting modern power-worship with the assumption that there is no world but this. . . .

6 If the Church has indeed lost the allegiance of the common people, she has a terrible responsibility. Yet more than fifty years ago, Leo XIII

inveighed in his encyclicals against the monstrous exploitation of man by man and complained that the majority of workers has been reduced to the condition of slaves.[2] In many dioceses priests refused to read that encyclical because they said it was 'sheer socialism'. . . .

7 The basis of the Church's defence of private property is that man has a natural right to enjoy the fruits of his labour. This is not at all the same thing as approving of unbridled capitalism. . . .

8 I can't agree with you that Bernanos is 'no more typical of Catholics than an albino Negro is typical of Negroes'. On a head count, Catholics of his type may well be in a minority. But they are the truest representatives of the real Catholic spirit and that current is growing stronger in the Church. We all wish that spirit were more obvious in the majority of our bishops but you will find it among the Dominicans and other orders, in innumerable obscure parish priests and among many of the laity. I wish it were Barbara Ward and not myself who was trying to answer your letter. . . .

9 But it's time I got back to immortality. The last paragraph of your letter raises such a number of tremendous questions that it needs a letter to itself. . . .

10 I don't see how the Church can possibly alter her *beliefs* to accommodate them to the temper of the 'modern mind'. Her whole justification in her own eyes is that she is the guardian of a truth committed to her by Christ and that she must continue to teach that truth whether men find it 'acceptable' or not. . . .

11 It is strange to me that you should seem to suggest Hinduism or Buddhism, both highly intellectual and philosophical religions, as alternatives to Christianity for the 'plain man'. In their corruption, they are liable to produce as much superstition and as much social injustice as any corruption of Christianity; at their best they demand a degree of discipline and training of which very few are capable. They require moreover a mental habit, almost a type of consciousness, which is not native to the western mind. . . . [She then suggested that Orwell would find the work of René Guénon, 'one of the greatest authorities on Hinduism,' interesting.]

12 I think you may misunderstand what is meant by 'personal' survival in Catholic teaching. . . . It doesn't mean 'warts and all'—exactly as we are here. Nor does it mean that the human personality is completely annihilated in God or Universal Being and only achieves 'immortality' at the price of total loss of identity.

But we believe that at baptism the soul receives the potentiality of being adopted into a higher order, of sharing the vision of God. It is like a creature that has the undeveloped capacity to live in another element. But before it can live in that element, endless adaptations have to be made. . . .

13 While entirely agreeing with you that the materialistic outlook leads to disaster, I don't see how you are going to inculcate a 'religious attitude' without a definite religion. Santayana says somewhere that to attempt to be religious without a religion is like trying to speak without a language.

14 I don't for one moment think that you attack Christian beliefs in a spirit of 'vulgar irreverence'. On the contrary, I am completely convinced of your sincerity and I wish all Christians were as sincere. I suppose the final test of one's sincerity in a belief is whether one is ready to risk one's life for it. . . .

15 Having gone so far, I may as well take in levitation and Chesterton.

16 *Levitation.* This seems to be a fairly well established phenomenon, though it is quite irrelevant to sanctity as such. It seems to occur also in people who are very far from being saints! But 'ecstacy' etc., are perfectly well-known among Buddhist, Hindu and Mahomedan mystics who have achieved a high degree of concentration. . . . Gordon Craig wrote somewhere that when Ellen Terry had been playing a part with complete absorption, he could lift her as easily as a small child, though normally he could not lift her at all. But, in considering a 'Cause' of canonisation, the question of whether or not the subject was supposed to have 'levitated' would have no relevance. The only thing that is in question is whether or not the subject achieved 'heroic sanctity'. . . .

17 *Chesterton.* I'm glad Chesterton didn't write the poem. He might conceivably answer that, in printing it, he would admit the legitimacy of jokes about hell, since hell was something one had the possibility of avoiding.

1. Antonia White (1899–1981), novelist and translator of more than thirty books from the French. In the 1930s she worked as fashion editor for the *Daily Mirror* and *Sunday Pictorial*, and as a copyrighter for the J. Walter Thompson advertising agency. She was in the BBC, 1940–43 (her pamphlet *The BBC at War* was published in 1941) and in the French section of the Political Intelligence Department of the Foreign Office, 1943–45. Her autobiographical novel, *Frost in May* (see *2838*), was published in 1933, and her daughters have published two biographies: Susan Chitty, *Now to My Mother: A Very Personal Memoir of Antonia White* (1985) and Lyndall Passerini Hopkinson, *Nothing to Forgive: A Daughter's Story of Antonia White* (1988). Sonia Orwell, who was a friend of Antonia White's (they went to the same convent school at Roehampton, though at different times), checked that none of Orwell's letters to Antonia White survived.
2. The encyclical was *Rerum Novarum* ('Of New Things'), 1891, on the abuses of capitalism.

2460. 'As I Please,' 22

Tribune, 28 April 1944

On the night in 1940 when the big ack-ack barrage was fired over London for the first time,[1] I was in Piccadilly Circus when the guns opened up, and I fled into the Cafe Royal to take cover. Among the crowd inside a good-looking, well-made youth of about twenty-five was making somewhat of a nuisance of himself with a copy of *Peace News*, which he was forcing upon the attention of everyone at the neighbouring tables. I got into conversation with him, and the conversation went something like this:

The youth: "I tell you, it'll all be over by Christmas. There's obviously going to be a compromise peace. I'm pinning my faith to Sir Samuel Hoare.

It's degrading company to be in, I admit, but still Hoare is on our side. So long as Hoare's in Madrid, there's always hope of a sell-out."

Orwell: "What about all these preparations that they're making against invasion—the pillboxes that they're building everywhere, the L.D.V.s,[1] and so forth?"

The youth: "Oh, that merely means that they're getting ready to crush the working class when the Germans get here. I suppose some of them might be fools enough to try to resist, but Churchill and the Germans between them won't take long to settle them. Don't worry, it'll soon be over."

Orwell: "Do you really want to see your children grow up Nazis?'

The youth: "Nonsense! You don't suppose the Germans are going to encourage Fascism in this country, do you? They don't want to breed up a race of warriors to fight against them. Their object will be to turn us into slaves. They'll encourage every pacifist movement they can lay hands on. That's why I'm a pacifist. They'll encourage people like me."

Orwell: "And shoot people like me?"

The youth: "That would be just too bad."

Orwell: "But why are you so anxious to remain alive?"

The youth: "So that I can get on with my work, of course."

It had come out in the conversation that the youth was a painter—whether good or bad I do not know; but, at any rate, sincerely interested in painting and quite ready to face poverty in pursuit of it. As a painter, he would probably have been somewhat better off under a German occupation than a writer or journalist would be. But still, what he said contained a very dangerous fallacy, now very widespread in the countries where totalitarianism has not actually established itself.

The fallacy is to believe that under a dictatorial government you can be free *inside*. Quite a number of people console themselves with this thought, now that totalitarianism in one form or another is visibly on the up-grade in every part of the world. Out in the street the loudspeakers bellow, the flags flutter from the rooftops, the police with their tommy-guns prowl to and fro, the face of the Leader, four feet wide, glares from every hoarding; but up in the attics the secret enemies of the regime can record their thoughts in perfect freedom—that is the idea, more or less. And many people are under the impression that this is going on now in Germany and other dictatorial countries.

Why is this idea false? I pass over the fact that modern dictatorships don't, in fact, leave the loopholes that the old-fashioned despotisms did; and also the probable weakening of the *desire* for intellectual liberty owing to totalitarian methods of education. The greatest mistake is to imagine that the human being is an autonomous individual. The secret freedom which you can supposedly enjoy under a despotic Government is nonsense, because your thoughts are never entirely your own. Philosophers, writers, artists, even scientists, not only need encouragement and an audience, they need constant stimulation from other people. It is almost impossible to think without talking. If Defoe had really lived on a desert island he could not have written *Robinson Crusoe*, nor would he have wanted to. Take away freedom of speech, and the creative faculties dry up. Had the Germans really got to England my acquaintance of the Cafe Royal would soon have found his painting deteriorating, even if the Gestapo had let him alone. And when the lid is taken off Europe, I believe one of the things that will surprise us will be to find how little worthwhile writing of any kind—even such things as diaries, for instance—have been produced in secret under the dictators.

Mr. Basil Henriques,[3] chairman of the East London juvenile court, has just been letting himself go on the subject of the Modern Girl. English boys, he says, are "just grand," but it is a different story with girls:

> "One seldom comes across a really bad boy. The war seems to have affected girls more than boys. . . . Children now went to the pictures several times a week and saw what they imagined was the high life of America, when actually it was a great libel on that country. They also suffer from the effects of listening through the microphone to wild raucous jitterbugging noises called music. . . . Girls of 14 now dress and talk like those of 18 and 19, and put the same filth and muck on their faces."

I wonder whether Mr. Henriques knows (a) that well before the other war it was already usual to attribute juvenile crime to the evil example of the cinematograph, and (b) that the Modern Girl has been just the same for quite 2,000 years?

One of the big failures in human history has been the age-long attempt to stop women painting their faces. The philosophers of the Roman Empire denounced the frivolity of the modern woman in almost the same terms as she is denounced today. In the fifteenth century the Church denounced the damnable habit of plucking the eyebrows. The English Puritans, the Bolsheviks, and the Nazis all attempted to discourage cosmetics, without success. In Victorian England rouge was considered so disgraceful that it was usually sold under some other name, but it continued to be used.

Many styles of dress from the Elizabethan ruff to the Edwardian hobble skirt, have been denounced from the pulpit, without effect. In the nineteen-twenties, when skirts were at their shortest, the Pope decreed that women improperly dressed were not to be admitted to Catholic churches; but somehow feminine fashions remained unaffected. Hitler's "ideal woman," an exceedingly plain specimen in a mackintosh, was exhibited all over Germany and much of the rest of the world, but inspired few imitators. I prophesy that English girls will continue to "put filth and muck on their faces" in spite of Mr. Henriques. Even in jail, it is said, the female prisoners redden their lips with the dye from the Post Office mail bags.

Just why women use cosmetics is a different question, but it seems doubtful whether sex attraction is the main object. It is very unusual to meet a man who does not think painting your fingernails scarlet is a disgusting habit, but hundreds of thousands of women go on doing it all the same. Meanwhile it might console Mr. Henriques to know that though make-up persists, it is far less elaborate than it used to be in the days when Victorian beauties had their faces "enamelled," or when it was usual to alter the contour of your cheeks by means of "plumpers," as described in Swift's poem, *On a Beautiful Young Nymph Going to Bed.*

1. 10 September 1940.
2. Local Defence Volunteers. On 13 May 1940, even before the withdrawal of British and Allied forces from the Continent through Dunkirk, Anthony Eden had proposed raising local volunteers for home defence. At the end of June 1940 they were renamed the Home Guard, a title Churchill suggested for such a force as early as October 1939 (*The Second World War*, II, 147–48; U.S.: *Their Finest Hour*, 166). They were initially poorly armed, and were even sometimes figures of fun. Though never called upon to face invading forces, they later manned anti-aircraft batteries, including the 'Z,' or rocket, batteries, which did see action.
3. Basil Henriques (1890–1961; Kt., 1955) was a distinguished and much-quoted magistrate. Among his books was *The Indiscretions of a Magistrate* (1950).

2461. To Philip Rahv

1 May 1944   Typewritten

10a Mortimer Crescent
London NW 6

Dear Rahv,

Thanks so much for your letter dated April 17th. It got here today, so the air mail is definitely looking up. I sent off my London letter on about April 17th, so that should certainly reach you before the end of May unless held up in the censorship. After I had sent it off it struck me there were several things in it the censorship might object to (on policy grounds, not security of course), but I haven't had any note from them to say they were stopping it, so I suppose it's all right. Your letter hadn't been opened by the censor, by the way.

I dare say the Dial people will have got my MS[1] by about now. As you say you're in touch with them, I wonder if you could ask them to let you have a look at it. I think you will agree it deserves to be printed, but its "message" is hardly a popular one nowadays. I am having hell and all to find a publisher for it here though normally I have no difficulty in publishing my stuff and in any case all publishers are now clamouring for manuscripts. A few weeks back a newspaper I write for regularly refused to print a book review of mine because it was anti-Stalin in tone.[2] Comically enough the Stalinists themselves haven't much influence in the press, but Stalin seems to be becoming a figure rather similar to what Franco used to be, a Christian gent whom it is not done to criticise. By some arrangement the Soviet government have made, most of the Russian propaganda books are published by Hutchinson's, a big octopus publisher who puts out not only very cheap tripe-novels but vicious anti-left pamphlets and semi-fascist stuff from Vansittart's followers.[3]

As to the Dial publishing other books of mine. Several have actually been published in the USA (they never sold much). The one that *ought* to be reprinted is my one about the Spanish civil war, but of course that's the most hopeless of all subjects now. I don't know whether the Penguin books are sold in the USA. My Burma novel which Harper's published in 1934 is being penguinised,[4] but if the Penguins don't get across the Atlantic it seems to me it is a book someone might reprint over there as Burma is a bit more in the news now. I believe the copyright is mine but could find out any way.° There are others that I think are worth reprinting as books, but the trouble is that they're too local to be of much interest in America. However, this autumn I intend to publish a book of reprinted literary essays. I would have done it before, but there are several more I want to write before issuing the book, and I haven't been able to do so because of being smothered under other work. However I should get them all done by the end of July, and perhaps the Dial would be interested in that book. I suppose it won't hurt if it's done here simultaneously as well.

Yours
Geo. Orwell

1. Of *Animal Farm*.
2. The review of Harold Laski's *Faith, Reason and Civilisation*, rejected by the *Manchester Evening News*; see *2434*.
3. Lord Vansittart (1881–1957), chief diplomatic adviser to the Foreign Secretary, 1938–41, and an outspoken critic of Germany and the Germans. In Orwell's pamphlet collection were several by Vansittart attacking Germany, including his *Black Record* (1941).
4. *Burmese Days*. It was not published in the United States until 19 January 1950, a few days before Orwell died.

2462. 'As I Please,' 23

Tribune, 5 May 1944

For anyone who wants a good laugh I recommend a book which was published about a dozen years ago, but which I only recently succeeded in getting hold of. This is I. A. Richards's *Practical Criticism*.

Although mostly concerned with the general principles of literary criticism, it also describes an experiment that Mr. Richards made with, or one should perhaps say *on*, his English students at Cambridge. Various volunteers, not actually students but presumably interested in English literature, also took part. Thirteen poems were presented to them, and they were asked to criticise them. The authorship of the poems was not revealed, and none of them was well enough known to be recognised at sight by the average reader. You are getting, therefore, specimens of literary criticism not complicated by snobbishness of the ordinary kind.

One ought not to be too superior, and there is no need to be, because the book is so arranged that you can try the experiment on yourself. The poems, unsigned, are all together at the end, and the authors' names are on a fold-over page which you need not look at till afterwards. I will say at once that I only spotted the authorship of two, one of which I knew already, and though I could date most of the others within a few decades, I made two bad bloomers, in one case attributing to Shelley a poem written in the nineteen-twenties. But still, some of the comments recorded by Dr. Richards are startling. They go to show that many people who would describe themselves as lovers of poetry have no more notion of distinguishing between a good poem and a bad one than a dog has of arithmetic.

For example, a piece of completely spurious bombast by Alfred Noyes gets quite a lot of praise. One critic compares it to Keats. A sentimental ballad from *Rough Rhymes of a Padre*, by "Woodbine Willie,"[1] also gets quite a good Press. On the other hand, a magnificent sonnet by John Donne gets a distinctly chilly reception. Dr. Richards records only three favourable criticisms and about a dozen cold or hostile ones. One writer says contemptuously that the poem "would make a good hymn," while another remarks, "I can find no other reaction except disgust." Donne was at that time at the top of his reputation and no doubt most of the people taking part in this experiment would have fallen on their faces at his name. D. H. Lawrence's poem *The Piano* gets many sneers, though it is praised by a minority. So also with a short poem by Gerard Manley Hopkins. "The worst poem I have ever read," declares one writer, while another's criticism is simply "Pish-posh!"

However, before blaming these youthful students for their bad judgment, let it be remembered that when some time ago somebody published a not very convincing fake of an eighteenth-century diary, the aged critic, Sir Edmund Gosse,[2] librarian of the House of Lords, fell for it immediately. And there was also the case of the Parisian art critics of I forget which "school," who went into rhapsodies over a picture which was afterwards discovered to have been painted by a donkey with a paintbrush tied to its tail.

Under the heading "We Are Destroying Birds that Save Us," the *News Chronicle* notes that "beneficial birds suffer from human ignorance. There is senseless persecution of the kestrel and barn owl. No two species of birds do better work for us."

Unfortunately it isn't even from ignorance. Most of the birds of prey are killed off for the sake of that enemy of England, the pheasant. Unlike the partridge, the pheasant does not thrive in England, and apart from the neglected woodlands and the vicious game laws that it has been responsible for, all birds or animals that are suspected of eating its eggs or chicks are systematically wiped out. Before the war, near my village in Hertfordshire, I used to pass a stretch of fence where the gamekeeper kept his "larder." Dangling from the wires were the corpses of stoats, weasels, rats, hedgehogs, jays, owls, kestrels and sparrowhawks. Except for the rats and perhaps the jays, all of these creatures are beneficial to agriculture. The stoats keep down the rabbits, the weasels eat mice, and so do the kestrels and sparrowhawks, while the owls eat rats as well. It has been calculated that a barn owl destroys between 1,000 and 2,000 rats and mice in a year. Yet it has to be killed off for the sake of this useless bird which Rudyard Kipling correctly described as "lord of many a shire."

We had to postpone announcing the results of the short story competition, but we are publishing the winning story next week. The runners-up will appear, I hope, in the two subsequent weeks.[3]

I will set forth my opinions about the English short story another week, but I will say at once that of the five or six hundred stories that were sent in, the great majority were, in my judgment, very bad. A fairly large number of competitors, more than I had expected, had a story to tell, but too many of them simply gave the bare bones of the story, making it into an anecdote, without character interest and usually written in a slovenly way. Others sent in entries which were written with more distinction, but had no interest or development in them—being, in fact, sketches and not stories. A dismayingly large number dealt with Utopias, or took place in Heaven, or brought in ghosts or magic or something of that kind. I do admit, however, that it is not easy to write a story which is about real people, and in which something happens, within the compass of 1,800 words, and I do not believe there is much hope of English short stories improving till our magazines again swell to Victorian size.

1. G. A. Studdert Kennedy (1883–1929), described in *G. A. Studdert Kennedy by his Friends* (1929) as 'an Army Chaplain of unconventional manners and speech,' was 'an effective platform speaker,' and also a model parish priest in Worcester (94). His nickname came from his generous distribution of a particular brand of cigarettes, Woodbines, to soldiers in the front line after becoming an army chaplain in December 1915. His *Rough Rhymes of a Padre* went into several editions (the sixth in 1918) and included poems used by him in his parish services. He was described also as driving 'straight through the deadening conventionalities of thought and life, as a Tank through barbed wire' (153).
2. Sir Edmund Gosse (1849–1928), literary scholar with a particular knowledge of Scandinavian literature, did much to promote the work of Ibsen in England. He also wrote prolifically on English literature and published several volumes of poetry. The work for which he is still remembered is *Father and Son*, published anonymously in 1907, which records his relations with his father, an eminent zoologist and Plymouth Brother. He was cruelly deceived by the 'Reading Sonnets,' a forgery produced by T. J. Wise and Harry Buxton-Forman purporting to be an edition of Elizabeth Barrett Browning's *Sonnets from the Portuguese*. This, the most outrageous of their skilful forgeries, was sold for a great price when news of its existence was leaked by Gosse.
3. In the section 'Ourselves,' *Tribune*, 28 April 1944, 5, the following announcement was made: 'George Orwell regrets that even after much overtime he has not completed reading all the entries submitted for the Short Story Competition. It is therefore not possible to publish the winning story in this issue.' It would appear that Orwell was having to cope with the competition single-handed, and he may have been the only judge.

2463. Review of *A Giant in the Age of Steel: The Story of General de Gaulle* by Alfred Hessenstein

Manchester Evening News, 5 May 1944[1]

It was probably necessary that General de Gaulle should be built up into a legendary figure, but this book, vulgar (in the literary sense) and expensive, is somehow very disquieting. Just to give one sample and then have done with it, here is the kind of language in which it is written:

"Victory! there is no other way, there never has been any other. . ."
"The flame goes on."
"France, whose head is 'bloody but unbowed,' will surely respond herself, De

Gaulle, her son, will bring her the weapon, and the people will eagerly seize it, rising as one man in the fight for liberty."

"With this sword he may turn the course of history."

The entire book is written in this style—not merely in inflated theatrical language (swords, banners, jackboots, clarion calls, and the like appear on every page), but in very short paragraphs, usually of one or at most two sentences which insult the reader by assuming that his attention will falter if he sees as much as an inch of solid print.[2] Moreover, all the way through there is the most vulgar emphasis on the personality of the General himself, with his "gigantic" stature, his "sonorous" voice, and the "faint smile that plays about his lips." It is all extremely unsympathetic, and even alarming.

If one sifts the facts out of the rubbish (it is not easy to extract a coherent story from this book which consists mainly of rhetoric and quotes largely of the texts of De Gaulle's speeches) it emerges as an unmistakable truth that General de Gaulle did his country and the world a very great service in 1940. History is not likely to forget that.

From this side of the Channel it was easy to see, even in 1940, that the odds against Germany were still heavy, but in France despair was almost general. And the "best" military opinion, openly voiced by Weygand, Darlan, and others, was that Britain would collapse in a fortnight. It is quite reasonably likely that if there had not been one commanding figure to rally resistance outside France and to give the conquered population a gleam of hope, Vichy France would have entered the war on the German side. And the resistance inside France undoubtedly began earlier and spread more rapidly because of the knowledge that Frenchmen elsewhere were continuing the fight. At the very least we owe the saving of thousands of British lives to De Gaulle, who was willing to stand by us in adversity, and who—luckily—had won himself enough renown in the Battle of France to be acceptable as a leader.

But that does not justify the extravagant claims made in this book and in other similar books that have appeared (for instance, Philippe Barres's "Charles de Gaulle"). To begin with, it is doubtful whether De Gaulle is really the all-foreseeing military genius that he is here represented as being. The claim that the German tank commanders learned their tactics from De Gaulle's teachings has been contested by people whose opinion is worth listening to.

Secondly, the debt we owe to De Gaulle does not make it any less a disaster that no politician of the first rank managed to escape from France at the time of the collapse. Count Hessenstein, incidentally, plays down all the French politicians, even Reynaud, and barely mentions Blum or Mandel. And he gives no publicity to the fact that Mandel and others only failed to escape because they were neatly trapped and imprisoned by the Vichy Government.

If the Free French movement could have had somebody like Blum or Mandel for its leader it would probably have had a coherent political programme. Nothing is stranger in this book than the author's vagueness about the future of France. Writing, apparently, while the Tunisian campaign was still happening he does show uneasiness over the deal with Darlan, but he gives no clear indication of what General de Gaulle's policy is or what he aims at doing when France is liberated.

Nor does he say anything about the General's political past. All we are told is that France must first be made free and then must be made strong—immensely strong: there is tremendous emphasis on the powerful mechanised forces, the fleets of aeroplanes and tanks, that France must and will have, and on the folly of preparing for peace in a world where war is the rule. (To quote the author, "Force alone can prevail against force. The sword must decide. The fate of France has always depended on the issue of combats.") And beyond that, the life of France is henceforth to be organised on "Christian principles," whatever those may be. So far as one can gather from this book, at any rate, De Gaulle's programme boils down to religion and tanks. And that is not an encouraging prospect. There have been so many leaders, from 1870 onwards, who have wanted to regenerate France by means of Christian principles and a big army.

The jacket of this book, bearing the photographs of General de Gaulle and a 50-ton tank, indicates its general tone.

Even the title of this book, *A Giant in the Age of Steel*, is not a good symptom at a time when humanity is suffering from too much steel and too many giants. Giants stamping on pygmies is the characteristic pattern of our age. It would be nice to catch a glimpse of a few ordinary-sized human beings again.

[Fee: £8.8.0; 3.5.44]

1. Orwell's reviews in the *Manchester Evening News* usually appeared on Thursdays, although there are a few exceptions. This review appeared on a Friday. On the previous day, where Orwell's review would have appeared (page 2, next to the leader column) was an article by J. H. Newsom, 'Bread and Butter for the Teacher.' A notice within a ruled box stated that Orwell's 'Life, People and Books' would appear on the following day. John Newsom (1910–1971, Kt., 1964) was County Education Officer for Hertfordshire, 1940–57.
2. Some of Orwell's contributions to the *Manchester Evening News* have very short paragraphs. These are probably a sub-editor's work. See, for example, *2572, n. 1, 2608, 2615*, and *2632*, and also headnote to *81*.

2464. Review of *This Changing World*, edited by J. R. M. Brumwell; *On Living in a Revolution* by Julian Huxley; *Reshaping Man's Heritage* by Various Authors

The Observer, 7 May 1944

We may be sure that when Noah was building the Ark someone was writing a book called THIS CHANGING WORLD, and though the manuscript will have perished in the Deluge it is possible to make a good guess at what it was like. It pointed with approval to recent scientific discoveries, denounced superstition and obscurantism, urged the need for radical educational reform and greater equality of the sexes, and probably had a chapter on the meaning of modern poetry. Its central thesis was that nothing is permanent but that everything is all for the best. The phrases "this is an age of transition" and "we live amid rapid and startling changes" occurred on almost every page, and perhaps the author remembered them with a certain bitterness as he went bubbling down into the dark waters.

The book now edited by Mr. Brumwell conforms to much the same pattern. In an introductory chapter Mr. Herbert Read notes that this is a changing world, and at the end, summing up the conclusions of the other contributors, he adds that the world is changing. In between are essays by C. H. Waddington, Karl Mannheim, J. D. Bernal, Franz Borkenau, Thomas Balogh, John Macmurray, Lewis Mumford, and others.[1] Of course, this list is a sufficient guarantee of the book's readability, at any rate in places, but it is astonishing how few of the contributors give the impression of writing about the actual world in which we are now living. Only Mr. Balogh, who insists on the impossibility of internal reforms while the world as a whole remains chaotic, and Dr. Borkenau, who traces the connection between democracy and totalitarianism, seem to have their feet anywhere near the ground. From very few of the others would you gather that the actual existence of civilisation is in danger.

Professor Bernal, for instance, writes on recent developments in science and the necessity for making the general public more scientific in outlook. He does not seem to see, or at least does not mention, that science itself is threatened by the world-wide trend towards dictatorship. Mr. Lewis Mumford does see this danger, but appears to think that it will right itself of its own accord. Dr. Darlington has some stimulating ideas on education, but hardly faces up to the question, "education by whom and for what?" Mr. John Summerson defends glass and concrete against "traditional" architecture. Dr. Macmurray thinks that the Christian religion will survive, but that in order to do so, it will have to change: unfortunately, he omits to say in what way it will change and what its new doctrines will be, if any. Miss Kathleen Raine weighs in with an essay on contemporary literature and supplies a list of thirty-five outstanding modern writers in which she includes herself while leaving out Shaw, Wells, Dreiser, Belloc, Pound, Koestler, and a few dozen others.

As you look at this book, with its vaguely modernistic jacket, its shiny photographs, its perky but inaccurate bibliography, and its general air of complacent progressiveness, it is hard to remember the atrocious reversal of history that is actually going on. The mass slaughter that has been happening for the past ten or fifteen years does not perhaps matter very much. All it means is that we happen to possess better weapons than our ancestors. The truly sinister phenomena of our time are the atomisation of the world, the increasing power of nationalism, the worship of leaders who are credited with divine powers, the crushing not only of freedom of thought but of the concept of objective truth, and the tendency towards oligarchical rule based on forced labour. That is the direction in which the world is changing, and it is the failure to discuss these subjects that makes it hard to take this book seriously.

Two other books which were probably in preparation when the waters of the Flood were gathering were ON LIVING IN A REVOLUTION and RE-SHAPING MAN'S HERITAGE. It should hardly be necessary to say in detail what the principal essay in Professor Huxley's book is about, since most of us have heard it rather often already. The "revolution" is the transition to a centralised economy, and Professor Huxley hopes that we shall achieve it democratically. Unfortunately, he does not explain with any precision how we are to set about this, and it is evident that, like the contributors to THIS CHANGING WORLD, he has not reckoned—perhaps is frightened to reckon—with the terrible power of the psychological forces now working against democracy, against rationalism, and against the individual. However, the book contains a good essay debunking racialism, and others on animal pests and Hebridean birds, subjects which are near to Professor Huxley's own heart, and on which he is eminently readable.

RESHAPING MAN'S HERITAGE is a collection of reprinted broadcasts by H. G. Wells, J. B. S. Haldane, J. C. Drummond, and others, and is concerned partly with food and agriculture, partly with medicine. There is a good talk on anaesthetics by L. J. Witts, and some useful information about rats by James Fisher. But the book as a whole has the sort of timid chirpiness that books of collected broadcasts seldom avoid.

[Fee: £7.7.0; 2.5.44]

1. A remarkable number of those mentioned in this review are featured in arrangements for broadcasts to India when Orwell was at the BBC, most of them directly with him: Read, Waddington, Bernal, Darlington, Macmurray, Haldane, Drummond—and, if tenuously, Fisher.

2465. To Charles Hamblett

8 May 1944   Typewritten

Tribune

Dear Mr. Hamblett,[1]
Following on the letter I've just sent, how about reviewing this? (It's ghastly tripe for the most part). I should think 800 words?

Yours sincerely,
[Signed] Geo. Orwell
George Orwell
Literary Editor.

'42 to '44 — Secker & Warburg[2]

1. Charles Hamblett (1919–), journalist, served in the RAF, 1939–42. He was on the editorial staff of the *Daily Herald*, 1944–45, and from 1946 was staff feature writer for *Illustrated*.
2. *'42 to '44: A Contemporary Memoir upon Human Behaviour During the Crisis of the World Revolution* by H. G. Wells. Hamblett's review was published in *Tribune* on 28 July 1944. Orwell reviewed Wells's book, in *The Observer*, 21 May 1944; see *2474*. The review by Michael Foot in the *Manchester Evening News* on 10 May 1944 was followed by a letter

complaining of the prohibitive cost of Wells's book; hence Orwell's article in the *Manchester Evening News*, 1 June 1944; see *2482*.

2466. To Leonard Moore

9 May 1944   Handwritten

10a Mortimer Crescent NW.6

Dear Mr Moore,

I have just seen Cape who is willing to publish "Animal Farm", so that is all right. I referred him to you for details of my existing contract with Gollancz. I don't really remember how it stands. Cape wants me to come to them, which I would be willing to do as I am fed up with this everlasting political business with Gollancz. Anyway, *if* Cape makes it a condition of publishing "Animal Farm" that I give them my future books, please close with that. I particularly want this book published on political grounds. But try in return to get Cape to agree to publish the book reasonably soon. As to the next projected book, ie. the reprinted pieces, I suppose it will not be difficult to arrange about that. I have 3 more essays contracted for, but these should all be done by the end of July, & then we can make the book up.

Yours sincerely
Eric Blair

P.S. I asked my friends on the "Partisan Review" to have a look at the MS. of "Animal Farm" & see what publisher would do if the Dial won't take it. I fancy if it's published here by a reputable publisher like Cape that would help it.

2467. 'As I Please,' 24

Tribune, 12 May 1944

Reading recently a batch of rather shallowly optimistic "progressive" books, I was struck by the automatic way in which people go on repeating certain phrases which were fashionable before 1914. Two great favourites are "the abolition of distance" and "the disappearance of frontiers." I do not know how often I have met with the statements that "the aeroplane and the radio have abolished distance" and "all parts of the world are now inter-dependent."

Actually, the effect of modern inventions has been to increase nationalism, to make travel enormously more difficult, to cut down the means of communication between one country and another, and to make the various parts of the world *less*, not more dependent on one another for food and manufactured goods. This is not the result of the war. The same tendencies had been at work ever since 1918, though they were intensified after the World Depression.

Take simply the instance of travel. In the nineteenth century some parts of the world were unexplored, but there was almost no restriction on travel. Up to 1914 you did not need a passport for any country except Russia. The European emigrant, if he could scrape together a few pounds for the passage, simply set sail for America or Australia, and when he got there no questions were asked. In the eighteenth century it had been quite normal and safe to travel in a country with which your own country was at war.

In our own time, however, travel has been becoming steadily more difficult. It is worth listing the parts of the world which were already inaccessible before the war started.

First of all, the whole of central Asia. Except perhaps for a very few tried Communists, no foreigner has entered Soviet Asia for many years past. Tibet, thanks to Anglo-Russian jealousy, has been a closed country since about 1912. Sinkiang, theoretically part of China, was equally un-get-atable. Then the whole of the Japanese Empire, except Japan itself, was practically barred to foreigners. Even India has been none too accessible since 1918. Passports were often refused even to British subjects—sometimes even to Indians!

Even in Europe the limits of travel were constantly narrowing. Except for a short visit it was very difficult to enter Britain, as many a wretched anti-Fascist refugee discovered. Visas for the U.S.S.R. were issued very grudgingly from about 1935 onwards. All the Fascist countries were barred to anyone with a known anti-Fascist record. Various areas could only be crossed if you undertook not to get out of the train. And along all the frontiers were barbed wire, machine-guns and prowling sentries, frequently wearing gasmasks.

As to migration, it had practically dried up since the nineteen-twenties. All the countries of the New World did their best to keep the immigrant out unless he brought considerable sums of money with him. Japanese and Chinese immigration into the Americas had been completely stopped. Europe's Jews had to stay and be slaughtered because there was nowhere for them to go, whereas in the case of the Czarist pogroms forty years earlier they had been able to flee in all directions. How, in the face of all this, anyone can say that modern methods of travel promote intercommunication between different countries, defeats me.

Intellectual contacts have also been diminishing for a long time past. It is nonsense to say that the radio puts people in touch with foreign countries. If anything, it does the opposite. No ordinary person ever listens in to a foreign radio; but if in any country large numbers of people show signs of doing so, the government prevents it either by ferocious penalties, or by confiscating short-wave sets, or by setting up jamming stations. The result is that each national radio is a sort of totalitarian world of its own, braying propaganda night and day to people who can listen to nothing else. Meanwhile, literature grows less and less international. Most totalitarian countries bar foreign newspapers and let in only a small number of foreign books, which they subject to careful censorship and sometimes issue in garbled versions. Letters going from one country to another are habitually tampered with on the way. And in many countries, over the past dozen years, history books have been rewritten in far more nationalistic terms than before, so that children may grow up with as false a picture as possible of the world outside.

The trend towards economic self-sufficiency ("autarchy") which has been going on since about 1930 and has been intensified by the war, may or may not be reversible. The industrialisation of countries like India and South America increases their purchasing power and therefore ought, in theory, to help world trade. But what is not grasped by those who say cheerfully that "all parts of the world are interdependent," is that they don't any longer *have* to be interdependent. In an age when wool can be made out of milk and rubber out of oil, when wheat can be grown almost on the Arctic Circle, when atebrin will do instead of quinine and Vit C tablets are a tolerable substitute for fruit, imports don't matter very greatly. Any big area can seal itself off much more completely than in the days when Napoleon's Grand Army, in spite of the embargo, marched to Moscow wearing British overcoats. So long as the world tendency is towards nationalism and totalitarianism, scientific progress simply helps it along.

Here are some current prices.

Small Swiss-made alarm clock, price before the war, 5s. or 10s.: present price, £3 15s. Second-hand portable typewriter, price before the war, £12 new: present price, £30. Small, very bad-quality coconut fibre scrubbing-brush, price before the war, 3d.: present price, 1s. 9d. Gas lighter, price before the war, about a 1s.: present price, 5s. 9d.

I could quote other similar prices. It is worth noticing that, for instance, the clock mentioned above must have been manufactured before the war at the old price. But, on the whole, the worst racket seems to be in second-hand goods—for instance, chairs, tables, clothes, watches, prams, bicycles and bed linen. On enquiry, I find that there is now a law against overcharging on second-hand goods. This comforts me a great deal just as it must comfort the 18 B'ers to hear about Habeas Corpus,[1] or Indian coolies to learn that all British subjects are equal before the law.

In Hooper's *Campaign of Sedan* there is an account of the interview in which General de Wympffen tried to obtain the best possible terms for the defeated French army. "It is to your interest," he said, "from a political standpoint, to grant us honourable conditions . . . A peace based on conditions which would flatter the *amour-propre* of the Army would be durable, whereas rigorous measures would awaken bad passions, and, perhaps, bring on an endless war between France and Prussia."

Here Bismarck, the Iron Chancellor, chipped in, and his words are recorded from his memoirs:

> "I said to him," he writes, "that we might build on the gratitude of a prince, but certainly not on the gratitude of a people—least of all on the gratitude of the French. That in France neither institutions nor circumstances were enduring; that governments and dynasties were constantly changing, and one need not carry out what the other had bound itself to do. . . . As things stood it would be folly if we did not make full use of our success."

The modern cult of "realism" is generally held to have started with Bismarck. That imbecile speech was considered magnificently "realistic" then, and so it would be now. Yet what Wympffen said, though he was only trying to bargain for terms, was perfectly true. If the Germans had behaved with ordinary generosity (ie. by the standards of the time) it might have been impossible to whip up the revanchiste spirit in France. What would Bismarck have said if he had been told that harsh terms now would mean a terrible defeat forty-eight years later? There is not much doubt of the answer: he would have said that the terms ought to have been harsher still. Such is "realism"—and on the same principle, when the medicine makes the patient sick, the doctor responds by doubling the dose.

J. F. Horrabin, cartoonist and cartographer, who had broadcast to India under Orwell's aegis, in 1942, out of which had developed the concept of 'The War of the Three Oceans,' took up Orwell's attack on 'shallowly optimistic progressive' authors in *Tribune*, 19 May 1944, and Orwell responded. Horrabin wrote:

As one of those "shallowly optimistic progressive" authors who has at various times enlarged upon such themes as the abolition of distance by modern inventions, the increasing interdependence of the present-day world, etc., etc., I naturally studied George Orwell's reflections on this subject with especial attention. But I am bound to say that I did not find his de-bunking of us shallow optimists particularly convincing—or very deep.

I fancy that most of us were quite well aware of all those not-so-cheerful aspects of the modern world over which he licks wry lips—the intensification of nationalism, the obstacles to travel, the limitation of the means of inter-national communication, and the attempts at autarchy on the part of various nations. Nobody, indeed, but a blind man could remain unconscious of such glaringly apparent facts.

But to assert, as Orwell does, that they are all "actually the effect of modern inventions" is, if I may be blunt, to talk shallow and petulant nonsense. They are, as every Socialist schoolboy knows, the result of determined efforts on the part of the social forces of reaction and privilege to put back the clock , and at all costs to retard tendencies which threaten the stability of their Old World Order.

No intelligent Socialist has ever talked or written about the disappearance of frontiers as if this was an already accomplished fact. What Socialists have stressed—and clearly must go on stressing—is that, in the world of today frontiers are, economically speaking, anachronisms; and that a fuller life for the mass of common men everywhere is only possible when, as economic barriers, frontiers are abolished.

I cannot believe that Orwell is not perfectly well aware of all this; and though I'm sure that constant re-examination and re-discussion of commonly accepted truths is desirable, lest they degenerate into mere clichés, I still think it a pity that a writer in a Socialist journal should deliberately make confusion worse confounded by substituting mere contradictoriness for argument. I seem to remember that, some years ago, Mr. St. John Ervine made a certain reputation for himself in a weekly column by precisely this method. But we have all to school ourselves to do without some of the little luxuries of the between-war world.

[*George Orwell answers*:]

Is Mr. Horrabin really certain that the obstacles to travel, international communication, etc., were caused solely by the "forces of reaction and privilege"? Before the war the country that guarded its national frontiers the most jealously of all was the U.S.S.R. Was this really due to "reaction and privilege"? The next most exclusive was probably Japan. Was Japan in any technical sense trying to "put back the clock"?

Scientific discovery, so long as it is misused, (a) makes weapons of war so destructive that actual national survival has to be a primary consideration: and (b) makes possible an interference with the individual that was quite unthinkable in previous ages. Am I not justified, therefore, in saying that every scientific advance speeds up the trend towards nationalism and dictatorship which is now going on? Let Mr. Horrabin look back at the prophecies which were being made of H. G. Wells and similar thinkers round about 1920, and see how many have been fulfilled.

1. The Habeus Corpus Act, 1679, was designed, among other things to stop people from being imprisoned on grounds of suspicion alone. The Emergency Powers (Defence) Acts enabled many regulations to be brought into force restricting peace-time rights. Thus, Regulation 18 gave the Home Secretary power to control the entry of British subjects into the UK and to forbid their leaving. Regulation 18B enabled aliens to be imprisoned on grounds that they might aid and comfort the enemy. The bitter irony of this was that large numbers of those imprisoned (often in internment camps on the Isle of Man) were those (such as Jews) fleeing persecution in Germany. The acts expired in February 1946, but various transitional acts were passed (against which the Freedom Defence Committee campaigned). However, 18B was abolished.

2468. Review of *Empire* by Louis Fischer

The Nation (New York), 13 May 1944

Imperialism means India, and in so short and "popular" a book Mr. Fischer is quite right to ignore the more complex colonial problems that exist in Africa and the Pacific. He is not trying to stimulate anti-British prejudice, and the uninformed reader would come away from this book with a true general picture as well as some quotable facts and figures.

As he perceives, the uninformed reader is the one most worth aiming at. No enlightened person needs any longer to be told that imperialism is an evil. The point Mr. Fischer is at pains to make clear is that it not only breeds war but impoverishes the world as a whole by preventing the development of backward areas. The "owner" of a colony usually does its best to exclude foreign trade; it strangles local industries—the British, to take only one instance, have deliberately prevented the growth of an automobile industry in India; and in self-protection it not only goes on the principle of "divide and rule" but more or less consciously fosters ignorance and superstition. In the long run it is not to the advantage, even in crude cash terms, of the ordinary Briton or American that India should remain in the Middle Ages; and the common people of both countries ought to realize this, for they are the only ones who are likely to do anything about it. No one in his senses imagines that the British ruling class will relinquish India voluntarily. The only hope lies in British and American public opinion, which at the time of the Cripps mission, for instance, could have forced a more generous offer upon the British government if it had understood the issues.

At the same time Mr. Fischer does oversimplify the Indian problem, even in terms of the very general picture that he is trying to give. To begin with, he does not say often enough or emphatically enough that India has no chance of freedom until some sort of international authority is established. In a world of national sovereignties and power politics it is improbable that even a British government of the left would willingly grant genuine independence to India. To do so would simply be to hand India over to some other power, which from either a selfish or an altruistic point of view is no solution. Secondly, in his anxiety to sound reasonable Mr. Fischer overplays the economic motive. It is not certain that increased prosperity for India would benefit the rest of the world *immediately*. Just suppose, he says, that 400,000,000 Indians all took to wearing shoes. Would not that mean a wonderful market for British and American shoe manufacturers? The Indians, however, might prefer to make their shoes for themselves, and as the Indian capitalist's idea of a living wage is two cents an hour, the effect of Indian competition on the Western standard of living might be disastrous. At present the West as a whole is exploiting Asia as a whole, and to right the balance may mean considerable sacrifices over a number of years. It is better to warn people of this and not lead them to imagine that honesty always pays in the financial sense.

The direct, assessable money profit that Britain draws from India is not enormous. If one divided it up amongst the British population it would only amount to a few pounds a year. But as Mr. Fischer rightly emphasizes, it is not divided among the population; it flows into the pockets of a few thousand persons who also control government policy and incidentally own all the newspapers. Up to date these people have been uniformly successful in keeping the truth about India from the British public. To enlighten the American public may perhaps be a little easier, since American interests are not so directly involved, and Mr. Fischer's book is not bad as a start. But he ought to supplement it by warning his readers of the difficult transition period that lies ahead, and also of the sinister forces, political and economic, that exist within India itself.

[Fee: £2.10.0; 15.4.44]

2469. To W. F. Stirling, Latin American Department, BBC

16 May 1944   Typewritten original

On 3 May 1944, W. F. Stirling asked Orwell to write a script for the Latin American Service of the BBC of some 1,400 words on political theories and European literature showing how modern political ideologies had had a direct effect on contemporary literature. The script was required by 21 June. It would then be translated, recorded, and broadcast a few days later. No fee was mentioned in the letter. Orwell replied:

Tribune

Dear Mr. Stirling,
All right, I'll let you have the article (1400 words) by June 21st.

Yours sincerely,
[Signed] Geo. Orwell
George Orwell.

2470. Review of *Parnell* by St. John Ervine

Manchester Evening News, 18 May 1944

Nationalist movements, especially those with a romantic colour to them, tend to be led by foreigners. There is probably a number of reasons for this, but a good and sufficient one is that it is difficult to idealise a country or a people that you know too much about.

Mr. St. John Ervine, himself an Ulsterman and no friend of the Southern Irish, perhaps overemphasises the part played by Englishmen and Scotsmen in Irish politics, but he does show that Parnell, the most gifted leader Ireland ever had, belonged both racially and culturally to the "English garrison" and had barely a drop of "native" Irish blood in his veins.

Almost everyone has heard of the tragic and sordid incident that brought Parnell's career to an end. Indeed it is difficult to remember his name without simultaneously remembering the names of Gladstone and Mrs. O'Shea. But the significant part of Parnell's short life was the fifteen years of feverish political activity in which he managed to give the Irish Nationalist movement a force and a unity it had never had before.

His personal disaster, and the cruelty and meanness with which his countrymen treated him, are bad enough to read about, but Mr. St. John Ervine rightly lays more stress on the wrecking of the Home Rule Bill and the long chain of evil consequences that has flowed out of it.

Parnell came of a family of Anglo-Irish landowners, and though he was not the eldest son he inherited a respectable fortune.

He was educated partly in England, spoke with an English accent, and was, of course, a Protestant. With his aristocratic background he had a considerable contempt for [the] rank and file of the Home Rule party, and it is recorded that in his youth, when out-at elbow Fenians came to sponge upon his mother, he sometimes kicked them down the front steps. But he had an implacable, lifelong hatred for England. It was not simply political opposition. He hated the English people, and could hardly stomach the idea of receiving English support; especially as the chief supporters of Home Rule were the Nonconformists, who, from Parnell's point of view, were "not gentlemen."

His actions were nearly always rational and extremely intelligent, but they sprang from subjective feelings which seem sometimes to have approached insanity. His mother, who was of American extraction, had the same insensate hatred of England (she made a special exception of the Queen, however) and infected all her children with it from their earliest years onward.

Parnell entered Parliament before he was 30 and within five years was the accepted leader of the Irish Parliamentary party. A few more years and he was known everywhere as "the uncrowned king of Ireland."

He had not only, by his skilful tactics, made the Parliamentary party into a force that even Gladstone feared, but he had won over all shades of Nationalist feeling to his side. Even the Fenians, who professed to despise constitutional methods, were ready to follow him, although he utterly refused to countenance violence.

By the late eighties it appeared almost certain that Home Rule would pass through Parliament. Gladstone seemed pledged to it. English Liberal opinion was coming round to it. And then there occurred an incident that strengthened Parnell's position all the more.

Some years earlier two members of the Government, Lord Frederick Cavendish and Thomas Henry Burke, had been murdered in Dublin by a gang who called themselves The Invincibles. The "Times" began publishing a series of articles which hinted that Parnell had some connection with the murder, and finally published a facsimile of a letter, seemingly signed by Parnell, and frankly approving of what had been done.

The letter was a forgery, and was easily exposed as such. Naturally this incident, which had an immense amount of publicity, increased Parnell's popularity and discredited the Conservatives, who had rashly accused him of conniving at murder.

Then suddenly everything crashed to the ground. Captain O'Shea, another Irish member, and a man of very doubtful character, filed a divorce suit, naming Parnell as co-respondent. Mrs. O'Shea had, in fact, been Parnell's mistress for nearly ten years.

She was unhappily married. He regarded her almost as his wife. And he did marry her when the divorce case was over. When the scandal broke English Nonconformist opinion swung against Parnell, his own party split, the majority demanding that he should resign from the chairmanship, and Gladstone refused to back him up.

The whole thing was a disgusting orgy of hypocrisy, English and Irish, for Parnell's association with Mrs. O'Shea had been widely known beforehand. Parnell refused to resign, and held meetings all over Ireland, but he had the priests against him, and his candidates were defeated in several by-elections.

For the time being the Nationalist movement was split into fragments.

Parnell could no doubt have united it again if he had lived long enough for the scandal to blow over, but he wore out his frail physique with electioneering, and died within a year.

A hundred and fifty thousand people followed his body to the grave, but Home Rule was a lost cause.

English rule in Ireland lasted another 30 years petering out in a civil war and a treaty which satisfied neither side.

There are passages in this book that any Irish Nationalist would object to—Mr. St. John Ervine is too free with his generalisations about "Celts," and he assumes without argument that De Valera's Government is the greatest calamity Ireland has ever known—but it is probably a reliable biography of Parnell, besides being extremely readable.

Mr. St. John Ervine tries to be fair to all the chief actors in the story, including the wretched Captain O'Shea, whose motives he probably interprets a good deal too generously. He began the book, he says, with a feeling of prejudice against Parnell, and ended it with a deep affection for him. He will awaken the same affection in most of his readers, though there is much in Parnell's career, especially the real reason for his hatred of England, that remains mysterious.

[Fee: £8.8.0; 17.5.44]

2470A. To Arthur Koestler, 18 May 1944: see Vol xx, last appendix.

2471. To Noel Willmett
       18 May 1944   Typewritten

10a Mortimer Crescent
London NW 6

Dear Mr Willmett,[1]
Many thanks for your letter. You ask whether totalitarianism, leader-worship etc. are really on the up-grade and instance the fact that they are not apparently growing in this country and the USA.

I must say I believe, or fear, that taking the world as a whole these things are on the increase. Hitler, no doubt, will soon disappear, but only at the expense of strengthening (a) Stalin, (b) the Anglo-American millionaires and (c) all sorts of petty fuhrers° of the type of de Gaulle. All the national movements everywhere, even those that originate in resistance to German domination, seem to take non-democratic forms, to group themselves round some superhuman fuhrer (Hitler, Stalin, Salazar, Franco, Gandhi, De Valera are all varying examples) and to adopt the theory that the end justifies the means. Everywhere the world movement seems to be in the direction of centralised economies which can be made to "work" in an economic sense but which are not democratically organised and which tend to establish a caste system. With this go the horrors of emotional nationalism and a tendency to disbelieve in the existence of objective truth because all the facts have to fit in with the words and prophecies of some infallible fuhrer. Already history has in a sense ceased to exist, ie. there is no such thing as a history of our own times which could be universally accepted, and the exact sciences are endangered as soon as military necessity ceases to keep people up to the mark. Hitler can say that the Jews started the war, and if he survives that will become official history. He can't say that two and two are five, because for the purposes of, say, ballistics they have to make four. But if the sort of world that I am afraid of arrives, a world of two or three great superstates which are unable to conquer one another, two and two could become five if the fuhrer wished it.[2] That, so far as I can see, is the direction in which we are actually moving, though, of course, the process is reversible.

As to the comparative immunity of Britain and the USA. Whatever the pacifists etc. may say, we have *not* gone totalitarian yet and this is a very hopeful symptom. I believe very deeply, as I explained in my book "The Lion and the Unicorn", in the English *people* and in their capacity to centralise their economy without destroying freedom in doing so. But one must remember that Britain and the USA haven't been really tried, they haven't known defeat or severe suffering, and there are some bad symptoms to balance the good ones. To begin with there is the general indifference to the decay of democracy. Do you realise, for instance, that no one in England under 26 now has a vote and that so far as one can see the great mass of people of that age don't give a damn for this? Secondly there is the fact that the intellectuals are more totalitarian in outlook than the common people. On the whole the English intelligentsia have opposed Hitler, but only at the price of accepting Stalin. Most of them are perfectly ready for dictatorial methods, secret police, systematic falsification of history[3] etc. so long as they feel that it is on "our" side. Indeed the statement that we haven't a Fascist movement in England largely means that the young, at this moment, look for their fuhrer elsewhere. One can't be sure that that won't change, nor can one be sure that the common people won't think ten years hence as the intellectuals do now. I *hope* they won't, I even trust they won't, but if so it will be at the cost of a struggle.[4] If one simply proclaims that all is for the best and doesn't point to the sinister symptoms, one is merely helping to bring totalitarianism nearer.

You also ask, if I think the world tendency is towards Fascism, why do I support the war. It is a choice of evils—I fancy nearly every war is that. I know enough of British imperialism not to like it, but I would support it against Nazism or Japanese imperialism, as the lesser evil. Similarly I would support the USSR against Germany because I think the USSR cannot altogether escape its past and retains enough of the original ideas of the Revolution to make it a more hopeful phenomenon than Nazi Germany. I think, and have thought ever since the war began, in 1936 or thereabouts, that our cause is the better, but we have to keep on making it the better, which involves constant criticism.

Yours sincerely,
[Signed] Geo. Orwell
George Orwell

1. In October 1972, Noel Willmett wrote from Cricklewood, London, to Bernard Crick describing the provenance of Orwell's letter. He is otherwise unidentified. Willmett was originally given the initials 'H. J.', possibly by association with the journalist H. J. Willmott, then working on a Cornish newspaper. Crick discusses the letter, 447–48. The letter has associations with *Nineteen Eighty-Four*; see *ns*. 2, 3, 4 below.
2. For Winston Smith's seeing four fingers as five at O'Brien's insistence, see *Nineteen Eighty-Four*, *CW*, IX, 270.
3. For Winston Smith's work on the falsification of history, see especially Part One, Section iv of *Nineteen Eighty-Four*, *CW*, IX, 40 ff.
4. '*If there is hope*, wrote Winston, *it lies in the proles*,' *Nineteen Eighty-Four*, *CW*, IX, 72, and elsewhere.

2472. William Lynch to *Tribune*

19 May 1944

William Lynch of Sacriston (a place-name the writer thought especially significant in the context of his letter, printing it in large capitals and underlining it), a small town about three miles north-west of the city of Durham, wrote to the Editors of *Tribune* on 19 May 1944. They did not print his letter, and it found its way to Orwell. The writer had been a collier for forty-three years, starting work when he was twelve; he had been unemployed for ten years and an old-age pensioner for nine. He was, therefore, seventy-four. He was a Roman Catholic and wrote about what he took to be *Tribune*'s policy and on matters of the day, all from a narrow, but passionate, Roman Catholic point of view. He was contemptuous of *Tribune*, relieved that, in his town of 8,000 people, there was only one copy to be found (in the local Miners' [Institute]), and he fiercely attacked its attitude. Although the letter is confused and often wildly off the mark (*Tribune* and the *Daily Worker* are seen as identical in attitude), and although it is written from a point of view with which Orwell would have had particularly little sympathy, it may have touched him at a number of points. The very unsophistication of the writer carried conviction.

Mr. Lynch condemned *Tribune* for its attitude to Franco, seeing him as 'a devout member of God's Holy Roman Catholic Church' and all who opposed him as Red Devils, sent by Stalin, 'the Soviet Antichrist.' But he then went on to contrast the way Franco had been called a criminal for using Moorish troops whilst Britain had been prepared to use Indians, the French Senegalese, and the Americans their blacks. He also contrasted Hitler's seizure of Belgium, Holland, and France with Stalin's incorporation of Lithuania, Estonia, and Poland. Why was the former condemned, he asked, but the latter silently passed over? From his experience as a miner, he argued that Ernest Bevin's scheme to recruit young men without a mining background to dig coal was doomed to failure: 30,000 Bevin Boys—'square pegs in round holes'—'will not add *50 tons* to the total output.'[1] Finally, he suggested to the Editors of *Tribune* that were they to go and live in the Utopia of Stalin's Russia, they would find it a Hell on Earth.

1. Mr. Lynch exaggerated, of course, but there was more than a germ of truth in what he said; see *2454, n. 2*. The British Bevin Boys should be distinguished from those similarly named from India; the latter were technical trainees; see *949, n. 2*.

2473. 'As I Please,' 25

Tribune, 19 May 1944

Miss Vera Brittain's[1] pamphlet, *Seed of Chaos*, is an eloquent attack on indiscriminate or "obliteration" bombing. "Owing to the R.A.F. raids," she says, "thousands of helpless and innocent people in German, Italian and German-occupied cities are being subjected to agonising forms of death and injury comparable to the worst tortures of the Middle Ages." Various well-known opponents of bombing, such as General Franco and Major-General Fuller, are brought out in support of this. Miss Brittain is not, however, taking the pacifist standpoint. She is willing and anxious to win the war, apparently. She merely wishes us to stick to "legitimate" methods of war and abandon civilian bombing, which she fears will blacken our reputation in the eyes of posterity. Her pamphlet is issued by the Bombing Restriction Committee, which has issued others with similar titles.

Now, no one in his senses regards bombing, or any other operation of war, with anything but disgust. On the other hand, no decent person cares tuppence for the opinion of posterity. And there is something very distasteful in accepting war as an instrument and at the same time wanting to dodge responsibility for its more obviously barbarous features. Pacifism is a tenable position, provided that you are willing to take the consequences. But all talk of "limiting" or "humanising" war is sheer humbug, based on the fact that the average human being never bothers to examine catchwords.

The catchwords used in this connection are "killing civilians," "massacre of women and children" and "destruction of our cultural heritage." It is tacitly assumed that air bombing does more of this kind of thing than ground warfare.

When you look a bit closer, the first question that strikes you is: Why is it worse to kill civilians than soldiers? Obviously one must not kill children if it is in any way avoidable, but it is only in propaganda pamphlets that every bomb drops on a school or an orphanage. A bomb kills a cross-section of the population; but not quite a representative selection, because the children and expectant mothers are usually the first to be evacuated, and some of the young men will be away in the army. Probably a disproportionately large number of bomb victims will be middle aged. (Up to date, German bombs have killed between six and seven thousand children in this country. This is, I believe, less than the number killed in road accidents in the same period.) On the other hand, "normal" or "legitimate" warfare picks out and slaughters all the healthiest and bravest of the young male population. Every time a German submarine goes to the bottom about fifty young men of fine physique and good nerve are suffocated. Yet people who would hold up their hands at the very words "civilian bombing" will repeat with satisfaction such phrases as "We are winning the Battle of the Atlantic." Heaven knows how many people our blitz on Germany and the occupied countries has killed and will kill, but you can be quite certain it will never come anywhere near the slaughter that has happened on the Russian front.

War is not avoidable at this stage of history, and since it has to happen it does not seem to me a bad thing that others should be killed besides young men. I wrote in 1937: "Sometimes it is a comfort to me to think that the aeroplane is altering the conditions of war. Perhaps when the next great war comes we may see that sight unprecedented in all history, a jingo with a bullet hole in him." We haven't yet seen that (it is perhaps a contradiction in terms), but at any rate the suffering of this war has been shared out more evenly than that of the last one was. The immunity of the civilian, one of the things that have made war possible, has been shattered. Unlike Miss Brittain, I don't regret that. I can't feel that war is "humanised" by being confined to the slaughter of the young and becomes "barbarous" when the old get killed as well.

As to international agreements to "limit" war, they are never kept when it pays to break them. Long before the last war the nations had agreed not to use gas, but they used it all the same. This time they have refrained, merely because gas is comparatively ineffective in a war of movement, while its use against civilian populations would be sure to provoke reprisals in kind. Against an enemy who can't hit back, e.g., the Abyssinians, it is used readily enough. War is of its nature barbarous, it is better to admit that. If we see ourselves as the savages we are, some improvement is possible, or at least thinkable.

A SPECIMEN of *Tribune's* correspondence:
TO THE JEW-PAID EDITOR,
TRIBUNE,
LONDON.
JEWS IN THE POLISH ARMY
YOU ARE CONSTANTLY ATTACKING OUR GALLANT POLISH ALLY BE CAUSE THEY KNOW HOW TO TREAT THE JEW PEST. THEY ALSO KNOW HOW TO TREAT ALL JEW-PAID EDITORS AND COMMUNIST PAPERS. WE KNOW YOU ARE IN THE PAY OF THE YIDS AND SOVIETS.

YOU ARE A FRIEND OF THE ENEMIES OF BRITAIN. THE DAY OF RECKONING IS AT HAND. BEWARE. ALL JEW PIGS WILL BE EXTERMINATED THE HITLER WAY—THE ONLY WAY TO GET RID OF THE YIDS.
PERISH JUDAH.
Typed on a Remington typewriter (postmark S.W.), and, what is to my mind an interesting detail, this is a carbon copy.

Anyone acquainted with the type will know that no assurance, no demonstration, no proof of the most solid kind would ever convince the writer of this that *Tribune* is *not* a Communist paper and *not* in the pay of the Soviet Government. One very curious characteristic of Fascists—I am speaking of amateur Fascists: I assume that the Gestapo are cleverer—is their failure to recognise that the parties of the Left are distinct from one another and by no means aiming at the same thing. It is always assumed that they are all one gang, whatever the outward appearances may be. In the first number of Mosley's *British Union Quarterly*, which I have by me (incidentally, it contains an article by no less a person than Major Vidkun Quisling), I note that even Wyndham Lewis speaks of Stalin and Trotsky as though they were equivalent persons. Arnold Lunn, in his *Spanish Rehearsal*, actually seems to suggest that Trotsky started the Fourth International on Stalin's instructions.

In just the same way, very few Communists, in my experience, will believe that the Trotskyists are not in the pay of Hitler. I have sometimes tried the experiment of pointing out that if the Trotskyists were in the pay of Hitler, or of anybody, they would occasionally have some money. But it is no use, it doesn't register. So also with the belief in the machinations of the Jews, or the belief, widespread among Indian nationalists, that all Englishmen, of whatever political colour, are in secret conspiracy with one another. The belief in the Freemasons as a revolutionary organisation is the strangest of all. In this country it would be just as reasonable to believe such a thing of the Buffaloes.[1a] Less than a generation ago, if not now, there were Catholic nuns who believed that at Masonic gatherings the Devil appeared in person, wearing full evening dress with a hole in the trousers for his tail to come through. In one form or another this kind of thing seems to attack nearly everybody, apparently answering to some obscure psychological need of our time.

Brittain replied to Orwell in *Tribune* on 23 June 1944; Orwell's response followed.

In his comments on my booklet, *Seed of Chaos*, George Orwell seems to assume that if pacifists do not succeed in preventing a war, they must throw up the sponge and acquiesce in any excesses which warmakers choose to initiate. This alone can explain his strange supposition that, because I protest against "saturation" bombing, I am "willing and anxious" to win the war by "legitimate" methods.

It is true that when war comes the pacifist has admittedly failed for the time being in his main purpose, but that does not exonerate him from any attempt to mitigate war's worst excesses. On the contrary, his very failure to prevent war makes its excesses his direct responsibility, which he would be "dodging" indeed if he were to sit back self-righteously excusing himself from the difficult endeavour to restrain the growth of barbarousness in his own community.

If Mr. Orwell had read my book with any care, he would have realised that the death of civilians is not my main concern, though direct attack on civilians does constitute an abandonment of the standard laid down for international conduct by international law. My chief concern is with the moral deterioration to which a nation condemns itself by the unrestrained infliction of cruelty; and with the setback to European civilisation which obliteration bombing must cause in addition to blockade and invasion. The century which followed the Thirty Years' War showed that there are degrees of chaos and privation which civilised values cannot survive.

Mr. Orwell's statement that "all talk of 'humanising' war is sheer humbug" is simply unhistorical. Prof. A. L. Goodhart (*What Acts of War Are Justifiable*, pp. 4–6)[2] describes the improvement in international morality owing to the reaction initiated by Grotius[3] against the horrors of the Thirty Years' War, and continues: "Further progress was made during the eighteen century with the result that the unrestrained cruelty of former times was in large part absent from the Napoleonic Wars." Even in this war there are depths to which the combatants have not yet descended—such as a general massacre of all prisoners,[4] bacteriological warfare, and the use of poison gas. Though gas, as Mr. Orwell alleges, may be ineffective in a war of movement, certain American voices have already suggested its use against the Japanese invaders of Pacific Islands. The fact that these voices have not been heeded means that the U.S.A. has not yet abandoned itself to the advocates of unrestrained cruelty—of whom, somewhat oddly, George Orwell appears to be one.

Vera Brittain

[George Orwell writes:]
(a) Is Miss Brittain not anxious to win the war? Is she willing to end it promptly in the only way in which it could be ended promptly—i.e., by stopping fighting and leaving Hitler in control of Europe? And if so, why did she not say so in her pamphlet?

(b) I did not say that agreements to humanise war cannot be made. I said they are not kept when it pays to break them. So also with treaties, non-aggression pacts, etc. That is the existing standard of political morality, and pious outcries from pacifists, etc., will not alter this while the *structure* of society remains what it is. We must either build a good society or continue to do evil. The "peace" to which Miss Brittain wants to return is ultimately based on the truncheon and the machine-gun. As to war, you cannot at present avoid it, nor can you genuinely humanise it. You can only, like the pacifists, set up a moral alibi for yourself while continuing to accept the fruits of violence. I would sooner be Air-Marshal Harris[5] than Miss Brittain, because he at least knows what he is doing.

(c) Why is gas or bacterial warfare worse than the ordinary kind? Certainly the results of gas are horrible, but as Miss Brittain was a nurse in the last war she will know what a shell wound in the intestines is like.

Orwell discussed the correspondence arising from his reply in 'As I Please,' 33, 14 July 1944; see *2507*.

1. Vera Mary Brittain (1896–1970), novelist particularly remembered for her moving account of her experiences as a nurse in World War 1, *Testament of Youth* (1933), that led to her becoming a pacifist. She also wrote a history of women from Queen Victoria to Queen Elizabeth II, *Lady into Woman* (1953), was on the Board of Directors of *Peace News*, of which Middleton Murry was editor, in 1944 and, in 1946, a Vice-President of the National Peace Council.

1a. Royal Antediluvian Order of Buffaloes, founded 1822 for social and charitable activities. They are mentioned in *A Clergyman's Daughter*, Vol. III P. 35, line 8 up.

2 *What Acts of War Are Justifiable?* by A. L. Goodhard (1940). Goodhart (1891–1978; Hon. KBE, 1948), born in New York, served in the U.S. Army in World War I. He was at this time Professor of Jurisprudence in the University of Oxford and editor of the *Law Quarterly Review*. The conclusion to this pamphlet tends to concentrate upon the shortcomings of the Germans. In World War I, Germany's disregard of international law as recognised by 'the civilized nations . . . contributed materially to her ultimate defeat'; in the current war, the Nazis were found guilty of 'indiscriminate aerial bombardment and unrestricted submarine warfare' (32). Goodhart argues that the history of the laws of war goes back to the Middle

Ages (though he does not mention Augustine); that there was a setback owing to the horrors of the Thirty Years' War; this led to a new development: Grotius's *De Jure Belli ac Pacis* [On the Law of War and Peace] in 1625, which 'did much to advance this by his attempt to state the general principles in concrete form' (4). The words quoted by Vera Brittain follow immediately. The tenor of Goodhart's conclusion (quoted above) does not quite tally with Vera Brittain's 'Even in this war . . .'

3. Hugo Grotius (1583–1645), jurist and scholar, was sentenced to life imprisonment in 1618 for leading opposition to Prince Maurice of Nassau, but he escaped three years later, hidden in a box of books. He wrote *De Jure Belli ac Pacis* whilst in exile in Paris.

4. The Russians did massacre prisoners; see *2912, n. 1*. Miss Brittain would not have known this when she wrote because the Germans were blamed.

5. Arthur 'Bomber' Harris (1892–1984; Bt., 1953) pursued a practice of 'area' bombing of Germany when head of Bomber Command from 1942. This approach was controversial, for it led to many civilian casualties, and it is significant that he was offered no more than a baronetcy for his wartime labours. It is probably fair to say that to many British people at the time, especially those who had suffered in the Blitz, Harris's methods seemed justified. Retribution, rather than cold appraisal, proved more appealing. Some sense of how many ordinary people felt can be gauged from a letter sent by the entertainer Joyce Grenfell, to her American mother. Miss Grenfell was a kind and gentle woman and a devoted Christian Scientist, yet she could write on 17 November 1940: 'Not that hate or reprisals do any good— all the same I'd like to see every single German mown down and exterminated—every bloody one of them! So there. And I wouldn't be above a nice spot of prolonged torture for the top boys' (*Darling Ma. Letters to Her Mother, 1932–1944*). In 1992, almost fifty years after the events, and seemingly reluctantly (and still controversially), a statue was erected in London, opposite St. Clement Danes Church, honouring Harris.

2474. Review of *'42 to '44: A Contemporary Memoir upon Human Behaviour During the Crisis of the World Revolution* by H. G. Wells

The Observer, 21 May 1944

The chief difficulty of writing a book nowadays is that pots of paste are usually sold without brushes. But if you can get hold of a brush (sometimes procurable at Woolworth's), and a pair of scissors and a good-sized blank book, you have everything you need. It is not necessary to do any actual writing. Any collection of scraps—reprinted newspaper articles, private letters, fragments of diaries, even "radio discussions" ground out by wretched hacks to be broadcast by celebrities—can be sold to the amusement-starved public. And even the paper shortage can be neutralised by—as in this case—issuing your book in a limited edition and selling it at an artificial price.

This seems to be the principle that Mr. Wells has followed. His book has gilt edges, which costs the reader an extra thirty shillings, but its contents are simply a sprawl. Quite largely it consists of a series of attacks on people who have shown insufficient enthusiasm for the document which Mr. Wells calls the "Universal Rights of Man." Other attacks (on the Catholic Church, for instance, the War Office, the Admiralty, and the Communist Party) do not seem to be occasioned by anything but bad temper. But in so far as the book has a unifying principle, it is the by now familiar idea that mankind must either develop a World State or perish.

What is very striking is that except in certain books in which he invoked a miracle, Mr. Wells has never once suggested how the World State is to be brought into being. This is to say that he has never bothered to wonder who the actual rulers of the world are, how and why they are able to hold on to power, and by what means they are to be evicted. In formulating the "Rights of Man," he does not even drop a hint as to how such a document could be disseminated in, say, Russia or China. Hitler he dismisses as simply a lunatic: that settles Hitler. He does not seriously inquire *why* millions of people are ready to lay down their lives for a lunatic, and what this probably betokens for human society. And in between his threats that *homo sapiens* must mend his ways or be destroyed he continues to repeat the slogans of 1900 as though they were self-evident truths.

For instance, it is startling to be told in 1944 that "the world is now one." One might as well say that the world is now flat. The most obvious fact about the contemporary world is that it is *not* one, and is becoming less and less of a unit every year, physically as well as psychologically.

In spite of some momentary misgivings, Mr. Wells is not ready to admit that his declaration of the "Rights of Man" is a purely Western document. Almost any Indian, for instance, would reject it at a glance. (One gathers from some angry "asides" that a number of Indians have rejected it already.) What is more serious, he is not ready to admit that even among scientists and thinkers generally the intellectual basis for world unity does not exist. He has not seen the red light of phrases like "Aryan chess" and "capitalistic astronomy." He still talks of the need for a world encyclopaedia, ignoring the fact that there are whole branches of knowledge upon which no sort of agreement exists or is at present possible. As for the increase in human equality which Mr. Wells also considers imperatively necessary, there is no sign that that is happening either.

Intermittently, of course, Mr. Wells does realise all this, but only as a nurse notices the unaccountable naughtiness of a child. And his response is the same as the nurse's—"Now, you'll take your nice medicine or the bogey-man'll come and eat you up." *Homo sapiens* must do what he is told or he will become extinct. "Knowledge or extinction. There is no other chance for man," says Mr. Wells. It is, however, very unlikely that man will become extinct except through some unforeseeable cosmic disaster. He has about doubled his numbers in the last century and is still probably on the increase, and no competing species is in sight. The ants, Mr. Wells's favourites, can hardly be taken seriously. Nor is there any reason to think that man or even, in the technical sense, civilisation will be destroyed by war. Wars do a great deal of local destruction, but probably lead to a net increase in the world's industrial plant. The picture that Mr. Wells drew long ago in "The War in the Air," of the world being plunged back into the Dark Ages by a few tons of bombs has turned out to be completely false. The machine culture thrives on bombs. The danger seemingly ahead of us is *not* extinction: it is a slave civilisation which, so far from being chaotic, might be horribly stable.

It is perhaps unnecessary to add that incoherent and—in places—annoying though it is, this book contains brilliant and imaginative passages. One expects that of Mr. Wells. More than any other writer, perhaps, he has altered the landscape of the contemporary mind. Because of him the moon seems nearer and the Stone Age more imaginable, and for that we are immeasurably in his debt. So perhaps we can forgive a few scrappy books, even at forty-two shillings a time, from the author of "The Time Machine," "The Island of Dr. Moreau," "Love and Mr. Lewisham," and about a dozen others.[1]

[Fee: £7.7.0; 16.5.44]

1. In an interview with Ian Angus on 2 January 1967, Inez Holden said that Wells wrote to *The Observer* about this review—information she had from Wells's daughter-in-law, Margery Wells. The letter was not published, possibly because it referred to Inez Holden, which would have puzzled readers, Wells having convinced himself that she was in some way connected with the adverse review. An indirect result of the review was that Inez Holden had to give up the mews flat of Wells's house in Hanover Square, where she had lived for three years after being bombed out of her own home in Albany Street. If Orwell took Wells to task, Charles Hamblett, who reviewed the book for *Tribune* at Orwell's request (see *2465*) was fiercely blunt. He begins by proposing to 'blow the gaff about Mr. Wells' and goes on: 'In a pompous preface he explains the high price and limited circulation (2,000 copies) by referring to his book as his ultimate philosophy, "strong meat for babes," its contents a long and difficult journey. Rubbish. The journey is neither long nor difficult,' and in that vein Hamblett continues.

2475. Publication of *The English People*

The English People, published in 1947, was commissioned in September 1943 by W. J. Turner (see *1743, n. 1*), Collins's General Editor for the series Britain in Pictures and also at that time literary editor of *The Spectator*. Orwell evidently completed his text by 22 May 1944, because he entered it in his Payments Book against that date with the note, 'Payment to be made later.' It is therefore included here, though the text as published (and reproduced here) was subjected to later amendment (e.g. the 1945 election, p. 209) but precise details are not known.

In a letter to Leonard Moore of 23 June 1945 (see *2682*) asking him to chase Collins for payment, Orwell describes the book as 'a piece of propaganda for the British Council'—the idea for the series actually emanated from the Ministry of Information—and states that Collins had wanted him to make changes to his text but he had refused to do so. Orwell recorded in his Payments Book that he received an advance of £20 on 14 July 1945. He wrote to Moore, also on 14 July 1947, outlining the hesitant progress of the book's production—he had corrected the proofs a year ago—and asking him to find out what was happening; see *3248*. *The English People* was published the following month, with some references updated, since publication had been so long delayed, and with twenty-five illustrations, eight of which were full-page colour plates. These were selected by the publisher; W. J. Turner may have vetted the final selection. All were modern, two-thirds of them having been drawn or painted between 1940 and 1946 by artists including Edward Ardizzone, Dame Laura Knight, L. S. Lowry, Henry Moore, and Feliks Topolski. Although Orwell probably played no part in the selection, John Minton's 'Hop Picking near Maidstone, Kent,' 1945, might have been chosen with him in mind.

No typescript has survived. This text is reproduced from the first edition.

For an account of this series, see Michael Carney, *Britain in Pictures: A History and a Bibliography*, 1995 and, for brief details, *2278, n. 1*.

ENGLAND AT FIRST GLANCE

In peacetime, it is unusual for foreign visitors to this country to notice the existence of the English people. Even the accent referred to by Americans as "the English accent" is not in fact common to more than a quarter of the population. In cartoons in Continental papers England is personified by an aristocrat with a monocle, a sinister capitalist in a top hat, or a spinster in a Burberry. Hostile or friendly, nearly all the generalisations that are made about England base themselves on the property-owning class and ignore the other forty-five million.

But the chances of war brought to England, either as soldiers or as refugees, hundreds of thousands of foreigners who would not normally have come here, and forced them into intimate contact with ordinary people. Czechs, Poles, Germans and Frenchmen to whom "England" meant Piccadilly and the Derby found themselves quartered in sleepy East Anglian villages, in northern mining towns, or in the vast working-class areas of London whose names the world had never heard until they were blitzed. Those of them who had the gift of observation will have seen for themselves that the real England is not the England of the guide-books. Blackpool is more typical than Ascot, the top hat is a moth-eaten rarity, the language of the B.B.C. is barely intelligible to the masses. Even the prevailing physical type does not agree with the caricatures, for the tall, lanky physique which is traditionally English is almost confined to the upper classes: the working classes, as a rule, are rather small, with short limbs and brisk movements, and with a tendency among the women to grow dumpy in early middle life.

It is worth trying for a moment to put oneself in the position of a foreign observer, new to England, but unprejudiced, and able because of his work to keep in touch with ordinary, useful, unspectacular people. Some of his generalisations would be wrong, because he would not make enough allowance for the temporary dislocations resulting from war. Never having seen England in normal times, he might underrate the power of class distinctions, or think English agriculture healthier than it is, or be too much impressed by the dinginess of the London streets or the prevalence of drunkenness. But with his fresh eyes he would see a great deal that a native observer misses, and his probable impressions are worth tabulating. Almost certainly he would find the salient characteristics of the English common people to be artistic insensibility, gentleness, respect for legality, suspicion of foreigners, sentimentality about animals, hypocrisy, exaggerated class distinctions, and an obsession with sport.

As for our artistic insensibility, ever-growing stretches of beautiful countryside are ruined by planless building, the heavy industries are allowed to convert whole counties into blackened deserts, ancient monuments are wantonly pulled down or swamped by seas of yellow brick, attractive vistas are blocked by hideous statues to nonentities—and all this without any *popular* protest whatever. When England's housing problem is discussed, its æsthetic aspect simply does not enter the mind of the average man. Nor is there any widespread interest in any of the arts, except perhaps music. Poetry, the art in which above all others England has excelled, has for more than a century had no appeal whatever for the common people. It is only acceptable when—as in some popular songs and mnemonic rhymes—it is masquerading as something else. Indeed the very word "poetry" arouses either derision or embarrassment in ninety-eight people out of a hundred.

Our imaginary foreign observer would certainly be struck by our gentleness: by the orderly behaviour of English crowds, the lack of pushing and quarrelling, the willingness to form queues, the good temper of harassed, overworked people like bus conductors. The manners of the English working class are not always very graceful, but they are extremely considerate. Great care is taken in showing a stranger the way, blind people can travel across London with the certainty that they will be helped on and off every bus and across every street. In wartime a few of the policemen carried revolvers, but England has nothing corresponding to the *gendarmerie*, the semi-military police living in barracks and armed with rifles (sometimes even with tanks and aeroplanes) who are the guardians of society all the way from Calais to Tokyo. And except for certain well-defined areas in half a dozen big towns there is very little crime or violence. The average of honesty is lower in the big towns than in the country, but even in London the newsvendor can safely leave his pile of pennies on the pavement while he goes for a drink. The prevailing gentleness of manners is a recent thing, however. Well within living memory it was impossible for a smartly dressed person to walk down Ratcliff Highway without being assaulted, and an eminent jurist, asked to name a typically English crime, could answer: "Kicking your wife to death."

There is no revolutionary tradition in England, and even in extremist political parties, it is only the middle-class membership that thinks in revolutionary terms. The masses still more or less assume that "against the law" is a synonym for "wrong." It is known that the criminal law is harsh and full of anomalies and that litigation is so expensive as always to favour the rich against the poor: but there is a general feeling that the law, such as it is, will be scrupulously administered, that a judge or magistrate cannot be bribed, that no one will be punished without trial. An Englishman does not believe in his bones, as a Spanish or Italian peasant does, that the law is simply a racket. It is precisely this general confidence in the law that has allowed a good deal of recent tampering with Habeas Corpus to escape public notice. But it also causes some ugly situations to end peacefully. During the worst of the London blitz the authorities tried to prevent the public from using the Tube stations as shelters. The people did not reply by storming the gates, they simply bought themselves penny-halfpenny tickets: they thus had legal status as passengers, and there was no thought of turning them out again.

The traditional English xenophobia is stronger among the working class than the middle class. It was partly the resistance of the Trade Unions that prevented a really large influx of refugees from the fascist countries before the war, and when the German refugees were interned in 1940, it was not the working class that protested. The difference in habits, and especially in food and language, makes it very hard for English working people to get on with foreigners. Their diet differs a great deal from that of any European nation, and they are extremely conservative about it. As a rule they will refuse even to sample a foreign dish, they regard such things as garlic and olive oil with disgust, life is unlivable to them unless they have tea and puddings. And the peculiarities of the English language make it almost impossible for anyone who has left school at fourteen to learn a foreign language after he has grown up. In the French Foreign Legion, for instance, the British and American legionaries seldom rise out of the ranks, because they cannot learn French, whereas a German learns French in a few months. English working people, as a rule, think it effeminate even to pronounce a foreign word correctly. This is bound up with the fact that the upper classes learn foreign languages as a regular part of their education. Travelling abroad, speaking foreign tongues, enjoying foreign food, are vaguely felt to be upper-class habits, a species of snobbery, so that xenophobia is reinforced by class jealousy.

Perhaps the most horrible spectacles in England are the Dogs' Cemeteries in Kensington Gardens, at Stoke Poges (it actually adjoins the churchyard where Gray wrote his famous *Elegy*) and at various other places. But there were also the Animals' A.R.P.[1] Centres, with miniature stretchers for cats, and in the first year of the war there was the spectacle of Animal Day being celebrated with all its usual pomp in the middle of the Dunkirk evacuation. Although its worst follies are committed by the upper-class women, the animal cult runs right through the nation and is probably bound up with the decay of agriculture and the dwindled birthrate. Several years of stringent rationing have failed to reduce the dog and cat population, and even in poor quarters of big towns the bird fanciers' shops display canary seed at prices ranging up to twenty-five shillings a pint.

Hypocrisy is so generally accepted as part of the English character that a foreign observer would be prepared to meet with it at every turn, but he would find especially ripe examples in the laws dealing with gambling, drinking, prostitution, and profanity. He would find it difficult to reconcile the anti-imperialistic sentiments which are commonly expressed in England with the size of the British Empire. If he were a continental European he would notice with ironical amusement that the English think it wicked to have a big army but see nothing wrong in having a big navy. This too he would set down as hypocrisy—not altogether fairly, for it is the fact of being an island, and therefore not needing a big army, that has allowed British democratic institutions to grow up, and the mass of the people are fairly well aware of this.

Exaggerated class distinctions have been diminishing over a period of about thirty years, and the war has probably speeded up the process, but newcomers to England are still astonished and sometimes horrified by the blatant differences between class and class. The great majority of the people can still be "placed" in an instant by their manners, clothes, and general appearance. Even the physical type differs considerably, the upper classes being on an average several inches taller than the working class. But the most striking difference of all is in language and accent. The English working class, as Mr. Wyndham Lewis has put it, are "branded on the tongue." And though class distinctions do not exactly coincide with economic distinctions, the contrast between wealth and poverty is very much more glaring, and more taken for granted, than in most countries.

The English were the inventors of several of the world's most popular games, and have spread them more widely than any other product of their culture. The word "football" is mispronounced by scores of millions who have never heard of Shakespeare or Magna Charta.° The English themselves are not outstandingly good at all games, but they enjoy playing them, and to an extent that strikes foreigners as childish they enjoy reading about them and betting on them. During the between-war years the football pools did more than any other one thing to make life bearable for the unemployed. Professional footballers, boxers, jockeys, and even cricketers enjoy a popularity that no scientist or artist could hope to rival. Nevertheless sport-worship is not carried to quite such imbecile lengths as one would imagine from reading the popular press. When the brilliant lightweight boxer, Kid Lewis, stood for Parliament in his native borough, he only scored a hundred and twenty-five votes.

These traits that we have enumerated are probably the ones that would strike an intelligent foreign observer first. Out of them he might feel that he could construct a reliable picture of the English character. But then probably a thought would strike him: is there such a thing as "the English character"? Can one talk about nations as though they were individuals? And supposing that one can, is there any genuine continuity between the England of to-day and the England of the past?

As he wandered through the London streets, he would notice the old prints in the bookshop windows, and it would occur to him that if these things are representative, then England must have changed a great deal. It is not much more than a hundred years since the distinguishing mark of English life was its brutality. The common people, to judge by the prints, spent their time in an almost unending round of fighting, whoring, drunkenness, and bull-baiting. Moreover, even the physical type appears to have changed. Where are they gone, the hulking draymen and low-browed prize-fighters, the brawny sailors with their buttocks bursting out of their white trousers, and the great overblown beauties with their swelling bosoms, like the figure-heads of Nelson's ships? What had these people in common with the gentle-mannered, undemonstrative, law-abiding English of to-day? Do such things as "national cultures" really exist?

This is one of those questions, like the freedom of the will or the identity of the individual, in which all the arguments are on one side and instinctive knowledge is on the other. It is not easy to discover the connecting thread that runs through English life from the sixteenth century onwards, but all English people who bother about such subjects feel that it exists. They feel that they understand the institutions that have come to them out of the past— Parliament, for instance, or sabbatarianism, or the subtle grading of the class system—with an inherited knowledge impossible to a foreigner. Individuals, too, are felt to conform to a national pattern. D. H. Lawrence is felt to be "very English," but so is Blake; Dr. Johnson and G. K. Chesterton are somehow the same kind of person. The belief that we resemble our ancestors—that Shakespeare, say, is more like a modern Englishman than a modern Frenchman or German—may be unreasonable, but by existing it influences conduct. Myths which are believed in tend to become true, because they set up a type, or "persona," which the average person will do his best to resemble.

During the bad period of 1940 it became clear that in Britain national solidarity is stronger than class antagonism. If it were really true that "the proletarian has no country," 1940 was the time for him to show it. It was exactly then, however, that class feeling slipped into the background, only reappearing when the immediate danger had passed. Moreover, it is probable that the stolid behaviour of the British town populations under the bombing was partly due to the existence of the national "persona"—that is, to their preconceived idea of themselves. Traditionally the Englishman is phlegmatic, unimaginative, not easily rattled: and since that is what he thinks he ought to be, that is what he tends to become. Dislike of hysteria and "fuss," admiration for stubbornness, are all but universal in England, being shared by everyone except the intelligentsia. Millions of English people willingly accept as their national emblem the bulldog, an animal noted for its obstinacy, ugliness, and impenetrable stupidity. They have a remarkable readiness to admit that foreigners are more "clever" than themselves, and yet they feel that it would be an outrage against the laws of God and Nature for England to be ruled by foreigners. Our imaginary observer would notice, perhaps, that Wordsworth's sonnets during the Napoleonic war might almost have been written during this one. He would know already that England has produced poets and scientists rather than philosophers, theologians, or pure theorists of any description. And he might end by deciding that a profound, almost unconscious patriotism and an inability to think logically are the abiding features of the English character, traceable in English literature from Shakespeare onwards.

THE MORAL OUTLOOK OF THE ENGLISH PEOPLE

For perhaps a hundred and fifty years, organised religion, or conscious religious belief of any kind, have had very little hold on the mass of the English people. Only about ten per cent of them ever go near a place of worship except to be married and buried. A vague theism and an intermittent belief in life after death are probably fairly widespread, but the main Christian doctrines have been largely forgotten. Asked what he meant by "Christianity," the average man would define it wholly in ethical terms ("unselfishness," or "loving your neighbour," would be the kind of definition he would give). This was probably much the same in the early days of the Industrial Revolution, when the old village life had been suddenly broken up and the Established Church had lost touch with its followers. But in recent times the Nonconformist sects have also lost much of their vigour, and within the last generation the Bible-reading which used to be traditional in England has lapsed. It is quite common now to meet with young people who do not know the Bible stories even as *stories*.

But there is one sense in which the English common people have remained more Christian than the upper classes, and probably than any other European nation. This is in their non-acceptance of the modern cult of power-worship. While almost ignoring the spoken doctrines of the Church, they have held on to the one that the Church never formulated, because taking it for granted: namely, that might is not right. It is here that the gulf between the intelligentsia and the common people is widest. From Carlyle onwards, but especially in the last generation, the British intelligentsia have tended to take their ideas from Europe and have been infected by habits of thought that derive ultimately from Machiavelli. All the cults that have been fashionable in the last dozen years, communism, fascism, and pacifism, are in the last analysis forms of power-worship. It is significant that in this country, unlike most others, the Marxist version of Socialism has found its warmest adherents in the middle class. Its methods, if not its theories, obviously conflict with what is called "*bourgeois* morality" (i.e., common decency), and in moral matters it is the proletarians who are "*bourgeois*."

One of the basic folk-tales of the English-speaking peoples is Jack the Giant-killer—the little man against the big man. Mickey Mouse, Popeye the Sailor, and Charlie Chaplin are all essentially the same figure. (Chaplin's films, it is worth noticing, were banned in Germany as soon as Hitler came to power, and Chaplin has been viciously attacked by English fascist writers.) Not merely a hatred of bullying, but a tendency to support the weaker side merely because it is weaker, are almost general in England. Hence the admiration for a "good loser" and the easy forgiveness of failures, either in sport, politics, or war. Even in very serious matters the English people do not feel that an unsuccessful action is necessarily futile. An example in the 1939–45 war was the campaign in Greece. No one expected it to succeed, but nearly everyone thought that it should be undertaken. And the popular attitude to foreign politics is nearly always coloured by the instinct to side with the under-dog.

An obvious recent instance was pro-Finnish sentiment in the Russo-Finnish war of 1940. This was genuine enough, as several by-elections fought mainly on this issue showed. Popular feeling towards the U.S.S.R. had been increasingly friendly for some time past, but Finland was a small country attacked by a big one, and that settled the issue for most people. In the American Civil War the British working classes sided with the North— the side that stood for the abolition of slavery—in spite of the fact that the Northern blockade of the cotton ports was causing great hardship in Britain. In the Franco-Prussian war, such pro-French sentiment as there was in England was among the working class. The small nationalities oppressed by the Turks found their sympathisers in the Liberal Party, at that time the party of the working class and the lower middle class. And in so far as it bothered with such issues at all, British mass sentiment was for the Abyssinians against the Italians, for the Chinese against the Japanese, and for the Spanish Republicans against Franco. It was also friendly to Germany during the period when Germany was weak and disarmed, and it is not surprising to see a similar swing of sentiment after the war.

The feeling that one ought always to side with the weaker party probably derives from the balance-of-power policy which Britain has followed from the eighteenth century onwards. A European critic would add that it is humbug, pointing in proof to the fact that Britain herself holds down subject populations in India and elsewhere. We don't, in fact, know what settlement the English common people would make with India if the decision were theirs. All political parties and all newspapers of whatever colour have conspired to prevent them from seeing the issue clearly. We do know, however, that they have sometimes championed the weak against the strong when it was obviously not to their own advantage. The best example is the Irish Civil War. The real weapon of the Irish rebels was British public opinion, which was substantially on their side and prevented the British Government from crushing the rebellion in the only way possible. Even in the Boer War there was a considerable volume of pro-Boer sentiment, though it was not strong enough to influence events. One must conclude that in this matter the English common people have lagged behind their century. They have failed to catch up with power politics, "realism," *sacro egoismo* and the doctrine that the end justifies the means.

The general English hatred of bullying and terrorism means that any kind of violent criminal gets very little sympathy. Gangsterism on American lines could not flourish in England, and it is significant that the American gangsters have never tried to transfer their activities to this country. At need, the whole nation would combine against people who kidnap babies and fire machine-guns in the street: but even the efficiency of the English police force really depends on the fact that the police have public opinion behind them. The bad side of this is the almost universal toleration of cruel and out-of-date punishments. It is not a thing to be proud of that England should still tolerate such punishments as flogging. It continues partly because of the widespread psychological ignorance, partly because men are only flogged for crimes that forfeit nearly everyone's sympathy. There would be an outcry if it were applied to non-violent crimes, or re-instituted for military offences. Military punishments are not taken for granted in England as they are in most countries. Public opinion is almost certainly opposed to the death penalty for cowardice and desertion, though there is no strong feeling against hanging murderers. In general the English attitude to crime is ignorant and old-fashioned, and humane treatment even of child offenders is a recent thing. Still, if Al Capone were in an English jail, it would not be for evasion of income tax.

A more complex question than the English attitude to crime and violence is the survival of puritanism and the world-famed English hypocrisy.

The English people proper, the working masses who make up seventy-five per cent of the population, are not puritanical. The dismal theology of Calvinism never popularised itself in England as it did for a while in Wales and Scotland. But puritanism in the looser sense in which the word is generally used (that is, prudishness, asceticism, the "kill-joy" spirit) is something that has been unsuccessfully forced upon the working class by the class of small traders and manufacturers immediately above them. In its origin it had a clear though unconscious economic motive behind it. If you could persuade the working man that every kind of recreation was sinful, you could get more work out of him for less money. In the early nineteenth century there was even a school of thought which maintained that the working man ought not to marry. But it would be unfair to suggest that the puritan moral code was mere humbug. Its exaggerated fear of sexual immorality, which extended to a disapproval of stage plays, dancing, and even bright-coloured clothes, was partly a protest against the real corruption of the later Middle Ages: there was also the new factor of syphilis, which appeared in England about the sixteenth century and worked frightful havoc for the next century or two. A little later there was another new factor in the introduction of distilled liquors—gin, brandy, and so forth—which were very much more intoxicating than the beer and mead which the English had been accustomed to. The "temperance" movement was a well-meant reaction against the frightful drunkenness of the nineteenth century, product of slum conditions and cheap gin. But it was necessarily led by fanatics who regarded not merely drunkenness but even the moderate drinking of alcohol as sinful. During the past fifty years or so there has even been a similar drive against tobacco. A hundred years ago, or two hundred years ago, tobacco-smoking was much disapproved of, but only on the ground that it was dirty, vulgar, and injurious to health: the idea that it is a wicked self-indulgence is modern.

This line of thought has never really appealed to the English masses. At most they have been sufficiently intimidated by middle-class puritanism to take some of their pleasures rather furtively. It is universally agreed that the working classes are far more moral than the upper classes, but the idea that sexuality is wicked in itself has no popular basis. Music-hall jokes, Blackpool postcards, and the songs the soldiers make up are anything but puritanical. On the other hand, almost no one in England approves of prostitution. There are several big towns where prostitution is extremely blatant, but it is completely unattractive and has never been really tolerated. It could not be regulated and humanised as it has been in some countries, because every English person feels in his bones that it is wrong. As for the general weakening of sex morals that has happened during the past twenty or thirty years, it is probably a temporary thing, resulting from the excess of women over men in the population.

In the matter of drink, the only result of a century of "temperance" agitation has been a slight increase in hypocrisy. The practical disappearance of drunkenness as an English vice has not been due to the anti-drink fanatics, but to competing amusements, education, the improvement in industrial conditions, and the expensiveness of drink itself. The fanatics have been able to see to it that the Englishman drinks his glass of beer under difficulties and with a faint feeling of wrong-doing, but have not actually been able to prevent him from drinking it. The pub, one of the basic institutions of English life, carries on in spite of the harassing tactics of Nonconformist local authorities. So also with gambling. Most forms of gambling are illegal according to the letter of the law, but they all happen on an enormous scale. The motto of the English people might be the chorus of Marie Lloyd's song, "A little of what you fancy does you good." They are not vicious, not even lazy, but they will have their bit of fun, whatever the higher-ups may say. And they seem to be gradually winning their battle against the kill-joy minorities. Even the horrors of the English Sunday have been much mitigated during the past dozen years. Some of the laws regulating pubs—designed in every case to discourage the publican and make drinking unattractive—were relaxed during the war. And it is a very good sign that the stupid rule forbidding children to enter pubs, which tended to dehumanise the pub and turn it into a mere drinking-shop, is beginning to be disregarded in some parts of the country.

Traditionally, the Englishman's home is his castle. In an age of conscription and identity cards this cannot really be true. But the hatred of regimentation, the feeling that your spare time is your own and that a man must not be persecuted for his opinions, is deeply ingrained, and the centralising processes inevitable in wartime, and still enforced, have not destroyed it.

It is a fact that the much-boasted freedom of the British press is theoretical rather than actual. To begin with the centralised ownership of the press means in practice that unpopular opinions can only be printed in books or in newspapers with small circulations. Moreover, the English people as a whole are not sufficiently interested in the printed word to be very vigilant about this aspect of their liberties, and during the last twenty years there has been much tampering with the freedom of the press, with no real popular protest. Even the demonstrations against the suppression of the *Daily Worker* [2] were probably stage-managed by a small minority. On the other hand, freedom of speech is a reality, and respect for it is almost general. Extremely few English people are afraid to utter their political opinions in public, and there are not even very many who want to silence the opinions of others. In peacetime, when unemployment can be used as a weapon, there is a certain amount of petty persecution of "reds," but the real totalitarian atmosphere, in which the State endeavours to control people's thoughts as well as their words, is hardly imaginable.

The safeguard against it is partly the respect for integrity of conscience, and the willingness to hear both sides, which can be observed at any public meeting. But it is also partly the prevailing lack of intellectuality. The English are not sufficiently interested in intellectual matters to be intolerant about them. "Deviations" and "dangerous thoughts" do not seem very important to them. An ordinary Englishman, Conservative, Socialist, Catholic, Communist, or what not, almost never grasps the full logical implications of the creed he professes: almost always he utters heresies without noticing it. Orthodoxies, whether of the Right or the Left, flourish chiefly among the literary intelligentsia, the people who ought in theory to be the guardians of freedom of thought.

The English people are not good haters, their memory is very short, their patriotism is largely unconscious, they have no love of military glory and not much admiration for great men. They have the virtues and the vices of an old-fashioned people. To twentieth-century political theories they oppose not another theory of their own, but a moral quality which must be vaguely described as decency. On the day in 1936 when the Germans re-occupied the Rhineland I was in a northern mining town. I happened to go into a pub just after this piece of news, which quite obviously meant war, had come over the wireless, and I remarked to the others at the bar, "The German army has crossed the Rhine." With a vague air of capping a quotation someone answered, "Parley-voo." No more response than that! Nothing will ever wake these people up, I thought. But later in the evening, at the same pub, someone sang a song which had recently come out, with the chorus—

> "For you can't do that there 'ere,
> No, you can't do that there 'ere;
> Anywhere else you can do that there,
> But you can't do that there 'ere!"

And it struck me that perhaps this was the English answer to fascism. At any rate it is true that it has not happened here, in spite of fairly favourable circumstances. The amount of liberty, intellectual or other, that we enjoy in England ought not to be exaggerated, but the fact that it did not markedly diminish in nearly six years of desperate war is a hopeful symptom.

The Political Outlook of the English People

The English people are not only indifferent to fine points of doctrine, but are remarkably ignorant politically. They are only now beginning to use the political terminology which has been current for years in Continental countries. If you asked a random group of people from any stratum of the population to define capitalism, socialism, communism, anarchism, Trotskyism, fascism, you would get mostly vague answers, and some of them would be surprisingly stupid ones.

But they are also distinctly ignorant about their own political system. During recent years, for various reasons, there has been a revival of political activity, but over a longer period the interest in party politics has been dwindling. Great numbers of adult English people have never in their lives bothered to vote in an election. In big towns it is quite common for people not to know the name of their M.P. or what constituency they live in. During the war years, owing to the failure to renew the registers, the young had no votes (at one time no one under twenty-nine had a vote), and did not seem much troubled by the fact. Nor does the anomalous electoral system, which usually favours the Conservative Party, though it happened to favour the Labour Party in 1945, arouse much protest. Attention focuses on policies and individuals (Chamberlain, Churchill, Cripps, Beveridge, Bevin) rather than on parties. The feeling that Parliament really controls events, and that sensational changes are to be expected when a new government comes in, has been gradually fading ever since the first Labour government in 1923.

In spite of many subdivisions, Britain has in effect only two political parties, the Conservative Party and the Labour Party, which between them broadly represent the main interests of the nation. But during the last twenty years the tendency of these two parties has been to resemble one another more and more. Everyone knows in advance that any government, whatever its political principles may be, can be relied upon not to do certain things. Thus, no Conservative government will ever revert to what would have been called Conservatism in the nineteenth century. No Socialist government will massacre the propertied class, nor even expropriate them without compensation. A good recent example of the changing temper of politics was the reception given to the Beveridge Report. Thirty years ago any Conservative would have denounced this as State charity, while most Socialists would have rejected it as a capitalist bribe. In 1944 the only discussion that arose was as to whether it would be adopted in whole or in part. This blurring of party distinctions is happening in almost all countries, partly because everywhere, except, perhaps, in the U.S.A., the drift is towards a planned economy, partly because in an age of power politics national survival is felt to be more important than class warfare. But Britain has certain peculiarities resulting from its being both a small island and the centre of an Empire. To begin with, given the present economic system, Britain's prosperity depends partly on the Empire, while all Left parties are theoretically anti-imperialist. Politicians of the Left are therefore aware—or have recently become aware—that once in power they choose between abandoning some of their principles or lowering the English standard of living. Secondly, it is impossible for Britain to go through the kind of revolutionary process that the U.S.S.R. went through. It is too small, too highly organised, too dependent on imported food. Civil war in England would mean starvation or conquest by some foreign power, or both. Thirdly and most important of all, civil war is not *morally* possible in England. In any circumstances that we can foresee, the proletariat of Hammersmith will not arise and massacre the *bourgeoisie* of Kensington: they are not different enough. Even the most drastic changes will have to happen peacefully and with a show of legality, and everyone except the "lunatic fringes" of the various political parties is aware of this.

These facts make up the background of the English political outlook. The great mass of the people want profound changes, but they do not want violence. They want to preserve their own standard of living, and at the same time they want to feel that they are not exploiting less fortunate peoples. If you issued a questionnaire to the whole nation, asking, "What do you want from politics?", the answer would be much the same in the overwhelming majority of cases. Substantially it would be: "Economic security, a foreign policy which will ensure peace, more social equality, and a settlement with India." Of these, the first is by far the most important, unemployment being an even greater nightmare than war. But few people would think it necessary to mention either capitalism or socialism. Neither word has much emotional appeal. No one's heart beats faster at the thought of nationalising the Bank of England: on the other hand, the old line of talk about sturdy individualism and the sacred rights of property is no longer swallowed by the masses. They know it is not true that "there's plenty of room at the top," and in any case most of them don't want to get to the top: they want steady jobs and a fair deal for their children.

During the last few years, owing to the social frictions arising out of the war, discontent with the obvious inefficiency of old-style capitalism, and admiration for Soviet Russia, public opinion has moved considerably to the Left, but without growing more doctrinaire or markedly bitterer. None of the political parties which call themselves revolutionary have seriously increased their following. There are about half a dozen of these parties, but their combined membership, even if one counts the remnants of Mosley's Blackshirts,[3] would probably not amount to 150,000. The most important of them is the Communist Party, but even the Communist Party, after twenty-five years of existence, must be held to have failed. Although it has had considerable influence at moments when circumstances favoured it, it has never shown signs of growing into a mass party of the kind that exists in France or used to exist in pre-Hitler Germany.

Over a long period of years, Communist Party membership has gone up or down in response to the changes in Russian foreign policy. When the U.S.S.R. is on good terms with Britain, the British Communists follow a "moderate" line hardly distinguishable from that of the Labour Party, and their membership swells to some scores of thousands. When British and Russian policy diverge, the Communists revert to a "revolutionary" line and membership slumps again. They can, in fact, only get themselves a worthwhile following by abandoning their essential objectives. The various other Marxist parties, all of them claiming to be the true and uncorrupted successors of Lenin, are in an even more hopeless position. The average Englishman is unable to grasp their doctrines and uninterested in their grievances. And in England the conspiratorial mentality which has been developed in police-ridden European countries is a great handicap. English people in large numbers will not accept any creed whose dominant notes are hatred and illegality. The ruthless ideologies of the Continent—not merely communism and fascism, but anarchism, Trotskyism, and even ultra-montane Catholicism—are accepted in their pure form only by the intelligentsia, who constitute a sort of island of bigotry amid the general vagueness. It is significant that English revolutionary writers are obliged to use a bastard vocabulary whose key phrases are mostly translations. There are no native English words for most of the concepts they are dealing with. Even the word "proletarian," for instance, is not English and the great majority of English people do not know what it means. It is generally used, if at all, to mean simply "poor." But even so it is given a social rather than an economic slant and most people would tell you that a blacksmith or a cobbler is a proletarian and that a bank clerk is not. As for the word "*bourgeois*," it is used almost exclusively by people who are of *bourgeois* origin themselves. The only genuinely popular use of the word is as a printer's term. It is then, as one might expect, anglicised and pronounced "boorjoyce."

But there is one abstract political term which is fairly widely used and has a loose but well-understood meaning attached to it. This is the word "democracy." In a way, the English people do feel that they live in a democratic country. Not that anyone is so stupid as to take this in a literal sense. If democracy means either popular rule or social equality, it is clear that Britain is not democratic. It is, however, democratic in the secondary sense which has attached itself to that word since the rise of Hitler. To begin with, minorities have some power of making themselves heard. But more than this, public opinion cannot be disregarded when it chooses to express itself. It may have to work in indirect ways, by strikes, demonstrations and letters to the newspapers, but it can and visibly does affect government policy. A British government may be unjust, but it cannot be quite arbitrary. It cannot do the kind of thing that a totalitarian government does as a matter of course. One example out of the thousands that might be chosen is the German attack on the U.S.S.R. The significant thing is not that this was made without a declaration of war—that was natural enough—but that it was made without any propaganda build-up beforehand. The German people woke up to find themselves at war with a country that they had been ostensibly on friendly terms with on the previous evening. Our own government would not dare to do such a thing, and the English people are fairly well aware of this. English political thinking is much governed by the word "They." "They" are the higher-ups, the mysterious powers who do things to you against your will. But there is a widespread feeling that "They," though tyrannical, are not omnipotent. "They" will respond to pressure if you take the trouble to apply it: "They" are even removable. And with all their political ignorance the English people will often show surprising sensitiveness when some small incident seems to show that "They" are overstepping the mark. Hence, in the midst of seeming apathy, the sudden fuss every now and then over a rigged by-election or a too-Cromwellian handling of Parliament.

One thing that is extremely difficult to be certain about is the persistence in England of monarchist sentiment. There cannot be much doubt that at any rate in the south of England it was strong and genuine until the death of King George V. The popular response to the Silver Jubilee in 1935 took the authorities by surprise, and the celebrations had to be prolonged for an extra week. At normal times it is only the richer classes who are overtly royalist: in the West End of London, for instance, people stand to attention for "God Save the King" at the end of a picture show, whereas in the poorer quarters they walk out. But the affection shown for George V at the Silver Jubilee was obviously genuine, and it was even possible to see in it the survival, or recrudescence, of an idea almost as old as history, the idea of the King and the common people being in a sort of alliance against the upper classes; for example, some of the London slum streeets bore during the Jubilee the rather servile slogan "Poor but Loyal." Other slogans, however, coupled loyalty to the King with hostility to the landlord, such as "Long Live the King. Down With the Landlord," or more often, "No Landlords Wanted" or "Landlords Keep Away." It is too early to say whether royalist sentiment was killed outright by the Abdication, but unquestionably the Abdication dealt it a serious blow. Over the past four hundred years it has waxed or waned according to circumstances. Queen Victoria, for instance, was decidedly unpopular during part of her reign, and in the first quarter of the nineteenth century public interest in the Royal Family was not nearly as strong as it was a hundred years later. At this moment the mass of the English people are probably mildly republican. But it may well be that another long reign, similar to that of George V, would revive royalist feeling and make it—as it was between roughly 1880 and 1936—an appreciable factor in politics.

THE ENGLISH CLASS SYSTEM

In time of war the English class system is the enemy propagandist's best argument. To Dr. Goebbels's charge that England is still "two nations," the only truthful answer would have been that she is in fact three nations. But the peculiarity of English class distinctions is not that they are unjust—for after all, wealth and poverty exist side by side in almost all countries—but that they are anachronistic. They do not exactly correspond to economic distinctions, and what is essentially an industrial and capitalist country is haunted by the ghost of a caste system.

It is usual to classify modern society under three headings: the upper class, or *bourgeoisie*, the middle class, or *petite bourgeoisie*, and the working class, or proletariat. This roughly fits the facts, but one can draw no useful inference from it unless one takes account of the subdivisions within the various classes and realises how deeply the whole English outlook is coloured by romanticism and sheer snobbishness.

England is one of the last remaining countries to cling to the outward forms of feudalism. Titles are maintained and new ones are constantly created, and the House of Lords, consisting mainly of hereditary peers, has real powers. At the same time England has no real aristocracy. The race difference on which aristocratic rule is usually founded was disappearing by the end of the Middle Ages, and the famous medieval families have almost completely vanished. The so-called old families are those that grew rich in the sixteenth, seventeenth, and eighteenth centuries. Moreover, the notion that nobility exists in its own right, that you can be a nobleman even if you are poor, was already dying out in the age of Elizabeth, a fact commented on by Shakespeare. And yet, curiously enough, the English ruling class has never developed into a *bourgeoisie* plain and simple. It has never become purely urban or frankly commercial. The ambition to be a country gentleman, to own and administer land and draw at least a part of your income from rent, has survived every change. So it comes that each new wave of parvenus, instead of simply replacing the existing ruling class, has adopted its habits, intermarried with it, and, after a generation or two, become indistinguishable from it.

The basic reason for this may perhaps be that England is very small and has an equable climate and pleasantly varied scenery. It is almost impossible in England, and not easy even in Scotland, to be more than twenty miles from a town. Rural life is less inherently boorish than it is in bigger countries with colder winters. And the comparative integrity of the British ruling class—for when all is said and done they have not behaved so contemptibly as their European opposite numbers—is probably bound up with their idea of themselves as feudal landowners. This outlook is shared by considerable sections of the middle class. Nearly everyone who can afford to do so sets up as a country gentleman, or at least makes some effort in that direction. The manor-house with its park and its walled gardens reappears in reduced form in the stockbroker's week-end cottage, in the suburban villa with its lawn and herbaceous border, perhaps even in the potted nasturtiums on the window-sill of the Bayswater flat. This widespread day-dream is undoubtedly snobbish, it has tended to stabilise class distinctions and has helped to prevent the modernisation of English agriculture: but it is mixed up with a kind of idealism, a feeling that style and tradition are more important than money.

Within the middle class there is a sharp division, cultural and not financial, between those who aim at gentility and those who do not. According to the usual classification, everyone between the capitalist and the weekly wage-earner can be lumped together as *"petite bourgeoisie."* This means that the Harley Street physician, the army officer, the grocer, the farmer, the senior civil servant, the solicitor, the clergyman, the schoolmaster, the bank manager, the speculative builder, and the fisherman who owns his own boat, are all in the same class. But no one in England feels them to belong to the same class, and the distinction between them is not a distinction of income but of accent, manners and, to some extent, outlook. Anyone who pays any attention to class differences at all would regard an army officer with £1,000 a year as socially superior to a shopkeeper with £2,000 a year. Even within the upper class a similar distinction holds good, the titled person being almost always more deferred to than an untitled person of larger income. Middle-class people are really graded according to their degree of resemblance to the aristocracy: professional men, senior officials, officers in the fighting services, university lecturers, clergymen, even the literary and scientific intelligentsia, rank higher than business men, though on the whole they earn less. It is a peculiarity of this class that their largest item of expenditure is education. Whereas a successful tradesman will send his son to the local grammar school, a clergyman with half his income will underfeed himself for years in order to send his son to a public school, although he knows that he will get no direct return for the money he spends.

There is, however, another noticeable division in the middle class. The old distinction was between the man who is "a gentleman" and the man who is "not a gentleman." In the last thirty years, however, the demands of modern industry, and the technical schools and provincial universities, have brought into being a new kind of man, middle class in income and to some extent in habits, but not much interested in his own social status. People like radio engineers and industrial chemists, whose education has not been of a kind to give them any reverence for the past, and who tend to live in blocks of flats or housing-estates where the old social pattern has broken down, are the most nearly classless beings that England possesses. They are an important section of society, because their numbers are constantly growing. The war, for instance, made necessary the formation of an enormous air force, and so you got thousands of young men of working-class origin graduating into the technical middle class by way of the R.A.F. Any serious reorganisation of industry now will have similar effects. And the characteristic outlook of the technicians is already spreading among the older strata of the middle class. One symptom of this is that intermarriage within the middle class is freer than it used to be. Another is the increasing unwillingness of people below the £2,000 a year level to bankrupt themselves in the name of education.

Another series of changes, probably dating from the Education Bill of 1871, is occurring in the working class. One cannot altogether acquit the English working class either of snobbishness or of servility. To begin with there is a fairly sharp distinction between the better-paid working class and the very poor. Even in socialist literature it is common to find contemptuous references to slum-dwellers (the German word *lumpenproletariat* is much used), and imported labourers with low standards of living, such as the Irish, are greatly looked down on. There is also, probably, more disposition to accept class distinctions as permanent, and even to accept the upper classes as natural leaders, than survives in most countries. It is significant that in the moment of disaster the man best able to unite the nation was Churchill, a Conservative of aristocratic origins. The word "Sir" is much used in England, and the man of obviously upper-class appearance can usually get more than his fair share of deference from commissionaires, ticket-collectors, policemen, and the like. It is this aspect of English life that seems most shocking to visitors from America and the Dominions. And the tendency towards servility probably did not decrease in the twenty years between the two wars: it may even have increased, owing chiefly to unemployment.

But snobbishness is never quite separable from idealism. The tendency to give the upper classes more than their due is mixed up with a respect for good manners and something vaguely describable as culture. In the South of England, at any rate, it is unquestionable that most working-class people want to resemble the upper classes in manners and habits. The traditional attitude of looking down on the upper classes as effeminate and "la-di-dah" survives best in the heavy-industry areas. Hostile nicknames like "toff" and "swell" have almost disappeared, and even the *Daily Worker* displays advertisements for "High-class Gentleman's Tailor." Above all, throughout southern England there is almost general uneasiness about the Cockney accent. In Scotland and northern England snobbishness about the local accents does exist, but it is not nearly so strong or widespread. Many a Yorkshireman definitely prides himself on his broad U's and narrow A's, and will defend them on linguistic grounds. In London there are still people who say "fice" instead of "face," but there is probably no one who regards "fice" as superior. Even a person who claims to despise the *bourgeoisie* and all its ways will still take care that his children grow up pronouncing their aitches.

But side by side with this there has gone a considerable growth of political consciousness and an increasing impatience with class privilege. Over a period of twenty or thirty years the working class has grown politically more hostile to the upper class, culturally less hostile. There is nothing incongruous in this: both tendencies are symptoms of the levelling of manners which results from machine civilisation and which makes the English class system more and more of an anachronism.

The obvious class differences still surviving in England astonish foreign observers, but they are far less marked, and far less real, than they were thirty years ago. People of different social origins, thrown together during the war in the armed forces, or in factories or offices, or as firewatchers and Home Guards, were able to mingle more easily than they did in the 1914–18 war. It is worth listing the various influences which—mechanically, as it were—tend to make Englishmen of all classes less and less different from one another.

First of all, the improvement in industrial technique. Every year less and less people are engaged in heavy manual labour which keeps them constantly tired and, by hypertrophying certain muscles, gives them a distinctive carriage. Secondly, improvements in housing. Between the two wars rehousing was done mostly by the local authorities, who have produced a type of house (the council house, with its bathroom, garden, separate kitchen, and indoor w.c.) which is nearer to the stockbroker's villa than it is to the labourer's cottage. Thirdly, the mass production of furniture which in ordinary times can be bought on the hire-purchase system. The effect of this is that the interior of a working-class house resembles that of a middle-class house very much more than it did a generation ago. Fourthly, and perhaps most important of all, the mass production of cheap clothes. Thirty years ago the social status of nearly everyone in England could be determined from his appearance, even at two hundred yards' distance. The working classes all wore ready-made clothes, and the ready-made clothes were not only ill-fitting but usually followed the upper-class fashions of ten or fifteen years earlier. The cloth cap was practically a badge of status. It was universal among the working class, while the upper classes only wore it for golf and shooting. This state of affairs is rapidly changing. Ready-made clothes now follow the fashions closely, they are made in many different fittings to suit every kind of figure, and even when they are of very cheap cloth they are superficially not very different from expensive clothes. The result is that it grows harder every year, especially in the case of women, to determine social status at a glance.

Mass-produced literature and amusements have the same effect. Radio programmes, for instance, are necessarily the same for everybody. Films, though often extremely reactionary in their implied outlook, have to appeal to a public of millions and therefore have to avoid stirring up class antagonisms. So also with some of the big-circulation newspapers. The *Daily Express*, for instance, draws its readers from all strata of the population. So also with some of the periodicals that have appeared in the past dozen years. *Punch* is obviously a middle- and upper-class paper, but *Picture Post* is not aimed at any particular class. And lending libraries and very cheap books, such as the Penguins, popularise the habit of reading and probably have a levelling effect on literary taste. Even taste in food tends to grow more uniform owing to the multiplication of cheap but fairly smart restaurants such as those of Messrs. Lyons.

We are not justified in assuming that class distinctions are actually disappearing. The essential structure of England is still almost what it was in the nineteenth century. But real differences between man and man are obviously diminishing, and this fact is grasped and even welcomed by people who only a few years ago were clinging desperately to their social prestige.

Whatever may be the ultimate fate of the very rich, the tendency of the working class and the middle class is evidently to merge. It may happen quickly or slowly, according to circumstances. It was accelerated by the war, and another ten years of all-round rationing, utility clothes, high income tax, and compulsory national service may finish the process once and for all. The final effects of this we cannot foresee. There are observers, both native and foreign, who believe that the fairly large amount of individual freedom that is enjoyed in England depends on having a well-defined class system. Liberty, according to some, is incompatible with equality. But at least it is certain that the present drift *is* towards greater social equality, and that that is what the great mass of the English people desire.

The English Language

The English language has two outstanding characteristics to which most of its minor oddities can be finally traced. These characteristics are a very large vocabulary and simplicity of grammar.

If it is not the largest in the world, the English vocabulary is certainly among the largest. English is really two languages, Anglo-Saxon and Norman-French, and during the last three centuries it has been reinforced on an enormous scale by new words deliberately created from Latin and Greek roots. But in addition the vocabulary is made much larger than it appears by the practice of turning one part of speech into another. For example, almost any noun can be used as a verb: this in effect gives an extra range of verbs, so that you have *knife* as well as *stab*, *school* as well as *teach*, *fire* as well as *burn*, and so on. Then again, certain verbs can be given as many as twenty different meanings simply by adding prepositions to them. (Examples are *get out of*, *get up*, *give out*, *take over*.) Verbs can also change into nouns with considerable freedom, and by the use of affixes such as *-y*, *-ful*, *-like*, any noun can be turned into an adjective. More freely than in most languages, verbs and adjectives can be turned into their opposites by means of the prefix *un-*. And adjectives can be made more emphatic or given a new twist by tying a noun to them: for example, *lily-white*, *sky-blue*, *coal-black*, *iron-hard*, etc.

But English is also, and to an unnecessary extent, a borrowing language. It readily takes over any foreign word that seems to fill a need, often altering the meaning in doing so. A recent example is the word *blitz*. As a verb this word did not appear in print till late in 1940, but it has already become part of the language. Other examples from the vast armoury of borrowed words are *garage, charabanc, alias, alibi, steppe, thug, role, menu, lasso, rendezvous, chemise.* It will be noticed that in most cases an English equivalent exists already, so that borrowing adds to the already large stock of synonyms.

English grammar is simple. The language is almost completely uninflected, a peculiarity which marks it off from almost all languages west of China. Any regular English verb has only three inflections, the third person singular, the present participle, and the past participle. Thus, for instance, the verb *to kill* consists of *kill, kills, killing, killed,* and that is all. There is, of course, a great wealth of tenses, very much subtilised in meaning, but these are made by the use of auxiliaries which themselves barely inflect. *May, might, shall, will, should, would* do not inflect at all, except in the obsolete second person singular. The upshot is that every person in every tense of such a verb as *to kill* can be expressed in only about thirty words including the pronouns, or about forty if one includes the second person singular. The corresponding number in, for instance, French would be somewhere near two hundred. And in English there is the added advantage that the auxiliaries which are used to make the tenses are the same in every case.

There is no such thing in English as declension of nouns, and there is no gender. Nor are there many irregular plurals or comparatives. Moreover, the tendency is always towards greater simplicity, both in grammar and syntax. Long sentences with dependent clauses grow more and more unpopular, irregular but time-saving formations such as the "American subjunctive" (*it is necessary that you go* instead of *it is necessary that you should go*) gain ground, and difficult rules, such as the difference between *shall* and *will*, or *that* and *which*, are more and more ignored. If it continues to develop along its present lines English will ultimately have more in common with the uninflected languages of East Asia than with the languages of Europe.

The greatest quality of English is its enormous range not only of meaning but of *tone*. It is capable of endless subtleties, and of everything from the most high-flown rhetoric to the most brutal coarseness. On the other hand, its lack of grammar makes it easily compressible. It is the language of lyric poetry, and also of headlines. On its lower levels it is very easy to learn, in spite of its irrational spelling. It can also for international purposes be reduced to very simple pidgin dialects, ranging from Basic to the "Bêche-de-mer" English used in the South Pacific.[4] It is therefore well suited to be a world lingua franca, and it has in fact spread more widely than any other language.

But there are also great disadvantages, or at least great dangers, in speaking English as one's native tongue. To begin with, as was pointed out earlier in this book, the English are very poor linguists. Their own language is grammatically so simple that unless they have gone through the discipline of learning a foreign language in childhood, they are often quite unable to grasp what is meant by gender, person, and case. A completely illiterate Indian will pick up English far faster than a British soldier will pick up Hindustani. Nearly five million Indians are literate in English and millions more speak it in a debased form. There are some tens of thousands of Indians who speak English as nearly as possible perfectly; yet the number of Englishmen speaking any Indian language perfectly would not amount to more than a few scores. But the great weakness of English is its capacity for debasement. Just because it is so easy to use, it is easy to use *badly*.

To write or even to speak English is not a science but an art. There are no reliable rules: there is only the general principle that concrete words are better than abstract ones, and that the shortest way of saying anything is always the best. Mere correctness is no guarantee whatever of good writing. A sentence like "an enjoyable time was had by all present" is perfectly correct English, and so is the unintelligible mess of words on an income-tax return. Whoever writes English is involved in a struggle that never lets up even for a sentence. He is struggling against vagueness, against obscurity, against the lure of the decorative adjective, against the encroachment of Latin and Greek, and, above all, against the worn-out phrases and dead metaphors with which the language is cluttered up. In speaking, these dangers are more easily avoided, but spoken English differs from written English more sharply than is the case in most languages. In the spoken tongue every word that can be omitted is omitted, every possible abbreviation is used. Meaning is conveyed quite largely by emphasis, though curiously enough the English do not gesticulate, as one might reasonably expect them to do. A sentence like *No, I don't mean that one, I mean that one* is perfectly intelligible when spoken aloud, even without a gesture. But spoken English, when it tries to be dignified and logical, usually takes on the vices of written English, as you can see by spending half an hour either in the House of Commons or at the Marble Arch.

English is peculiarly subject to jargons. Doctors, scientists, business men, officials, sportsmen, economists, and political theorists all have their characteristic perversion of the language, which can be studied in the appropriate magazines from the *Lancet* to the *Labour Monthly*. But probably the deadliest enemy of good English is what is called "standard English." This dreary dialect, the language of leading articles, White Papers, political speeches, and B.B.C. news bulletins, is undoubtedly spreading: it is spreading downwards in the social scale, and outwards into the spoken language. Its characteristic is its reliance on ready-made phrases—*in due course, take the earliest opportunity, warm appreciation, deepest regret, explore every avenue, ring the changes, take up the cudgels, legitimate assumption, the answer is in the affirmative*, etc. etc.—which may once have been fresh and vivid, but have now become mere thought-saving devices, having the same relation to living English as a crutch has to a leg. Anyone preparing a broadcast or writing a letter to *The Times* adopts this kind of language almost instinctively, and it infects the spoken tongue as well. So much has our language been weakened that the imbecile chatter in Swift's essay on *Polite Conversation* (a satire on the upper-class talk of Swift's own day) would actually be rather a good conversation by modern standards.

This temporary decadence of the English language is due, like so much else, to our anachronistic class system. "Educated" English has grown anæmic because for long past it has not been reinvigorated from below. The people likeliest to use simple concrete language, and to think of metaphors that really call up a visual image, are those who are in contact with physical reality. A useful word like *bottleneck*, for instance, would be most likely to occur to someone used to dealing with conveyor belts: or again, the expressive military phrase *to winkle out* implies acquaintance both with winkles and with machine-gun nests. And the vitality of English depends on a steady supply of images of this kind. It follows that language, at any rate the English language, suffers when the educated classes lose touch with the manual workers. As things are at present, nearly every Englishman, whatever his origins, feels the working-class manner of speech, and even working-class idioms, to be inferior. Cockney, the most widespread dialect, is the most despised of all. Any word or usage that is supposedly Cockney is looked on as vulgar, even when, as is sometimes the case, it is merely an archaism. An example is *ain't*, which is now abandoned in favour of the much weaker form *aren't*. But *ain't* was good enough English eighty years ago, and Queen Victoria would have said *ain't*.

During the past forty years, and especially the past dozen years, English has borrowed largely from American, while America has shown no tendency to borrow from English. The reason for this is partly political. Anti-British feeling in the United States is far stronger than anti-American feeling in England, and most Americans dislike using a word or phrase which they know to be British. But American has gained a footing in England partly because of the vivid, almost poetic quality of its slang, partly because certain American usages (for instance, the formation of verbs by adding *-ise* to a noun) save time, and most of all because one can adopt an American word without crossing a class barrier. From the English point of view American words have no class label. This applies even to thieves' slang. Words like *stooge* and *stool-pigeon* are considered much less vulgar than words like *nark* and *split*. Even a very snobbish English person would probably not mind calling a policeman a *cop*, which is American, but he would object to calling him a *copper*, which is working-class English. To the working classes, on the other hand, the use of Americanisms is a way of escaping from Cockney without adopting the B.B.C. dialect, which they instinctively dislike and cannot easily master. Hence, especially in the big towns, working-class children now use American slang from the moment that they learn to talk. And there is a noticeable tendency to use American words even when they are not slang and when an English equivalent already exists: for instance, *car* for *tram*, *escalator* for *moving staircase*, *automobile* for *motor-car*.

This process will probably continue for some time. One cannot check it simply by protesting against it, and in any case many American words and expressions are well worth adopting. Some are necessary neologisms, others (for instance, *fall* for *autumn*) are old words which we ought never to have dropped. But it ought to be realised that on the whole American is a bad influence and has already had a debasing effect.

To begin with, American has some of the vices of English in an exaggerated form. The interchangeability of different parts of speech has been carried further, the distinction between transitive and intransitive verbs tends to break down, and many words are used which have no meaning whatever. For example, whereas English alters the meaning of a verb by tacking a preposition on to it, the American tendency is to burden every verb with a preposition that adds nothing to its meaning (*win out, lose out, face up to,* etc.). On the other hand, American has broken more completely than English with the past and with literary traditions. It not only produces words like *beautician*, *moronic*, and *sexualise*, but often replaces strong primary words by feeble euphemisms. For instance, many Americans seem to regard the word *death* and various words that go with it (*corpse, coffin, shroud*) as almost unmentionable. But above all, to adopt the American language whole-heartedly would probably mean a huge loss of vocabulary. For though American produces vivid and witty turns of speech, it is terribly poor in names for natural objects and localities. Even the streets in American cities are usually known by numbers instead of names. If we really intended to model our language upon American we should have, for instance, to lump the lady-bird, the daddy-long-legs, the sawfly, the water-boatman, the cockchafer, the cricket, the death-watch beetle and scores of other insects all together under the inexpressive name of *bug*. We should lose the poetic names of our wild flowers, and also, probably, our habit of giving individual names to every street, pub, field, lane, and hillock. In so far as American is adopted, that is the tendency. Those who take their language from the films, or from papers such as *Life* and *Time*, always prefer the slick time-saving word to the one with a history behind it. As to accent, it is doubtful whether the American accent has the superiority which it is now fashionable to claim for it. The "educated" English accent, a product of the last thirty years, is undoubtedly very bad and is likely to be abandoned, but the average English person probably speaks as clearly as the average American. Most English people blur their vowel sounds, but most Americans swallow their consonants. Many Americans pronounce, for instance, *water* as though it had no T in it, or even as though it had no consonant in it at all, except the w. On the whole we are justified in regarding the American language with suspicion. We ought to be ready to borrow its best words, but we ought not to let it modify the actual structure of our language.

However, there is no chance of resisting the American influence unless we can put new life into English itself. And it is difficult to do this while words and idioms are prevented from circulating freely among all sections of the population. English people of all classes now find it natural to express incredulity by the American slang phrase *sez you*. Many would even tell you in good faith that *sez you* has no English equivalent. Actually it has a whole string of them—for instance, *not half, I don't think, come off it, less of it, and then you wake up*, or simply *garn*. But most of these would be considered vulgar: you would never find an expression like *not half* in a *Times* leader, for instance. And on the other hand, many necessary abstract words, especially words of Latin origin, are rejected by the working class because they sound public-schoolish, "tony," and effeminate. Language ought to be the joint creation of poets and manual workers, and in modern England it is difficult for these two classes to meet. When they can do so again—as, in a different way, they could in the feudal past—English may show more clearly than at present its kinship with the language of Shakespeare and Defoe.

THE FUTURE OF THE ENGLISH PEOPLE

This is not a book about foreign politics, but if one is to speak of the future of the English people, one must start by considering what kind of world they will probably be living in and what special part they can play in it.

Nations do not often die out, and the English people will still be in existence a hundred years hence, whatever has happened in the meantime. But if Britain is to survive as what is called a "great" nation, playing an important and useful part in the world's affairs, one must take certain things as assured. One must assume that Britain will remain on good terms with Russia and Europe, will keep its special links with America and the Dominions, and will solve the problem of India in some amicable way. That is perhaps a great deal to assume, but without it there is not much hope for civilisation as a whole, and still less for Britain itself. If the savage international struggle of the last twenty years continues, there will only be room in the world for two or three great powers, and in the long run Britain will not be one of them. It has not either the population or the resources. In a world of power politics the English would ultimately dwindle to a satellite people, and the special thing that it is in their power to contribute might be lost.

But what is the special thing that they could contribute? The outstanding and—by contemporary standards—highly original quality of the English is their habit of *not killing one another*. Putting aside the "model" small states, which are in an exceptional position, England is the only European country where internal politics are conducted in a more or less humane and decent manner. It is—and this was true long before the rise of fascism—the only country where armed men do not prowl the streeets and no one is frightened of the secret police. And the whole British Empire, with all its crying abuses, its stagnation in one place and exploitation in another, at least has the merit of being internally peaceful. It has always been able to get along with a very small number of armed men, although it contains a quarter of the population of the earth. Between the wars its total armed forces amounted to about 600,000 men, of whom a third were Indians. At the outbreak of war the entire Empire was able to mobilise about a million trained men. Almost as many could have been mobilised by, say, Rumania. The English are probably more capable than most peoples of making revolutionary changes without bloodshed. In England, if anywhere, it would be possible to abolish poverty without destroying liberty. If the English took the trouble to make their own democracy work, they would become the political leaders of western Europe, and probably of some other parts of the world as well. They would provide the much-needed alternative to Russian authoritarianism on the one hand and American materialism on the other.

But to play a leading part the English have got to know what they are doing, and they have got to retain their vitality. For this, certain developments are needed within the next decade. These are a rising birthrate, more social equality, less centralisation and more respect for the intellect.

There was a small rise in the birthrate during the war years, but that is probably of no significance, and the general curve is downwards. The position is not quite so desperate as it is sometimes said to be, but it can only be put right if the curve not only rises sharply, but does so within ten or at most twenty years. Otherwise the population will not only fall, but, what is worse, will consist predominantly of middle-aged people. If that point is reached, the decline may never be retrievable.

At bottom, the causes of the dwindled birthrate are economic. It is nonsense to say that it has happened because English people do not care for children. In the early nineteenth century they had an extremely high birthrate, and they also had an attitude towards children which now seems to us unbelievably callous. With very little public disapproval, children as young as six were sold into the mines and factories, and the death of a child, the most shocking event that modern people are able to imagine, was looked on as a very minor tragedy. In a sense it is true that modern English people have small families because they are too fond of children. They feel that it is wrong to bring a child into the world unless you are completely certain of being able to provide for him, and at a level not lower than your own. For the last fifty years, to have a big family has meant that your children must wear poorer clothes than others in the same group, must have less food and less attention, and probably must go to work earlier. This held good for all classes except the very rich and the unemployed. No doubt the dearth of babies is partly due to the competing attraction of cars and radios, but its main cause is a typically English mixture of snobbishness and altruism.

The philoprogenitive instinct will probably return when fairly large families are already the rule, but the first steps towards this must be economic ones. Half-hearted family allowances will not do the trick, especially when there is a severe housing shortage, as there is now. People should be better off for having children, just as they are in a peasant community, instead of being financially crippled, as they are in ours. Any government, by a few strokes of the pen, could make childlessness as unbearable an economic burden as a big family is now: but no government has chosen to do so, because of the ignorant idea that a bigger population means more unemployed. Far more drastically than anyone has proposed hitherto, taxation will have to be graded so as to encourage child-bearing and to save women with young children from being obliged to work outside the home. And this involves readjustment of rents, better public service in the matter of nursery schools and playing grounds, and the building of bigger and more convenient houses. It also probably involves the extension and improvement of free education, so that the middle-class family shall not, as at present, be crushed out of existence by impossibly high school fees.

The economic adjustments must come first, but a change of outlook is also needed. In the England of the last thirty years it has seemed all too natural that blocks of flats should refuse tenants with children, that parks and squares should be railed off to keep the children out of them, that abortion, theoretically illegal, should be looked on as a peccadillo, and that the main aim of commercial advertising should be to popularise the idea of "having a good time" and staying young as long as possible. Even the cult of animals, fostered by the newspapers, has probably done its bit towards reducing the birthrate. Nor have the public authorities seriously interested themselves in this question till very recently. Britain to-day has a million and a half less children than in 1914, and a million and a half more dogs. Yet even now, when the government designs a prefabricated house, it produces a house with only two bedrooms—with room, that is to say, for two children at the most.

When one considers the history of the years between the wars, it is perhaps surprising that the birthrate has not dropped more catastrophically than it has. But it is not likely to rise to the replacement level until those in power, as well as the ordinary people in the street, come to feel that children matter more than money.

The English are probably less irked by class distinctions, more tolerant of privilege and of absurdities like titles, than most peoples. There is nevertheless, as I have pointed out earlier, a growing wish for greater equality and a tendency, below the £2,000 a year level, for surface differences between class and class to disappear. At present this is happening only mechanically and quite largely as a result of the war. The question is how it can be speeded up. For even the change-over to a centralised economy, which, except, possibly, in the United States, is happening in all countries under one name or another, does of itself guarantee greater equality between man and man. Once civilisation has reached a fairly high technical level, class distinctions are an obvious evil. They not only lead great numbers of people to waste their lives in the pursuit of social prestige, but they also cause an immense wastage of talent. In England it is not merely the ownership of property that is concentrated in a few hands. It is also the case that all power, administrative as well as financial, belongs to a single class. Except for a handful of "self-made men" and Labour politicians, those who control our destinies are the product of about a dozen public schools and two universities. A nation is using its capacities to the full when any man can get any job that he is fit for. One has only to think of some of the people who have held vitally important jobs during the past twenty years, and to wonder what would have happened to them if they had been born into the working class, to see that this is not the case in England.

Moreover, class distinctions are a constant drain on morale, in peace as well as in war. And the more conscious, the better educated, the mass of the people become, the more this is so. The word "They," the universal feeling that "They" hold all the power and make all the decisions, and that "They" can only be influenced in indirect and uncertain ways, is a great handicap in England. In 1940 "They" showed a marked tendency to give place to "We," and it is time that it did so permanently. Three measures are obviously necessary, and they would begin to produce their effect within a few years.

The first is a scaling-up and scaling-down of incomes. The glaring inequality of wealth that existed in England before the war must not be allowed to recur. Above a certain point—which should bear a fixed relation to the lowest current wage—all incomes should be taxed out of existence. In theory, at any rate, this has happened already, with beneficial results. The second necessary measure is greater democracy in education. A completely unified system of education is probably not desirable. Some adolescents benefit by higher education, others do not, there is need to differentiate between literary and technical education, and it is better that a few independent experimental schools should remain in existence. But it should be the rule, as it is in some countries already, for all children to attend the same schools up to the age of twelve or at least ten. After that age it becomes necessary to separate the more gifted children from the less gifted, but a uniform educational system for the early years would cut away one of the deepest roots of snobbery.

The third thing that is needed is to remove the class labels from the English language. It is not desirable that all the local accents should disappear, but there should be a manner of speaking that is definitely national and is not merely (like the accent of the B.B.C. announcers) a copy of the mannerisms of the upper classes. This national accent—a modification of Cockney, perhaps, or of one of the northern accents—should be taught as a matter of course to all children alike. After that they could, and in some parts of the country they probably would, revert to the local accent, but they should be able to speak standard English if they wished to. No one should be "branded on the tongue." It should be impossible, as it is in the United States and some European countries, to determine anyone's status from his accent.

We need, too, to be less centralised. English agriculture revived during the war, and the revival may continue, but the English people are still excessively urban in outlook. Culturally, moreover, the country is very much over-centralised. Not only is the whole of Britain in effect governed from London, but the sense of locality—of being, say, an East Anglian or a West Countryman as well as an Englishman—has been much weakened during the past century. The ambition of the farm labourer is usually to get to a town, the provincial intellectual always wants to get to London. In both Scotland and Wales there are nationalist movements, but they are founded on an economic grievance against England rather than on genuine local pride. Nor is there any important literary or artistic movement that is truly independent of London and the university towns.

It is uncertain whether this centralising tendency is completely reversible, but a good deal could be done to check it. Both Scotland and Wales could and should be a great deal more autonomous than they are at present. The provincial universities should be more generously equipped and the provincial press subsidised. (At present nearly the whole of England is "covered" by eight London newspapers. No newspaper with a large circulation, and no first-class magazine, is published outside London.) The problem of getting people, and especially young, spirited people, to stay on the land would be partly solved if farm labourers had better cottages and if country towns were more civilised and cross-country bus services more efficient. Above all, local pride should be stimulated by teaching in the elementary schools. Every child ought as a matter of course to learn something of the history and topography of its own county. People ought to be proud of their own locality, they ought to feel that its scenery, its architecture and even its cookery are the best in the world. And such feelings, which do exist in some areas of the North but have lapsed throughout the greater part of England, would strengthen national unity rather than weaken it.

It has been suggested earlier that the survival of free speech in England is partly the result of stupidity. The people are not intellectual enough to be heresy-hunters. One does not wish them to grow less tolerant, nor, having seen the results, would one want them to develop the political sophistication that prevailed in pre-Hitler Germany or pre-Pétain France. But the instincts and traditions on which the English rely served them best when they were an exceptionally fortunate people, protected by geography from major disaster. In the twentieth century the narrow interests of the average man, the rather low level of English education, the contempt for "highbrows" and the almost general deadness to æsthetic issues, are serious liabilities.

What the upper classes think about "highbrows" can be judged from the Honours Lists. The upper classes feel titles to be important: yet almost never is any major honour bestowed on anyone describable as an intellectual. With very few exceptions, scientists do not get beyond baronetcies, or literary men beyond knighthoods. But the attitude of the man in the street is no better. He is not troubled by the reflection that England spends hundreds of millions every year on beer and the football pools while scientific research languishes for lack of funds; or that we can afford greyhound tracks innumerable but not even one National Theatre. Between the wars England tolerated newspapers, films, and radio programmes of unheard-of silliness, and these produced further stupefaction in the public, blinding their eyes to vitally important problems. This silliness of the English press is partly artificial, since it arises from the fact that newspapers live off advertisements for consumption goods. During the war the papers grew very much more intelligent without losing their public, and millions of people read papers which they would have rejected as impossibly "highbrow" some years ago. There is, however, not only a low general level of taste, but a widespread unawareness that æsthetic considerations can possibly have any importance. Rehousing and town-planning, for instance, are normally discussed without even a mention of beauty or ugliness. The English are great lovers of flowers, gardening and "nature," but this is merely a part of their vague aspiration towards an agricultural life. In the main they see no objection to "ribbon development" or to the filth and chaos of the industrial towns. They see nothing wrong in scattering the woods with paper bags and filling every pool and stream with tin cans and bicycle frames. And they are all too ready to listen to any journalist who tells them to trust their instincts and despise the "highbrow."

One result of this has been to increase the isolation of the British intelligentsia. English intellectuals, especially the younger ones, are markedly hostile to their own country. Exceptions can, of course, be found, but it is broadly true that anyone who would prefer T. S. Eliot to Alfred Noyes despises England, or thinks that he ought to do so. In "enlightened" circles, to express pro-British sentiments needs considerable moral courage. On the other hand, during the past dozen years there has been a strong tendency to develop a violent nationalistic loyalty to some foreign country, usually Soviet Russia. This must probably have happened in any case, because capitalism in its later phases pushes the literary and even the scientific intellectual into a position where he has security without much responsibility. But the philistinism of the English public alienates the intelligentsia still further. The loss to society is very great. It means that the people whose vision is acutest—the people, for instance, who grasped that Hitler was dangerous ten years before this was discovered by our public men—are hardly able to make contact with the masses and grow less and less interested in English problems.

The English will never develop into a nation of philosophers. They will always prefer instinct to logic, and character to intelligence. But they must get rid of their downright contempt for "cleverness." They cannot afford it any longer. They must grow less tolerant of ugliness, and mentally more adventurous. And they must stop despising foreigners. They are Europeans and ought to be aware of it. On the other hand they have special links with the other English-speakers overseas, and special imperial responsibilities, in which they ought to take more interest than they have done during these past twenty years. The intellectual atmosphere of England is already very much livelier than it was. The war scotched if it did not kill certain kinds of folly. But there is still need for a conscious effort at national re-education. The first step towards this is an improvement in elementary education, which involves not only raising the school-leaving age but spending enough money to ensure that elementary schools are adequately staffed and equipped. And there are immense educational possibilities in the radio, the film, and—if it could be freed once and for all from commercial interests—the press.

These, then, appear to be the immediate necessities of the English people. They must breed faster, work harder, and probably live more simply, think more deeply, get rid of their snobbishness and their anachronistic class distinctions, and pay more attention to the world and less to their own backyards. Nearly all of them already love their country, but they must learn to love it intelligently. They must have a clear notion of their own destiny and not listen either to those who tell them that England is finished or to those who tell them that the England of the past can return.

If they can do that they can keep their feet in the post-war world, and if they can keep their feet they can give the example that millions of human beings are waiting for. The world is sick of chaos and it is sick of dictatorship. Of all peoples the English are likeliest to find a way of avoiding both. Except for a small minority they are fully ready for the drastic economic changes that are needed, and at the same time they have no desire either for violent revolution or for foreign conquests. They have known for forty years, perhaps, something that the Germans and the Japanese have only recently learned, and that the Russians and the Americans have yet to learn: they know that it is not possible for any one nation to rule the earth. They want above all things to live at peace, internally and externally. And the great mass of them are probably prepared for the sacrifices that peace entails.

But they will have to take their destiny into their own hands. England can only fulfil its special mission if the ordinary English in the street can somehow get their hands on power. We were told very frequently during the war years that this time, when the danger was over, there should be no lost opportunities, no recurrence of the past. No more stagnation punctuated by wars, no more Rolls-Royces gliding past dole queues, no return to the England of the Distressed Area, the endlessly stewing teapot, the empty pram, and the Giant Panda. We cannot be sure that this promise will be kept. Only we ourselves can make certain that it will come true, and if we do not, no further chance may be given to us. The past thirty years have been a long series of cheques drawn upon the accumulated good will of the English people. That reserve may not be inexhaustible. By the end of another decade it will be finally clear whether England is to survive as a great nation or not. And if the answer is to be "Yes," it is the common people who must make it so.[5]

1. Air Raid Precautions.
2. The Communist newspaper the *Daily Worker* was banned from 22 Janury 1941 to 6 September 1942; see Orwell's War-time Diary, *749, 22.1.41.*
3. The British Union of Fascists.
4. Orwell gives an example of bêche-de-mer in the last paragraph of 'As I Please,' 80, 4 April 1947; see *3208.*
5. As Charles Humana, in *Freedom,* 18 October 1947, pointed out, *The English People* was generally very favourably reviewed: 'Strangely enough, despite the party line of the various journals, they were all unanimous on this occasion. Nationalism had transcended all.' Humana's review, whilst not quite coming down hard, did provide the most perceptive comments. He would have preferred to ignore this book, 'coming so soon after the profundity of *Animal Farm,* as a natural weakening to temptation despite the promptings of higher reason.' But, had the reviewers connived or been fooled, and also the editor (W. J. Turner) of this 'prestige building series'? He went on, 'Orwell has cleverly produced out of his top hat a definite political pamphlet. The message that goes hand in hand with his carefully compiled lists of virtues and faults of the English people is one that he has been peddling in his more obvious political writings.' That message was, briefly, 'that of Britain leading a European bloc in the face of the Russo-American stalemate.' Nevertheless, Humana thought 'a little fresh air should be allowed into the stuffy basement' and invoked Henry Miller. For all the claims to gentleness, not killing one another inordinately, being considerate and peace-loving, one should recall, as did Orwell, 'the traditional faults of the Englishman . . . hypocrisy and line shooting.' We should remember 'that even a Nigerian bushman will lose his suspicion in the face of kindness and become sullen and unfriendly when exploited.' Nor, concluded Humana, should we forget 'the example of progressive writers who, temporarily we hope, fail to remember all this.' In his notes for his literary executor written in the last year of his life (see *3728*), Orwell included *The English People* among four works not to be reprinted; the others were *A Clergyman's Daughter, Keep the Aspidistra Flying,* and *The Lion and the Unicorn.* The last line is echoed in *Nineteen Eighty-Four:* 'If there was hope it *must* lie in the proles (*CW,* IX, 72).

2475A. To Lydia Jackson

23 May 1944   Typewritten

Tribune

Dear Lydia,
Would you like to review this (say 600 words)?[1] It may be quite interesting and you would be able to judge how far it is authentic. By the way, we pay for reviews now (a little).

Yours
[Signed] Eric.[2]

1. Probably *Before the Storm: The Recollections of I. M. Maisky.* This was published in *Tribune* on 18 August 1944. Ivan Mikhailovich Maisky (1884–1975) was Soviet Ambassador in London

during the war. He pressed hard for the launching of a Second Front to relieve pressure on the Russians and argued at the Yalta Conference (4–11 February 1945) on Stalin's behalf that Germany should pay the Soviet Union reparations after the war.

2. Although Orwell continued to use the name 'George' when signing-off letters to Lydia Jackson, at least until 1947, he had used the name 'Eric' when writing to her before the war (for example, *534A*) and he chiefly used the name 'Eric' from this date. This signature is a scrawl; it is certainly not 'George' but just could be the initials 'EB.' However, 'Eric' is most likely and this scrawl is so interpreted here and elsewhere. See also *3402A, n. 7.*

2476. To Leonard Moore

24 May 1944   Typewritten

10a Mortimer Crescent
London NW 6

Dear Mr Moore,
Thanks for your letter. Yes, Cape's offer sounds all right,[1] so I should close with it. The only thing is, would it be possible to get some stipulation about the date when the book is to be published? I don't want it to be held up for a year or something like that, and as it is so short I should think he ought to be able to do it fairly soon.

Yours sincerely
Eric Blair

1. To publish *Animal Farm.*

2477. To A. S. Umpleby, JP

25 May 1944   Typewritten

Tribune

Dear Mr. Umpleby,[1]
Many thanks for the copy of C. A. Hinks's[2] poem, and the Yorkshire dialect poems. I am sending them for review to Rayner Heppenstall, another Yorkshire writer who is at present in the army.

Yours truly,
[Signed] Geo. Orwell
George Orwell,
Literary Editor.

1. A. S. Umpleby was station-master of Darlington railway station and a local magistrate.
2. C. A. Hinks was a solicitor in Darlington, Yorkshire. His poem, *The Summing Up* (1943), 1,156 lines, described the trial of Everyman before a jury and judge, the latter summing up the arguments of prosecuting and defending counsel. The case hinged on 'the central social and psychological dilemma of wishing to remain an idealist, either as a nation or as an individual, in a world governed by purely property values' (as the publisher's description explained). No verdict is given; the poem ends with the dismissal of the 'jury of historians / in the quiet of

your peaceful times' to consider its verdict. The kernel of Hinks's own verdict is indicated by a plea that 'For such a high and consecrated purpose / let there arise some commonwealth of citizens, / scorched with devotion to the general health, / uncorrupted and untaught of property . . .' (lines 894–97). Heppenstall reviewed the poem with four other books in *Tribune*, 18 August 1944. One of these was by Umpleby—*A Bo'ddin O'Cowls*; the others were a collection produced by the Yorkshire Dialect Society, *Yorkshire Dialect Poems*; W. J. Halliday, *History and Aims*; and Albert Mackie, *Sing a Sang o' Scotland*. (*Tribune* misspelled Mackie as Mackay and *Sang* as *Song*).

2478. 'As I Please,' 26

Tribune, 26 May 1944

I was talking the other day to a young American soldier, who told me—as quite a number of others have done—that anti-British feeling is completely general in the American army. He had only recently landed in this country, and as he came off the boat he asked the Military Policeman on the dock, "How's England?"

"The girls here walk out with niggers," answered the M.P. "They call them American Indians."

That was the salient fact about England, from the M.P.'s point of view. At the same time my friend told me that anti-British feeling is not violent and there is no very clearly-defined cause of complaint. A good deal of it is probably a rationalisation of the discomfort most people feel at being away from home. But the whole subject of anti-British feeling in the United States badly needs investigation. Like anti-semitism, it is given a whole series of contradictory explanations, and again like anti-semitism, it is probably a psychological substitute for something else. *What* else is the question that needs investigating.

Meanwhile, there is one department of Anglo-American relations that seems to be going well. It was announced some months ago that no less than 20,000 English girls had already married American soldiers and sailors, and the number will have increased since. Some of these girls are being educated for their life in a new country at the "Schools for Brides of U.S. Servicemen" organised by the American Red Cross. Here they are taught practical details about American manners, customs and traditions—and also, perhaps, cured of the widespread illusion that every American owns a motor car and every American house contains a bathroom, a refrigerator and an electric washing-machine.

The May number of the *Matrimonial Post and Fashionable Marriage Advertiser* contains advertisements from 191 men seeking brides and over 200 women seeking husbands. Advertisements of this type have been running in a whole series of magazines since the 'sixties or earlier, and they are nearly always very much alike. For example:

"Bachelor, age 25, height 6 ft. 1 in., slim, fond of horticulture, animals, children, cinema, etc., would like to meet lady, age 27 to 35, with love of flowers, nature, children, must be tall, medium build, Church of England."

The general run of them are just like that, though occasionally a more unusual note is struck. For instance:

"I'm 29, single, 5 ft. 10 in., English, large build, kind, quiet, varied intellectual interests, firm moral background (registered unconditionally as absolute C.O.), progressive, creative, literary inclinations. A dealer in rare stamps, income variable but quite adequate. Strong swimmer, cyclist, slight stammer occasionally. Looking for the following rarity, amiable, adaptable, educated girl, easy on eye and ear, under 30, Secretary type or similar, mentally adventurous, immune to mercenary and social incentives, bright sense of genuine humour, a reliable working partner. Capital unimportant, character vital."

The thing that is and always has been striking in these advertisements is that nearly all the applicants are remarkably eligible. It is not only that most of them are broad-minded, intelligent, home-loving, musical, loyal, sincere and affectionate, with a keen sense of humour and, in the case of women, a good figure; in the majority of cases they are financially O.K. as well. When you consider how fatally easy it is to get married, you would not imagine that a 36-year-old bachelor, "dark hair, fair complexion, slim build, height 6 ft., well educated and of considerate, jolly and intelligent disposition, income £1,000 per annum and capital," would need to find himself a bride through the columns of a newspaper. And ditto with "Adventurous young woman, Left-wing opinions, modern outlook" with "fairly full but shapely figure, medium colour curly hair, grey-blue eyes, fair skin, natural colouring, health exceptionally good, interested in music, art, literature, cinema, theatre, fond of walking, cycling, tennis, skating and rowing." Why does such a paragon have to advertise?

It should be noted that the *Matrimonial Post* is entirely above-board and checks up carefully on its advertisers.

What these things really demonstrate is the atrocious loneliness of people living in big towns. People meet for work and then scatter to widely separated homes. Anywhere in inner London it is probably exceptional to know even the names of the people who live next door.

Years ago I lodged for a while in the Portobello Road.[1] This is hardly a fashionable quarter, but the landlady had been lady's maid to some woman of title and had a good opinion of herself. One day something went wrong with the front door and my landlady, her husband and myself were all locked out of the house. It was evident that we should have to get in by an upper window, and as there was a jobbing builder next door I suggested borrowing a ladder from him. My landlady looked somewhat uncomfortable.

"I wouldn't like to do that," she said finally. "You see we don't know him. We've been here fourteen years, and we've always taken care not to know the people on either side of us. It *wouldn't do*, not in a neighbourhood like this. If you once begin talking to them they get familiar, you see."

So we had to borrow a ladder from a relative of her husband's, and carry it nearly a mile with great labour and discomfort.

1. In 1927 Orwell went to live at 22 Portobello Road, next door to Ruth Pitter (at number 24),

who found him these lodgings; his landlady was Mrs. Edwin Craig. The builder lived at number 20. The three houses are illustrated in Thompson, 23.

2479. To The Royal Literary Fund

26 May 1944   Handwritten

10a Mortimer Crescent London NW.6

Dear Sir,

I am asked to write to you on behalf of the Anglo-Indian writer Cedric Dover, who I believe is in severe financial straits. I wrote to you on his behalf last year[1] & I believe you were good enough to make him a grant, but I know him to be a writer of promise & I think he is deserving of help. He is one of the very few Eurasian writers who have yet appeared, & his books "Half-Caste" & "Hell in the Sunshine" have drawn the attention of many people to the colour problem. He has another book, "Brown Phoenix", coming out some time this year. He also contributed some valuable pieces to "Talking to India", a book of radio talks published by Allen & Unwin's for the Indian Section of the BBC. I am asking E. M. Forster, who also knows his work, to write to you as well.

Yours truly
George Orwell

1. See 13 May 1943, *2078*.

2480. To Leonard Moore

27 May 1944   Typewritten

10a Mortimer Crescent
London NW 6

Dear Mr Moore,

I had not realised that you were negotiating for a Penguin of "Keep the Aspidistra Flying." I don't think I can allow this book to be reprinted, or "A Clergyman's Daughter" either. They are both thoroughly bad books and I would much rather see them go out of print. The Penguin people did say something to me in their last letter about reprinting some other or others of my books, but I took them to be referring to "Coming Up for Air." Couldn't they do that one instead? I should like that to be reprinted, and I should imagine that from their point of view it would be a better speculation than the other. I am sorry you have had this trouble for nothing, but I did not realise what was under way. It wouldn't do me any good to have those two books revived. The other one that deserves reprinting is the Spanish book, but of course that is no use at present.

I have heard from the Dial people who say they will wire as soon as the MS arrives. I note their letter took 5 weeks in getting here, so presumably the MS won't have taken less. If by any chance it should have been lost on the way I have a spare copy.

I am at work now on my essay on Dali. After that I have one more long essay to do and then we could go ahead with the book of reprints. I have, however, tentatively arranged to do two other essays, one on Arthur Koestler, and one on women's weekly papers,[1] and it might be well to wait so as to put those in as well.

Yours sincerely
Eric Blair

1. No essay on women's weekly papers was published and no script has survived.

2481. 'Benefit of Clergy: Some Notes on Salvador Dali'
Intended for *Saturday Book*, 4, 1944

'Benefit of Clergy' is entered in Orwell's Payments Book against 1 June 1944. He was paid £25 for the essay, although, as he explained in a note when it was published, in 1946, in *Critical Essays* (and the U.S. edition, *Dickens, Dali & Others*, 1946), it did not appear in copies of the *Saturday Book* which were intended for distribution to the public. '"Benefit of Clergy" made a sort of phantom appearance in the *Saturday Book* for 1944. The book was in print when its publishers, Messrs Hutchinson, decided that this essay must be suppressed on grounds of obscenity. It was accordingly cut out of each copy, though for technical reasons it was impossible to remove its title from the table of contents.'

Orwell's own copy of the *Saturday Book* (and a few others that eluded Hutchinson's censors) included the essay, and it is from that copy that this essay is reproduced here. In *Critical Essays* it appeared in a slightly different form. Most of the changes were almost certainly the work of whoever at Secker & Warburg styled the book for publication. Double quotation marks are made single and single double; italicised titles sometimes are changed to roman; and there are some slight changes in punctuation and capitalisation. One or two errors crept into the 1946 text. The *Saturday Book* text reproduced here (apart from the correction of the spelling of homosexuality) contains punctuation and capitalisation that are probably closer to Orwell's typescript. Capitalisation of 'Civil War' is almost certainly not Orwell's (see his typescript for 'Arthur Koestler.' *2548*), and he was prone to omitting the first comma, or both, in constructions such as 'And, after all,' a practice found in the *Saturday Book* but not in *Critical Essays*, where the punctuation is more formal. Textual variants are given in the notes at the end of the essay; inversions of quotations marks are not recorded. The expression 'benefit of clergy' derives from the time when clergy were exempted from trial by a secular court when charged with a felony. In 'As I Please,' 58, 9 February 1945 (see *2616*), Orwell comments ironically on the failure of reviewers to notice the excision of his contribution. However, since the copies of *Saturday Book*, 4 that have survived, which include 'Benefit of Clergy,' may be review copies, his irony may not be justified.

Autobiography is only to be trusted when it reveals something disgraceful. A man who gives a good account of himself is probably lying, since any life when viewed from the inside is simply a series of defeats. However, even the most flagrantly dishonest book (Frank Harris's autobiographical writings are an example) can without intending it give a true picture of its author. Dali's recently-published[1] Life★ comes under this heading. Some of the incidents in it are flatly incredible, others have been re-arranged and romanticised, and not merely the humiliation but the persistent *ordinariness* of everyday life has been cut out. Dali is even by his own diagnosis narcissistic, and his autobiography is simply a strip-tease act conducted in pink limelight. But as a record of fantasy, of the perversion of instinct that has been made possible by the machine age, it has great value.

Here then[2] are some of the episodes in Dali's life, from his earliest years onward. Which of them are true and which are imaginary hardly matters: the point is that this is the kind of thing that Dali would have *liked* to do.

When he is six years old there is some excitement over the appearance of Halley's comet:

'Suddenly one of my father's office clerks appeared in the drawing-room doorway and announced that the comet could be seen from the terrace. . . . While crossing the hall I caught sight of my little three-year-old sister crawling unobtrusively through a doorway. I stopped, hesitated a second, then gave her a terrible kick in the head as though it had been a ball, and continued running[3] carried away with a "delirious joy" induced by this savage act. But my father, who was behind me, caught me and led me down into his office, where I remained as a punishment till dinner time.'[4]

A year earlier than this Dali had 'suddenly, as most of my ideas occur'[5] flung another little boy off a suspension bridge. Several other incidents of the same kind are recorded, including (this was when he was twenty-nine years old) knocking down and trampling on a girl 'until they had to tear her, bleeding, out of my reach.'

When he is about five he gets hold of a wounded bat which he puts into a tin pail. Next morning he finds that the bat is almost dead and is covered with ants which are devouring it. He puts it in his mouth, ants and all, and bites it almost in half.

When he is adolescent a girl falls desperately in love with him. He kisses and caresses her so as to excite her as much as possible, but refuses to go further. He resolves to keep this up for five years (he calls it his 'five year[6] plan'), enjoying her humiliation and the sense of power it gives him. He frequently tells her that at the end of five years he will desert her, and when the time comes he does so.

Till well into adult life he keeps up the practice of masturbation, and likes to do this, apparently, in front of a looking-glass. For ordinary purposes he is impotent, it appears, till the age of thirty or so. When he first meets his future wife, Gala, he is greatly tempted to push her off a precipice. He is aware that

★ *The Secret Life of Salvador Dali* (the Dial Press, New York) [Orwell's footnote].

there is something that she wants him to do to her, and after their first kiss the confession is made:

'I threw back Gala's head, pulling it by the hair, and, trembling with complete hysteria, I commanded,
'"Now tell me what you want me to do with you! But tell me slowly, looking me in the eye, with the crudest, the most ferociously erotic words that can make both of us feel the greatest shame!"
'. . . Then,[7] Gala, transforming the last glimmer of her expression of pleasure into the hard light of her own tyranny, answered,
'"I want you to kill me!"'

He is somewhat disappointed by this demand, since it is merely what he wanted to do already. He contemplates throwing her off the bell-tower of the Cathedral of Toledo, but refrains from doing so.

During the Spanish civil war[8] he astutely avoids taking sides and makes a trip to Italy. He feels himself more and more drawn towards the aristocracy, frequents smart salons,[9] finds himself wealthy patrons, and is photographed with the plump Vicomte de Noailles, whom he describes as his 'Maecenas.' When the European war[10] approaches he has one preoccupation only: how to find a place which has good cookery and from which he can make a quick bolt if danger comes too near. He fixes on Bordeaux, and duly flees to Spain during the Battle of France. He stays in Spain long enough to pick up a few anti-red atrocity stories, then makes for America. The story ends in a blaze of respectability. Dali, at thirty-seven, has become a devoted husband, is cured of his aberrations, or some of them, and is completely reconciled to the Catholic Church. He is also, one gathers, making a good deal of money.

However, he has by no means ceased to take pride in the pictures of[11] his Surrealist period, with titles like *The Great Masturbator, Sodomy of a Skull with a Grand Piano,*[12] etc. There are reproductions of these all the way through the book. Many of Dali's drawings are simply representational and have a characteristic to be noted later. But from his Surrealist paintings and photographs the two things that stand out are sexual perversity and necrophilia. Sexual objects and symbols—some of them well-known,[13] like our old friend the high-heeled slipper, others, like the crutch and the cup of warm milk, patented by Dali himself—recur over and over again, and there is a fairly well-marked excretory motif as well. In his painting *Le Jeu Lugubre,*[14] he says, 'the drawers bespattered with excrement were painted with such minute and realistic complacency that the whole little surrealist[15] group was anguished by the question: Is he coprophagic or not?' Dali adds firmly that he is *not,* and that he regards this aberration as 'repulsive,' but it seems to be only at that point that his interest in excrement stops. Even when he recounts the experience of watching a woman urinate standing up, he has to add the detail that she misses her aim and dirties her shoes. It is not given to any one person to have all the vices, and Dali also boasts that he is not homosexual, but otherwise he seems to have as good an outfit of perversions as anyone could wish for.

However, his most notable characteristic is his necrophilia. He himself freely admits to this, and claims to have been cured of it. Dead faces, skulls, corpses of animals occur fairly frequently in his pictures, and the ants which devoured the dying bat make countless reappearances. One photograph shows an exhumed corpse, far gone in decomposition. Another shows the dead donkeys putrefying on top of grand pianos which formed part of the Surrealist film *Le Chien Andalou*. Dali still looks back on these donkeys with great enthusiasm:[16]

> 'I "made up" the putrefaction of the donkeys with great pots of sticky glue which I poured over them. Also I emptied their eye sockets and made them larger by hacking them out with scissors. In the same way I furiously cut their mouths open to make the white rows[17] of their teeth show to better advantage, and I added several jaws to each mouth so that it would appear that although the donkeys were already rotting they were vomiting up a little more of their own death, above those other rows of teeth formed by the keys of the black pianos.'

And finally there is the picture—apparently some kind of faked photograph—of 'Mannequin rotting in a taxicab.' Over the already somewhat bloated face and breast of the [18] apparently dead girl, huge snails are crawling. In the caption below the picture Dali notes that these are Burgundy snails—that is, the edible kind.

Of course, in this long book of 400 quarto pages there is more than I have indicated, but I do not think that I have given an unfair account of its moral atmosphere and mental scenery. It is a book that stinks. If it were possible for a book to give a physical stink off its pages, this one would—a thought that might please Dali, who before wooing his future wife for the first time rubbed himself all over with an ointment made of goat's dung boiled up in fish glue. But against this has to be set the fact that Dali is a draughtsman of very exceptional gifts. He is also, to judge by the minuteness and the sureness of his drawings, a very hard worker. He is an exhibitionist and a careerist, but he is not a fraud. He has fifty times more talent than most of the people who would denounce his morals and jeer at his paintings. And these two sets of facts, taken together, raise a question which for lack of any basis of agreement seldom gets a real discussion.

The point is that you have here a direct, unmistakable assault on sanity and decency: and even—since some of Dali's pictures would tend to poison the imagination like a pornographic postcard—on life itself. What Dali has done and what he has imagined is debatable, but in his outlook, his character, the bedrock decency of a human being does not exist. He is as anti-social as a flea. Clearly, such people are undesirable, and a society in which they can flourish has something wrong with it.

Now, if you showed this book, with its illustrations, to Lord Elton, to Mr Alfred Noyes, to *The Times* leader-writers who exult over the 'eclipse of the highbrow,' in fact to any 'sensible' art-hating English person,[19] it is easy to imagine what kind of response you would get. They would flatly refuse to see any merit in Dali whatever. Such people are not only unable to admit that what is morally degraded can be aesthetically right, but their real demand of every artist is that he shall pat them on the back and tell them that thought is unneccessary. And they can be especially dangerous at a time like the present, when the Ministry of Information and the British Council put power into their hands. For their impulse is not only to crush every new talent as it appears, but to castrate the past as well. Witness the renewed highbrow-baiting that is now going on in this country and America, with its outcry not only against Joyce, Proust,[20] and Lawrence, but even against T. S. Eliot.

But if you talk to the kind of person who *can* see Dali's merits, the response that you get is not as a rule very much better. If you say that Dali, though a brilliant draughtsman, is a dirty little scoundrel, you are looked upon as a savage. If you say that you don't like rotting corpses, and that people who do like rotting corpses are mentally diseased, it is assumed that you lack the aesthetic sense. Since 'Mannequin rotting in a taxicab' is a good composition (as it undoubtedly is), it cannot be a disgusting, degrading picture:[21] whereas Noyes, Elton, etc., would tell you that because it is disgusting it cannot be a good composition. And between these two fallacies there is no middle position: or [22] rather, there is a middle position, but we seldom hear much about it. On the one side, *Kulturbolschevismus*: on the other (though the phrase itself is out of fashion) 'Art for Art's sake.' Obscenity is a very difficult question to discuss honestly. People are too frightened either of seeming to be shocked, or of seeming not to be shocked, to be able to define the relationship between art and morals.

It will be seen that what the defenders of Dali are claiming is a kind of *benefit of clergy*. The artist is to be exempt from the moral laws that are binding on ordinary people. Just pronounce the magic word 'Art,' and everthing is O.K. Rotting corpses with snails crawling over them are O.K.; kicking little girls on the head is O.K.; even a film like *L'Age d'Or* is O.K.* It is also O.K. that Dali should batten on France for years and then scuttle off like a rat as soon as France is in danger. So long as you can paint well enough to pass the test, all shall be forgiven you.

One can see how false this is if one extends it to cover ordinary crime. In an age like our own, when the artist is an altogether exceptional person, he must be allowed a certain amount of irresponsibility, just as a pregnant woman is. Still, no one would say that a pregnant woman should be allowed to commit murder, nor would anyone make such a claim for the artist, however gifted. If Shakespeare returned to the earth to-morrow, and if it were found that his favourite recreation was raping little girls in railway carriages, we should not tell him to go ahead with it on the ground that he might write another *King Lear*. And[23] after all, the worst crimes are not always the punishable ones. By encouraging necrophilic reveries one probably does quite as much harm as by, say, picking pockets at the races. One ought to be able to hold in one's head simultaneously the two facts that Dali is a good draughtsman and a disgusting human being. The one does not invalidate or, in a sense, affect the

* Dali mentions *L'Age d'Or* and adds that its first public showing was broken up by hooligans, but he does not say in detail what it was about. According to Henry Miller's account of it, it showed among other things some fairly detailed shots of a woman defaecating [Orwell's footnote].

other. The first thing that we demand of a wall is that it shall stand up. If it stands up[24] it is a good wall, and the question of what purpose it serves is separable from that. And yet even the best wall in the world deserves to be pulled down if it surrounds a concentration camp. In the same way it should be possible to say, 'This is a good book or a good picture, and it ought to be burned by the public hangman.' Unless one can say that, at least in imagination, one is shirking the implications of the fact that an artist is also a citizen and a human being.

Not, of course, that Dali's autobiography, or his pictures, ought to be suppressed. Short of the dirty postcards that used to be sold in Mediterranean seaport towns, it is doubtful policy to suppress anything, and Dali's fantasies probably cast useful light on the decay of capitalist civilisation. But what he clearly needs is diagnosis. The question is not so much *what* he is as *why* he is like that. It ought not to be in doubt that he is a diseased intelligence, probably not much altered by his alleged conversion, since genuine penitents, or people who have returned to sanity, do not flaunt their past vices in that complacent way. He is a symptom of the world's illness. The important thing is not to denounce him as a cad who ought to be horsewhipped, or to defend him as a genius who ought not to be questioned, but to find out *why* he exhibits that particular set of aberrations.

The answer is probably discoverable in his pictures, and those I myself am not competent to examine. But I can point to one clue which perhaps takes one part of the distance. This is the old-fashioned, over-ornate, Edwardian style of drawing to which Dali tends to return[25] when he is not being Surrealist. Some of Dali's drawings are reminiscent of Dürer, one (p. 113) seems to show the influence of Beardsley, another (p. 269) seems to borrow something from Blake. But the most persistent strain is the Edwardian one. When I opened this[26] book for the first time and looked at its innumerable marginal illustrations, I was haunted by a resemblance which I could not immediately pin down. I fetched up at the ornamental candlestick at the beginning of Part I (p. 7). What did this thing remind me of? Finally I tracked it down. It reminded me of a large, vulgar, expensively got-up edition of Anatole France (in translation) which must have been published about 1913.[27] That had ornamental chapter headings and tailpieces after this style. Dali's candlestick displays at one end a curly fish-like creature that looks curiously familiar (it seems to be based on the conventional dolphin), and at the other is the burning candle. This candle, which recurs in one picture after another, is a very old friend. You will find it, with the same picturesque gouts of wax arranged on its sides, in those phoney electric lights done up as candlesticks which are popular in sham-Tudor country hotels. This candle, and the design beneath it, convey at once an intense feeling of sentimentality. As though to counteract this[28] Dali has spattered a quill-ful of ink all over the page, but without avail. The same impression keeps popping up on page after page. The design at the bottom of page 62, for instance, would nearly go into *Peter Pan*. The figure on page 224, in spite of having her cranium elongated into an immense sausage-like shape, is the witch of the fairy-tale books. The horse on page 234 and the unicorn on page 218 might be illustrations to James

Branch Cabell. The rather pansified drawings of youths on pages 97, 100,[29] and elsewhere convey the same impression. Picturesqueness keeps breaking in. Take away the skulls, ants, lobsters, telephones,[30] and other paraphernalia, and every now and again you are back in the world of Barrie, Rackham, Dunsany and *Where the Rainbow Ends*.

Curiously enough, some of the naughty-naughty touches in Dali's autobiography tie up with the same period. When I read the passage I quoted at the beginning, about the kicking of the little sister's head, I was aware of another phantom resemblance. What was it? Of course! *Ruthless Rhymes for Heartless Homes* by Harry Graham. Such rhymes were very popular round about 1912, and one that ran:

> *Poor little Willy is crying so sore,*
> *A sad little boy is he,*
> *For he's broken his little sister's neck*
> *And he'll have no jam for tea.*

might almost have been founded on Dali's anecdote. Dali, of course, is aware of his Edwardian leanings, and makes capital out of them, more or less in a spirit of pastiche. He professes an especial affection for the year 1900, and claims that every ornamental object of 1900 is full of mystery, poetry, eroticism, madness, perversity, etc. Pastiche, however, usually implies a real affection for the thing parodied. It seems to be, if not the rule, at any rate distinctly common for an intellectual bent to be accompanied by a non-rational, even childish urge in the same direction. A sculptor, for instance, is interested in planes and curves, but he is also a person who enjoys the physical act of mucking about with clay or stone. An engineer is a person who enjoys the feel of tools, the noise of dynamos and the smell of oil. A psychiatrist usually has a leaning towards some sexual aberration himself. Darwin became a biologist partly because he was a country gentleman and fond of animals. It may be, therefore, that Dali's seemingly perverse cult of Edwardian things (for example[31] his 'discovery of the 1900 subway entrances') is merely the symptom of a much deeper, less conscious affection. The innumerable, beautifully executed copies of textbook illustrations, solemnly labelled 'le rossignol,' 'une montre'[32] and so on, which he scatters all over his margins, may be meant partly as a joke. The little boy in knickerbockers playing with a diabolo on page 103 is a perfect period piece. But perhaps these things are also there because Dali can't help drawing that kind of thing, because it is to that period and that style of drawing that he really belongs.

If so, his aberrations are partly explicable. Perhaps they are a way of assuring himself that he is not commonplace. The two qualities that Dali unquestionably possesses are a gift for drawing and an atrocious egoism. 'At seven,' he says in the first paragraph of his book, 'I wanted to be Napoleon. And my ambition has been growing steadily ever since.' This is worded in a deliberately startling way, but no doubt it is substantially true. Such feelings are common enough. 'I knew I was a genius,' somebody once said to me, 'long before I knew what I was going to be a genius *about*.' And suppose that you have nothing in you except your egoism and a dexterity that goes no higher than the elbow:[33] suppose that your real gift is for a detailed, academic, representational style of drawing, your real *métier* to be an illustrator of scientific textbooks. How then do you become Napoleon?

There is always one escape: *into wickedness.* Always do the thing that will shock and wound people. At five, throw a little boy off a bridge, strike an old doctor across the face with a whip and break his spectacles—or, at any rate, dream about doing such things. Twenty years later, gouge the eyes out of dead donkeys with a pair of scissors. Along those lines you can always feel yourself original. And after all, it pays! It is much less dangerous than crime. Making all allowance for the probable suppressions in Dali's autobiography, it is clear that he has not had to suffer for his eccentricities as he would have done in an earlier age. He grew up into the corrupt world of the nineteen-twenties, when sophistication was immensely widespread and every European capital swarmed with aristocrats and rentiers who had given up sport and politics and taken to patronising the arts. If you threw dead donkeys at people[34] they threw money back. A phobia for grasshoppers—which a few decades back would merely have provoked a snigger—was now an interesting 'complex' which could be profitably exploited. And when that particular world collapsed before the German Army, America was waiting. You could even top it all up with religious conversion, moving at one hop and without a shadow of repentance from the fashionable salons[35] of Paris to Abraham's bosom.

That, perhaps, is the essential outline of Dali's history. But why his aberrations should be the particular ones they were, and why it should be so easy to 'sell' such horrors as rotting corpses to a sophisticated public—those are questions for the psychologist and the sociological critic. Marxist criticism has a short way with such phenomena as Surrealism. They are 'bourgeois decadence' (much play is made with the phrases 'corpse poisons' and 'decaying rentier class'), and that is that. But though this probably states a fact, it does not establish a connection. One would still like to know *why* Dali's leaning was towards necrophilia (and not, say, homosexuality),[36] and *why* the rentiers and the aristocrats should buy his pictures instead of hunting and making love like their grandfathers. Mere moral disapproval does not get one any further. But neither ought one to pretend, in the name of 'detachment,' that such pictures as 'Mannequin rotting in a taxicab' are morally neutral. They are diseased and disgusting, and any investigation ought to start out from that fact.

Readings after the square bracket are those in *Critical Essays* unless stated otherwise.
1. recently-published] recently published
2. Here then] Here, then,
3. running] running,
4. dinner time] dinner-time
5. occur'] occur",
6. five year] five-year
7. Then,] Then
8. civil war] Civil War
9. salons] *salons*

10. war] War
11. of] if
12. Titles in *Critical Essays* are roman within quotation marks, and that may represent what was in Orwell's typescript.
13. well-known] well known
14. *Le Jeu Lugubre*] "Le Jeu Lugubre." *Note that* Le Chien Andalou *in the next paragraph is in italics in both versions.*
15. surrealist] Surrealist
16. enthusiasm:] enthusiasm.
17. white rows] rows
18. the] an
19. highbrow,' . . . person,] highbrow"— . . . person—
20. Proust,] Proust
21. picture:] picture;
22. position: or] position; or,
23. And] And,
24. up] up,
25. return] revert
26. this] the
27. 1913] 1914. *If this were a deliberate change to 1914 because that was the precise date, it would be expected that 'about' would have been cut.*
28. this] this,
29. 100,] 100
30. telephones,] telephones
31. example] example,
32. 'le rossignol,' 'une montre'] *le rossignol, une montre*
33. elbow:] elbow;
34. people] people,
35. salons] *salons*
36. homosexuality] homosecuality *in* Saturday Book

2482. 'Are Books Too Dear?'

Manchester Evening News, 1 June 1944

H. G. Wells's *'42 and '44: A Contemporary Memoir upon Human Behaviour During the Crisis of the World Revolution* was adversely reviewed by Orwell in *The Observer* (see *2474*); by Charles Hamblett in *Tribune* (see *2465*); and by Michael Foot in the *Manchester Evening News*. Not only was the content of the book criticised, but so was its price and the fact that it was issued in a limited edition of 2,000 copies. This led to a lively argument in the public and trade press. The *Manchester Evening News* published a letter from James C. Smith on 16 May 1944 headed '2 Guinea Book':
    The review by Mr. Foot of H. G. Well's° book " '42 to '44" omitted one adjective—the word is "prohibitive." I wanted this book, but . . . I decided that his gospel is° become too exclusive.
    It is an act of contempt by Mr. Wells to do this both to the people who could find two guineas and never read him and to those who could find only two shillings and read him avidly.
    I should like to say to him ". . . why, even poor Tom Paine never took money at all for his pamphlets, so why should you charge me two guineas. . . ."
In this contribution to the *Manchester Evening News* for 1 June, Orwell did not review a book but wrote this general article.

The decision of Mr. H. G. Wells to publish his recent book " '42 to '44," in a limited edition at the stiff price of two guineas has set many people talking about the expensiveness of books, and whether it is necessary or justifiable. The subject is an extremely important one, but before discussing it it is perhaps worth mentioning in passing that the price of this particular book was not a financial "stunt" on Mr. Wells's part. Even if he took half the receipts he would only get about £1,000, which is not a great deal for so well-known a writer. He would have made about as much from a sale of 10,000 copies at a normal price.

In any discussion of the price of books one must take two propositions as axiomatic. One is that the more the public reads—provided that it is not reading sheer trash—the better. The other is that it is undesirable that writers should starve to death. And it is important to realise that they *would* starve, or at least would have to find other means of support, if cheap books were the rule instead of the exception.

In peace time the average book—a novel, say—is published at seven and sixpence. That is the price on the jacket, but the wholesale price is five shillings: if it is sold in a shop the bookseller takes half a crown. Out of that seven and sixpence the author's share is usually in the neighbourhood of a shilling. This means that he gets £50 (but in practice it is always less than £50, because of agents' fees and the like) on each 1,000 copies sold. Few novelists are capable of turning out more than one book a year, so that to make the very modest income of £250 a year one has to sell at least 5,000 copies of each book. And authors who are not "established" don't as a rule sell 5,000 copies: it is quite common for a writer's first book to sell only six or seven hundred.

It will be seen that from the author's point of view seven and sixpence is none too high a price. It *is* high, however, from the point of view of the public, especially as English books are on the whole none too well bound and extremely ugly to look at. And so general is the feeling that books are too expensive that many people are in the habit of proclaiming (usually with a certain air of pride) that they "never buy a book." This, however, is a delusion. Everyone who reads does buy books, indirectly, by means of library subscriptions.

If you take only one book a week out of a twopenny library you are paying for at least one new book a year, and a fraction of what you pay to the rates also goes on books for the public library. It is, in fact, the libraries and not the book-buying public that keeps the writer and publisher alive.

But while cheapness in new books is not desirable, there is an obvious need for cheap reprints. England has always been fairly well supplied with cheap reprints of "classics" (the Everyman Library, the World's Classics, etc.), but in 1935 John Lane tried, with the Penguin books, the seemingly unhopeful experiment of reprinting contemporary books at the very low price of sixpence.

Earlier attempts to do this had usually failed. The Penguin books were an instant success, partly because by 1935 the reading public had greatly expanded, partly because Lane's had the imagination to choose their books well and to produce them with legible print and an attractive cover.

The success of the Penguins has led innumerable people to say: "If they can produce a book as well as this for sixpence, why should one normally have to pay 15 times as much? Why shouldn't new books as well as old ones come out in sixpenny form?"

The answer is that this *would* be possible, but only at the price of robbing the writer of his independent status. If all books were sixpence (or, as in wartime, ninepence) each, there would never be enough of them sold to give writers a livelihood.

Books, like any other kind of merchandise, have their saturation point. If you are a person who normally spends £10 a year on books, you may, perhaps, get 30 new books for your money. If you laid it all out in Penguins you would get 400—and after all, who wants to buy 400 books every year?

In all probability you would spend, say, £2 on books and keep the rest for gramophone records. Meanwhile the writer could not keep alive, for whereas he gets about a shilling on each copy of a seven and sixpenny book, he gets only a farthing on a Penguin. Most Penguins bring their authors only £50, and £100 is a maximum. And though it is true that some books take only a couple of months to write, between six months and a year would be an average time.[1]

In pre-war France, as in most European countries, books were very cheap. A new book usually cost about 1s. 6d. or 2s., and as the library system was not so well developed as it is here, a book was considered to have done well if it sold 2,000 copies. The result was that only a very small number of writers could live by books alone. The others had to live off government grants and literary prizes, with all the racketeering that that implies, or by selling themselves as publicists to some political party. In totalitarian countries the writer's economic problem is solved, but only by turning him into a mouthpiece of the regime, to the destruction of his creative powers as well as his honesty.

Our literature over the past 20 years has had very grave faults, but these have not arisen from the writer's economic status. Writers have had greater freedom of expression than ever before, and at the same time they have been answerable to the general public rather than to a "patron" or the State. This can only happen so long as royalties are fairly high, and books, therefore, fairly expensive. Moreover, if books are very cheap it is impossible to produce them in great variety. A 6d. book does not pay unless it sells in scores of thousands, so that all-round cheapness in books would inevitably mean that fewer titles were produced and fewer new writers got a chance.

There is admittedly racketeering over certain books that possess snob appeal, but in general there is no case for reducing the price of *new* books. On the other hand we do deserve better selections of cheap reprints. It is a disgraceful thing that—to name only one instance—you cannot get the complete unabridged works of Swift without paying several pounds for them.

And since our books are expensive, they ought to be (and easily could be) better physical objects. They ought to be as durable as American books and as pleasant to look at as French ones.

But seven and sixpence, or in war time half a guinea, is not an unreasonable price for a book. It enables the writer to stay alive and to preserve fragments of his honesty. And after all, even with books at seven and sixpence you can take half a dozen of them out of the library for a shilling. In what other department of life will a shilling buy so much?

[Fee: £8.8.0; 30.5.44]

Orwell's article was reprinted in an abridged form (but omitting only the first paragraph) in *Synopsis*, Vol. 5, No. 2, Autumn 1944. It was followed by an editor's note which made two points. It asked why, if a retail return of one-third on a book costing three shillings was adequate, it was necessary to take three shillings of a book costing nine shillings. Only a little more capital but no additional labour was involved. It also suggested that as there was a snobbery about new books, a first edition should be sold at, say, 15s.0 for the first six months, 10s.0 for the next six, and then at whatever price would bring 'a fair return to all its producers.'

The abridged article in *Synopsis* was then printed in *The News & Book Trade Review and Stationers' Gazette*, Vol. 107, No. 38, 16 September 1944. The article was followed by a 'close analysis of four retail bookseller's° trading accounts' and a table showing how for the first six books sold there was no gross profit, the capital involved not even being replaced. It concluded that 'taking an average size bundle of ten books of one title at the price suggested by Mr. George Orwell the capital involved by the purchase amounts for° fifty shillings.' Orwell's article was read by the publisher Stanley Unwin, who wrote on 18 September to congratulate him. It was refreshing, he said, to encounter an author who understood the economics of the problem from the author's angle. He assumed Orwell's strictures about the poor binding and ugliness of English books referred to war-time production. He thought British books before the war were as durable as those produced in America and pleasanter to look at than most French books. He also maintained that early attempts at 'sixpennies' were not failures. They only failed when too many titles were produced, so that sales per title were inadequate. He asked Orwell to come to see him and said he hoped he had received a copy of his pamphlet *Publishing in Peace & War*. See also *2557*.

1. See also Orwell's review of the third batch of ten Penguin books, 5 March 1936, *290*, especially the first and last paragraphs and for estimates of Orwell's receipts from publishing, 1928–45, P. Davison, 'Orwell: Balancing the Books,' *The Library*, VI, 16 (1994), 77–98. Orwell's receipts (after agent's commission) from sales of the Penguin *Down and Out in Paris and London* (1940) were probably £91, and from the Penguin *Burmese Days* (1944), £148. Two guineas in 1944 would be equivalent to about £45 in 1996.

2483. 'As I Please,' 27

Tribune, 2 June 1944

An extract from the Italian radio, about the middle of 1942, describing life in London:

"Five shillings were given for one egg yesterday, and one pound sterling for a kilogram of potatoes. Rice has disappeared, even from the Black

Market, and peas have become the prerogative of millionaires. There is no sugar on the market, although small quantities are still to be found at prohibitive prices."

One day there will be a big, careful, scientific enquiry into the extent to which propaganda is believed. For instance, what is the effect of an item like the one above, which is fairly typical of the Fascist radio? Any Italian who took it seriously would have to assume that Britain was due to collapse within a few weeks. When the collapse failed to happen, one would expect him to lose confidence in the authorities who had deceived him. But it is not certain that that is the reaction. For quite long periods, at any rate, people can remain undisturbed by obvious lies, either because they simply forget what is said from day to day or because they are under such a constant propaganda bombardment that they become anaesthetised to the whole business.

It seems clear that it pays to tell the truth when things are going badly, but it is by no means certain that it pays to be consistent in your propaganda. British propaganda is a good deal hampered by its efforts not to be self-contradictory. It is almost impossible, for instance, to discuss the colour question in a way that will please both the Boers and the Indians. The Germans are not troubled by a little thing like that. They just tell everyone what they think he will want to hear, assuming, probably rightly, that no one is interested in anyone else's problems. On occasion their various radio stations have even attacked one another.

One which aimed at middle-class Fascists used sometimes to warn its listeners against the pseudo-left Worker's Challenge, on the ground that the latter was "financed by Moscow."

Another thing that that enquiry, if it ever takes place, will have to deal with is the magical properties of names. Nearly all human beings feel that a thing becomes different if you call it by a different name. Thus when the Spanish civil war broke out the B.B.C. produced the name "Insurgents" for Franco's followers. This covered the fact that they were rebels while making rebellion sound respectable. During the Abyssinian war Haile Sellassie was called the Emperor by his friends and the Negus by his enemies. Catholics strongly resent being called Roman Catholics. The Trotskyists call themselves Bolshevik-Leninists but are refused this name by their opponents. Countries which have liberated themselves from a foreign conqueror or gone through a nationalist revolution almost invariably change their names, and some countries have a whole series of names, each with a different implication. Thus the U.S.S.R. is called Russia or U.S.S.R. (neutral or for short), Soviet Russia (friendly) and Soviet Union (very friendly). And it is a curious fact that of the six names by which our own country is called, the only one that does not tread on somebody or other's toes is the archaic and slightly ridiculous name "Albion."

Wading through the entries for the Short Story Competition,[1] I was struck once again by the disability that English short stories suffer under in being all cut to a uniform length. The great short stories of the past are of all lengths from perhaps 1,500 words to 20,000. Most of Maupassant's stories, for

245

instance, are very short, but his two masterpieces, *Boule de Suif* and *La Maison de Madame Tellier*, are decidedly long. Poe's stories vary similarly. D. H. Lawrence's *England, My England*, Joyce's *The Dead*, Conrad's *Youth*, and many stories by Henry James, would probably be considered too long for any modern English periodical. So, certainly, would a story like Mérimée's *Carmen*. This belongs to the class of "long short" stories which have almost died out in this country, because there is no place for them. They are too long for the magazines and too short to be published as books. You can, of course, publish a book containing several short stories, but this is not often done because at normal times these books never sell.

It would almost certainly help to rehabilitate the short story if we could get back to the bulky nineteenth-century magazine, which had room in it for stories of almost any length. But the trouble is that in modern England monthly and quarterly magazines of any intellectual pretensions don't pay. Even the *Criterion*, perhaps the best literary paper we have ever had, lost money for sixteen years before expiring.

Why? Because people were not willing to fork out the seven and sixpence that it cost. People won't pay that much for a mere magazine. But why then will they pay the same sum for a novel, which is no bulkier than the *Criterion*, and much less worth keeping? Because they don't pay for the novel directly. The average person never buys a new book, except perhaps a Penguin. But he does, without knowing it, buy quite a lot of books by paying twopences into lending libraries. If you could take a literary magazine out of the library just as you take a book, these magazines would become commercial propositions and would be able to enlarge their bulk as well as paying their contributors better. It is book-borrowing and not book-buying that keeps authors and publishers alive, and there seems no good reason why the lending library system should not be extended to magazines. Restore the monthly magazine—or make the weekly paper about a quarter of an inch fatter—and you might be able to restore the short story. And incidentally the book-review, which for lack of elbow room has dwindled to a perfunctory summary, might become a work of art again, as it was in the days of the *Edinburgh* and the *Quarterly*.

After reading the *Matrimonial Times* last week I looked in the Penguin *Herodotus* for a passage I vaguely remembered about the marriage customs of the Babylonians. Here it is:

> Once a year in each village the maidens of an age to marry were collected altogether into one place, while the men stood round them in a circle. Then a herald called up the damsels one by one and offered them for sale. He began with the most beautiful. When she was sold for no small sum of money, he offered for sale the one who came next to her in beauty . . . The custom was that when the herald had gone through the whole number of the beautiful damsels, he should then call up the ugliest and offer her to the men, asking who would agree to take her with the smallest marriage portion. And the man who offered to take the smallest sum had her assigned to him. The marriage portions were furnished by the money paid

for the beautiful damsels, and thus the fairer maidens portioned out the uglier.

This custom seems to have worked very well and Herodotus is full of enthusiasm for it. He adds, however, that, like other good customs, it was already going out round about 450 B.C.

Four months later, on 13 October 1944, *Tribune* published the following letter from D.R. Brewley, a soldier serving in the Royal Electrical and Mechanical Engineers:

EFFECTS OF PROPAGANDA

I have just read one of the many interesting articles which George Orwell writes under the heading of "As I Please," which refers to the debatable effect which extensive propaganda has amongst the people. The article refers to the Italian radio quoting fantastic food prices in London when the enemy stood at the gates of Alexandria. It is perhaps a coincidence that this matter was brought up in an Italian household which entertained me recently, and I thought you might be interested in a first-hand impression on this subject.

First I will indicate briefly the status of the Italian family in question. They could be compared with a high-class middleman's family, the householder being a small land controller, formerly a captain in the Italian army. His daughter, a young woman, was a school teacher, formerly a secretary to the local Fascist Italian chief. The family was well educated and their opinions are worthy of note.

They firmly believe that England was almost finished in 1942 and that we were preparing for an armistice when Alexandria fell. They seem to imagine that it was a stroke of fate and good fortune for us that Americans came to our assistance and reversed the position at El Alamein. The extensive propaganda over a period of years has led them to believe that the British could never possess a really good army, and on equal terms could be licked by German and Italian soldiers; but we are fortunate to have so much outside assistance as regards planes and men from the Americans and negroes, etc. The people realise gross exaggerations were applicable in the Fascist regime, but even when they deduct a high percentage of over-statements the net result is still far from the truth, and no amount of reason and sensible arguments will alter their convictions.

As regards the English army being "no bona," I reminded them of Wavell and his 30,000, and in connection with American help re planes, I quoted the occasion in 1940 when a handful of English fighters fought off the enemy air armada. Many Italians believe that London is virtually wiped out, and although I have not ventured to suggest that bombing is of no consequence, I have referred to Italian areas of devastation, particularly in connection with railways, which will certainly prevent them from ever making war on the Eskimos for quite a long time.

The points I raised did not strike home, however, and it seems that it will take a long, gradual sensible education to bring Italian minds which are soaked with propaganda to realise the true facts and formulate a reasonable view of the situations under review.

I hesitate to consider who is likely to promote a sensible post-war education for the Italians when I think of the Badoglio Gas King in charge, and the presence of surrounding local Fascist chiefs free to live an ordinary life, for what is to stop them reinstating their dictatorship with propaganda under another heading, maybe altering the sense of the word democracy? Education in Italy was barred to those who were not Fascists, the net result being that all reasonably educated people are doped with poisonous propaganda, and it seems that before our work is finished we should help to organise some re-education, so that a post-war system does not arise and become influenced by minds which are already warped.

The danger of extensive propaganda, as I see it, is an enemy equal to Prussian militarism, but it needs a far better man than me to suggest an effective answer to this menace.

1. For details of this competition, which Orwell organised for *Tribune*, see 'As I Please,' 6, 7 January 1944, *2401, n. 1.*

2484. 'Survey of "Civvy Street"'

The Observer, 4 June 1944

The surveys undertaken by Mass-Observation[1] from the beginning of the war onwards have revealed many different moods, but nearly all have suggested that Britain suffers from too little government rather than too much. Cheque after cheque has been drawn on the accumulated good will of the British people, but very little positive guidance has been given. They know what they are fighting against, but they have not been clearly told what they are fighting *for* or what the post-war world will probably be like. The new survey, like some previous ones, gives warning that their patience and hopefulness may not be inexhaustible.

Although specifically concerned with demobilisation, it also deals with re-employment and reconstruction. It reveals not only widespread cynicism about "after the war" but also a surprising vagueness. Thus, when a cross-section of the public were asked in November, 1943, "whether the Government had announced any policy of post-war reconstruction," only 16 per cent. thought it had. The corresponding percentage had actually been higher two years earlier. Most disquieting is the return to the 1918 frame of mind. Great numbers are convinced that "it will be just like last time," and, as their memories of last time are not happy ones, the effects on morale are potentially bad.

Disbelief in the future is especially strong in the armed forces and among the Civil Defence workers. The soldiers (this is somewhat less marked in the women's services) want above all things to get out of uniform as soon as the war is over, and a number of people even think that there will be great discontent if demobilisation is not achieved rapidly. They know that the process of demobilisation is complicated, but are not confident that it will be done fairly or intelligently (memories of "last time" are a heavy liability here), and, even more serious, they have no clear idea as to how long it ought to take. Meanwhile countless soldiers cherish a private dream that they, as individuals, will somehow be able to get out of it when the fighting stops. The possible effects of this kind of thing in the immediate post-war period are obvious. They can only be countered by a clear statement from the Government which will let people know just how long they will be expected to stay in uniform, and why.

So also with post-war employment. According to the Mass-Observers' findings, a majority still expect large-scale unemployment after the war—another legacy from "last time." At the same time there is a growing consciousness that unemployment is an unnecessary evil. It is probably significant that the number of people expecting unemployment to return has not markedly altered over several years: there is no strong belief that our economic system will be radically changed. In general the feeling seems to be that most of our problems are soluble, but that the mysterious and all-powerful "They" will prevent anything from being done. The result is increasing apathy and a determination—of course accentuated by sheer fatigue as the war continues—to sit back and have a good rest as soon as the guns stop firing.

It is a sign of the general lack of confidence in the future that in 1943, out of a random sample of Londoners, 46 per cent. thought that there would be another world war after this one, and 19 per cent. thought there might be. The majority of these thought that this new war would happen within 25 years. Faith in all the main political parties has dwindled, and there is a confused desire for more vigorous leadership combined with more genuine democracy.

Yet how ready for effort and sacrifice most people are, when they are given a good reason, can be seen in their attitude towards war-time controls. Nearly all of these have been accepted readily: even the withdrawal of white bread was approved by a four to one majority. Other more drastic measures, not actually put into force, would be generally approved. For example, the Mass-Observers found a ten to one majority in favour of Government ownership of essential industries, and seven to one in favour of nationalisation of the mines.

Controls are even welcomed for their own sake, as having an equalising effect. On the whole, whenever the Government acts positively and explains what it is doing, even if what it is doing is to take something away, the people seem to respond. Certain events, such as the delay about "Beveridge," and even the release of Mosley, have deeply shaken public confidence, but it is the failure to explain, to give a picture of the future, that apparently does the most harm.

It is unfortunate that much of the work done by Mass-Observation should have to be financed by a private body which naturally only wants reports on a rather limited range of subjects. The present survey has one very serious omission: this is that it makes no reference to the war against Japan. The subject of demobilisation is complicated by the fact that Japan will almost certainly go on fighting, perhaps for years, after Germany is defeated. But the main conclusions reached by the Mass-Observers can hardly be questioned.

Political consciousness has expanded greatly during the war, while belief in the existing leadership has shrunk. The belief that planned reconstruction is *possible* has grown, while the belief that it is *likely* has made no headway. There is a gap between the leaders and the led, and the deadly word "They" saps confidence and encourages anarchic individualism. It is important that that gap should be closed before the war ends. For, as the Mass-Observers point out, it will need as great an effort to win the peace as to win the war, and the people may shrink from making it unless they have a better notion than at present of where they are going.

[Fee: £7.7.0; 30.5.44]

1. In his Payments Book (see *2831*), Orwell describes this as an article; it was, however, prompted by *The Journey Home* by Mass Observation, published for the Advertising Service Guild by John Murray.

2484A. To Lydia Jackson

5 June 1944   Typewritten

Tribune

Dear Lydia,
Thanks so much for the article on Malyshkin, which I'll be glad to use.[1] It will have to wait over for some weeks though.

Yours,
[Signed] Eric.

1. 'A Tender Bolshevik: A Sketch of A. G. Malyshkin' was published by *Tribune* on 18 August 1944.

2485. To Leonard Moore

8 June 1944   Typewritten

10a Mortimer Crescent
London NW 6

Dear Mr Moore,
Many thanks for your letter.[1] It is awkward about Gollancz. I don't however remember anything in that contract about *full-length* novels. As I remember it, it simply referred to my next three works of fiction (you could verify that

from the contract.) If so, "Animal Farm" which is certainly a work of fiction (and any way what is "full-length") would be one of them. But even so there is one more novel to be accounted for. Do you think it would be possible to arrange with Cape that Gollancz had the refusal of my next novel (or two novels if "Animal Farm" doesn't count), on the understanding that all other works went to Cape, including novels after the Gollancz contract ran out? In that case I should only be going away from Cape for one or at most two books. (Incidentally, I don't know when I shall write another novel. This doesn't seem a propitious time for them.)[2] I shouldn't in any case go to Gollancz again for non-fiction books. His politics change too fast for me to keep up with them. Could you find out what Cape thinks about that?

Meanwhile how do we stand about the book of reprints? Cape could have that too if he wants it. But the Dickens essay, which I should *like* to reprint, was in a Gollancz book. Has he the copyright of that, or have I? I have only one more essay to do, then I can start assembling the book.[3]

I am sorry about "Keep the Aspidistra Flying", but I don't think it worth reprinting a book I don't care about. If you tell Lane's I don't want that one done I dare say they'll be readier to close with "Coming up for Air."[4]

I hope it will be O.K. with Cape and this book won't have to start on its rounds once again. I do want it to see the light this year if possible.

Yours sincerely
E. A. Blair

1. Jonathan Cape wrote to Victor Gollancz on 26 May 1944 to say that he was inclined to publish *Animal Farm*, and to publish Orwell's future work. He wished to know whether that would be acceptable to Gollancz. On 1 June, Gollancz wrote to Moore, pointing out that he had a contract dated 1 February 1937 to publish three novels by Orwell, only one of which, *Coming Up for Air*, had been delivered. He argued that his rejection of *Animal Farm* did not affect that agreement. Moore then wrote to Orwell—his letter has not been traced—and this is Orwell's response. See Fredric Warburg, *All Authors Are Equal* (1973), 47–50, and also Michael Howard, *Jonathan Cape, Publisher* (1977)
2. This does not mean, of course, that Orwell was not thinking about and planning for what was to become *Nineteen Eighty-Four*.
3. Against this paragraph is a barely decipherable annotation: 'Get stuff together. Get Gollancz to agree.' The paragraph referring to *Keep the Aspidistra Flying* is scored with two lines in the margin and *Coming Up for Air* is underlined twice.
4. Penguin Books did not publish *Coming Up for Air* in Orwell's lifetime. It was reprinted in the first of Secker's Uniform series in May 1948 and next printed in the United States, the first edition in that country, by Harcourt, Brace, in January 1950, the month Orwell died.

2486. 'As I Please,' 28

Tribune, 9 June 1944

Arthur Koestler's recent article in *Tribune*[1] set me wondering whether the book racket will start up again in its old vigour after the war, when paper is plentiful and there are other things to spend your money on.

Publishers have got to live, like anyone else, and you cannot blame them for advertising their wares, but the truly shameful feature of literary life before the war was the blurring of the distinction between advertisement and criticism. A number of the so-called reviewers, and especially the best known ones, were simply blurb writers. The "screaming" advertisement started some time in the nineteen-twenties, and as the competition to take up as much space and use as many superlatives as possible became fiercer, publishers' advertisements grew to be an important source of revenue to a number of papers. The literary pages of several well-known papers were practically owned by a handful of publishers, who had their quislings planted in all the important jobs. These wretches churned forth their praise— "masterpiece," "brilliant," "unforgettable" and so forth—like so many mechanical pianos. A book coming from the right publishers could be absolutely certain not only of favourable reviews, but of being placed on the "recommended" list which industrious book-borrowers would cut out and take to the library the next day.

If you published books at several different houses you soon learned how strong the pressure of advertisement was. A book coming from a big publisher, who habitually spent large sums on advertisement, might get fifty or seventy-five reviews: a book from a small publisher might get only twenty. I knew of one case where a theological publisher, for some reason, took it into his head to publish a novel. He spent a great deal of money on advertising it. It got exactly four reviews in the whole of England, and the only full-length one was in a motoring paper, which seized the opportunity to point out that the part of the country described in the novel would be a good place for a motoring tour. This man was not in the racket, his advertisements were not likely to become a regular source of revenue to the literary papers, and so they just ignored him.

Even reputable literary papers could not afford to disregard their advertisers altogether. It was quite usual to send a book to a reviewer with some such formula as, "Review this book if it seems any good. If not, send it back. We don't think it's worth while to print simply damning reviews."

Naturally, a person to whom the guinea or so that he gets for the review means next week's rent is not going to send the book back. He can be counted on to find something to praise, whatever his private opinion of the book may be.

In America even the pretence that hack-reviewers read the books they are paid to criticise has been partially abandoned. Publishers, or some publishers, send out with review copies a short synopsis telling the reviewer what to say. Once, in the case of a novel of my own, they misspelt the name of one of the characters. The same misspelling turned up in review after review. The so-called critics had not even glanced into the book—which, nevertheless, most of them were boosting to the skies.

A phrase much used in political circles in this country is "playing into the hands of." It is a sort of charm or incantation to silence uncomfortable truths. When you are told that by saying this, that or the other you are "playing into the hands of " some sinister enemy, you know that it is your duty to shut up immediately.

For example, if you say anything damaging about British imperialism, you are playing into the hands of Dr. Goebbels. If you criticise Stalin you are playing into the hands of the *Tablet* and the *Daily Telegraph*. If you criticise Chiang-Kai-Shek you are playing into the hands of Wang Ching Wei—and so on, indefinitely.

Objectively this charge is often true. It is always difficult to attack one party to a dispute without temporarily helping the other. Some of Gandhi's remarks have been very useful to the Japanese. The extreme Tories will seize on anything anti-Russian, and don't necessarily mind if it comes from Trotskyist instead of right-wing sources. The American imperialists, advancing to the attack behind a smoke-screen of novelists, are always on the look-out for any disreputable detail about the British Empire. And if you write anything truthful about the London slums, you are liable to hear it repeated on the Nazi radio a week later. But what, then, are you expected to do? Pretend there are no slums?

Everyone who has ever had anything to do with publicity or propaganda can think of occasions when he was urged to tell lies about some vitally important matter, because to tell the truth would give ammunition to the enemy. During the Spanish civil war, for instance, the dissensions on the Government side were never properly thrashed out in the left-wing Press, although they involved fundamental points of principle. To discuss the struggle between the Communists and the Anarchists, you were told, would simply give the *Daily Mail* the chance to say that the Reds were all murdering one another. The only result was that the left-wing cause as a whole was weakened. The *Daily Mail* may have missed a few horror stories because people held their tongues, but some all-important lessons were not learned, and we are suffering from the fact to this day.

1. In *Tribune*, 28 April 1944, Koestler had written an article in the form of a letter to a young corporal who had written to ask for advice as to which book reviewers could be taken as reliable guides. Koestler pointed out the dismal standards of criticism prevailing in most of the press.

2487. Review of *Burma Surgeon* by Gordon S. Seagrave; *India Since Cripps* by Horace Alexander

The Observer, 11 June 1944

Up to date the Burma campaign of 1942 has not been well documented. Sensational and inaccurate books have been published by American journalists, while better-informed manuscripts from British and Burmese sources have failed to find publishers, because it is felt that the public is not interested in Burma except as a land of snakes, tigers, elephants, and pagodas. The political background of the campaign has been largely ignored or misrepresented. Dr. Seagrave's book is valuable because the events it describes begin in 1922 and the Japanese invasion is placed in its proper setting. Moreover, being written by a missionary, and a medical missionary at that, it is exceptionally free from political partisanship. Dr. Seagrave's experiences have not given him any reason for idealising either the Burmese, the British, the Indians, the Chinese, or the wild tribes, and though his manner of writing is often tiresome his book deserves to be read.

Dr. Seagrave was born into a family of missionaries and spoke Karen from his earliest childhood onwards. When, however, after being educated in the United States, he returned to Burma, it was as a medical and not a religious missionary. With almost no money, with a set of worn-out instruments, and with, at first, no trained assistance, he set up his hospital at Namkham, in the wild country where the Burma road was later to be built. Life for years after that was an unending struggle not only against disease but against filth, ignorance, and poverty. Malaria flourished in its most deadly form, goitre was common, venereal diseases almost equally common. There were also periodical outbreaks of plague. Dr. Seagrave had to build his hospital and his nurses' quarters with stones procured from the nearest river bed, and he had to raise money wherever he could find it, from the British Government, from the Shan chieftains, and even from the primitive villagers whom he attended. A twenty- mile ride over roadless mountains, followed by three hours' work on a difficult childbirth, might be rewarded by a fee of one rupee. It was, he says,

> surgery with waste-basket instruments. Orthopaedic surgery without an X-ray. Urological surgery without a cystoscope. Surgery without any actual cautery except a stray soldering-iron. Surgery without electricity. Medicine without a laboratory, and without medicines, often.

He did, however, have in his favour the incredible insensitiveness to pain of the Mongolian peoples which allowed him to use rough-and-ready methods and effect some surprising cures which were useful in winning him a reputation.

But Dr. Seagrave's greatest achievement was in the training of nurses. Such nurses as then existed in Burma were mostly drawn from among the Christian Karens, but Dr. Seagrave drew his recruits from all races, including the almost savage Kachins who inhabit the mountain ranges in the north of Burma. He had to give them their entire training from the rudiments upwards, and to do this in three or four different languages, teaching himself Burmese in the process. After years of work he had a brilliant team of nurses, trained to take responsibility and to refuse no matter what job, however dirty, and so used to working together that even experienced observers could not tell to which race each girl belonged.

Throughout most of the Burma campaign they were attached to General Stilwell's Chinese Army, and won golden opinions for themselves. "Seagrave's Burmese nurses" as they were inaccurately called—actually there was only one Burmese among them—were known throughout the British, Chinese, and American forces. All the ambulance units were overwhelmed with work, and Dr. Seagrave even found it possible to entrust simple surgical operations to his nurses. Some of them were cut off by the Japanese advance, but the majority retreated into India with the army, their tiny bodies standing the fatigue of the long march suprisingly well.

Dr. Seagrave is mainly concerned with medical matters, but such remarks as he makes on the Burmese political situation are probably reliable. His estimate of the Burmese attitude towards the war is much the same as that of some other observers—about ten per cent. actively pro-Japanese, another ten per cent. pro-British, and the rest neutral and primarily anxious to remain alive. He gives evidences of Burmese fifth-column activity—also of a good deal of shooting of fifth columnists by the Chinese—and confirms other accounts of the fearful effects of bombing on the wooden towns of Burma. His book ends with a note that Namkham has been visited by American bombers and his nurses' home presumably destroyed.

Dr. Seagrave's chronicle ends in 1942 and to some extent INDIA SINCE CRIPPS carries on the story. The peculiarly stupid deadlock now existing in India dates from the Burma campaign, and now that the danger of a Japanese invasion of India has obviously receded, a satisfactory settlement might be achieved if the initiative came from this country. Mr. Alexander's book is a useful popularly-written account of the existing situation. Quite rightly, since he is addressing a British audience, he stresses the Indian rather than the British case and shows that even when Indian politicians have acted foolishly their chronic suspicion of British motives is not unpardonable.

[Fee: £7.7.0; 7.6.44]

2488. To Leading Aircraftman C. Hopkins

14 June 1944   Typewritten

Tribune

Dear Mr. Hopkins,

I liked your sketch and shall be glad to use it, but it will have to wait over for some time. We have a lot of material in hand and are working it off in rotation.[1]

Yours truly,
[Signed] Geo. Orwell
George Orwell,
Literary Editor

1. This story has not been traced. A story, 'It's a Lovely Day to Die,' by G. Thurston Hopkins was published in *Tribune* on 11 August 1944, but, apart from the wrong initials, it seems to be written by a soldier, not by an aircraftman.

2489. Review of *Robert Cain* by William Russell

Manchester Evening News, 15 June 1944

The present is not a good time in which to write a novel, and it is a fact that most of the novels worth reading that have appeared in this country during the past few years had been written before the blitz and were in any case the work of foreigners.

War-time Britain has produced nothing of the calibre of "For Whom the Bell Tolls" or "Darkness at Noon," for instance. But even before the war there were, from the point of view of a novelist, certain advantages in being an American, and this powerful though rather immature and uneven novel brings some of them out.

It is a story of the southern States, and its essential theme is the attitude of the whites towards the negroes. Its hero is a boy with an inferiority complex, horribly sat upon by an oafish father. His reaction, a quite natural one in a little southern cotton town where the white inhabitants have never really abandoned the slave-owning habit of mind, is to develop a secret sympathy with the "niggers." It would not be, by our standards, a very deep sympathy; he never goes so far as to stop calling them "niggers," for instance, but he does feel a kind of incoherent rage at the way they are treated, and at the age of 17 he is sacked from his job and has to leave the town after uttering his opinions too freely. Earlier than this he has had a strong impulse to make friends with a mulatto boy, but has lacked the moral courage to do so.

He goes to St. Louis, and after much suffering gets a job in a steel mill, later on getting six months' imprisonment for various violent acts committed in a strike. Some of his adventures are less credible than others, but in their violence and their sudden vicissitudes one can see the advantages that contemporary American life offers to a novelist.

To begin with America is a big country, existing at many different levels of civilisation, and things happen cruelly and dramatically.

Colour feeling, for instance, is not merely a matter of quiet snobbery, as it is even in India. There are still lynchings and race riots. When Robert's mulatto friend Jim marries a white girl in St. Louis and then has the temerity to go back to his native town he is promptly shot by a gang of white men who have the law on their side and who are quite certain that they are doing the right thing in wiping out a racial insult.

Nor is the American class system rigid enough to confine every citizen to a single walk of life. Robert is not following a very unusual pattern when he first grows up in a fairly comfortable southern family, then freezes on a bench in a park in St. Louis, then works as an unskilled mill hand, then when his father dies goes home to manage the farm. Moreover, the predicament of the sensitive person isolated among ignorant boors is very much more painful in America than in England if only because America is so very much bigger.

Anyone who has read Sinclair Lewis's "Main Street" will notice certain resemblances of mood in "Robert Cain."

The struggles of enlightenment against reaction, of labour against capital, of coloured against white, and of young against old are all very much fiercer in America than in England, and American novels of the last twenty years have undoubtedly benefited from this. An English novel at the same intellectual level as this one would almost inevitably be less eventful.

When it leaves the negroes for familiar themes, Robert's psychological development becomes convincing,[1] though this is partly because the English edition of the book has been heavily bowdlerised.

In St. Louis, when his sense of inferiority is still so acute that he has not even succeeded in finding himself a job, he meets a lonely girl in the park, and, after much prodding on her part, marries her.

It now turns out that he is impotent. This seems somewhat arbitrary, but it is not really so—it arises from a boyhood incident which has been censored into unintelligibility in the English edition. (Incidentally, another advantage of being an American is that you can print words that make English proof-readers scatter query-marks all over the margin of the copy.) Robert's impotence is cured in the end, but his real psychological cure is effected when his father dies. He returns to his native town just in time to see, and vainly try to prevent, the lynching of his mulatto friend Jim.

He is still, so he imagines, in violent revolt against the white community and their barbarous attitude to "niggers."

But he is also the inheritor of his father's cotton plantation, and unaffectedly relieved at his father's death—his inferiority complex is slain at last, and his real character, which is not altogether an amiable one, begins to emerge.

At first he makes feeble efforts to be an enlightened employer and treat his negroes like human beings. The only result is that the bank refuses credits and he is forced to sell off a quarter of his land. Very soon he develops into just the same kind of employer as all the others, with the same attitude towards the "niggers."

The "niggers" are a kind of animal, needing firm handling tempered by occasional charity—a present of a worn-out pair of trousers, say, or a quid of chewing tobacco. To get all the work you can out of them, and pay them just as little as will keep them alive, is as much a matter of course as it would be with a horse or a mule.

Before long Robert begins to prosper: war is approaching, the price of cotton is going up. The local society has forgotten his past misdeeds and taken him back to its bosom. "Two of the married women had already made passes at him"—in spite of which, when the book ends, he is on the point of seducing a negro girl. As for the colour problem, his final reflection is "they are right about the niggers; you have to keep the niggers in line."

If the book has a moral it is that it is better to be a lonely and persecuted individual—even at the price of a crippling inferiority complex—than to be too well integrated with your environment. This is not a novel of the first rank, but it is an unusual one, and its author's future development will be worth watching.[2]

[Fee: £8.8.0; 13.6.44]

1. Perhaps 'unconvincing' was intended.
2. William Richard Russell (1915–) published *A Wind Is Rising* (1946) and *Strayhorn* (1948). Orwell reviewed his play *Cellar* in the *Manchester Evening News*, 20 December 1945 (see *2822*). In 1962 Russell published a non-fiction work, *Berlin Embassy*. *Robert Cain* was first published in 1942.

2490. 'As I Please,' 29

Tribune, 16 June 1944

Several times, by word of mouth and in writing, I have been asked why I do not make use of this column for an onslaught on the Brains Trust.[1] "For Christ's sake take a crack at Joad," one reader put it. Now, I would not deny that the Brains Trust is a very dismal thing. I am objectively anti-Brains Trust, in the sense that I always switch off any radio from which it begins to emerge. The phoney pretence that the whole thing is spontaneous and uncensored, the steady avoidance of any serious topic and concentration on questions of the "Why do children's ears stick out" type, the muscular-curate heartiness of the question-master, the frequently irritating voices, and the thought of incompetent amateur broadcasters being paid ten or fifteen shillings a minute to say "Er—er—er," are very hard to bear. But I cannot feel the same indignation against this programme as many of my acquaintances seem to do, and it is worth explaining why.

By this time the big public is probably growing rather tired of the Brains Trust, but over a long period it was a genuinely popular programme. It was listened to not only in England, but in various other parts of the world, and its technique has been adopted by countless discussion groups in the Forces and Civil Defence. It was an idea that "took on," as the saying goes. And it is not difficult to see why. By the standards of newspaper and radio discussion prevailing in this country up to about 1940, the Brains Trust was a great step forward. It did at least make some show of aiming at free speech and at intellectual seriousness, and though latterly it has had to keep silent about "politics and religion," you could pick up from it interesting facts about birds' nest soup or the habits of porpoises, scraps of history and a smattering of philosophy. It was less obviously frivolous than the average radio programme. By and large it stood for enlightenment, and that was why millions of listeners welcomed it, at any rate for a year or two.

It was also why the blimps loathed it, and still do. The Brains Trust is the object of endless attacks by right-wing intellectuals of the G. M. Young–A. P. Herbert type (also Mr. Douglas Reed), and when a rival brains trust under a squad of clergymen was set up, all the blimps went about saying how much better it was than Joad and company. These people see the Brains Trust as a symbol of freedom of thought, and they realise that, however silly its programmes may be in themselves, their tendency is to start people thinking. You or I, perhaps, would not think of the B.B.C. as a dangerously subversive organisation, but that is how it is regarded in some quarters, and there are perpetual attempts to interfere with its programmes. To a certain extent a man may be known by his enemies, and the dislike with which all right-thinking people have regarded the Brains Trust—and also the whole idea of discussion groups, public or private—from the very start, is a sign that there must be something good in it. That is why I feel no strong impulse to take a crack at Dr. Joad, who gets his fair share of cracks anyway. I say rather: just think what the Brains Trust would have been like if its permanent members had been (as they might so well have been) Lord Elton, Mr. Harold Nicholson and Mr. Alfred Noyes.

The squabble in the House about *Your M.P.*, was perhaps less disgusting than it might have been, since after all Brendan Bracken[2] did announce that he was not going to ban the book for export; but it was a bad symptom all the same. Mr. Beverley Baxter[3] is not the most effective of the many guns now firing in the counter-attack of the Conservative Party—indeed he is less like a gun than a home-made mortar with a strong tendency to blow up—but it is significant that he should have the impudence to make the remarks he did. He wanted the book banned on the ground (a) that the author had been in prison, (b) that it was "scurrilous," and (c) that it "might disturb our relations with Russia." Of these, (a) is a simple appeal to prejudice, while (b) and (c) boil down to saying that the book is a reminder of what the record of the Conservative Party has actually been. I have my own quarrel with books like *Your M.P.*, but at least this book is almost entirely a compilation of admitted facts, all of them easily verifiable. A great deal of it could be dug out of Hansard, which is available to anyone who can pay the sixpence a day. But, as Mr. Baxter realises, *Your M.P.* will be read by tens of thousands who would never think of looking into Hansard or even into *Who's Who*. Therefore, ban the book from export, and if possible discredit it in this country as well. It will never do to let people know who our Conservative M.P.s are, what shares they own, how they have voted on crucially important issues, and what they said about Hitler before we went to war with him. Heaven knows the Conservative Party have enough reason for wanting to keep their record dark. But a couple of years ago they did not have the nerve to say so, and there lies the difference.

Also, Brendan Bracken in his reply said that the book contained a "venomous attack" on Sir Arnold Wilson[4] who "with the greatest gallantry gave his life for his country," the implication being that Sir Arnold Wilson's death in action made it improper to criticise him.

Sir Arnold Wilson was a brave and honourable man. When the policy he had supported came to ruin he was ready to face the consequences. In spite of his age he insisted on joining the RAF., and was killed in battle. I can think of plenty of other public figures who have behaved less well. But what has that to do with his pre-war record, which was mischievous in the extreme? His newspaper, the *Hitchin Mercury*,[5] was a frankly pro-Fascist paper and buttered up the Nazi regime almost to the last. Are we supposed to believe that if a man dies well his previous actions cease to have results?

One cannot buy magazines from abroad nowadays, but I recommend anyone who has a friend in New York to try and cadge a copy of *Politics*, the new monthly magazine, edited by the Marxist literary critic, Dwight Macdonald. I don't agree with the policy of this paper, which is anti-war (not from a pacifist angle), but I admire its combination of highbrow political analysis with intelligent literary criticism. It is sad to have to admit it, but we have no monthly or quarterly magazines in England to come up to the American ones—for there are several others of rather the same stamp as *Politics*. We are still haunted by a half-conscious idea that to have æsthetic sensibilities you must be a Tory. But of course the present superiority of American magazines is partly due to the war. Politically, the paper in this country most nearly corresponding to *Politics* would be, I suppose, the *New Leader*. You have only to compare the get-up, the style of writing, the range of subjects and the intellectual level of the two papers, to see what it means to live in a country where there are still leisure and wood-pulp.

On 21 July 1944 *Tribune* published a reader's letter which gave the following comparison of the prices of books reviewed in *Tribune* with those in literary reviews:

George Orwell's recent note on the literary value of Socialist publications in America shows a useful sidelight on the weakness of *Tribune* here! Take a look at its Book Reviews and see how many of them are of new Penguins, pamphlets, or books that we all can afford, obtain through a library, or at least borrow. I have been comparing the literary reviews (*Spectator*, *Time and Tide*, and *New Statesman*) for some weeks with *Tribune*, and find that the average price of the books reviewed is the lower in the "literaries" than the "political" journal! And the general appeal, fiction as well as non-fiction, is wider, too, in your contemporaries.

Now, readers, don't you also agree with me that we want to appeal to our "allies" and come down to earth from heaven?

S. H. Hassell

1. 'The Brains Trust' was a popular BBC programme, led by Dr C. E. M. Joad (1891–1953), head of the Department of Psychology and Philosophy, Birkbeck College, University of London, with a panel of experts which discussed questions submitted by listeners. Among the panelists there was usually someone less 'expert' but supposedly gifted with down-to-earth common-sense. Ruth Pitter (1897–1992), a poet and a friend of Orwell's when he was struggling to become a writer (see *139, n. 1*), was one such. In September 1942, Orwell reported to the BBC Eastern Service Committee that C. E. M. Joad would contribute to its broadcasts (see *1469*) and he was later engaged by Orwell.
2. Brendan Bracken (1901–1958; Viscount Bracken, 1952), politician and publisher, entered Parliament as a Conservative in 1929 and was a close associate of Churchill's in the 1930s and during the war. Among his more important offices of state was that of Minister of Information from 1941. He was one of the three political chiefs of the Political Warfare Executive.
3. Beverley Baxter (1891–1964; Kt., 1954), Canadian-born journalist, author, and critic, entered Parliament in 1935 as a Conservative. He had served in the Canadian army in World War I and in World War II was Controller of Aircraft Factory Cooperation under Lord Beaverbrook (also a Canadian).
4. Sir Arnold Wilson (1884–1940) was a Conservative M.P. who before the war actively supported Hitler and Mussolini. He was also an author, publicist, and administrator. When war was declared, although he held the rank of lieutenant-colonel and was over age for flying duties, he took a commission in the RAF as a pilot officer air gunner. He was killed in action.
5. There was no such paper as the *Hitchin Mercury*. Orwell has confused the *Hertfordshire Mercury and County Press* and the *Hertfordshire Express and Hitchin, Letchworth and Stevenage Gazette*, which, in July 1938, became the *Hertfordshire and Bedfordshire Express*. The former newspaper had little to do with Orwell's part of Hertfordshire, which was covered by the second journal. This not only published much of what Wilson said, but also reported highlights of the ILP Summer Schools at Letchworth, 1936–38.

2491. To [W. F. Stirling, Latin American Department], BBC

19 June 1944   Handwritten

Tribune

Dear Sir,

I am sorry to say I have lost the letter in which I was commissioned to write this script (it was to be of 1400 words & to be in by June 21st), so I am directing it to the English Region, hoping it will be sent on to the right quarter.

Yours faithfully,
George Orwell

> Orwell had agreed to write a script on political theories and European literature showing how modern political ideologies had had a direct effect on contemporary literature (see *2469* and *2497*). His letter is annotated (presumably by W. F. Stirling of the Latin American Department of the BBC, who had requested the script): 'Miss H. / Dear Mr   ). / Many thanks for your excellent script. It is being broadcast on Wednesday June 28th. / Yours sinc°— —.' This reply was sent on 26 June. On 4 July, Betty Medus, Latin American Programme Executive, wrote to Miss B. H. Alexander of the Copyright Department asking her to negotiate a fee for this fifteen-minute talk. Unfortunately, the script has not been traced in either its English or Spanish version.

2492. 'As I Please,' 30

Tribune, 23 June 1944

The week before last *Tribune* printed a centenary article on Gerald° Manley Hopkins, and it was only after this that the chance of running across an April number of the American *Nation* reminded me that 1944 is also the centenary of a much better-known writer—Anatole France.

When Anatole France died, twenty years ago, his reputation suffered one of those sudden slumps to which highbrow writers who have lived long enough to become popular are especially liable. In France, according to the charming French custom, vicious personal attacks were made upon him while he lay dying and when he was freshly dead. A particularly venomous one was written by Pierre Drieu la Rochelle, afterwards to become a collaborator of the Nazis. In England, also, it was discovered that Anatole France was no good. A few years later than this a young man attached to a weekly paper (I met him afterwards in Paris and found that he could not buy a tram ticket without assistance) solemnly assured me that Anatole France "wrote very bad French." France was, it seemed, a vulgar, spurious and derivative writer whom everyone could now "see through." Round about the same time, similar discoveries were being made about Bernard Shaw and Lytton Strachey: but curiously enough all three writers have remained very readable, while most of their detractors are forgotten.

How far the revulsion against Anatole France was genuinely literary I do not know. Certainly he had been overpraised, and one must at times get tired of a writer so mannered and so indefatigably pornographic. But it is unquestionable that he was attacked partly from political motives. He may or may not have been a great writer, but he was one of the symbolic figures in the politico-literary dogfight which has been raging for a hundred years or more. The clericals and reactionaries hated him in just the same way as they hated Zola. Anatole France had championed Dreyfus, which needed considerable courage, he had debunked Joan of Arc, he had written a comic history of France; above all, he had lost no opportunity of poking fun at the Church. He was everything that the clericals and revanchists, the people who first preached that the Boche must never be allowed to recover and afterwards sucked the blacking off Hitler's boots, most detested.

I do not know whether Anatole France's most characteristic books, for instance, *La Rôtisserie de la Reine Pédauque*, are worth re-reading at this date. Whatever is in them is really in Voltaire. But it is a different story with the four novels dealing with Monsieur Bergeret. Besides being extremely amusing these give a most valuable picture of French society in the 'nineties and the background of the Dreyfus case. There is also *Crainquebille*, one of the best short stories I have ever read, and incidentally a devastating attack on "law and order."[1]

But though Anatole France could speak up for the working class in a story like *Crainquebille*, and though cheap editions of his works were advertised in Communist papers, one ought not really to class him as a Socialist. He was willing to work for Socialism, even to deliver lectures on it in draughty halls, and he knew that it was both necessary and inevitable, but it is doubtful whether he subjectively wanted it. The world, he once said, would get about as much relief from the coming of Socialism as a sick man gets from turning over in bed. In a crisis he was ready to identify himself with the working class, but the thought of a Utopian future depressed him, as can be seen from his book, *La Pierre Blanche*. There is an even deeper pessimism in *Les Dieux Ont Soif*, his novel about the French Revolution. Temperamentally he was not a Socialist but a Radical. At this date that is probably the rarer animal of the two, and it is his Radicalism, his passion for liberty and intellectual honesty, that give their special colour to the four novels about Monsieur Bergeret.

I have never understood why the *News-Chronicle*, whose politics are certainly a very pale pink—about the colour of shrimp paste, I should say, but still pink—allows the professional Roman Catholic "Timothy Shy" (D. B. Wyndham Lewis) to do daily sabotage in his comic column. In Lord Beaverbrook's *Express* his fellow-Catholic "Beachcomber" (J. B. Morton) is, of course, more at home.[2]

Looking back over the twenty years or so that these two have been on the job, it would be difficult to find a reactionary cause that they have not championed. Pilsudski, Mussolini, appeasement, flogging, Franco, literary censorship—between them they have found good words for everything that any decent person instinctively objects to. They have conducted endless propaganda against Socialism, the League of Nations and scientific research. They have kept up a campaign of abuse against every writer worth reading, from Joyce onwards. They were viciously anti-German until Hitler appeared, when their anti-Germanism cooled off in a remarkable manner. At this moment, needless to say, the especial target of their hatred is Beveridge.[3]

It is a mistake to regard these two as comics pure and simple. Every word they write is intended as Catholic propaganda, and some at least of their co-religionists think very highly of their work in this direction. Their general "line" will be familiar to anyone who has read Chesterton and kindred writers. Its essential note is denigration of England and of the Protestant countries generally. From the Catholic point of view this is necessary. A Catholic, at least an apologist, feels that he *must* claim superiority for the Catholic countries, and for the Middle Ages as against the present, just as a Communist feels that he must in all circumstances support the U.S.S.R. Hence the endless jibing of "Beachcomber" and "Timothy Shy" at every English institution—tea, cricket, Wordsworth, Charlie Chaplin, kindness to animals, Nelson, Cromwell and what-not. Hence also "Timothy Shy's" attempts to rewrite English history and the snarls of hatred that escape him when he thinks of the defeat of the Spanish Armada. (How it sticks in his gizzard, that Spanish Armada! As though anyone cared, at this date!). Hence, even, the endless jeering at novelists, the novel being essentially a post-Reformation form of literature at which on the whole Catholics have not excelled.

From either a literary or a political point of view these two are simply the leavings on Chesterton's plate. Chesterton's vision of life was false in some ways, and he was hampered by enormous ignorance, but at least he had courage. He was ready to attack the rich and powerful, and he damaged his career by doing so. But it is the peculiarity of both "Beachcomber" and "Timothy Shy" that they take no risks with their own popularity. Their strategy is always indirect. Thus, if you want to attack the principle of freedom of speech, do it by sneering at the Brains Trust, as if it were a typical example. Dr. Joad won't retaliate! Even their deepest convictions go into cold storage when they become dangerous. Earlier in the war, when it was safe to do so, "Beachcomber" wrote viciously anti-Russian pamphlets, but no anti-Russian remarks appear in his column these days. They will again, however, if popular pro-Russian feeling dies down. I shall be interested to see whether either "Beachcomber" or "Timothy Shy" reacts to these remarks of mine. If so, it will be the first recorded instance of either of them attacking anyone likely to hit back.[4]

The correspondence columns of *Tribune* for 7 July were much taken up by long letters from George Richards and H. McCormack and a shorter letter from Anthony Sylvestre arising from Orwell's discussion of 'Timothy Shy' and 'Beachcomber.' Richards (who said that he 'read Orwell with relish. His column has got teeth in it') thought that in criticising the blimpish element in their ideological make-up 'one comes up against a difficulty that is thoroughly characteristic of our tangled times, which is that nearly all the people who hold the right opinions do so for the wrong reasons!' McCormack maintained:

Beachcomber is a Roman Catholic diehard, less scholarly than the academic Timothy Shy and much more mendacious. His anti-Soviet slanders are not in evidence these days since his boss's lies about dirty Russian butter, Russian famine, and Russian slavery were eliminated from the *Express*. But whilst Beaverbrook has changed his tune, we merely have a foxy silence from Beachcomber. . . .

The erudite Shy is less annoying because he does occasionally burlesque the more blatant incongruities of our society. But he certainly dislikes progressive organisations, modern science and novelists who don't fit in with his mediaeval scholasticism.

Sylvestre wrote:

There is considerable justification for George Orwell's attack on "Timothy Shy" and "Beachcomber," but it contains the unpleasant implication that they are what they are by virtue of their being Catholics. The inaccuracy of this is twofold.

First, the Faith cannot be held responsible for the politics, literary opinions, philosophy—Descartes was a Catholic—or morals of the faithful, not only laymen, but priests, bishops and Popes.

Second, D. B. Wyndham Lewis, J. B. Morton and those other gentlemen so aptly labelled by Mr. Orwell as "the leavings on Chesterton's plate" are hardly representative of contemporary Catholic intellectuals. They have nothing in common but their faith with such Catholics as Maritain, Dalbiez, David Jones, Graham Sutherland, Graham Greene, Kathleen Raine and Antonia White. Neither will we find anything of the Chesterton aftermath among the intellectuals of the priesthood, of whom such men as Frs. Victor White. Gervase Mathew, Gerald Vann, or Conrad Pepler, O.P., or Fr. M. J. D'Arcy, S. J., are representative. We may find pacifism among these, but certainly not High Toryism or literary conservatism.

A short letter on 21 July 1944 from Alan Leavett attempted to give the debate a different slant:

Beachcomber is sorely belaboured by your correspondents.

I hold no brief for his politico-religious views but surely the discussion in your columns is incomplete without a tribute to the irresistibly topsy-turvy world he has created in "By The Way." Much can be forgiven to the creator of Mr. Justice Cocklecarrot and those ubiquitous Red-Bearded Dwarfs.

1. *Crainquebille* was adapted as a radio play by Orwell and broadcast in the BBC's Eastern Service on 11 August 1943; see *2230*.

2. The 'Beachcomber' column in the *Daily Express* was started by D. B. Wyndham Lewis (1891–1969) and continued from 1924 by J. B. Morton (1893–1979), a fellow Roman Catholic. Wyndham Lewis then contributed a column under the pen-name 'Timothy Shy' to the *News Chronicle*. Both authors produced a fair amount of comic and nonsense writing, but both also wrote biographical studies and Morton wrote fiction. On a number of occasions Orwell made pejorative references to these columnists. In his Wigan Pier Diary, *287, 27.2.36*, he refers to 'the Chesterton-Beachcomber type of writer' who is 'always in favour of private ownership and against Socialist legislation and "progress" generally'; and see 'Politics vs. Literature,' *3089*.
3. William Beveridge (see *1896, n. 6*) was the author of the *Report on Social Insurance and Allied Services*, known as the *Beveridge Report* (1942), which laid the foundations of the Welfare State in Britain.
4. Neither did.

2493. To Mrs. Gerry Byrne (Amy Charlesworth)

23 June 1944   Handwritten

10a Mortimer Crescent NW 6 (or "Tribune")

Dear Mrs Byrne,[1]
Many thanks for your letter. I would certainly like to have lunch with you & your husband when you are in town. I am at the Tribune office Mondays, Tuesdays & Fridays, otherwise at my home address (MAI 4579) but my movements are rather variable on those days. I'll try & find a copy of "Burmese Days" for you. These Penguins are sold out as soon as published nowadays, but I believe I have a few copies somewhere.

Your sincerely
Eric Blair

1. Mrs. Gerry Byrne (1904–1945) had written to Orwell as Amy Charlesworth from Flixton, near Manchester, on 6 October 1937; see *384, n. 1*. She had married first when young, had two children, and left her husband because he struck here so often. She then trained as a health visitor and remarried (possibly the crime reporter Gerald Byrne).

2494. To Leonard Moore

24 June 1944   Typewritten

10a Mortimer Crescent
London NW 6

Dear Mr Moore,
It is a pity about Cape's.[1] I rang up T. S. Eliot, telling him the circumstances, and shall give him the other copy of the MS on Monday. I have no doubt Eliot himself would be on my side in this matter, but, as he says, he might not be able to swing the rest of the board of Faber's.

About the contract with Gollancz. If 30,000 words is not "full-length", what does amount to full-length?[2] Is an actual amount of words named in our existing contract? If not, could we get from Gollancz a definite statement as to what he considers a full-length work of fiction. It is clearly very unsatisfactory to have this clause in the contract without a clear definition of it.

Yours sincerely
Eric Blair

1. Jonathan Cape wrote to Victor Gollancz on 26 May 1944 to say that he was inclined to publish *Animal Farm* (see *2485, n. 1*). His principal reader, Daniel George, and C. V. Wedgwood, then working for Cape, both strongly urged publication. However, on 16 June 1944, Cape wrote to Leonard Moore to say he would not publish the book. He did have some anxiety about Orwell having to offer his next two works of fiction to Gollancz, but the basis for the rejection was the representation made to him by 'an important official in the Ministry of Information' whom he had consulted. He had come to the conclusion that it would be 'highly ill-advised to publish [it] at the present time,' partly because it was not a generalised attack on dictatorships but was aimed specifically at the Soviets, and partly because the 'choice of pigs as the ruling caste' would be especially offensive. (Crick gives the full text of this letter, with background details, 454–56.) Inez Holden, in a letter to Ian Angus of 27 May 1967, summarised Cape's reason for the rejection and Orwell's reaction: 'He said he couldn't publish that as he was afraid "Stalin wouldn't like it". George was amused at this. I will quote what he said on this: "Imagine old Joe (who doesn't know one word of any European language) sitting in the Kremlin reading 'Animal Farm' and saying 'I don't like this'"'. For Daniel George's response to Orwell's 'Confessions of a Book Reviewer' and for an extract from his report, see *2992*.
2. Annotated in Moore's office: 'Agreement only states "full-length."'

2495. Review of *The Sociology of Literary Taste* by L. L. Schucking

The Observer, 25 June 1944

This learned but rather rambling essay sets out to explain the variation in literary taste from one age to another, and to show why it is that even a writer such as Shakespeare, who is generally in favour, is admired for totally different reasons in different periods.

Literary taste can be explained either as a reflection of current social conditions, or as something created from above, as it were, by writers of outstanding talent. In other words, one can regard either the author or the public as the dominant factor. Dr. Schucking, while conceding a great deal to the influence of individual writers, literary cliques and enterprising publishers, takes the second position. Artists, in general, produce what is required of them, and changes in technique may be produced by quite crudely mechanical causes. For example, it seems that the reason—at any rate the immediate reason—why English novels grew shorter at the beginning of the 'nineties was a decision of the lending libraries. The three-volume novel had become uneconomic, and so it had to go. Even such things as shortage or abundance of paper can affect literary form.

Probably the most interesting passages in Dr. Schucking's book are those that trace the connection between classicism and an aristocratic society. It is not merely that "good form" is best appreciated in a small homogeneous society, while half-educated people are nearly always repelled by what seems to them the coldness and emptiness of classicism. It is also that the aristocrat objects to emotional violence, and on the other hand to naturalism, because he knows that they are dangerous to his own kind:

His life is dominated by tradition, which in his view is bound to be powerful because his whole existence is dependent on inheritance. Property, which is a further condition of his existence, implies a permanent temptation to the enjoyment of life, an enjoyment which is refined by the inherited feeling for form; form acquires further an extraordinary importance from the fact that it is the precise means of social differentiation . . . : His characteristic style of living, and the external claims based upon it, further make him anti-individualistic and promote the creation of types. The complete exposure of the life of the emotions, like all that is ruthless in expression, is thus bound to be unattractive to him. It is always revealing things that must at all costs be suppressed.

Dr. Schucking probably rather over-stresses the advantage, from the writer's point of view, of a middle-class as against an aristocratic society. But it is true that in capitalist society the dependence of the artist on his patrons has been less direct and humiliating than in previous ages. As Dr. Schucking points out, the appearance of the commercial publisher was an important turning-point in the history of literature. As soon as books began to be published by subscription, the writer was the servant of a caste rather than an individual, and when they became ordinary commercial speculations he was only answerable to the amorphous big public, which did not know very well what it wanted and would, or at any rate might, listen respectfully to the critics.

One result of this was an improvement in the status of the artist. In previous ages the artist had been simply a rather expensive and superior kind of servant: the poet who appears as a character in "Timon of Athens" is represented as a sponging hanger-on. It was only in the nineteenth century, when the artist had been economically emancipated, that he could begin to take an inflated view of himself and indulge in such theories as "art for art's sake." But what he could or could not write was still partly determined by non-literary considerations, among which Dr. Schucking lists the current notion of sexual ethics, the normal size of the family circle, the prevalence or otherwise of the café-going habit, the arbitrary decisions of publishers, and also the writer's own flair for publicity. The conclusion seems to be that the artist, at any rate the writer, fares best under old-style capitalism but remains in essence a tradesman, dominated in the last resort by his customers.

In explaining literary fashion Dr. Schucking does not, perhaps, allow enough weight to tradition and sheer imitation, and he says very little about the effect on any national literature of the structure of its language. English verse, for instance, must owe some of its characteristics to the fact that the English language lacks rhymes. It was also unfortunate that this book should, apparently, have been written before the rise of Hitler, or at any rate before 1933.[1] Totalitarianism affects the artist, and especially the writer, more intimately than any other class of person. In effect, the "patron" has come back again, but he is a patron enormously less civilised, less tolerant, less individual and more powerful than in the past.

It is not very pleasant to read about the out-at-elbow poets who had to dance attendance while "my lord" consumed his morning chocolate, but "my lord" was probably not a harder master than Dr. Goebbels, or even the M.O.I., and his literary taste was probably better. What the position of the artist would be in a democratic Socialist régime is still uncertain and much disputed. We do not, indeed, yet know to what extent freedom of thought is separable from economic independence. Dr. Schucking might well follow up his present book with a consideration of that subject.

[Fee: £7.7.0; 22.6.44]

1. It was published in German in Munich in 1923 and in an enlarged edition in Leipzig in 1931.

2495A. To Lydia Jackson

26 June 1944   Typewritten

Tribune

Dear Lydia,
Would you like to do a short note (300 words) on this?[1]

Yours,
[Signed] George

[Postscript] Polish Folk-Lore Stories—Polish Pubs. committee°

1. The review of *Polish Folk-Lore Stories* was published in *Tribune* on 22 September 1944

2495B. 'The World Goes By'

On 27 June, Miss I. D. Benzie, a talks producer in the BBC Home Division, wrote to G. R. Barnes, Director of Talks, asking if there would be any objection to discussing possible scripts for the programme 'The World Goes By' with George Orwell. Barnes annotated her memorandum, 'Depends what on. But no objection in principle' ('no objection' replacing 'none,' which was scored through). A search of the files at the BBC Archive and an examination of some thirty lists of speakers in the file 'The World Goes By,' does not reveal Orwell's name, and there are no letters or internal correspondence referring to him.

2496. To T. S. Eliot

28 June 1944   Handwritten

10a, Mortimer Crescent NW.6 (Or "Tribune" CEN 2572)

Dear Eliot,

This MS.[1] has been blitzed which accounts for my delay in delivering it & its slightly crumpled condition, but it is not damaged in any way.

I wonder if you could be kind enough to let me have Messrs. Faber's decision fairly soon. If they are interested in seeing more of my work, I could let you have the facts about my existing contract with Gollancz, which is not an onerous one nor likely to last long.

If you read this MS. yourself you will see its meaning which is not an acceptable one at this moment, but I could not agree to make any alterations except a small one at the end which I intended making any way. Cape or the MOI, I am not certain which from the wording of his letter,[2] made the imbecile suggestion that some other animal than the pigs might be made to represent the Bolsheviks. I could not of course make any change of that description.

Yours sincerely
Geo. Orwell

Could you have lunch with me one of the days when you are in town?

1. Of *Animal Farm*.
2. Presumably from Leonard Moore, reporting on Cape's 19 June 1944 letter; see *2494*.

2497. 'Political Theories and European Literature'

BBC Broadcast, 28/29 June 1944

Orwell's fifteen-minute talk was broadcast in the Latin-American Service early in the morning of 29 June 1944 at 02.45 DBST. No script has been traced. The talk was translated into Spanish by J. Tuya Videl and read by W. G. Cain. The Spanish title is not given in PasB. Orwell was not sent a contract until 6 July 1944; he signed it that same day; see *2500*.

2498. Review of *From One Generation to Another* by Hilda Martindale, CBE

Manchester Evening News, 29 June 1944

To become a factory inspector does not sound a very thrilling achievement, but its unusualness depends partly on the sex of the person in question, and also on the date. Miss Hilda Martindale was one of the first women factory inspectors to be appointed in this country, and afterwards held one of the highest posts in her department. Behind that rather prosaic statement there lies a story of feminine struggle stretching far back into the nineteenth century—for Miss Martindale is almost more interested in her mother's history than her own.[1]

At the beginning of her book there is a photograph of her mother in old age; a grim but handsome face, belonging obviously to a woman of character. Miss Spicer (as her maiden name was) had been born into a wealthy nonconformist family, and like her near-contemporary, Florence Nightingale, she became dissatisfied in early adult life with the idle meaningless existence that a woman of the richer classes was then expected to lead.

This dissatisfaction persisted in spite of a happy marriage and the birth of two children, and she became one of the pioneers of the women's suffrage movement. Her great aim in life was to see men and women regarded as the same kind of animal—once, when approached by a clergyman who was opening a home for fallen women, she told him that if he opened a home for fallen men she would subscribe to it—and to make it possible for girls to follow any profession that suited them instead of being tied down to a few "ladylike" pursuits.

Among the innumerable girls to whom she gave help and advice was an eager, intelligent, overworked shop assistant of 16 named Margaret Bondfield.[2] Mrs. Martindale did not live long enough to see female suffrage become a reality, but unlike some of her fellow-workers she did not lose her faith in the Liberal party.

The Liberals, from Gladstone onwards, tended to be tepid or evasive on the subject of female emancipation, and it was out of disappointment with the behaviour of the Liberal Government that the "militant" suffragette movement arose. It is interesting to learn that as early as the 'nineties female suffrage was opposed inside the Liberal party on the ground that if women were given votes they would vote Conservative.

Miss Hilda Martindale's official career began about 1895. Much the most interesting thing in her book is the revelation that the kind of sweating and child labour that we associate with the early days of the Industrial Revolution persisted in England till almost the beginning of the last war. At different times she was investigating conditions in the pottery trade, the textile industries, the dressmaking trade, and many others, both in England and in Ireland, and everywhere she found atrocious things happening.

In the Potteries, for instance, children as young as 12 worked long hours carrying lumps of clay weighing 60 or 70 pounds, while among adults lead poisoning was extremely common and was regarded as something unavoidable, like the weather. In Ireland the highly skilled lace-makers earned round about a penny an hour, and the Truck Act which had been passed 70 years earlier[3] was flagrantly disregarded. Lace-making was a cottage industry, and orders were farmed out to an "agent" who in most cases was also the local shopkeeper and publican. As far as possible he paid his work people in goods instead of money, grossly overcharging for everything, and kept them permanently in debt to him.

The prosecutions which Miss Martindale instituted generally failed, because no one dared to give evidence against the "agent." But the worst sweating of all seems to have happened in the workshops of "court" dressmakers in London. When some urgent order, for a wedding or something of the kind, had to be completed the sempstresses might be kept on the job for 60 or 70 hours continuously. The laws against Sunday work and child labour were a dead letter. If a factory inspector arrived unexpectedly the girls were simply bundled into an attic, or anywhere else where they would be out of sight, and the employer was able to declare that no law was being infringed.

The enormous supplies of cheap female labour that were available made it very difficult to combat these conditions. Any girl who complained against her employer knew that she would be dismissed, and Miss Martindale had to proceed chiefly on the evidence of anonymous letters.

On one occasion she received information that the girls in a certain shop were being kept at work on Sunday. When she arrived there she was assured that the girls were all at their homes, and was shown round the empty workrooms. She promptly jumped into a hansom cab and made a tour of all the girls' homes, the addresses of which she had procured beforehand.

They were, in fact, all at work, and had been hidden somewhere or other while Miss Martindale made her visit. Miss Martindale is convinced that industrial conditions have enormously improved over the last 40 years, and when one reads of her experiences—especially when one reads the pathetic ill-spelt letters she used to receive from working girls—it is impossible not to agree.

Wages, working hours, protection against accident and industrial diseases and also the treatment of children are very different from what they were 40 years ago, although there has been no basic change in the economic system. Miss Martindale thinks that the improvement, at any rate so far as women are concerned, dates from the last war, when women for the first time were employed in large numbers in industry including trades previously reserved for men, and made their first acquaintance with trade unions.

It was, incidentally, the Boer War that had first made the Government realise that the national physique was deteriorating as a result of industrial conditions, and the present war has probably worked another improvement in the status of labour.

Evidently war has its compensations since military efficiency is not compatible with underfeeding, overwork, or even illiteracy.

Parts of this book are rather slow going, but it is an informative book, and a remarkably good-tempered one. Herself a feminist and the daughter of an even more ardent feminist, Miss Martindale has none of that bitter anti-masculine feeling that feminist writers used to have. Her own career, and the self-confidence and independence of outlook that she evidently showed from the very start, bear out her claim that women are the equals of men in everything except physical strength.

[Fee: £8.8.0; 28.6.44]

1. Hilda Martindale (1875–1952), a civil servant, was born into a great Liberal-Nonconformist family, but her father and one sister (there were three children, not two, as Orwell says; the

surviving sister became one of the first women surgeons) died before she was born. She was appointed deputy chief inspector after years of devoted work against opposition and with little support from the magistracy. She also fought for equal opportunities for women in the Civil Service. When, some years after her retirement in 1937, a woman became principal assistant secretary in charge of all general establishment work, she wrote, 'Now indeed my desire was fulfilled.' She also did much to establish the Home Office Industrial Museum (*DNB*).

2. Margaret Bondfield (1873–1953), trade union leader and first woman cabinet minister, as Minister of Labour in Ramsay MacDonald's second administration, 1929. She was the first woman Privy Councillor.

3. The Truck Acts were passed in 1831, 1887, and 1896 and were designed to stop the practice of paying employees' wages in goods instead of money.

2499. 'As I Please,' 31

Tribune, 30 June 1944

I notice that apart from the widespread complaint that the German pilotless planes "seem so unnatural" (a bomb dropped by a live airman is quite natural, apparently), some journalists are denouncing them as barbarous, inhumane, and "an indiscriminate attack on civilians."[1]

After what we have been doing to the Germans over the past two years, this seems a bit thick, but it is the normal human response to every new weapon. Poison gas, the machine-gun, the submarine, gunpowder, and even the crossbow were similarly denounced in their day. Every weapon seems unfair until you have adopted it yourself. But I would not deny that the pilotless plane, flying bomb, or whatever its correct name may be, is an exceptionally unpleasant thing, because, unlike most other projectiles, it gives you time to think. What is your first reaction when you hear that droning, zooming noise? Inevitably, it is a hope that the noise *won't stop*. You want to hear the bomb pass safely overhead and die away into the distance before the engine cuts out. In other words, you are hoping that it will fall on somebody else. So also when you dodge a shell or an ordinary bomb—but in that case you have only about five seconds to take cover and no time to speculate on the bottomless selfishness of the human being.

It cannot be altogether an accident that nationalists of the more extreme and romantic kind tend not to belong to the nation that they idealise. Leaders who base their appeal on *"la patrie,"* or *"the fatherland"* are sometimes outright foreigners, or else come from the border-countries of great empires. Obvious examples are Hitler, an Austrian, and Napoleon, a Corsican, but there are many others. The man who may be said to have been the founder of British jingoism was Disraeli, a Spanish Jew, and it was Lord Beaverbrook, a Canadian, who tried to induce the unwilling English to describe themselves as Britons. The British Empire was largely built up by Irishmen and Scotsmen, and our most obstinate nationalists and imperialists have frequently been Ulstermen. Even Churchill, the leading exponent of romantic patriotism in our own day, is half an American. But not merely the men of action, but even the theorists of nationalism are frequently foreigners.

Pan-Germanism, for instance, from which the Nazis later took many of their ideas, was largely the product of men who were not Germans: for instance, Houston Chamberlain, an Englishman, and Gobineau, a Frenchman. Rudyard Kipling was an Englishman, but of a rather doubtful kind. He came from an unusual Anglo-Indian background (his father was curator of the Bombay Museum), he had spent his early childhood in India, and he was of small stature and very dark complexion which caused him to be wrongly suspected of having Asiatic blood. I have always held that if we ever have a Hitler in this country he will be, perhaps, an Ulsterman, a South African, a Maltese, a Eurasian, or perhaps an American—but, at any rate, not an Englishman.

Two samples of the English language:

1. Elizabethan English:

While the pages are at their banqueting, I keep their mules, and to someone I cut the stirrup-leather of the mounting side, till it hangs by a thin strap or thread, that when the great puff-guts of the counsellor or some other hath taken his swing to get up, he may fall flat on his side like a porker, and so furnish the spectators with more than a hundred francs' worth of laughter. But I laugh yet further, to think how at his homecoming the master-page is to be swinged like green rye, which makes me not to repent what I have bestowed in feasting them.

(Thomas Urquhart: Translation of Rabelais.)

2. Modern American:

The phase of detachment may be isolated from its political context and in the division of labour become an end in itself. Those who restrict themselves to work only such segments of intellectual endeavour may attempt to generalise them, making them the basis for political and personal orientation. Then the key problem is held to arise from the fact that social science lags behind physical science and technology, and political and social problems are a result of this deficiency and lag. Such a position is inadequate.

(American highbrow magazine.)

Six million books, it is said, perished in the blitz of 1940, including a thousand irreplaceable titles. Most of them were probably no loss, but it is dismaying to find how many standard works are now completely out of print. Paper is forthcoming for the most ghastly tripe, as you can see by glancing into any bookshop window, while all the reprint editions, such as the Everyman Library, have huge gaps in their lists. Even so well-known a work of reference as Webster's dictionary is no longer obtainable unless you run across a copy second-hand. About a year ago I had to do a broadcast on Jack London. When I started to collect the material I found that those of his books that I most wanted had vanished so completely that even the London Library could not produce them. To get hold of them I should have had to go to the British Museum reading-room, which in these days is not at all easy of access. And this seems to me a disaster, for Jack London is one of those border-line writers whose works might be forgotten altogether unless somebody takes the trouble to revive them. Even *The Iron Heel* was distinctly a rarity for some years, and was only reprinted because Hitler's rise to power made it topical.

He is remembered chiefly by *The Iron Heel*, and—in totally different circles—by books like *White Fang* and *The Call of the Wild*, in which he exploited a typically Anglo-Saxon sentimentality about animals. But there were also *The People of the Abyss*, his book about the London slums, *The Road*, which gives a wonderful picture of the American hoboes, and *The Jacket*, which is valuable for its prison scenes. And above all there are his short stories. When he is in a certain vein—it is chiefly when he is dealing with American city life—Jack London is one of the best short-story writers the English-speaking peoples have had. There is a story called *Just Meat*, about two burglars who get away with a big haul, and then simultaneously poison one another with strychnine, which sticks very vividly in my memory. *Love of Life*, the last story that was read to Lenin when he was dying, is another wonderful story, and so is *A Piece of Steak*, which describes the last battle of a worn-out prizefighter. These and other similar stories benefit by the strong streak of brutality that London had in his nature. It was this also that gave him a subjective understanding of Fascism which Socialists do not usually have, and which made *The Iron Heel* in some ways a true prophecy.

Or am I overrating those short stories? I may be, for it is many years since I have set eyes on them. Two of those I have named above were included in a book called *When God Laughs*. So far as I can discover this book has simply ceased to exist, and if anyone has a copy to sell I should be glad to hear of it.

1. Writing in his column in *Reynold's News* on 9 July 1944, Tom Driberg (see *1931, n. 1*) commented that though he always enjoyed Orwell's column in *Tribune*, he disagreed strongly with this paragraph. He went on: 'An intelligent man like Orwell really oughtn't to talk like a Peace Pledger. There is surely an appreciable difference in principle between these flying bombs, which are necessarily aimed only vaguely and may fall anywhere, and RAF raids, which do kill thousands of civilians incidentally but are aimed *primarily*—for reasons of economy and strategy if not humanity—at military and industrial targets. Our side [the political left] shouldn't give such loopholes to the Right.' The following Sunday, he reported that his comment had 'excited 24 letters—of which 22 agreed with Orwell, accused me of "hypocrisy" and "peddling official dope." Well, well . . .' The 'pilotless plane' was the V-1; see *2501, n. 1*.

2500. Contract for 'Political Theories and European Literature'

6 July 1944

On 6 July 1944, Miss B. H. Alexander, of the BBC Copyright Department, wrote to Orwell suggesting a fee of ten guineas for the talk he had given on 28/29 June for the Latin American Service (see *2469* and *2497*). She enclosed a contract. Orwell annotated her letter, 'Contract signed herewith   Geo. Orwell   6.7.44' and signed the contract, also dating it 6 July. The letter was addressed to Orwell at *Tribune* and, in those days, despite the war, it was quite practicable for a letter to be delivered on the day that it was posted.[1] Orwell sent the Latin American Service a postcard on 15 July.

Received with thanks cheque for £10–10–0

Geo. Orwell

1. Joyce Grenfell records that a letter she posted in Burnham in the morning was delivered in Windsor by 5:00 P.M. (*Darling Ma*, 28 September 1941).

2501. 'As I Please,' 32

Tribune, 7 July 1944

When the Caliph Omar destroyed the libraries of Alexandria he is supposed to have kept the public baths warm for eighteen days with burning manuscripts, and great numbers of tragedies by Euripides and others are said to have perished, quite irrecoverably. I remember that when I read about this as a boy it simply filled me with enthusiastic approval. It was so many less words to look up in the dictionary—that was how I saw it. For, though I am only forty-one, I am old enough to have been educated at a time when Latin and Greek were only escapable with great difficulty, while "English" was hardly regarded as a school subject at all.

Classical education is going down the drain at last, but even now there must be far more adults who have been flogged through the entire extant works of Aeschylus, Sophocles, Euripides, Aristophanes, Virgil, Horace and various other Latin and Greek authors, than have read the English masterpieces of the eighteenth century. People pay lip service to Fielding and the rest of them, of course, but they don't read them, as you can discover by making a few inquiries among your friends. How many people have even read *Tom Jones*, for instance? Not so many have even read the later books of *Gulliver's Travels*. *Robinson Crusoe* has a sort of popularity in nursery versions, but the book as a whole is so little known that few people are even aware that the second part (the journey through Tartary) exists. Smollett, I imagine, is the least read of all. The central plot of Shaw's play, *Pygmalion*, is lifted straight out of *Peregrine Pickle*, and I believe that no one has ever pointed this out in print, which suggests that few people can have read the book. But what is strangest of all is that Smollett, so far as I know, has never been boosted by the Scottish Nationalists, who are so careful to claim Byron for their own. Yet Smollett, besides being one of the best novelists the English-speaking races have produced, *was* a Scotsman, and proclaimed it openly at a time when being so was anything but helpful to one's career.

> Life in the civilised world.
> (The family are at tea.)
> Zoom-zoom-zoom!
> "Is there an alert on?"
> "No, it's all clear."
> "I thought there was an alert on."
> Zoom-zoom-zoom!
> "There's another of those things coming!"

"It's all right, it's miles away."

Zoom-zoom-ZOOM!

"Look out, here it comes! Under the table, quick!"

Zoom-zoom-zoom!

"It's all right, it's getting fainter."

Zoom-zoom-ZOOM!

"It's coming back!"

"They seem to kind of circle round and come back again. They've got something on their tails that makes them do it. Like a torpedo."

ZOOM-ZOOM-ZOOM!

"Christ! It's bang overhead!"

Dead silence.

"Now get *right* underneath. Keep your head well down. What a mercy baby isn't here!"

"Look at the cat! He's frightened too."

"Of course animals *know*. They can feel the vibrations."

BOOM!

"It's all right, I told you it was miles away."

(Tea continues.)[1]

I see that Lord Winterton,[2] writing in the *Evening Standard*, speaks of the "remarkable reticence (by no means entirely imposed by rule or regulation) which Parliament and Press alike have displayed in this war to avoid endangering national security" and adds that it has "earned the admiration of the civilised world."

It is not only in war time that the British Press observes this voluntary reticence. One of the most extraordinary things about England is that there is almost no official censorship, and yet nothing that is acutely offensive to the governing class gets into print, at least in any place where large numbers of people are likely to read it. If it is "not done" to mention something or other, it just doesn't get mentioned. The position is summed up in the lines by (I think) Hilaire Belloc:[3]

> You cannot hope to bribe or twist
> Thank God! the English journalist:
> But seeing what the man will do
> Unbribed, there is no reason to.

No bribes, no threats, no penalties—just a nod and a wink and the thing is done. A well-known example was the business of the Abdication. Weeks before the scandal officially broke, tens or hundreds of thousands of people had heard all about Mrs. Simpson, and yet not a word got into the Press, not even into the *Daily Worker*, although the American and European papers were having the time of their lives with the story. Yet I believe there was no definite official ban: just an official "request" and a general agreement that to break the news prematurely "would not do." And I can think of other instances of good news stories failing to see the light although there would have been no penalty for printing them.

Nowadays this kind of veiled censorship even extends to books. The M.O.I. does not, of course, dictate a party line or issue an index expurgatorius. It merely "advises." Publishers take manuscripts to the M.O.I., and the M.O.I. "suggests" that this or that is undesirable, or premature, or "would serve no good purpose." And though there is no definite prohibition, no clear statement that this or that must not be printed, official policy is never flouted.[4] Circus dogs jump when the trainer cracks his whip, but the really well-trained dog is the one that turns his somersault when there is no whip. And that is the state we have reached in this country thanks to three hundred years of living together without a civil war.

Here is a little problem sometimes used as an intelligence test.

A man walked four miles due south from his house and shot a bear. He then walked two miles due west, then walked another four miles due north and was back at his home again. What was the colour of the bear?

The interesting point is that—so far as my own observations go—men usually see the answer to this problem and women do not.[5]

1. Orwell is describing the V-1 (Vergeltungswaffe-1; Revenge Weapon-1) or 'buzz-bomb' or 'doodlebug,' as it was nicknamed. These flying bombs had no pilot and carried about 2,000 lbs. (900 kg.) of explosives. Their design was started secretly in 1936. The first was fired on the night of 13–14 June 1944, seven days after the Normandy landings and continued intermittently until the end of March 1945. In all, 9,251 were fired at southern England. Of these, 4,621 were destroyed, 630 being shot down by the RAF. About 5,500 people were killed and some 16,000 injured; damage was considerable but not of a kind to undermine war production. The buzz of the bomb cut out as the bomb lost power and fell silently to earth to explode on impact. They did not circle around as suggested in Orwell's dialogue. Inez Holden, in her *Summer Journal*, wrote, 'I tried to finish the short story I had been writing for L.'s paper. The general conditions are bad for work. Flying bombs produce a mood of frustration and guilt. One stops work as they go over and after the engine has cut out and the explosion is ended, a feeling of guilt follows because one knows that the bomb has "fallen on someone else"' (*Leaves in the Storm: A Book of Diaries . . . with a Running Commentary*, edited by Stefan Schimanski and Henry Treece, 1947, 245). Thompson has an illustration of a V-1 about to crash in Drury Lane, London, 1944. An illustration of the sound-track of the buzz, the ensuing silence, and the explosion was printed in the *Evening Standard*, 20 November 1944, 5, with a picture of an explosion caused by a V-1. taken from the top of the University of London Senate House (Minitru of *Nineteen Eighty-Four*).
2. See *1241, n. 4*.
3. It is, in fact, from *The Uncelestial City* by Humbert Wolfe (1885–1940), poet and satirist.
4. Orwell had in mind the reason given by Cape for rejecting *Animal Farm*; see *2494, n. 1*.
5. In response to an anguished request from G. A. Weller, *Tribune*, 28 July, Orwell gave this answer (though the outward and inward journeys had become two instead of four miles): "The bear was white. The man travelled two miles south, then two miles west, then two miles north, and was back at his house again. In any ordinary locality these movements would have brought him to a spot two miles west of his house. Evidently he lived at the North Pole. Therefore, the bear must have been a polar bear."

2502. Review of *In a Strange Land: Essays by Eric Gill*
The Observer, 9 July 1944

An uneasy awareness that medievalism is a by-product of industrialism seems to underlie much of Eric Gill's writing. With more grip on reality than Chesterton, who was saying much the same thing in a more flamboyant way, he gave the same impression of constantly nagging away at a half-truth and evading every real criticism that could be brought against him. But it must be allowed to both of them that the half-truth they got hold of was an unpopular one and therefore worthy of emphasis.

In this little book of collected essays and lectures, Gill is presenting his usual thesis: the fundamental evil of industrial society. The good life is well-nigh impossible, and the arts are mostly dead, because we live in an age in which the workman is not master of his own work. He is simply a cog in an enormous machine, performing over and over again some mechanical task of which he does not know the meaning and in which he has no interest except the wage he receives for it. His creative instincts have to be satisfied, if at all, outside his working hours, and they are constantly perverted by the mass-produced goods that capitalism forces upon him. True civilisation, Gill thinks, can only return when people choose their own work and do it in their own time, and when they are conscious of being free agents while possessing a common body of belief. This much one might accept, even though Gill makes the usual parochial claim that the common belief of humanity must be *Christian* belief, and even though his dislike of factory production is illogically mixed up with ideas about currency reform and the special wickedness of bankers.

But however much one may agree with Gill's indictment, he has no real remedy to offer. Naturally his programme is a return to peasant ownership, hand production, and, in general, to an idealised version of the Middle Ages. But there are two insuperable objections to this, neither of which he really meets. One is that the world is so manifestly not going in that direction that to wish for it is like wishing for the moon. Elsewhere in his writings, though not in this book, Gill does admit this and seems to realise that the way to a simpler life must lead through greater complexity. The other objection is that Gill and all similar thinkers have no real notion of what a non-industrial society would be like, nor, indeed, much idea of the meaning of work.

Much the best thing in this book is a diary of a trip to Ireland in 1919. As a Catholic convert, slightly Anglophobe and in love with peasant society, Gill is naturally inclined to idealise Ireland, and he does so even to the extent of claiming that the Irish country people are less ugly than the English. But whenever he encounters an Irish working man, for instance a trade union organiser, he notes with dismay that the Irishmen seem to have the same outlook as their English colleagues. That is, they think in terms of mechanisation, efficiency, shorter hours, and higher wages, and are not much interested in the sacredness of private property. "They appear," he says, "to be quite content to promote a co-operative commonwealth in which there shall be no individual ownership or responsibility—i.e., the factory system in public instead of private hands." Elsewhere in the book he explains this by saying that the working man has taken over his employer's system of values. What he does not see is that the working man's attitude is founded on hard experience. Middle-class people hardly have the right to question it.

The point is well brought out in a bit of dialogue in Shaw's "Man and Superman" between the sentimental Octavius and the chauffeur, 'Enery Straker:

> *Octavius*: "I believe in the dignity of labour."
> *Straker*: "That's because you never done any, Mr. Octavius."

Eric Gill, a sculptor, obviously thinks of manual labour as being of its nature creative labour, and in thinking of the past he tends to forget the lower strata of the population. The world he imagines is a world of craftsmen—owner-farmers, carpenters, handloom weavers, stonemasons, and the like—and it is also a world almost without machinery. But, of course, in a world without machinery the average person is not a craftsman but a serf, or as near it as makes no difference. The job of getting food out of the soil without machinery is so laborious that it necessarily reduces large numbers of people almost to the status of animals, and we forget this aspect of pre-industrial life precisely because the poorest classes were too worn out by drudgery to leave much record behind them. In many primitive countries to-day, the ordinary person is toiling like a slave from the age of about ten onwards, and even his seeming aesthetic superiority is probably only due to lack of opportunity. Nothing could really improve his situation except the machinery, the division of labour, and the centralised economy which Gill so much dislikes.

The book also contains an address delivered to the Peace Pledge Union, an essay on clothes, and some remarks on Ruskin and on the painter, David Jones. Gill was a pacifist, at any rate towards the end of his life, and in spite of his theories about land-ownership and cottage industries, he toyed with the idea of Socialism. But the central thing in him was his hatred of the machine. He was right, no doubt, in his denunciations of present-day society, but wrong in looking for a quick way out, and like all people who hanker for the past, he could not altogether escape affectation and pretty-prettiness. Not to be arty and crafty, not to resemble William Morris—naturally this was his claim. But one does not reject one's own age without paying the penalty, and the price Gill paid can be seen in the carvings outside Broadcasting House, in the woodcuts that adorn this book, and in his over-simplified way of writing.

[Fee: £7.7.0; 7.7.44]

2502A. To Arthur Koestler, 10 July 1944: see Vol xx, last appendix.

2503. To Rayner Heppenstall

11 July 1944   Typewritten

Tribune

Dear Rayner,

I think we shall have to modify slightly your review of Barzun's book.[1] I don't think it's fair to drag up Roy Campbell's past[2] as he has greatly changed his views, nor to say that Eliot has kept silent about this war when he has been acting for the British Council for the last two years. Could you make these alterations? You might find other instances, e.g. Arthur Bryant.[3]

Yours,
George

P.S. Would you like to review some more Scottish Nationalism?

1. Jacques Barzun, *Romanticism and the Modern Ego*; Orwell reviewed this book for *The Observer*, 23 July 1944; see *2517*. Heppenstall's review appeared in *Tribune* on 27 October 1944.
2. Roy Campbell (1901–1957), poet born in South Africa, came to Europe when seventeen. Orwell refers to his supporting Franco during the Spanish civil war as reporter and propagandist. See also *2314, n. 1* and *2511*.
3. Sir Arthur Bryant (1899–1985), conservatively-inclined historian, published (among many books). *The Spirit of Conservatism* (1929) and *Stanley Baldwin: A Tribute* (1937). He had recently published *Unfinished Victory*, on Germany, 1918–33 (1940), *The Years of Endurance, 1793–1812* (1942), and *Years of Victory, 1802–12* (1944; New York, 1945). Of *Unfinished Victory*, Kenneth Rose said 'Goebbels himself could not have composed a more ingratiating apologia for the Nazis. Anti-semitism is a recurrent theme,' yet he received 'a whole chestful of decorations,' including a knighthood and the Companion of Honour (*Sunday Telegraph*, 1 August 1993). See also *2511*.

2504. Review of *Art and Scientific Thought* by Martin Johnson

Manchester Evening News, 13 July 1944

There are some books that get nowhere, but do at least get there by interesting routes. This book is decidedly one of them, and anyone who can face some rather clumsy writing and a jungle of prefaces almost recalling the "Tale of a Tub" will come away with quite a quantity of miscellaneous and unusual information. But it seems doubtful whether he will come away with any clearer idea than before of the relationship between art and science—which is a pity, for, as the author perceives, the subject is vitally important.

Dr. Johnson is rightly concerned over the fact that the arts and the exact sciences have diverged until they seem to have no common basis[1] and hardly even seem to be dealing with the same universe. The mental world of the artist is still largely in the pre-machine age, while the scientist, as such, is not expected to have the smallest æsthetic sensibility. Figures like Leonardo da Vinci, equally at home in both camps, do not exist in the modern world.

And Dr. Johnson might have added that this dichotomy is made worse by the fact that the average man, in our own age, sides as a matter of course with the scientist and would not be conscious of any loss if certain of the arts—for instance, poetry—disappeared altogether. This much is ably set forth in the opening chapters, but when the last page is reached the question is hardly further advanced.

Dr. Johnson merely suggests, rather tentatively, that the reconciliation between science and art (and also science and religion) may be achieved via symbolism. The rest of the book, though arranged upon an elaborate pattern, is a series of enormous digressions, displaying very unusual erudition but leaving the main subject very much where it was.

Still, parts of it are fascinating reading. First of all there is a long disquisition on ancient Chinese jade carvings, and then another on the twelfth-century statues on the portals of Chartres Cathedral. Then there is a chapter on Russian ballet, then another on Mr. Walter de la Mare's poetry, and then some really first-rate chapters on the early astronomers of China and the Middle East. These probably contain information which one could not get from any ordinarily accessible book, and certainly they are excellent reading.

It appears that in mediæval Arabia and Persia, as earlier in Greece and earlier still in China, that now-extinct figure, the artist-scientist, existed, and mathematics was intensively studied in Bagdad at a time when our own ancestors were not much better than savages. Under the Caliph al Mamun, in A.D. 820, the circumference of the earth was calculated with fair accuracy, and in the thirteenth century the Mongol conqueror, Kublai Khan, maintained a staff of learned men from all over Asia and Eastern Europe for the study of astronomy.

In this section Dr. Johnson points out a fact which is of great interest in itself and which probably has a bearing on the relationship between art and science. This is that the incorrect astronomical theories of Ptolemy survived for many centuries because they were æsthetically satisfying. Greeks, Arabs, and Chinese were all fascinated by a picture of the universe in which all the heavenly bodies moved in circles.

The ellipse on which the planets actually move seemed to them an uninteresting figure, and it was left to the comparatively vulgar Europeans of the Renaissance to construct a true picture of the solar system. There are also admirable chapters on Leonardo da Vinci, who was not only a painter and draughtsman of the first rank but one of the most intellectually adventurous people who have ever lived. Not many of Leonardo's paintings have survived, but there exist many note books containing hundreds of his drawings, and these show him to have been acquainted with the whole body of scientific knowledge that existed in his own time. He even anticipated many modern inventions and discoveries, among which Dr. Johnson lists aeroplanes, submarines, and the use of steam for motive power.

He may have discovered independently that the earth goes round the sun. In his case, obviously, scientific curiosity and æsthetic sensibility did not clash. But whether such a man could exist in our own day is more doubtful, because of a difficulty which Dr. Johnson does mention, but does not discuss at length. This is, that scientific knowledge has now swollen beyond manageable limits.

One must be a specialist if one is to know anything at all about A.D. 1500, when Leonardo lived, or centuries earlier in Bagdad and Damascus, when it was possible for one man to absorb all the knowledge that existed, or at least to have a nodding acquaintance with it. Now, when it would need a lifetime of work merely to learn all that is known about marine fishes, or radio, or chemotherapy, or ballistics, it is clearly not possible, and even the full-time scientific worker is often completely ignorant about branches of science other than his own. The artist can at best have only a smattering of a few of the sciences, while the scientist's necessarily rigid training often leads him to despise the imagination. It is difficult to imagine anyone genuinely combining the two rôles.

There is a possible clue in the affinity that seems to exist between certain arts and certain sciences. Apart from the well-known fact that mathematicians are nearly always musical, it seems to be true that biologists are usually sensitive to literature. Dr. Johnson hardly touches on this, and does not, indeed, offer any positive solution except for some rather vague hints about symbolism. This is an unsatisfactory book, but incidentally an interesting one, well worth dipping into for the knowledge it so irrelevantly displays.

[Fee: £8.8.0; 12.7.44]

1. The original has 'oasis'.

2505. T. S. Eliot to Orwell

13 July 1944

On 13 July 1944, Miss Sheldon of Faber & Faber wrote on T. S. Eliot's behalf returning the manuscript of *Animal Farm* to Orwell. She said Orwell would be receiving a personal letter from Eliot, 'direct from the country.' Eliot wrote on the same day on Faber & Faber headed notepaper:

Dear Orwell,
I know that you wanted a quick decision about "Animal Farm": but the minimum is two directors' opinions, and that can't be done under a week. But for the importance of speed, I should have asked the Chairman to look at it as well. But the other director is in agreement with me on the main points. We agree that it is a distinguished piece of writing; that the fable is very skilfully handled, and that the narrative keeps one's interest *on its* own plane—and that is something very few authors have achieved since Gulliver.

On the other hand, we have no conviction (and I am sure none of the other directors would have) that this is the right point of view from which to criticise the political situation at the present time. It is certainly the duty of any publishing firm which pretends to other interests and motives than mere commercial prosperity, to publish books which go against the current of the moment: but in each instance that demands that at least one member of the firm should have the conviction that this is the thing that needs saying at the moment. I can't see any reason of prudence or caution to prevent anybody from publishing this book—if he believed in what it stands for.

Now I think my own dissatisfaction with this apologue is that the effect is simply one of negation. It ought to excite some sympathy with what the author wants, as well as sympathy with his objections to something: and the positive point of view, which I take to be generally Trotskyite, is not convincing. I think you split your vote, without getting any compensating stronger adhesion from either party—i.e. those who criticise Russian tendencies from the point of view of a purer communism, and those who, from a very different point of view, are alarmed about the future of small nations. And after all, your pigs are far more intelligent than the other animals, and therefore the best qualified to run the farm—in fact, there couldn't have been an Animal Farm at all without them: so that what was needed, (someone might argue), was not more communism but more public-spirited pigs.

I am very sorry, because whoever publishes this, will naturally have the opportunity of publishing your future work: and I have a regard for your work, because it is good writing of fundamental integrity.

Miss Sheldon will be sending you the script under separate cover.

Yours sincerely,
T. S. Eliot

2506. Orwell's Flat Bombed

28 June 1944

On 28 June 1944, Orwell and his wife were bombed out of their flat in Mortimer Crescent. They first moved into Inez Holden's house, 106 George Street, London, W.1; Inez Holden was away, ill. In a letter to Leonard Moore, 3 October 1944, Orwell described 27b Canonbury Square, London, N.1 as 'my permanent address.' In the intervening weeks he gave his address as care of the *Tribune* office.

In her *Summer Journal* (see *2501, n. 1*), Inez Holden wrote: 'George [Orwell] telephoned. He had been planning to get his books up from the country [Wallington] for some time. At last he managed it, but now his house has been broken up by blast. The place is no longer habitable, but he goes each day to rummage in the rubble to recover as many books as possible and wheel them away in a wheel-barrow. He makes this journey from Fleet Street during his lunch hour' (245). Mortimer Crescent to Fleet Street is about four miles each way. Thompson illustrates Mortimer Crescent and Canonbury Square (60 and 92).

2507. 'As I Please,' 33

Tribune, 14 July 1944

Among the mail Orwell received following 'As I Please,' 25, 19 May 1944 (see *2473*), and which led to this 'As I Please' (though not the 'quite violent ones' mentioned in his first sentence), were letters from A. Clark Smith and Gerald Brenan dated 25 and 26 June 1944 respectively. Clark Smith wondered, if the war 'became an affair of bacterial and chemical warfare . . . and a string of other atrocities,' whether Orwell 'would not recognise any difference from that and the present fighting and would do nothing about it.' Vera Brittain, he wrote, saw 'the barbarism getting worse' and was 'merely asking people who are not pacifists to think about what they are doing.' Did Air Marshal (Bomber) Harris 'know what he was doing? Did the man who blew up the Ruhr dam know what he was doing? I doubt it. . . . You oppose capitalism but you accept the fruits of capitalism.' He concluded by quoting from Bernard Shaw's play *Geneva*, giving part of a speech by the Judge of the High Court of the League in which he addressed Heads of State: 'You have reduced one another to such a condition of terror that there is no atrocity which will make you recoil and say that you will die rather than commit it.' Pacifism might not spring from freedom and democracy, but, wrote Clark Smith, 'it has a lot to do with the dignity and nobility of man.'

Gerald Brenan, who said he was not a pacifist but an ex-soldier, argued that war had always been humanized. He asked Orwell two questions: Did he advocate using gas against German cities? Did he advocate killing all German prisoners who were convinced Nazis? Such steps would hasten the end of the war. If Orwell agreed with taking these steps, then 'we shall all know where he stands'; if not, 'let him have the common honesty to withdraw what he first said.'

Orwell's reponse was given in this 'As I Please.'

I have received a number of letters, some of them quite violent ones, attacking me for my remarks on Miss Vera Brittain's anti-bombing pamphlet. There are two points that seem to need further comment.

First of all there is the charge, which is becoming quite a common one, that "we started it." i.e. that Britain was the first country to practise systematic bombing of civilians. How anyone can make this claim, with the history of the past dozen years in mind, is almost beyond me. The first act in the present war—some hours, if I remember rightly, before any declaration of war passed—was the German bombing of Warsaw. The Germans bombed and shelled the city so intensively that, according to the Poles, at one time 700 fires were raging simultaneously. They made a film of the destruction of Warsaw, which they entitled "Baptism of Fire" and sent all round the world with the object of terrorising neutrals.

Several years earlier than this the Condor Legion, sent to Spain by Hitler, had bombed one Spanish city after another. The "silent raids" on Barcelona in 1938 killed several thousand people in a couple of days. Earlier than this the Italians had bombed entirely defenceless Abyssinians and boasted of their exploits as something screamingly funny. Bruno Mussolini wrote newspaper articles in which he described bombed Abyssinians "bursting open like a rose," which, he said, was "most amusing." And the Japanese ever since 1931, and intensively since 1937, have been bombing crowded Chinese cities where there are not even any A.R.P. arrangements, let alone any A.A. guns or fighter aircraft.

I am not arguing that two blacks make a white, nor that Britain's record is a particularly good one. In a number of "little wars" from about 1920 onwards the R.A.F. has dropped its bombs on Afghans, Indians and Arabs who had little or no power of hitting back. But it is simply untruthful to say that large-scale bombing of crowded town areas, with the object of causing panic, is a British invention. It was the Fascist states who started this practice, and so long as the air war went in their favour they avowed their aims quite clearly.

The other thing that needs dealing with is the parrot cry "killing women and children." I pointed out before, but evidently it needs repeating, that it is probably somewhat better to kill a cross section of the population than to kill only the young men. If the figures published by the Germans are true, and we have really killed 1,200,000 civilians in our raids, that loss of life has probably harmed the German race somewhat less than a corresponding loss on the Russian front or in Africa and Italy.

Any nation at war will do its best to protect its children, and the number of children killed in raids probably does not correspond to their percentage of the general population. Women cannot be protected to the same extent, but the outcry against killing women, if you accept killing at all, is sheer sentimentality. Why is it worse to kill a woman than a man? The argument usually advanced is that in killing women you are killing the breeders, whereas men can be more easily spared. But this is a fallacy based on the notion that human beings can be bred like animals. The idea behind it is that since one man is capable of fertilising a very large number of women, just as a prize ram fertilises thousands of ewes, the loss of male lives is comparatively unimportant. Human beings, however, are not cattle. When the slaughter caused by a war leaves a surplus of women, the enormous majority of those women bear no children. Male lives are very nearly as important, bio-logically, as female ones.

In the last war the British Empire lost nearly a million men killed, of whom about three-quarters came from these islands. Most of them will have been under thirty. If all those young men had had only one child each we should now have an extra 750,000 people round about the age of 20. France, which lost much more heavily, never recovered from the slaughter of the last war, and it is doubtful whether Britain has fully recovered, either. We can't yet calculate the casualties of the present war, but the last one killed between ten and twenty million young men. Had it been conducted, as the next one will perhaps be, with flying bombs, rockets and other long-range weapons which kill old and young, healthy and unhealthy, male and female impartially, it would probably have damaged European civilisation somewhat less than it did.

Contrary to what some of my correspondents seem to think, I have no enthusiasm for air raids, either ours or the enemy's. Like a lot of other people in this country, I am growing definitely tired of bombs. But I do object to the hypocrisy of accepting force as an instrument while squealing against this or that individual weapon, or of denouncing war while wanting to preserve the kind of society that makes war inevitable.

I note in my diary for 1940 an expectation that commercial advertisements will have disappeared from the walls within a year. This seemed likely enough at the time, and a year or even two years later the disappearance seemed to be actually happening, though more slowly than I had expected. Advertisements were shrinking both in numbers and size, and the announcements of the various Ministries were more and more taking their place both on the walls and in the newspapers. Judging from this symptom alone, one would have said that commercialism was definitely on the downgrade.

In the last two years, however, the commercial ad., in all its silliness and snobbishness, has made a steady comeback. In recent years I consider that the most offensive of all British advertisements are the ones for Rose's Lime Juice, with their "young squire" motif and their P. G. Wodehouse dialogue.

"I fear you do not see me at my best this morning, Jenkins. There were jollifications last night. Your young master looked upon the wine when it was red and also upon the whisky when it was yellow. To use the vulgar phrase, I have a thick head. What do you think the doctor would prescribe, Jenkins?"

"If I might make so bold, sir, a glass of soda water with a dash of Rose's Lime Juice would probably have the desired effect."

"Go to it, Jenkins! You were always my guide, philosopher and friend," etc., etc., etc.

When you reflect that this advertisement appears, for instance in every theatre programme, so that every theatre-goer is at any rate assumed to have a secret fantasy life in which he thinks of himself as a young man of fashion with faithful old retainers, the prospect of any drastic social change recedes perceptibly.

There are also the hair-tonic adverts. which tell you how Daphne got promotion in the W.A.A.F.S. thanks to the neatness and glossiness of her hair. But these are misleading as well as whorish, for I seldom or never pass a group of officers in the W.A.R.E.N.S.[1] without having cause to reflect that, at any rate, promotion in the women's services has nothing to do with looks.

Vera Brittain sent *Tribune* a long letter dated August 1944 and headed, 'Vera Brittain, George Orwell, Night Bombing and "What DID happen."' This energetically, if not always coherently, repeated the case against the heavy bombing of Germany, in the course of which she offered a review of the stages of the war as she saw them. Orwell, she wrote, might 'find self-satisfaction if lecturing down to Miss V. Brittain for telling a Truth, like so many of our "Bull-dog breed", who boasted of the "thrashing" they proposed giving the Huns if they "dared to put a foot on British soil". (That was in 1940!).' She made great play of the fact that Britain had made a night raid on Germany before the Germans made night raids on Britain. [Vera Brittain was correct in that on 25 August 1940 the RAF raided Berlin, and the first night alert in London was not until the next night; the first fire-bomb raid on London was on 28 August. However, the Berlin raid was partly in retaliation for the daylight bombing offensive mounted by the Germans from 11 August, and partly to disprove Goering's claim that Berlin would remain immune from attack.] Despite the 1,000-bomber raids, Germany, Vera Brittain said, had been able to retaliate with flying-bomb raids. These could 'raise the entire country to debris' and it was vital 'to Negotiate like Rational Beings (what we should have done in the first instance).' She feared Russia becoming 'any more powerful & we a 5th rate power' but that was 'no excuse for pretending Hitler is not the Leader he is & of which we remain bankrupt.' She directed this remark at Winston Churchill, whom she called 'Windbag Churchill.' *Tribune* did not publish the letter. The original was among Orwell's papers at his death. For later comments by Orwell on this subject, see his review of B. H. Liddell Hart's, *The Revolution in Warfare*, 4 April 1946, *2960*.

1. The women's branches of the armed services: Women's Auxiliary Air Force, Auxiliary Territorial Service, Women's Royal Naval Service.

2508. John Middleton Murry to Orwell

11 July 1944

John Middleton Murry wrote to Orwell on 11 July 1944 saying that someone had written to him to draw his attention to Orwell's review 'Gandhi in Mayfair' (*Horizon*, September 1943; see *2257*), and in particular to the statement 'One realizes . . . when one sees Middleton Murry praising the Japanese invasion of China.' Murry's correspondent had asked for an explanation. Murry was certain Orwell must have misinterpreted something he had said, and he remarked, a little wryly, 'You are rather given to taking pot-shots at me, nowadays.' He suggested that Orwell tackle his position frontally by writing a straight review of his new book, *Adam and Eve*. 'Knock it to pieces by all means. That will be much better for us both than setting up a dummy J.M.M. and knocking bits off that. I have no doubt that you want to be fair to me. Let this be the opportunity,' for he had packed into *Adam and Eve* practically all he had to say.

He enclosed the letter from his correspondent 'and the contribution which accompanied it,' because he thought Orwell would be interested in both. He asked for them to be returned, so it is not possible to identify the correspondent with certainty. However, in the Berg Collection in the New York Public Library, in addition to Murry's letter, is his draft. On its verso is a draft of what may have been intended as a final paragraph of the letter to Orwell, omitted intentionally or by accident. One version of the draft begins, 'We rejoice to hear that Dr Salter[1] . . . ,' which suggests a more public statement than would be appropriate for a private letter, but the second, and completed, draft refers to Dr. Salter's rooms having been severely damaged by a flying bomb, and concludes, 'His innumerable friends will rejoice to hear that he is safe.' This version might have been intended for Orwell. The nearest guess, therefore, to Murry's correspondent is Salter.

1. Dr. Alfred Salter (1873–1945) was for a long time a sponsor of the Peace Pledge Union and for a while its Joint Treasurer. Except for a brief interval, he was Labour M.P. from 1922 until he

retired at the 1945 General Election. He had a distinguished career at Guy's Hospital and London University, then joined the Society of Friends and settled in Bermondsey as a 'poor man's doctor.' He was elected to the London County Council in 1905.

2509. To John Middleton Murry

14 July 1944   Typewritten

Tribune

Dear Murry,

Thanks for your letter. I have not the text by me, but you wrote in an article in the "Adelphi" something that ran more or less as follows:

"We are in the habit of describing the war between Japan and China as though it were a war in the European sense. But it is nothing of the kind, because the average Chinese expects to be conquered. That is what the history of thousands of years has taught him to expect. China will absorb Japan, and Japan will energise China. And so also with India."

If this is not praise and encouragement of the Japanese invasion of China, and an invitation to the Japanese to go on and invade India, I don't know what it is. It takes no account of what has been happening in China since 1912 and uses exactly the same argument ("these people are used to being conquered") that was always brought forward to justify our own rule in India. In any case its moral is, "don't help the Chinese."

As to the general charge of "praising violence" which your correspondent refers to. Many remarks you have made in recent years seem to me to imply that you don't object to violence if it is violent enough. And you certainly seem or seemed to me to prefer the Nazis to ourselves, at least so long as they appeared to be winning.

If you'll send the book along I'll naturally be glad to give it a notice, but I *might* have to turn it over to someone else, though I'll do it myself if possible. I am smothered under work, and also I've been bombed out and we have a very young baby,[1] all of which adds to one's work.

Yours,
[Signed] Geo. Orwell
George Orwell

1. In June 1944 Orwell and his wife had adopted a three-week-old boy, who was christened Richard Horatio Blair. Both Richard and Horatio were Blair family names, but the Richard also referred to Richard Rees. Richard was fetched from Newcastle in the week of 15–21 October (see *2528A headnote*).

2510. 'The Eight Years of War: Spanish Memories'

The Observer, 16 July 1944

The Spanish Civil War, curtain-raiser of the present struggle and one of the most tragic as well as one of the most sordid events that modern Europe has seen, began eight years ago next Friday.

The issue of the Spanish war was decided outside Spain, and by the time that it was a year old realistic observers were able to see that the elected government could not win unless there were some radical change in the European situation. In the first period of the war, which lasted just under a year, the struggle was essentially between Franco's professional soldiers and Moors on the one side and the hurriedly-raised militias of peasants and factory workers on the other.

In this period honours were about even, and no objective of first-rate importance changed hands.

Franco, however, was being reinforced on a massive scale by the Axis Powers, while the Spanish Government was receiving only sporadic doles of arms from Soviet Russia and the help of a few thousand foreign volunteers, mostly refugee Germans. In June, 1937, the resistance of the Basques collapsed and the balance of forces tipped heavily against the Government.

In the meantime, however, the Government had quelled the revolutionary disorder of early days, smoothed out the struggles between factions, and trained its raw forces. Early in 1938 it had a formidable army, able to fight on for the year or so that food supplies would last out.

Dr. Negrin and the other rulers of Government Spain probably realised that they could not win by their own efforts, but they were justified in fighting on, since the political outlook in Europe still might change. The obviously approaching world war might break out during 1938; the British Government might abandon its policy of non-intervention.

Neither event happened, and towards the end of 1938 the Russians withdrew their help. Government Spain had long been hungry, and was now definitely starving.

As the Fascist forces drove across Catalonia, hordes of refugees streamed into France, machine-gunned by Italian aeroplanes and interned behind barbed-wire as soon as they arrived.

Early in 1939 Franco entered Madrid, and used his victory with the utmost ruthlessness. All political parties of the Left were suppressed, and countless people executed or imprisoned. If recent reports are true, half a million people, or 2 per cent. of the population of Spain, are still in concentration camps.

The story is a disgusting one, because of the sordid behaviour of the Great Powers and the indifference of the world at large. The Germans and Italians intervened in order to crush Spanish democracy, to seize a strategic keypoint for the coming war, and, incidentally, to try out their bombing planes on helpless populations.

The Russians doled out a small quantity of weapons and extorted the maximum of political control in return. The British and French simply looked the other way while their enemies triumphed and their friends were destroyed. The British attitude is the hardest to forgive, because it was foolish as well as dishonourable.

It had been obvious from the start that any foreign country which supplied arms to the Spanish Government could control or at least influence that Government's policy. Instead, the British preferred to make sure that Franco and Hitler should win, and at the same time that the affection and gratitude of the Spanish people should be earned by Russia and not by Britain.

For a year or more the Spanish Government was effectively under Russian control, mainly because Russia was the only country to come to the rescue. The growth of the Spanish Communist Party from a few thousands to a quarter of a million was directly the work of the British Tories.

There has been a strong tendency to push these facts out of sight and even to claim Franco's hostile "non-belligerency" as a triumph for British diplomacy. Rather should the true history of the Spanish war be kept always in mind as an object-lesson in the folly and meanness of Power Politics. Nothing, indeed, redeems its story except the courage of the fighting-men on both sides, and the toughness of the civilian population of Loyalist Spain, who for years endured hunger and hardship unknown to us at the worst moments of war.

[Fee: £7.7.0; 15.7.44]

2511. To Rayner Heppenstall

17 July 1944   Typewritten

Tribune

Dear Rayner,
Thanks for the alterations in the review. I finally sent the Scottish books to someone else (they didn't look much good) but am sending you something which *may* be interesting, though I haven't examined it. It is a printing of the first Draft of "Portrait of the Artist"[1] which I suppose someone rescued from the w.p.b.

I thought you would have seen the answers to your anti-Scotland review,[2] but they were so damn silly they weren't worth answering any way. The only bright remark was "I spit in Mr Heppenstall's eye," which I suppose the writer hasn't actually done, up to date.

Eliot has been working for the British Council for a couple of years. He has also written at least once for "British Ally," the British propaganda paper published in Moscow. To judge by his private conversation he has definitely changed some of his political views though he hasn't made any public pronouncement yet. Roy Campbell (I don't know him but I have mutual friends) stayed on in Spain after Franco won and was so disgusted by the resulting regime that he has become definitely anti-Fascist. He was acting as a paid firewatcher for some time, then he joined the army where I think he still is. Arthur Bryant is one of the big guns of the Conservative intelligentsia. He was the one who said during the Spanish war that "the sawing off of a Conservative tradesman's legs is a commonplace in Republican Spain", a phrase which stuck in my memory.

I'd like very much to get down and see you, but it's difficult to get out of town. What with my work, our flat being blitzed, and a very young baby, life is pretty full now. Look me up (Tribune is the best address) any time you're in town.

Yours
[Signed] Eric
George Orwell

1. *Stephen Hero: Part of the first draft of 'A Portrait of the Artist as a Young Man,'* edited by Theodore Spencer (1944). Though so titled, it proved not to be the first draft. This took the form of a 2,000-word short story which was submitted to a Dublin journal but rejected and which Joyce then laid aside. It is reproduced in *The Workshop of Daedalus: James Joyce and the Raw Materials for A Portrait of the Artist as a Young Man*, edited by Robert Scholes and Richard M. Kain (Evanston, 1965), 60–68. Orwell's 'which I suppose someone rescued from the w[aste] p[aper] b[asket]' is indicative of his attitude to his own draft manuscripts. Heppenstall reviewed *Stephen Hero* in *Tribune*, 15 September 1944.
2. Of *Poetry Scotland*, No. 1, edited by Maurice Lindsay, *Tribune*, 7 April 1944.

2512. To Z. A. Bokhari

18 July 1944   Handwritten

Tribune

Dear Bokhari,

I'm sorry I didn't answer your letter earlier[1] but I have been blitzed out & this has put all my correspondence etc. back. I am afraid I cannot possibly undertake a b'cast any time in the near future. I am smothered under work. Possibly later in the year if you have a long series going. Sorry!

Yours
E. A. Blair

1. Z. A. Bokhari, Indian Programme Organiser, under whom Orwell worked at the BBC, first wrote to Orwell on 2 June 1944. He said, 'Following in your footsteps, in our English programmes to India, we have started a monthly 13½ minute broadcast under the general title "New Writing"' and asked Orwell if he would like to contribute. He received no answer and wrote again on 14 July specifying 12 September as the date for Orwell's broadcast. He made a number of specific suggestions. Would Orwell like to discuss "new tendencies, or new books, or the lack of new books—and you know here what I mean by new books? Can real creative work be done while the world consists of partisans? Why haven't we been able to produce a Rupert Brooke? Why are the creative writers turning into literary commentators? These are just vague suggestions, and I am sure you will be able to improve upon them considerably."

2513. To Leonard Moore

18 July 1944   Handwritten

Care of "Tribune" 222 Strand WC.2

Dear Mr Moore,

Thanks for your letter. The Dial people had written to me independently. I have wired to my friends of the "Partisan Review" asking them to get hold of the MS. & advise me about it. I don't know what they meant about my sending them something else—I hadn't promised to do so. I fancy from Joel's letter that he had not grasped what the book was about, but of course the "Partisan Review" people will do so.

Meanwhile could you send me the copy of the MS. that you have. Faber's replied in much the same sense as Cape's. Warburg again says he wants to see it & would publish it if he can see his way to getting the paper, but that is a big "if". If that falls through I am not going to tout it round further publishers, which wastes time & may lead to nothing, but shall publish it myself as a pamphlet at 2/–.[1] I have already half-arranged to do so & have got the necessary financial backing.[2] With the demand for books there is now, & the strings I can pull in one or two papers, I have no doubt we should get our money back, though probably not make much profit. You understand that it is important to get this book into print, & this year if possible.

I think I told you I have been bombed out so "Tribune" is the safest address.

Yours sincerely
Eric Blair

1. This was to be in association with Paul Potts. Orwell was to pay the printer, and Potts would supply the paper from his quota for the Whitman Press. Potts had actually got so far as travelling twice to Bedford to see the printer. See his *Dante Called You Beatrice*, 76–77. Although the Lilly Library letters at Indiana University had not then been made public and were therefore not available to him, Crick gives an excellent account in chapter 14 of *George Orwell: A Life* of the vicissitudes experienced in the publication of *Animal Farm*.
2. Shelden states that Orwell discussed with David Astor 'the possibility of borrowing £200 to pay the costs'; Orwell did not explain what the book was about, and Astor did not ask but agreed to make the loan (403–04; U.S., 368); no source is given.

2514. 'As I Please,' 34

Tribune, 21 July 1944

I have just found my copy of Samuel Butler's *Note-books*, the full edition of the first series, published by Jonathan Cape in 1921. It is twenty years old and none the better for having gone through several rainy seasons in Burma, but at any rate it exists, which is all to the good, for this is another of those well-known books which have now ceased to be procurable. Cape's later produced an abridged version in the *Traveller's Library*, but it is an unsatisfactory abridgment, and the second series which was published about 1934 does not contain much that is of value. It is in the first series that you will find the story of Butler's interview with a Turkish official at the Dardanelles, the description of his method of buying new-laid eggs and his endeavours to photograph a seasick bishop, and other similar trifles which in a way are worth more than his major works.

Butler's main ideas now seem either to be unimportant, or to suffer from wrong emphasis. Biologists apart, who now cares whether the Darwinian theory of evolution, or the Lamarckian version which Butler supported, is the correct one? The whole question of evolution seems less momentous than it did, because, unlike the Victorians, we do not feel that to be descended from animals is degrading to human dignity. On the other hand, Butler often makes a mere joke out of something that now seems to us vitally important. For example:

"The principal varieties and sub-varieties of the human race are not now to be looked for among the Negroes, the Circassians, the Malays or the American aborigines, but among the rich and the poor. The difference in physical organisation between these two species of man is far greater than that between the so-called types of humanity. The rich man can go from (New Zealand) to England whenever he feels inclined. The legs of the other are by an invisible fatality prevented from carrying him beyond certain narrow limits. Neither rich nor poor can yet see the philosophy of the thing, or admit that he who can tack a portion of one of the P. & O. boats on to his identity is a much more highly organised being than he who cannot."

There are innumerable similar passages in Butler's work. You could easily interpret them in a Marxist sense, but the point is that Butler himself does not do so. Finally his outlook is that of a Conservative, in spite of his successful assaults on Christian belief and the institution of a family. Poverty is degrading: therefore, take care not to be poor—that is his reaction. Hence the improbable and unsatisfying ending of *The Way of All Flesh*, which contrasts so strangely with the realism of the earlier parts.

Yet Butler's books have worn well, far better than those of more earnest contemporaries like Meredith and Carlyle, partly because he never lost the power to use his eyes and to be pleased by small things, partly because in the narrow technical sense he wrote so well. When one compares Butler's prose with the contortions of Meredith or the affectations of Stevenson, one sees what a tremendous advantage is gained simply by not trying to be clever. Butler's own ideas on the subject are worth quoting:

"I never knew a writer yet who took the smallest pains with his style and was at the same time readable. Plato's having had seventy shies at one sentence is quite enough to explain to me why I dislike him. A man may, and ought to, take a great deal of pains to write clearly, tersely and euphoniously: he will write many a sentence three or four times over—to do much more than this is worse than not rewriting at all: he will be at great pains to see that he does not repeat himself, to arrange his matter in the way that shall best enable the reader to master it, to cut out superfluous words and, even more, to eschew irrelevant matter: but in each case he will be thinking not of his own style but of his reader's convenience. . . . I should like to put it on record that I never took the smallest pains with my style, have never thought about it, and do not know or want to know whether it is a style at all or whether it is not, as I believe and hope, just common, simple, straightforwardness. I cannot conceive how any man can take thought for his style without loss to himself and his readers."

Butler adds characteristically, however, that he had made considerable efforts to improve his handwriting.

An argument that Socialists ought to be prepared to meet, since it is brought up constantly both by Christian apologists and by neo-pessimists such as James Burnham, is the alleged immutability of "human nature." Socialists are accused—I think without justification—of assuming that Man is perfectible, and it is then pointed out that human history is in fact one long tale of greed, robbery and oppression. Man, it is said, will always try to get the better of his neighbour, he will always hog as much property as possible for himself and his family. Man is of his nature sinful, and cannot be made virtuous by act of Parliament. Therefore, though economic exploitation can be controlled to some extent, the classless society is for ever impossible.

The proper answer, it seems to me, is that this argument belongs to the Stone Age. It presupposes that material goods will always be desperately scarce. The power-hunger of human beings does indeed present a serious problem, but there is no reason for thinking that the greed for mere wealth is a permanent human characteristic. We are selfish in economic matters because we all live in terror of poverty. But when a commodity is not scarce, no one tries to grab more than his fair share of it. No one tries to make a corner in air, for instance. The millionaire as well as the beggar is content with just so much air as he can breathe. Or, again, water. In this country we are not troubled by lack of water. If anything we have too much of it, especially on Bank Holidays. As a result water hardly enters into our consciousness. Yet in dried-up countries like North Africa, what jealousies, what hatreds, what appalling crimes the lack of water can cause! So also with any other kind of goods. If they were made plentiful, as they so easily might be, there is no reason to think that the supposed acquisitive instincts of the human being could not be bred out in a couple of generations. And after all, if human nature never changes, why is it that we not only don't practise cannibalism any longer, but don't even want to?

Another brain-tickler.

A business-man was in the habit of going home by a suburban train which left London at seven-thirty. One evening the night watchman, who had just come on duty, stopped him and said:—

"Excuse me, sir, but I'd advise you not to go by your usual train tonight. I dreamed last night that the train was smashed up and half the people in it were killed. Maybe you'll think I'm superstitious, but it was all so vivid that I can't help thinking it was meant as a warning."

The business-man was sufficiently impressed to wait and take a later train. When he opened the newspaper the next morning he saw that, sure enough, the train *had* been wrecked and many people killed. That evening he sent for the night watchman and said to him:—

"I want to thank you for your warning yesterday. I consider that you saved my life, and in return I should like to make you a present of thirty pounds. In addition, I have to inform you that you are sacked. Take a week's notice from today."

This was an ungrateful act, but the business-man was strictly within his rights. Why?[1]

1. Orwell did not give the answer to this conundrum in a later issue of *Tribune*. The reason was, of course, that in order to dream of the wreck the watchman must have been asleep on duty.

2515. To Rayner Heppenstall

21 July 1944   Typewritten

Tribune

Dear Rayner,
Herewith that book.[1] About 600 words perhaps? I'd like you very much to draw little Richard's horoscope.[2] He was born on May 14th. I thought I had told you, however, that he is an adopted child. Does that make any difference to the horoscope? Don't forget to look me up if you do get to town. The above is the safest address for the time being.

Yours
Eric

1. Presumably the book in Orwell's letter of 17 July 1944; see *2511*.
2. For this horoscope, see *2558*.

2516. To John Middleton Murry

21 July 1944   Typewritten

Tribune

Dear Murry,
I am sorry I did not return your correspondent's letter, which is herewith.

I haven't the reference (all my papers are in store), but you will find it if you look through the files of the "Adelphi", and I do not think it will be found to differ much from what I quoted. Nor can I agree that such a statement is not pro-Japanese both objectively and, to all appearances, subjectively. Ditto with many other statements of yours, eg. your remarks about Hess[1] soon after his arrival. You are wrong, however, in thinking that I have made use of you as a scapegoat. I think I have only mentioned you in print twice, once in this article in "Horizon",[2] the other time in the "Adelphi" in the review I did for you of Alex Comfort's novel.[3] You are wrong also in thinking that I dislike wholehearted pacifism, though I do think it mistaken. What I object to is the circumspect kind of pacifism which denounces one kind of violence while endorsing or avoiding mention of another. Your own failure to make a clear statement about the Russo-German war is the kind of thing I mean. I can respect anyone who is willing to face unpopularity, however much I may disagree with him.

Your sincerely
[Signed] Geo. Orwell
George Orwell

1. Rudolf Hess (1894–1987), Nazi official, second to Goering as Hitler's successor, flew to Scotland on 10 May 1941, allegedly bearing peace proposals. He was interned in Britain, and, in 1946, sentenced to life imprisonment by the international war crimes tribunal at Nuremberg. An argument has since raged as to whether this was the genuine Rudolf Hess.
2. Orwell's review of Lionel Fielden's *Beggar My Neighbour*; see *2257*.
3. Orwell's review of Alex Comfort's *No Such Liberty*; see *855.*

2517. Review of *Romanticism and the Modern Ego* by Jacques Barzun

The Observer, 23 July 1944

When one's ears are full of the wailing of sirens and the boom of distant explosions, the news that Rousseau was *not* the father of totalitarianism is apt to seem unexciting. And yet the issues that Mr. Barzun is discussing in this learned and polemical book are of great importance, and without making up one's mind upon them one cannot have any clear picture of the post-war world.

Briefly, Mr. Barzun's aim is to defend romanticism against the now common charge that by exalting passion as against reason it has led directly to modern power-worship and the Absolute State. He makes out a very strong case, but it suffers by being too narrowly defined. To begin with he treats ideas almost as though they were unconnected with economic conditions, and hardly raises the question of *why* the classical or the romantic outlook should prevail in different epochs. Secondly, the very use of such terms as "classical" and "romantic" ties the controversy to the schoolroom, whereas what is at issue is the much wider question of progress and original sin.

He himself does indeed recognise that "romantic" is a much-abused word. A table of quotations at the end of the book shows over fifty different usages (it is applied, for instance, to Napoleon, to the Middle Ages, to almost any female film star, to royalism, to republicanism, to Catholicism, to Protestantism, to reactionaries, revolutionaries, saints, highwaymen, cosmetics, ruined castles, and what-not). Worse yet, the distinction between classical and romantic art is reliable only within rather narrow limits, roughly 1650 to 1850, and even then there are individuals, Byron for instance, who seem to have a foot in both camps. In our own day the words "classical" and "romantic" have changed their meaning, or at least have become very much subtilised. Thus Mr. T. S. Eliot ranks as classical while, say, A. E. Housman would be regarded as romantic, but Pope or Dr. Johnson would probably have failed to notice the distinction.

On his own ground, that is to say, the eighteenth and nineteenth centuries, Mr. Barzun certainly has the better of his adversaries. He is able to show that the unfortunate Rousseau preached almost none of the ideas popularly attributed to him, and that the German Romantics and the English poets of the early nineteenth century have been similarly traduced. He rightly insists on the energy and intellectual curiosity of the whole Romantic movement, and on the inter-connection between classicism and an aristocratic society.

Louis XIV., he points out, was at least as great a tyrant as Napoleon, and was worshipped at least as slavishly, and it needs a great deal of juggling to derive modern authoritarianism from the Romantic cult of the individual. On the other hand, he hardly inquires *why* our own age should have seen a revival of the yearning for authority, together with a rejection of the Romantic values. He speaks of the

> prevailing search for a single truth, a single religion, a single allegiance. Whether Marxist or Thomist or Anglican or neo-classicist, or Fascist or Falangist, the universal cry seems to be: "Give us a dogma, give us a leader." If we add to this the doctrinal scholasticism of these groups, the preciosity and religiosity of its artistic standard-bearers, together with their united drive on romanticism, we have the clearest evidence we could desire for the prophecy that a new classical age is in the making, that we already live and breathe in the classicist atmosphere.

This is largely true, though there are enough exceptions to spoil it as a generalisation. Mr. Barzun is quite right in denouncing the Marxists, neo-Thomists, and other enemies of freedom of thought, and in pointing out that their own attack on romanticism is a species of bluff. Their real aim is the destruction of liberty, and they consequently argue that any extension of liberty must lead to slavery. But he does not discuss the deeper reasons for their attitude, nor does he set forth his case in plain enough terms. Very broadly, two principles are at work. One is the belief that human beings are by nature fairly decent and that a society founded on justice and liberty could be fairly easily established. The other is the belief that Man can only be trusted to behave himself when he is gagged and handcuffed. Clearly, the second belief prevails at this moment, and equally clearly Mr. Barzun is on the other side. But he would be a more effective champion of liberty if he bothered less about defending Rousseau and attacking Boileau.

If one uses the labels "classical" and "romantic" to mean authoritarian and libertarian—and this is practically what Mr. Barzun does—the many exceptions distract the average reader's attention from the main issue. For example, Voltaire is a classical writer and Carlyle a romantic one. Therefore Carlyle was a friend of liberty and Voltaire its enemy—which is ridiculous. One could think of countless similar objections. Exasperated by rivals who would like to wipe out at one stroke the poems of Wordsworth and the principles of the French Revolution, Mr. Barzun has made himself the almost uncritical champion of Romanticism in all its aspects. The result is a certain amount of muddle and, at times, an avoidance of awkward but important questions. But, though this is an unsatisfactory book, much of it is well worth reading.

[Fee: £7.7.0; 20.7.44]

2518. To Dwight Macdonald

23 July 1944   Typewritten original

Care of the "Tribune"

Dear Macdonald,

I must thank you very much for sending the copies of "Politics", which I have greatly enjoyed. I gave you a small write-up, the best I could find space for, in my column in "Tribune", and have lent the copies to various friends. I have no doubt you could work up a British circulation, but you know how it is now about sending money out of this country. I found when trying to increase the British circulation of PR that though it would have been quite easy to find subscribers there was literally no way for them to pay their subscriptions. You can't even do it by means of exchanging with an English magazine, because the government always demands the dollars for any English magazines sold in the USA beyond a very small number. I think sooner or later it *may* be possible to pull a wire about this via the British Council. I keep trying to contact Eliot about both PR and Politics, but he's hardly ever in town nowadays, especially as his flat has been blitzed (so has mine incidentally—hence the above address.)

I have *at last* got round to beginning that article about "No Orchids for Miss Blandish." I think it'll be much too long for Politics but I'll send you a copy as soon as done and I dare say you'll be able to use bits of it. I want to go into the thing at some length because I think it's important. I'm sorry about this long delay after my promise, but you can't conceive the time-wasting of life in London nowadays, especially as the expensiveness of life now forces one to be constantly doing hackwork. That other article I suggested long ago, about the Spanish war, was finally given to the "New Road" crew—much to my subsequent annoyance because the little beasts cut it about without informing me. However, the Miss Blandish one really will be done quite soon now.

I was interested to see that the May number of Politics reviews Laski's "Faith, Reason and Civilization", and I thought it might amuse you to see the review I wrote of it when first published. This review was written for the Manchester Evening news, the evening paper of the Manchester Guardian (generally looked on as the only truthful paper in England), for which I write once every fortnight. The editor refused to print it, evidently because of its anti-Stalin implications. If you look through it you will see that I have gone about as far as was consistent with ordinary honesty *not* to say what pernicious tripe the book is, and yet my remarks were too strong even for the Manchester Evening News. This will give you an idea of the kind of thing you can't print in England nowadays.[1] Yet this isn't due to the Stalinists, who aren't much regarded nowadays. Editors will print nothing anti-Russian because of the supposed Russomania of the general public and also because of the complaints which the Soviet government is constantly raising about the British press.

I hope politics is going well.

Yours
[Signed] Geo. Orwell
George Orwell

P.S. Did you know George Padmore[2] is a Negro? I noticed you didn't mention it.

1. In the November 1944 issue of *Politics* (1, No. 10), Macdonald, in his 'Comment' column, quoted from Orwell's letter at length in a section subtitled 'Russomania in England.' He said Orwell's quarrel with Laski is that

   Laski shuts his eyes to "purges, liquidations, the dictatorship of a minority, suppression of criticism and so forth." Orwell also takes to pieces Laski's phoney analogy of Stalin's Russia with the early Christian church. That such a review, agreeing with Laski on the main point—the socialist nature of the USSR today—and merely venturing to make the criticisms any honest and intelligent reviewer would have to make of Laski's book—that such a review should be too hot for a paper like *The Manchester Evening News* shows how seriously the feats of the Red Army have misled English public opinion about Russia. (It will be recalled that *The Manchester Guardian*—and the English liberal press in general—was much more honest and critical about the Moscow Trials than our own liberal journals; the *Guardian* in particular threw its columns open to Trotsky himself.)

   One reason for the present Russomania in British° is, of course, the universal feeling that the Red Army "saved" England—as it probably did—coupled with admiration for Russian military strength. And from such admiration it is a short step to the conclusion that a nation which performs so effectively on the battlefield must be pretty wonderful behind the lines. Another reason is perhaps less obvious: that the English workers and middleclass are fed up with private capitalism and put their post-war hopes in some kind of socialism. In this mood, it is easy to feel sympathetic—from a safe distance—to Russia. Finally, one must add the agreement of both workingclass and big business on a high degree of state intervention into the economic process after the war. The Government's recent White Paper on Employment Policy opened with the statement "The Government accept as one of their primary aims and responsibilities the maintenance of a high and stable level of employment after the war." Over here it is not the state which proclaims this responsibility but "private enterprise", notably the business-financed Committee for Economic Development. Thus if there are less illusions about Russia over here, and more freedom to criticise Stalinism in the general press, this fortunate state of affairs is largely due to the more reactionary temper of public opinion. Such are the paradoxes that arise when the hopes of progressives are pinned, by default, on a great anti-progressive force.

   In England the paradoxes are even more fantastic. . . .

2. Orwell is referring to Padmore's name in a list of contributors to *Politics*, May 1944, which stated, 'George Padmore's article ['The New Imperialism, III: Anglo-American Condominium'] originally appeared in the English monthly *Left*. He is a leading English socialist writer, and a specialist on Africa and other colonial areas.' Padmore, a West Indian, had been expelled from the Comintern in 1934. This was his first contribution to *Politics*. His article 'The Story of Viet Nam,' *Politics*, December 1946, the issue in which Orwell's 'Catastrophic Gradualism' appeared (see 2778), attracted long letters from Victor Serge (see *1046, n. 7*) and Saul Mendelson in *Politics*, March–April 1947. Among the points made, Serge expressed surprise that Padmore, 'an I.L.P. militant of many years' standing' had omitted to inform readers of *Politics* that the Vietnamese leader, Ho Chi Minh, was a Communist and had given 'only in the vaguest terms Ho Chi Minh's connection with Moscow.' In his reply, Padmore argued that the issue in Viet Nam was a struggle for national independence and that 'Moscow is really very remote from Hanoi.' He could not see 'anything but a totalitarian outlook in the French desire to reconquer Viet Nam,' and it shocked him that there had been 'no popular manifestation by way of sympathetic strike or mass demonstration on the part of the French workers, who so recently were themselves suppressed under the totalitarian yoke of Nazism. . . . French workers . . . tacitly or expressly, condone French totalitarianism.' Padmore, whose real name was Malcolm Ivan Meredith Nurse, was born in Trinidad in 1903. He joined the Communist Party in the United States in 1927 and went to the Soviet Union in 1939. He

founded the Pan-African Federation in 1944 and later became an adviser to Kwame Nkrumah (1909–1972), President of Ghana. He died in London in 1959 of acute dysentery and was buried in Ghana.

2519. London Letter, 24 July 1944[1]

Partisan Review, Fall 1944

There is very little political news. All the currents seem to be moving in the same directions as when I wrote to you last—public opinion moving leftward, the Right nevertheless consolidating its power owing to the weakness of the Labour leaders, and the minor left-wing parties quarreling among themselves. It seems to be taken for granted that there will be a general election before the end of the year, and most people assume that the Labour Party is going to fight the election independently, which I cannot believe: at least I cannot believe that they will make a serious effort to win it. The Conservatives, though continuing to disillusion the public by their every act, now feel strong enough to disclaim responsibility for their past mistakes. Many books and articles partially rehabilitating Chamberlain are being published, and a section of the Conservative party, probably financed by Beaverbrook, has started a new paper which appears three times a week (in theory one is not allowed to start new periodicals but there are ways of evading this) and is taking a militantly anti-Socialist line.

There is violent competition by all parties to cash in on the popularity of the USSR. The pinks deprecate any criticism of the USSR on the ground that it "plays into the hands of the Tories," but on the other hand the Tories seem to be the most pro-Russian of the lot. From the point of view of the M.O.I. and the B.B.C. the only two people who are completely sacrosanct are Stalin and Franco. I imagine that the Russians themselves regard the Tories as their real friends in this country. It may possibly be of some significance that the Soviet press recently made a sharp attack on a group of very Russophile leftwing M.P.'s who had made the suggestion that the flying bombs were manufactured in Spain. These M.P.'s included D. N. Pritt,[2] the alleged "underground" Communist who has been perhaps the most effective pro-Soviet publicist in this country.

Common Wealth continues to score impressive votes at by-elections but is not gaining much in membership and seems to be less and less definite in its policy. It is not even certain whether it intends, as previously advertised, to fight 150 seats at the forthcoming general election, or simply to make local arrangements with acceptable Labour candidates. People inside the party complain that it is infested by middling business-men of the "managerial" type who are resigned to a centralised economy and foresee good pickings in it for themselves. The Communists, who for a short period were opposing the Government and even collaborated with Common Wealth at one or two elections, seem to be swinging to the support of the Conservatives. There have been some faint indications that attempts may be made to revive the almost-extinct Liberal Party. Otherwise there are no political developments, i.e., in the narrower sense, that I can discern.

Domestic issues continue to occupy most people's attention. India, for instance, has almost dropped out of the news. The chief subjects of discussion are demobilization, re-housing and, for those who are a little longer-sighted, the birth-rate. The housing shortage, already serious, is going to be appalling as soon as the troops come home, and the Government proposes to cope with it by means of prefabricated steel houses which are reasonably convenient but so small as only to have room for one-child families. In theory these temporary shacks are to be scrapped after three years, but everyone assumes that in practice the new houses will not be forthcoming. It is widely recognized that our birth-rate cannot be expected to rise significantly unless people have houses to live in and that re-housing on a big scale is impossible while private property rights are respected. It would be impossible to rebuild London, for instance, without buying out tens of thousands of ground-landlords at fantastic prices. The Conservatives, who are on the whole more concerned about the birth-rate situation than the Left, are at the same time fighting the landlord's battles for him, and try to solve the problem by preaching to the working class the duty of self-sacrifice and the wickedness of birth-control. The Left tends to evade this problem, partly because small families are still vaguely associated with enlightenment, partly because of a certain unwillingness to recognize, or at any rate to say publicly, that a sudden rise in the birth-rate (it has got to rise drastically within ten or twenty years if our population is to be kept up) would mean a drop in the standard of living. There is a vague belief that "Socialism" would somehow make people philoprogenitive again, and much praise of the high Russian birth-rate, without, however, any serious examination of the Russian vital statistics. This is only one of the basic questions that the Left habitually ignores, others being the relation between ourselves and the coloured peoples of the Empire, and the dependence of British prosperity on trade and foreign investments. The Tories are far more willing to admit that these problems exist, though unable to produce any real solution. Very nearly all English leftwingers, from Labourites to Anarchists, have the outlook of people who neither want nor expect power. The Tories are not only more courageous, but they don't make extravagant promises and have no scruples about breaking the promises they do make.

Other highly unpopular subjects are postwar mobility of labour, postwar continuation of food rationing, etc., and the war against Japan. People will, I have no doubt, be ready to go on fighting until Japan is beaten, but their capacity for simply *forgetting* these years of warfare that lie ahead is surprising. In conversation, "When the war stops" invariably means when Germany packs up. The last Mass Observation report shows a considerable recrudescence of 1918 habits of thought. Everyone expects not only that there will [be] a ghastly muddle over demobilization, but that mass unemployment will promptly return. No one wants to remember that we shall have to keep living for years on a wartime basis and that the switch-over to peacetime production and the recapture of lost markets may entail as great an effort as the war itself. Everyone wants, above all things, a rest. I overhear very little discussion of the wider issues of the war, and I can't discern much popular interest in the kind of peace we should impose on Germany. The newspapers of the Right and Left are outdoing one another in demanding a vindictive peace. Vansittart[3] is now a back number; indeed the more extreme of his one-time followers have brought out a pamphlet denouncing him as pro-German.

The Communists are using the slogan, "Make Germany Pay" (the diehard Tory slogan of 1918) and branding as pro-Nazi anyone who says either that we should make a generous peace or that publication of reasonable peace-terms would hasten the German collapse. The peace-terms that they and other Russophiles advocate are indeed simply a worse version of the Versailles Treaty against which they yapped for twenty years. Thus the dog returns to his vomit, or more exactly to somebody else's vomit. But once again, I can't see that ordinary people want anything of the kind, and if past wars are any guide the troops will all come home pro-German. The implications of the fact that the common people are Russophile but don't want the sort of peace that the Russians are demanding haven't yet sunk in, and leftwing journalists avoid discussing them. The Soviet government now makes direct efforts to interfere with the British press. I suppose that for sheer weariness and the instinct to support Russia at all costs the man-in-the-street might be brought to approve of an unjust peace, but there would be a rapid pro-German reaction, as last time.

There are a few social developments, which again take the same directions as I reported before. Evening dress (i.e., for men) is gradually reappearing. The distinction between first class and third class on the railways is being enforced again.[4] Two years ago it had practically lapsed. Commercial advertisements, which I told you a year or so back were rapidly disappearing, are definitely on the up-grade again, and make use of the snobbery motif more boldly. The Home Guard still exists in as great numbers as before, but is employed largely on the AA guns and seems now to have no political colour of one kind or the other. It now consists to a great extent of youths who are conscripted in at 16 or 17.[5] For boys younger than this there are various cadet corps and the Air Training Corps, and even for young girls a uniformed formation named vaguely the Girls' Training Corps. All this is something quite new in English life, pre-military training having been practically confined to the middle and upper classes before the war. Everything grows shabbier and more rickety. Sixteen people in a railway carriage designed for ten is quite common. The countryside has quite changed its face, the once green meadows having changed into cornfields, and in the remotest places one cannot get away from the roar of airplanes, which has become the normal background noise, drowning the larks.

There are very few literary developments to report. After nine months as a literary editor I am startled and frightened by the lack of talent and vitality. The crowd who are grouped about *New Road, Now* and *Poetry, London*—and

I suppose these are "the movement" in so far as there is one—give me the impression of fleas hopping among the ruins of a civilization. There are endless anthologies and other scissor-and-paste books, and enormous output of unreadable pamphlets from every kind of political party and religious body, in spite of the paper shortage. On the other hand innumerable standard books are out of print and unobtainable. Attempts are constantly being made in short-lived reviews to revivify the various regional literatures, Scottish, Welsh, Irish and Northern Irish. These movements always have a strong nationalist and separatist tinge, sometimes bitterly anti-English, and will print anything however bad which is politically O.K. But the various nationalisms are so to speak interchangeable. The leading Anglophobes all contribute to one another's papers, and the London pacifist intellectuals pop up in all of them. There are also signs, which I haven't been able to investigate yet, that Australian literature is at last getting on its own feet.

No more news to speak of. This has been a foul summer, everything happening at the wrong time and hardly any fruit. I have been tied so tight to this beastly town that for the first time in my life I have not heard a cuckoo this year. . . .[6] After the wail of the siren comes the zoom-zoom-zoom of the bomb, and as it draws nearer you get up from your table and squeeze yourself into some corner that flying glass is not likely to reach. Then BOOM!, the windows rattle in their sockets, and you go back to work. There are disgusting scenes in the Tube stations at night, sordid piles of bedding cluttering up the passageways and hordes of dirty-faced children playing round the platforms at all hours. Two nights ago, about midnight, I came on a little girl of five "minding" her younger sister, aged about two. The tiny child had got hold of a scrubbing brush with which she was scrubbing the filthy stones of the platform, and then sucking the bristles. I took it away from her and told the elder girl not to let her have it. But I had to catch my train, and no doubt the poor little brat would again be eating filth in another couple of minutes. This kind of thing is happening everywhere. However, the disorganization and consequent neglect of children hasn't been serious compared with 1940.

George Orwell

[Fee: £2.2.0; 24.7.44]

1. This is the date in Orwell's Payments Book.
2. For D. N. Pritt, *see 2393, 3600, n, 10,* and Orwell's list of crypto-Communists and fellow travellers, *3732.*
3. For Lord Vansittart, see *758, n. 1* and 'London Letter', 1 January 1942, *913* (first section).
4. In the mid nineteenth century there were four classes of railway travel: first, second, third, and parliamentary. In World War II only first and third classes were run. These are now called first and standard.
5. Orwell refers again to conscription into the Home Guard in *2564.* It seems very doubtful whether this was applied to those under eighteen, and the experience of those who recall service in the Home Guard suggests that conscription was unknown to them.
6. Ellipsis as in the original: nothing has been left out of this edition.

2520. To Ivor Brown

24 July 1944   Handwritten

TRIBUNE

Dear Ivor Brown,[1]
This is to introduce Paul Potts,[2] whose work you perhaps know. He is anxious to do some reviewing & I think could be of use to you. He is a Canadian & could therefore deal with books touching on Canada, but he also has special knowledge of Eire, & of films.

Yours sincerely
Geo. Orwell

1. Ivor Brown (1891–1974), editor of *The Observer*, 1942–48 and its drama critic, 1929–54. See also *1480, n. 2.*
2. See *1971, n. 1.*

2521. 'As I Please,' 35

Tribune, 28 July 1944

Some years ago, in the course of an article about boys' weekly papers,[1] I made some passing remarks about women's papers—I mean the twopenny ones of the type of *Peg's Paper*, often called "love books." This brought me, among much other correspondence, a long letter from a woman who had contributed to and worked for the *Lucky Star*, the *Golden Star*, *Peg's Paper*, *Secrets*, the *Oracle*, and a number of kindred papers. Her main point was that I had been wrong in saying that these papers aim at creating wealth fantasy. Their stories are "in no sense Cinderella stories" and do not exploit the "she married her boss" motif. My correspondent adds:

"Unemployment is mentioned—quite frequently. . . . The dole and the trade union are certainly never mentioned. The latter may be influenced by the fact that the largest publishers of these women's magazines are a non-union house. One is never allowed to criticise the system, or to show up the class struggle for what it really is, and the word Socialist is *never* mentioned—all this is perfectly true. But it might be interesting to add that class feeling is not altogether absent. The rich are often shown as mean, and as cruel and crooked money-makers. The rich and idle beau is nearly always planning marriage without a ring, and the lass is rescued by her strong, hard-working garage hand. Men with cars are generally 'bad' and men in well-cut, expensive suits are nearly always crooks. The ideal of most of these stories is *not* an income worthy of a bank manager's wife, but a life that is 'good.' A life with an upright, kind husband, however poor, with babies and a 'little cottage.' The stories are conditioned to show that the meagre life is not so bad really, as you are at least honest and happy, and that riches bring trouble and false friends. The poor are given moral values to aspire to as something within their reach."

There are many comments I could make here, but I choose to take up the point of the moral superiority of the poor being combined with the non-mention of trade unions and Socialism. There is no doubt that this is deliberate policy. In one woman's paper I actually read a story dealing with a strike in a coal-mine, and even in that connection trade unionism was not mentioned. When the U.S.S.R. entered the war one of these papers promptly cashed in with a serial entitled "Her Soviet Lover," but we may be sure that Marxism did not enter into it very largely.

The fact is that this business about the moral superiority of the poor is one of the deadliest forms of escapism the ruling class have evolved. You may be downtrodden and swindled, but in the eyes of God you are superior to your oppressors, and by means of films and magazines you can enjoy a fantasy existence in which you constantly triumph over the people who defeat you in real life. In any form of art designed to appeal to large numbers of people, it is an almost unheard of thing for a rich man to get the better of a poor man. The rich man is usually "bad," and his machinations are invariably frustrated. "Good poor man defeats bad rich man" is an accepted formula, whereas if it were the other way about we should feel that there was something very wrong somewhere. This is as noticeable in films as in the cheap magazines, and it was perhaps most noticeable of all in the old silent films, which travelled from country to country and had to appeal to a very varied audience. The vast majority of the people who will see a film are poor, and so it is politic to make a poor man the hero. Film magnates, Press lords and the like amass quite a lot of their wealth by pointing out that wealth is wicked.

The formula "good poor man defeats bad rich man" is simply a subtler version of "pie in the sky." It is a sublimation of the class struggle. So long as you can dream of yourself as a "strong, hard-working garage hand" giving some moneyed crook a sock on the jaw, the *real* facts can be forgotten. That is a cleverer dodge than wealth fantasy. But, curiously enough, reality does enter into these women's magazines, not through the stories but through the correspondence columns, especially in those papers that give free medical advice. Here you can read harrowing tales of "bad legs" and hemorrhoids, written by middle-aged women who give themselves such pseudonyms as "A Sufferer," "Mother of Nine," and "Always Constipated." To compare these letters with the love stories that lie cheek by jowl with them is to see how vast a part mere day-dreaming plays in modern life.

I have just been reading Arthur Koestler's novel *The Gladiators*, which describes the slave rebellion under Spartacus, about 70 B.C. It is not one of his best books, and, in any case, any novel describing a slave rebellion in antiquity suffers by having to stand comparison with *Salammbo*,° Flaubert's great novel about the revolt of the Carthaginian mercenaries. But it reminded me of how tiny is the number of slaves of whom anything whatever is known. I myself know the names of just three slaves—Spartacus himself, the fabulous Æsop, who is supposed to have been a slave, and the philosopher Epictetus, who was one of those learned slaves whom the Roman plutocrats liked to have among their retinue. All the others are not even names. We don't, for instance—or at least I don't—know the name of a single one of the myriads of human beings who built the Pyramids. Spartacus, I suppose, is much the most widely known slave there ever was. For five thousand years or more civilisation rested upon slavery. Yet when even so much as the name of a slave survives, it is because he did not obey the injunction "resist not evil," but raised violent rebellion. I think there is a moral in this for pacifists.

In spite of the appalling overcrowding of the trains (16 people in a carriage designed for 10 is fairly normal nowadays), I note that the distinction between first and third class is definitely coming back. Earlier in the war it almost lapsed for a while. If you were crowded out of the third class you went as a matter of course into the first, and no questions were asked. Now you are invariably made to pay the difference in fare—at least, if you sit down—even though it would have been quite impossible to find a place anywhere else in the train. (You can, I believe, travel in a first-class carriage with a third-class ticket if you choose to stand up the whole way.) A few years ago the railway companies would hardly have dared to enforce this distinction. By such small symptoms (another, by the way, is that evening suits are beginning to come out of their moth balls) you can judge how confident the higher-ups are and how insolent they feel it safe to be.

We published last week part of a very truculent letter about the anti-war poem entitled *The Little Apocalypse of Obadiah Hornbooke*,[2] with the comment, "I am surprised that you publish it." Other letters and private comments took the same line.

I do not, any more than our correspondent, agree with "Obadiah Hornbooke," but that is not a sufficient reason for not publishing what he writes. Every paper has a policy, and in its political sections it will press that policy, more or less to the exclusion of all others. To do anything else would be stupid. But the literary end of a paper is another matter. Even there, of course, no paper will give space to direct attacks on the things it stands for. We wouldn't print an article in praise of anti-semitism, for instance. But granted the necessary minimum of agreement, literary merit is the only thing that matters.

Besides, if this war is about anything at all, it is a war in favour of freedom of thought. I should be the last to claim that we are morally superior to our enemies, and there is quite a strong case for saying that British imperialism is actually worse than Nazism. But there does remain the difference, not to be explained away, that in Britain you are relatively free to say and print what you like. Even in the blackest patches of the British Empire, in India, say, there is very much more freedom of expression than in a totalitarian country. I want that to remain true, and by sometimes giving a hearing to unpopular opinions, I think we help it to do so.

Orwell's reaction to fiction for the working class was taken up in *Tribune* for 11 August 1944 by Walter Tyrer.

I was interested to see George Orwell return to the subject of working-class periodicals, and I notice that, as usual, he is unable to see the trees for the wood. I have written some fifteen million words in this field, and I have never been aware of a Press Lord at my elbow dictating the subtle and cynical policy he describes.

I look on myself as an entertainer in the class of the clown who balances on a ladder or the juggler who keeps seven billiard balls in the air. I am not aware of doing anyone any harm and I probably haven't done them much good, but if I wished to be smug I might claim that I have given a great many people some pleasure.

Orwell and similar persecution-mongers are curiously related in viewpoint to the Dictators and great financiers, for they always seem to see people in the mass and remain unaware of the desires and emotions of the individual. I believe that people seek colour and romance from natural inclination and not because of any deep-lying frustration. I think that even in the numbered, badged and inspector-harassed Utopias (all different) to which our Orwells would lead us, young people would still be urgently interested in falling in love, marrying, having babies, for these things are the expression of a force older and more powerful than any conception of cloud-capped towers above communal dormitories.

It is true that the Trade Unions do not figure prominently in working-class fiction, any more than the Insurance Companies and Building Societies loom very large in the light novels that are the sustenance of the middle classes, although these institutions probably play an equally important part in their lives. Tropical islands, gypsies, murders on lonely farms, offer more entertainment, so those are the things of which we write.

Do we fiction writers argue that happiness lies in human relationships rather than the acquisition of wealth? I think we do, but no one tells us to say it. Most authors and artists believe it; watch the way they handle money when they have any. But there is no conspiracy behind all this. After all, would it really be very clever of the Press lords to insist, as Orwell says, that all rich men are wicked? Wouldn't this tend to stimulate the class hatred which might threaten their ascendancy?

Maybe we are "escapist." Perhaps that is the story-teller's justification. I'm willing to bet that in that organised world of concrete and chromium communities to which our Orwells want to lead us there would be a tremendous demand for "escapist" literature about the dear old days when people lived private lives in little homes.

1. See 598.
2. 'The Little Apocalypse of Obadiah Hornbooke,' pseudonym of Alex Comfort, appeared in *Tribune*, 30 June 1944. 'Letter to an American Visitor,' another poem by Comfort under the pseudonym Obadiah Hornbooke appeared in *Tribune* on 4 June 1943 and was answered by Orwell with 'As One Non-Combatant to Another' on 18 June 1943; see 2137 and 2138. *Tribune* spelt Hornbooke as Hornbrook.

2522. Review of *English Diaries of the Nineteenth Century*, edited by James Aitken

Manchester Evening News, 28 July 1944

The diary is not a lost art, as various recently published diaries of soldiers and Civil Defence workers go to show. But it seems unlikely that we now have, in England, any diarists of quite the type of Lord Shaftesbury, or Dorothy Wordsworth, or Mary Shelley, or various others who are gathered together in this recent Pelican. Take, for instance, this typical extract from the diary of Hurrell Froude, one of the leading spirits in the early days of the Oxford Movement:

> "*November 12, 1826*: Felt ashamed that my trowsers were dirty whilst sitting next . . . but resolved not to hide them. This sort of shame about what we ourselves esteem matters of indifference, because they do not seem so to other people, bring home to our minds what depravity it proves in us to pay so little attention to what we know is serious."

Or this equally typical one from William Charles Macready, the famous actor-manager:

> "*January 22, 1833*: Not altogether dissatisfied with the labour of to-day, though I might have done my duty better by rising earlier. My walk to London was real enjoyment from the beauty of the day: my thoughts, too, were not idle, for I went through several scenes of 'Othello.' Taking into consideration the employment of my time in the study of that character, the benefit of the air and exercise, and the money saved in my walk, I cannot set down the three hours and a half it cost me as misused or laid out to waste."

Very few modern people would bother to write down such trifles. A battle or a blitz may seem worth recording, but we are probably less interested in the tiny details of our behaviour than were the Victorians. At any rate, our consciences weigh less heavily upon us, our sense of the sinfulness of pleasure is less acute. Froude, for instance, seems to have felt himself in danger of damnation every time he enjoyed his dinner. But it was exactly this hypertrophied moral sense that turned so many nineteenth-century English men and women into industrious diarists. Nearly every action seemed to them significant. And though they recorded many absurdities they also added valuable footnotes to history and sometimes made dramatic stories out of what, by modern standards, would seem very uneventful lives.

This volume necessarily consists of short extracts, since it deals with 22 diarists in all. They range from Queen Victoria (on her first trip to the Highlands, with her beloved husband Prince Albert, who pays the Scots the highest honour he knows by saying that they "look like Germans") to the humble Emily Shore, daughter of an unbeneficed clergyman, who died at 19 and hardly met any eminent people, but, nevertheless, contributes some of the best passages in the book. All of them are genuine diarists, except, perhaps, William Cobbett, whose rural rides were written expressly for publication and should be regarded as a sort of political pamphlet in diary form.

For the historical information that can be extracted from them, no doubt the most important contributors are Lord Shaftesbury, Fulke Greville (who was Clerk of the Council in Ordinary during three reigns), and Lord Colchester, who was for 15 years Speaker of the House of Commons. From these, as from the furious tirades of Cobbett, we get a reminder of how very black the state of England was in the earlier part of the nineteenth century.

The industrial revolution had broken up the old village life, and millions of human beings had been herded together in conditions of dirt, misery, ignorance and moral degradation such as we now find it difficult to imagine. Up to 1848 Chartism was a serious force, terrifying to the Conservatives and dismaying even to Radicals like Shaftesbury. Even the discreet Greville remarks that violent revolution would hardly be suprising, considering how the working classes in the new industrial areas are forced to live.

Epidemics which killed thousands of people were constantly breaking out in the big towns. The most usual disease was cholera, but in 1837 Emily Shore notes the appearance of a new malady "which they call an influenza," and which rapidly spread all over the country.[1]

However, not all the entries in these diaries tell of disasters. Dorothy Wordsworth, sister of the poet, seems to have led an exceptionally happy, well-integrated life in her peaceful corner of the Lake District. Although her first entry is made in 1800 there is hardly a single reference to the Napoleonic War. Her time is completely filled up with household cares, gardening, watching birds, picking wild flowers, helping passing beggars and, above all, copying out William's poems for him.

"*May 21st, 1802*: A very warm, gentle morning; a little rain. William wrote two sonnets on Buonaparte, after I had read Milton's sonnets to him."

"*May 29th, 1802*: William finished poem on going for Mary. I wrote it out. . . . A sweet day. We nailed up the honeysuckles, and hoed the scarlet beans."

There are many such references to individual poems, and it would be a fascinating job to identify them. Even the leech-gatherer, afterwards to be famous, appears as a beggar casually met on the road, and supplies the interesting information that the price of leeches has risen from half a crown a hundred to thirty shillings.

Also represented are Byron, Sir Walter Scott, Thomas Moore, Ford Madox Ford[2] (one of the founders of the Pre-Raphaelite School), the unfortunate painter Benjamin Haydon, and various others. There is also Henry Crabb Robinson, a queer creature but in some ways a very typical Englishman, whose life, published about 10 years ago,[3] is worth dipping into. In his enormous lifetime (1775 to 1867) Robinson did almost nothing, but he knew everybody, kept in touch with every new development, and carefully entered all the current gossip in a diary which he kept for 56 years.

It is recorded of him that he was the first man in England to use a safety-razor, and that when chloroform was discovered he promptly had himself chloroformed to see what it was like. In 1812 we already find him reading Blake's poems, which at that date were known to very few people. It is interesting to learn, however, that Wordsworth, who was Robinson's friend, was also an admirer of Blake and regarded him "as having in him the elements of poetry much more than either Byron or Scott."

This is a good ninepennyworth, its effect—and no doubt its object—is to whet the reader's appetite rather than satisfy it. Few people could read through this book without wanting to learn more of at least one of the diarists represented; and since most of these people's works are not easily obtainable, the Pelican Library would do well to follow this volume up with another series of extracts.

[Fee: £8.8.0; 27.7.44]

1. Although the word goes back to 1504, its use in England for the contagious illness which still afflicts us dates from 1743. There were two 'true influenza' epidemics in the nineteenth century, 1847–48 and 1889, but the word was used, as nowadays, to describe any serious headcold (OED).
2. Orwell has confused the author Ford Madox Ford (1873–1939) with the painter Ford Madox Brown (1821–1893).
3. Edith J. Morley, *The Life and Times of Henry Crabb Robinson*, reviewed by Orwell in *The Adelphi*, October 1935; see *256*.

2523. 'Propaganda and Demotic Speech'

Persuasion, Summer Quarter, 1944, 2, No. 2

Against 28 April 1944, the day of its completion or despatch, Orwell's Payments Book notes this essay as an article of 2,250 words for which he was paid £15.15.0. The issue of *Persuasion* for the Summer Quarter of 1944 includes an illustration of the *Manchester Guardian* dated 28 June 1944, so publication must have been late rather than early in the summer quarter. The article's placement here is necessarily approximate.

The article has at its head in bold sans serif type this statement:

The bloodless jargon of Government spokesmen seems deliberately to avoid clear, popular, everyday language. This remoteness from the average man's vocabulary and understanding is equally characteristic of newspaper editorials, political broadcasts, and left-wing manifestos. Little wonder the public is unconcerned and apathetic about many of the vital political issues of the day.

The article is decorated with small reproductions of four posters: 'Food is a Munition of War—Don't Waste It' (for the British Ministry of Food); a French soldier shouting 'On les aura!' for the second French War Loan; Kitchener and the slogan 'Your Country Needs You'; and a line of marching Japanese soldiers. There was also, within the article, a large (and rather poor) drawing of a man in a trilby hat speaking into twin microphones with the insignia 'GB', evidently intended to represent the Gaumont–British newsreel commentator, E. V. H. Emmett[1]. In a box was this comment, headed 'Voice of the news-reel':

Even uncritical cinema audiences are made restive and irritable by the pompous, facetious, and dreary voices of the weekly news-reel commentators. Only their shortness (8 mins.) and excellent camera work stifle complaints. Intelligent Englishmen are frequently humiliated by overseas reactions to these "typical English voices." Brilliant exception to this uniform mediocrity is E. V. H. Emmett, of Gaumont–British News, whose lively, sparkling and inspired descriptions are in such striking contrast. Avoiding the affected "Oxford accent" and the lifeless B.B.C. voice, Emmett's style could well serve as a model for news broadcasters and news-reel commentators.

When I was leaving England for Morocco at the end of 1938, some of the people in my village (less than fifty miles from London)[2] wanted to know whether it would be necessary to cross the sea to get there. In 1940, during General Wavell's African campaign, I discovered that the woman from whom I bought my rations thought Cyrenaica was in Italy. A year or two ago a friend of mine, who had been giving an A.B.C.A. lecture to some A.T.s,[3] tried the experiment of asking them a few general knowledge questions: among the answers he got were, (a) that there are only six Members of Parliament, and (b) that Singapore is the capital of India. If there were any point in doing so I could give many more instances of this kind of thing. I mention these three, simply as a preliminary reminder of the ignorance which any speech or piece of writing aimed at a large public has to take into account.

However, when you examine Government leaflets and White Papers, or leading articles in the newspapers, or the speeches and broadcasts of politicians, or the pamphlets and manifestos of any political party whatever, the thing that nearly always strikes you is their remoteness from the average man. It is not merely that they assume non-existent knowledge: often it is right and necessary to do that. It is also that clear, popular, everyday language seems to be instinctively avoided. The bloodless dialect of Government spokesmen (characteristic phrases are: in due course, no stone unturned, take the earliest opportunity, the answer is in the affirmative) is too well known to be worth dwelling on. Newspaper leaders are written either in this same dialect or in an inflated bombastic style with a tendency to fall back on archaic words (peril, valour, might, foe, succour, vengeance, dastardly, rampart, bulwark, bastion) which no normal person would ever think of using. Left-wing political parties specialise in a bastard vocabulary made up of Russian and German phrases translated with the maximum of clumsiness. And even posters, leaflets and broadcasts which are intended to give instructions, to tell people what to do in certain circumstances, often fail in their effect. For example, during the first air raids on London, it was found that innumerable people did not know which siren meant the Alert and which the All Clear. This was after months or years of gazing at A.R.P. posters. These posters had described the Alert as a "warbling note": a phrase which made no impression, since air-raid sirens don't warble, and few people attach any definite meaning to the word.

When Sir Richard Acland, in the early months of the war, was drawing up a Manifesto to be presented to the Government, he engaged a squad of Mass

Observers to find out what meaning, if any, the ordinary man attaches to the high-sounding abstract words which are flung to and fro in politics. The most fantastic misunderstandings came to light. It was found, for instance, that most people don't know that "immorality" means anything besides sexual immorality.* One man thought that "movement" had something to do with constipation. And it is a nightly experience in any pub to see broadcast speeches and news bulletins make no impression on the average listener, because they are uttered in stilted bookish language and, incidentally, in an upper-class accent. At the time of Dunkirk I watched a gang of navvies eating their bread and cheese in a pub while the one o'clock news came over. Nothing registered: they just went on stolidly eating. Then, just for an instant, reporting the words of some soldier who had been hauled aboard a boat, the announcer dropped into spoken English, with the phrase, "Well, I've learned to swim this trip, anyway!" Promptly you could see ears being pricked up: it was ordinary language, and so it got across. A few weeks later, the day after Italy entered the war, Duff-Cooper announced that Mussolini's rash act would "add to the ruins for which Italy has been famous." It was neat enough, and a true prophecy, but how much impression does that kind of language make on nine people out of ten? The colloquial version of it would have been: "Italy has always been famous for ruins. Well, there are going to be a damn' sight more of them now." But that is not how Cabinet Ministers speak, at any rate in public.

Examples of futile slogans, obviously incapable of stirring strong feelings or being circulated by word of mouth, are: "Deserve Victory," "Freedom is in Peril. Defend it with all your Might," "Socialism the only Solution," "Expropriate the Expropriators," "Austerity," "Evolution not Revolution," "Peace is Indivisible." Examples of slogans phrased in spoken English are: "Hands off Russia," "Make Germany Pay," "Stop Hitler," "No Stomach Taxes," "Buy a Spitfire," "Votes for Women." Examples about mid-way between these two classes are: "Go To It," "Dig for Victory," "It all depends on ME," and some of Churchill's phrases, such as "the end of the beginning," "soft underbelly," "blood, toil, tears and sweat," and "never was so much owed by so many to so few." (Significantly, in so far as this last saying has been repeated by word of mouth, the bookish phrase *in the field of human conflict* has dropped out of it.) One has to take into account the fact that nearly all English people dislike anything that sounds high-flown and boastful. Slogans like "They shall not pass," or "Better to die on your feet than live on your knees," which have thrilled continental nations, seem slightly embarrassing to an Englishman, especially a working man. But the main weakness of propagandists and popularisers is their failure to notice that spoken and written English are two different things.

When recently I protested in print against the Marxist dialect which makes use of phrases like "objectively counter-revolutionary left-deviationism" or "drastic liquidation of petty-bourgeois elements," I received indignant

---

* In spite of this, Common Wealth has adopted the astonishingly feeble slogan: "What is morally wrong cannot be politically right" [Orwell's footnote].

letters from lifelong Socialists who told me that I was "insulting the language of the proletariat." In rather the same spirit, Professor Harold Laski devotes a long passage in his last book, *Faith, Reason and Civilisation*, to an attack on Mr. T. S. Eliot, whom he accuses of "writing only for a few." Now Eliot, as it happens, is one of the few writers of our time who have tried seriously to write English as it is spoken. Lines like—

"And nobody came, and nobody went,
But he took in the milk and he paid the rent"[4]

are about as near to spoken English as print can come. On the other hand, here is an entirely typical sentence from Laski's own writing:

"As a whole, our system was a compromise between democracy in the political realm—itself a very recent development in our history—and an economic power oligarchically organised which was in its turn related to a certain aristocratic vestigia still able to influence profoundly the habits of our society."

This sentence, incidentally, comes from a reprinted lecture; so one must assume that Professor Laski actually stood up on a platform and spouted it forth, parenthesis and all. It is clear that people capable of speaking or writing in such a way have simply forgotten what everyday language is like. But this is nothing to some of the other passages I could dig out of Professor Laski's writings, or better still, from Communist literature, or best of all, from Trotskyist pamphlets. Indeed, from reading the Left-wing press you get the impression that the louder people yap about the proletariat, the more they despise its language.

I have said already that spoken English and written English are two different things. This variation exists in all languages, but is probably greater in English than in most. Spoken English is full of slang, it is abbreviated wherever possible, and people of all social classes treat its grammar and syntax in a slovenly way. Extremely few English people ever button up a sentence if they are speaking extempore. Above all, the vast English vocabulary contains thousands of words which everyone uses when writing, but which have no real currency in speech: and it also contains thousands more which are really obsolete but which are dragged forth by anyone who wants to sound clever or uplifting. If one keeps this in mind, one can think of ways of ensuring that propaganda, spoken or written, shall reach the audience it is aimed at.

So far as writing goes, all one can attempt is a process of simplification. The first step—and any social survey organisation could do this for a few hundreds or thousands of pounds—is to find out which of the abstract words habitually used by politicians are really understood by large numbers of people. If phrases like "unprincipled violation of declared pledges" or "insidious threat to the basic principles of democracy" don't mean anything to the average man, then it is stupid to use them. Secondly, in writing one can keep the spoken word constantly in mind. To get genuine spoken English on to paper is a complicated matter, as I shall show in a moment. But if you habitually say to yourself, "Could I simplify this? Could I make it more like speech?," you are not likely to produce sentences like the one quoted from Professor Laski above: nor are you likely to say "eliminate" when you mean kill, or "static water" when you mean fire tank.

Spoken propaganda, however, offers greater possibilities of improvement. It is here that the problem of writing in spoken English really arises.

Speeches, broadcasts, lectures and even sermons are normally written down beforehand. The most effective orators, like Hitler or Lloyd George, usually speak extempore, but they are very great rarities. As a rule—you can test this by listening at Hyde Park Corner—the so-called extempore speaker only keeps going by endlessly tacking one cliché on to another. In any case, he is probably delivering a speech which he has delivered dozens of times before. Only a few exceptionally gifted speakers can achieve the simplicity and intelligibility which even the most tongue-tied person achieves in ordinary conversation. On the air extempore speaking is seldom even attempted. Except for a few programmes, like the Brains Trust, which in any case are carefully rehearsed beforehand, every word that comes from the B.B.C. has been written down, and is delivered exactly as written. This is not only for censorship reasons: it is also because many speakers are liable to dry up at the microphone if they have no script to follow. The result is the heavy, dull, bookish lingo which causes most radio-users to switch off as soon as a talk is announced. It might be thought that one could get nearer to colloquial speech by dictating than by writing; but actually, it is the other way about. Dictating, at any rate to a human being, is always slightly embarrassing. One's impulse is to avoid long pauses, and one necessarily does so by clutching at the ready-made phrases and the dead and stinking metaphors (ring the changes on, ride rough-shod over, cross swords with, take up the cudgels for) with which the English language is littered. A dictated script is usually less life-like than a written one. What is wanted, evidently, is some way of getting ordinary, slipshod, colloquial English on to paper.

But is this possible? I think it is, and by a quite simple method which so far as I know has never been tried. It is this: Set a fairly ready speaker down at the microphone and let him just talk, either continuously or intermittently, on any subject he chooses. Do this with a dozen different speakers, recording it every time. Vary it with a few dialogues or conversations between three or four people. Then play your recordings back and let a stenographer reduce them to writing: not in the shortened, rationalised version that stenographers usually produce, but word for word, with such punctuation as seems appropriate. You would then—for the first time, I believe—have on paper some authentic specimens of spoken English. Probably they would not be readable as a book or a newspaper article is readable, but then spoken English is not meant to be read, it is meant to be listened to. From these specimens you could, I believe, formulate the rules of spoken English and find out how it differs from the written language. And when writing in spoken English had become practicable, the average speaker or lecturer who has to write his material down beforehand could bring it far closer to his natural diction, make it more essentially speakable, than he can at present.

Of course, demotic speech is not solely a matter of being colloquial and avoiding ill-understood words. There is also the question of accent. It seems certain that in modern England the "educated" upper-class accent is deadly to any speaker who is aiming at a large audience. All effective speakers in recent times have had either cockney or provincial accents. The success of Priestley's broadcasts in 1940 was largely due to his Yorkshire accent, which he probably broadened a little for the occasion. Churchill is only a seeming exception to this rule. Too old to have acquired the modern "educated" accent, he speaks with the Edwardian upper-class twang which to the average man's ear sounds like cockney. The "educated" accent, of which the accent of the B.B.C. announcers is a sort of parody, has no asset except its intelligibility to English-speaking foreigners. In England the minority to whom it is natural don't particularly like it, while in the other three-quarters of the population it arouses an immediate class antagonism. It is also noticeable that where there is doubt about the pronunciation of a name, successful speakers will stick to the working-class pronunciation even if they know it to be wrong. Churchill, for instance, mispronounced "Nazi" and "Gestapo" as long as the common people continued to do so. Lloyd George during the last war rendered "Kaiser" as "Kayser," which was the popular version of the word.

In the early days of the war the Government had the greatest difficulty in inducing people to bother to collect their ration books. At parliamentary elections, even when there is an up-to-date register, it often happens that less than half of the electorate use their votes. Things like these are symptoms of the intellectual gulf between the rulers and the ruled. But the same gulf lies always between the intelligentsia and the common man. Journalists, as we can see by their election forecasts, never know what the public is thinking. Revolutionary propaganda is incredibly ineffective. Churches are empty all over the country. The whole idea of trying to find out what the average man thinks, instead of assuming that he thinks what he ought to think, is novel and unwelcome. Social surveys are viciously attacked from Left and Right alike. Yet some mechanism for testing public opinion is an obvious necessity of modern government, and more so in a democratic country than in a totalitarian one. Its complement is the ability to speak to the ordinary man in words that he will understand and respond to.

At present propaganda only seems to succeed when it coincides with what people are inclined to do in any case. During the present war, for instance, the Government has done extraordinarily little to preserve morale: it has merely drawn on the existing reserves of good-will. And all political parties alike have failed to interest the public in vitally important questions—in the problem of India, to name only one. But some day we may have a genuinely democratic government, a government which will want to tell people what is happening, and what must be done next, and what sacrifices are necessary, and why. It will need the mechanisms for doing so, of which the first are the right words, the right tone of voice. The fact that when you suggest finding out what the common man is like, and approaching him accordingly, you are either accused of being an intellectual snob who wants to "talk down to" the

315

masses, or else suspected of plotting to establish an English Gestapo, shows how sluggishly nineteenth-century our notion of democracy has remained.

[Fee: £15.15.0; 28.4.44]

1. There is a good account of newsreel comentators of this period in Anthony Aldgate, *Cinema and History: British Newsreels and the Spanish Civil War* (1979). For E. V. H. (Ted) Emmett, see especially 32, 41, 122–25, 132–33, and 158–9. Emmett was in the advantageous position of cutting Gaumont's stories so that picture and commentary always matched – he had himself worked as a film cutter (41).
2. Wallington, near Baldock, Hertfordshire.
3. Army Bureau of Current Affairs and (Women's) Auxiliary Territorial Service, 1938–48.
4. From 'Sweeney Agonistes: Fragment of an Agon.' Orwell is probably quoting from memory and the quotation is not quite accurate (see also *2538, n. 21*). Eliot's text reads:

> This went on for a couple of months
> Nobody came
> And nobody went
> But he took in the milk and he paid the rent.

2524. To Rayner Heppenstall

2 August 1944   Typewritten

Tribune

Dear Rayner,
I've just been to look for Fowler's shop in Ludgate Circus. It appears it's been blitzed. Do you know somewhere else where one can get the book?[1]

Yours,
[Signed] Eric
Eric

1. Not identified; presumably a book Heppenstall had asked Orwell to obtain for him.

2525. To W. J. Strachan

2 August 1944   Typewritten

Tribune

Dear Mr. Strachan,
I think I can use the poem "The Grey Sleepers," but it will have to wait over for some time. I have a lot of stuff in hand.[1]

Yours truly,
[Signed] Geo. Orwell
George Orwell
Literary Editor

1. Published in *Tribune*, 3 November 1944.

2526. 'As I Please,' 36

Tribune, 4 August 1944

Apropos of saturation bombing, a correspondent who disagreed with me very strongly added that he was by no means a pacifist. He recognised, he said, that "the Hun had got to be beaten." He merely objected to the barbarous methods that we are now using.

Now, it seems to me that you do less harm by dropping bombs on people than by calling them "Huns." Obviously one does not want to inflict death and wounds if it can be avoided, but I cannot feel that mere killing is all-important. We shall all be dead in less than a hundred years, and most of us by the sordid horror known as "natural death." The truly evil thing is to act in such a way that peaceful life becomes impossible. War damages the fabric of civilisation not by the destruction it causes (the net effect of a war may even be to increase the productive capacity of the world as a whole), nor even by the slaughter of human beings, but by stimulating hatred and dishonesty. By shooting at your enemy you are not in the deepest sense wronging him. But by hating him, by inventing lies about him and bringing children up to believe them, by clamouring for unjust peace terms which make further wars inevitable, you are striking not at one perishable generation, but at humanity itself.

It is a matter of observation that the people least infected by war hysteria are the fighting soldiers. Of all people they are the least inclined to hate the enemy, to swallow lying propaganda or to demand a vindictive peace. Nearly all soldiers—and this applies even to professional soldiers in peace time—have a sane attitude towards war. They realise that it is disgusting, and that it may often be necessary. This is harder for a civilian, because the soldier's detached attitude is partly due to sheer exhaustion, to the sobering effects of danger, and to continuous friction with his own military machine. The safe and well-fed civilian has more surplus emotion, and he is apt to use it up in hating somebody or other—the enemy if he is a patriot, his own side if he is a pacifist. But the war mentality is something that can be struggled against and overcome, just as the fear of bullets can be overcome. The trouble is that neither the Peace Pledge Union nor the Never Again Society know the war mentality when they see it. Meanwhile, the fact that in this war offensive nicknames like "Hun" have not caught on with the big public seems to me a good omen.[1]

What has always seemed to me one of the most shocking deeds of the last war was one that did not aim at killing anyone—on the contrary, it probably saved a great many lives. Before launching their big attack at Caporetto, the Germans flooded the Italian army with faked Socialist propaganda leaflets in which it was alleged that the German soldiers were ready to shoot their officers and fraternise with their Italian comrades, etc., etc. Numbers of Italians were taken in, came over to fraternise with the Germans, and were made prisoner—and, I believe, jeered at for their simple-mindedness. I have heard this defended as a highly intelligent and humane way of making war—which it is, if your sole aim is to save as many skins as possible. And yet a trick like that damages the very roots of human solidarity in a way that no mere act of violence could do.

I see that the railings are returning—only wooden ones, it is true, but still railings—in one London square after another. So the lawful denizens of the squares can make use of their treasured keys again, and the children of the poor can be kept out.

When the railings round the parks and squares were removed, the object was partly to accumulate scrap iron, but the removal was also felt to be a democratic gesture. Many more green spaces were now open to the public, and you could stay in the parks till all hours instead of being hounded out at closing time by grim-faced keepers. It was also discovered that these railings were not only unnecessary but hideously ugly. The parks were improved out of recognition by being laid open, acquiring a friendly, almost rural look that they had never had before. And had the railings vanished permanently, another improvement would probably have followed. The dreary shrubberies of laurel and privet—plants not suited to England and always dusty, at any rate in London—would probably have been grubbed up and replaced by flower beds. Like the railings, they were merely put there to keep the populace out. However, the higher-ups managed to avert this reform, like so many others, and everywhere the wooden palisades are going up, regardless of the wastage of labour and timber.

When I was in the Home Guard we used to say that the bad sign would be when flogging was introduced. That has not happened yet, I believe, but all minor social symptoms point in the same direction. The worst sign of all— and I should expect this to happen almost immediately if the Tories win the General Election—will be the reappearance in the London streets of top hats not worn by either undertakers or bank messengers.

We hope to review before long—and meanwhile I take the opportunity of drawing attention to it—an unusual book called *Branch Street*, by Marie Paneth. The author is or was a voluntary worker at a children's club, and her book reveals the almost savage conditions in which some London children still grow up. It is not quite clear, however, whether these conditions are to any extent worse as a result of the war. I should like to read—I suppose some such thing must exist somewhere, but I don't know of it—an authoritative account of the effect of the war on children. Hundreds of thousands of town children have been evacuated to country districts, many have had their schooling interrupted for months at a time, others have had terrifying experiences with bombs (earlier in the war, a little girl of eight, evacuated to a Hertfordshire village, assured me that she had been bombed out seven times), others have been sleeping in Tube shelters, sometimes for a year or so at a stretch. I would like to know to what extent the town children have adapted themselves to country life—whether they have grown interested in birds and animals, or whether they simply pine to be back among the picture-houses— and whether there has been any significant increase in juvenile crime. The children described by Mrs. Paneth sound almost like the gangs of "wild children" who were a by-product of the Russian Revolution.[2]

318

Back in the eighteenth century, when the India muslins were one of the wonders of the world, an Indian king sent envoys to the court of Louis XV. to negotiate a trade agreement. He was aware that in Europe women wield great political influence, and the envoys brought with them a bale of costly muslins, which they had been instructed to present to Louis's mistress. Unfortunately their information was not up to date: Louis's not very stable affections had veered, and the muslins were presented to a mistress who had already been discarded. The mission was a failure, and the envoys were decapitated when they got home.

I don't know whether this story has a moral, but when I see the kind of people that our Foreign Office likes to get together with, I am often reminded of it.

1. Orwell's antipathy toward the Peace Pledge Union brought forth a well-written rebuke from Michael Sorensen, serving on the Ambulance Train based at Godalming Goods Station, Surrey, and dated 6 August 1944. He ironically asked Orwell to continue to vilify the P.P.U. (of which he was a member), so clearing the air for saying what, from a pacifist, 'would probably be denounced as "mawkish."' In addition to making the pacifist case, he argued that Orwell knew that 'a socialist pacifist is after the same sort of world as you: you know that he breaks with you only regarding the method of attaining it: why, then, the venom?' The letter was not published, but remained among Orwell's papers at his death.
2. For some very unaffected comments on receiving evacuees, see Joyce Grenfell's letters to her mother in *Darling Ma*, 4 and 18 September and 2 October 1939. There were homes for unbilletable children. Elisaveta Fen (see *534A*) records in her *A Russian's England* that she was appointed Assistant Matron of such a home in Oxford in June 1941 (465).

2527. To John Middleton Murry

5 August 1944 Typewritten

Murry responded to Orwell's letter of 21 July on 2 August. He said he was glad he was mistaken in thinking Orwell had made a scapegoat of him, but he took up Orwell's remark that he had failed to make a clear statement about the Russo-German war and asked Orwell if he could make one. He continued:

I think that Soviet Russia is probably a little less horrible by my standard of the good political society than Nazi Germany: but I am not *sure* about that. Whether Germany beats Russia or Russia beats Germany is from my point of view (i.e. considering what good will accrue to the human values I set store by) almost a matter of indifference. I have made that statement, or something like it, many times.

I have also said that I am glad that Russia has driven the Germans out of Russia. I cannot quite reconcile these two statements. The former is more a sober rational judgment, the latter more an instinctive feeling. They co-exist in me.

That I have failed to make a clear statement on the Russo-German war is therefore true. But you put it forward as evidence of "a circumspect kind of pacifism which denounces one kind of violence while endorsing or avoiding mention of another." This charge appears to me quite unwarranted.

Dear Murry,

Thanks for your letter of the 2nd. What I meant by not making "a clear statement about the Russo-German war" is that while advocating pacifism you have never, so far as I know, stated that the *Russians* ought not to defend themselves, and in such of your writings as I have read you have distinctly avoided the whole subject of the Russo-German war altogether. If I remember correctly, the next five or the next six numbers of the Adelphi following on the German invasion of the USSR did not even mention that Germany and Russia were at war. You also wrote in a tone of what I could only interpret as approval when the Russians invaded Poland in the early weeks of the war. The impression left by all that you have written about this—and I am by no means alone in inferring this—is that war is all right for Russians and perhaps for Germans and Japanese, but all wrong for us and the Americans. I simply do not see how you square this with pacifism. If it is wrong for one nation to defend its national sovereignty, then it is wrong for all nations. If it is right for any nation, then pacifism is nonsense.

As to "circumspect kind of pacifism". The issue of Russia comes in here again. You say to me, in a letter, that you are not even certain that the USSR is a less horrible phenomenon than Nazi Germany, and that which defeats the other is almost a matter of indifference to you. But in your published writings, so far as I know, you have written in a consistently approving tone of the USSR and invariably compared it with this country to our own disadvantage. You described the USSR as "the only *inherently* peaceful country", and you have even defended its intellectual totalitarianism on the ground that the same thing exists here in veiled forms. You also never raised your voice against such horrors as the purges of 1936–9, and you have used quite unnecessarily euphemistic terms about mass deportations of kulaks, etc. Judging by what I have read of them, I cannot reconcile your published statements with what you have written to me personally. And I cannot escape the impression that you avoid or gloze over the whole subject of Russian militarism and internal totalitarianism because it not only conflicts with your declared pacifism but because to speak clearly about it would also involve you in the only kind of unpopularity an intellectual cares about.

Of course, fanatical Communists and Russophiles generally can be respected, even if they are mistaken. But for people like ourselves, who suspect that something has gone very wrong with the Soviet Union, I consider that willingness to criticise Russia and Stalin is *the* test of intellectual honesty. It is the only thing that from a literary intellectual's point of view is really dangerous. If one is over military age or physically unfit, and if one lives one's life inside the intelligentsia, it seems to me nonsense to say that it needs any courage to refuse military service or to express any kind of antinomian opinions. To do so only gets one into trouble with the blimps, and who cares what they say? In any case the blimps hardly interfere. The thing that needs courage is to attack Russia, the only thing that the greater part of the British intelligentsia now believe in. The very tender way in which you have handled Stalin and his regime, compared with your denunciations of, say, Churchill, seems to me to justify the word "circumspect." If you are genuinely anti-violence you ought to be anti-Russian at least as much as you are anti-British. But to be anti-Russian makes enemies, whereas the other doesn't—ie. not such enemies as people like us would care about.

I don't agree with pacifism, but I judge the sincerity of pacifists by the subjects they avoid. Most pacifists talk as though the war were a meaningless bombing match between Britain and Germany, with no other countries involved. A courageous pacifist would not simply say "Britain ought not to bomb Germany." Anyone can say that. He would say, "The Russians should let the Germans have the Ukraine, the Chinese should not defend themselves against Japan, the European peoples should submit to the Nazis, the Indians should not try to drive out the British." Real pacifism would involve all of that: but one can't say that kind of thing and also keep on good terms with the rest of the intelligentsia. It is because they consistently avoid mentioning such issues as these, while continuing to squeal against obliteration bombing etc., that I find the majority of English pacifists so difficult to respect.

Yours sincerely
Geo. Orwell

2528. Review of *The Dragon Beards versus the Blue Prints* by Hsiao Ch'ien[1]

The Observer, 6 August 1944

Readers of Mr. Hsiao Ch'ien's earlier book, ETCHING OF A TORMENTED AGE, will remember that many of the problems it dealt with were curiously familiar. Chinese intellectuals who have grown up since the Revolution appear to have gone through much the same phases as their contemporaries in Europe, though not necessarily in the same order. In China, as in England, poets who would not have known which end to milk a cow wrote praises of the country life, others wrote proletarian literature which the proletariat was unable to understand, and the rival claims of propaganda and pure art were savagely disputed. In his present book (most of the essays in it have been delivered as lectures or broadcasts) Mr. Hsiao carries on the story, but here he is concerned less exclusively with literature and more with the impact of the machine age on Chinese culture as a whole.

As he points out, the machine came to Asia suddenly and disturbingly. "The London 'buses of today are a development of your Victorian horse-omnibus, and who knows, perhaps the next development will be air transport over London, with aerial conductresses shouting 'Hold tight, we're taking off!' But the motor 'buses in Hong-kong° or Shanghai have no tradition behind them. Your wireless sets are, in a way, the successors of your pianolas and your musical boxes . . . but the wireless sets in China seem just like miracles dropped from heaven." There was the additional fact (writing for an English audience, Mr. Hsiao is too polite to emphasise this) that for some decades the Chinese experienced the benefits of Western civilisation chiefly in the form of bullets. It was not unnatural that they should go through a period of violent hostility to machinery as such. Earlier than this they had simply despised Western science as the uninteresting product of barbarians. In the seventeenth century—

"When a German astrologer, Schell, tried to introduce the Solar calendar into China, he was first rebuked by native scholars, and finally died in prison of a broken heart. . . . A scholar of the time, Yang Kwang-hsien, wrote. 'We would rather live without an accurate calendar, than adopt an alien one. Without an accurate calendar, we may miscalculate the cycle of the moon, or miss an eclipse, but the Empire will prosper just the same.' "

This attitude was excusable at a time when China was visibly more civilised than the West (at a time, for instance, when Orientals washed themselves and Europeans did not), but far later, when China was already in imminent danger of conquest, Chinese sages were still producing delightful arguments to prove that machines were no good. In the mid-nineteenth century Wang Jen Chiu wrote:

"What is a steamship but the clumsiest of ships, and field guns but the clumsiest of cannons? The virtue of a ship lies in its speed, and the best cannons should be easily manoeuvrable. Now, these barbarous ships cannot sail an inch without being fed with coal, and their guns cannot be raised or moved without involving several hands. If one meets a brave soldier in the battlefield who rushes at one with bloody sword, he cannot but be killed."

It might almost be Marshal Pétain debunking the tank. However, the ships and the guns proved all too efficient, and after a period of obstinate conservatism the Chinese changed their attitude to the machine and began to develop what Mr. Hsiao describes as "blind admiration." Scientific studies became immensely popular, but the tendency was to concentrate on what was narrowly utilitarian. Young men studied animal husbandry rather than biology, ship-building rather than general engineering. Only comparatively recently was it realised that the Western technical achievements were based on theoretic studies of no immediate value.

Naturally the question that exercises Mr. Hsiao Ch'ien is: will the ancient Chinese culture be able to survive China's transformation into a modern mechanised state? It is perhaps an even more pressing question for the rest of the world, for if China should take the same road as Japan the results would hardly bear thinking about. China already manufactures machine guns, and will no doubt be manufacturing bombing planes before long. Mr. Hsiao is convinced, however—and he can quote many statements to support him—that his countrymen have no liking for a merely materialistic civilisation, and that their artistic traditions are too deeply rooted to be destroyed by the machine. Meanwhile China has to exist in the modern world, and does not enjoy being told that pigtails are more picturesque than steel helmets. But she would gladly return to her "dragon beards" (that is, to Chinese calligraphy, and the leisurely culture that it implies), if she could be reasonably secure from outside interference.

Apart from the essays dealing with the arrival of the machine, there is one dealing with the influence of Ibsen and Bernard Shaw on the Chinese theatre, and another dealing with recent Chinese literature. The Chinese vernacular theatre seems to have started with direct imitation of European models and in its early days to have been inseparable from propaganda. One author wrote of his own work: "Although the play is aesthetically immature, I am glad to say that I have touched on matrimony and rural bankruptcy, the two up-to-date social problems confronting us." Both Ibsen and Bernard Shaw were immensely valued as "problem playwrights," though *Mrs. Warren's Profession* caused a scandal in Shanghai as late as 1921. Later there was a reaction in favour of sentimental love-dramas, and later still in favour of "proletarian" plays. It is interesting to learn that the very first plays to be adapted for the Chinese theatre were *La Dame aux Camélias* and *Uncle Tom's Cabin*. *Uncle Tom's Cabin*, incidentally, had the effect of convincing the Chinese that "Westerners were not all callous."

This is a slight book, but well worth the hour or so that it takes to read. It would have been better in places if Mr. Hsiao Ch'ien were not over-anxious to avoid giving offence. Europe has not behaved well towards Asia, and in certain contexts it is necessary to say so. The publishers are to be congratulated on the make-up of the book, which is printed on the kind of hand-made paper which most of us have not seen for several years.

[Fee: £10.0.0; 2.8.44]

1. Hsiao Ch'ien (Xiao Qian) undertook some work for the BBC under Orwell's aegis early in 1941; see *919, n. 1*. In 1995, his translation into Chinese of Joyce's *Ulysses* was published.

2528A. Eileen to Lydia Jackson

Wednesday [9? August 1944]   Typewritten with handwritten
postscript

Ministry of Food,
Portman Court,
Portman Square,
London, W. 1

Richard Blair was born on 14 May 1944 in the Newcastle upon Tyne area. In June he was adopted by the Orwells and in that month Eileen gave up her job at the Ministry of Food; see Crick, 463–64. Although the letter is typed on Ministry of Food headed paper, it must have been written in August 1944. The flat in Canonbury Square, which the Orwells were to rent, was not in their possession when the letter was written. Eileen qualifies its being theirs by saying, 'at least references are being taken up.' On 15 August, Orwell told Leonard Moore that they were taking the flat at the end of August (*2533*) and on 29 August he told him that the flat would be theirs on 1 September but they would probably move in only on 9 September (*2539*). The letter must therefore have been written in August 1944 and a little before the 15th, by when, presumably, their references had proved acceptable. This would indicate that the journey north was to take place on Thursday 17 August and that Eileen hoped to visit Lydia Jackson at the Orwell's cottage in Wallington (where Lydia Jackson was staying, as she did from time to time – see *3255A*) during the period of Saturday to Monday, 12 to 14 August. This would imply that the letter was written on Wednesday 9 August 1944. In her letter, Eileen writes, 'When and if Richard comes'; he was not, therefore, then with them. It seems possible, therefore, that one reason for the journey north (presumably to Greystone, Carlton, near Stockton-on-Tees, County Durham, Gwen O'Shaughnessy's family home, some twenty-five miles south of Newcastle upon Tyne) was to see Richard. There is no indication as to whether or not Orwell went north with Eileen. Richard is first referred to in a letter by Orwell when writing to Rayner Heppenstall on 4 October 1944 (*2558*). Writing to Mrs Gerry Byrne on Saturday, 28 October 1944 (*2569*), Orwell says he fetched Richard 'last week,' that is between 15 and 21 October. See also *2566A*. It is possibly significant that in his London Letter, tentatively dated here October 1944 (*2553*), when referring to current shortages, Orwell mentions teats for babies' feeding bottle.

Dear Lydia,

I didn't know where to write to you and indeed I don't know whether this is a very good idea because one of Gwen's letters to Florrie[1] took ten days in transit. However we'll *hope*.

So far as I can see the cottage is going to repeat its Disney act. *Two* babies are now supposed to be going into residence, one with a mother and father the other with a mother (fortunately the father is in Normandy or somewhere). I pity them but it's satisfactory to have the space so well used. Mrs. Horton[2] has seen the space now so it's her responsibility. And about that, I thought I might come down for an hour or two while you're there and pack away some of our oddments – papers chiefly. I've arranged that the old tin trunk can stay locked but I think it would be a good idea to put it in the bottom of the larder (if it'll go) and also that the linen chest will be used for our things or yours. They're providing their own linen of course and will bring it in something in which it can be kept. I expect they will move most of the furniture about and the two passage rooms will go into use again. By the way, do you . . .° (There was a long interruption on the telephone and I can't at all remember what this important enquiry was.)

But I have remembered what I really wanted to write to you about. It was a confession. Lettice Cooper[3] and her sister went down to the cottage for the week-end. Barbara the sister is in the act of recovering from a nervous breakdown and this life is not good for her. She won't go away without Lettice and Lettice couldn't free herself for the week-end until just before it came. Then she did but of course it was too late to make any ordinary arrangements. They had a *lovely* time they say. Mrs. Anderson[4] swore she would clean on Tuesday and I hope she did but Lettice has a curious liking for housewifery and doubtless did clean quite well herself; the real crisis was about the sheets as usual – they carried one but couldn't well do more than that. Anyway I hope you don't mind. It seemed a pity to have the place empty for the bank holiday and I couldn't contact you. Seeing how much they enjoyed it and how well they looked I rather hoped that all these babies wouldn't like the place after all. It would be fun to send people down all the time and I don't think it need have been empty for a night for the rest of the summer anyway. But of course it won't be *empty*!

Can I come to tea? It's a bit of a job because we are going North with Gwen on the 17th to help with the luggage primarily. But I could manage Saturday or Monday—or Sunday I suppose but the travelling back is so ungodly. It'll have to be a compressed trip because we are also more or less in the act of moving. We have a flat in Canonbury Square—at least references are now being taken up and we shall have it unless the bombs beat us to the post which is rather likely. It's a top floor flat and there have been numbers of bombs in the vicinity though the square itself has lost nothing but a window or two. I rather like it, in fact in some ways I like it very much indeed. The outlook is charming and we have a flat roof about three yards by two which seems full of possibilities. Disadvantage is that to get to it you climb an uncountable number of stone stairs—to get to the flat I mean; to get to the roof you climb one of those fire-escape ladders with very small iron rungs. I don't know how Richard will be managed if the bombing ever stops. I thought we might have a crane and sling and transport him the way they do elephants in the films but George thinks this unsuitable.

Which day? With preference Saturday or Monday. No. Posts being as they are, I think I'll come on Saturday unless I hear to the contrary, and hope to see you. I expect I shan't get on the bus anyway but I'll come some time in the afternoon and leave in the late afternoon, having put away the papers and possibly collected one or two things. When and if Richard comes I'll be wanting a few things but probably the best thing to do will be to leave them for the moment in the linen chest so that they don't get bombed before they're used. I meant to brood on this when I went over with Mrs. Horton but she had to get back and we only had half an hour in the cottage which didn't leave much time for brooding.

See you on Saturday I hope.

With love
Eilee.[5]

[Handwritten postscript] (One thing I want to do *with* you is to check up on the things you want out of the garden. Kay wants you to have the crops of course but she'd better be forewarned so that the apple disaster isn't repeated the day they arrive.

[In left-hand margin:] Also I want to arrange to buy the coal and the Calor Gas.

1. Gwen O'Shaughnessy was Eileen's sister-in-law. Like her husband, Laurence O'Shaughnessy (killed at Dunkirk), she was a doctor. Florrie has not been identified. She may have been a neighbour at Carlton, Stockton-on-Tees.
2. Mrs Horton was evidently the new tenant of The Stores at Wallington, but see 2712 and 3255A.
3. Lettice Cooper (1897–1994), novelist and biographer, worked during the war at the Ministry of Food and had just resigned her post there. Her novels include *The Lighted Room* (1925), *The Ship of Truth* (1930), *Private Enterprise* (1931), and *Black Bethlehem* (1947), in which Ann is said to be based on Eileen Blair. In her memoir 'Eileen Blair,' Lettice Cooper records, 'I met Eileen

when she joined the Public Relations Division of the Ministry of Food . . . She came in some months after Dunkirk. . . . She looked after the Kitchen Front Broadcasts' (*PEN Broadsheet*, No. 17 Autumn 1984). A perceptive and touching account of Eileen (and to a lesser extent of her husband) was written by Miss Cooper for the Orwell Archive; it is printed in *Orwell Remembered*, 162–66; in this she describes how Orwell read each instalment of *Animal Farm* to her each evening 'and she used to come in and tell us next morning how it was getting on, she knew at once it was a winner.' See also *Remembering Orwell*, 116–17, 130–32, 144–45, and 196–97. Lettice Cooper underwent psychoanalysis and Orwell's knowledge of the subject may have come from her.

4. Mrs Anderson was one of the Orwells' neighbours at Wallington; she often looked after their affairs in their absence.

5. Eileen signs off with an indecipherable scrawl. She possibly writes 'With best wishes/Eilee.' but it is a little more likely that it is 'With love/Eilee.'—and the degree of scrawl is indicated by interpretations that see two and three words here. What is clear is that there is no final 'n' to 'Eilee', which may have been what she was familiarly called at the Ministry of Food.

2529. Review of *The Porch and The Stronghold*[1] by Richard Church

Manchester Evening News, 10 August 1944

One advantage of the novel, as a literary form, is that you can stuff very nearly anything into it. Fragments of old diaries, scraps of conversation overheard in the street, unpublished poems, disquisitions on politics or life in general, miscellaneous information on every subject from botany to tin-mining—with a very little ingenuity they can all be pressed into service.

Subject-matter too trivial, too scandalous, or too recondite to be used in any kind of essay or casual article can always be woven into fiction. And indeed, at a time like the present, when the art of pure story-telling is in a bad way, the best passages in many novels are those in which the author forgets about his characters and turns aside to discuss some irrelevant subject which he really understands.

Certainly that is true of these two reprinted novels by Mr. Richard Church. Their plots are non-existent and their characters improbable, but they do impart, on the side as it were, some valuable or, at any rate, interesting scraps of information.

"The Stronghold" is a sequel to "The Porch" (which, by the way, was given the Femina Vie-Heureuse Prize in 1938), and the central character all the way through is a young man named John Quickshott, who is employed as a clerk in the Customs Department, but whose ambition is to become a doctor. He has a fellow–clerk named Mouncer, who is a poet, and who dies at the end of the first volume, having first awakened the affections of a young woman, who ultimately marries John.

John does, in the end, after heroic struggles and much neglect of his official duties, succeed in passing his medical examinations. The stronger personality of Mouncer, even after death, imposes itself on John and Dorothy (the heroine) and keeps them apart, and the ghost is only laid when John is launched on his medical career and Mouncer's posthumously published poems score a great success.

That is the plot, if it can be called a plot, but towards the end the story simply goes to pieces and many of the incidents are quite meaningless. And the writing is surprisingly slovenly, phrases like "he sold the majority of his mother's furniture," or (notice the mental confusion of this) "he unloaded 30 or 40 pots of one-pound jam jars" occurring all over the place.

Yet certain passages in these two stories, perhaps 50 or 100 pages in all, are well worth reading. These are, needless to say, the passages dealing with the Customs Department (of which Mr. Church evidently has inside knowledge)[2] and with John's experiences as a medical student. Here you come upon concrete facts which you would probably not be able to find out for yourself, and their irrelevance to the main story hardly seems to matter.

There is much curious information about the goings-on in the Customs-house, the activities of tea-tasters, analysts and the like, but the most revealing thing is the way in which it is taken for granted that a minor Civil Servant will have no interest in his job.

Everyone either has some all-absorbing hobby or is studying for some examination by which he may hope to get out of the Civil Service, and in either case he steals all the time he can from his official tasks.

The Chiefs of the Department cannot officially countenance this, but even they are rather gratified when some junior clerk publishes a book, or obtains his B.Sc., or in some other way demonstrates that he has been using the Government's time for his own purposes.

John Quickshott, at the age of eighteen, enters his Majesty's Service without a trace of illusion or enthusiasm. He arrives late at the office on his very first day, and within a week or so is dodging work with the best of them. His friend Bembridge, a student of music and botany, spends hours of every day on his two hobbies, hurriedly slipping a blotter over his notebooks when the head clerk enters the room.

Work is bondage, life begins where work ends—that seems to be the attitude in the lower grades of the Civil Service, at any rate according to Mr. Church's picture of it.

It is a little difficult to believe John Quickshott would have made a successful doctor, but one or two scenes from his student days (these, no doubt, also drawn from personal experience) are convincing and interesting. There is a shocking description of an operation for cancer of the breast. This is a good example of the kind of mental junk for which there is always room in a novel. Presented with this description as a piece of "reportage," the editor of almost any kind of periodical would reject it at sight. In a novel it seems acceptable, even though it has no organic connection with the story.

The book also contains three descriptions of accouchements (two babies and one calf), all of them occurring in highly unfavourable circumstances. One of them, incidentally, happens during an air raid—in 1916.

The second of these two novels was written just before the present war, and deals with the opening years of the last war. Certain passages in it have an amusing period flavour, especially the descriptions of the Zeppelin raids—which, in the light of more recent experiences, seem rather unimpressive.

These novels were worth reprinting, but to say this is to say that English fiction is at a very low ebb. Probably this state of affairs, like Mrs. Carlyle's toothache, will not be permanent. The German end of the war should be over within a year, the paper situation will presumably improve within a year of that, and simultaneously the younger writers, or some of them, will be released from the Forces, and the older ones from the propaganda jobs under which they are now smothered.

When that happens we may hope for a reasonably large output of good novels again. But at present it is a lamentable fact that when a novel worth reading appears in this country it is in most cases either a reissue of something published before 1939 or, like "Darkness at Noon" and "Flight to Arras," a translation from some foreign language or, like "For Whom the Bell Tolls,"[3] the work of an American.

[Fee: £8.8.0; 9.8.44]

1. This is the way the title is printed, but it represents two novels which form the first parts of a trilogy: *The Porch* (1937), *The Stronghold* (1939), and *The Room Within* (1940).
2. Richard Church (1893–1972), poet, novelist, and essayist, did make a career in the Civil Service, but later became an adviser to a publisher. A prolific writer, he became President of the English Association. He published three volumes of autobiography, in 1955, 1957, and 1964, and was awarded the *Sunday Times* Gold Medal in 1955 for the first, which tells how, from modest beginnings (he was a postman's son), his life was transformed by his love of poetry.
3. By Arthur Koestler, Antoine de Saint-Exupéry, and Ernest Hemingway respectively. *The Flight to Arras* (1942) is not a novel; it describes author's experience as a pilot in 1940.

2530. 'As I Please,' 37

Tribune, 11 August 1944

A few days ago a West African wrote to inform us that a certain London dance hall had recently erected a "colour bar," presumably in order to please the American soldiers who formed an important part of its clientele. Telephone conversations with the management of the dance hall brought us the answers: (a) that the "colour bar" had been cancelled, and (b) that it had never been imposed in the first place; but I think one can take it that our informant's charge had some kind of basis. There have been other similar incidents recently. For instance, during last week a case in a magistrate's court brought out the fact that a West Indian Negro working in this country had been refused admission to a place of entertainment when he was wearing Home Guard uniform. And there have been many instances of Indians, Negroes and others being turned away from hotels on the ground that "we don't take coloured people."

It is immensely important to be vigilant against this kind of thing, and to make as much public fuss as possible whenever it happens. For this is one of those matters in which making a fuss can achieve something. There is no kind of legal disability against coloured people in this country, and, what is more, there is very little popular colour feeling. (This is not due to any inherent virtue in the British people, as our behaviour in India shows. It is due to the fact that in Britain itself there is no colour problem.)

The trouble always arises in the same way. A hotel, restaurant or what-not is frequented by people who have money to spend and who object to mixing with Indians or Negroes. They tell the proprietor that unless he imposes a colour bar they will go elsewhere. They may be a very small minority, and the proprietor may not be in agreement with them, but it is difficult for him to lose good customers; so he imposes the colour bar. This kind of thing cannot happen when public opinion is on the alert and disagreeable publicity is given to any establishment where coloured people are insulted. Anyone who knows of a provable instance of colour discrimination ought always to expose it. Otherwise the tiny percentage of colour-snobs who exist among us can make endless mischief, and the British people are given a bad name which, as a whole, they do not deserve.

In the nineteen-twenties, when American tourists were as much a part of the scenery of Paris as tobacco kiosks and tin urinals, the beginnings of a colour bar began to appear even in France. The Americans spent money like water; and restaurant proprietors and the like could not afford to disregard them. One evening, at a dance in a very well-known café, some Americans objected to the presence of a Negro who was there with an Egyptian woman. After making some feeble protests, the proprietor gave in, and the Negro was turned out.

Next morning there was a terrible hullabaloo and the cafe proprietor was hauled up before a Minister of the Government and threatened with prosecution. It had turned out that the offended Negro was the Ambassador of Haiti. People of that kind can usually get satisfaction, but most of us do not have the good fortune to be ambassadors, and the ordinary Indian, Negro or Chinese can only be protected against petty insult if other ordinary people are willing to exert themselves on his behalf.

Readers of this week's *Tribune* will notice that Mr. Reginald Reynolds,[1] reviewing *What the German Needs*, repeats and appears to believe a story about British troops advancing to the attack behind the cover of civilian hostages. His authority for it is a casual undated reference to the *News-Chronicle*.

Now, this business of advancing behind a screen of civilian hostages is a very old favourite in the history of war propaganda. The Germans were accused of doing it in 1914, and again in 1940. But would Mr. Reynolds believe it if it were told about Germans? I very much doubt it. He would at once reject it as an "atrocity story," which it is. As it happens, his quoted authority, the *News-Chronicle*, reported last week from the Normandy front another time-honoured atrocity—dipping women in petrol and setting fire to them. (This has been a steady favourite in the wars of the last thirty years. Ideally the women should be nuns. The *News-Chronicle* made them school-mistresses, which is perhaps the next best thing.) I feel pretty certain that Mr. Reynolds would reject that one too. It is only when these tales are told about our own side that they become, from the point of view of a war-resister, true or at any rate credible; just as for a blimp they only become true when told about the enemy.

I doubt whether the war-resister's attitude is any better than the blimp's, and in essentials I don't even think it is different. During recent years many pacifists and other war-resisters have assured me that all the tales of Nazi atrocities—the concentration camps, the gas vans, the rubber truncheons, the castor oil and all the rest of it—are simply lies emanating from the British Government. Or, alternatively, they are not lies, but then we do exactly the same ourselves. All that is said about the enemy is "war propaganda," and war propaganda, as we know from the experience of 1914–18, is invariably untruthful.

God knows there was enough lying in 1914–18, but I do urge that this time there is a radical difference. For it is not the case this time that the atrocity stories have only appeared since the war started. On the contrary, there were far more of them during the period 1933–39. During that time the whole civilised world looked on in horror at the things that were done in the Fascist countries. Nor did these stories emanate from the British Government, or from any Government.

It was everywhere the Socialists and Communists who believed them and circulated them. The concentration camps, the pogroms and all the rest of it were believed in by the whole of the European Left, including the majority of pacifists. They were also believed in by the hundreds of thousands of refugees who fled from the Fascist countries. If it is true *now*, therefore, that the tales of Nazi outrages are all lies, we have to accept one of two things. Either (a) between the years 1933–39 some tens of millions of Socialists and some hundreds of thousands of refugees suffered a mass hallucination about concentration camps, or (b) atrocities happen in peace time, but stop as soon as war breaks out.

I submit that both of these are incredible, and that the case against the Nazis must be substantially true. Nazism is a quite exceptionally evil thing, and it has been responsible for outrages quite unparalleled in recent times. It is definitely worse than British Imperialism, which has plenty of crimes of its own to answer for. Not to accept this seems to me merely unrealistic.

There is a point at which incredulity becomes credulity. "The Duke of Bedford," a young pacifist[2] writes to me, "knows—I assure you that this is so—that Hitler is a good man, and he would like to have a talk with him in order to bring out what is best in him." I suggest on the contrary that Hitler is *not* a good man, and that there is a large body of evidence to support this. I don't know, of course, whether the Duke of Bedford is correctly reported. But if he is, then I see no significant difference between his outlook and that of any fat-headed *Daily Telegraph* reader who cries out against doodle-bugs while not caring a damn for the starvation of millions of Indians.

This 'As I Please' drew responses on three fronts. The Duke of Bedford wrote to *Tribune* on 20 August to say that 'Mr. Orwell's young friend who stated that I knew that Hitler was a "good" man seems to be under a misapprehension. I should not apply the term "good" to any prominent statesman at present on the axis° or on the Allied side.' He argued that no matter how bad some of a man's actions might be you could not tell what he was truly like until 'you have tested his response to generous, unexpected practical friendliness on occasions where there has been no element of compulsion or bargaining.' He wrote from many years' experience in attempting the 'reclamation' of difficult people, including criminals. The letter was not published.

A second unpublished letter, from C. Jack (the signature is not quite clear), was headed 'George Orwell & "What the Germans needs.°"' Its burden, in a somewhat confused outpouring, was that it was 'sheer nonsense' to suggest that Nazi outrages were 'definately° worse' than the crimes of British Imperialism. He maintained that the war had been the Allies' responsibility for the way the Germans had been treated in 1919. 'This war could not have occurred but of° our own co-operation & foreign policy & so we should pay most of the costs & penalties.' A summary makes the writer's case more forcefully than does his letter.

Orwell's comment on his friend Reginald Reynolds's dismissive review of E. O. Lorimer's *What the German Needs* (which Reynolds concluded by saying that Allen and Unwin should feel ashamed of publishing such drivel), led to this letter from Reynolds, which was included in *Tribune* for 25 August 1944:

George Orwell's comment on my review in a recent number of *Tribune* gives sharp emphasis to Pilate's question. I think Orwell and I would agree on two propositions: (1) That real "atrocities" do occur, and (2) that hatred, inventiveness and exaggeration account for others.

I have, I believe, an unusually rich collection of atrocity stories, relating to many times and places. It would be larger had I not, some years ago, foolishly destroyed a whole trunkful of Indian stories (about the British), because I felt that they were not useful evidence. I was (and still am) more impressed by the less spectacular admissions implicit in Government White Papers and news items in "sound" capitalist journals etc. Being unable to wash my hands of the matter (like Pilate), I sought truth *where it was in nobody's visible interests to lie*. For example, there were once sensational atrocity stories about Russia, in newspapers hardly unbiassed, and these same papers should carry no more weight with us now that they have discovered all Russians to be angels and all Germans to be devils. But if such a paper, a respectable imperialist organ, tells me how many Indians have been flogged in the past year, I see no reason to suppose that it is deliberately defaming the British Empire. Indeed, one is driven to the conclusion that Fleet Street chivalry is often rather proud of such achievements.

Yet I do owe your readers an apology. Like many Londoners, I have been somewhat disorganised by the war. My files, hastily salvaged from an attic flat with a hole in the roof, are scattered and badly mixed up. Hence my undated reference to the *News-Chronicle*. But to satisfy Mr. Orwell I have with some trouble, unearthed the cutting I had in mind: and I find, to my horror and shame, that it was from the *Daily Telegraph*. The date was October 27, 1938, and the relevant passage from Arthur Merton's dispatch runs as follows:—

"We formed a convoy of a dozen vehicles led by an armoured car and a 'mine-sweeper'—an ordinary taxi in which had been placed two 'oozlebats.' This is a typical British soldier's corruption of the Arabic word 'Aisabit,' meaning rebel bands. The men were carried as hostages to avert the mining of our route."

The *Daily Telegraph* was, however, no more friendly than the *News-Chronicle* to Arab rebels: so why should the story have been invented? It may or may not be considered "atrocious"—the best test is to imagine our reaction to similar conduct on the part of the Germans. . . . The story was not forgotten because on the day that I read it I had been considering the comments of a nineteenth century historian on similar devices in the Middle Ages. He explained that, though barbarous by modern standards and unknown in his own time, such things were O.K. to the benighted mediæval mind. If my friend George Orwell wants this reference too, I am willing to spend a morning at the British Museum to satisfy him.

1. Despite Orwell's attitude towards pacifists and this disagreement, Orwell and Reynolds (see *560, 2.8.39, n. 4*) remained good friends, later collaborating on *British Pamphleteers* (1948). For Reynolds, see *1061, n. 1*.
2. This was Roy Walker; see *2259, n. 1* and *2372*. It looks as if Orwell was quoting here from memory. Walker wrote that the 'Duke of Bedford who really does—I can assure you it is so— understand Hitler, knows he has a good heart, and wants to bring out the best in him—by talking to him in a nice friendly way.' For the Duke of Bedford, see *913 n. 6* and *n. 7*.

2531. To John Middleton Murry

11 August 1944   Typewritten

On 9 August, Murry wrote to Orwell in response to his letter of 5 August. It not only explained a lot, he said, 'but it is a staggerer.' It had never occurred to him that Orwell could regard him 'as uncritically or circumspectly pro-Soviet.' He said he could furnish a series of weekly comments in *Peace News* which were 'severely, but I hope not unfairly, critical of the U.S.S.R.' He was, he said, completely nonplussed by this criticism. 'The only atom of support for your case that I can think of is that I did once write that the U.S.S.R. is "the only inherently peaceful nation." By that I meant that it was the only nation whose economic system did not reinforce the natural tendency of the human being towards war. . . . Now I am much more inclined to the idea that no economic structure of itself makes for peace.' He sent Orwell his two most recent references to Russia in *Peace News* (28 July and 4 August 1944), and concluded by referring to another point raised by Orwell. He did not, as a pacifist, say no nation ought to defend itself. This was because he did not see 'any real good in a nation refusing to defend itself except out of pacifist conviction. Here I agree with Gandhi. In so far as people still believe in defending themselves as a nation, they had better do it than shirk the job.'

Care of *Tribune*

Dear Murry,

Thanks for the copy of "Peace News," and your letter. I must apologise very deeply for attacking you on the score of your attitude to the USSR. I seldom see "Peace News" and did not know that you had taken this line, and I was going on what you used to say earlier on, eg. at the time of the Russian invasion of Poland and before the war. It is also unquestionable—as you yourself point out in this issue—that many pacifists regard Russia as sacrosanct and keep silent on this issue while denouncing the rest of the allied war effort, and I wrongly assumed that you would be doing so too. I ought to have kept up with your utterances and I am very sorry that I should have written you an almost abusive letter founded on out of date information. I know only too well what sort of trouble it gets one into to write anything anti-Stalin at this date, and I admire your courage in doing so. Fortunately I had not accused you in print of doing this particular thing—ie. attacking militarism but making an exception of the Red Army. As to my remarks about pacifism in general, I don't think I can withdraw anything. I hold to my opinion that it acts objectively in favour of violence and tends to turn into power-worship. But even here I may perhaps have been attributing to you too much of the outlook of the younger intellectual pacifists, some of whom seem to me completely corrupted. I wonder if you would send me a copy of your new book, "Adam and Eve," when it comes out, and I could do something about it in my column in the "Tribune."[1] In that way I could get over the difficulty of finding time to do it. Meanwhile please accept my apologies for misjudging your attitude.

Yours sincerely
Geo. Orwell

P.S. Do you ever see my column in the "Tribune?" You must not think that because I "support" the war and don't disapprove of bombing I am in favour of reprisals, making Germany pay, etc, etc. You may not understand this, but I don't think it matters killing people so long as you do not hate them. I also think that there are times when you can only show your feeling of brotherhood for somebody else by killing him, or trying to. I believe most ordinary people feel this and would make a peace in that sense if they had any say in the matter. There has been very little popular resistance to this war, and also very little hatred. It is a job that has to be done.

On 30 August 1944, Murry wrote to Orwell asking him to write an article of 800 words for *Peace News* to indicate 'the basic provisions which you consider indispensable to a lasting peace.' 'If you think a lasting peace a practical impossibility, will you say why.' Orwell did not respond to Murry's request.

1. Orwell reviewed *Adam and Eve* in the *Manchester Evening News*, 19 October 1944 (see *2565*), and there is a passing reference to the book in 'As I Please,' 46, 27 October 1944; see *2568*. See also Orwell's review of Max Plowman's Letters, *Manchester Evening News*, 7 December 1944, *2589*.

2532. On *Branch Street* by Marie Paneth[1]

The Observer, 13 August 1944

A valuable piece of sociological work has been done by Mrs. Marie Paneth, the Austrian authoress, whose book, "Branch Street," recently published by Allen and Unwin, brought to light some rather surprising facts about the slum conditions still existing here and there in the heart of London.

For nearly two years Mrs. Paneth has been working at a children's play centre in a street which she chooses to conceal under the name of Branch Street. Though not far from the centre of London it happens to be a "bad" quarter, and it is quite clear from her descriptions that when she first went there the children were little better than savages. They did, indeed, have homes of sorts, but in behaviour they resembled the troops of "wild children" who were a by-product of the Russian civil war. They were not only dirty, ragged, undernourished and unbelievably obscene in language and corrupt in outlook, but they were all thieves, and as intractable as wild animals.

A few of the girls were comparatively approachable, but the boys simply smashed up the play centre over and over again, sometimes breaking in at night to do the job more thoroughly, and at times it was even dangerous for a grown-up to venture among them single-handed.

It took a long time for this gentle, grey-haired lady, with her marked foreign accent, to win the children's confidence. The principle she went on was never to oppose them forcibly if it could possibly be avoided, and never to let them think that they could shock her. In the end this seems to have worked, though not without some very disagreeable experiences. Mrs. Paneth believes that children of this kind, who have had no proper home life and regard grown-ups as enemies, are best treated on the "libertarian" principles evolved by Homer Lane, Mr. A. S. Neill, and others.

Though not a professional psychologist, Mrs. Paneth is the wife of a doctor, and has done work of this kind before. During the last war she worked in a children's hospital in Vienna and later in a children's play centre in Berlin. She describes the "Branch Street" children as much the worst she has encountered in any country. But, speaking as a foreign observer, she finds that nearly all English children have certain redeeming traits: she instances the devotion which even the worst child will show in looking after a younger brother or sister.

It is also interesting to learn that these semi-savage children, who see nothing wrong in stealing and flee at the very sight of a policeman, are all deeply patriotic and keen admirers of Mr. Churchill.

It is clear from Mrs. Paneth's account that "Branch Street" is simply a forgotten corner of the nineteenth century existing in the middle of a comparatively prosperous area. She does not believe that the conditions in which the children live have been made much worse by the war. (Incidentally, various attempts to evacuate these children were a failure: they all came under the heading of "unbilletable.")

It is impossible to talk to her or read her book without wondering how many more of these pockets of corruption exist in London and other big towns. Mrs. Paneth has managed to keep in touch with some of the children who were previously under her care and have now gone to work. With such a background they have neither the chance of a worth-while job nor, as a rule, the capacity for steady work. At best they find their way into some blind-alley occupation, but are more likely to end up in crime or prostitution.

The surprise which this book caused in many quarters is an indication of how little is still known of the under side of London life. The huge slum areas that existed within living memory have been cleared up, but in a smaller way there is obviously still a great deal to do. Mrs. Paneth was astonished and gratified that her book, which casts a very unfavourable light on this country, received no hostile criticism.

Probably that is a sign that public opinion is becoming more sensitive to the problem of the neglected child. In any case it would be difficult to read the book without conceiving an admiration for its author, who has carried out a useful piece of civilising work with great courage and infinite good-temper.

But "Branch Street" still exists, and it will go on creating wild and hopeless children until it has been abolished and rebuilt along with the other streets that have the same atmosphere.

[Fee: £8.0.0; 11.8.44]

1. This article was headed, presumably by a member of *The Observer*'s staff, 'The Children Who Cannot be Billeted.' See also *2526* and *2526, n. 2*.

2533. To Leonard Moore

15 August 1944   Handwritten

Care of the° *Tribune*

Dear Mr Moore,

Thanks for your letter of 14th August. Yes, it is O.K. about Gollancz retaining the rights of "Wigan Pier".

I think Warburg is going to publish "Animal Farm"—I say "I think", because although W. has agreed to do so there *may* be a slip-up about the paper. But so long as we can lay hands on the paper he will do it. So that will save me from the trouble of doing it myself.

I am now doing that essay I spoke to you of,[1] & I shall then be able to compile the book of essays, but I shall have to find someone to do the typing as I have not time to do it myself.

We are, I think, taking a flat in Islington at the end of this month, & I will let you have the address when we move in.

Yours sincerely
E. A. Blair

1. 'Raffles and Miss Blandish' was completed on 28 August 1944, according to Orwell's Payments Book. It was published in *Horizon*, October 1944 (see *2538*), and in *Politics*, November 1944, with the additional title, 'The Ethics of the Detective Story.'

2534. 'As I Please,' 38

Tribune, 18 August 1944

Appropos° of my remarks on the railings round London squares, a correspondent writes:

"Are the squares to which you refer public or private properties? If private, I suggest that your comments in plain language advocate nothing less than theft and should be classed as such."

If giving the land of England back to the people of England is theft, I am quite happy to call it theft. In his zeal to defend private property, my correspondent does not stop to consider how the so-called owners of the land got hold of it. They simply seized it by force, afterwards hiring lawyers to provide them with title deeds. In the case of the enclosure of the common lands, which was going on from about 1600 to 1850, the land-grabbers did not even have the excuse of being foreign conquerors; they were quite frankly taking the heritage of their own countrymen, upon no sort of pretext except that they had the power to do so.

Except for the few surviving commons, the high roads, the lands of the National Trust, a certain number of parks, and the sea shore below high-tide mark, every square inch of England is "owned" by a few thousand families. These people are just about as useful as so many tapeworms. It is desirable that people should own their own dwelling-houses, and it is probably desirable that a farmer should own as much land as he can actually farm. But the ground landlord in a town area has no function and no excuse for existence. He is merely a person who has found out a way of milking the public while giving nothing in return. He causes rents to be higher, he makes town planning more difficult, and he excludes children from green spaces: that is literally all that he does, except to draw his income. The removal of the railings in the squares was a first step against him. It was a very small step, and yet an appreciable one, as the present move to restore the railings shows. For three years or so the squares lay open, and their sacred turf was trodden by the feet of working-class children, a sight to make dividend-drawers gnash their false teeth. If that is theft, all I can say is, so much the better for theft.[1]

I note that once again there is serious talk of trying to attract tourists to this country after the war. This, it is said, will bring in a welcome trickle of foreign currency. But it is quite safe to prophesy that the attempt will be a failure. Apart from the many other difficulties, our licensing laws, and the artificial price of drink, are quite enough to keep foreigners away. Why should people who are used to paying sixpence for a bottle of wine visit a country where a pint of beer costs a shilling? But even these prices are less dismaying to foreigners than the lunatic laws which permit you to buy a glass of beer at half-past ten while forbidding you to buy it at twenty-five past, and which have done their best to turn the pubs into mere boozing shops by excluding children from them.

How downtrodden we are in comparison with most other peoples is shown by the fact that even people who are far from being "temperance" don't seriously imagine that our licensing laws could be altered. Whenever I suggest that pubs might be allowed to open in the afternoon, or to stay open till midnight, I always get the same answer—"The first people to object would be the publicans. *They* don't want to have to stay open twelve hours a day." People assume, you see, that opening hours, whether long or short, must be regulated by the law, even for one-man businesses. In France, and in various other countries, a café proprietor opens or shuts just as it suits him. He can keep open the whole twenty-four hours if he wants to; and, on the other hand, if he feels like shutting his café and going away for a week, he can do that too. In England we have had no such liberty for about a hundred years, and people are hardly able to imagine it.

England is a country that *ought* to be able to attract tourists. It has much beautiful scenery, an equable climate, innumerable attractive villages and medieval churches, good beer, and foodstuffs of excellent natural taste. If you could walk where you chose instead of being fenced in by barbed wire and "Trespassers will be prosecuted" boards, if speculative builders had not been allowed to ruin every pleasant view within ten miles of a big town, if you could get a drink when you wanted it at a normal price, if an eatable meal in a country inn were a normal experience, and if Sunday were not artificially made into a day of misery, then foreign visitors might be expected to come here. But if those things were true England would no longer be England, and I fancy that we shall have to find some way of acquiring foreign currency that is more in accord with our national character.

In spite of my campaign against the jackboot—in which I am not operating single-handed—I notice that jackboots are as common as ever in the columns of the newspapers. Even in the leading articles in the *Evening Standard*, I have come upon several of them lately. But I am still without any clear information as to what a jackboot is. It is a kind of boot that you put on when you want to behave tyrannically: that is as much as anyone seems to know.

Others beside myself have noted that war, when it gets into the leading articles, is apt to be waged with remarkably old-fashioned weapons. Planes and tanks do make an occasional appearance, but as soon as an heroic attitude has to be struck, the only armaments mentioned are the sword ("We shall not sheathe the sword until," etc., etc.), the spear, the shield, the buckler, the trident, the chariot and the clarion. All of these are hopelessly out of date (the chariot, for instance, has not been in effective use since about A.D. 50), and even the purpose of some of them has been forgotten. What is a buckler, for instance? One school of thought holds that it is a small round shield, but another school believes it to be a kind of belt. A clarion, I believe, is a trumpet, but most people imagine that a "clarion call" merely means a loud noise.

One of the early Mass Observation reports, dealing with the coronation of George VI., pointed out that what are called "national occasions" always seem to cause a lapse into archaic language. The "ship of state," for instance, when it makes one of its official appearances, has a prow and a helm instead of having a bow and a wheel, like modern ships. So far as it is applied to war, the motive for using this kind of language is probably a desire for euphemism. "We will not sheathe the sword," sounds a lot more gentlemanly than "We will keep on dropping block-busters," though in effect it means the same.

One argument for Basic English is that by existing side by side with Standard English it can act as a sort of corrective to the oratory of statesmen and publicists. High-sounding phrases, when translated into Basic, are often deflated in a surprising way. For example, I presented to a Basic expert the sentence, "He little knew the fate that lay in store for him"—to be told that in Basic this would become "He was far from certain what was going to happen." It sounds decidedly less impressive, but it means the same. In Basic, I am told, you cannot make a meaningless statement without its being apparent that it is meaningless—which is quite enough to explain why so many schoolmasters, editors, politicians and literary critics object to it.

1. On the subject of claiming what seemed to be public as private property, Betty Lilly wrote to *Tribune*, 1 September 1944, to say that those who lived on the shores of Lake Windermere were charged ten shillings a year for each post which supported the landing pier by the Lonsdale Estate Office. Lord Lonsdale claimed the whole of the lake bottom. When people protested and threatened a lawsuit, 'the earl briefed every barrister on the Northern Circuit, and so the case was dropped.'

2. A letter from Dorothy V. Carter was published in *Tribune* on 25 August suggesting that to assist the pacification of the German people, Germans should be forbidden to wear boots. Though her friends laughed at her proposition, she was, she said, serious. 'To be shod in heavy boots gives anyone a tough feeling. . . . They shout and tend to bully. They don't care about quiet, decent living.' Orwell initiated his 'campaign against the jackboot' in 'As I Please,' 16, 17 March 1944, see *2435*.

2535. Review of *Milton: Man and Thinker* by Denis Saurat[1]

The Observer, 20 August 1944

This book, with all its learning, does not remove the impression that Milton, considered as anything except a poet, was an uninteresting person. It cannot be said that his life was uneventful: he went blind, he was twice married, and in the period of the Commonwealth he played an important part by answering, more or less officially, the leading pamphleteers of Europe. He also had the courage to continue writing anti-Royalist pamphlets when the Restoration was obviously imminent. And yet somehow Professor Saurat's claim that Milton was a "profound thinker" as well as a "marvellous poet" does not seem to be justified. Milton is remembered by his phraseology: it is difficult to feel that he added anything to our stock of ideas.

Professor Saurat has very little to say about Milton's private life, and not a great deal about his political outlook. The main emphasis of the book is religious. Milton's creed, it seems, was a kind of Deism or pantheism, definitely heretical even by Puritan standards. He did not believe in the duality of body and soul, and therefore only doubtfully believed in individual immortality. As he saw it, the Fall and the Atonement were a struggle that took place anew in every human being, and it was a struggle between reason and passion rather than between good and evil. In this scheme of things the doctrine of the Atonement in its Christian form had no place, and Milton does not even mention the Crucifixion in "Paradise Regained." Implicit in his outlook is the belief that the Kingdom of Heaven will be finally established on this earth, as was also believed by the ancient Hebrews before the doctrine of the immortality of the soul took root.

Professor Saurat accepts Blake's dictum that Milton "was of the Devil's party without knowing it,"[2] but adds that "he was also of God's party, and, what is more important, he knew it." "Paradise Lost" is a dramatisation of his own struggle, moral and political. The story of the Fall, which is different from the Biblical version, sets forth his own view of sexual ethics, while the relationship between Adam and Eve ("He for God only, she for God in him") emphasises the necessary subjection of Woman. There are indeed passages in "Paradise Lost" in which it is difficult not to feel that Milton is writing "at" his first wife. Professor Saurat does not say this, but he does say that Milton's subject-matter is in one way or another always himself. His political opinions sprang very directly out of his subjective feelings. Persecution made him a champion of liberty, but on the other hand he was not in favour of toleration for those he seriously disagreed with, such as the Catholics. He believed in democracy until he found that the common people were not of his way of thinking. Professor Saurat admits Milton's egotism and his tendency to base his theories on personal motives, but turns this into a virtue:

> But we may as well think . . . what a powerful personality was here, a personality which, in the exercise of its normal needs, was brought up against everything that was arbitrary in the laws and customs of the time! This man was under no necessity to think in order to discover the abuses of the social order; all he had to do was to live, and he naturally came to stumble against every prejudice and to trip against every error. He was naively surprised, and wondered why everyone did not think as he did. His egotism and his pride were so deep that they acted as hardly conscious natural forces, as though human nature, trammelled, bound, and imprisoned in all other men, had held to its free course in Milton alone.

This is ingenious, but when one remembers, for instance, that Milton only became an advocate of divorce when he wanted to dissolve his own marriage, it hardly seems to hold water.

This is, of course, a book about Milton as a thinker and not as a writer, but one cannot help feeling that a little more should have been made of the fact that Milton was a poet. For his outstanding characteristic, which cannot be left out of any full account of him, is his sheer skill with words. It is fair to call it unique, not only because it has never been successfully imitated, in spite of some well-marked stylistic tricks, but because, far more than in most great poets, it is independent of meaning. Many of Milton's best verbal effects are got by monstrously irrelevant digressions, lists of names, and sheer trivialities, things like—

> *the barren plains*
> *Of Sericana, where Chineses drive*
> *With sails and wind their cany wagons light.*

If Milton did a service to the human intellect, it was not by writing pamphlets against Salmasius but by weaving noble words round comparatively simple thoughts. For instance:—

> *I did but prompt the age to quit their clogs,*
> *By the known rules of ancient liberty,*
> *When straight a barbarous noise environs me*
> *Of owls and cuckoos, asses, apes and dogs.*

Over a period of 300 years, how many defenders of free speech must have drawn strength from that line, "By the known rules of ancient liberty"! However, perhaps Professor Saurat will write another book about Milton, considered this time as a poet.

[Fee: £10.0.0; 17.8.44]

1. This footnote appeared in *The Observer*: 'The first edition of this book was published in French in 1920 and in English in 1925. One section is now published for the first time in English.'
2. From *The Marriage of Heaven and Hell*, Blake's 'Note' to 'The Voice of the Devil.'

2535A. To Lydia Jackson

23 August 1944   Typewritten

Tribune

Dear Lydia,
Can you do us a short note (say 300 words) indicating whether this is any good?[1]

I have some other things of yours in hand but they will be published in due course.[2]

Yours,
[Signed] Eric.

1. Possibly *Elementary Russian Grammar* (on one sheet) by Dr I. Freiman. Lydia Jackson's 200-word notice appeared in *Tribune* on 10 November 1944.
2. The only item that can be identified is her review of *Polish Folk-Lore Stories*, published on 22 September 1944; see *2495A*.

2536. Review of *South of the Congo* by Selwyn James
Manchester Evening News, 24 August 1944

It is pointed out in the Bible that prophets are always wrong ("Whether there be prophecies, they shall fail," the text runs[1]), but it is difficult to believe that the prophets of the ancient world can have been so consistently wrong as the modern ones have been. Looking back through the torrent of political literature that has poured from the presses since 1935, it is very hard to recall a single correct prediction and only too easy to remember the most astonishing howlers.

The trouble at this particular moment is that whereas events move at lightning speed the process of printing and publishing has been slowed down by paper shortage, lack of labour, and the general disorganisation caused by the war. Any book that you read now is likely to have been written in 1943, if not earlier.

Even where there are not gross errors any political book published nowadays is likely to suffer from a certain distortion, thanks to the inevitable shifting of the world-picture between the time of writing and the time of publication.

Mr. Selwyn James's book—internal evidence suggests it was written early in 1943—comes out of this test rather better than most, but suffers from the fact that between now and then it has become obvious that an Axis victory is impossible.

His book is a survey of the various states, colonies, and protectorates that make up Southern Africa, and at the time of writing it was inevitable that he should overrate the dangers of an Axis invasion and the strategic importance of South Africa as a whole.

At that time the Mediterranean was almost closed to Allied shipping, and the Japanese were still on the offensive, though it was an error even then to state, as Mr. James does, that they had "obtained control of the Indian Ocean." And the pro-Nazi factions among the South African Dutch still looked upon Hitler as the saviour of the world, and said so openly.

Probably, therefore, Mr. James's picture is a good deal too gloomy—the immediate political prospect is not so desperate as he makes it appear. But the long-term problems of Africa are still unsolved, and it is for his frank and popularly written account of these that his book is worth reading.

The basic fact about Africa is racial exploitation. The native African, robbed of most of his lands and debarred nearly everywhere from education and political rights, lives in atrocious poverty, but at the same time the exploiting white population is a resident population and too numerous to be simply ejected.

The Boer farmer looks on Africa as his country. He has no wish to get rich quick or to go back to Europe, he wants only to live a patriarchal life on his primitive farm, and he longs passionately to get rid of the British and the Jews.

At the same time he has not the slightest notion of treating the native African as a human being, and the secession of South Africa from the British Empire would inevitably result in the African being pushed down into even greater degradation.

Mr. James points out, however, that the behaviour of the British on the spot is not much better than that of the Boers. The most violent political hatred can be sunk when it is a question of combining against the blacks, and the highly paid white industrial workers have no sense of solidarity with their black comrades.

British colonial policy, however, in so far as it is answerable to public opinion in Britain, is slightly more enlightened, and it is exactly this fact that has allowed the Nazi propagandists to make so big an impression on the Boer Nationalists.

Except perhaps in the Belgian Congo (50 years ago scene of unheard-of atrocities, but now comparatively well run), it cannot be said that the native Africans, anywhere south of Equatorial Africa, have been given a fair deal, but it is at any rate true that the protectorates of Bechuanaland, Swaziland and Basutoland are anxious to remain under the direct protection of the British crown and not to be "incorporated" in the neighbouring territories.

In every area the Kaffirs and other native tribes have been pushed off the best lands; even the protectorates are largely desert.

On top of this they are burdened with taxes which it is impossible for them to pay out of the proceeds of their tiny farms, or from the miserable wages which they earn as agricultural labourers. The taxes are imposed less, perhaps, for their own sake than as a way of keeping up the supply of cheap labour for the gold and diamond mines.

It is in the towns that conditions are worst. The huge "native quarters" are more sordid and disgusting than we can imagine. Mr. James says he was actually afraid to go into some of the huts he saw. Tuberculosis and other diseases are general, and infant mortality rises as high as 50 per cent (in England the corresponding figure is about 14 per cent).

The big towns also have their white proletariat, the "poor whites," mostly of Dutch extraction, who give its mass following to the Ossewa Brandwag, the South African Fascist Party, with a programme which is viciously anti-native, anti-British, anti-Semitic, and anti-Democratic.

And, of course, there is not even the pretence that black and white are equal before the law. The colour bar is so strict that even sexual intercourse between an African and a European is punishable by imprisonment.

Mr. James has a good word for missionaries, who have done what little has been done to provide the Kaffirs with schools and colleges.

But in general the Christian religion has not brought the African much good—a fact recognised in the Kaffir saying "previously the white man had the Bible and we had the land, now we have the Bible and the white man has the land."

Though lightly written, this is essentially a depressing book. It leaves the impression that the problems of Africa cannot be solved without generations of suffering and, probably, terrible bloodshed.

But too many others have given similar testimony to leave any doubt that Mr. James's general thesis is correct, even if his fears of Nazi penetration have been shown to be exaggerated.

[Fee: £8.8.0; 23.8.44]

1. 'Charity never faileth: but whether there be prophecies, they shall fail,' 1 *Corinthians*, 13.8.

2537. 'As I Please,' 39

Tribune, 25 August 1944

A certain amount of material dealing with Burma and the Burma campaign has been passed on to me by the India-Burma Association, which is an unofficial body representing the European communities in those countries, and standing for a "moderate" policy based on the Cripps proposals.

The India-Burma Association complains with justice that Burma has been extraordinarily ill-served in the way of publicity. Not only has the general public no interest in Burma, in spite of its obvious importance from many points of view, but the authorities have not even succeeded in producing an attractive booklet which would tell people what the problems of Burma are and how they are related to our own. Newspaper reports of the fighting in Burma, from 1942 onwards, have been consistently uninformative, especially from a political point of view. As soon as the Japanese attack began the newspapers and the B.B.C. adopted the practice of referring to all the inhabitants of Burma as "Burmans," even applying this name to the quite distinct and semi-savage peoples of the far north. This is not only about as accurate as calling a Swede an Italian, but masks the fact that the Japanese find their support mostly among the Burmese proper, the minorities being largely pro-British. In the present campaign, when prisoners are taken, the newspaper reports never state whether they are Japanese or whether they are Burmese and Indian partisans—a point of very great importance.

Almost all the books that have been published about the campaign of 1942 are misleading. I know what I am talking about, because I have had most of them to review. They have either been written by American journalists with no background knowledge and a considerable anti-British bias, or by British officials who are on the defensive and anxious to cover up everything discreditable. Actually, the British officials and military men have been blamed for much that was not their fault, and the view of the Burma campaign held by left wingers in this country was almost as distorted as that held by the blimps. But this trouble arises because there is no official effort to publicise the truth. For to my knowledge manuscripts do exist which give valuable information, but which, for commercial reasons, cannot find publishers.

I can give three examples. In 1942 a young Burman[1] who had been a member of the Thakin (extreme Nationalist) party and had intrigued with the Japanese fled to India, having changed his mind about the Japanese when he saw what their rule was like. He wrote a short book which was published in India under the title of *What Happened In Burma* and which was obviously authentic in the main. The Indian Government in its negligent way sent exactly two copies to England. I tried to induce various publishers to re-issue it, but failed every time: they all gave the same reason—it was not worth wasting paper on a subject which the big public was not interested in. Later a Major Enriquez, who has published various travel books dealing with Burma, brought to England a diary covering the Burma campaign and the retreat into India. It was an extremely revealing—in places a disgracefully

343

revealing—document, but it suffered the same fate as the other book. At the moment I am reading another manuscript which gives valuable background material about Burma's history, its economic conditions, its system of land tenure, and so forth. But I would bet a small sum that it won't be published either, at any rate until the paper shortage lets up.

If paper and money are not forthcoming for books of this kind—books which may spill a lot of beans but do help to counteract the lies put about by Axis sympathisers—then the Government must not be surprised if the public knows nothing about Burma and cares less. And what applies to Burma applies to scores of other important but neglected subjects.

Meanwhile here is a suggestion. Whenever a document appears which is not commercially saleable but which is likely to be useful to future historians, it should be submitted to a committee set up by, for instance, the British Museum. If they consider it historically valuable they should have the power to print off a few copies and store them for the use of scholars. At present a manuscript rejected by the commercial publishers almost always ends up in the dustbin. How many possible correctives to accepted lies must have perished in this way!

At a time when muck floods the bookshops while good books go out of print. I was rather glad to see recently that one or two of Leonard Merrick's novels have been re-issued in a cheap edition.

Leonard Merrick is a writer who seems to me never to have quite had his due. He was not trying to be anything but a popular writer, he has many of the characteristic faults of the pre-1914 period, and he takes almost for granted the middle-class values of that time. But his books are not only sincere, they have the fascination that belongs to all books which deal with the difficulty of earning a living. The most characteristic of them are about struggling artists, usually actors, but Art with a big A hardly enters: everything centres round the ghastly effort to pay the rent and remain "respectable" at the same time. Ever since reading Leonard Merrick, the horrors of a travelling actor's life— the Sunday journeys and draughty ill-lit theatres, the catcalling audiences, the theatrical lodgings presided over by "Ma," the white china chamberpot and the permanent smell of fried fish, the sordid rivalries and love affairs, the swindling manager who disappears with all the takings in the middle of the tour—have had their own special corner in my mind.

To anyone who wants to try Leonard Merrick, I would say: lay off the Paris books, which are William J. Locke-ish and tiresome, and read either *The Man Who Was Good, The House of Lynch* or *The Position of Peggy Harper*.[2] In a different vein, but also worth reading, is *The Worldlings*.

I wish some botanist among my readers would give me a clear ruling about the name of the weed with a pink flower which grows so profusely on blitzed sites.

I was brought up to call this plant Willowherb. Another similar but distinct plant, which grows in marshy places, I was taught to call Rosebay or French Willow. But I notice that Sir William Beach Thomas, writing in the *Observer*, calls the plant on the blitzed sites Rosebay Willowherb, thus combining the two names. The only wildflower book I have consulted gives no help. Other people who have referred to the plant seem to use all three names interchangeably. I should like the point cleared up, if only for the satisfaction of knowing whether a Nature Correspondent of fifty years' standing can be wrong.[3]

1. Maung Thein Pe; for details of the author and his book see *2236, n. 1.* See also Orwell's note to G. E. Harvey, 18 August 1943, *2240.*
2. Orwell wrote an introduction for a reprint of *The Position of Peggy Harper* late in 1945; this was to be published by Eyre and Spottiswoode but the project was abandoned. For Orwell's introduction, see *2957.*
3. See 'As I Please,' 41, *2547,* and also *n. 2* to the letter to R. S. R. Fitter, *2544.* The nature correspondent was William Beach Thomas; see *2439, n. 1.*

2538. 'Raffles and Miss Blandish'

28 August 1944;   *Horizon,* October 1944;   *Politics,* November 1944

Orwell's Payments Book records that this essay was completed on 28 August 1944 and that his fee from *Horizon,* in which the essay was published in October 1944, was £13.0.0. The essay was then titled 'The Ethics of the Detective Story from Raffles to Miss Blandish.' Two letters to Dwight Macdonald, editor of *Politics,* indicate changes made by Orwell for fear of libel (see 5 September 1944, *2545)* and how the essay had been censored by *Horizon* for political reasons (see 15 September 1944, *2550).* The two censorship cuts mentioned in the second letter (see *ns. 51* and *54* at the end of this item) were restored when the essay was reprinted in *Critical Essays* (London, 1946), and in the same collection of essays when published the same year in New York by Reynal & Hitchcock under the title *Dickens, Dali and Others: Studies in Popular Culture.* Neither of these editions restored the readings given by Orwell in his letter of 5 September (see *ns. 26, 31,* and *42* below).

Macdonald published the essay in *Politics* in November 1944 without making verbal cuts or modifications, and it is that version, with three exceptions, which is reproduced here. *Politics* gave the main title of the essay as 'The Ethics of the Detective Story' and made Orwell's title a sub-title; this seems to have no authority and is not reproduced here. Macdonald may have modified Orwell's typescript to suit his magazine's style but seems to have made fewer changes than were made for *Horizon* and *Critical Essays.* (One obvious non-Orwell form in *Critical Essays* is the use of 'To-day' for 'Today' (see *n. 61).* *Horizon* uses single instead of double quotations marks and =ize for =ise; these variants are not listed here.)

Two readings in this version, neither of which Orwell mentions anywhere, are: the change from *Lady—Don't Turn Over* (which appears in *Politics)* to *Miss Callaghan comes to Grief* (which appears in *Horizon,* the two essay collections, and the page proofs of the first impression of *Critical Essays;* see *n. 43);* and the change from 'left a trail of broken bones up and down Australia' (which appears in *Politics, Horizon,* and the page proofs of *Critical Essays)* to 'practised body-line bowling in Australia,' an alteration made in what is almost certainly the hand of Roger Senhouse (the director of Secker & Warburg who dealt with Orwell's work) to those page proofs; see *n. 14*. The book which drew James Hadley Chase's work to the attention of the authorities, and led to the withdrawal of *No Orchids for Miss Blandish*, was not *Lady – Don't Turn Over*. The latter was not, as popularly believed, written by Chase, but by Darcy Glinto (Harold Ernest Kelly), and it was published in May 1940, eighteen months after *No Orchids for Miss Blandish*. It was incorrect that Harold Larwood left a trail of broken bones round Australia as a result of his bowling technique; so that change, and the correct title of the book, appear in this text. These corrections of fact were probably made by Orwell, but they may have been proposed by others; if the latter, there is no reason to suppose that they did not have his approval. The amendment of 'suppressed' (see *n. 42*) does seem to have had Orwell's approval. He says in his letter to Macdonald of 5 September that it is probably better to change 'ultimately suppressed' ('ultimately' does not appear in any of the surviving texts) because the book may have been withdrawn voluntarily. 'Withdrawn' is therefore preferred. The change made to the note on Raffles as a murderer (see *n. 24*) shows clearly that Orwell did make corrections to the 1946 edition (which he dated 1945, the year he wrote these notes).

Orwell's own notes are indicated here by asterisks, and they are placed at the foot of the relevant page. Other notes, mainly variant readings, are at the end. All verbal variants are noted, as are significant changes in punctuation, capitalisation, and other accidentals. House-styling changes made for *Horizon* are not listed. The *Horizon* changes given in *ns. 27* and *48* are not likely to be Orwell's. One or two minor changes have been made to this text where *Horizon* or *Critical Essays* is more grammatically or lexically accurate; see, for example, *ns. 2* and *17*. These few changes are all noted. In textual notes, *Hor = Horizon*; *Pol = Politics*; *CrE = Critical Essays*; *DD&O = Dickens, Dali and Others*. Except for *n. 47*, readings in *DD&O* are not recorded, because that edition has no independent authority. *Critical Essays* was first published in February 1946; the second impression, May 1946, has been collated here. In the 'Etcetera' section of 'Comment' in *Politics* for November 1944, Dwight Macdonald included this note about the censorship of Orwell's essay by *Horizon*:

> 'George Orwell's article on detective-story ethics in this issue is being published simultaneously in the English literary monthly, *Horizon*. Not the full text, however. The editors of *Horizon* insisted on cutting out one passage entirely: ". . . and accounts, for instance, for the positive delight with which many English intellectuals greeted the Nazi-Soviet pact." And they altered another: in the reference to "the countless English intellectuals who kiss the arse of Stalin" the last five words are replaced by "worship dictators." (Incidentally completely changing Orwell's meaning.) This kind of panicky self-censorship is evidence of the degree to which the English intelligentsia has succumbed to Russomania (cf. also Orwell's experience with the *Manchester Guardian* noted earlier in this department).'[1]

About a page of this essay (taken from the *Horizon* text) was quoted by John Hampson (with Orwell's permission) in *Penguin New Writing*, 27, Spring 1946; see *2859*. A version was published in Polish in *Kultura* (Paris), 9–10, Sept–Oct 1948.

Nearly half a century after his first appearance, Raffles, "the amateur cracksman," is still one of the best-known[2] characters in English fiction. Very few people would need telling that he played cricket for England, had bachelor chambers in the Albany and burgled the Mayfair houses which he also entered as a guest. Just for that reason he and his exploits make a suitable background against which to examine a more modern crime story such as *No Orchids for Miss Blandish*.[3] Any such choice is necessarily arbitrary—I might equally well have chosen *Arsène*[4] *Lupin*, for instance—but at any rate *No Orchids* and the Raffles books* have the common quality of being crime stories which play the limelight on the criminal rather than the policeman. For sociological purposes they can be compared. *No Orchids* is the 1939 version of glamourised crime, *Raffles* the 1900 version. What I am concerned with here is the immense difference in moral atmosphere between the two books, and the change in the popular attitude that this probably implies.

At this date, the charm of *Raffles* is partly in the period atmosphere, and partly in the technical excellence of the stories. Hornung was a very conscientious and, on his level,[5] a very able writer. Anyone who cares for sheer efficiency must admire his work. However, the truly dramatic thing about Raffles, the thing that makes him a sort of by-word[6] even to this day (only a few weeks ago, in a burglary case, a magistrate referred to the prisoner as "a Raffles in real life"), is the fact that he is *a gentleman*. Raffles is presented to us—and this is rubbed home in countless scraps of dialogue and casual remarks—not as an honest man who has gone astray, but as a public-school man who has gone astray. His remorse, when he feels any, is almost purely social:[7] he has disgraced "the old school," he has lost his right to enter "decent society," he has forfeited his amateur status and become a cad. Neither Raffles nor Bunny[8] appears to feel at all strongly that stealing is wrong in itself, though Raffles does once justify himself by the casual remark that "the distribution of property is all wrong anyway." They think of themselves not as sinners but as renegades, or simply as outcasts. And the moral code of most of us is still so close to Raffles's[9] own that we do feel his situation to be an especially ironical one. A West End clubman[10] who is really a burglar! That is almost a story in itself, is it not? But how if it were a plumber or a greengrocer who was really a burglar? Would there be anything inherently dramatic in that? No—although the theme of the "double life," of respectability covering crime, is still there. Even Charles Peace[11] in his clergyman's dog-collar seems somewhat less of a hypocrite than Raffles in his Zingari[12] blazer.

Raffles, of course, is good at all games, but it is peculiarly fitting that his chosen game should be cricket. This allows not only of endless analogies between his cunning as a slow bowler and his cunning as a burglar, but also helps to define the exact nature of his crime. Cricket is not in reality a very popular game in England—it is nowhere near so popular as football, for instance—but it gives expression to a well-marked trait in the English character, the tendency to value "form" or "style" more highly than success. In the eyes of any true cricket-lover it is possible for an innings of ten runs to be "better" (i.e.[13] more elegant) than an innings of a hundred runs: cricket is also one of the very few games in which the amateur can excel the

---

* *Raffles, A Thief in the Night* and *Mr. Justice Raffles*, by E. W. Hornung. The third of these is definitely a failure, and only the first has the true Raffles atmosphere. Hornung wrote a number of crime stories, usually with a tendency to take the side of the criminal. A successful book in rather the same vein as *Raffles* is *Stingaree* [Orwell's footnote].

professional. It is a game full of forlorn hopes and sudden dramatic changes of fortune, and its rules are so ill-defined that their interpretation is partly an ethical business. When Larwood, for instance, practised body-line bowling in Australia[14] he was not actually breaking any rule: he was merely doing something that was "not cricket." Since cricket takes up a lot of time and is rather expensive to play, it is predominantly an upper-class game,[15] but for the whole nation it is bound up with such concepts as "good form," "playing the game", etc., and it has declined in popularity just as the tradition of "don't hit a man when he's down" has declined. It is not a twentieth-century game, and nearly all modern-minded people dislike it. The Nazis, for instance, were at pains to discourage cricket, which had gained a certain footing in Germany before and after the last war. In making Raffles a cricketer as well as a burglar[16] Hornung was not merely providing him with a plausible disguise; he was also drawing the sharpest moral contrast that he was able to imagine.

Raffles, no less than *Great Expectations* or *Le Rouge et le Noir*, is a story of snobbery, and it gains a great deal from the precariousness of Raffles's social position. A cruder writer would have made the "gentleman burglar" a member of the peerage, or at least a baronet. Raffles, however, is of upper-middle-class[17] origin and is only accepted by the aristocracy because of his personal charm. "We were in Society but not of it," he says to Bunny towards the end of the book; and "I was asked about for my cricket." Both he and Bunny accept the values of "Society" unquestioningly, and would settle down in it for good if only they could get away with a big enough haul. The ruin that constantly threatens them is all the blacker because they only doubtfully "belong." A duke who has served a prison sentence is still a duke, whereas a mere man-about town[18] if once disgraced, ceases to be "about town" for evermore. The closing chapters of the book, when Raffles has been exposed and is living under an assumed name, have a twilight-of-the-gods[19] feeling, a mental atmosphere rather similar to that of Kipling's poem, *Gentleman Rankers*:[20]

> A trooper of the forces—
> I, who kept my own six horses! etc.

Raffles now belongs irrevocably to the "cohorts of the damned."[21] He can still commit successful burglaries, but there is no way back into Paradise, which means Piccadilly[22] and the M.C.C.[23] According to the public-school code there is only one means of rehabilitation: death in battle. Raffles dies fighting against the Boers (a practiced reader would foresee this from the start), and in the eyes of both Bunny and his creator this cancels his crimes.

Both Raffles and Bunny, of course, are devoid of religious belief, and they have no real ethical code, merely certain rules of behaviour which they observe semi-instinctively. But it is just here that the deep moral difference between *Raffles* and *No Orchids* becomes apparent. Raffles and Bunny, after all, are gentlemen, and such standards as they do have are not to be violated. Certain things are "not done," and the idea of doing them hardly arises. Raffles will not, for example, abuse hospitality. He will commit a burglary in a house where he is staying as a guest, but the victim must be a fellow-guest and not the host. He will not commit murder,* and he avoids violence wherever possible and prefers to carry out his robberies unarmed. He regards friendship as sacred, and is chivalrous though not moral in his relations with women. He will take extra risks in the name of "sportsmanship," and sometimes even for aesthetic reasons. And above all he is intensely patriotic. He celebrates the Diamond Jubilee ("For sixty years, Bunny, we've been ruled over by absolutely the finest sovereign the world has ever seen") by despatching to the Queen, through the post, an antique gold cup which he has stolen from the British Museum. He steals, from partly political motives, a pearl which the German Emperor is sending to one of the enemies of Britain, and when the Boer War begins to go badly his one thought is to find his way into the fighting line. At the front he unmasks a spy at the cost of revealing his own identity, and then dies gloriously by a Boer bullet. In this combination of crime and patriotism he resembles his near-contemporary Arsène[25] Lupin, who also scores off the German Emperor and wipes out his very dirty past by enlisting in the Foreign Legion.

It is important to note that by modern standards Raffles's crimes are very petty ones. Four hundred pounds' worth of jewelry seems to him an excellent haul. And though the stories are convincing in their physical detail, they contain very little sensationalism—very few corpses, hardly any blood, no sex crimes, no sadism, no perversions of any kind. It seems to be the case that the crime story, at any rate on its higher levels, has greatly increased in bloodthirstiness during the past twenty years. Some of the early detective stories do not even contain a murder. The Sherlock Holmes stories, for instance, are not all murders, and some of them do not even deal with an indictable crime. So also with the John Thorndyke stories, while of the Max Carrados stories only a minority are murders. Since 1918, however, a detective story not containing a murder has been a great rarity, and the most disgusting details of dismemberment and exhumation are commonly exploited. Some of the Peter Wimsey stories, for instance, seem to point to definite necrophilia.[26] The Raffles stories, written from the angle of the criminal, are much less anti-social than many modern stories written from the angle of the detective. The main impression that they leave behind is of boyishness. They belong to a time when people had standards, though they happened to be foolish standards. Their key phrase is "not done." The line that[27] they draw between good and evil is as senseless as a Polynesian taboo, but at least, like the taboo, it has the advantage that everyone accepts it.

So much for *Raffles*. Now for a header into the cesspool. *No Orchids for Miss Blandish*, by James Hadley Chase, was published in 1939 but seems to have enjoyed its greatest popularity in 1940, during the Battle of Britain and the blitz. In its main outlines its story is this:

Miss Blandish, the daughter of a millionaire, is kidnapped by some

---

* 1945. Actually Raffles does kill one man and is more or less consciously responsible for the death of two others. But all three of them are foreigners and have behaved in a very reprehensible manner. He also, on one occasion, contemplates murdering a blackmailer. It is, however, a fairly well-established convention in crime stories that murdering a blackmailer "doesn't count" [Orwell's footnote].[24]

gangsters who are almost immediately surprised and killed off by a larger and better organised gang. They hold her to ransom and extract half a million dollars from her father. Their original plan had been to kill her as soon as the ransom-money[28] was received, but a chance keeps her alive. One of the gang is a young man named Slim[29] whose sole pleasure in life consists in driving knives into other people's bellies. In childhood he has graduated by cutting up living animals with a pair of rusty scissors. Slim is sexually impotent, but takes a kind of fancy to Miss Blandish. Slim's mother, who is the real brains of the gang, sees in this the chance of curing Slim's impotence, and decides to keep Miss Blandish in custody till Slim shall have succeeded in raping her. After many efforts and much persuasion, including the flogging of Miss Blandish with a length of rubber hosepipe, the rape is achieved. Meanwhile Miss Blandish's father has hired a private detective, and by means of bribery and torture the detective and the police manage to round up and exterminate the whole gang. Slim escapes with Miss Blandish and is killed after a final rape, and the detective prepares to restore Miss Blandish to her family. By this time, however, she has developed such a taste for Slim's caresses* that she feels unable to live without him, and she jumps out of the window of a skyscraper.[30]

Several other points need noticing before one can grasp the full implications of this book. To begin with its central story is an impudent plagiarism of William Faulkner's novel, Sanctuary.[31] Secondly it is not, as one might expect, the product of an illiterate hack, but a brilliant piece of writing, with hardly a wasted word or a jarring note anywhere. Thirdly, the whole book, récit[32] as well as dialogue, is written in the American language:[33] the author, an Englishman who has (I believe) never been in the United States, seems to have made a complete mental transference to the American underworld. Fourthly, the book sold, according to its publishers, no less than half a million copies.

I have already outlined the plot, but the subject-matter is much more sordid and brutal than this suggests. The book contains eight full-dress murders, an unassessable number of casual killings and woundings, an exhumation (with a careful reminder of the stench), the flogging of Miss Blandish, the torture of another woman with redhot[34] cigarette ends, a strip-tease act, a third-degree scene of unheard-of cruelty, and much else of the same kind. It assumes great sexual sophistication in its readers (there is a scene, for instance, in which a gangster, presumably of masochistic tendency, has an orgasm in the moment of being knifed), and it takes for granted the most complete corruption and self-seeking as the norm of human behaviour. The detective, for instance, is almost as great a rogue as the gangsters, and actuated by nearly the same motives. Like them, he is in pursuit of "five hundred grand." It is necessary to the machinery of the story that Mr. Blandish should be anxious to get his daughter back, but apart from

* 1945. Another reading of the final episode is possible. It may mean merely that Miss Blandish is pregnant. But the interpretation I have given above seems more in keeping with the general brutality of the book [Orwell's footnote].

this such things as affection, friendship, good-nature[35] or even ordinary politeness simply do not enter. Nor, to any great extent, does normal sexuality. Ultimately only one motive is at work throughout the whole story: the pursuit of power.

It should be noticed that the book is not in the ordinary sense pornography. Unlike most books that deal in sexual sadism, it lays the emphasis on the cruelty and not on the pleasure. Slim, the ravisher of Miss Blandish, has "wet, slobbering lips": this is disgusting, and it is meant to be disgusting. But the scenes describing cruelty to women are comparatively perfunctory. The real high-spots of the book are cruelties committed by men upon other men: above all the third-degreeing of the gangster, Eddie Schultz, who is lashed into a chair and flogged on the windpipe with truncheons, his arms broken by fresh blows as he breaks loose. In another of Mr. Chase's books, *He Won't Need It Now*, the hero, who is intended to be a sympathetic and perhaps even noble character, is described as stamping on somebody's face, and then, having crushed the man's mouth in, grinding his heel round and round in it. Even when physical incidents of this kind are not occurring, the mental atmosphere of these books is always the same. Their whole theme is the struggle for power and the triumph of the strong over the weak. The big gangsters wipe out the little ones as mercilessly as a pike gobbling[36] up the little fish in a pond; the police kill off the criminals as cruelly as the angler kills the pike. If ultimately one sides with the police against the gangsters it is merely because they are better organised and more powerful, because, in fact, the law is a bigger racket than crime. Might is right: vae victis.[37]

As I have mentioned already, *No Orchids* enjoyed its greatest vogue in 1940, though it was successfully running as a play till some time later. It was, in fact, one of the things that helped to console people for the boredom of being bombed. Early in the war the *New Yorker* had a picture of a little man approaching a news-stall littered with papers with such headlines as GREAT TANK BATTLES IN NORTHERN FRANCE, BIG NAVAL BATTLE IN THE NORTH SEA, HUGE AIR BATTLES OVER THE CHANNEL, etc. etc.[38] The little man is saying, "*Action Stories*, please." That little man stood for all the drugged millions to whom the world of the gangsters and the prize-ring is more "real," more "tough" than such things as wars, revolutions, earthquakes, famines and pestilences. From the point of view of a reader of *Action Stories*, a description of the London blitz, or of the struggles of the European underground parties, would be "sissy stuff." On the other hand some puny gun-battle in Chicago, resulting in perhaps[39] half a dozen deaths, would seem genuinely "tough." This habit of mind is now extremely widespread. A soldier sprawls in a muddy trench, with the machine-gun bullets crackling a foot or two overhead and whiles away his intolerable boredom by reading an American gangster story. And what is it that makes that story so exciting? Precisely the fact that people are shooting at each other with machine-guns![40] Neither the soldier nor anyone else sees anything curious in this. It is taken for granted that an imaginary bullet is more thrilling than a real one.

The obvious explanation is that in real life one is usually a passive victim, whereas in the adventure story one can think of oneself as being at the centre of events. But there is more to it than that. Here it is necessary to refer again to the curious fact of *No Orchids* being written—with technical errors, perhaps, but certainly with considerable skill—in the American language.

There exists in America an enormous literature of more or less the same stamp as *No Orchids*. Quite apart from books, there is the huge array of "pulp magazines," graded so as to cater for different kinds of fantasy but nearly all having much the same mental atmosphere. A few of them go in for straight pornography[41] but the great majority are quite plainly aimed at sadists and masochists. Sold at threepence a copy under the title of Yank Mags,* these things used to enjoy considerable popularity in England, but when the supply dried up owing to the war, no satisfactory substitute was forthcoming. English imitations of the "pulp magazine" do now exist, but they are poor things compared with the original. English crook films, again, never approach the American crook film in brutality. And yet the career of Mr. Chase shows how deep the American influence has already gone. Not only is he himself living a continuous fantasy-life in the Chicago underworld, but he can count on hundreds of thousands of readers who know what is meant by a "clipshop" or the "hotsquat," do not have to do mental arithmetic when confronted by "fifty grand," and understand at sight a sentence like "Johnnie was a rummy and only two jumps ahead of the nut-factory." Evidently there are great numbers of English people who are partly Americanised in language and, one ought to add, in moral outlook. For there was no popular protest against *No Orchids*. In the end it was withdrawn,[42] but only retrospectively, when a later work, *Miss Callaghan comes to Grief*[43] brought Mr. Chase's books to the attention of the authorities. Judging by casual conversations at the time, ordinary readers got a mild thrill out of the obscenities in *No Orchids*, but saw nothing undesirable in the book as a whole. Many people, incidentally, were under the impression that it was an American book re-issued[44] in England.

The thing that the ordinary reader *ought* to have objected to—almost certainly would have objected to, a few decades earlier—was the equivocal attitude towards crime. It is implied throughout *No Orchids* that being a criminal is only reprehensible in the sense that it does not pay. Being a policeman pays better, but there is no moral difference, since the police use essentially criminal methods. In a book like *He Won't Need It Now* the distinction between crime and crime-prevention practically disappears. This is a new departure for English sensational fiction, in which till recently there has always been a sharp distinction between right and wrong and a general agreement that virtue must triumph in the last chapter. English books glorifying crime (modern crime, that is—pirates and highwaymen are different) are very rare. Even a book like *Raffles*, as I have pointed out, is governed by powerful taboos, and it is clearly understood that Raffles's crimes must be expiated sooner or later. In America, both in life and fiction,

---

* They are said to have been imported into this country as ballast, which accounted for their low price and crumpled appearance. Since the war the ships have been ballasted with something more useful, probably gravel [Orwell's footnote].

the tendency to tolerate crime, even to admire the criminal so long as he is successful, is very much more marked. It is, indeed, ultimately this attitude that has made it possible for crime to flourish upon so huge a scale. Books have been written about Al Capone that are hardly different in tone from the books written about Henry Ford, Stalin, Lord Northcliffe and all the rest of the "log cabin to White House" brigade. And switching back eighty years, one finds Mark Twain adopting much the same attitude towards the disgusting bandit Slade, hero of twenty-eight murders, and towards the Western desperadoes generally. They were successful, they "made good," therefore he admired them.

In a book like *No Orchids* one is not, as in the old-style crime story, simply escaping from dull reality into an imaginary world of action. One's escape is essentially into cruelty and sexual perversion. *No Orchids* is aimed at the power-instinct which *Raffles* or the Sherlock Holmes stories are not. At the same time[45] the English attitude towards crime is not so superior to the American as I may have seemed to imply. It too[46] is mixed up with power-worship, and has become more noticeably so in the last twenty years. A writer who is worth examining is Edgar Wallace, especially in such typical books as *The Orator* and the Mr. J. G. Reeder stories. Wallace was one of the first crime-story writers to break away from the old tradition of the private detective and make his central figure a Scotland Yard official. Sherlock Holmes is an amateur, solving his problems without the help and even, in the earlier stories, against the opposition of the police. Moreover, like Dupin,[47] he is essentially an intellectual, even a scientist. He reasons logically from observed fact, and his intellectuality is constantly contrasted with the routine methods of the police. Wallace objected strongly to this slur, as he considered it, on Scotland Yard, and in several newspaper articles he went out of his way to denounce Holmes by name. His own ideal was the detective-inspector who catches criminals not because he is intellectually brilliant but because he is part of an all-powerful organisation. Hence the curious fact that in Wallace's most characteristic stories the "clue" and the "deduction" play no part. The criminal is always defeated either[48] by an incredible coincidence, or because in some unexplained manner the police know all about the crime beforehand. The tone of the stories makes it quite clear that Wallace's admiration for the police is pure bully-worship. A Scotland Yard detective is the most powerful kind of being that he can imagine, while the criminal figures in his mind as an outlaw against whom anything is permissible, like the condemned slaves in the Roman arena. His policemen behave much more brutally than British policemen do in real life—they hit people without provocation, fire revolvers past their ears to terrify them,[49] and so on—and some of the stories exhibit a fearful intellectual sadism. (For instance, Wallace likes to arrange things so that the villain is hanged on the same day as the heroine is married.) But it is sadism after the English fashion: that is to say it is unconscious, there is not overtly any sex in it, and it keeps within the bounds of the law. The British public tolerates a harsh criminal law and gets a kick out of monstrously unfair murder trials: but still that is better, on any count, than tolerating or admiring crime. If one must worship a bully, it is better

353

that he should be a policeman than a gangster. Wallace is still governed to some extent by the concept of "not done." In *No Orchids* anything is "done" so long as it leads on to power. All the barriers are down, all the motives are out in the open. Chase is a worse symptom than Wallace, to the extent that all-in wrestling is worse than boxing, or Fascism is worse than capitalist democracy.

In borrowing from William Faulkner's *Sanctuary*, Chase only took the plot; the mental atmosphere of the two books is not similar. Chase really derives from other sources, and this particular bit of borrowing is only symbolic. What it symbolises is the vulgarisation of ideas which is constantly happening, and which probably happens faster in an age of print. Chase has been described as "Faulkner for the masses," but it would be more accurate to describe him as Carlyle for the masses. He is a popular writer—there are many such in America, but they are still rarities in England—who has caught up with what it is now fashionable to call "realism," meaning the doctrine that might is right. The growth of "realism" has been the great feature of the intellectual history of our own age. Why this should be so is a complicated question. The interconnection between sadism, masochism, success-worship, power-worship, nationalism and totalitarianism is a huge subject whose edges have barely been scratched, and even to mention it is considered somewhat indelicate. To take merely the first example that comes to mind, I believe no one has ever pointed out the sadistic and masochistic element in Bernard Shaw's work, still less suggested that this probably has some connection with Shaw's admiration for dictators.[50]

Fascism is often loosely equated with sadism, but nearly always by people who see nothing wrong in the most slavish worship of Stalin. The truth is, of course, that the countless English intellectuals who kiss the arse of Stalin[51] are not different from the minority who give their allegiance to Hitler or Mussolini, nor from[52] the efficiency experts who preached "punch," "drive," "personality" and "learn to be a Tiger Man" in the nineteen-twenties, nor from the older generation of intellectuals, Carlyle, Creasey and the rest of them, who bowed down before German militarism. All of them are worshipping power and succcessful cruelty. It is important to notice that the cult of power tends to be mixed up with a love of cruelty and wickedness *for their own sakes*. A tyrant is all the more admired if he happens to be a bloodstained crook as well, and "the end justifies the means" often becomes, in effect, "the means justify themselves provided they are dirty enough." This idea colours the outlook of all sympathisers with totalitarianism, and accounts, for instance, for the positive delight with which many English intellectuals greeted the Nazi-Soviet pact. It was a step only doubtfully useful to the USSR, but it was entirely unmoral, and for that reason to be admired:[53] the explanations of it, which were numerous and self-contradictory, could come afterwards.[54]

Until recently the characteristic adventure stories of the English-speaking peoples have been stories in which the hero fights *against odds*. This is true all the way from Robin Hood to Popeye[55] the Sailor. Perhaps the basic myth of the Western world is Jack the Giant Killer.[56] But to be brought up to date this should be renamed Jack the Dwarf Killer,[57] and there already exists a considerable literature which teaches, either overtly or implicitly, that one should side with the big man against the little man. Most of what is now written about foreign policy is simply an embroidery on this theme, and for several decades such phrases as "play[58] the game," "don't[59] hit a man when he's down" and "it's[60] not cricket" have never failed to draw a snigger from anyone of intellectual pretensions. What is comparatively new is to find the accepted pattern according to which (a) right is right and wrong is wrong, whoever wins, and (b) weakness must be respected, disappearing from popular literature as well. When I first read D. H. Lawrence's novels, at the age of about twenty, I was puzzled by the fact that there did not seem to be any classification of the characters into "good" and "bad." Lawrence seemed to sympathise with all of them about equally, and this was so unusual as to give me the feeling of having lost my bearings. Today[61] no one would think of looking for heroes and villains in a serious novel, but in lowbrow fiction one still expects to find a sharp distinction between right and wrong and between legality and illegality. The common people, on the whole, are still living in the world of absolute good and evil from which the intellectuals have long since escaped. But the popularity of No Orchids and the American books and magazines to which it is akin shows how rapidly the doctrine of "realism" is gaining ground.

Several people, after reading No Orchids, have remarked to me, "It's pure Fascism." This is a correct description, although the book has not the smallest connection with politics and very little with social or economic problems. It has merely the same relation to Fascism as, say, Trollope's novels have to nineteenth-century capitalism. It is a daydream appropriate to a totalitarian age. In his imagined world of gangsters Chase is presenting, as it were, a distilled version of the modern political scene, in which such things as mass bombing of civilians, the use of hostages, torture to obtain confessions, secret prisons, execution without trial, floggings with rubber truncheons, drownings in cesspools, systematic falsification of records and statistics, treachery, bribery and quislingism are normal and morally neutral, even admirable when they are done in a large and bold way. The average man is not directly interested in politics, and when he reads he wants the current struggles of the world to be translated into a simple story about individuals. He can take an interest in Slim and Fenner as he could not in the GPU and the Gestapo. People worship power in the form in which they are able to understand it. A twelve-year-old boy worships Jack Dempsey. An adolescent in a Glasgow slum worships Al Capone. An aspiring pupil at a business college worships Lord Nuffield. A New Statesman reader worships Stalin. There is a difference in intellectual maturity, but none in moral outlook. Thirty years ago the heroes of popular fiction had nothing in common with Mr. Chase's gangsters and detectives, and the idols of the English liberal intelligentsia were also comparatively sympathetic figures. Between Holmes and Fenner on the one hand, and between Abraham Lincoln and Stalin on the other, there is a similar gulf.

One ought not to infer too much from the success of Mr. Chase's books. It is possible that it is an isolated phenomenon, brought about by the mingled boredom and brutality of war. But if such books should definitely acclimatise themselves in England, instead of being merely a half-understood import from America, there would be good grounds for dismay. In choosing *Raffles* as a background for *No Orchids*,[62] I deliberately chose a book which by the standards of its time was morally equivocal. Raffles, as I have pointed out, has no real moral code, no religion, certainly no social consciousness. All he has is a set of reflexes—the nervous system, as it were, of a gentleman. Give him a sharp tap on this reflex or that (they are called "sport," "pal," "woman," "king and country" and so forth), and you get a predictable reaction. In Mr. Chase's book there are no gentlemen, and no taboos. Emancipation is complete, Freud and Macchiavelli have reached the outer suburbs. Comparing the schoolboy atmosphere of the one book with the cruelty and corruption of the other, one is driven to feel that snobbishness, like hypocrisy, is a check upon behaviour whose value from a social point of view has been underrated.

1. See *2518, n. 1.*
2. best-known] best known   *Pol*
3. *No Orchids for Miss Blandish was James Hadley Chase's first book and was written when he was working for a book wholesaler. It was published in May 1939, and by the time Orwell wrote his essay had sold over a million copies. Chase's real name was René Brabazon Raymond (1906–1985); he wrote some eighty books, using various pseudonyms.*
4. *Arsène*] Arsene   *Pol, CrE*
5. and, on his level,] and on his level   *Hor, CrE*
6. by-word] byword   *CrE*
7. social:] social;   *CrE*
8. Bunny] his Bunny   *Hor; altered in page proofs of CrE*
9. Raffles's] Raffles'   *CrE*
10. clubman] club man   *CrE*
11. *Charles Peace (1832–1879), petty criminal and murderer. In 1876 he killed Police Constable Cook, but another man was charged and found guilty of murder. In 1878 he murdered Alfred Dyson. Arrested in the act of burglary, he was tried for Dyson's murder and found guilty. He confessed to having killed Cook, and the man originally charged, William Habron, was given a free pardon. Peace was executed in 1879. His exploits entered popular myth and he was the subject of an early silent film.*
12. Zingari] *properly, I Zingari (Italian, the Gypsies); an exclusive English cricket club founded in 1845 which has no home ground and so travels away to all its matches*
13. i.e.] i.e.,   *Hor, i.e.   CrE*
14. practised body-line bowling in Australia] left a trail of broken bones up and down Australia   *Pol; left . . . Australia, Hor; altered in page proofs of CrE (in Senhouse's hand)*
15. *Had Orwell stayed in Wigan beyond March 1936 he would have realised that cricket is anything but a predominantly upper-class game. The leagues of Lancashire and Yorkshire in particular were not and are not the preserves of the upper classes.*
16. burglar] burglar,   *Hor. CrE*
17. upper-middle-class] upper-middle class   *Pol, Hor*
18. man-about-town] man-about-town,   *Hor*   man about town,   *CrE*
19. twilight-of-the-gods] twilight of the gods; a Wagnerian reference (as at XII/97, line 1)   *Hor, CrE*
20. *Gentleman Rankers:*] *Gentleman Rankers,   Hor. The title should be hyphenated.*
21. A trooper . . . kept] Yes, a trooper of the forces— / Who has kept   *CrE. These lines, from Barrack-room Ballads (1892 or 1893), should be printed as a single line as as 'Yes, a trooper of the forces who has run his own six horses,'—no exclamation point. Orwell doubtless quoted (and perhaps 'corrected' himself) from memory. Compare 2523, n. 3. 'cohorts of the damned' from Gentleman Rankers.*
22. *Raffles allegedly lived in Albany, Piccadilly, though Hornung locates Albany incorrectly. Albany is*

often referred to as 'Paradise in Piccadilly.' For Raffles at Albany, see Harry Furniss, Paradise in Piccadilly *(1925), 163–71, published by John Lane, The Bodley Head, from Albany, whence a decade later he launched Penguin Books. Ernest William Hornung (1866–1921) was a journalist and prolific author. See 600, n. 4.*

23. M.C.C.] *Marylebone Cricket Club, then the ruling body of English and international cricket, responsible for the rules of the game and situated at Lord's Cricket Ground, the 'headquarters of cricket.' Membership is restricted.*

24. *This note originally read:* 'He does once contemplate murdering a blackmailer. It is, however, a fairly well established convention in crime stories that murdering a blackmailer "doesn't count." '

25. Arsène] Arsene *Pol. Compare n. 3 added in page proofs of CrE*

26. seem to point to definite necrophilia] centre round macabre practical jokes played with corpses *Hor;* display an extremely morbid interest in corpses *CrE. The Lord Peter Wimsey stories were written by Dorothy L. Sayers (1893–1957).*

27. that] *omitted in Hor*

28. ransom-money] ransom money *Hor*

29. Slim] Slim, *Hor, CrE*

30. skyscraper] sky-scraper *CrE*

31. is an impudent plagiarism] bears a very marked resemblance to *Hor, CrE; and see 2545. D. Streatfeild,* A Study of Two Worlds: Persephone, *1959, offers a psychological analysis of* No Orchids for Miss Blandish *(and refers also to* Animal Farm *and* Nineteen Eighty-Four*). He remarks, 'William Faulkner's* Sanctuary *was published in 1931, eight years earlier than* No Orchids, *and, unlike as the two works are in many respects, the parallels between them are striking' (35). There is a comment on Orwell's essay on* No Orchids *on 43.*

32. récit] recit *Pol;* récit *Hor*

33. language:] language; *CrE*

34. redhot] red-hot *Hor, CrE*

35. good-nature] good nature *Hor, CrE*

36. gobbling] gobbles *Hor*

37. vae victis] *væ victis Hor, CrE.* 'Woe to the vanquished.'

38. etc. etc.] etc., etc. *Pol. The omission of the comma was a typical Orwell form.*

39. in perhaps] perhaps in *Hor*

40. machine-guns] machine guns *Pol. The hyphenated form was used by Orwell.*

41. pornography] pornography, *Hor, CrE*

42. withdrawn] suppressed *Pol. Orwell regarded 'withdrawn' as a more accurate explanation: see headnote and 2545.*

43. Miss Callaghan comes to Grief] Lady, Don't Turn Over *Pol. Since the page proofs of the first impression of CrE have* Miss Callaghan comes to Grief, *this change must have been made in the setting copy for CrE. (Glinto's book-title should have a dash, not a comma, after* Lady.*)*

44. re-issued] reissued *Hor, CrE. Orwell favoured the hyphenated form.*

45. time] time, *Hor*

46. It too] It, too, *Hor*

47. DD&O *has* 'Lupin.' *Orwell annotated his copy of this edition giving the correct reading. For another reference to Orwell's annotations, see headnote to 'Rudyard Kipling,' 948.*

48. either] *omitted in Hor*

49. them,] them *CrE*

50. dictators.] *Hor and CrE run on to next paragraph.*

51. who kiss the arse of Stalin] who worship dictators *Hor. See headnote and 2550.*

52. the minority . . . nor from] *omitted in Hor. See headnote.*

53. admired:] admired, *CrE*

54. This idea colours the outlook . . . could come afterwards.] This idea colours the outlook of all sympathizers with totalitarianism in any of its forms. *Hor. See headnote.*

55. Popeye] Pop-eye *CrE*

56. Giant Killer] Giant-killer *CrE*

57. Dwarf Killer] Dwarf-killer *CrE*

58. play] Play *CrE*

59. don't] Don't *CrE*

60. it's] It's *CrE*
61. Today] To-day *CrE. Orwell regularly used the unhyphenated form.*
62. *Orchids*,] *Orchids Hor, CrE*

2539. To Leonard Moore

29 August 1944 Handwritten

Care of the "Tribune"

Dear Mr Moore,
I have just seen Warburg. He has definitely arranged to publish "Animal Farm" about March 1945, so perhaps you can get in touch with him about the contract. He is willing to pay an advance of £100, half of this to be paid about Christmas of this year.[1] I shall give him an option on all my future books, but this can be arranged in such a way as not to tie me down if for some special reason I want to take a book elsewhere. I have finished the final essay for the book of essays, & as soon as possible I will get the whole thing typed & send you a copy. Warburg presumably won't be able to do it till some time next year, but meanwhile we should make an attempt at an American edition. The Dial Press have asked to see this book & I more or less promised to send it to them.[2]

Yours sincerely
E. A. Blair

P.S. My address as from Sept. 1st will be

1 Canonbury Square[3]
Islington
London N.1

but I probably shan't move in there till Sept. 8th, so "Tribune" is the safest address for the time being.

1. Orwell's Payments Book shows that at an unspecified date he received £45 royalty from Secker & Warburg. This would be half £100 less 10% agent's commission.
2. Orwell's letter has been annotated, showing that Moore wrote to Secker & Warburg on 1 September. There is a note to telephone Secker's and to check 'Blair's last a/c.' There is also an annotation of Gollancz's royalty levels, the last part of which cannot be deciphered: 'Gollancz 10% 2,000 15% 3,000 20% [undecipherable].'
3. The figure one is unclear; Orwell's address was to be 27B Canonbury Square.

2540. Burma: Interview by G. B. Pittock-Buss

New Vision, 19, Autumn 1944[1]

One of the very few good things arising from modern war is the increase in geographical knowledge. This 'global' war has made us familiar with the names of many places of which we previously knew nothing. As a result of Japanese domination we have had to brush up our scanty knowledge of the East.

Three years ago, Burma sprang into the news as British Eastern possessions began to fall. The prime minister, a 'moderate' named U Saw, came to this country to plead for independence. His curious name made the headlines even if people failed to realise the political significance of his mission. When I asked George Orwell, well-known socialist writer, author of *Burmese Days* and formerly a police official in Burma, what he thought of U Saw and his country, he told me that although the prime minister transferred his attentions to the Japanese when he found the British were unwilling to declare Burma free, he was not among the most pro-Japanese element of the country. Just before the outbreak of war in the Far East he made (in London) a declaration that Burma would support the Allied cause, and earlier, when the Japanese occupied Indo-China, he had advocated that the British should occupy Siam. But he demanded Dominion status for Burma which corresponded to the wishes of his countrymen and was the least that any nationalist politician could demand. When this failed he probably made contact with the Japanese. Although an able man with a genuine popular following, he was of doubtful honesty, and in approaching the Japanese he may have been influenced by the belief that an Axis victory was inevitable. He was arrested and is still in internment in some unknown place.

Mr. Orwell told me that although the spirit of nationalism has always been strong in Burma, it has failed to a great degree to find adequate expression politically. From the time of the capture of Mandalay onwards there has been intermittently a spirit of resistance to British rule, which has sometimes expressed itself in outbreaks of violence. Much of this violence was inspired by a genuinely nationalist spirit and not by mere bands of terrorists.

When Burma was left out of the Montagu-Chelmsford reforms[2] there were strong protests throughout the land and it was at this stage that the modern nationalist parties began to grow. A reformed constitution was adopted in 1923, when a legislative council was introduced, 80 of its 103 members being elected on a limited property franchise. This franchise gave the vote to some two million people, about 23 per cent. of the population. A further change in the constitution took place in 1937, providing for a Senate and a House of Representatives, half the Senate being chosen by the Governor.

Normally Burma is a country with a reasonably good standard of living, Mr. Orwell told me. Extreme wealth and extreme poverty are seldom to be found, and, apart from the rich land around the Irrawaddy delta, much of the country is still owned by the peasants; either individually or communally. In the years before Burma was separated from India, however, there was great unrest and the collapse of rice prices caused serious agrarian problems. In 1930 rioting broke out and a real rebellion began against British rule. Fundamentally the causes were economic, but the nationalist element became increasingly strong.

The political demand for nationalism found its most active form in the Thakin movement, which, in turn, formed a youth section called the

Domba Asi Avon (We Burmans League). In the Thakin movement, as in other organisations, there was a tendency to regard anything anti-British with sympathy, and the result was that a section of the politically-conscious community tended to view Japan's imperial designs with favour. They considered that Burma's future would be brighter within Japan's sphere of influence than under the British, and they were prepared to assist, or at any rate not to hinder, Japan in its plans. Some of them may have been definitely pro-Japanese in sentiment: others imagined—wrongly of course, but such illusions are inevitable in a subject people—that they could use the Japanese to get rid of the British, and then somehow get rid of the Japanese.

However, as Mr. Orwell pointed out to me, this pro-Japanese aspect has been grossly exaggerated. In his estimation perhaps 10,000 Burmans were actively pro-Japanese, another 10,000 actively pro-British, and the rest apathetic to any form of alien rule. It is necessary to be careful to see that generalisations about the attitude of the Burmans are not allowed to sway public opinion when the Japanese have been expelled from the country.

I asked Mr. Orwell if he had any knowledge of conditions in Burma under Japanese rule. He pointed out that very little reliable information is available. One politician, Paw Tun, has escaped to India and is now the British puppet Burman statesman. Ba Maw, who was in prison for making seditious speeches when the Japanese over-ran Burma, was released by the British before they retreated and is now the Japanese puppet Burman statesman.

Mr. Orwell told me he is inclined to think the Burmans will have been cured of any partiality they may have felt for Japanese rule. Their standard of living must undoubtedly have declined as the Japanese economy will not have allowed for the import of the small luxuries which raised the average living standard before the war. It is not likely, however, that there has been any serious food problem. Even in dealing with this situation generalisations must be avoided. For example, war correspondents have spoken of the pro-British attitude of the villagers in the North West who have been liberated by Allied troops, or with whom the Allies have been in contact. But Burma is a country of many races. The tribes of the North and North West are traditionally pro-British, having been used to serving in the British armies for generations. On the whole they are at a lower stage of culture than the Burmese proper. Their attitude, therefore, cannot in any way be taken as representative of the whole country.

Indeed, despite distaste for Japanese rule, Mr. Orwell thinks that the Allied bombing of Burman towns as part of the offensive against the Japanese may well have turned the people even more strongly against the British. Politically, at least, this may have been a bad blunder. The effects of bombing in the all-wood Burman towns cannot be imagined by Europeans; a handful of incendiaries would turn a town into a blazing inferno and force thousands of innocent civilians to be burnt to death. The Burmans saw their towns and villages destroyed and their people killed and maimed by the Japanese; they cannot look kindly upon the process being repeated by the British as part of the struggle for 'liberation'.

The present war situation indicates that before long a full-scale assault will be launched against the Japanese in Burma. What will follow the expulsion of the Japanese troops? Inevitably there will be considerable chaos and robber bands will, for a time, seek to pillage the country. The inexperienced and often corrupt Burmese politicians will be unable to cope with the situation—if, indeed, they are given a chance—and the military administration, in Mr. Orwell's view, may well pave the way for a return to direct rule. This would be accompanied by an announcement that constitutional government would be restored when the situation was under control. Probably the promise will be made that Dominion status will be granted after a lapse of years. Unless a very definite and fairly short time limit is set, we may assume that 'direct rule' will continue indefinitely under the plea that Burma is not yet fit for self-government.

The British dare not offer any form of independence to Burma, because they know it would be accepted. Within the country they have no communal problems to play upon. The Burmese people, who constitute three-quarters of the population, are united in their national consciousness and their religion and the only possibility for an imperial government is to steer clear of any promises of self-determination. Had the Cripps proposals been extended to Burma, for example, they would have been accepted without hesitation. So the offer was not made.

British interests in Burma are extremely strong and Britain's precarious position in the post-war world indicates that the strongest possible control will be retained. It is essential to Burma's future as a free and independent nation that it should be in strong and friendly alliance with China and on good terms with India. Fortunately for the British, the Chinese are viewed with hatred and fear by many Burmans. The powerful economic position of the small Chinese community in Burma has already provoked riots and the new China's tendency towards imperialism has, not without some reason, given the Burmans cause for misgiving. The Indians are also extremely unpopular, partly because they lower the standard of living. If Burma is to develop as a free political entity, these barriers of distrust must be broken down.

The present British fancy for Eastern 'development' is the creation of a Southern Asiatic Federation, and when the impossibility of continuing to hold Burma by naked direct rule becomes apparent, this plan is likely to be pushed. Culturally such a federation is admirable, for there is considerable affinity between the people to be brought together, but strategically it would be helpless. Oddly enough, for its existence it would have to depend upon a major Western power, such as Britain.

The future of Burma, therefore, is not bright at the moment, but when the Japanese have been defeated it may be that the necessity of Sino-Burman and Indo-Burman co-operation may win through despite all the machinations of the imperialists.

1. It has not been possible to date when Orwell gave this interview or when this issue of *New Vision* appeared. The British Library date-stamp, 21 May 1945, is well after that for the Winter/

Spring 1945 issue (9 April 1945), which was announced in the Autumn issue as due for publication on 19 February. The Autumn issue mentions a debate in the House of Commons on 27 September 1944. It may have been published in December 1944. This interview is not logged in Orwell's Payments Book.

2. The Montagu-Chelmsford Report, 1918, prepared by Edwin Samuel Montagu, a Liberal MP and Secretary of State for India, 1917–22, and Lord Chelmsford, Viceroy of India, 1916–21, made recommendations for constitutional reform in India. These allowed for limited control by Indians of provincial affairs and were a step towards Indian self-government. Although in 1886 the British had made Burma a part of India (to the great distaste of the Burmans), they refused to apply the Montagu-Chelmsford reforms in Burma. This led to considerable unrest from 1920 until constitutional reforms were enacted in 1923. Orwell served in Burma when unrest was at its height.

2541. 'As I Please,' 40

Tribune, 1 September 1944

'As I Please,' 40, was prompted in the first place by the Warsaw Uprising (August to October 1944), and more particularly by the controversy that surrounded it and the response of the press and intellectuals. *Tribune* devoted an editorial on 11 August to analysing 'Who Deserted Warsaw?' Its argument centred on the failure of the Allies to supply arms to what might be termed people's armies, whether in Italy, France, or Poland, whilst willing enough to recognise the value of the efforts of such forces in aiding the Allied cause. The Allies, *Tribune* complained, thought it 'a mistake to divert any large quantities of arms in order to assist the civilian uprisings. They think only in terms of disciplined armies, of marching columns, of ordered attacks.' There were other dimensions to the controversy. The Polish government-in-exile, in London, was regarded by some of *Tribune*'s readers and correspondents as reactionary; it was argued that there was a tactical war between left and right to gain power in Poland after the war, and whilst that might well seem likely, what was less certain was whether either side was willing to sacrifice, coldheartedly and cynically, the 50,000-strong Warsaw Home Army under General Tadeusz Komorowski (known as 'Bor') to achieve political ends. Most crucial was the attitude of the Soviets. The Russian army, close in the last days of July 1944, had not then crossed the river separating their forces from Warsaw. At this moment, the Poles in Warsaw rose and took command of most of their city. Whether they were prompted to rise at that moment by the Russians was not known to those writing in the English press at the time. It did become clear that the Russian army held back. On 18 August 1944, *Tribune* included this information in its regular feature 'What's Happening.'

Stalin's Promise

More details of the battle inside Warsaw have now reached us. It would seem that the advancing spearhead of the Red Army reached the outer suburbs of Warsaw when it was counterattacked from the north by German Panzer Divisions rushed to the defence of Warsaw. This Russian force had no choice but to retire. In the meantime it is reported a Red Army liaison officer contacted the Partisans in the city and after surveying the situation sent urgent appeals for help to the Soviet Government. As a result of this Stalin has promised the Polish Premier that help would be sent to the fighting workingmen of Warsaw as soon as was humanly possible. Fighting is still going on, the people of Warsaw are still on their feet, and there is hope that they may yet be sustained in their great endeavour.

Meantime a controversy has broken out in this country about the nature of the rising. *The Daily Worker* first said that it was all imagination. Then correspondents have written to us to say that it was criminally provoked by the Poles in London to create a *fait accompli* when the Russians entered the city. Poles, on the other hand, say that the Russians deliberately paused before reaching Warsaw so as to let the non-Communist Poles stew in their own juice.

We can say now that this last charge is not true. The reason for the Soviet delay was in the first place military (the German counter-attack mentioned) due to a lamentable absence of co-ordination between the Polish Forces in Warsaw, the Soviet liaison officer and Marshal Rokossovsky. It would seem that General Bor, the Commander of the Poles in Warsaw, is to blame for this.

Moscow's Appeal to Warsaw

Finally, the charge that the rising was provoked by the London Government. This charge is incorrect in so far as the Polish Patriots in Moscow, also broadcast to the people of Warsaw to rise and fight. On July 29 the Union of Polish Patriots addressed the following appeal to Warsaw:

"Join battle with the Germans. This time for decisive action. Strike a mortal blow at the beast of Prussian militarism. The hour of action has arrived for Warsaw. Struggle in the streets, in the factories, the houses, the stores, and hasten the moment of final liberation."

This appeal was answered. It is no use for Communists or Liberals to say that the rising was premature. Risings cannot be set like stop-watches. Marx commented on the Paris Commune, that it was historically premature, but having broken out it was deserving of the fullest help. This is the position in Warsaw today; it may be that in a dozen other cities tomorrow. Europe is so near the brink that even the most general appeal to rise will be answered. Those who issue these appeals should be fully conscious of this responsibility.

On 1 September 1944, Orwell entered the controversy with 'As I Please,' 40.

It is not my primary job to discuss the details of contemporary politics, but this week there is something that cries out to be said. Since, it seems, nobody else will do so, I want to protest against the mean and cowardly attitude adopted by the British press towards the recent rising in Warsaw.

As soon as the news of the rising broke, the *News-Chronicle* and kindred papers adopted a markedly disapproving attitude. One was left with the general impression that the Poles deserved to have their bottoms smacked for doing what all the Allied wirelesses had been urging them to do for years past, and that they would not be given and did not deserve to be given any help from outside. A few papers tentatively suggested that arms and supplies might be dropped by the Anglo-Americans, a thousand miles away: no one, so far as I know, suggested that this might be done by the Russians, perhaps twenty miles away. The *New Statesman*, in its issue of August 18, even went so far as to doubt whether appreciable help could be given from the air in such circumstances. All or nearly all the papers of the Left were full of blame for the "*émigré*" London Government which had "prematurely" ordered its followers to rise when the Red Army was at the gates. This line of thought is adequately set forth in a letter to last week's *Tribune* from Mr. G. Barraclough. He makes the following specific charges:—

(1) The Warsaw rising was "not a spontaneous popular rising," but was "begun on orders from the soi-disant Polish Government in London."

(2) The order to rise was given "without consultation with either the British or Soviet Governments," and "no attempt was made to co-ordinate the rising with Allied action."

(3) The Polish resistance movement is no more united round the London Government than the Greek resistance movement is united round King George of the Hellenes. (This is further emphasised by frequent use of the words "*émigré*," "soi-disant," etc., applied to the London Government.)

(4) The London Government precipitated the rising in order to be in possession of Warsaw when the Russians arrived, because in that case "the bargaining position of the *émigré* Government would be improved." The London Government, we are told, "is ready to betray the Polish people's cause to bolster up its own tenure of precarious office," with much more to the same effect.

No shadow of proof is offered for any of these charges, though (1) and (2) are of a kind that could be verified and may well be true. My own guess is that (2) is true and (1) partly true. The third charge makes nonsense of the first two. If the London Government is not accepted by the mass of the people in Warsaw, why should they raise a desperate insurrection on its orders? By blaming Sosnokowski and the rest for the rising, you are automatically assuming that it is to them that the Polish people looks for guidance. This obvious contradiction has been repeated in paper after paper, without, so far as I know, a single person having the honesty to point it out. As for the use of such expressions as "*émigré*," it is simply a rhetorical trick. If the London Poles are *émigrés*, so are the Polish National Committee of Liberation, besides the "free" Governments of all the occupied countries. Why does one become an *émigré* by emigrating to London and not by emigrating to Moscow?

Charge No. (4) is morally on a par with the *Osservatore Romano's* suggestion that the Russians held up their attack on Warsaw in order to get as many Polish resisters as possible killed off. It is the unproved and unprovable assertion of a mere propagandist who has no wish to establish the truth, but is simply out to do as much dirt on his opponent as possible. And all that I have read about this matter in the press—except for some very obscure papers and some remarks in *Tribune*, the *Economist* and the *Evening Standard*—is on the same level as Mr. Barraclough's letter.

Now, I know nothing of Polish affairs and even if I had the power to do so I would not intervene in the struggle between the London Polish Government and the Moscow National Committee of Liberation. What I am concerned with is the attitude of the British intelligentsia, who cannot raise between them one single voice to question what they believe to be Russian policy, no matter what turn it takes, and in this case have had the unheard-of meanness to hint that our bombers ought not to be sent to the aid of our comrades fighting in Warsaw. The enormous majority of Left-wingers who swallow the policy put out by the *News-Chronicle*, etc., know no more about Poland than I do. All they know is that the Russians object to the London Government and have set up a rival organisation, and so far as they are concerned that settles the matter. If tomorrow Stalin were to drop the Committee of Liberation and recognise the London Government, the whole British intelligentsia would flock after him like a troop of parrots. Their attitude towards Russian foreign policy is not "Is this policy right or wrong?" but "This is Russian policy: how can we make it appear right?" And this attitude is defended, if at all, solely on grounds of power. The Russians are powerful in Eastern Europe, we are not: therefore we must not oppose them. This involves the principle, of its nature alien to Socialism, that you must not protest against an evil which you cannot prevent.

I cannot discuss here why it is that the British intelligentsia, with few exceptions, have developed a nationalistic loyalty towards the U.S.S.R. and are dishonestly uncritical of its policies. In any case, I have discussed it elsewhere. But I would like to close with two considerations which are worth thinking over.

First of all, a message to English Left-wing journalists and intellectuals generally. "Do remember that dishonesty and cowardice always have to be paid for. Don't imagine that for years on end you can make yourself the boot-licking propagandist of the Soviet regime, or any other regime, and then suddenly return to mental decency. Once a whore, always a whore."

Secondly, a wider consideration. Nothing is more important in the world today than Anglo-Russian friendship and co-operation, and that will not be attained without plain speaking. The best way to come to an agreement with a foreign nation is *not* to refrain from criticising its policies, even to the extent of leaving your own people in the dark about them. At present, so slavish is the attitude of nearly the whole British press that ordinary people have very little idea of what is happening, and may well be committed to policies which they will repudiate in five years' time. In a shadowy sort of way we have been told that the Russian peace terms are a super-Versailles, with partition of Germany, astronomical reparations, and forced labour on a huge scale. These proposals go practically uncriticised, while in much of the Left-wing press hack-writers are even hired to extol them. The result is that the average man has no notion of the enormity of what is proposed. I don't know whether, when the time comes, the Russians will really want to put such terms into operation. My guess is that they won't. But what I do know is that if any such thing were done, the British and probably the American public would never support it when the passion of war had died down. Any flagrantly unjust peace settlement will simply have the result, as it did last time, of making the

British people unreasonably sympathetic with the victims. Anglo-Russian friendship depends upon there being a policy which both countries can agree upon, and this is impossible without free discussion and genuine criticism *now*. There can be no real alliance on the basis of "Stalin is always right." The first step towards a real alliance is the dropping of illusions.

Finally, a word to the people who will write me letters about this. May I once again draw attention to the title of this column and remind everyone that the Editors of *Tribune* are not necessarily in agreement with all that I say, but are putting into practice their belief in freedom of speech?

[NOTE.—This column was written some days before the appearance of Vernon Bartlett's article in the *News Chronicle* of August 29, which gives at any rate a hint of disagreement with the policy prevailing throughout the press.]

On the same day that Orwell's 'As I Please,' 40, appeared—1 September 1944—*Tribune* published, in 'What's Happening,' another comment on the situation in Warsaw, and Lucjan Blit, a Socialist member of the Warsaw City Council, then resident in Edgware, North London, wrote at length on who had deserted Warsaw.

Soviets and Warsaw
Last Wednesday, for the first time since June, 1941, Soviet policy had a bad Press in London. This followed the announcement that the Soviet authorities had refused facilities for Allied planes based in the West to fly supplies to Warsaw and bomb German targets in the city, and then land and re-fuel on Soviet territory. This was further aggravated by broadcasts from Warsaw that the Soviet authorities are arresting and imprisoning officers and men of the Polish "Home Army" who refuse to accept the Moscow Polish Committee and enter its armed forces. At the same time, the newly liberated Poles in Eastern Poland, who have survived the five years German rule, are being called up by the new Polish authorities and often sent to distant parts within a few days of liberation. This treatment meted out to an Ally stands in striking contrast to the generous and correct attitude adopted by the Soviets to their enemies of yesterday in Rumania and also towards Finland.

It is therefore no explanation to suggest, as does the *Daily Worker*, that this public concern expressed now by all sections of British opinion is based on nothing more than sinister anti-Soviet intrigues. It is no help to the Soviets to suggest this. Public feeling goes much deeper. The battle of Warsaw, the tremendous though isolated resistance now in its fifth week at the end of five years of war, with liberation so near, has deeply touched public sentiment.

Polish Home Army
Nor is that all. The announcement which was made by the British and American Governments recognising the Polish Home Army as part of the Polish Army in this country was clearly intended to give protection against vicious German reprisals. But it was more than that. It was revealed in

London on Tuesday that the Polish Committee in Moscow (clearly not without consent from the Soviet authorities) had dropped leaflets in Warsaw threatening punishment and execution of the men they described as the guilty leaders of the uprising.

The British recognition of the Polish Home Army challenges this extraordinary step taken by Moscow, and it is no use blinking at the fact that there is now a strong difference of opinion between London and Washington on the one side and Moscow on the other. The more clearly Moscow understands that this is not a case of a small anti-Soviet clique taking a stand, but that it represents the great majority of public opinion in this country, the speedier a settlement will be carried about.° It is not the first time that Stalin has revised a policy which had been driven beyond the limit by hotheads inside the Soviet administration.

All the same, it is also clear that anti-Soviet elements in America and in this country will utilise this genuine public feeling to further their anti-Soviet plans. Similarly there are reactionary Poles who do not possess the decency to shrink from using the crisis in Warsaw for their own ends by issuing appeals not only for Warsaw from its radio station, but also for a Polish Vilna and Polish Lwow. Poles ought to be clear about this. So long as they are concerned with the genuine relief of Warsaw's terrible plight they have the whole of Western opinion behind them, but the moment they permit reactionary elements to exploit this sentiment for their own anti-Soviet ends they will lose most of this support in Europe and America.

Lucjan Blit wrote:

Who Deserted Warsaw?

I should like to express my complete agreement with Mr. G. Barraclough's statement in his letter published in *Tribune* of August 25, saying that the question, "Who Deserted Warsaw?" "once raised, cannot be ignored."

Never before has the Polish Government in London been given such moral and political support in *Tribune* as in Mr. Barraclough's letter, which states categorically that the rising of the people of Warsaw, which has already lasted for a month, is no "spontaneous popular rising," but "began on orders from the soi-disant Polish Government in London." Even the most uncritical supporters of this Government did not go as far as that in stressing the influence of this Government on the events inside Poland.

But I am not particularly interested in criticism levelled against the Polish Government in London. I myself belong to a party which, while recognising the legality of this Government, retains a critical attitude towards it, because, side by side with Socialist and Peasant Party representatives, it includes certain reactionary elements. But that seems to be the fate of all wartime coalition Governments.

However, from the Socialist point of view, I cannot find an excuse for those who have created a common front against the fighters of the Warsaw barricades.

When I was still on the territory of the Soviet Union (until August, 1942), I heard again and again appeals sent by a radio station situated somewhere on the Volga and calling on the people of Poland to start an armed rising on Polish soil against the Nazi invader. At that time Soviet troops were about 800 miles away from those people and that soil, and were engaged in hard fighting against the then victorious hordes of the invader.

But on July 30, 1944, the victorious Soviet armies were only a few miles from Warsaw. Once again there were appeals for a rising. Mr. Barraclough and others think that, in spite of all this, the Poles should not have started the rising, that they should have conducted some diplomatic negotiations, that they should have waited "until the Russian forces had advanced in strength beyond the Vistula." But Warsaw lies on both sides of the Vistula. And if her people were to rise at all they could not have waited until the Russians were "beyond it."

I do not know who gave the order to rise. But I do know who forms the overwhelming majority of those fighting for the freedom of my city. It is the Socialist workers from Wola, Powisle and Zoliborz.[1] It is my comrades from the Smocza Street, who have survived the massacre of the Ghetto. For 60 years every generation of Warsaw workers has shed its blood on the barricades. In the course of this war they have fought alone three times. Several times they were told to wait. But not for once did they listen to voices of opportunists. Now they fight again, fully and tragically aware of their being left alone.

A few miles away there is a powerful Allied army. In spite of several appeals the people of Warsaw did not receive any help from them, neither material nor even moral. On the contrary. The assistance sent to them by the Western Allies has been insignificant—rather symbolic than anything else.

Cynicism is an almost automatic product of every decaying system. It was rampant in the ancient Roman Empire and in France before the Great Revolution. The cynicism of a "less ideological war" is supposed to pave the way for a victory of reaction in a deadly tired Europe.

The wave of cynicism did not reach those fighting in Warsaw, Paris or Milan. That is why they are able to fight. What is the future and the hope for us all if people calling themselves progressive and Socialist, when having to choose between fighters for freedom and the cynicism of the diplomacy of the strong choose the latter?

A lengthy correspondence followed and, despite the pressure on space, *Tribune* gave it full vent. Orwell's attitude was discussed and so was the attitude of the Soviet Union. On 8 September, the following four letters were published.

I suppose the reason "British intelligentsia have developed a nationalistic loyalty towards the U.S.S.R." is that the U.S.S.R. is the one organisation that has been founded, developed and preserved wholly by intelligence. Arthur Koestler, in *Darkness at Noon*, says of the leaders of the revolution:

"Each one knew more about the philosophy of law, political economy and statesmanship than all the high-lights in the professorial chairs of the universities of Europe. The discussions at the congress during the Civil War had been on a level never before in history attained by a political body."

I do not know which of the panaceas for human ills Mr. Orwell prefers, the liberalism, social democracy or plutodemocracy that between them made ready in Italy for Mussolini, in Austria for Dolfuss, in Spain for Franco, in Germany for Hitler, in France for the fall of France, and in this country avoided the same function only by combining into a near-totalitarian regime; but if I were a member of the "British intelligentsia" I would think twice before committing myself to any of them. I would rather be a whore in the house of reality than a housemaid to ghosts.

John Armstrong

As a long-standing reader and supporter of the *Tribune* and its policy I must confess that I am greatly perturbed at the attitude you are adopting over the recent uprising in Warsaw, an attitude which I cannot too strongly condemn. I am sure that when the military history of this war is written these events within Warsaw will be seen to have little or no significance. Their political implications may have profound and disastrous results for the future of mankind.

In regard to your reference that for the first time since 1941 Soviet policy had a bad press in London, my mind immediately recalls two previous occasions (not to mention the Zinoviev Letter, the first and second Trotskyist trials, hypothetical religious persecutions, the rancid butter infamy, *ad infinitum*), namely, the occupation of Eastern Poland and the Finnish war, when the Capitalist Press and its satellites endeavoured, by the utmost nonsense, to split the British working class movements, and involve us in a war with the Soviet Union.

Only a knave or a fool, or a Tory lunatic, would deny that on these two occasions the strategy of the Supreme Command of the Red Army and the foreign policy of the Kremlin were correct. Therefore, the point we must always remember, in relation to Press campaigns in this country against the Soviet Union, is that there is a dangerous motive behind them. The only time for us to be wary of Soviet foreign policy is when it is most loudly praised by the *Catholic Herald*, the *Daily Sketch* and the *Telegraph*. In any case it would be beneath my political and scientific dignity to ally myself with the stinking politics and propaganda of the Vatican.

Our first duty to the working classes of all countries, in view of the classic example of recent events in Italy, is to ensure that at all costs Socialism achieves victory over Capitalism. The nearness of British and American and Russian armies to German territory makes this task more vital and imminent. I feel sure that, along with myself, you would be one of the last persons consciously to assist those elements in this country and in America whose one desire is to bring about the destruction of the Soviet Union. I would point out that at this critical stage of the present world crisis there can be no middle course. Those who are not with the Soviets are against them. From at least a scientific viewpoint I am convinced that future peace is indissolubly linked with the Soviet Union. In any case, I feel sure that no Socialist can ally himself with the new and omnipotent mythology, "Browderism,"[2] leaving Socialism to some new sort of evolution, and convince himself that neo-Fascist states and the U.S.S.R. can now live peacefully together for the rest of time.

If it is at all necessary, and I personally do not feel it is, to answer the charge that the Soviet Union has deserted the Polish patriots within Warsaw, the supporters of the reactionary Polish Government in London, such as Mr. Blit and Mr. Orwell, would do well to consider the following points:

1. The charge that the Soviet authorities had refused facilities for allied planes, based in the west, to fly supplies to Warsaw and bomb German targets in the city on a shuttle service has since been denied by the British and American authorities, *vide* the *Times*. In any case, has it occurred to anyone, including Mr. Blit, that this would be a military impossibility?

2. If anyone deserted the workers at the barricades at Warsaw it was those officials who, in 1939, loudly declaring that the defence of Warsaw would be more epic than the defence of Madrid, five days later left those same workers at the barricades to their fate.

3. Who but a military adventurer or a political knave would give an order for a revolt without first ensuring that (a) his followers were sufficiently equipped in arms and supplies; (b) the revolt was timed to coincide with grand strategy?

4. The general strategy of the Red Army Supreme Command is the destruction of the Wehrmacht. As it was demonstrated by the late General Vatutin at Kiev that frontal assault on river cities is a military blunder,[3] I see no reason why an exception should be made of Warsaw. Only a military nincompoop would, therefore, have given the order for an uprising until the city had been outflanked, when the Red Army rear and front assault would have taken place.

5. The Supreme Command of the Red Army had undoubtedly made its plans for the present summer campaign by not later than October of last year. Since there was no trustworthy Polish government in existence at that time the present uprising in Warsaw or, indeed, in any part of Poland could not have been considered as a military possibility.

C. A. Aplin, B.Sc., F.R.S.G.

George Orwell's experiences in the Spanish war, in which he served in a "Trotskyite" formation, seem to have roused in him a pathological hatred not only of the U.S.S.R. but of all the Left-wing intellectuals who do not share his opinions.

In the course of a sort of papal encyclical, arrogantly addressed "to English Left-wing journalists and intellectuals *generally*," he exhorts us to "remember that dishonesty and cowardice always have to be paid for. Don't imagine that for years on end you can make yourself the boot-licking propagandist of the Soviet régime, or any other régime, and then suddenly return to mental decency. Once a whore, always a whore."

Apart from two or three independent dailies and one Sunday paper, the "Left-wing Press" in this country means, for practical purposes, the *New Statesman, Tribune* and the *Daily Worker*. If we omit *Tribune* and discount the *Daily Worker*, which Mr. Orwell would probably regard as prostituted to Moscow, it only leaves the *New Statesman* as a possible field for those "hack-writers," hired to extol Russian policies at the expense of their honour, to whom he refers.

It happens that the *New Statesman*, whose chastity I have hitherto considered above suspicion, deals editorially in last week's issue with the Warsaw tragedy and also prints a long cable from its correspondent in Poland. The leader gives an impartial résumé of the most authoritative information at present available, while the message cabled from Lublin contains a full report of the interview which British and American correspondents have had with Morawski, General Rola-Zymierski and other members of the Polish Committee of Liberation. As both these statements contradict Mr. Orwell's unfounded assertions, the hired "hack-writers" responsible for them must be, by his definition, cowardly boot-licking whores, guilty of what he describes as "unheard of meanness."

Evidently my old-fashioned ideas of what constitutes "mental decency" conflict with Mr. Orwell's. I consider his article a disgrace to the profession he has so recently condescended to join and an insult to readers of *Tribune*.

As for nearly 30 years I have had the honour to belong to the group of writers to whom his "message" is addressed, I should like to add a word of warning to any beginners who may be taken in by his exposure of our venality. If they want to sell their virtue profitably they should turn not Left but Right. It is Catholic Fascist boot-licking and Anti-Soviet propaganda that produce the big money—and the Mayfair invitations to meet Foreign Office high-ups and fascinating Polish Counts.

Douglas Goldring[4]

I would say that Mr. Orwell was not justified in including the *New Statesman and Nation* among the papers which he suggested licked the boots of Moscow. The *New Statesman and Nation* has repeatedly said that it regards friendship with the U.S.S.R. as a most important single object of international policy after the war, but that it believes that this object will not be best attained by sycophancy. On the contrary, it believes that we should do well to state our genuine differences and that we win respect in Moscow by doing so. Only agreements based on common understanding will last. If we accept settlements in fear of causing offence without genuinely approving of them the only result will be their repudiation at a later date with disastrous consequences to our relations with Russia.

We have urged the importance of a Soviet-British alliance throughout the pre-war years and also have been strongly critical of the U.S.S.R. on many occasions. Without going back into past history, we recall recently the *New Statesman and Nation* was attacked by *Isvestia*° for discussing development on Federal lines in South-Eastern Europe, and we believe that the subsequent discussion had good results in clearing up the misunderstanding. Again, the *New Statesman and Nation* stated strong disagreement with the policy, said to be sponsored by the U.S.S.R., of "compensating" Poland with large tracts of purely German territory.

Kingsley Martin,
Editor, New Statesman and Nation[5]

Two more letters were published in *Tribune* on 15 September:

I read the letter in *Tribune* of September 8 from my namesake, C. A. Aplin, with mixed feelings. Pleasure at finding myself not to be the only representative of the Clan Aplin within the Left was sadly marred when I read what my distant relative (as I suppose him to be) had to say!

For the sake of clarity, let us first clear up the points which are not at issue, at any rate so far as the Left is concerned:

1. The Sosnokowski clique and its political allies represent all that is reactionary within contemporary Polish life. They are the heirs to the violently anti-Socialist, anti-Soviet, pro-Fascist forces that ruled Poland for so many years up to the outbreak of war;

2. The Polish "Government" in London bases its legal claim to represent the Polish people on a constitution that was, in effect, forced on the Polish people in what has now become the classical Fascist method;

3. On the other hand, the same "Government" is formed of representatives of all the major parties in Poland with, as far as one can judge from the reports we are allowed to receive, the endorsement of the Parties' membership in Poland. The exception to this is the Communist Party whose strength it is difficult to determine. (I am not concerned here with views on the desirability of such a Coalition, though my own views are emphatically opposed to the principles involved.)

4. The Warsaw rising was primarily the responsibility of Sosnokowski with the backing of the London "Government." On the other hand, whether it was "Routine propaganda" or not, the fact remains that Soviet Union radio stations called upon Polish workers and peasants to rise in revolt and therefore strengthened the call to rise issued from London. I think it will be generally agreed that the rising must have consisted in large measure of Warsaw workers who belonged to one or other sections of the Left;

5. How far the British and American Governments are involved in the call to rise is difficult to determine. But these two Imperialist Governments attempted to send some help, and I find it hard to believe that they would not have preferred to send their 'planes from nearby Soviet bases than to have to send them on the suicidal route that was chosen. If that much is conceded, then it must be conceded, too, that those Governments would have approached the Soviet Government for permission to use such bases.

Now for some points on which there is probably disagreement as between those who believe that the Soviet Union is something sacred and not to be criticised, and those who believe that critical discussion is the only way to secure clarity. (It is so easy to use a facile phrase such as Mr. C. A. Aplin's "Those who are not with the Soviets are against them"; one of the difficulties is to render oneself sufficiently malleable to keep attuned. For instance, when "Soviet foreign policy" (again quoting my namesake) "is most loudly praised by the *Catholic Herald*, the *Daily Sketch* and the *Telegraph*," should we be with or against?) However, to return to the points at issue:

1. The Polish masses, Jewish and Gentile, are traditionally and understandably anti-*Russian*, though not necessarily anti-Soviet. This was understood by Lenin and an appreciation of the necessity to break down this barrier would be a help today;

2. In this war the Polish masses have suffered more than any other national group. The overwhelming proportion of this suffering came from the Germans; some came from the Soviet forces, and military necessity is poor comfort to sufferers;

3. The Warsaw rising could not have held out so long without the support of the masses. Some form of assistance from the Soviets, or even from Soviet soil, would have done much to allay anti-*Russian* feeling; failure inevitably intensified that feeling and strengthened the anti-*Soviet* propaganda of the reactionaries;

4. When "routine propaganda" incessantly calls for a rising, when a supposedly liberating army is not far away, when hell has reigned for five years in a great city, and when finally the accepted leadership calls for a rising, are the masses enclosed in that city and without means to find out the nicer points of Soviet strategy and tactics supposed to be able to judge whether the time is ripe, whether their city has been out-flanked? And if some of the responsibility is on the shoulders of a military "nincompoop," does that justify sacrificing those masses to their death without so much as a gesture from their Socialist comrades, Russian or otherwise? It appears to me that every Internationalist Socialist should, rather, remember with regret the all [but?] inadequate help that continued to go to the Spanish workers when their battle was obviously lost and resolve to exploit every means to help those magnificent working-class fighters of Warsaw;

5. It is significant that, according to reports, the Socialists in the London "Government" are moving into an open anti-Soviet position and that the President-designate, lately arrived from the struggle in Poland, is also reported to hold the same views. I know little of those "Socialists"; they may be of the same calibre as the "Socialists" in the British War Cabinet and may therefore be of little use in the Socialist regeneration of their country. Or they may be sound men who are being driven into intransigeance. What matters, either way, is that this crisis is building up bitter opposition to the Soviet Union among its neighbours. That is scarcely the road leading to Socialist Internationalism.

There is much more one would like to say, but *Tribune* has to work to

Paper Control limits! May I add as a personal footnote that I left the I.L.P. after some 20 years' membership because I found myself in violent disagreement with their war policy following the Nazi attack on the Soviet Union.

John Aplin

In your last issue John Armstrong, in defence of Russian policy, quotes from my novel, "Darkness at Noon," a passage extolling the virtues of the old Bolshevik Guard. Mr. Armstrong, an excellent painter and political nitwit, seems not to have realised that the theme of the book he quotes is the liquidation of that old guard by Russia's present rulers, and that praise of the victim aggravates the charge against the killer.

I don't believe in polemics in correspondence columns, but as I have been quoted in defence of the Russian attitude towards the Warsaw maquis, you will permit me to say that I consider it as one of the major infamies of this war which, though committed by different methods, will rank for the future historian on the same ethical level with Lidice.[6]

Arthur Koestler

On 22 September, two last letters were published:

It is a pity that Mr. [C. A.] Armstrong, Mr. Aplin and Mr. Goldring did not feel themselves able to comment on Orwell's article without talking about "George Orwell's experiences in the Spanish war, in which he served in a 'Trotskyite' formation," and "the supporters of the reactionary Polish Government in London, such as . . . Mr. Orwell," and "I do not know which of the panaceas for human ills Mr. Orwell prefers." Your correspondents are all using, consciously or unconsciously, a technique by which Orwell's remarks are discredited in advance. Orwell is obviously not a supporter of the London Polish Government, and whatever "panacea" he may prefer is nothing to do with his article.

These letters express that admiration for Stalin's policy and tactics which is shared equally by Left intellectuals and Churchill; only Mr. Aplin, who clouds his letter with a mass of irrelevancies (e.g., "In regard to your reference that for the first time since 1941 Soviet policy had a bad press . . . my mind immediately recalls" no fewer than six occasions *before* 1941 when the U.S.S.R. had a bad press) makes direct reference to the subject of Orwell's article. Mr. Armstrong admires the "reality" of the U.S.S.R., which, he says (and he gives the high authority of a remark in a novel for it) has been "preserved wholly by intelligence." But what can be more "real" than Nazism and who is more "intelligent" than Goebbels? Mr. Goldring must be aware that in view of the strict Soviet censorship, reports on hand-outs given by the Polish Committee of National Liberation must be viewed with some reserve; and why does he leave out of consideration in his letter the "two or three independent dailies and one Sunday paper" which he characterises as Left-wing? When it is obviously those papers that Orwell was writing about?

I do not wish to associate myself with Orwell's attitude to the Warsaw tragedy: I wish only to stress the sterility of this "Those who are not with the Soviets are against them" attitude, which is used by all your correspondents except Mr. Kingsley Martin in discussing this matter. The intellectual has a right (and indeed a duty) to make such observations when he feels them necessary; and they are not answered simply by using the cat-calls of "Trotskyite" or "reactionary."

Julian Symons[7]

May I congratulate Mr. Orwell and Mr. Service on their comments on the Polish-Soviet question in a recent *Tribune*. What a relief to find one English paper which has sufficient guts to stand up to ill-informed public opinion. The British Press seems to have returned to a pre-Munich outlook. Then, no one dared criticise the Germans. Now it is the Russians who must not be criticised.

The *New Statesman* recently compared the Polish Government to that of Vichy. What an incredible insult to a government which, for five years, has organised and controlled a superb Underground Movement, working actively against the Germans.

They have tremendous faith in us. I pray God we may not betray their confidence. We will never do this if we remain true to the moral principles which are the basis of Socialism.

Bryan Matheson

Liddell Hart argues that perhaps the Soviet government did not want to see the Poles take the lead in freeing their capital from the Germans, and so become inspired to adopt a more independent attitude. On the other hand, he says, there was 'a remarkable German rally' at the beginning of August and 'the much wider extent of the Russian check at this time indicates that military factors could well have been more decisive than political considerations' (*History of the Second World War*, 610–11; U.S.: 583). What may undermine that conclusion is the fact (given by Liddell Hart in a footnote) that Russia refused 'to allow American bombers from Western Europe to land on Soviet airfields after dropping supplies to the Poles in Warsaw.' In order to provide limited assistance to the Poles, 'British and Polish pilots flew from Italy and back on such missions, but at such extreme range their efforts, courageous though they were, could hardly affect the issue' (611; U.S.: 583). As the verbal conflict raged in London, based on partial information, the Polish Home Army fought a bitter and bloody battle unavailingly. Tens of thousands were killed; after nine weeks, the remnants surrendered on 2 October 1944. It was not until 17 January 1945 that the Soviets and the Polish First Army re-entered Warsaw. By then the Germans had deported about 600,000 people—almost the whole population—to concentration camps.

1. Powísle is a district of central Warsaw adjacent to the Old City and fronting the river Vistula; Wola and Zoliborz are two of the seven districts into which Warsaw is divided.
2. After Earl Russell Browder (1891–1973), General Secretary of the U.S. Communist Party, 1930–45. When, in 1936, the Department of State refused to join a diplomatic mediation initiative to end the Spanish civil war, he said, 'Let us ask Jefferson where he stands on this issue!' a question still posed from time to time, as it was at the Democratic Convention in New

York in 1992. Browder was the Communist Party candidate for President of the United States in 1936 and 1940, but his policies led to his being expelled from the party in 1946.

3. The Russian generals Vatutin, Koniev, and Rokossovsky launched an attack on the Dnieper front in the late summer of 1943. By the end of September they had reached the river from Dnepropetrovsk in the south, and beyond Kiev to the north towards the Pripet. According to Liddell Hart, 'crossings were quickly made at a wide range of points, and bridgeheads established. . . . The ease with which crossings had been gained by the Russians was helped by their commanders' skill and boldness in exploiting the potentialities of space.' Koniev made crossings at many places simultaneously instead of concentrating efforts at Kremenchug, and 'similar methods enabled Vatutin to gain a series of footholds north of Kiev that were subsequently linked up' (515; U.S.: 493). Kiev fell to Vatutin on 6 November 1943.

4. Douglas Goldring (1887–1960), journalist, editor, university teacher, 1925–27, critic, and novelist. In his notes about fellow-travellers, Orwell showed how little respect he had for Goldring, describing him as probably venal; and note Goldring's reference to Orwell's 'exposure of our venality.' See 3732.

5. It is just possible that Kingsley Martin's protest took a more formal turn: see Orwell's letter to Dwight Macdonald, 15 October 1946, 3097, n. 3.

6. The Czech village of Lidice was 'removed from the map' and its population shot or moved to concentration camps (where most died) in revenge for the assassination of Reinhard Heydrich, Reich "Protector" in Czechoslovakia. See also Orwell's War-time Diary, 11.6.42, 1218 and 1218, n. 1, and his Weekly News Review, 13 June 1942, 1219.

7. Julian Symons (1912–1994) poet, novelist, and critic, and later a distinguished crime writer, became one of Orwell's friends. See 913, n. 5.

2542. Review of *Selections from the Works of Gerrard Winstanley*, edited by Leonard Hamilton, with an Introduction by Christopher Hill

The Observer, 3 September 1944

Every successful revolution has its June Purge. A moment always comes when the party which has seized power crushes its own Left Wing and then proceeds to disappoint the hopes with which the revolution started out. The dictators of the past, however, lacked modern thoroughness in silencing their opponents, and the defeated minorities of one revolution after another have left behind residues of thought which have gradually coalesced into the modern Socialist movement. Even the poor, humble English Diggers, as these pamphlets show, were able in their few years of activity to disseminate ideas which may have contributed to Spanish Anarchism and may even have remotely influenced such thinkers as Gandhi.

Winstanley, who it seems was not the originator of the Digger movement but was its chief publicist, was born in Wigan in 1609 and was for a while a cloth merchant in London. He was ruined by the Civil War. In 1649 he and twenty or thirty others took over and began cultivating some waste land on St. George's Hill, near Cobham, forming themselves into a self-supporting community on what would now be called Communist-Anarchist lines. In this community there was to be no money, no trade, no inequality, no idle persons, no priests, and as far as possible no law. As Winstanley saw it, the land of England had once belonged to the common people and had been unjustly taken from them, and the best way to get it back was for bodies of landless men to form colonies which would act as an example to the mass of the nation. At the beginning he was simple enough to imagine that even the landlords could ultimately be won over to the Anarchist programme. But ideas similar to his own were evidently widespread, as other colonies of Diggers were started in various parts of the country at about the same time.

Needless to say, the Diggers were swiftly crushed. The parvenu gentry who had won the civil war were willing enough to divide the lands of the Royalists among themselves, but they had no intention of setting up an egalitarian society, and they saw the danger of allowing such experiments as Winstanley's to succeed. The Diggers were beaten up, their crops were trampled on, their stock was taken away from them by means of law suits in which packed juries imposed impossible damages. Troops of soldiers sent to deal with them tended to be sympathetic—this was the period of the revolt of the Levellers in the army—but the gentry won and the Digger movement was effectively finished by 1652. Winstanley vanishes from history about 1660.

It is clear from these pamphlets that, though a visionary, Winstanley was by no means a fool. He did not expect his ideas to be accepted immediately, and he was ready to modify them at need. After his experiment had failed he submitted to Cromwell a quite detailed and practical programme from which the earlier extravagances had been eliminated. This makes provision for laws, magistrates and foreign trade, even, in spite of his pacifist tinge, for a standing army and the death penalty for certain offences. But the central idea is still the same—a society founded on brotherhood and co-operation, with no profit-making, and, for internal purposes, no money. "Everyone shall put to their hands to till the earth and bring up cattle, and the blessing of the earth shall be common to all; when a man hath need of any corn or cattle, take from the next store-house he meets with *Acts, iv, 32.*"

Winstanley's thought links up with Anarchism rather than Socialism because he thinks in terms of a purely agricultural community living at a low level of comfort, lower than was even then strictly necessary. Not foreseeing the machine, he states that a man cannot be rich except by exploiting others, but it is evident that, like Mr. Gandhi, he also values simplicity for its own sake. Moreover, he clings to a belief which seems to haunt all thinkers of the Anarchist type—the belief that the wished-for Utopia has already existed in the past. The land did once belong to the common people, but has been taken away from them. According to Winstanley, this happened at the Norman Conquest, which in his eyes is the cardinal fact in English history. The essential struggle is the struggle of the Saxon common people against the Frenchified upper class. In every pamphlet, almost in every paragraph, he refers to the defeated Royalists as "Normans." But alas! he could see only too clearly that the victors of the civil war were themselves developing "Norman" characteristics:

"And you zealous preachers and professors of the City of London, and you great officers and soldiery of the army, where are all your victories over the Cavaliers, that you made such a blaze in the land, in giving God thanks for, and which you begged in your fasting days and morning exercises? Are they all sunk into the Norman power again, and must the old prerogative laws stand? What freedom did you then give thanks for? Surely that you had killed him that rode upon you, that you may get up into his saddle to ride upon others. Oh, thou City, thou hypocritical City! Thou blindfold, drowsy England, that sleeps and snorts in the bed of covetousness, awake, awake! The enemy is upon thy back, he is ready to scale the walls and enter possession, and wilt not look out?"

If only our modern Trotskyists and Anarchists—who in effect are saying the same thing—could write prose like that! This is not a book that can be read through at one sitting, but it is a book to buy and keep. Mr. Hill's short introduction is useful and interesting.

[Fee: £10.0.0; 31.8.44]

In *The New Leader* for 16 September 1944, Reg Groves[1] discussed Winstanley and the way he had been reviewed, especially by Orwell.

The newly-published "Selections from the Works of Gerrard Winstanley" has, on the whole, had a respectful press—respectful but puzzled. Like mourners at the funeral of a stranger, the commentators take off their hats but stand by uncomfortably not quite sure what to say. And among them is Mr. George Orwell, who, trying to find a kindly thing to say, decides, it seems, that though Winstanley lived in the seventeenth century he can get respect in the twentieth century only by wearing one of our party labels.

    Winstanley's thought, wrote Orwell, in his able, lively review in the "Sunday Observer," *links up with Anarchism rather than Socialism because he thinks in terms of a purely agricultural community living at a low level of comfort, lower than was even then strictly necessary. Not foreseeing the machine he states that a man cannot be rich except by exploiting others.* . . . To classify Winstanley an "Anarchist" is, even on historical grounds, wrong. Long after the introduction of machinery the English socialist movement sought the way to a better social order by founding agricultural communities, so that Winstanley is neither peculiar nor Anarchist because he tried to do the same thing. Indeed the one consistent belief in all the English rebel movements has been that land and labour are the ultimate sources of all wealth, that labour's only hope of lasting freedom and equality was in getting possession of, and access to, the land.

Groves went on to discuss how Winstanley's political teaching centred on the choice open to men. Whereas the Commonwealth had fought for 'a goodly society,' it set about enclosing land and engaging in the activities of the merchant class. However, men could take another road: 'the way of useful labour, of the full use of the land and a sharing of its fruits.' He concluded:

In this sense Winstanley towers above our present-day theorists. The "left" to-day has no beliefs, only a few political catchwords. Our doctrines have no roots and will not abide. There is another sentence in the same review that may help us to see what is wrong, a sentence that (almost worthy to be put alongside the classic "poor but honest") epitomises the modern view. Mr. Orwell, wishing, I am sure to remove what he thought might be a slur on Winstanley's character, wrote: *though a visionary Winstanley was by no means a fool.* Truly we have lost something; perhaps it is too far away now to recapture, though glimpses of it come now and again to trouble us, in the writings and sayings of the old English rebels. Maybe with their help we shall one day bridge the gulf dug by the industrial revolution and, by looking afresh at the lives and works of these men, bring nearer the day of righteousness for which they worked.

Orwell was evidently upset by Groves's comments, and in *The New Leader* for 28 October the following letter from Groves was printed (which incidentally provides further evidence that some of Orwell's *Observer* reviews were cut. See Orwell's letter to Liddell Hart, 12 August 1942, *1379*, regarding his review of Philippe Barrès's *Charles de Gaulle*).

Dear Comrade,—George Orwell has written me about my *New Leader* article commenting on his review of the Winstanley book.

The article criticised his apparent indifference to the visionary side of Winstanley's writings. On the review as published the criticism was justified. But it seems that certain passages were—for space reasons—omitted from Mr. Orwell's review and that in these passages he wrote on this very point. Not knowing about these omissions I stressed the criticism too heavily.

I should be glad if you would publish this so that your readers will know that this part of the article was unintentionally unfair to Mr. Orwell.

1. Reg Groves (1908–) is described by Crick as an agitator and author and personally abrasive. He was one of the first British Trotskyists and had immediately preceded Orwell at the Westropes' bookshop. They had met but did not know each other well. Groves described *Homage to Catalonia* as 'the best thing that ever happened to us' (Crick, 270, 611, 363). He died in the 1980s.

2543. To T. S. Eliot
5 September 1944   Typewritten

27B Canonbury Square
Islington
N 1

Dear Eliot,
Have you seen the new New York monthly paper "Politics" which is a sort of dissident offshoot from the "Partisan Review" which you used to write for? Dwight Macdonald the editor asked me whether you would like it and I said you would, so he'll probably send you a copy.

I am going away for the second half of September,[1] but can you have lunch some day early in October, any day from the 3rd onwards? You might let me know at the above or at "Tribune." Warburg is going to do that book you saw but he probably can't get it out till early next year because of paper.[2]

Yours
[Signed] Geo. Orwell
George Orwell

1. It is not known where Orwell went. It was thought that he paid his first visit to Jura in September 1945 (*CEJL*, iv, 582), but Eileen's letter to him of 21 March 1945 (*2638*) makes it plain that the renting and repair of Barnhill were in train. On 18 August 1945, Orwell told Herbert Read that he would be away from about 10 September to arrange renting Barnhill and to have repairs started (*2725*). It looks, therefore, as if Orwell made his first visit to Jura in September 1944, not 1945, as was previously thought. David Astor (see *891 n. 1* and *1195, n. 5*), realising how exhausted Orwell was by the end of the war, wanted to arrange a holiday for him and he asked Orwell if he would like him to try to 'get him in' to stay in the northern part of the Isle of Jura. He recalls in *Remembering Orwell*, 'my family had a property in the central part of the island. I used to walk to the northern part. It's the most beautiful part of the island and certainly the most lonely and remote'; he knew some families there and offered to get in touch with them. Orwell was attracted by the idea; and so Astor wrote to the McKinnon family. At first Janet McKinnon replied that they could not take a guest, but Astor wrote again, and again, and it was agreed. Orwell went north, and at first Astor heard nothing. He then learned that Orwell had found an empty farmhouse—'an extremely uncomfortable place to live'—and had asked the landowner if he could rent it. The empty farmhouse was Barnhill, owned by Robin Fletcher and his wife, Margaret. 'For a person in delicate health it was a crazy place to live . . . but he was very independent . . . [and] I didn't know how ill he was' (160–70); and see 170–74 for a description by Margaret Fletcher Nelson of Orwell's arrival in May 1946

2. Eliot replied on 15 September. He had not seen *Politics* but hoped Dwight Macdonald would send him a copy. He asked Orwell to telephone on his return so they could arrange a time when Orwell and Eileen could lunch with him. And he said he was glad Warburg was to publish *Animal Farm*.

2544. To R. S. R. Fitter

5 September 1944   Typewritten

Tribune

Dear Mr. Fitter,[1]
Many thanks for the information re Willowherb.[2]

I don't think we could undertake a regular "nature" feature. We haven't the space and I doubt whether enough of our readers are interested in the subject.

Yours sincerely,
[Signed] Geo. Orwell
George Orwell
Literary Editor

1. Richard Sidney Richmond Fitter (1913–) was at this time a member of the operational research staff of Coastal Command (1942–45) and editor of the *London Naturalist* (1942–45). He had previously worked for Political and Economic Planning (1936–40) and Mass Observation (1940–42) and later was assistant editor of *Countryman* (1946–59) and editor of *Kingfisher* (1965–72). He wrote and edited many nature books.

2. Orwell wrote about this in 'As I Please,' 41, 8 September 1944; see *2547*.

2545. To Dwight Macdonald

5 September 1944   Typewritten

27B Canonbury Square
Islington
London N 1

Dear Macdonald,

I only yesterday received your letter dated August 5th, so I suppose the mails have got bad again. You will have had my Miss Blandish article by this time. I hope you don't mind "Horizon" also printing it, and also, if you are using it, making one or two minor alterations which might prevent a libel action. The alterations are (I haven't got a copy of the MS so don't know pages):

"Miss B." is "an impudent plagiarism of Faulkner's 'Sanctuary.'" I think we should alter "is an impudent plagiarism" to "bears a very striking resemblance to." Of course it is a plagiarism but one couldn't necessarily prove it in court.

"Miss B." was "ultimately suppressed." Probably better to alter to "withdrawn from circulation." It disappeared when "Lady Don't Turn Over" was suppressed, but this may have been done voluntarily.

Some of the Dorothy Sayers books described as displaying "necrophilia." Better to alter to "morbid interest in corpses" or whatever phrase would fit in.

I merely suggest these alterations which I am going to make in the English version, but of course use your own judgement. I believe the libel laws aren't so stiff in the USA. Bringing libel actions is quite a lucrative profession over here.[1]

The best address for Eliot is Care of Faber & Faber, 24 Russell Square, London, WC1. I have told him about "Politics" and I am sure he would like it and might write something for you. He is very busy what with publishing and being a stooge for the British Council. With ref to that review I sent you. I think the USSR *is* the dynamo of world Socialism so long as people believe in it.[2] I think that if the USSR were conquered by some foreign country the working class everywhere would lose heart, for the time being at least, and the ordinary stupid capitalists who have never lost their suspicion of Russia would be encouraged. I think the fact that the Germans have failed to conquer Russia has given prestige to the idea of Socialism. For that reason I wouldn't want to see the USSR destroyed and think it ought to be defended if necessary. But I want people to become disillusioned about it and to realise that they must build their own Socialist movement without Russian interference, and I want the existence of democratic Socialism in the West to exert a regenerative influence upon Russia. I suppose that if the working class everywhere had been taught to be as anti-Russian as the Germans had been made, the USSR would simply have collapsed in 1941 or 1942, and God knows what things would then have come out from under their stones. After that Spanish business I hate the Stalin regime perhaps worse than you do, but I think one must defend it as against people like Franco, Laval etc. But the present state of censorship here is ghastly. I have had hell and all about that anti-Stalin book of mine, which is really only a little squib. However, Warburg is going to publish it, but not till early next year because of paper.

I'm glad "Politics" is going well. I'll make further enquiries about how people can take out subs, but so far everyone has told me you can't send money out for that purpose. If we do quote anything—thanks for the permission—I'll see that it's acknowledged.

The above is my address from now on.

Yours,
Geo. Orwell

1. Macdonald ignored these proposed changes, and the original version of Orwell's essay was published in *Politics*. The changes were made in *Horizon* and in the essay when printed in book form in England in 1945 and in the United States in 1946. The surviving text has 'In the end' not 'ultimately'; was Orwell writing from memory or referring to a draft version he had retained? For the preference for 'withdrawn,' see headnote to *2538*.
2. The area of the letter which includes the latter part of the reference to T. S. Eliot and the first part of what Orwell thought of the USSR is ringed and attention drawn to it by a marginal line and arrow. Presumably this was done in Macdonald's office. The review mentioned was probably that rejected by the *Manchester Evening News* (of Harold Laski's *Faith, Reason and Civilization*); see *2518, n. 1*.

2546. 'How Long is a Short Story'

Manchester Evening News, 7 September 1944

Anybody who has been connected with the book trade knows that collections of short stories are poor sellers, and anyone who has edited a magazine knows at least part of the reason—that good, short stories, good enough to be worth reprinting and collecting in volume form, are very hard to come by.

The book-borrowers who ask the librarian for "a nice book" and add in the same breath, "not short stories, please," are, on the whole, justified.

But by their attitude they help to push the average level of the short story even lower. For writers, like everyone else, have to live, and since it is notorious that books of this kind don't sell, talent tends to drift elsewhere.

The besetting fault of English short stories to-day is lifelessness. On the higher levels—in "new writing," shall we say—the so-called story is almost always not a story.

Nothing happens in it. There is no surprise, no development, and usually not enough distinction of writing to compensate for lack of incident. There are exceptions, of course—for instance, Mr. V. S. Pritchett's "Sense of Humour," Mr. Christopher Isherwood's "Farewell to Berlin",[1] and one or two Army stories by Mr. Maclaren-Ross.

On the lower levels the story still has a "plot," but it has been mechanically constructed and bears the same relation to real life as a clockwork mouse does to a living one.

It was not always so. Only a few decades ago H. G. Wells, Somerset

Maugham, W. W. Jacobs, D. H. Lawrence, and others, were writing short stories which were masterpieces on their different levels.

And though the decline of the English short story may have complex social causes, it also has mechanical and economic causes which are fairly easy to point out. Mr. H. G. Wells once made the illuminating remark that he could write short stories as long as he had a market for them. Round about the turn of the century "The Strand" and other magazines happened to have a public for intelligent stories, and Mr. Wells turned them out one after another. They are collected under various titles, and quite twenty of them are of outstanding brilliance. The best of all, perhaps, are "A Slip Under the Microscope"[2] and "Miss Winchelsea's Heart."

But what caused the drying-up of that market which stimulated Mr. Wells to some of his best work? One reason, almost certainly, is the reduced size and neater make-up of modern magazines. Stories have to be cut all to a length, and in weekly papers, particularly, it is a length into which a story with any character-interest can hardly be crammed. In the fat and disorderly magazines of the Victorian Age, "Chambers's Papers For the People," for instance, or "All The Year Round"—there was room for contributions of almost any length. The story-writer had elbow room.

Here is a list of outstanding short stories—and there is no need to go outside the English language for them:

"The Purloined Letter," by Edgar Allan Poe.
"The Man that Corrupted Hadleyburg," by Mark Twain.
"The Fox," by D. H. Lawrence.
"Heart of Darkness," by Joseph Conrad.
"The Dead," by James Joyce.
"Love of Life," by Jack London.
"The Plattner Story," by H. G. Wells.
"Rain," by Somerset Maugham.
"Baa, Baa, Black Sheep," by Rudyard Kipling.
"Lord Arthur Savile's Crime," by Oscar Wilde.

These stories are of varying length, but in general they would be too long for modern magazines.

Certain stories which are universally admitted to be masterpieces, for instance, Lawrence's "England, my England," could not be fitted into any modern English periodical, but would be too short to be printed as a separate book. There has never been much market in England for the "long-short" story, called in France the "Nouvelle"—Prosper Merimee's "Carmen" is an outstanding example—probably because the lending libraries consider them bad value.

Stories of odd lengths can be published several together in one volume, but, as we have seen, such books do not sell. They do not sell because for a dozen years or more they have usually been dull, and they have been dull because the cramped magazines (which often do not pay too well) do not attract talent towards this particular art-form.

If you examine the best English short stories of the past, the thing that strikes you about most of them is how leisurely they are. Kipling's "Drums

383

of the Fore and Aft," for example, starts off with pages and pages of mere talk. The Sherlock Holmes stories would be rejected by most modern editors on the ground that they are too long, have too much padding, and are too slow in getting off the mark. But of course it is the padding that gives these stories life—the character of Holmes, for instance, being built up almost entirely by irrelevant scraps of conversation.

On the other hand there have been gifted writers whose stories are exceedingly short; Katharine Mansfield is an example. A short story is anything between a thousand and twenty thousand words, and to do his best a writer should be able to rove freely between those limits.

Russian literature has probably owed much to the enormous size of Russian magazines, which could accommodate, for instance, the separate stories in Dostoievski's "Letters from the Underworld."[3]

And even so laconic a writer as Maupassant wrote some stories, such as "La Maison de Madame Tellier," which would be uncomfortably long by modern standards.

Also, writers need to be paid. The superiority of contemporary American short-story writers (for instance, Damon Runyan, Dorothy Parker, and, to step back 15 years, Ring Lardner) is at any rate partly due to the fact that American magazines pay "good money." A writer of fiction cannot confine himself entirely to periodicals—it is hard to build up a public in that way—but it is necessarily in periodicals that new talent is first discovered.

Therefore fatter, and it should be added, more enterprising magazines are the first step towards restoring the prestige and the readability of the English short story.

There are other forms of literature which have also suffered by curtailment. In the days of the old "quarterly review," when it was normal for a book review to be 15 pages long, reviewing had a literary quality it seldom has nowadays.

Elbow room cannot create talent, but at least it allows a writer to follow a good idea when he has one—whereas if he is told as he frequently is in these days to "keep it down to fifteen hundred words," he is likely to produce either a grey and eventless little sketch, or else an unlifelike anecdote with a slick surprise (which the experienced reader has foreseen all along) in the last sentence.[4]

[Fee: £8.8.0; 6.9.44]

1. The *Manchester Evening News* printed these titles as 'V. S. Pritchett's sense of humour, Mr. Christopher Isherwood's farewell to Berlin.' *Synopsis* (see *n. 4*) printed the titles as corrected here.
2. 'A Slip Under the Microscope' was adapted for broadcasting by Orwell and transmitted in the BBC's Eastern Service on 6 October 1943; see *2297*.
3. Presumably *Notes from Underground* (1864), as it is now better known. But the ten sections are hardly ten short stories, though the whole work might be called a novella. The importance of this work for *Nineteen Eighty-Four* has been pointed out by, among others, William Steinhoff in *George Orwell and the Origins of 1984* (1975); see especially 173–75, where Steinhoff points to Dostoievski's use of the formula $2 + 2 = 5$ and man's unwillingness to renounce real suffering. Steinhoff mentions earlier occurences of this formula known to Orwell, for example, Eugene

Lyons's *Assignment in Utopia* (1937), although not that in Sterne's *Tristram Shandy*, a copy of which Orwell owned.

4. Reprinted in full in *Synopsis*, Winter 1944, with the corrections given in *n. 1*. No payment for republication is listed by Orwell in his Payments Book.

2547. 'As I Please,' 41

Tribune, 8 September 1944

For a book of 32 pages, Sir Osbert Sitwell's *A Letter to My Son* contains a quite astonishing quantity of invective. I imagine that it is the invective, or rather the eminence of the people it is directed against, that has led Sir Osbert to change his publisher. But in among passages that are sometimes unfair and occasionally frivolous, he manages to say some penetrating things about the position of the artist in a modern centralised society. Here, for instance, are some excerpts:—

"The true artist has always had to fight, but it is, and will be, a more ferocious struggle for you, and the artists of your generation, than ever before. The working man, this time, will be better looked after, he will be flattered by the press and bribed with Beveridge schemes, because he possesses a plurality of votes. But who will care for you or your fate, who will trouble to defend the cause of the young writer, painter, sculptor, musician? And what inspiration will you be offered when theatre, ballet, concert-hall lie in ruins, and, owing to the break in training, there are no great executant artists for several decades? Above all, do not underestimate the amount and intensity of genuine ill-will that people will feel for you; not the working man, for though not highly educated he has a mild respect for the arts and no preconceived notions, not the few remaining patricians, but the vast army between them, the fat middle classes and the little men. And here I must make special mention of the civil servant as enemy. . . . At the best, you will be ground down between the small but powerful authoritarian minority of art directors, museum racketeers, the chic, giggling modistes who write on art and literature, publishers, journalists and dons (who will, to do them justice, try to help you, if you will write as they tell you)—and the enormous remainder, who would not mind, who would indeed be pleased, if they saw you starve. For we English are unique in that, albeit an art-producing nation, we are not an art-loving one. In the past the arts depended on a small number of very rich patrons. The enclave they formed has never been re-established. The very name 'art-lover' stinks. . . . The privileges you hold to-day, then, as an artist, are those of Ishmael, the hand of every man is against you. Remember, therefore, that outcasts must never be afraid."

These are not my views. They are the views of an intelligent Conservative who underrates the virtues of democracy and attributes to feudalism certain advantages which really belong to capitalism. It is a mistake, for instance, to yearn after an aristocratic patron. The patron could be just as hard a master as the B.B.C., and he did not pay your salary so regularly. François Villon had, I suppose, as rough a time as any poet in our own day, and the literary man starving in a garret was one of the characteristic figures of the eighteenth century. At best, in an age of patronage you had to waste time and talent on revolting flatteries, as Shakespeare did. Indeed, if one thinks of the artist as an Ishmael, an autonomous individual who owes nothing to society, then the golden age of the artist was the age of capitalism. He had then escaped from the patron and not yet been captured by the bureaucrat. He could—at any rate a writer, a musician, an actor and perhaps even a painter could— make his living off the big public, who were uncertain of what they wanted and would to a great extent take what they were given. Indeed, for about a hundred years it was possible to make your livelihood by openly insulting the public, as the careers of, say, Flaubert, Tolstoy, D. H. Lawrence, and even Dickens show.

But all the same there is much in what Sir Osbert Sitwell says. Laissez-faire capitalism is passing away, and the independent status of the artist must necessarily disappear with it. He must become either a spare-time amateur or an official. When you see what has happened to the arts in the totalitarian countries, and when you see the same thing happening here in a more veiled way through the M.O.I., the B.B.C. and the film companies—organisations which not only buy up promising young writers and geld them and set them to work like cab-horses, but manage to rob literary creation of its individual character and turn it into a sort of conveyor-belt process—the prospects are not encouraging. Yet it remains true that capitalism, which in many ways was kind to the artist and the intellectual generally, is doomed and is not worth saving any way. So you arrive at these two antithetical facts: (1) Society cannot be arranged for the benefit of artists; (2) without artists civilisation perishes. I have never yet seen this dilemma solved (there must be a solution), and it is not often that it is honestly discussed.[1]

I have before me an exceptionally disgusting photograph, from the *Star* of August 29, of two partially undressed women, with shaven heads and with swastikas painted on their faces, being led through the streets of Paris amid grinning onlookers. The *Star*—not that I am picking on the *Star*, for most of the press has behaved likewise—reproduces this photograph with seeming approval.

I don't blame the French for doing this kind of thing. They have had four years of suffering, and I can partially imagine how they feel towards the collaborators. But it is a different matter when newspapers in this country try to persuade their readers that shaving women's heads is a nice thing to do. As soon as I saw this *Star* photograph, I thought, "Where have I seen something like this before?" Then I remembered. Just about ten years ago, when the Nazi regime was beginning to get into its stride, very similar pictures of humiliated Jews being led through the streets of German cities were exhibited in the British press—but with this difference, that on that occasion we were not expected to approve.

Recently another newspaper published photographs of the dangling corpses of Germans hanged by the Russians in Kharkov,[2] and carefully informed its readers that these executions had been filmed and that the public would shortly be able to witness them at the news theatres. (Were children admitted, I wonder?)

There is a saying of Nietzsche which I have quoted before (not in this column, I think), but which is worth quoting again:—

He who fights too long against dragons becomes a dragon himself: and if thou gaze too long into the abyss, the abyss will gaze into thee.

"To long," in this context, should perhaps be taken as meaning "after the dragon is beaten."

The correspondents who wrote in answer to my query about the weed which grows on blitzed sites are too numerous to thank individually, but I would like to thank them collectively. The upshot is that Sir William Beach Thomas was right. The plant *is* called Rosebay Willowherb.[3] The name of the other plant I referred to is not completely certain, but as there are, it seems, nine kinds of willowherb, this must be one of them. As a piece of information which may be useful at a time when whisky costs twenty-seven shillings a bottle, I pass on the statement of one of my correspondents that "an infusion of the whole plant is extremely intoxicating." If anyone is brave enough to try this, I shall be interested to learn the results.

Tribune for 22 September 1944 published a letter from a member of the Amalgamated Engineering Union and a letter from a 'Young Writer.' The latter was taken up by several correspondents in *Tribune*, 6 October 1944. Orwell reverted to this correspondence in 'As I Please,' 44; see *2562*.

How much longer must your readers be affronted by the quite patent pro-Fascist, neo-Jesuit posturings of George Orwell? He writes in the wrong periodical. Like the late Lord Haldane, his spiritual home lies elsewhere.

He protests against the *Star* pictures of some collaborationist (whores—Orwell's pet phrase) being shown in British news sheets.

He carefully fails to mention the *much more* disgusting pictures of Allied troops being used in Paris to protect these traitors and murderers of their countrymen and countrywomen.

Protection being given to treason-mongers by Allied troops at a time when flying bombs were killing innocent London civilians.

In this connection it is interesting to note that the alleged Liberal paper[4]—stable companion to the *Star*— refused to print letters of protest, or to even mention they had received any protest of this misuse of Allied soldiers at a time when black murder was raining down on London, and no "effective *protection*" given to the British citizens.

The suggestion was made that Allied troops would be much more usefully employed in *attacking* the flying bomb sites than acting as strong-arm boys in defending French Quislings and collaborators, or showing the flag to the people of Paris, who had freed themselves *before the arrival of Eisenhower*.

Perhaps George Orwell will go to the next step: use the columns of *Tribune* for advocating a set of safe peace proposals for the Romish-German warmongers.

He should team up with the Reber-Murphy-Kirkpatrick crowd, or go out to organise a Friends of the Vatican League.

Frank Smith, A.E.U.[5]

Outlook for Young Writers

I think our young writers are lucky to have such a stout champion as Sir Osbert Sitwell, whose *Letter to My Son* has already upset the pinheads, a sure proof that he has rung the bell! George Orwell also deserves thanks for his observations upon the problems which the little book raises so graphically. But cannot a Socialist literary-political review like *Tribune* give some space so that the question of how a writer or artist can *live* in society can be honestly thrashed out? What is the Labour solution? Should all the younger writers give up writing and devote all their energies to bringing about a Socialist society which would have a place for them as creative artists, and a status above that of a garret-genius? Or should they rub along as best they can accepting the patronage of the B.B.C., M.O.I., Rank, E.N.S.A., C.E.M.A.[6] and any other governmental or industrial set-up that offers to "buy" them up?

I am afraid the careers of our better-known contemporary men of letters offer little help. T. S. Eliot, Herbert Read, Richard Church, John Lehmann, and others seem to have solved the problem by turning publishers themselves. George Orwell, Cyril Connolly, Peter Quennell, John Betjeman, Philip Toynbee, Alan Hodge by turning columnists. Others have taken to "editing" pictorial series, bookstall miscellanies, or have become minor critics of art, radio, theatre and music or have turned journalists and political commentators. Few are professional writers in the sense that Thomas Hardy, W. B. Yeats etc., were; E. M. Forster, Robert Graves, Sean O'Casey perhaps are exceptions. Only people enjoying private incomes can take a £25 advance from a publisher and feel they are facing up to a present day writer's life.

What can be done? This is a question which should seriously exercise the Labour Party, for I fear the younger writers generally (if sardonically!) feel that they get more sympathy from out and out Conservatives than from the Progressive Parties. I have heard two or three confess that they prefer the arch-Tory—"a sentimental blimp has something more attractive about him than a text-book party member." Fabians might do worse than read T. S. Eliot's essay on "The Responsibility of the Man of Letters in the Cultural Restoration of Europe" in *The Norseman* for August, 1944. Dealing with "questions which arise when the freedom of the man of letters is menaced," Eliot writes: "I have in mind also the dangers which may come from official encouragement and patronage of the arts; the dangers to which men of letters would be exposed, if they became, in their professional capacity, servants of the State. Modern governments are very much aware of the new invention "cultural propaganda," even when the governors are not remarkably sensitive to culture; and, however necessary cultural propaganda may be under modern conditions, we must be alert to the fact that all propaganda can be perverted.

Young Writer

To anyone conditioned by suggestions in *Tribune* that the Labour Party should do something about Socialism, there is something rather quaint in "Young Writer's" suggestion that the Left should start worrying seriously about the personal quandary of the writer.

Before you are inundated with analyses of the status of the artist in Soviet Russia, I should like to suggest that "Young Writer's" letter is a bad starting point for a discussion. He confuses the issue by basing his arguments on several outsize misconceptions.

For one thing, he seems to think that writing and doing other more economically steady work are mutually exclusive.

It is quite feasible to write and devote oneself to Socialism whilst accepting the patronage of the B.B.C., M.O.I., Rank or C.E.M.A. (though when he includes E.N.S.A. in this category I am with him). I'm not saying that this is an ideal way to go about one's life, but I think he should admit it can be done.

He names a string of writers who are publishers or columnists (many are temporary civil servants as well) as if they no longer wrote in consequence; and he forgets that an ivory castle is not perpetually inspiring to most writers, and that a little contact with the coarser ways of making a living is rarely harmful to the Muse, even if the nostrils do react.

He raises the word propaganda as a bogey, rather as if the soul of any creative type who lowers himself to doing "cultural propaganda" is bound to be perverted. I always thought that artists were supposed to have a pretty keen sense of what is right and wrong—to be able to smell the rose no matter what the name.

Perhaps good judgment and perception are not the strongest points in anyone who finds Conservatives more sympathetic than the Progressive parties. Well, it may be true, put like that—equating individuals with parties. Of course, most Conservatives have had a good education and can often be better company than strict proletarians. To woo Conservatism in consequence is not my idea of logic.

I don't think a party line can solve the personal dilemma which lies behind the letter. "Young Writer" should admit that E. M. Forsters are rarities, however society is ordered. He might also admit that editors, critics and commentators are not necessarily to be sniffed at, and often continue to write, quite well at that.

The artist lives in relation to the contemporary demand for his work—whether he has a private patron, a State patron or faces up to the capitalist rough and tumble supply and demand. The smaller the Muse the smaller the demand—the only way out is some minor form of prostitution, part time. The same thing would almost certainly happen with the State as patron, at any rate to someone. Even so, there are more safeguards in State patronage; and if I am right in detecting a Left leaning in the letter, I cannot see that our cause is served by confusing attractive sentimental blimps versus text-book party members with Capitalism versus Socialism.

P. Philips Price

"Young Writer" in *Tribune* of September 22 raises some points of interest to all of us. In our opinion the young writer in present society should neither abandon writing in favour of direct political action, nor should he look for patronage. At any rate, organisations such as C.E.M.A. extend help, not patronage, and a means whereby we can struggle for a fuller use of our gifts.

The solution is in the young writer's own hands, in his typewriter and pen, but most of all in his guts. He can contribute best to the solution of the problem by *writing*.

But his creation may reach nobody. The solution again is in the writer's own hands. There are young writers all over the world clamouring to be heard, and for all of them the solution is the same as for young workers in other arts and trades, namely, "Unity."

The Bristol Writers' Association is tackling the job by creating a Writers' Co-operative—a productive body.

One of its jobs will be to publish the work of the young writer of today, and the old and young writer of tomorrow. In this organisation the reader and writer have a common meeting place. The profits of the writer's genius return to him. His audience also have a direct reward for buying the writer's work.

So the young writer turns publisher as in the case of the authors mentioned by your correspondent. But in a collective rather than in an individual way which will bring better rewards and results.

The "can't be dones" have had their say, but the Bristol Writers' Association is doing it.

The problems of Socialist writers can be solved in a Socialist way.

W. R. Hutton
Miles Carpenter

George Orwell wrote in *Tribune*: "Society cannot be arranged for the benefit of artists; without artists civilisation perishes. I have never yet seen this dilemma solved."

But there is no such dilemma to be solved! The world could exist quite comfortably without artists. Incidentally, I have not noticed that artists are more civilised *in their lives* than ordinary people!

If I remember rightly, it was Plato who said that the best rulers of the Republic would be *the philosophers*. Philosophers are generally kindly, unwarlike, conscientious, thoughtful individuals. They have no desire to rule despotically, or to gain land and wealth at the expense of others.

If every man was a philosopher the world would be at peace, and thus be encouraged to become civilised. Judging from the present state of affairs the world is certainly *not* civilised; as civilisation does not yet exist it cannot "perish," whether artists flourish or not.

D. M. C. Granville

1. Sitwell sent Orwell a copy of his book inscribed 'For George Orwell, with best wishes, even though he might not agree with all the sentiments, from Osbert Sitwell, August 1944'; see *3734*. Orwell again discussed *A Letter for My Son* in 'As I Please,' 44; see *2562*; see also 'Authors Deserve a New Deal,' *2697*.
2. The hangings were the result of the first war crimes trial. A Ukrainian was also sentenced to death. See 'As I Please,' 5, 31 December 1943, *2398*, *n. 1*.
3. Orwell had asked the name of this plant in 'As I Please,' 39, 25 August 1944; see *2537*. See also his letter to R. S. R. Fitter, *2544*. There are many plants called willowherb—among them yellow loosestrife, members of the Epilobium family (evening primrose), and almost certainly what is intended in this context, the purple-spiked willowherb. This plant was referred to at the time by those unfamiliar with botanical names as 'the bomb-site plant.' It now grows prolifically in even famous gardens.
4. Smith refers to the *News Chronicle*, a morning daily; the *Star* was one of three London evening papers published each weekday. Both ceased publication on 17 October 1960.
5. Amalgmated Engineering [Trade] Union. Orwell did not refer to the women as whores.
6. The British Broadcasting Corporation; the Ministry of Information; J. Arthur Rank; Entertainments National Service Association (which organised entertainment for the armed forces); Council for the Encouragement of Music and the Arts (which became the Arts Council). Lord Rank (1888–1972), as he became, was an industrialist particularly associated with flour milling who, through his work as a Methodist lay preacher, took an interest in the production of religious films for Methodist Sunday schools. His first commercial film, *The Turn of the Tide*, was made in 1935 and from that developed his control of two of the three major British cinema chains and a film-producing organisation based on Denham Studios, intended to rival Hollywood, at least in Britain.

2548. 'Arthur Koestler'

11 September 1944   Typescript

This essay exists, unusually, as a typescript. The typewriter-face and the style of the typing (which includes page-slip and X-ing out with capital Xs) strongly suggest that Orwell was the typist. His name and address at Canonbury Square are typed at the head of the first page of the script. At the end is the date: '1944.' According to his Payments Book, the essay was completed on 11 September 1944. It appeared in *Focus*, *Critical Essays* (1946) and *Dickens, Dali & Others* (1946). In his 'Note' to *Critical Essays* (6), Orwell said that the essay 'was written for *Focus*, but it will probably not have appeared there before this book is published.' That proved so. Although the issue was dated Winter 1946, it was published in January or February 1947.

Apart from house-styling and some changes in punctuation, each publication made verbal changes to the typescript—over a score in all; more in *Focus* than in *Critical Essays*. Only one of these coincides (see *n. 4*) but another, *n. 13*, is an alteration to the same effect though worded differently. It is likely that Roger Senhouse, a director of Secker & Warburg, prepared a copy of the typescript for *Critical Essays*, and either of the two editors of *Focus*, Balachandra Rajan or Andrew Pearse, for *Focus*. These changes probably had Orwell's formal or tacit approval. The typescript has been reproduced here with the verbal changes made for the second impression of *Critical Essays*; the first impression and the page proofs for that impression (in the Orwell Archive, University College London) have been consulted.

The readings in *Dickens Dali & Others* are not separately noted except for five which differ from those recorded for *Critical Essays* (see *ns. 4, 13, 14, 16, 23*). The placement of the circumflex in Salammbô is an error (at one stage or another every vowel was adorned with this mark, and Orwell omitted it from his typescript). The other four readings in DD&O follow the typescript; this arises from the fact that copy for CrE and DD&O was prepared from separate copies of the manuscript. Writing to Moore on 23 January 1945 (see 2607), Orwell said, 'Herewith the MS. of the book of essays to send to the USA. I am giving Warburg the other copy.' No other changes have been deliberately made except for the addition of an omitted 'the' (in square brackets) and for the silent correction of a mistyping—'spycho-analyst.' It will be noted that Orwell's typescript has lower-case 'c' and 'w' in 'Spanish civil war' but that the printed text capitalises these. Orwell spells 'today' and 'leftwing(er)' without hyphens, and id est is represented by 'ie'—all forms commonly found in his manuscripts and typewriting. The editorial notes, mainly textual, follow the essay. They do not list the use of single quotation marks in Focus nor 'ise' for 'ize' in Critical Essays. TS = typescript; CrE = Critical Essays; DD&O = Dickens, Dali, and Others; F = Focus. The second impression of Critical Essays, May 1946, was collated.

One striking fact about English literature during the present century is the extent to which it has been dominated by foreigners—for example, Conrad, Henry James, Shaw, Joyce, Yeats, Pound and Eliot. Still, if you chose to make this a matter of national prestige and examine our achievement in the various branches of literature, you would find that England made a fairly good showing[1] until you came to what may be roughly described as political writing, or pamphleteering. I mean by this the special class of literature that has arisen out of the European political struggle since the rise of Fascism. Under this heading novels, autobiographies, books of "reportage," sociological treatises and plain pamphlets can all be lumped together, all of them having a common origin and to a great extent the same emotional atmosphere.

Some of the outstanding figures in this school of writers are Silone, Malraux, Salvemini, Borkenau, Victor Serge[2] and Koestler himself. Some of these are imaginative writers, some[3] not, but they are all alike in that they are trying to write contemporary history, but unofficial history, the kind[4] that is ignored in the textbooks[5] and lied about in the newspapers. Also they are all alike in being continental Europeans. It may be an exaggeration, but it cannot be a very great one, to say that whenever a book dealing with totalitarianism appears in this country, and still seems[6] worth reading six months after publication, it is a book translated from some foreign language. English writers, over the past dozen years, have poured forth an enormous spate of political literature, but they[7] have produced almost nothing of aesthetic value, and very little of historical value either. The Left Book Club, for instance, has been running ever since 1936. How many of its chosen volumes can you even remember the names of? Nazi Germany, Soviet Russia, Spain, Abyssinia, Austria, Czechoslovakia—all that these and kindred subjects have produced, in England, are slick books of reportage, dishonest pamphlets in which propaganda is swallowed whole and then spewed up again, half digested, and a very few reliable guidebooks[8] and textbooks. There has been nothing resembling, for instance, *Fontamara* or *Darkness at Noon*, because there is almost no English writer to whom it has happened to see totalitarianism from the inside. In Europe, during the past decade and more, things have been happening to middle-class people which in England do not even happen to the working class. Most of the European writers I mentioned above, and scores of others like them, have been obliged to break the law in order to engage in politics at all:[9] some of them have thrown bombs and fought in street battles,[10] many have been in prison or the concentration camp, or fled across frontiers with false names and forged passports. One cannot imagine, say, Professor Laski indulging in activities of that kind. England is lacking, therefore, in what one might call concentration-camp literature. The special world created by secret police forces, censorship of opinion, torture and frame-up trials is, of course, known about and to some extent disapproved of, but it has made very little emotional impact. One result of this is that there exists in England almost no literature of disillusionment about the Soviet Union. There is the attitude of ignorant disapproval, and there is the attitude of uncritical admiration, but very little in between. Opinion on the Moscow sabotage trials, for instance, was divided, but divided chiefly on the question of whether the accused were guilty. Few people were able to see that whether justified or not[11] the trials were an unspeakable horror. And English disapproval of the Nazi outrages has also been an unreal thing, turned on and off like a tap according to political expediency. To understand such things one has to be able to imagine oneself as the victim, and for an Englishman to write *Darkness at Noon* would be as unlikely an accident as for a slave-trader to write *Uncle Tom's Cabin*.

Koestler's published work really centres about the Moscow trials. His main theme is the decadence of revolutions owing to the corrupting effects of power, but the special nature of the Stalin dictatorship has driven him back into a position not far removed from pessimistic Conservativism.[12] I do not know how many books he has written in all. He is a Hungarian whose earlier books were written in German,[13] and five books have been published in England: *Spanish Testament*, *The Gladiators*, *Darkness at Noon*, *Scum of the Earth*,[14] and *Arrival and Departure*. The subject matter of all of them is similar, and none of them ever escapes for more than a few pages from the atmosphere of nightmare. Of the five books, the action of three takes place entirely or almost entirely in prison.

In the opening months of the Spanish civil war [15] Koestler was the *News-Chronicle's*[16] correspondent in Spain, and early in 1937 he was taken prisoner when the Fascists captured Malaga. He was nearly shot out of hand, then spent some months imprisoned in a fortress, listening every night to the roar of rifle fire, [17] as batch after batch of Republicans was executed, and being most of the time in acute danger of execution himself. This was not a chance adventure which "might have happened to anybody," but was in accordance with Koestler's life style. A politically indifferent person would not have been in Spain at that date, a more cautious observer would have got out of Malaga before the Fascists arrived, and a British or American newspaper-man[18] would have been treated with more consideration. The book that

393

Koestler wrote about this, *Spanish Testament*, has remarkable passages, but apart from the scrappiness that is usual in a book of reportage, it is definitely false in places. In the prison scenes Koestler successfully establishes the nightmare atmosphere which is, so to speak, his patent, but the rest of the book is too much coloured by the Popular Front orthodoxy of the time. One or two passages even look as though they had been doctored for the purposes of the Left Book Club. At that time Koestler still was, or recently had been, a member of the Communist Party, and the complex politics of the civil war made it impossible for any Communist[19] to write quite honestly about the internal struggle on the Government side. The sin of nearly all leftwingers[20] from 1933 onwards is that they have wanted to be anti-Fascist[21] without being anti-totalitarian. In 1937 Koestler already knew this, but did not feel free to say so. He came much nearer to saying it—indeed, he[22] did say it, though he put on a mask to do so—in his next book, *The Gladiators*, which was published about a year before the war and for some reason attracted very little attention.

The Gladiators is in some ways an unsatisfactory book. It is about Spartacus, the Thracian gladiator who raised a slaves' rebellion in Italy round about 65 B.C., and any book on such a subject is handicapped by challenging comparison with *Salammbô*.[23] In our own age it would not be possible to write a book like *Salammbô* even if one had the talent. The great thing about[24] *Salammbô*, even more important than its physical detail, is its utter mercilessness. Flaubert could think himself into the stony cruelty of antiquity, because in the mid-nineteenth century one still had peace of mind. One had time to travel in the past. Nowadays the present and the future are too terrifying to be escaped from, and if one bothers with history it is in order to find modern meanings there. Koestler makes Spartacus into an allegorical figure, a primitive version of the proletarian dictator. Whereas Flaubert has been able, by a prolonged effort of the imagination, to make his mercenaries truly pre-Christian, Spartacus is a modern man dressed up. But this might not matter if Koestler were fully aware[25] of what his allegory means. Revolutions always go wrong—that is the main theme. It is on the question of *why* they go wrong that he falters, and his uncertainty enters into the story and makes the central figures enigmatic and unreal.

For several years the rebellious slaves are uniformly successful. Their numbers swell to a hundred thousand, they overrun great areas of southern[26] Italy, they defeat one punitive expedition after another, they ally themselves with the pirates who at that time were the masters of the Mediterranean, and finally they set to work to build a city of their own, to be named the City of the Sun. In this city human beings are to be free and equal, and above all they are to be happy: no slavery, no hunger, no injustice, no floggings, no executions.[27] It is the dream of a just society which seems to haunt the human imagination ineradicably and in all ages, whether it is called the Kingdom of Heaven or the classless society, or whether it is thought of as a Golden Age which once existed in the past and from which we have degenerated. Needless to say[28] the slaves fail to achieve it. No sooner have they formed themselves into a community than their way of life turns out to be as unjust, laborious and fear-ridden as any other. Even the cross, symbol of slavery, has to be revived for the punishment of malefactors. The turning point[29] comes when Spartacus finds himself obliged to crucify twenty of his oldest and most faithful followers. After that the City of the Sun[30] is doomed, the slaves split up and are defeated in detail, the last fifteen thousand of them being captured and crucified in one batch.

The serious weakness of this story is that the motives of Spartacus himself are never made clear. The Roman lawyer Fulvius, who joins[31] the rebellion and acts as its chronicler, sets forth the familiar dilemma of ends and means. You can achieve nothing unless you are willing to use force and cunning, but in using them you pervert your original aims. Spartacus, however, is not represented as power-hungry, nor on the other hand[32] as a visionary. He is driven onwards by some obscure force which he does not understand, and he is frequently in two minds as to whether it would not be better to throw up the whole adventure and flee to Alexandria while the going is good. The slaves' republic is in any case wrecked rather by hedonism than by the struggle for power. The slaves are discontented with their liberty because they still have to work, and the final break-up happens because the more turbulent and less civilized slaves, chiefly Gauls and Germans, continue to behave like bandits after the republic has been established. This may be a true account of events—naturally we know very little about the slave rebellions of antiquity—but by allowing the Sun City to be destroyed because[33] Crixus the Gaul cannot be prevented from looting and raping, Koestler has faltered between allegory and history. If Spartacus is the prototype of the modern revolutionary—and obviously he is intended as that—he should have gone astray because of the impossibility of combining power with righteousness. As it is, he is an almost passive figure, acted upon rather than acting, and at times not convincing. The story partly fails because the central problem of revolution has been avoided, or at least[34] has not been solved.[35]

It is again avoided in a subtler way in the next book, Koestler's masterpiece, Darkness at Noon. Here however[36] the story is not spoiled, because it deals with individuals and its interest is psychological. It is an episode picked out from a background that does not have to be questioned. Darkness at Noon describes the imprisonment and death of an Old Bolshevik, Rubashov, who first denies and ultimately confesses to crimes which he is well aware he has not committed. The grown-upness, the lack of surprise or denunciation, the pity and irony with which the story is told show the advantage, when one is handling a theme of this kind, of being a European. The book reaches the stature[37] of tragedy, whereas an English or American writer could at most have made it into a polemical tract. Koestler has digested his material and can treat it on the aesthetic level. At the same time his handling of it has a political implication, not important in this case but likely to be damaging in later books.

Naturally the whole book centres round one question: Why did Rubashov confess? He is not guilty—that is, not guilty of anything except the essential crime of disliking the Stalin regime. The concrete acts of treason in which he is supposed to have engaged are all imaginary. He has not even been tortured, or not very severely. He is worn down by solitude, toothache, lack of tobacco, bright lights glaring in his eyes, and continuous questioning,[38] but these in themselves would not be enough to overcome a hardened revolutionary. The Nazis have previously done worse to him without breaking his spirit. The confessions obtained in the Russian state[39] trials are capable of three explanations:—[40]

(1) That the accused were guilty.

(2) That they were tortured, and perhaps blackmailed by threats to relatives and [41] friends.

(3) That they were actuated by despair, mental bankruptcy and the habit of loyalty to the Party.

For Koestler's purpose in Darkness at Noon (1) is ruled out, and though this is not the place to discuss the Russian purges, I must add that what little verifiable evidence there is suggests that the trials of the Old Bolsheviks were frame-ups. If one assumes that the accused were not guilty—at any rate, not guilty of the particular things they confessed to—then (2) is the common-sense[42] explanation. Koestler, however, plumps for (3), which is also accepted by the Trotskyist Boris Souvarine,[43] in his pamphlet Cauchemar en URSS. Rubashov ultimately confesses because he cannot find in his own mind any reason for not doing so. Justice and objective truth have long[44] ceased to have any meaning for him. For decades he has been simply the creature of the Party, and what the Party now demands is that he shall confess to non-existent crimes. In the end, though he has had to be bullied and weakened first, he is somewhat proud of his decision to confess. He feels superior to the poor Czarist officer who inhabits the next cell and who talks to Rubashov by tapping on the wall. The Czarist officer is shocked when he learns that Rubashov intends to capitulate. As he sees it from his "bourgeois" angle, everyone ought to stick to his guns, even a Bolshevik. Honour, he says, consists in doing what you think right. "Honour is to be useful without fuss", Rubashov taps back; and he reflects with a certain satisfaction that he is tapping with his pince-nez while[45] the other, the relic of the past, is tapping with a monocle.

Like Bukharin, Rubashov is "looking out upon black darkness." What is there, what code, what loyalty, what notion of good and evil, for the sake of which he can defy the Party and endure further torment? He is not only alone, he is also hollow. He has himself committed worse crimes than the one that is now being perpetrated against him. For example, as a secret envoy of the Party in Nazi Germany, he has got rid of disobedient followers by betraying them to the Gestapo. Curiously enough, if he has any inner strength to draw upon, it is the memories of his boyhood when he was the son of a landowner. The last thing he remembers, when he is shot from behind, is the leaves of the poplar trees on his father's estate. Rubashov belongs to the older generation of Bolsheviks that was largely wiped out in the purges. He is aware of art and literature, and of the world outside Russia. He contrasts sharply with Gletkin, the young GPU[46] man who conducts his interrogation, and who is the typical "good party man," completely without scruples or curiosity, a thinking gramophone. Rubashov, unlike Gletkin, does not have the

Revolution as his starting point.[47] His mind was not a blank sheet when the party[48] got hold of it. His superiority to the other is finally traceable to his bourgeois origin.

One cannot, I think, argue that *Darkness at Noon* is simply a story dealing with the adventures of an imaginary individual. Clearly it is a political book, founded on history and offering an interpretation of disputed events. Rubashov might be Trotsky, Bukharin, Rakovsky[49] or some other relatively civilized figure among the Old Bolsheviks. If one writes about the Moscow trials one must answer the question, "Why did the accused confess?",[50] and which answer one makes is a political decision. Koestler answers, in effect, "Because these people had been rotted by the Revolution which they served," and in doing so he comes near to claiming that revolutions are of their nature bad. If one assumes that the accused in the Moscow trials were made to confess by means of some kind of terrorism, one is only saying that one[51] particular set of revolutionary leaders has gone astray. Individuals, and not the situation, are to blame. The implication of Koestler's book, however, is that Rubashov in power would be no better than Gletkin: or rather, only better in that his outlook is still partly pre-revolutionary. Revolution, Koestler seems to say, is a corrupting process. Really enter into the Revolution and you must end up as either Rubashov or Gletkin. It is not merely that "power corrupts": so also do the ways of attaining power. Therefore, all efforts to regenerate society *by violent means* lead to the cellars of the Ogpu. Lenin leads to Stalin, and would have come to resemble Stalin if he had happened to survive.

Of course, Koestler does not say this quite explicitly, and perhaps is not altogether conscious of it. He is writing about darkness, but it is darkness at what ought to be noon. Part of the time he feels that things might have turned out differently. The notion that so-and-so[52] has "betrayed," that things have only gone wrong because of individual wickedness, is ever-present in leftwing thought. Later, in *Arrival and Departure*, Koestler swings over much further towards the anti-revolutionary position, but in between these two books there is another, *Scum of [the] Earth*, which is straight autobiography and has only an indirect bearing upon the problems raised by *Darkness at Noon*. True to his life style,[53] Koestler was caught in France by the outbreak of war,[54] and, as a foreigner and a known anti-fascist,[55] was promptly arrested and interned by the Daladier Government.[56] He spent the first nine months of war mostly in a prison camp, then, during the collapse of France, escaped and travelled by devious routes to England, where he was once again thrown into prison as an enemy alien. This time he was soon released, however. The book is a valuable piece of reportage, and together with a few other scraps of honest writing that happened to be produced at the time of the debacle, it is a reminder of the depths that bourgeois democracy can descend to. At this moment, with France newly liberated and the witch-hunt after collaborators[57] in full swing, we are apt to forget that in 1940 various observers on the spot considered that about 40 per cent of the French population was either actively pro-German or completely apathetic. Truthful war books are never acceptable to non-combatants, and Koestler's book did not have a very good reception. Nobody came well out of it—neither the bourgeois politicians, whose idea of conducting an anti-fascist war was to jail every leftwinger they could lay hands on, nor the French Communists, who were effectively pro-Nazi and did their best to sabotage the French war effort,[58] nor the common people, who were just as likely to follow mountebanks like Doriot[59] as responsible leaders. Koestler records some fantastic conversations with fellow-victims in the concentration camp,[60] and adds that till then, like most middle-class Socialists and Communists,[61] he had never made contact with real proletarians, only with the educated minority. He draws the pessimistic conclusion: "Without education of the masses, no social progress; without social progress, no education of the masses." In *Scum of the Earth* Koestler ceases to idealise the common people. He has abandoned Stalinism, but he is not a Trotskyist either. This is the book's real link with *Arrival and Departure*, in which what is normally called a revolutionary outlook is dropped, perhaps for good.

Arrival and Departure is not a satisfactory book. The pretence that it is a novel is very thin; in effect it is a tract purporting to show that revolutionary creeds are rationalisations of neurotic impulses. With all too neat a symmetry, the book[62] begins and ends with the same action—a leap into a foreign country. A young ex-Communist who has made his escape from Hungary jumps ashore in Portugal, where he hopes to enter the service of Britain, at that time the only power fighting against Germany. His enthusiasm is somewhat cooled by the fact that the British consulate is uninterested in him and almost[63] ignores him for a period of several months, during which his money runs out and other astuter refugees escape to America. He is successively tempted by the World in the form of a Nazi propagandist, the Flesh in the form of a French girl, and—after a nervous breakdown—the Devil in the form of a psycho-analyst. The psycho-analyst drags out of him the fact that his revolutionary enthusiasm is not founded on any real belief in historical[64] necessity, but on a morbid guilt complex arising from an attempt in early childhood to blind his baby brother. By the time that he gets an opportunity of serving the Allies he has lost all reason for wanting to do so, and he is on the point of leaving for America when his irrational impulses seize hold of him again. In practice he cannot abandon the struggle. When the book ends he is floating down in a parachute over the dark landscape of his native country, where he will be employed as a secret agent of Britain.

As a political statement (and the book is not much more), this is insufficient. Of course it is true in many cases, and it may be true in all cases, that revolutionary activity is the result of personal maladjustment. Those who struggle against society are, on the whole, those who have reason to dislike it, and normal healthy[65] people are no more attracted by violence and illegality then they are by war. The young Nazi in *Arrival and Departure* makes the penetrating remark that one can see what is wrong with the leftwing movement by the ugliness of its women. But[66] after all, this does not invalidate the Socialist[67] case. Actions have results, irrespective of their motives. Marx's ultimate motives may well have been envy and spite, but this does not prove that his conclusions were false. In making the hero of *Arrival and Departure* take his final decision from a mere instinct not to shirk action and danger, Koestler is making him suffer a sudden loss of intelligence. With such a history as he has behind him, he would be able to see that certain things have to be done, whether our reasons for doing them are "good" or "bad." History has to move in a certain direction, even if it has to be pushed that way by neurotics. In *Arrival and Departure* Peter's idols are overthrown one after the other. The Russian Revolution has degenerated, Britain, symbolised by the aged consul with gouty fingers, is no better, the international class-conscious proletariat is a myth. But the conclusion (since, after all, Koestler and his hero "support" the war) ought to be that getting rid of Hitler is still a worthwhile[68] objective, a necessary bit of scavenging in which motives are almost irrelevant.

To take a rational political decision one must have a picture of the future. At present Koestler seems[69] to have none, or rather to have two which cancel out. As an ultimate objective he believes in the Earthly Paradise, the Sun State which the gladiators set out to establish, and which has haunted the imagination of Socialists, Anarchists[70] and religious heretics for hundreds of years. But his intelligence tells him that the Earthly Paradise is receding into the far distance and that what is actually ahead of us is bloodshed, tyranny and privation. Recently he described himself as a "short-term pessimist." Every kind of horror is blowing up over the horizon, but somehow it will all come right in the end. This outlook is probably gaining ground among thinking people: it results from the very great difficulty, once one has abandoned orthodox religious belief, of accepting life on earth as inherently miserable, and on the other hand[71] from the realisation that to make life livable[72] is a much bigger problem than it recently seemed. Since about 1930 the world has given no reason for optimism whatever. Nothing is in sight except a welter of lies, hatred, cruelty and ignorance, and beyond our present troubles loom vaster ones which are only now entering into the European consciousness. It is quite possible that man's major problems will *never* be solved. But it is also unthinkable! Who is there who dares to look at the world of today[73] and say to himself, "It will always be like this: even in a million years it cannot get appreciably better?" So you get the quasi-mystical belief that for the present there is no remedy, all political action is useless,[74] but that somehow, somewhere in space and time, human life will cease to be the miserable brutish thing it now is.

The only easy way out is that of the religious believer, who regards this life merely as a preparation for the next. But few thinking people now believe in life after death, and the number of those who do is probably diminishing. The Christian churches[75] would probably not survive on their own merits if their economic basis were destroyed. The real problem is how to restore the religious attitude while accepting death as final. Men can only be happy when they do not assume that the object of life is happiness. It is most unlikely, however, that Koestler would accept this. There is a well-marked hedonistic strain in his writings, and his failure to find a political position after breaking with Stalinism is a result of this.

The Russian Revolution, the central event in Koestler's life, started out with high hopes. We forget these things now, but a quarter of a century ago it was confidently expected that the Russian Revolution would lead to Utopia. Obviously this has not happened. Koestler is too acute not to see this, and too sensitive not to remember the original objective. Moreover, from his European angle he can see such things as purges and mass deportations for what they are: he is not, like Shaw or Laski, looking at them through the wrong end of the telescope. Therefore he draws the conclusion: This is what revolutions lead to. There is nothing for it except to be a "short-term pessimist," ie.[76] to keep out of politics, make a sort of oasis within which you and your friends can remain sane, and hope that somehow things will be better in a hundred years. At the basis of this lies his hedonism, which leads him to think of the Earthly Paradise as desirable. Perhaps, however, whether desirable or not, it isn't possible. Perhaps some degree of suffering is ineradicable from human life, perhaps the choice before Man is always a choice of evils, perhaps even the aim of Socialism is not to make the world perfect but to make it better. All revolutions are failures, but they are not all the same failure. It is his unwillingness to admit this that has led Koestler's mind temporarily into a blind alley and that makes *Arrival and Departure* seem shallow compared with the earlier books.

1. good showing] good-showing   *F*
2. *For Silone, see 856, n. 1; Malraux, 210, n. 2 and 856, n. 1; Serge, 1046, n. 7; Franz Borkenau, 628, n. 12; Orwell reviewed his* The Spanish Cockpit, *31 July 1937 (see 379), his* The Communist International, *22 September 1938 (see 485), and* The Totalitarian Enemy, *4 May 1940 (see 620). Professor Gaetano Salvemini (1873–1957) wrote on Italy and against Fascism. Among his books translated into English are* The Fascist Dictatorship in Italy *(New York, c. 1927),* The Fate of Trade Unions under Fascism *(with other writers) (New York, 1937), Italian Fascism (published by Victor Gollancz, 1938), Historian and Scientist: An Essay on the Nature of History and the Social Sciences (Cambridge, MA, 1939),* The Frontiers of Italy *(New York, 1944), and* The French Revolution *(London, 1954). A pamphlet he published in 1942 (reprinting an article that had appeared in* Common Sense*) might have interested Orwell particularly:* Our Allies Inside Italy: *instead of inspiring them, our short-short-wave broadcasts are the laughing stock of Italy. See also 524, n. 1.*
3. some] others   *F*
4. kind] kind of thing   TS
5. textbooks] text-books   *CrE (and elsewhere in the essay)*
6. seems] seem   *F*
7. they] *omitted in F*
8. guidebooks] guide-books   *F; also hyphenated in CrE but with* 'guide-' *at end of line*
9. all:] all;   *CrE*
10. street battles] street-battles   *CrE*
11. that . . . not] that, . . . not,   *CrE*
12. Conservatism] conservatism   *F*
13. whose earlier books were written in German] who usually writes in German (some of his books have been very ably translated by his wife)   TS *(with passage in parenthesis crossed out, probably by Orwell)*; whose earlier books were in German   *F*; who usually writes in German   DD&O *(as TS before amendment)*
14. *Scum of the Earth*] *The Scum of the Earth*   TS, DD&O
15. civil war] Civil War   *F, CrE (and elsewhere). Orwell invariably used lower-case initial letters for this phrase; see headnote.*
16. *News-Chronicle's*] *News Chronicle's*   F, CrE; DD&O *follows TS*
17. rifle fire] rifle-fire   *F*

18. newspaperman] newspaper man   *CrE*
19. Communist] communist   *F (and elsewhere)*
20. leftwingers] left-wingers   *F, CrE (and elsewhere)*
21. anti-Fascist] anti-fascist   *F. Contrast n. 55.*
22. he] *omitted in F*
23. *Salammbô*] *Salammbo*   TS *(and elsewhere)*; *DD&O has* Salâmmbo. *As the page proofs show, when first set, CrE left* Salammbô *unaccented; the proofs were marked to place a circumflex over the first 'a'; the correct position was introduced in the second impression.*
24. about] in   TS, *F*
25. aware] certain   *F*
26. southern] Southern   *F, CrE*
27. executions] crucifixions   *F*
28. say] say,   *F, CrE*
29. turning point] turning-point   *F, CrE*
30. City of the Sun] Sun City   *F*
31. joins] joins in   *F*
32. nor on the other hand] nor, on the other hand,   *CrE*
33. because] chiefly because   *F*
34. or at least] or, at least,   *CrE*
35. solved] resolved   *F*
36. Here however] Here, however,   *F, CrE*
37. stature] status   TS, *F*
38. questioning,] questioning;   *F*
39. state] State   *CrE*
40. explanations:—] explanations: *F, CrE*
41. and] or   *F*
42. commonsense] common-sense   *F, CrE*
43. *Boris Souvarine's* Cauchemar en U.R.S.S. (1937) *was reprinted from* La Revue de Paris. *Souvarine's* The Third International *was published in English by the British Socialist Party, probably in 1921. His* Stalin: A Critical Survey of Bolshevism *was published in New York, 1939, in a translation by C. L. R. James.*
44. long] long since   *F*
45. pince-nez while] pince-nez, whereas   *F*
46. GPU] G.P.U.   *CrE; set in page proofs of CrE as* 'Ogpu' *but marked to be changed to* 'G.P.U.'
47. starting point] starting-point   *F, CrE*
48. party] Party   *F*
49. Rakovsky] Rakovsky,   *F*
50. confess?] confess   *F*
51. that one] that that   TS, *F, and page proofs of CrE, which marked change to* 'that one'
52. so-and-so] So-and-so   *CrE*
53. life style] life-style   *F*
54. war,] war   *CrE*
55. anti-fascist] anti-Fascist   *CrE. Contrast n. 21.*
56. Government] government   *F*
57. collaborators] collaborationists   *F*
58. effort,] effort;   *F*
59. Doriot] *See 1116, n. 19.*
60. concentration camp] demobilization camps   *F*
61. middle-class Socialists and Communists] Socialists and Communists   *TS*; socialists and communists   *F*
62. book] books   *F*
63. almost] almost completely   *F*
64. historical] historic   TS, *F*
65. normal healthy] healthy normal   *F*
66. But] But,   *F*
67. Socialist] socialist   *F (and elsewhere)*
68. worthwhile] worth-while   *CrE*

69. seems] appears   TS, F
70. Anarchists] anarchists   F, CrE
71. hand] hand,   CrE
72. livable] liveable   F, CrE
73. today] to-day   F, CrE. *The unhyphenated form is invariably used by Orwell.*
74. useless] hopeless   F
75. churches] Churches   F
76. ie.] i.e.   F; i.e.   CrE. *The typescript's form is invariably used by Orwell.*

2548A. To Lydia Jackson

11 September 1944   Typewritten

Tribune

Dear Lydia,
Would you like to review this (about 500 words)? I don't know whether it is
any good, but as it is Polish I thought it would perhaps be up your street.

Yours,
[Signed] Eric.

[Postscript] "G for Genevieve",—Polish Book Depot[1]

1. A short notice of *G for Genevieve* by Flight-Lieutenant Herbert was published in *Tribune* on 29
   December 1944, signed Elisaveta Fen

2549. 'As I Please,' 42

Tribune, 15 September 1944

About the end of 1936, as I was passing through Paris on the way to Spain, I
had to visit somebody at an address I did not know, and I thought that the
quickest way of getting there would probably be to take a taxi. The taxi-
driver did not know the address either. However, we drove up the street and
asked the nearest policeman, whereupon it turned out that the address I was
looking for was only about a hundred yards away. So I had taken the taxi-
driver off the rank for a fare which in English money was about threepence.

The taxi-driver was furiously angry. He began accusing me, in a roaring
voice and with the maximum of offensiveness, of having "done it on
purpose." I protested that I had not known where the place was, and that I
obviously would not have taken a taxi if I had known. "You knew very
well!" he yelled back at me. He was an old, grey, thick-set man, with ragged
grey moustaches and a face of quite unusual malignity. In the end I lost my
temper, and, my command of French coming back to me in my rage, I
shouted at him, "You think you're too old for me to smash your face in.
Don't be too sure!" He backed up against the taxi, snarling and full of fight, in
spite of his sixty years.

Then the moment came to pay. I had taken out a ten-franc note. "I've no change!" he yelled as soon as he saw the money. "Go and change it for yourself!"

"Where can I get change?"

"How should I know? That's your business."

So I had to cross the street, find a tobacconist's shop and get change. When I came back I gave the taxi-driver the exact fare, telling him that after his behaviour I saw no reason for giving him anything extra; and after exchanging a few more insults we parted.

This sordid squabble left me at the moment violently angry, and a little later saddened and disgusted. "Why do people have to behave like that?" I thought.

But that night I left for Spain. The train, a slow one, was packed with Czechs, Germans, Frenchmen, all bound on the same mission. Up and down the train you could hear one phrase repeated over and over again, in the accents of all the languages of Europe—*là-bas* (down there). My third-class carriage was full of very young, fair-haired, underfed Germans in suits of incredible shoddiness—the first *ersatz* cloth I had seen—who rushed out at every stopping-place to buy bottles of cheap wine and later fell asleep in a sort of pyramid on the floor of the carriage. About halfway down France the ordinary passengers dropped off. There might still be a few nondescript journalists like myself, but the train was practically a troop train, and the countryside knew it. In the morning, as we crawled across southern France, every peasant working in the fields turned round, stood solemnly upright and gave the anti-Fascist salute. They were like a guard of honour, greeting the train mile after mile.

As I watched this, the behaviour of the old taxi-driver gradually fell into perspective. I saw now what had made him so unnecessarily offensive. This was 1936, the year of the great strikes, and the Blum government was still in office. The wave of revolutionary feeling which had swept across France had affected people like taxi-drivers as well as factory workers. With my English accent I had appeared to him as a symbol of the idle, patronising foreign tourists who had done their best to turn France into something midway between a museum and a brothel. In his eyes an English tourist meant a bourgeois. He was getting a bit of his own back on the parasites who were normally his employers. And it struck me that the motives of the polyglot army that filled the train, and of the peasants with raised fists out there in the fields, and my own motive in going to Spain, and the motive of the old taxi-driver in insulting me, were at bottom all the same.

The official statement on the doodle-bug, even taken together with Churchill's earlier statement, is not very revealing, because no clear figures have been given of the number of people affected. All we are told is that on average something under thirty bombs have hit London daily. My own estimate, based simply on such "incidents" as I have witnessed, is that on average every doodle-bug hitting London makes thirty houses uninhabitable, and that anything up to five thousand people have been rendered homeless daily. At that rate between a quarter and half a million people will have been blitzed out of their homes in the last three months.

It is said that good billiard-players chalk their cues before making a stroke, and bad players afterwards. In the same way, we should have got on splendidly in this war if we had prepared for each type of blitz before and not after it happened. Shortly before the outbreak of war an official, returning from some conference with other officials in London, told me that the authorities were prepared for air-raid casualties of the order of 200,000 in the first week. Enormous supplies of collapsible cardboard coffins had been laid in, and mass graves were being dug. There were also special preparations for a great increase in mental disorders. As it turned out the casualties were comparatively few, while mental disorders, I believe, actually declined. On the other hand, the authorities had failed to foresee that blitzed people would be homeless and would need food, clothes, shelter and money. They had also, while foreseeing the incendiary bomb, failed to realise that you would need an alternative water supply if the mains were burst by bombs.

By 1942 we were all set for the blitz of 1940. Shelter facilities had been increased, and London was dotted with water tanks which would have saved its historic buildings if only they had been in existence when the fires were happening. And then along came the doodle-bug, which, instead of blowing three or four houses out of existence, makes a large number uninhabitable, while leaving their interiors more or less intact. Hence another unforeseen headache—storage of furniture. The furniture from a doodle-bugged house is nearly always salvaged, but finding places to put it in, and labour to move it, has been almost too much for the local authorities. In general it has to be dumped in derelict and unguarded houses, where such of it as is not looted is ruined by damp.[1]

The most significant figures in Duncan Sandys's[2] speech were those dealing with the Allied counter-measures. He stated, for instance, that whereas the Germans shot off 8,000 doodle-bugs, or something under 8,000 tons of high explosive,[3] we dropped 100,000 tons of bombs on the bases, besides losing 450 aeroplanes and shooting off hundreds of thousands or millions of A.A. shells. One can only make rough calculations at this date, but it looks as though the doodle-bug may have a big future before it in forthcoming wars. Before writing it off as a flop, it is worth remembering that artillery scored only a partial success at the battle of Crécy.[4]

1. There was, in fact, a fairly efficient service based on 'Rest Centres' (often schools not in use because the children had been evacuated), which tried to deal with the shock felt by those who had been bombed out, to find them somewhere to live, and to provide them with clothes and furniture. Part of the work involved was recovering furniture from bombed houses. However, when raids were intense the service was very badly stretched and the staff, who worked at least twenty-four hours on and twenty-four hours off, became exhausted.
2. Duncan Sandys (1908–1987; Baron Duncan-Sandys, 1974), Conservative politician, served in the army; was wounded, and discharged in 1941. An M.P., 1935–74, he held a number of offices of state. At this time he was chairman of a War Cabinet Committee responsible for defence against flying bombs. He married Winston Churchill's daughter Diana in 1935; the marriage was dissolved in 1960.
3. For the V-1, or doodlebug, see *2501, n. 1*. Each carried about 2,000 pounds of explosive (900 kg).
4. At the Battle of Crécy, 1346, Edward III routed a large French army near Abbeville. His success was a result of tactics perfected against the Scotch and archers armed with longbows

(not artillery) capable of firing ten arrows a minute, which could pierce the armour of cavalrymen.

2550. To Dwight Macdonald

15 September 1944   Typewritten

Dear Macdonald,
Re. that article. After the cuts which I myself suggested because of the libel danger, "Horizon", who have the other copy, have insisted on some cuts on political grounds.[1] They fear that "Horizon" might be banned from the USSR where it sells a few score of copies. There's no earthly reason why you should follow suit, but I thought it might amuse you to know what the cuts are, as an example of the kind of thing considered unprintable in England nowadays. It ties up with that review I sent you a copy of.
The passages are:
"The truth is, of course, that the countless English intellectuals who kiss the arse of Stalin."
Altered to "worship dictators."
". . . and accounts, for instance, for the positive delight with which many English intellectuals greeted the Nazi-Soviet pact . . . could come afterwards."
Cut right out. (The first alteration reminds me of when I was in the BBC and someone in writing a literary talk used the word "copulation." I said "You'll never get that past the censorship", and altered it to "fornication." The Censorship altered it to "indulgence in base passions.")[2]
In reviewing "The Lion & the Unicorn" you rather took me to task for despising the English intelligentsia.[3] After this kind of thing don't you think I have some justification?

Yours
[Signed] Geo. Orwell
George Orwell

1. Macdonald did not make these cuts when 'Raffles and Miss Blandish' was published in *Politics*, though changes and cuts were made to the version in *Horizon*. See headnote and textual notes to *2538*.
2. Compare the change required of 'copulating' in *The Road to Wigan Pier*, *CW*, V, 228 and 231, 16/16.
3. Macdonald reviewed *The Lion and the Unicorn* in *Partisan Review*, March-April 1942. It was, he said, in its virtues and its defects 'typical of English leftwing political writing.' Its approach to politics was literary rather than technical, that of the amateur, not the professional.' That had its advantages, especially Orwell's ability to deal with much that Marxists had wrongly excluded, and what he described as 'a *human* quality to Orwell's political writing.' But the defects were, Macdonald thought, also marked. Orwell's scope was broad but none too deep, he described when he should analyse, he posed questions too impressionistically, used terms vaguely, made sweeping generalisations, and had an appalling innocence of scientific criteria. The passage that Orwell specifically refers to reads: 'He reacts so violently against the admittedly great defects of the leftwing intellectual tradition of the last two decades as to deny himself as an intellectual. . . . Orwell is bitterly hostile to both internationalism and

405

intellectualism, preaching the virtues of patriotism and denouncing "Europeanized intellectuals." ' Macdonald concluded his review by regretting the lack of a Searchlight Series in the United States; it was, he thought, an ideal medium for political pamphleteering.

2551. Review of *The American Problem* by D. W. Brogan
The Observer, 17 September 1944

It is uncertain what Professor Brogan intended to achieve by this book, which seems to fall mid-way between being a popular history of the United States and a forecast of American behaviour in the post-war world. His book, "The English People,"[1] written a year or two ago, had a clear enough purpose. It was obviously written "at" America, with the object of explaining the British social system and allaying anti-British prejudice, and its—on the whole—too favourable tone was therefore understandable. But the present book, presumably written to enlighten British readers, also gives the impression that Professor Brogan had an American rather than a British public in mind. The issues that are soft-pedalled are the ones that American opinion is sensitive about, and though the British reader will carry away many picturesque facts, he gets no clear answer to the questions that he is likeliest to ask about the United States at this moment.

The main emphasis of the book is historical. Professor Brogan rightly lays great stress upon the enormous achievement, quite unparalleled in human history, of colonising the North American continent, and on the "frontier" habit of mind which persisted after the frontier had ceased to exist. He also has some penetrating things to say about the position of American women, their civilising influence in the early days when the West was opened up, and the effects on American industry of their struggle for emancipation. He is also good on regional differences, and on the American climate and its effects on character, architecture and much else. But on the whole it is either marginal things of this kind that he is discussing, or else very large and vague issues: the immediate concrete problems are only mentioned in passing, if at all.

For instance, in discussing the American governmental machine, Professor Brogan gives a lot of details about the working of Congress, and utters some wide generalisations about the American love of oratory, but he hardly answers the question which almost any Englishman would ask—namely, what sections of the population, and what economic interests, do the two main parties represent? Again, though he has some good passages on American agriculture and the position of the farmer, he says very little about the economic structure of American society, the distribution of wealth, the trade unions, the ownership of the Press, and the popularity or otherwise of collectivist theories. Nor does he definitely say whether class distinctions are increasing or decreasing. The Negro problem is very lightly skated over. Professor Brogan does give a few pages to the Negroes, but only in connection with the backwardness of the South as a whole, and it is only in a couple of parentheses that he mentions that millions of Negroes are both half-starved and disenfranchised.

The thing, of course, that Professor Brogan is talking about and about [2] is American isolationism. Will the Americans, or will they not, give the world the moral lead it is waiting for and play their part in building a sane society? No doubt he is right to leave the answer open, but not, surely, to imply that it is merely a question of the Americans becoming less fixated on internal affairs and more aware that the outside world exists and is dangerous. The ignorant isolationism of the American mother who does not want "our boys" killed in foreign wars is not the main danger. The United States, now the greatest world power, will presumably have an active foreign policy after the war; the question is whether it will be an enlightened and unselfish policy. There are symptoms and tendencies which may help to give an answer, but Professor Brogan does not mention them, or barely mentions them.

For example, he says almost nothing about American imperialism, actual or potential. Nor does he discuss the meaning of the swing towards the Republican Party which appears to have been going on during the past year or two. Nor—this indeed is a question which involves Britain as much as the United States, but which obviously should not have been left out of account—does he say anything about the problems of migration, and especially the migration of the coloured peoples. And he is exceedingly cautious on the subject, all-important from our point of view, of anti-British feeling. Even when he mentions it, he is content to give the well-worn historical explanation and does not point to the fact that different sections of American society are anti-British for different and incompatible reasons. Professor Brogan seems to hint that the less we interfere in American affairs the better, and there he is probably right. But it is still important to us to know what the Americans think about us, and to what extent traditional and cultural hostilities are a cover for something else. Professor Brogan's witty manner of writing and his ability to drag in recondite illustrations for nearly everything that he says do not compensate for his avoidance of essentials.

In general this is a "get together" book. Though it is full of digressions, its main aim seems to be to convince the British public that the United States is a powerful and important country whose faults are those of youth, and with whom we should do well not to quarrel. This was hardly worth saying. Britain cannot afford to quarrel with America and there is very little popular anti-American feeling. On the other hand we could do with some expert information about American policy, internal and external: Professor Brogan is probably qualified to give it, but the fact that he always has at least one eye on a possible American reader prevents him from doing so.

[Fee: £10.0.0; 15.9.44]

1. Orwell reviewed *The English People* anonymously in *The Listener*, 27 May 1943; see *2099*.
2. 'talking about and about': although at first sight this might seem like an error in setting, Orwell typed 'about it and about' in the typescript of his rejected review of *Faith, Reason and Civilisation*; see *2434* and *2434, n 2*; 'about it and about' appears in stanza 27 of Fitzgerald's *The Rubáiyat of Omar Khayyám*; see also IV/281, line 11.

2552. 'Tobias Smollett: Scotland's Best Novelist'

Tribune, 22 September 1944[1]

"Realism," a much abused word, has at least four current meanings, but when applied to novels it normally means a photographic imitation of everyday life. A "realistic" novel is one in which the dialogue is colloquial and physical objects are described in such a way that you can visualise them. In this sense almost all modern novels are more "realistic" than those of the past, because the describing of everyday scenes and the construction of natural-sounding dialogue are largely a matter of technical tricks which are passed on from one generation to another, gradually improving in the process. But there is another sense in which the stilted, artificial novelists of the eighteenth century are more "realistic" than almost any of their successors, and that is in their attitude towards human motives. They may be weak at describing scenery, but they are extraordinarily good at describing scoundrelism. This is true even of Fielding, who in *Tom Jones* and *Amelia* already shows the moralising tendency which was to mark English novels for a hundred and fifty years. But it is much truer of Smollett, whose outstanding intellectual honesty may have been connected with the fact that he was not an Englishman.

Smollett is a picaresque novelist, a writer of long, formless tales full of farcical and improbable adventures. He derives to some extent from Cervantes, whom he translated into English and whom he also plagiarised in *Sir Lancelot Greaves*. Inevitably a great deal that he wrote is no longer worth reading, even including, perhaps, his most-praised book, *Humphrey Clinker,*° which is written in the form of letters and was considered comparatively respectable in the nineteenth century, because most of its obscenities are hidden under puns. But Smollett's real masterpieces are *Roderick Random* and *Peregrine Pickle*, which are frankly pornographic in a harmless way and which contain some of the best passages of sheer farce in the English language.

Dickens, in *David Copperfield*, names these two books among his childhood favourites, but the resemblance sometimes claimed as existing between Smollett and Dickens is very superficial. In *Pickwick Papers*, and in several others of Dickens's early books, you have the picaresque form, the endless travelling to and fro, the fantastic adventures, the willingness to sacrifice no matter what amount of probability for the sake of a joke; but the moral atmosphere has greatly altered. Between Smollett's day and Dickens's there had happened not only the French Revolution, but the rise of a new industrial middle class, Low Church in its theology and puritanical in its outlook. Smollett writes of the middle class, but the mercantile and professional middle class, the kind of people who are cousins to a landowner and take their manners from the aristocracy.

Duelling, gambling and fornication seem almost morally neutral to him. It so happens that in private life he was a better man than the majority of writers. He was a faithful husband who shortened his life by overworking for the sake of his family, a sturdy republican who hated France as the country of the Grand Monarchy, and a patriotic Scotsman at a time when—the 1745 rebellion being a fairly recent memory—it was far from fashionable to be a Scotsman. But he has very little sense of sin. His heroes do things, and do them on almost every page, which in any nineteenth-century English novel would instantly call forth vengeance from the skies. He accepts as a law of nature the viciousness, the nepotism and the disorder of eighteenth-century society, and therein lies his charm. Many of his best passages would be ruined by any intrusion of the moral sense.

Both *Peregine Pickle* and *Roderick Random* follow roughly the same course. Both heroes go through great vicissitudes of fortune, travel widely, seduce numerous women, suffer imprisonment for debt, and end up prosperous and happily married. Of the two, Peregrine is somewhat the greater blackguard, because he has no profession—Roderick is a naval surgeon, as Smollett himself had been for a while—and can consequently devote more time to seductions and practical jokes. But neither is ever shown acting from an unselfish motive, nor is it admitted that such things [as] religious belief, political conviction or even ordinary honesty are serious factors in human affairs.

In the world of Smollett's novels there are only three virtues. One is feudal loyalty (Roderick and Peregrine each have a retainer who is faithful through thick and thin), another is masculine "honour," i.e., willingness to fight on any provocation, and another is female "chastity," which is inextricably mixed up with the idea of capturing a husband. Otherwise anything goes. It is nothing out of the way to cheat at cards, for instance. It seems quite natural to Roderick, when he has got hold of £1,000 from somewhere, to buy himself a smart outfit of clothes and go to Bath posing as a rich man, in hopes of entrapping an heiress. When he is in France and out of a job, he decides to join the army, and as the French army happens to be the nearest one, he joins that, and fights against the British at the battle of Dettingen: he is nevertheless ready soon afterwards to fight a duel with a Frenchman who has insulted Britain.

Peregrine devotes himself for months at a time to the elaborate and horribly cruel practical jokes in which the eighteenth century delighted. When, for instance, an unfortunate English painter is thrown into the Bastille for some trifling offence and is about to be released, Peregrine and his friends, playing on his ignorance of the language, let him think that he has been sentenced to be broken on a wheel. A little later they tell him that this punishment has been commuted to castration, and then extract a last bit of fun out of his terrors by letting him think that he is escaping in disguise when he is merely being released from the prison in the normal way.

Why are these petty rogueries worth reading about? In the first place because they are funny. In the Continental writers from whom Smollett derived there may be better things than the description of Peregrine Pickle's adventures on the Grand Tour, but there is nothing better of that particular kind in English. Secondly, by simply ruling out "good' motives and showing no respect whatever for human dignity, Smollett often attains a truthfulness that more serious novelists have missed. He is willing to mention things which do happen in real life but are almost invariably kept out of fiction.

Roderick Random, for instance, at one stage of his career, catches a venereal disease—the only English novel-hero, I believe, to whom this has happened. And the fact that Smollett, in spite of his fairly enlightened views, takes patronage, official jobbery and general corruption for granted gives great historical interest to certain passages in his books.

Smollett had been for a while in the Navy, and in *Roderick Random* we are given not only an unvarnished account of the Cartagena expedition, but an extraordinarily vivid and disgusting description of the inside of a warship, in those days a sort of floating compendium of disease, discomfort, tyranny and incompetence. The command of Roderick's ship is for a while given to a young man of family, a scented homosexual fop who has hardly seen a ship in his life, and who spends the whole voyage in his cabin to avoid contact with the vulgar sailormen, almost fainting when he smells tobacco. The scenes in the debtors' prison are even better. In the prisons of those days, a debtor who had no resources might actually starve to death unless he could keep alive by begging from more fortunate prisoners. One of Roderick's fellow-prisoners is so reduced that he has no clothes at all, and preserves decency as best he can by wearing a very long beard. Some of the prisoners, needless to say, are poets, and the book includes a self-contained story, "Mr. Melopoyn's Tragedy," which should make anyone who thinks aristocratic patronage a good basis for literature think twice.

Smollett's influence on subsequent English writers has not been as great as that of his contemporary, Fielding. Fielding deals in the same kind of boisterous adventure, but his sense of sin never quite leaves him. It is interesting, in *Joseph Andrews*, to watch Fielding start out with the intention of writing a pure farce, and then, in spite of himself as it were, begin punishing vice and rewarding virtue in the way that was to be customary in English novels until almost yesterday. Tom Jones would fit into a novel by Meredith, or for that matter by Ian Hay,[2] whereas Peregrine Pickle seems to belong to a more European background. The writers nearest to Smollett are perhaps Surtees and Marryat, but when sexual frankness ceased to be possible, picaresque literature was robbed of perhaps half of its subject matter. The eighteenth-century inn where it was almost abnormal to go into the right bedroom was a lost dominion.

In our own day various English writers—Evelyn Waugh, for instance, and Aldous Huxley in his early novels—drawing on other sources, have tried to revive the picaresque tradition. One has only to watch their eager efforts to be shocking, and their readiness to be shocked themselves—whereas Smollett was merely trying to be funny in what seemed to him the natural way—to see what an accumulation of pity, decency and public spirit lies between that age and ours.

1. Orwell was on holiday for the second half of September (see letter to T. S. Eliot, 5 September 1944, 2543). There was no 'As I Please' for 22 and 29 September, but on the first of these dates he contributed this essay on Smollett.
2. Ian Hay (John Hay Beith) (1876–1952), novelist and dramatist, is probably best remembered for the well-turned light comedies based on his novels: *A Safety Match* (1911, produced 1921), *The Middle Watch* (1930, produced 1931), *The Midshipmaid* (1933, produced 1931), and

Housemaster (1936, as novel and play). He wrote a famous 'unofficial chronicle' of Kitchener's Army, *The First Hundred Thousand* (1915).

2553. London Letter

Partisan Review, Winter 1944–45   Written October (?) 1944

This London Letter is not noted in Orwell's Payments Book, so its position is conjectural. However, it is likely to have been written in October 1944 because, at the very end of the Letter, Orwell speaks of the Home Guard being stood down; in his article 'Home Guard Lessons for the Future,' *The Observer*, 15 October 1944 (see *2564*), he refers to the disbanding of the Home Guard.

An undated letter written to Orwell on behalf of the Senior Press Censor, Postal Sub-Section, Ministry of Information, states that the following passage was deleted from his 'letter' addressed to the Editor of *Partisan Review*: 'since here in L. there is no new development except the rocket bombs (very unpleasant, but there are only about half a dozen of them a day) which have replaced the doodle-bugs.'

The doodlebug, or flying bomb, was the V-1 (see *2501*, *n. 1*). It was followed by the V-2, another 'Vergeltungswaffe' or 'reprisal (or revenge) weapon,' and a genuine rocket. The first of these was fired at Paris on 6 September 1944; two days later the first of some 3,000 to be launched at England was fired. A similar number was aimed at Belgium. V-1s and V-2s each carried about 2,000 pounds (900 kilograms) of high explosive.

The censor made the cut because of anxiety about the public's reaction to yet another fearsome weapon at a time when people were particularly war-weary; it was felt that the less publicity given to this new weapon the better. The cut appears to have been made from the end of the second sentence of the final paragraph of the Letter. By the time Orwell wrote 'As I Please,' 50, 1 December 1944 (see *2586*), he was able to mention the existence of the V-2, provided, as he put it, it was not described 'too minutely.'

Dear Editors,

It is close on four years since I first wrote to you, and I have told you several times that I would like to write one letter which should be a sort of commentary on the previous ones. This seems to be a suitable moment.

Now that we have seemingly won the war and lost the peace, it is possible to see earlier events in a certain perspective, and the first thing I have to admit is that up to at any rate the end of 1942 I was grossly wrong in my analysis of the situation. It is because, so far as I can see, everyone else was wrong too that my own mistakes are worth commenting on.

I have tried to tell the truth in these letters, and I believe your readers have got from them a not too distorted picture of what was happening at any given moment. Of course there are many mistaken predictions (e.g., in 1941 I prophesied that Russia and Germany would go on collaborating and in 1942 that Churchill would fall from power), many generalizations based on little or no evidence, and also, from time to time, spiteful or misleading remarks about individuals. For instance, I particularly regret having said in one letter that Julian Symons "writes in a vaguely Fascist strain"—a quite unjustified statement based on a single article which I probably misunderstood. But this kind of thing results largely from the lunatic atmosphere of war, the fog of lies and misinformation in which one has to work and the endless sordid controversies in which a political journalist is involved. By the low standards now prevailing I think I have been fairly accurate about facts. Where I have gone wrong is in assessing the relative importance of different *trends*. And most of my mistakes spring from a political analysis which I had made in the desperate period of 1940 and continued to cling to long after it should have been clear that it was untenable.

The essential error is contained in my very first letter, written at the end of 1940, in which I stated that the political reaction which was already visibly under weigh "is not going to make very much ultimate difference." For about eighteen months I repeated this in various forms again and again. I not only assumed (what is probably true) that the drift of popular feeling was towards the Left, but that it would be quite impossible to win the war without democratizing it. In 1940 I had written, "Either we turn this into a revolutionary war, or we lose it," and I find myself repeating this word for word as late as the middle of 1942. This probably colored my judgment of actual events and made me exaggerate the depth of the political crisis in 1942, the possibilities of Cripps as a popular leader and of Common Wealth as a revolutionary party, and also the socially levelling process occurring in Britain as a result of the war. But what really matters is that I fell into the trap of assuming that "the war and the revolution are inseparable." There were excuses for this belief, but still it was a very great error. For after all we have not lost the war, unless appearances are very deceiving, and we have not introduced Socialism. Britain is moving towards a planned economy, and class distinctions tend to dwindle, but there has been no real shift of power and no increase in genuine democracy. The same people still own all the property and usurp all the best jobs. In the United States the development appears to be *away* from Socialism. The United States is indeed the most powerful country in the world, and the most capitalistic. When we look back at our judgments of a year or two ago, whether we "opposed" the war or whether we "supported" it, I think the first admission we ought to make is that *we were all wrong*.

Among the British and American intelligentsia, using the word in a wide sense, there were five attitudes towards the war:

(1) The war is worth winning at any price, because nothing could be worse than a Fascist victory. We must support any regime which will oppose the Nazis.

(2) The war is worth winning at any price, but in practice it cannot be won while capitalism survives. We must support the war, and at the same time endeavor to turn it into a revolutionary war.

(3) The war cannot be won while capitalism survives, but even if it could, such a victory would be worse than useless. It would merely lead to the establishment of Fascism in our own countries. We must overthrow our own government before lending our support to the war.

(4) If we fight against Fascism, under no matter what government, we shall inevitably go Fascist ourselves.

(5) It is no use fighting, because the Germans and the Japanese are bound to win anyway.

Position (1) was taken by radicals everywhere, and by Stalinists after the entry of the USSR. Trotskyists of various colors took either position (2) or position (4). Pacifists took position (4) and generally used (5) as an additional argument. (1) merely amounts to saying, "I don't like Fascism," and is hardly a guide to political action: it does not make any prediction about what will happen. But the other theories have all been completely falsified. The fact that we were fighting for our lives has not forced us to "go Socialist," as I foretold that it would, but neither has it driven us into Fascism. So far as I can judge, we are somewhat further away from Fascism than we were at the beginning of the war. It seems to me very important to realize that we have been wrong, and say so. Most people nowadays, when their predictions are falsified, just impudently claim that they have been justified, and squeeze the facts accordingly. Thus many people who took the line that I did will in effect claim that the revolution has already happened, that class privilege and economic injustice can never return, etc., etc. Pacifists claim with even greater confidence that Britain is already a Fascist country and indistinguishable from Nazi Germany, although the very fact that they are allowed to write and agitate contradicts them. From all sides there is a chorus of "I told you so," and complete shamelessness about past mistakes. Appeasers, Popular Front-ers, Communists, Trotskyists, Anarchists, Pacifists, all claim—and in almost exactly the same tone of voice—that *their* prophecies and no others have been borne out by events. Particularly on the Left, political thought is a sort of masturbation fantasy in which the world of facts hardly matters.

But to return to my own mistakes. I am not here concerned with correcting those mistakes, so much as with explaining why I made them. When I suggested to you that Britain was on the edge of drastic political changes, and had already made an advance from which there could be no drawing back, I was not trying to put a good face on things for the benefit of the American public. I expressed the same ideas, and much more violently, in books and articles only published at home. Here are a few samples:

"The choice is between Socialism and defeat. We must go forward, or perish." "Laissez-faire capitalism is dead." "The English revolution started several years ago, and it began to gather momentum when the troops came back from Dunkirk." "With its present social structure England cannot survive." "This war, unless we are defeated, will wipe out most of the existing class privileges." "Within a year, perhaps even within six months, if we are still unconquered, we shall see the rise of something that has never existed before, a specifically *English* Socialist movement." "The last thing the British ruling class wants is to acquire fresh territory." "The real quarrel of the Fascist powers with British imperialism is that they know that it is disintegrating." "The war will bankrupt the majority of the public schools if it continues for another year or two." "This war is a race between the consolidation of Hitler's empire and the growth of democratic consciousness."

And so on and so on. How could I write such things? Well, there is a clue in the fact that my predictions, especially about military events, were by no means always wrong. Looking back through my diaries and the news commentaries[1] which I wrote for the BBC over a period of two years, I see that I was often right as against the bulk of the leftwing intelligentsia. I was right to the extent that I was not defeatist, and after all the war has not been lost. The majority of leftwing intellectuals, whatever they might say in print, were blackly defeatist in 1940[2] and again in 1942. In the summer of 1942, the turning-point of the war, most of them held it as an article of faith that Alexandria would fall and Stalingrad would not. I remember a fellow broadcaster, a Communist saying to me with a kind of passion, "I would bet you anything, *anything*, that Rommel will be in Cairo in a month." What this person really meant, as I could see at a glance, was, "I *hope* Rommel will be in Cairo in a month." I myself didn't hope anything of the kind, and therefore I was able to see that the chances of holding on to Egypt were fairly good. You have here an example of the wish-thinking that underlies almost all political prediction at present.

I could be right on a point of this kind, because I don't share the average English intellectual's hatred of his own country and am not dismayed by a British victory. But just for the same reason I failed to form a true picture of political developments. I hate to see England either humiliated or humiliating anybody else. I wanted to think that we would not be defeated, and I wanted to think that the class distinctions and imperialist exploitation of which I am ashamed would not return. I over-emphasized the anti-Fascist character of the war, exaggerated the social changes that were actually occurring; and under-rated the enormous strength of the forces of reaction. This unconscious falsification colored all my earlier letters to you, though perhaps not the more recent ones.

So far as I can see, all political thinking for years past has been vitiated in the same way. People can foresee the future only when it coincides with their own wishes, and the most grossly obvious facts can be ignored when they are unwelcome. For example, right up to May of this year the more disaffected English intellectuals refused to believe that a Second Front would be opened. They went on refusing while, bang in front of their faces, the endless convoys of guns and landing craft rumbled through London on their way to the coast. One could point to countless other instances of people hugging quite manifest delusions because the truth would be wounding to their pride. Hence the absence of reliable political prediction. To name just one easily isolated example: Who foresaw the Russo–German pact of 1939? A few pessimistic Conservatives foretold an agreement between Germany and Russia, but the wrong kind of agreement, and for the wrong reasons. So far as I am aware, no intellectual of the Left, whether Russophile or Russophobe, foresaw anything of the kind. For that matter, the Left as a whole failed to foresee the rise of Fascism and failed to grasp that the Nazis were dangerous even when they were on the verge of seizing power. To appreciate the danger of Fascism the Left would have had to admit its own shortcomings, which was too painful: so the whole phenomenon was ignored or misinterpreted, with disastrous results.

The most one can say is that people can be fairly good prophets when their wishes are realizable. But a truly objective approach is almost impossible, because in one form or another almost everyone is a nationalist. Leftwing intellectuals do not think of themselves as nationalists, because as a rule they transfer their loyalty to some foreign country, such as the USSR, or indulge it in a merely negative form, in hatred of their own country and its rulers. But their outlook is essentially nationalist, in that they think entirely in terms of power politics and competitive prestige. In looking at any situation they do not say, "What are the facts? What are the probabilities," but, "How can I make it appear to myself and others that my faction is getting the better of some rival faction?" To a Stalinist it is *impossible* that Stalin could ever be wrong, and to a Trotskyist it is equally impossible that Stalin could ever be right. So also with Anarchists, Pacifists, Tories or what-have-you. And the atomization of the world, the lack of any real contact between one country and another, makes delusions easier to preserve. To an astonishing extent it is impossible to discover what is happening outside one's own immediate circle. An illustration of this is that no one, so far as I know, can calculate the casualties in the present war within ten millions. But one expects governments and newspapers to tell lies. What is worse, to me, is the contempt even of intellectuals for objective truth so long as their own brand of nationalism is being boosted. The most intelligent people seem capable of holding schizophrenic beliefs, of disregarding plain facts, of evading serious questions with debating-society repartees, or swallowing baseless rumors and of looking on indifferently while history is falsified. All these mental vices spring ultimately from the nationalistic habit of mind, which is itself, I suppose, the product of fear and of the ghastly emptiness of machine civilization. But at any rate it is not surprising that in our age the followers of Marx have not been much more successful as prophets than the followers of Nostradamus.

I believe that it is possible to be more objective than most of us are, but that it involves a *moral* effort. One cannot get away from one's own subjective feelings, but at least one can know what they are and make allowance for them. I have made attempts to do this, especially latterly, and for that reason I think the later ones among my letters to you, roughly speaking from the middle of 1942 onwards, give a more truthful picture of developments in Britain than the earlier ones. As this letter has been largely a tirade against the leftwing intelligentsia, I would like to add, without flattery, that judging from such American periodicals as I see, the mental atmosphere in the USA is still a good deal more breathable than it is in England.

I began this letter three days ago. World-shaking events are happening all over the place, but in London nothing new.[3] The change-over from the blackout to the so-called dim-out[4] has made no difference as yet. The streets are still inky dark. On and off it is beastly cold and it looks as though fuel will be very short this winter. People's tempers get more and more ragged, and shopping is a misery. The shopkeepers treat you like dirt, especially if you want something that happens to be in short supply at the moment. The latest shortages are combs and teats for babies' feeding bottles. Teats have been actually unprocurable in some areas, and what do exist are made of reconditioned rubber. At the same time contraceptives are plentiful and made of good rubber. Whisky is rarer than ever, but there are more cars on the roads, so the petrol situation must have let up a little. The Home Guard has been stood down and firewatching greatly reduced. More U.S. soldiers have looked me up, using PR as an introduction. I am always most happy to meet any reader of PR. I can generally be got at the *Tribune*, but failing that my home number is CAN 3751.

George Orwell

1. From the way that Orwell expresses this, it would seem that he kept some, at least, of the scripts he wrote for the Eastern Service Newsletters, just as he kept his diaries.
2. Contrast the defeatist (but possibly jocular) undated note at *619*.
3. At this point, Orwell's reference to the V-2 appears to have been censored. See headnote.
4. In the autumn of 1944, strict blackout regulations were relaxed, and a low level of lighting was permitted, since manned bombing flights were then rare. V-1s and V-2s did not depend on direct land sightings

2554. Review of *Burma Pamphlets*: 1. *Burma Background* by V. R. Pearn, 2. *Burma Setting* by O. H. K. Spate, 3. *Buddhism in Burma* by G. Appleton; *Burma* by Ma Mya Sein; *Wings Over Burma* by Kenneth Hemingway; *Wingate's Raiders* by Charles J. Rolo

The Observer, 1 October 1944

Until very recently Burma has been so badly publicised in this country that it has been difficult even for the most thoughtful newspaper readers to form any opinion about it. The campaign of 1942 was inadequately reported, there has been as nearly as possible no information about what is happening under Japanese rule, and nothing has been divulged about Britain's post-war intentions towards Burma. Nor has there been much reliable information about Burma's background problems and its relations with China and India. The newly-published Burma Pamphlets—they appear to have been printed and perhaps planned in India—are therefore a useful departure, and may help public opinion to exert itself in favour of a reasonable settlement when the Japanese have been evicted.

Of the three that have so far appeared, *Burma Background*—a brief history of the country from the eleventh century onwards—is probably the most useful, but *Burma Setting* fills up a number of gaps by giving a picture of the day-to-day life of the country and describing its climatic conditions and natural resources. *Buddhism in Burma*, which gives the appearance of having been written by a Christian missionary, is less useful from the point of view of the average reader, as it concentrates on the doctrinal side of Buddhism and does not say enough about the extremely important political and social activities of the Burmese priesthood.

Ma Mya Sein's pamphlet (what a novelty, by the way, to find something about Burma written by a Burmese!) overlaps to some extent with the other three. The author has had a distinguished public career in Burma and is, one gathers, a very moderate Nationalist. She gives a general survey of the country, with as much reference as is necessary to its past history, and is at pains to emphasise that in spite of its numerous races Burma is a natural unit and capable of full nationhood. Unlike the writers in the other series, she touches on present-day politics and adds the warning that "any attempt to reconstruct Burma after the war can only succeed if it gets full nationalist sympathy behind it."

The other two books are not concerned with political problems, though "Wingate's Raiders" does throw some indirect light upon them. *Wings Over Burma*—an account of the heroic effort of the small group of R.A.F., and the A.V.G.,[1] to fight off the Japanese invasion—is a tale of continued battles against odds, ending triumphantly some time in 1943, when the Allies began to gain mastery in the air, and the unfortunate Burma towns, already partly destroyed by the Japanese, began to get their second dose of bombing and machine-gunning from the skies. It is full of technical slang, but vivid and readable. *Wingate's Raiders* is a more schoolboyish type of book, obviously written with the object of building round Brigadier-General Wingate[2] the same kind of legend as surrounds Gordon and T. E. Lawrence; but its detailed account of Wingate's methods should be valuable to students of guerrilla warfare.

The book does not deal with Wingate's part in the successful operations against Myitkyina in 1944, in which he met his death. It is chiefly concerned with his preliminary raid into Japanese-occupied territory a year earlier. Lord Wavell, who remembered Wingate's achievements in Palestine and Abyssinia, brought him to Burma in 1942, when the campaign was already lost, but while there was still time to study the Japanese tactics in jungle warfare.

Wingate saw that the British and Indians, apart from being outnumbered and ill-supported in the air, were hopelessly hampered by being tied to mechanised transport. The more lightly equipped Japanese could move round them and cut their communications at will. He set himself to produce an even more mobile force, which would use the game-tracks where the Japanese used the cart-tracks, and which could be supplied entirely by air, and therefore be quite independent of lines of communication. Any man who was medically fit, he said, could be made into a good jungle fighter. And in the event his mixed force of British, Indians, and Burmese—the British were mostly second-line troops who had seen no fighting before—penetrated hundreds of miles into strongly occupied territory, did an immense amount of damage, and got out again, having suffered terribly from hunger and hardship, but with comparatively few battle casualties.

As Lord Wavell says in his foreword, this expedition had no strategic aim except the secondary one of taking the pressure off the Kachin levies who were still beleaguered at Fort Hertz; but it was invaluable experience and prepared the way for Wingate's airborne descent on the Japanese rear at Katha[3] a year later. Wingate's originality of mind is apparent in his every action.

It is interesting to notice that the column seems to have been received almost everywhere in friendly fashion by the Burmese villagers—a sign, perhaps, that after a year of occupation the Japanese promises were already wearing thin.

[Fee: £10.0.0; 29.9.44]

1. American Volunteer Group, popularly known as the Flying Tigers. This force of pilots and supporting mechanics was raised by a retired U.S. Air Force General, Claire Lee Chennault (1890–1958). They had fewer than fifty planes at any one time and only some seventy pilots. Yet, operating in primitive conditions about 150 miles from Rangoon, they proved remarkably effective. From December 1941 to July 1942 they brought down some 300 Japanese planes for certain and destroyed perhaps as many more.
2. General Orde Charles Wingate (1903–1944) led forces deep into Japanese-held Burmese territory in February 1943 and March 1944. His degree of success was bitterly disputed. Traditional military authority was disturbed by his unconventional methods and personal behaviour—eating raw onions as if they were fruit—but he attracted extraordinary devotion and certainly showed that Japanese forces could be beaten in the depths of the jungle. He had made his reputation training Zionist guards during the Arab Revolt in Palestine in 1936 and since then has been held in high regard in Israel. John Keegan and Andrew Wheatcroft conclude his entry in their *Who's Who in Military History* (1976) by suggesting 'he is perhaps best seen as a prophet of doom: his strategic ideas supplied the French . . . with the germ of the plan for the [disastrous] Dien Bien Phu operation.' As Orwell suspected he would, he has become a legend.
3. Orwell served at Katha from 23 December 1926 until he left Burma in July 1927. It provided a basis for Kyauktada in *Burmese Days*.

2555. To T. S. Eliot

3 October 1944   Typewritten

Tribune

Dear Eliot,

I think you replied while I was away to a letter of mine. Can you have lunch some day this month? I forget which are your days in town. Mondays, Tuesdays and Fridays are my best days. How about for instance the 16th, 17th, or 20th?

Yours sincerely,
[Signed] Geo. Orwell
George Orwell

P.S. Have you seen the current Partisan Review?

Eliot replied on 11 October, apologising for his tardiness. He explained that he was ordinarily in London only three days a week and he could not manage the dates Orwell had suggested. He proposed 16 November and renewed the invitation to Eileen to join him for lunch with Orwell. Orwell's reply has not been traced.

2556. To Leonard Moore

3 October 1944   Handwritten

CANONBURY 27B Canonbury Square Islington London N. 1

Dear Mr Moore,

Many thanks for your letters. I think the terms with Warburg are quite satisfactory. I am now collating the stuff for my book of reprints & shall get it typed. Warburg wants to publish it but presumably cannot do so before next autumn or so. But I will send one copy straight off to the U.S.A. & have another try at the Dial Press, as they expressed a desire to see it.

Yours sincerely
E. A. Blair

P.S. The above is now my *permanent* address.[1]

1. After Orwell and Eileen were bombed out of their flat in Mortimer Crescent, 14 July 1944, they stayed in Inez Holden's house, 106 George Street, London W.1. The letter has been annotated in Moore's office: 'note address'; over that is written, 'done.' Orwell also printed CANONBURY in case his handwriting was unclear.

2557. To Stanley Unwin

3 October 1944   Typewritten

Tribune

Dear Mr. Unwin,

Many thanks for your letter of September 18th, which I've only just had as I've been away.

Yes, I got your pamphlet[1] and am going to refer to it in my column when I can get space to do so.

Your sincerely,
[Signed] Geo. Orwell
George Orwell

1. *Publishing in Peace & War*; see end note to 'Are Books Too Dear?,' *2482*.

2558. To Rayner Heppenstall

4 October 1944   Original

Tribune

Dear Rayner,

I don't seem to have had books by either Rosamund Lehmann or Alex Comfort. Of course they may come along later. I'm sending you "Transformation (2)",[1] which may have some interesting stuff in it.

I understand that Richard (not Christopher—his names are Richard Horatio) was born about 11 a.m. on May 14th 1944.[2]

Yours,
Eric

1. The 'little magazine' *Transformation* was edited by Stefan Schimanski and Henry Treece. It appeared annually from 1943 to 1947. Treece was associated with Orwell's work at the BBC. Three of his poems were read by John Atkins in 'Voice,' 1, 11 August 1942. For Schimanski, see *1615, n. 1*; for Treece, *1327, n. 1*. In the event, Heppenstall did not review *Transformation*, 2. Presumably, despite his desire for 'plenty of books' to review (see *n. 2*), he did not find it worth reviewing and sent it back. It was reviewed by C. H. (Charles Hamblett?) under the heading 'Shorter Notices' on 22 December 1944.
2. Information required so that Richard's horoscope, which Heppenstall had offered to cast (see *2515*), could be prepared. Heppenstall wrote on 14 October enclosing the horoscope. He said, however, that he seemed to have lost the technique and feeling for casting a horoscope and had 'scarcely bothered with Adam's' (his son's). He asked if Eliot's *Four Quartets* was available for review and, indeed, for 'plenty of books'; also, whether Orwell was doing his (Heppenstall's) 'anti-nationalist article.' Neither Heppenstall nor anyone else reviewed *Four Quartets* in *Tribune* in 1944; see also *2563, n. 1*.

2559. Review of *Four Quartets* by T. S. Eliot

Manchester Evening News, 5 October 1944

The four long poems contained in this book—"Burnt Norton," "East Coker," "The Dry Salvages," and "Little Gidding"—were all published as separate pamphlets between 1936 and 1942,[1] and they rightly attracted a great deal of attention and criticism.

Nevertheless, after several years in which to get them into perspective, it is still a little difficult to be sure what to think of them.

The difficulty is in deciding whether the unlyrical and, one might also say, deliberately unpoetical way of writing which Mr. Eliot has developed in the last 10 years, is an improvement on his earlier manner. At this date his early poems, which can be found in the collected edition also published by Fabers, hardly need introduction.

Once vilified as a "high-brow" and accused of writing in deliberately obscure language for the benefit of a small clique of initiates, Mr. Eliot has become almost a popular writer. Even the obscurity which some of the early poems do certainly display springs chiefly from literary allusions, which can be tracked down with a little thought and a few works of reference.

Perhaps the best-known poem of all, the love song of Alfred J. Prufrock°, is written in extremely simple language, and in this and other poems, notably "Sweeney Agonistes," Mr. Eliot has made one of the few serious efforts that have been made in our time to get spoken English on to paper. And certainly no poet writing in English in this century, except, perhaps, W. B. Yeats, has rivalled him for sheer verbal beauty.

To quote simply one out of countless passages that lodge themselves in the memory:

And the lost heart stiffens and rejoices
In the lost lilac and the lost sea voices,
And the weak spirit quickens to rebel
For the bent golden-rod and the lost sea smell,
Quickens to recover
The cry of quail and whirling plover,
And smell renews the salt savour of the sandy earth.

That passage comes from "Ash Wednesday," which will have been written about 1928,[2] and marks the turning-point between Mr. Eliot's two manners.

It is significant that in his earlier poems there are many passages that one easily remembers by heart—and the test, at any rate of lyric poetry, is whether one remembers it by heart, or, at least, whether one wants to do so. This quality has largely departed from the later poems. But the subject matter has also changed, and one cannot consider the two changes independently.

Most of Mr. Eliot's early poems were, quite frankly, poems of decay. They were a sort of ironical elegy on a dying civilisation. The Sweeney poems are a verse counterpart of James Joyce's "Ulysses," while "Prufrock" is, among other things, a devastating picture of the modern over-civilised intellectual.

The four last poems, however, are poems of belief—though not, apparently, a very spontaneous kind of belief. Curiously enough, in spite of an obviously sincere effort to be explicit and not to put verbal difficulties in the way, it is not so easy to say what these poems are about.

Their titles are the names of places (three in England, one in America) with which Mr. Eliot has ancestral connections, and their[3] substance is a devout but rather gloomy musing on the subject of death and immortality.

Making use of various contexts he is trying to talk his readers (and perhaps himself) out of time and into eternity. Essentially, these poems are a profession of faith by someone who has only reached that faith by a considerable intellectual effort.

As Mr. Eliot explicitly states in the poems, this entails an abandonment of ordinary literary aims. "So here I am, in the middle way, having had 20 years—20 years largely wasted, the years of *l'entre deux guerres*—trying to learn to use words, and every attempt is a wholly new start, and a different kind of failure because one has only learnt to get the better of words for the thing one no longer has to say, or the way in which one is no longer disposed to say it. And so each venture is a new beginning, a raid on the inarticulate with shabby equipment always deteriorating in the general mess of imprecision of feeling, undisciplined squads of emotion." [4]

Essentially the same idea is repeated in a number of different forms. He is not trying to be "poetical" any longer. "The poetry does not matter," he says. One can respect this abandonment of literary vanity while still feeling that much has been lost in the process.

There are considerable passages in these poems which—precisely because Mr. Eliot is trying very hard to convey an exact meaning—are so prosaic in language that if they were printed as prose one would never know that they had originally been intended as verse.

And where the verse breaks into rhyme it frequently has a sort of metallic tinkle that even the slickest of the earlier poems never had. But it would be unfair to say that the old magic is never there. For example:

> Oh, dark, dark, dark. They all go into the dark,
> The vacant interstellar spaces, the vacant into the vacant,
> The captains, merchant bankers, eminent men of letters,
> The generous patrons of art, the statesmen and the rulers,
> Distinguished civil servants, chairmen of many committees,
> Industrial lords and petty contractors, all go into the dark,
> And dark the sun and moon,
> And the Almanach de Gotha,
> And the Stock Exchange Gazette, the directory of directors,
> And cold the sense and lost the motive of action.[5]

And at least anyone who reads these poems will never forget the phrase "At the still point of the turning world," nor, probably, the line "Time and the bell have buried the day."[6]

It is difficult not to feel that Mr. Eliot lost a great deal by embracing the Anglo-Catholic version of the Christian religion, and that he would have done better to go on chronicling the decay of a civilisation which he frankly dislikes.

Curiously enough he had not only more power but more gaiety when he despaired of life than now, when he is at least trying to see a meaning in it.

But one cannot simply dismiss these poems as failures. For Mr. Eliot is one of those writers who "grow upon you," as the saying goes. Plenty of people who found him unreadable or unintelligible in 1920 were worshipping him by 1930, and in a few years' time we may be discovering that his later manner, from which so much of the old grace of language seems to have departed, is not a mistake after all.

There are very few writers now alive who are better worth taking trouble over. And even the reader who is disappointed by this particular book will not have wasted his time if the list of previous works on the dust-jacket leads him to the discovery of "Prufrock," or the "Waste Land," or "Sweeney Agonistes."

[Fee: £8.0.0; 4.10.44]

1. 'Burnt Norton' was first published in Eliot's *Collected Poems*, 1936, and 'East Coker' in a supplement to *New English Weekly*, Easter 1940; 'The Dry Salvages' and 'Little Gidding' were published as pamphlets in 1941 and 1942 respectively.
2. 'Ash Wednesday' was published complete in 1930, but three sections had already been published: I in *Commerce*, Spring 1928; II in *Saturday Review of Literature*, December 1927; and III in *Commerce*, Autumn 1929. Each had a title omitted from the complete poem. The passage Orwell quotes is from VI. The original has no punctuation whatsoever, not even a final full-point. It should be 'the whirling plover' and that should be followed by two lines: 'And the blind eye creates / The empty forms between the ivory gates.' As so often when Orwell gets his quotations wrong, one suspects that it is, paradoxically, because he 'knows' the text and quotes from memory, but the lines had not quite perfectly lodged themselves in his memory (as Orwell put it).
3. 'their' set as 'that.'
4. The passage quoted and set as prose is, of course, verse. It is the first eleven lines of part V of

'East Coker.' The lines should break after: twenty years—, *guerres*—, attempt, failure, words, which, venture, inarticulate, deteriorating, feeling. It is extremely unlikely that the compositor would have set as prose what Orwell typed as verse—the section quoted later in the review (from the opening of part III of 'East Coker') is not only presented as verse but set in italic. Further, the capital letters for words that start all lines but the first have been set in lower case and, as a final touch, the word 'twenty,' given twice, is set in figures. Orwell has, evidently, played a subtle trick on the reader (likely then to be unfamiliar with 'East Coker'), demonstrating what he argues in the next section of his review, that, printed as prose, one might not know that this was verse so prosaic is the language.

5. From the opening of part III of 'East Coker.' The first words should be: 'O dark dark dark'; the seventh line should read: 'And dark the Sun and Moon, and the Almanach de Gotha' with no comma at the end; 'Directory of Directors' should be capitalised.

6. From 'Burnt Norton,' II and IV. 'At the still point . . .' appears in both sections.

2560. 'As I Please,' 43

Tribune, 6 October 1944

By permission of a correspondent, I quote passages from a letter of instruction which she recently received from a well-known school of journalism.[1] I should explain that when she undertook her "course" the instructor asked her to supply the necessary minimum of information about her background and experience, and then told her to write a couple of specimen essays on some subject interesting to her. Being a miner's wife, she chose to write about coal-mining. Here is the reply she got from someone calling himself the "Assistant Director of Studies."[2] I shall have to quote from it at some length:

"I have read your two exercises with care and interest. You should have a good deal to write about. But do be careful of getting a bee in your bonnet. Miners are not the only men who have a hard time. How about young naval officers, earning less than a skilled miner—who must spend three or four years from home and family, in ice or the tropics? How about the many retired folks on a tiny pension or allowance, whose previous £2 or £3 have been reduced by *half* by the income tax? We all make sacrifices in this war—and the so-called upper classes are being hard hit indeed.

"Instead of writing propaganda for Socialist newspapers you will do better to describe—for the housewives—what life is like in a mining village. Do not go out of your way to be hostile to owners and managers—who are ordinary fellow-creatures—but, if you must air a grievance, do so tolerantly, and fit it in with your plot or theme.

"Many of your readers will be people who are not in the least inclined to regard employers as slave drivers and capitalist villains of society. . . . Write simply and naturally, without any attempt at long words or sentences. Remember that your task is to *entertain*. No reader will bother after a hard day's work to read a list of somebody else's woes. Keep a strict eye on your inclination to write about the 'wrongs' of mining. There are *millions* of people who will not forget that miners did strike while our sons and husbands were fighting the Germans. Where would the miners be if the troops had refused to fight? I mention this to help you keep a sense of perspective. I advise you against writing very controversial things. They are hard to sell. A plain account of mining life will stand a far better chance. . . . the average reader is willing to read facts about other ways of life—but unless he is a fool or knave, he will not listen to *one-sided* propaganda. So forget your grievances, and tell us something of how *you* manage in a typical mining village. One of the women's magazines will, I'm sure, consider a housewife's article on that subject."

My correspondent, who, it seems, had agreed in advance to pay £11 for this course, sent the letter on to me with the query: Did I think that her instructor was trying to influence her to give her writings an acceptable political slant? Was an attempt being made to talk her out of writing like a Socialist?

I do think so, of course, but the implications of this letter are worse than that. This is not a subtle capitalist plot to dope the workers. The writer of that slovenly letter is not a sinister plotter but simply an ass (a female ass, I should say by the style)[3] upon whom years of bombing and privation have made no impression. What it demonstrates is the unconquerable, weed-like vitality of pre-war habits of mind. The writer assumes, it will be seen, that the only purpose of journalism is to tickle money out of the pockets of tired business men, and that the best way of doing this is to avoid telling unpleasant truths about present-day society. The reading public, so he (or she) reasons, don't like being made to think: therefore don't make them think. You are after the big dough, and no other consideration enters.

Anyone who has had anything to do with "courses" in free-lance journalism, or has even come as near to them as studying the now-defunct *Writer*[4] and the *Writer's and Artist's Yearbook*, will recognise the tone of that letter. "Remember that your task is to *entertain*." "No reader will bother after a hard day's work to read a list of somebody else's woes," and "I advise you against writing very controversial things. They are hard to sell." I pass over the fact that even from a commercial point of view such advice is misleading. What is significant is the assumption that nothing ever changes, that the public always will be and always must be the same mob of nitwits wanting only to be doped, and that no sane person would sit down behind a typewriter with any other object than to produce saleable drivel.

When I started writing, about fifteen years ago, various people—who, however, didn't succeed in getting £11 out of me in return—gave me advice almost identical with what I have quoted above. Then too, it seemed, the public did not want to hear about "unpleasant" things like unemployment, and articles on "controversial" subjects were "hard to sell." The dreary sub-world of the free-lance journalist, the world of furnished bed-sitting rooms, hired typewriters and self-addressed envelopes, was entirely dominated by the theory that "your task is to entertain." But at that time there was some excuse. To begin with, there was widespread unemployment, and every newspaper and magazine was besieged by hordes of amateurs struggling frantically to earn odd guineas; and in addition the Press was incomparably sillier than it is now, and there was some truth in the claim that editors would not print "gloomy" contributions. If you looked on writing as simply and solely a way of making money, then cheer-up stuff was probably the best line. What is depressing is to see that for the —— school of journalism the world has stood still. The bombs have achieved nothing. And, indeed, when I read that letter I had the same feeling that the pre-war world is back upon us as I had a little while ago when, through the window of some chambers in the Temple, I watched somebody—with great care and evident pleasure in the process—polishing a top hat.

It is superfluous to say that long railway journeys are not pleasant in these days, and for a good deal of the discomfort that people have to suffer, the railway companies are not to blame. It is not their fault that there is an enormous to-and-fro of civilian traffic at a time when the Armed Forces are monopolising most of the rolling stock, nor that an English railway carriage is built with the seeming object of wasting as much space as possible. But journeys which often entail standing for six or eight hours in a crowded corridor could be made less intolerable by a few reforms.

To begin with, the First Class nonsense should be scrapped once and for all. Secondly, any woman carrying a baby should have a priority right to a seat. Thirdly, waiting rooms should be left open all night. Fourthly, if timetables cannot be adhered to, porters and other officials should be in possession of correct information, and not, as at present, tell you that you will have to change when you won't, and vice versa. Also—a thing that is bad enough in peace time but is even worse at this moment—why is it that there is no cheap way of moving luggage across a big town? What do you do if you have to move a heavy trunk from Paddington to Camden Town? You take a taxi. And suppose you can't afford a taxi, what do you do then? Presumably you borrow a handcart, or balance the trunk on a perambulator. Why are there not cheap luggage-vans, just as there are buses for human passengers? Or why not make it possible to carry luggage on the Underground?

This evening, as King's Cross discharged another horde of returned evacuees, I saw a man and woman, obviously worn out by a long journey, trying to board a bus. The woman carried a squalling baby and clutched a child of about six by the other hand; the man was carrying a broken suitcase tied with rope and the elder child's cot. They were refused by one bus after another. Of course, no bus could take a cot on board. How could it be expected to? But, on the other hand, how were those people to get home? It ended by the woman boarding a bus with the two children, while the man trailed off carrying the cot. For all I know he had a five-mile walk ahead of him.

In war time one must expect this kind of thing. But the point is that if those people had made the same journey, similarly loaded, in peace time, their predicament would have been just the same. For

The rain it raineth every day
Upon the just and unjust feller,
But more upon the just because
The unjust has the just's umbrella.

Our society is not only so arranged that if you have money you can buy luxuries with it. After all, that is what money is for. It is also so arranged that if you don't have money you pay for it at every hour of the day with petty humiliations and totally unnecessary discomforts—such as, for instance, walking home with a suitcase cutting your fingers off when a mere half-crown would get you there in five minutes.

1. Orwell's correspondent was Mrs. Ada Dodd who lived near Bridgend, Glamorgan. She had two boys and two girls and, writing on 14 September to thank Orwell for his kind advice, said she did not suppose she would be able to achieve anything by her writing, but 'as things are today in the mining Industry I see no outlook for the vast majority of miner's° children other than to be caught in the same vicious circle of poverty, injustice & bitterness, that we, their parents have been caught in.' She longed to be able to write about the evils of coal mining and in the hope of bettering the future for miners' children refused to be persuaded by her instructor to write contrary to her beliefs. The 'well-known school of journalism' was the London School of Journalism. Ironically, it advertised regularly in *Tribune*. Its advertisement for 27 October 1944 took as its theme Orwell's subject of 8 September and 13 October, under the headline 'Where are the Writers of To-morrow?' Some wit in *Tribune*'s magazine make-up department placed one of the School's advertisements on the same page as 'As I Please,' 47, 3 November 1944; see *2573*. See also the letter from E. R. Ward about advertisements in *Tribune* for another writing school, *2579*. The London School of Journalism advertised in *Tribune* on 15 February 1946, a 'new Course by L. A. G. Strong, the famous author and broadcaster.' Under the heading, 'Make Your Writing Pay in 1991,' the LSJ still advertised in the national press in that year. The advertisement stated that the school had been established in 1920 and offered correspondence and tutorial courses, the latter being recognised by the Home Office. Successful students were awarded the LSJ diploma. The school offered short-story, television, and radio courses for writers.
2. He signed himself J. H. B. Peel.
3. 'a female ass . . . by the style': note 'while our sons and husbands were fighting the Germans.'
4. The *Writer* was not defunct: Orwell apologised for his error in 'As I Please,' 48 (see *2579*).

2561. To Daniel George

Monday [9 October 1944][1]   Handwritten

Tribune

Dear Daniel George,[2]
How about Friday (13th—I suppose you meant this week?) at Antoine's at 1.15 pm?

Yours
Geo. Orwell

1. It is likely that this letter was written in connexion with Orwell's duties as literary editor of *Tribune*. In that case, there was only one Friday, 13, when he was in London whilst in that post—October 1944. Monday was the ninth. The 13th fell on a Friday in July 1945, but on 24 July he wrote to Kathleen Raine that he was not working for *Tribune* any more, 'at least for the time being.'
2. Daniel George Bunting (1890–1967), essayist and poet; chief reader for Jonathan Cape. He reported favourably on *Animal Farm*, although 'its real purpose is not clear. Publication is a matter of policy. I cannot myself see any serious objection to it' (Crick, 455, quoting Michael S. Howard, *Jonathan Cape, Publisher*, 1971, 179). In 'As I Please,' 47, 3 November 1944 (see

2573), Orwell, discussing how reviewing is to be reorganised in *Tribune*, says, 'Daniel George's novel reviews will not be affected.'

2561A. To Lydia Jackson
11 October 1944   Typewritten

Tribune

Dear Lydia,
Thanks for the review.[1] I hope to see the one of the Polish book soon.[2] We *aren't* on the phone yet (you know how long it takes to get it put in), but the address is 27B, Canonbury Square, N.1., a 2d. ride for you on the 30 bus.

Yours,
[Signed] Eric.

1. All Lydia Jackson's reviews and articles (signed Elisaveta Fen) published in 1944 and until the end of March 1945 have been identified and allocated to Orwell's letters requesting reviews except for *Stalin and Eternal Russia* by Walter Kolarz. No letter survives offering this book for review. It may be referred to here but the review was published by *Tribune* only two days later, 13 October. Possibly Orwell's letter of the 11th was intended to be written earlier. If this does not refer to the review of Kolarz's book, whatever is referred to was not published.
2. As Orwell specifies 'the Polish Book,' this presumably refers to *G for Genevieve*; see *2548A*.

2562. 'As I Please', 44
Tribune, 13 October 1944

Sir Osbert Sitwell's little book, and my remarks on it, brought in an unusually large amount of correspondence,[1] and some of the points that were raised seem to need further comment.

One correspondent solved the whole problem by asserting that society can get along perfectly well without artists. It can also get along without scientists, engineers, doctors, bricklayers or road-menders—for the time being. It can even get along without sowing next year's harvest, provided it is understood that everyone is going to starve to death in about twelve months' time.

This notion, which is fairly widespread and has been encouraged by people who should know better, simply restates the problem in a new form. What the artist does is not immediately and obviously necessary in the same way as what the milkman or the coalminer does. Except in the ideal society which has not yet arrived, or in very chaotic and prosperous ages like the one that is just ending, this means in practice that the artist must have some kind of patron—a ruling class, the Church, the State, or a political party. And the question "Which is best?" normally means "Which interferes least?"

Several correspondents pointed out that one solution is for the artist to have an alternative means of livelihood. "It is quite feasible," says Mr. P. Philips Price, "to write and devote oneself to Socialism whilst accepting the patronage of the B.B.C., M.O.I., Rank or C.E.M.A. . . . the only way out is some minor form of prostitution, part time." The difficulty here is that the practice of writing or any other art takes up a lot of time and energy. Moreover, the kind of job that a writer gets in war-time, if he is not in the Forces (or even if he is—for there is always P.R.),[2] usually has something to do with propaganda. But this is itself a kind of writing. To compose a propaganda pamphlet or a radio feature needs just as much work as to write something you believe in, with the difference that the finished product is worthless. I could give a whole list of writers of promise [3] or performance who are now being squeezed dry like oranges in some official job or other. It is true that in most cases it is voluntary. They want the war to be won, and they know that everyone must sacrifice something. But still the result is the same. They will come out of the war with nothing to show for their labours and with not even the stored-up experience that the soldier gets in return for his physical suffering.

If a writer is to have an alternative profession, it is much better that it should have nothing to do with writing. A particularly successful holder of two jobs was Trollope, who produced two thousand words between seven and nine o'clock every morning before leaving for his work at the Post Office. But Trollope was an exceptional man, and as he also hunted three days a week and was usually playing whist till midnight, I suspect that he did not overwork himself in his official duties.

Other correspondents pointed out that in a genuinely Socialist society the distinction between the artist and the ordinary man would vanish. Very likely, but then no such society yet exists. Others rightly claimed that State patronage is a better guarantee against starvation than private patronage, but seemed to me too ready to disregard the censorship that this implies. The usual line was that it is better for the artist to be a responsible member of a community than an anarchic individualist. The issue, however, is not between irresponsible "self-expression" and discipline; it is between truth and lies.

Artists don't so much object to *æsthetic* discipline. Architects will design theatres or churches equally readily, writers will switch from the three-volume novel to the one-volume, or from the play to the film, according to the demand. But the point is that this is a political age. A writer inevitably writes—and less directly this applies to all the arts—about contemporary events, and his impulse is to tell what he believes to be the truth. But no government, no big organisation, will pay for the truth. To take a crude example: can you imagine the British Government commissioning E. M. Forster to write *A Passage to India*? He could only write it because he was *not* dependent on State aid. Multiply that instance by a million, and you see the danger that is involved—not, indeed, in a centralised economy as such, but in our going forward into a collectivist age without remembering that the price of liberty is eternal vigilance.[4]

Recently I was told the following story, and I have every reason to believe that it is true.

Among the German prisoners captured in France there are a certain number of Russians. Some time back two were captured who did not speak Russian or any other language that was known either to their captors or their fellow-prisoners. They could, in fact, only converse with one another. A professor of Slavonic languages, brought down from Oxford, could make nothing of what they were saying. Then it happened that a sergeant who had served on the frontiers of India overheard them talking and recognised their language, which he was able to speak a little. It was Tibetan! After some questioning, he managed to get their story out of them.

Some years earlier they had strayed over the frontier into the Soviet Union and been conscripted into a labour battallion, afterwards being sent to western Russia when the war with Germany broke out. They were taken prisoner by the Germans and sent to North Africa; later they were sent to France, then exchanged into a fighting unit when the Second Front opened, and taken prisoner by the British. All this time they had been able to speak to nobody but one another, and had no notion of what was happening or who was fighting whom.

It would round the story off neatly if they were now conscripted into the British Army and sent to fight the Japanese, ending up somewhere in Central Asia, quite close to their native village, but still very much puzzled as to what it is all about.

An Indian journalist sends me a cutting of an interview he had with Bernard Shaw. Shaw says one or two sensible things and does state that the Congress leaders ought not to have been arrested, but on the whole it is a disgusting exhibition. Here are some samples:—

Q. — Supposing you were a National leader of India. How would you have dealt with the British? What would have been your methods to achieve Indian independence?

A. — Please do not suppose a situation that can never happen. The achievement of Indian independence is not my business.

Q. — What do you think is the most effective way of getting the British out of India? What should the Indian people do?

A. — Make them superfluous by doing their work better. Or assimilate them by cross-fertilisation. British babies do not thrive in India.

What kind of answers are those to give to people who are labouring under a huge and justified grievance? Shaw also refuses to send birthday greetings to Gandhi, on the ground that this is a practice he never follows, and advises the Indian people not to bother if Britain repudiates the huge credit balance which India has piled up in this country during the war. I wonder what impression this interview would give to some young Indian student who has been a couple of years in jail and has dimly heard of Bernard Shaw as one of Britain's leading "progressive" thinkers? Is it surprising if even very level-headed Indians are liable to a recurrent suspicion that "all Englishmen are the same"?

1. *A Letter to My Son*; see 'As I Please,' 41, 8 September 1944, *2547*, and ensuing correspondence.
2. Public Relations.

3. On 27 October, *Tribune* published a letter from someone who signed himself 'Writer' concerning what he or she took to be the real enemies of promise. They were 'publishers ("Barabbas was a publisher"), publishers' readers (often arty-tarty public school "Communists"), the hell of the book-reviewing racket and the society that revolves around it, and the Authors' Society and the P.E.N. Club!' Reviewing had reached a new low in wartime, Writer said, and the future for the younger author might be a 'real Trade Union,' a new Writers' Union, or co-operative publishing.

4. 'The condition upon which God hath given liberty to man is eternal vigilance', John Philpot Curran, Dublin, 1790.

2563. To Rayner Heppenstall

13 October 1944   Typewritten

Tribune

Dear Rayner,

We should like it very much if you would become one of our regular reviewers. It would in all probability mean doing an article once every two or three months, but not in regular rotation. I will explain what it is that we want to do.

We feel that the practice of giving shortish reviews to a large number of books each week is unsatisfactory, and we intend to have each week a leading review of anything up to 1500 words, dealing with some current book which for one reason or another deserves serious criticism. With this much space to dispose of one can not only give a full criticism of the book in hand but make one's article a worth-while piece of writing in itself. The reason why we cannot keep to a regular rotation is that we must send each book to the reviewer who seems most suitable.[1] We should be able to give about a fortnight's notice. The fee for these articles will be 3 guineas.

A stamped addressed envelope is enclosed. I should be obliged if you would let me know as early as possible whether you are interested in this.

Yours truly,
[Signed] Geo. Orwell
George Orwell

1. Orwell announced the replanning of the way book reviewing was to be organised in 'As I Please,' 47, 3 November 1944 (see 2573), and listed there those who would contribute the kind of reviews described in this letter to Heppenstall. It was a list of 'first-rate . . . reviewers' in addition to those who had written fairly frequently for *Tribune* in the past. On 3 November, Heppenstall reviewed in *Tribune*, *Selected Poems of Friedrich Hölderlin* (translated by J. B. Leisham), *The Best Poems of 1943*, and Edith Sitwell's *Green Song and Other Poems*. He thought *Green Song* 'may be first-rate' and the finest book of verse he had read since the outbreak of war, 'unless perhaps I have to except *Little Chipping*° or whatever the last of T. S. Eliot's long topographical rhapsodies is called.' On 17 November, *Tribune* published a letter from W. L. Hutton condemning Heppenstall as a reviewer of poetry: 'No one who knows anything of prosody could write of stress and classical metres in the slap-happy way that Heppenstall does. . . . Surely, Heppenstall knows that the quantity of one to two of vowel values of classical verse is not found in English?' He concluded: 'George Orwell promises us better reviews and announces his team. Heppenstall's name is not among them, so I have great hopes of the promise being fulfilled. Heppenstall's pronouncements are like that of the celebrated James Pigg who, when asked to discover what kind of a night it was, stuck his head in a cupboard and said that it was hellish dark and smelled of cheese. It would be better for

Heppenstall to honestly announce his ignorance of poetry in general rather than to flaunt his feigned ignorance of Eliot's last poem in particular.' Orwell may have decided that Heppenstall's silly remark about *Four Quartets* and Hutton's letter disqualified Heppenstall from reviewing Eliot's poem. See. *2558, n. 2.*

2563A. **To Arthur Koestler**, 13 October 1944: see Vol xx, last appendix.

2563B. **[Ivor Brown] to Dr Thomas Jones, CH**, 14 October 1944: see Vol. xx, Appendix 15

2564. 'Home Guard Lessons for the Future'

The Observer, 15 October 1944

Now that the danger of any serious attempt at German invasion has obviously passed, the Home Guard can be safely disbanded, and it becomes possible to see its activities in perspective and even to draw some general inferences about part-time irregular armies.

We do not know how the Home Guard would have fought if it had been called upon: almost certainly it would have given a good account of itself any time after 1941, and would have had a considerable nuisance value even in 1940. As things turned out its functions were purely preventive,[1] and granted that its existence did help to make the Germans think twice about invasion, it gave extraordinarily good value at very low cost to the community as a whole. It is worth reflecting on the amount of extra work than can be safely demanded of the citizens of a democratic State, without effective compulsion and almost without pay.

The ordinary Home Guard private who is now retiring after four years' service will certainly not have given up less than 1,200 hours of his spare time: more probably it would be about 4,000 hours, or many more in the case of an officer. During those four years he will have been paid, in fees for guard duties (similar to those paid to fire-watchers) round about £35.

Otherwise he will have cost the community nothing except his uniform, a certain amount of ammunition, and wear and tear of weapons, the rent of a few premises, and the salaries of a very few Regular Army instructors. And, in addition, during the second two years of its existence the Home Guards has given valuable preliminary training to tens of thousands of youths who would later enter the Regular Forces.

More important, symptomatically, than the cheapness of an army of this type is its voluntary character. Conscription was introduced after about two years, but it was probably aimed at getting younger recruits and was not strictly necessary for the purpose of keeping up number. Between a million and two million men had been raised by voluntary means. Moreover, at the beginning discipline rested entirely upon good will. Officers and N.C.O.s had no power of coercion whatever. Later, legal penalties were introduced for absenteeism and indiscipline, but they were a very weak substitute for military punishments, and they were applied in only a few cases. There were many units where no prosecution was ever instituted, and some unit commanders announced from the start that they did not intend to make use of their legal powers.

If one asks, "What held the Home Guard together?" the answer can only be, "The Germans." The idea behind it was simply the primitive instinct to defend one's native soil, and to an astonishing extent it failed throughout its four years to develop any political colour. Foreign-born recruits remarked with surprise that they listened to scores of lectures on military technique, but never to one on the origins of the war. The inherited or early acquired patriotism on which the Home Guard depended is not necessarily inexhaustible even in Britain, and it is possible to point out ways in which a force of this kind could probably be made more effective should it be needed again.

Briefly, such a force should be, and probably could be, more democratic and more conscious of what the war is about. It should be more exactly aware of its own aims, military as well as political. The Home Guard suffered from the start from an uncertainty as to whether it was a guerrilla force or an adjunct to the Regular Army. And it would have been more democratic as well as more efficient if it had had a higher proportion of paid personnel. In the absence of paid instructors the commissioned ranks were frequently filled by people with fairly large incomes, so that the Home Guard mirrored the existing class-structure even more exactly than the Regular Army. In the circumstances of a foreign invasion these things could be serious weaknesses. But they are all remediable, and meanwhile the Home Guard has played its part, both as military force and as a political symptom. No authoritarian State would have dared to distribute weapons so freely.

[Fee: £10.0.0; 13.10.44]

1. The Home Guard did man many anti-aircraft batteries, especially 'Z' (rocket) batteries.

2565. Review of *Adam and Eve* by John Middleton Murry[1]

Manchester Evening News, 19 October 1944

Anyone who looks for a way out of the nightmare in which we are now living is apt to find himself caught in a dilemma which can be stated thus—men will not get better while their environment remains what it is, but the environment will not improve unless men get better.

Society needs to be regenerated, but the regeneration must be done by individuals whom society has already corrupted. Since progress does happen (for after all, we are probably better than we were in the Stone Age, or even in the Dark Ages) it is likely that this vicious circle is not quite so vicious as it looks, but no thinking person pretends that the problem is easy. At the least, it involves deciding whether laws matter more than men, or bodies more than souls.

The Marxists (of whom Mr. Middleton Murry was one until fairly recently) will have no truck with individual regeneration. According to them a corrupt society *must* produce corrupt individuals. Mr. Murry, over a period of about half a dozen years, has moved in the opposite direction, till he has reached the point of asserting that civilisation can only be saved by very small bodies of men and women who deliberately set themselves apart and live as far as possible outside the control of the State. Mass action is useless, everything must start with the individual and with the natural unit of the family.

"Sex," says Mr. Murry, "is at the bottom of all." From families in which the man and the woman genuinely love one another, and in which the children grow up in an atmosphere free from fear, it may be possible to build up small self-contained communities to act as the nuclei of a new civilisation, like the Christian monasteries after the collapse of the Roman Empire.

Translated into concrete terms, this means pacifist anarchist colonies, supporting themselves by agriculture. If such colonies can remain in being and produce happy and well-adjusted human beings, they may act as an example to the community as a whole and draw it back towards a simpler, saner and more essentially religious form of life.

Mr. Murry is not advocating a return to the "noble savage," or even to the Middle Ages. He knows that machine-production has come to stay, and he has no objection to using the machine, provided that it is merely to save brute labour and not to cheat the creative impulses of the human being.

At present it is almost true that man is the slave of the machine. In peace-time it cuts him off from the chance of creative work, in war it gives him such frightful powers of destruction that his very existence as a species is menaced.

But he has no escape from the machine, because he has no conscious objective except a "high standard of living," meaning a rapid rate of production. For the evils produced by a mechanised society he can think of no remedy except a still higher degree of mechanisation—whereas, says Mr. Murry, if he believed in God, loved his wife and enjoyed working with his hands, a "high standard of living" would seem comparatively irrelevant to him.

So far as Mr. Murry's diagnosis is negative it is easy to agree with it, or at least to feel sympathetic with it. But his positive suggestions are less easy to accept, especially when one remembers that Mr. Murry was advocating different and even opposite remedies with equal confidence only a few years ago.

One obvious difficulty is the conflict between his pacifism and his desire to escape totalitarianism of the Nazi kind. So far as can be gathered from this book, Mr. Murry refuses unequivocally to "support" the war, and in fact he has for some years been editor of "Peace News" and one of the ablest exponents of the pacifist case. At the same time he admits that Britain is not so far gone on the road to totalitarianism as various European countries, and even that the kind of anarchist colonies that he hopes to see established would have no chance if the Nazis were to triumph.

"The new community cannot hope to prosper and expand, or even survive, in the python embrace of a full totalitarian State. But in this country, where full totalitarianism runs directly counter to the political and religious ethos of society, it can hope for toleration and assistance enough to make headway."

This is quite true. Communities of the sort that Mr. Murry advocates do exist here and there in Britain,[2] and the Government tolerates them, though, perhaps, not very gladly. In a totalitarian State they would be simply wiped out—indeed, they could never have been established in the first place.

But how does this square with pacifism? For if the first indispensable necessity is political toleration, and if you can get a little of this in Britain and none at all in Germany, surely you must, at all costs, prevent Britain from being conquered?

Mr. Murry does not answer this question, but from time to time it silently intrudes itself, and probably leads Mr. Murry to overstate parts of his case. One claim which he makes, and which is habitually made by nearly all pacifists, is that as a result of fighting totalitarianism by violence we have "gone totalitarian" ourselves.

Before the war it was reasonable to expect this, but it is doubtful whether it has happened. Indeed, the non-appearance in England of a genuinely totalitarian outlook, and the comparative absence of hate propaganda (it was far worse in 1914–18) are encouraging symptoms. Again, Mr. Murry probably overstresses the "dehumanising" effects of the machine. Before being certain that the machine has taken the flavour out of life one would have to know a great deal more than we actually do about the common people of past ages.

It is quite possible that a modern factory-worker is more individual, more intelligent, happier, and more amiable than, say, a mediæval serf or a Roman slave. In general, Mr. Murry shows a tendency to squeeze the facts and to accept doubtful evidence when it suits his case.

But this is an interesting book and a good antidote to the current notion that we should all be perfectly happy if we could get rid of Hitler and then go back to 1939 with shorter working hours and no unemployment. There is a postscript by "Eve," which might well have been omitted.

[Fee: £8.0.0; 18.10.44]

1. Orwell had asked John Middleton Murry on 11 August 1944 (see *2531*) for a copy of *Adam and Eve*, saying he might be able to discuss it in 'As I Please.' Murry wanted Orwell to read his book because it encapsulated so many of his ideas. In addition to this review, there is some discussion of *Adam and Eve* in 'As I Please,' 46, 27 October 1944; see *2568*.

2. Orwell's son, Richard, would stay with such a Community (Whiteway) in 1949; see *3592*, n. 1.

2566. 'As I Please,' 45

Tribune, 20 October 1944

Reading recently a book on Brigadier-General Wingate,[1] who was killed early this year in Burma, I was interested to note that Wingate's "Chindits," who marched across Upper Burma in 1943, were wearing not the usual clumsy and conspicuous pith helmets, but slouch hats like those worn in the Gurkha regiments. This sounds a very small point, but it is of considerable social significance, and twenty or even ten years ago it would have been impossible. Nearly everyone, including nearly any doctor, would have predicted that large numbers of these men would perish of sunstroke.

Till recently the Europeans in India had an essentially superstitious attitude towards heat apoplexy, or sunstroke as it is usually called. It was supposed to be something dangerous to Europeans but not to Asiatics. When I was in Burma I was assured that the Indian sun, even at its coolest, had a peculiar deadliness which could only be warded off by wearing a helmet of cork or pith. "Natives," their skulls being thicker, had no need of these helmets, but for a European even a double felt hat was not a reliable protection.

But why should the sun in Burma, even on a positively chilly day, be deadlier than in England? Because we were nearer to the equator and the rays of the sun were more perpendicular. This astonished me, for obviously the rays of the sun are only perpendicular round about noon. How about the early morning, when the sun is creeping over the horizon and the rays are parallel with the earth? It is exactly then, I was told, that they are at their most dangerous. But how about the rainy season, when one frequently does not see the sun for days at a time? Then of all times, the old-stagers told me, you should cling to your topi. (The pith helmet is called a "topi," which is Hindustani for "hat.") The deadly rays filter through the envelope of cloud just the same, and on a dull day you are in danger of forgetting it. Take your topi off in the open for one moment, even for one moment, and you may be a dead man. Some people, not content with cork and pith, believed in the mysterious virtues of red flannel and had little patches of it sewn into their shirts over the top vertebra. The Eurasian community, anxious to emphasise their white ancestry, used at that time to wear topis even larger and thicker than those of the British.

My own disbelief in all this dated from the day when my topi was blown off my head and carried away down a stream, leaving me to march bareheaded all day without ill-effects. But I soon noticed other facts that conflicted with the prevailing belief. To begin with some Europeans (for instance sailors working in the rigging of ships) did habitually go bareheaded in the sun. Again, when cases of sunstroke occurred (for they do occur), they did not seem to be traceable to any occasion when the victim had taken his hat off. They happened to Asiatics as well as to Europeans; and were said to be commonest among stokers on coal-burning ships, who were subjected to fierce heat but not to sunshine. The final blow was the discovery that the topi, supposedly the only protection against the Indian sun, is quite a recent invention. The early Europeans in India knew nothing of it. In short, the whole thing was bunkum.

But why should the British in India have built up this superstition about sunstroke? Because an endless emphasis on the differences between the "natives" and yourself is one of the necessary props of imperialism. You can only rule over a subject race, especially when you are in a small minority, if you honestly believe yourself to be racially superior, and it helps towards this if you can believe that the subject race is *biologically* different. There were quite a number of ways in which Europeans in India used to believe, without any evidence, that Asiatic bodies differed from their own. Even quite considerable anatomical differences were supposed to exist. But this nonsense about Europeans being subject to sunstroke, and Orientals not, was the most cherished superstition of all. The thin skull was the mark of racial superiority, and the pith topi was a sort of emblem of imperialism.

That is why it seems to me a sign of the changing times that Wingate's men, British, Indians and Burmese alike, set forth in ordinary felt hats. They suffered from dysentery, malaria, leeches, lice, snakes and Japanese, but I do not think any cases of sunstroke were recorded. And above all, there seems to have been no official protest and no feeling that the abandonment of the topi was a subtle blow at white prestige.

In Mr. Stanley Unwin's recent pamphlet, *Publishing in Peace and War*,[2] some interesting facts are given about the quantities of paper allotted by the Government for various purposes. Here are the present figures:—

Newspapers . . . . . . 250,000 tons
H.M. Stationery Office 100,000 ,,
Periodicals   (nearly)   50,000 ,,
Books . . . . 22,000 ,,

A particularly interesting detail is that out of the 100,000 tons allotted to the Stationery Office, the War Office gets no less than 25,000 tons, or more than the whole book trade put together.

I haven't personally witnessed, but I can imagine, the kind of wastage of paper that goes on in the War Office and the various ministries. I know what happens in the B.B.C. Would you credit, for instance, that of every radio programme that goes out on the air, even the inconceivable rubbish of cross-talk comedians, at least six copies are typed—sometimes as many as fifteen copies? For years past all this trash has been filed somewhere or other in enormous archives.[3] At the same time paper for books is so short that even the most hackneyed "classic" is liable to be out of print, many schools are short of textbooks, new writers get no chance to start and even established writers have to expect a gap of a year or two years between finishing a book and seeing it published. And incidentally the export trade in English books has been largely swallowed up by America.

This part of Mr. Unwin's pamphlet is a depressing story. He writes with justified anger of the contemptuous attitude towards books shown by one Government department after another. But in fact the English as a whole, though somewhat better in this respect than the Americans, have not much reverence for books. It is in the small countries, such as Finland and Holland, that the book-consumption per head is largest. Is it not rather humiliating to be told that a few years before the war a remote town like Reykjavik had a better display of *British* books than any English town of comparable size?

1. *Wingate's Raiders* by Charles J. Rolo, reviewed by Orwell in *The Observer*, 1 October 1944; see *2554*; for Wingate, see *2554, n. 2*.
2. See *2557*.
3. Many of these typescripts (including some of Orwell's) are now to be found in the BBC's Written Archive, Caversham.

2566A. To Lydia Jackson

23 October 1944   Typewritten

Tribune

Dear Lydia,

Thanks so much for the review.[1]

I think you'll find us at home almost any evening. (You know the address—27B Canonbury Square. 30 bus takes you there). We can't go out at night much because of the baby.

Yours,
[Signed] George

1. Possibly the short notice (it was of only 200 words) of *Elementary Russian Grammar* (on one sheet) by Dr I. Freiman; see *2535A*. It was published on 10 November.

2567. Unpublished Review of *Beyond Personality* by C. S. Lewis

The Observer, Mid-October 1944?[1]

According to the blurb on the dust jacket a distinguished critic[2] wrote of "The Screwtape Letters," "I do not hesitate to compare Mr. Lewis's achievement with 'Pilgrim's Progress'." Here is a sample, entirely representative, from the present book:

> "Well, even on the human level, you know, there are two kinds of pretending. There's a bad kind, where the pretence is *instead of* the real thing; as when a man pretends he's going to help you instead of really helping you. But there's also a good kind, where the pretence *leads up to* the real thing. When you're not feeling particularly friendly but know you ought to be, the best thing you can do, very often, is to put on a friendly manner and behave as if you were a nicer chap than you actually are. And in a few minutes as we've all noticed, you will be *really* feeling friendlier than you were. Very often the only way to get a quality is to start behaving as if you had it already. That's why children's games are so important. They're always pretending to be grown-ups—playing soldiers, playing shop. But all the time, they are hardening their muscles and sharpening their wits, so that the pretence of being grown-ups helps them to grow up in earnest."

One could be forgiven for not detecting any resemblance to "Pilgrim's Progress" here. On the other hand, where has one read something like this before? Of course! In "For Sinners Only"![3] There is the same lavish use of italics, the same intimate little asides ("you know," "mind you," and "I'm going to be brutally frank"), the same abbreviations and Edwardian slang ("awfully," "jolly well," "specially" for "especially," "awful cheek," and so forth) all aimed at persuading the suspicious reader that one can be a Christian and a "decent chap" at the same time. The essays that make up this book were originally delivered as broadcasts, and one must make some allowance for that fact; but the English language is a great betrayer of motives, and the uneasy geniality with which Mr. Lewis writes is not a good symptom. Who has not observed some well-meaning muscular curate, only too anxious to be a "man among men," broadminded on the subject of alcohol, robustly tolerant of a "damn" and even a "bloody," and yet wearing permanently a guilty look in his eyes? In his heart he knows that ordinary people will never accept him as a friend until he turns his collar the other way round. The same impression is conveyed by this book, and beneath Mr. Lewis's man-to-man approach there is an obvious consciousness not only that the great mass of the people is alienated, perhaps for ever, from the Christian Church but that the Church itself must be somehow to blame for this.

These essays set out to be a popular exposition of Theology. Mr. Lewis belongs in the same line of descent as all the silly-clever apologists for the Faith who spring ultimately from W. H. Mallock.[4] The most telling argument of these people is always to point out that every heresy has been uttered before (with the implication that it has also been refuted before), and "all this atheism is really awfully old-fashioned, you know." Mr. Lewis gets in the usual side-kick at "all these people who turn up every few years with some patent simplified religion of their own." But the technique has changed a little. Some indefensible positions have been quietly abandoned (Mr. Lewis appears to accept the theory of Evolution, "refuted" by nearly every popular Christian apologist 15 years ago), and the woolliness which the B.B.C. imposes upon its speakers prevents any doctrinal precision or the raising of any really painful problem.

The other change is that Mr. Lewis seems a little more conscious than his forerunners used to be that the non-Christian portion of the world also exists. The visible fact that Christians are not better than other people he gets over by assuming it to mean merely that Christians, as individuals, are not more amiable than other people. He does tone down, by implication, the doctrine of *extra ecclesiam nulla salus*.[5] At the beginning we are told that individual religious experience is not enough, that there is also need of a Church, a priesthood, and a clear body of doctrine. Our ancestors, or some of them, followed this up with the quite logical inference that the heathen are damned. But we are growing too squeamish for that nowadays, and besides, the heathen are too numerous. A thousand million Asiatics are not Christians and do not want to be, yet they are not morally worse than ourselves and are manifestly more religious in outlook. Mr. Lewis comes to terms with this fact by admitting that there are many different roads to salvation and that a man may in effect be a Christian without knowing it. But in that case what is the function of the Christian Church and of the theologians whose wisdom Mr. Lewis tells us to prefer to our own?

Books of this kind are endemic in England. Their brisk assumption that unbelief is outmoded, and their reactionary political implications, always get them a lot of praise, but somehow they make no difference. The drift away from the churches, and the decay of the religious attitude to life, continue. One has only to look out of the nearest window to see that this is a disaster, but it is inevitable so long as the real reasons for it are not faced. The function of Mr. Lewis and his kind is to cover those reasons up or dispose of them with debating-society repartees. But 50 years of effort in this direction have achieved very little.

1. In 'As I Please,' 46, 27 October 1944 (see *2568*), Orwell says he had read C. S. Lewis's *Beyond Personality* 'A week or two ago'; that would be very soon after it had been published. He reviewed the book for *The Observer*, but his review was not published presumably on the advice of Dr Thomas Jones (see *2563B*, XX, Appendix 15). The review is printed here from a galley-proof. There is no record in Orwell's Payments Book that this review was submitted, so it cannot be dated precisely. It is possible that the review was intended for 10 December 1944. From mid-August to 26 November 1944, reviews or articles appear fortnightly, then none until after 24 December; so there is none at 10 December. However, a review appears out of this fortnightly sequence on 31 December; this may have made up Orwell's quota of reviews and articles, replacing whatever should have appeared on 10 December. Since the date is not known, the review is printed here next to the 'As I Please' which refers to Lewis's book.
2. W. J. Turner, with whom Orwell worked on *The English People*; see *1743, n. 1.*
3. By A. J. Russell, published in 1932. It is an account of the Oxford Group Movement, followers of Frank Buchman (1878–1961), an American-born evangelist. The Movement, also known as Moral Re-Armament, was founded in Oxford in 1921. See also *2571, n. 1.*
4. W. H. Mallock (1849–1923), novelist who successfully imitated Peacock (in *The New Republic*, 1877) and *Candide* (in *The New Paul and Virginia*, 1878). His *Social Equality* (1882) defended inequality and wealth, and for this he was attacked by Bernard Shaw in *Socialism and Superior Brains* (1910). He also wrote an autobiography, *Memoirs of Life and Literature* (1920). He was described in 1894 by Percy Russell as 'one of the pioneers of the contemporary religious novel' (*A Guide to British and American Novels*, 197).
5. Properly: *salus extra ecclesiam non est*—no salvation exists outside the church (St Augustine). Also quoted by Orwell in *2309.*

2568. 'As I Please,' 46

Tribune, 27 October 1944

Reading, a week or two ago, Mr. C. S. Lewis's recently-published book, *Beyond Personality* (it is a series of reprinted broadcasts on theology), I learned from the blurb on the dust jacket that a critic who should, and indeed does, know better had likened an earlier book, *The Screwtape Letters*, to *The Pilgrim's Progress*. "I do not hesitate to compare Mr. Lewis's achievement with *Pilgrim's Progress*" were his quoted words. Here is a sample, entirely representative, from the later book:—

> "Well, even on the human level, you know, there are two kinds of pretending. There's a bad kind, where the pretence is *instead of* the real thing, as when a man pretends he's going to help you instead of really helping you. But there's also a good kind, where the pretence *leads up to* the real thing. When you're not feeling particularly friendly but know you ought to be, the best thing you can do, very often, is to put on a friendly manner and behave as if you were a much nicer chap than you actually are. And in a few minutes, as we've all noticed, you will be *really* feeling friendlier than you were. Very often the only way to get a quality is to start behaving as if you had it already. That's why children's games are so

439

important. They're always pretending to be grown-ups—playing soldiers, playing shop. But all the time they are hardening their muscles and sharpening their wits, so that the pretence of being grown-ups helps them in earnest."

The book is like this all the way through, and I think most of us would hesitate a long time before equating Mr. Lewis with Bunyan. One must make some allowance for the fact that these essays are reprinted broadcasts, but even on the air it is not really necessary to insult your hearers with homey little asides like "you know" and "mind you," or Edwardian slang like "awfully," "jolly well," "specially" for "especially," "awful cheek," and so forth. The idea, of course, is to persuade the suspicious reader, or listener, that one can be a Christian and a "jolly good chap" at the same time. I don't imagine that the attempt would have much success, and in any case the cotton wool with which the B.B.C. stuffs its speakers' mouths makes any real discussion of theological problems impossible, even from an orthodox angle. But Mr. Lewis's vogue at this moment, the time allowed to him on the air and the exaggerated praise he has received, are bad symptoms and worth noticing.

Students of popular religious apologetics will notice early in the book a side-kick at "all these people who turn up every few years with some patent simplified religion of their own," and various hints that unbelief is "out of date," "old-fashioned," and so forth. And they will remember Ronald Knox[1] saying much the same thing fifteen years ago, and R. H. Benson[2] twenty or thirty years before that, and they will know in which pigeonhole Mr. Lewis should be placed.

A kind of book that has been endemic in England for quite sixty years is the silly-clever religious book, which goes on the principle not of threatening the unbeliever with Hell, but of showing him up as an illogical ass, incapable of clear thought and unaware that everything he says has been said and refuted before. This school of literature started, I think, with W. H. Mallock's *New Republic*, which must have been written about 1880, and it has had a long line of practitioners—R. H. Benson, Chesterton, Father Knox, "Beachcomber" and others, most of them Catholics, but some, like Dr. Cyril Alington[3] and (I suspect) Mr. Lewis himself, Anglicans. The line of attack is always the same. Every heresy has been uttered before (with the implication that it has also been refuted before); and theology is only understood by theologians (with the implication that you should leave your thinking to the priests). Along these lines one can, of course, have a lot of clean fun by "correcting loose thinking" and pointing out that so-and-so is only saying what Pelagius said in A.D. 400 (or whenever it was),[4] and has in any case used the word transubstantiation in the wrong sense. The special targets of these people have been T. H. Huxley, H. G. Wells, Bertrand Russell, Professor Joad, and others who are associated in the popular mind with Science and Rationalism. They have never had much difficulty in demolishing them—though I notice that most of the demolished ones are still there, while some of the Christian apologists themselves begin to look rather faded.

One reason for the extravagant boosting that these people always get in the Press is that their political affiliations are invariably reactionary. Some of them were frank admirers of Fascism as long as it was safe to be so. That is why I draw attention to Mr. C. S. Lewis and his chummy little wireless talks, of which no doubt there will be more. They are not really so unpolitical as they are meant to look. Indeed they are an outflanking movement in the big counter-attack against the Left which Lord Elton, A. P. Herbert, G. M. Young, Alfred Noyes and various others have been conducting for two years past.[5]

I notice that in his new book, *Adam and Eve*, Mr. Middleton Murry instances the agitation against Mosley's release from internment as a sign of the growth of totalitarianism, or the totalitarian habit of mind, in this country. The common people, he says, still detest totalitarianism: but he adds in a later footnote that the Mosley business has shaken this opinion somewhat. I wonder whether he is right.

On the face of it, the demonstrations against Mosley's release were a very bad sign. In effect people were agitating against Habeas Corpus.[6] In 1940 it was a perfectly proper action to intern Mosley, and in my opinion it would have been quite proper to shoot him if the Germans had set foot in Britain. When it is a question of national existence, no government can stand on the letter of the law: otherwise a potential quisling has only to avoid committing any indictable offence, and he can remain at liberty, ready to go over to the enemy and act as their gauleiter as soon as they arrive. But by 1943 the situation was totally different. The chance of a serious German invasion had passed, and Mosley (though possibly he may make a comeback at some future date—I won't prophesy about that) was merely a ridiculous failed politician with varicose veins. To continue imprisoning him without trial was an infringement of every principle we are supposedly fighting for.

But there was also strong popular feeling against Mosley's release, and not, I think, for reasons so sinister as Mr. Murry implies. The comment one most frequently heard was "They've only done it because he's a rich man," which was a simplified way of saying "Class privilege is on the up-grade again." It is a commonplace that the political advance we seemed to make in 1940 has been gradually filched away from us again. But though the ordinary man sees this happening, he is curiously unable to combat it: there seems to be nowhere to take hold. In a way, politics has stopped. There has been no general election, the elector is conscious of being unable to influence his M.P., Parliament has no control over the Government. You may not like the way things are going, but what exactly can you do about it? There is no concrete act against which you can plausibly protest.

But now and again something happens which is obviously symptomatic of the general trend—something round which existing discontents can crystallise. "Lock up Mosley" was a good rallying cry. Mosley, in fact, was a symbol, as Beveridge still is[7] and as Cripps was in 1942.[8] I don't believe Mr. Murry need bother about the implications of this incident. In spite of all that has happened, the failure of any genuinely totalitarian outlook to gain ground

441

among the ordinary people of this country is one of the most surprising and encouraging phenomena of the war.

Orwell's discussion of Lewis's apologetics was attacked in *Tribune* on 3 November by Sylvia Barrett (1914–), whose memoir of her progress from atheism to Christianity was published in 1968 as *Beyond the Wilderness*. William Empson, Orwell's colleague at the BBC, responded on 10 November, and he was backed by 'Francophil' on 17 November; Francophil includes an attack on the forthcoming issue of *Fontaine* in which Orwell's essay 'Grandeur et décadence du roman policier anglais' appeared. That attack is discussed in the headnote to Orwell's essay; see *2357*.

My concern for truth and justice, as well as a keen appreciation of the merits of Mr. C. S. Lewis, compels me to protest against the intellectual sleight-of-hand practised by Mr. George Orwell in his reference to this very clear-headed and fair-minded writer.

Mr. Orwell begins by taking W. J. Turner to task for likening *The Screwtape Letters* to *The Pilgrim's Progress*. He proceeds to take a brief passage from a reprinted broadcast talk, out of its context and without reference to its subject matter, and to demolish the *literary* style of this admittedly *colloquial* extract. Having done so, he proceeds to the completely unrelated conclusion that *The Screwtape Letters*, which happens to be a *literary* work and therefore couched in a quite different style, is not as good as *The Pilgrim's Progress*.

Having satisfactorily disposed of the B.B.C. Fireside Chat style which he finds so irritating, Mr. Orwell continues with a few generalisations about other Christian apologists, the upshot of which is that C. S. Lewis is only saying much the same as G. K. Chesterton, Ronald Knox, and others. It is perfectly true that for the past half century these admirable writers have been trying to din much the same facts into our thick heads; but unfortunately it appears that either Mr. Orwell has never seriously read any of their books, or he has been handicapped by a bee in his bonnet buzzing so loudly as to deafen him to other sounds, for he has completely reversèd the main implication of their work. Far from saying that theology is only understood by theologians and that you should leave your thinking to the priests, these writers have been engaged in a Socratic struggle to bring theology down from the clouds to the market-place.

As for Mr. Orwell's statement that the "rationalists" whom he names as having been the targets of these Christian apologists are still there while their attackers are beginning to look rather faded, I wonder if C. S. Lewis, for instance, really looks any more faded than Bertrand Russell? G. K. Chesterton, of course, suffers under the material handicap of being dead, but I notice that his books seem to be in rather greater demand than those of H. G. Wells—at any rate, when I try to buy one it always seems to be "reprinting."

The assertion that "these people's political affiliations are invariably reactionary" is particularly choice if it is intended to refer to Chesterton. It is hard to believe that a political writer of Mr. Orwell's status is really ignorant of the firebrand activities of the weekly paper which was run by G. K., his brother Cecil, and Hilaire Belloc, especially the conspicuous part it played in the showing up of the notorious Marconi shares scandal and its determined fight against monopoly. Of Mr. Lewis's "political affiliations," if any, I know nothing, and they are not indicated in any of his books, apart from a general impression that he regards political extremes of either colour as equal and opposite errors, and dislikes totalitarianism of either the Left or the Right (this may be clearly seen from *The Pilgrim's Regress*, published as long ago as 1933, at which time Mr. Orwell may consider that it was still "safe" to admire Fascism).

Such clumsy attacks on religion do a double disservice to the cause which Mr. Orwell has at heart. Firstly, they cannot fail to cast grave doubt on his intellectual honesty and reliability as a critic; and secondly, their only possible result if they were successful would be to kill the goose that lays the golden eggs. No social or economic system, however efficiently planned, can hope to succeed any better than the present one without vastly more good will than is current in the world today, and there is only one ultimate source for that good will. Lasting social justice will only be achieved when the majority of human beings have learned to love their neighbours with a love which is quite independent of personal likings and such love has its only firm and sure foundation in the faith that even the most apparently unattractive of human beings has an irreplaceable value in the eyes of his Creator. When this faith dies, the sense of the brotherhood of man cannot survive for more than a limited period, and there are signs in the recent outbreak of bestiality in Europe and Asia that this limited period is now coming to an end.

Sylvia Barrett

About George Orwell and the letter from Sylvia Barrett, saying that his attacks on popular apologists for Christianity are clumsy, dishonest, and on a wrong literary foot.

Orwell's quotation from C. S. Lewis, she said, was a complaint about broadcasting colloquial style which unfairly proceeded to assume that the content must be bad because the style was. C. S. Lewis wrote a wonderful book, *The Allegory of Love* (about the history of medieval allegory) when he was content to be a scholar; I think his first book as a Christian apologist was *The Problem of Pain*, in which he says that wild animals don't live for ever, but maybe pet animals do, because their owners have taught them to feel nicely. This was long before he started broadcasting. His style went wrong because his thoughts became silly, and the distinction that Sylvia Barrett wants to make is therefore false.

Orwell said that the apologists were always reactionary in political affiliations, and Sylvia Barrett says this is absurd because of Chesterton, a Liberal. Chesterton was a splendid writer, full of true prophecies about how Europe would go after his death, and unless the word is used as an empty insult it is absurd to pretend that he didn't end up in favour of Mussolini, and therefore as a Fascist; the reasons were decent ones, but he made no bones about the choice. He wanted a Catholic small-holding peasantry, and that was where it took him.

Sylvia Barrett then widens her net and says that there is no hope for the world unless everybody becomes Christian (I don't think she would really object to this summary of her formula) because otherwise there won't be enough goodwill. This is difficult to refute because it is hard to say that there has ever been enough goodwill inside or outside or before or after the Christian communities. But it is a very harmful idea that the Chinese and the Russians (to name the major cases) are bound to be untrustworthy allies because they don't profess this religion; they haven't got holy thoughts like we have, so we must be ready to cheat them in advance. This nasty little bit of salesmanship for Christianity keeps cropping up. Anyone who has lived in non-Christian countries without prejudice knows how obscure, if not downright false, the argument would become on examination; and meanwhile it is one of the main roads to the next war.

W. Empson[9]

I wholly share William Empson's sentiments about the regrettable deterioration of C. S. Lewis's literary work since he took to writing religious propaganda for the B.B.C., and I am glad there are still some critics left whose standards are untarnished by wartime propagandist build-ups, especially as it is rumoured that C. S. Lewis has been tipped as the next King's Professor at Cambridge in succession to Quiller-Couch,[10] because of his "religious soundness," which is said to appeal to the Prime Minister's Patronage Secretary as well as to such Cambridge figures as G. M. Trevelyan.

Christian salesmanship nearly always tends to unfairness and nastiness, and it seems strange that it is allowed to seep into so much of our literary propaganda in this war when one considers some of the political, social and literary philosophies of some of these people *together* with their attitude towards the war. I cannot see why our literary propagandists in the more cultural Ministries are actually encouraged to propagand° themselves, their own personal attitudes, their friends, their clique, etc., as frequently happens.

Surely it's about time there was some check to this? A good article on the more vulgar propagandists has already appeared in *Persuasion*; perhaps *Tribune* could follow up examining the predilections of Norman Collins, George Barnes, R. A. Scott-James, Phyllis Bentley, C. Day Lewis, Grafton Greene, Eric Gillett, etc., etc.

A good instance of our present literary propaganda is an announcement of a forthcoming English number of *Fontaine*, sponsored by various Government departments: a volume of 500 pages, edited by Miss Kathleen Raine and Miss Antonia White, both Catholics. Besides contributions by Miss Raine and Miss White themselves, this historic "panorama" "represents" the younger writers and poets by no less than ten people who could and have indeed qualified for a religious anthology. But of the "living" writers engaged in this war not one is deemed worthy of inclusion.

I wonder if the French will appreciate such a tribute under the sign of Liberty—the most complete possible?

Francophil

1. Monsignor Ronald Knox (1888–1957), Roman Catholic priest, essayist, and, unofficially, spokesman for Roman Catholicism in Britain. Orwell wrote of 'the tittering Knox' in a review of *Medieval Religion* by Christopher Dawson in 1934 (see *214*).
2. Monsignor Robert Hugh Benson (1871–1914), eminent preacher and prolific author of religious books and novels. Among the latter were *The Light Invisible* (1903), *The King's Achievement* (1905), *The Sentimentalists* (1906), *A Winnowing* (1910), *The Coward* (1912), and *Come Rack! Come Rope!* (1912); the last of these was reprinted many times.
3. The Reverend Cyril Alington (1872–1955), headmaster of Eton, 1917–33 (when Orwell was there). On retiring from Eton he was appointed Dean of Durham Cathedral. He had been a teacher at Eton, 1899–1908, where he won a very high reputation. He wrote several novels and detective stories, a study of the political party system (*Twenty Years*, 1921), memoirs, and religious books (including *Elementary Christianity*, 1927).
4. Orwell's date is right; Pelagius lived from about 360 to 420. He was excommunicated for heresy in 418.
5. In 'Politics vs. Literature: An Examination of *Gulliver's Travels*' (see *3089*), Orwell likens Swift's 'perverse Toryism' to a position akin to that of the 'innumerable silly-clever Conservatives' of his own day, and many of the names he quotes—A. P. Herbert, G. M. Young, Lord Elton, W. H. Mallock, Monsignor Ronald Knox—are referred to there. The indulgence in 'clean fun' at the expense of those such as Bertrand Russell, and, by implication, C. E. M. Joad (through the medium of his participation in 'The Brains Trust') is also mentioned. These names are annotated at *3089*.
6. For Habeas Corpus and the internment regulations (18B), see *2467*, *n. 1*.
7. For Beveridge, representing the Welfare State, see *2492*, *n. 3*.
8. Sir Stafford Cripps (1889–1952), lawyer and politician of unusual rectitude. In 1942 he went on a mission to India (then comprising India and Pakistan) to attempt to obtain total Indian support for the war on the understanding that self-government would follow when the war was over. The mission failed, and Cripps attributed that to the behind-the-scenes work of Mahatma Gandhi. There were those in Britain who were relieved he had not succeeded (for example L. S. Amery).
9. William Empson (1906–1984; Kt., 1979), poet, scholar, critic, was Professor of English Literature at Tokyo University, 1931–34, and at Peking, 1937–39 and 1947–53. He joined the BBC with Orwell; see *845*, *n. 3*.
10. He was appointed Professor of Mediæval and Renaissance Literature in 1954.

2569. To Mrs. Gerry Byrne (née Charlesworth)

28 October 1944   Typewritten

27B Canonbury Square
Islington
London N 1

Dear Mrs Byrne,[1]

I hope you will forgive me for having delayed so long in answering your letter. I have been away again, and also somewhat distraught with the move into here, which is now more or less accomplished except that there are no carpets on the floor and as far as I can see won't be for a long time.

I went up to Newcastle and fetched the baby back last week. It is no joke travelling with a child now, but we had good luck about porters etc.[2] and he was very good all through the journey. He has settled down nicely in his new home. My wife has at last managed to get out of her job at the Ministry of Food,[3] so she can be at home all day and we don't have to make use of the day nursery.

We should love to come down one week-end, but I think not in the very near future because there is still so much to do here and my wife wants to get quite used to looking after the baby. But we'd love to come in say about a month's time, if you care to suggest a date and I can arrange so that it doesn't clash with firewatching or anything. I'd like to show you the baby (his name is Richard) and get your opinion on him. I'm no judge but I think he is a very nice child and quite forward for his age, especially as he was very tiny at first.

Please remember me to your husband.

Yours sincerely
Geo. Orwell

1. Mrs. Gerry Byrne wrote to Orwell in 1937, then as Mrs. Amy Charlesworth; see *384*. She had trained to be a health worker, and it may partly have been for that reason that Orwell wanted her to see Richard. It is not known if this visit was made.
2. See Orwell's comments on rail travel, porters, and carrying luggage in 'As I Please,' 43, 6 October 1944, *2560*.
3. Wartime regulations controlled movement into and out of employment.

2570. Review of *Verdict on India* by Beverley Nichols

The Observer, 29 October 1944

It is fair to say that this book does not read as though it were intended to make mischief, but that is the effect it will probably have. Mr. Nichols spent about a year in India—as an unofficial visitor, he insists—travelling all over the country and interviewing Indians of every description, from maharajahs to naked mendicants. When he got there the menace of a Japanese invasion still loomed large and the "Quit India" campaign was in full swing. A little later there was the Bengal famine, of which he records some horrifying details. In a slapdash way he has obviously tried very hard to get at the truth, and his willingness to disclose scandals, together with frank, even violent, partisanship in Indian internal affairs, will cause much offence among Indians. It would not even be surprising if this book, like "Mother India,"[1] provoked a whole series of counterblasts.

Mr. Nichols's essential quarrel is with Hinduism. He detests the Hindu religion itself—its cow-worship, the obscene carvings in the temples, its caste-system, and the endless superstitions which war against science and enlightenment—but above all he is politically anti-Hindu. He is an advocate of Pakistan, which he believes will certainly be established by one means or another, and his favourite Indian politician is Mr. Jinnah. Much of what he says is true, but his way of saying it, and the things he leaves out, may mislead some people and will certainly antagonise countless others.

The thing Mr. Nichols never really gets round to admitting is that India's major grievance against Britain is justified. The British are still in India long after the Indians have ceased to want them there. If one keeps that in mind, much of Mr. Nichols's indictment of the Congress politicians can be accepted. India's immediate problems will not be solved by the disappearance of the British, and the Nationalist propaganda which declares every existing evil to be a direct result of British rule is dishonest as well as hysterical. As Mr. Nichols is aware—indeed, too much aware—this propaganda is lapped up by well-meaning Liberals in this country and America who are all the readier to accept what Indian apologists tell them because they have no real interest in Indian problems. Many of Mr. Nichols's points would have been well worth making if only he could have made them in a better-tempered way.

It is quite true that Hindu-Moslem antagonism is played down in Nationalist propaganda and that the Moslem end of the case seldom gets a fair hearing outside India. Again, it is true that the Congress Party is not the idealistic Left-Wing organisation which western Liberals imagine it to be, but has considerable resemblances to the Nazi Party and is backed by sinister business men with pro-Japanese leanings. Again, it is true that pro-Indian and anti-British propaganda habitually skates over huge problems such as Untouchability and ignores or misrepresents the positive achievements of the British in India. One could make a whole list of similar points on which Mr. Nichols is probably in the right. But he does not see that the appalling atmosphere of Indian politics, the hysteria, the lies, the pathological hatred, suspicion, and credulity, is itself the result of wounded national pride. He observes with some acuteness the mentality of a subject people, but talks of it as though it were innate or simply the product of the Hindu religion.

For instance, he has an undisguised contempt for the army of half-educated youths, picking up a precarious living from journalism and litigation, who are the noise-makers of the Nationalist movement. He barely admits that the existence of this huge unemployed intelligentsia is a commentary on British educational methods, or that these people might develop a more grown-up mentality if they had real responsibilities to face.

A more serious mistake is that he repeatedly attacks Mr. Gandhi, for whom he has an unconquerable aversion. Mr. Gandhi is an enigmatic character, but he is obviously not a plain crook, which is what Mr. Nichols seems to imply, and even his endless self-contradictions may be simply a form of sincerity. Throughout nearly the whole of Mr. Nichols's book, indeed, there is an air of prejudice and irritation which weakens even his justified criticisms.

Mr. Nichols is not unwilling to admit that the British in India have faults, especially social faults (he says, exaggerating slightly, that no European ever says "Thank you" to an Indian), and towards the end he makes some constructive suggestions. The British, he considers, both should, and will, quit India in the fairly near future. It would have created a very much better impression if he had said this on the first page of the book. Morally, he says, there is no case for our remaining there after the war is won, though it was, as he rightly emphasises, an absurdity to ask Britain simply to hand India over to the Japanese. His formula is "Divide and Quit"—that is, we are to recognise Indian independence, but make sure that Pakistan is established first. This is perhaps a thinkable solution, and if the Moslem League has the following that Mr. Nichols claims for it, it might help to avert civil war after the British power is withdrawn.

[Fee: £10.0.0; 26.10.44]

1. *Mother India* by Katherine Mayo, an American, was published in New York and London in 1927. It exposed, with great frankness 'the worst plague spots in the social customs and practices that still prevail behind the purdah', in particular the way women were treated in India, economic waste, 'cruelty to animals involved in the worship of the cow', and 'poisonously insanitary conditions . . . in the most sacred shrines and cities' (*Times Literary Supplement*, 28 July 1927). Books by at least ten authors were published in reply. In its review of *Unhappy India*, by Lajpat Ral (Calcutta), and *India: Its Character*, by J. A. Chapman (Oxford), the *TLS* said that Miss Mayo's 'facts were largely true, but their presentation was sometimes distorted' (23 August 1928).

2571. To Tom Driberg

30 October 1944   Handwritten

"Tribune"

Dear Mr Driberg,[1]
I wonder if you could let me have the name of that Oxford magazine you referred to in your column yesterday?[2] I am interested in that kind of thing, particularly in the overlap which I know does exist between pacifism & antisemitism.

Yours sincerely
Geo. Orwell

1. Thomas Edward Neil Driberg (1905–1976; Baron Bradwell, 1975), journalist and author, was on the editorial staff of the *Daily Express*, 1928–43. At this time, he was also a contributor to the Labour-inclined Sunday paper *Reynold's News*; war correspondent, 1944–45, and in Korea, 1950. An Independent M.P., 1942–45, Labour M.P., 1945–55, 1959–74; and from 1949 a member of the National Executive Committee of the Labour Party. Among his books are studies of the British Fascist leader, Oswald Mosley; Lord Beaverbrook, for whom he worked for many years as the *Daily Express* columnist 'William Hickey'; the spy Guy Burgess; the journalist Hannen Swaffer; and Frank Buchman and the Moral Re-Armament Movement. Assertions were made that he conveyed information to the Russians over a long period, and it was also suggested that he was a double agent. No charges were laid.
2. See note to Orwell's letter to Driberg of 4 November, *2574*.

2572. Review of *The Warden* by Anthony Trollope; *Silas Marner* by George Eliot; *Public Faces* by Harold Nicolson; *Seducers in Ecuador* by V. Sackville-West; *Les Dieux ont Soif* by Anatole France; *Hitler et le Christianisme* by Edmond Vermeil

Manchester Evening News, 2 November 1944

In Ripon Cathedral you can see—or could see a few years ago—a sight irresistibly reminiscent of the fairy story of "The Three Bears." It is (or was) the stalls of the Dean and Chapter. At one end of the row was the Dean's stall, with an enormous plush cushion and a folio Bible; then came the Canons' stalls, in descending order, each with cushion a little thinner and Bible a little smaller than the last; and down at the bottom was a stall for the Rural Dean, who had only a strip of Brussels carpet to sit on and a duodecimo Bible.

It was some such spectacle that led Anthony Trollope to evolve the enormous saga of clerical life that is contained in the Barchester novels. For Trollope was not a very active churchman, and his remarkably convincing portraits of Church dignitaries came out of his imagination and were not caricatures of individuals, as they were widely believed to be at the time.

He himself says that he hit on the idea almost accidentally while strolling through a cathedral and speculating idly on the kind of life that was led there.

Some of Trollope's best work lies outside the Barchester series. There is "Orley Farm," for instance, which contains one of the most brilliant descriptions of a lawsuit in English fiction, and "The Three Clerks," and Trollope's fascinating "Autobiography."

"The Small House at Allington," which is perhaps his most perfect novel, has only indirect connections with the town of Barchester itself.[1]

Trollope wrote with equal facility of politics, fox-hunting and professional life, and by the end there were not many activities in his imaginary county of Barsetshire (it might, perhaps, be Somersetshire) which he had not covered. But it is by the clerical series that he is best known, and "The Warden," the earliest in this vein, is also probably the most successful.

In "The Warden" the central idea is so brilliant that it would have succeeded in far less skilful hands than Trollope's.

In Barchester there is an almshouse for 12 indigent old men, supported by a fund left for that purpose by some charitable person in the Middle Ages. The Warden of the almshouse, Mr. Harding, is a gentle old clergyman, devoted to his paupers and his violin[2] and completely happy in his post.

There is, however, something morally and legally doubtful about the whole position. The mediæval benefactor had bequeathed to his charity the rent of two fields, which are now covered with house property and have become extremely valuable. As a result the Church is drawing a comfortable revenue from the charity, and the Warden is receiving a salary of £800 a year, while the twelve old paupers are only receiving a dole of 1s. 6d. a day.

It is one of those abuses which happen in the first place through accident and then become sanctified by time. An interfering young reformer named John Bold (Trollope likes to give his characters appropriate names) finds out the facts and sets a lawsuit on foot. A tremendous three-sided conflict ensues between Bold, Mr. Harding, and Mr. Harding's formidable son-in-law, Archdeacon Grantley, who is to feature largely in later novels. In the end the lawsuit is called off, partly because Bold has become engaged to Mr. Harding's younger daughter, but not before poor old Mr. Harding, unwilling to take money which perhaps does not belong to him, has resigned his job. The twelve paupers are left somewhat worse off than before.

It is essentially the same situation as arises in Ibsen's play, "An Enemy of the People," but whereas in Ibsen's hands it becomes a brutal and almost farcical exposure of human meanness, Trollope turns it into a good-tempered comedy in which, on the whole, the honours lie with the clergy and not with their opponents.

Trollope was a shrewd critic, but no reformer. A time-honoured abuse, he held, is frequently less bad than its remedy. He builds Archdeacon Grantley up into a thoroughly odious character, and is well aware of his odiousness, but he still prefers him to John Bold (Bold is hurriedly killed off between "The Warden" and "Barchester Towers"), and the book contains a scarcely veiled attack on Charles Dickens, whose reforming zeal he found it hard to sympathise with.

But it is because he did not disapprove of existing society that Trollope could record it so minutely and yet so entertainingly. He is pre-eminent among English novelists for the accuracy of his detail as well as for his charm. This is one of his best works and one of the most notable of recent Penguins.

George Eliot's "Silas Marner" is heavy going after Trollope, but she will always have her devoted band of followers.

Harold Nicolson's "Public Faces"—it is a political fantasy written in 1932, and dealing with events in 1939, but extravagantly unlike anything that has actually happened—is a tiresome book, and it is hard to see why it was reprinted.

Miss Sackville-West's book consists of two "long short" stories. The name-story is a frigid and rather pointless fantasy, but the other, a tale of sixteenth-century Holland, has a sort of unearthly charm, like that of a fairy story.

In these bookless days, when the most hackneyed "classic" is liable to be unobtainable, even second-hand, life would be appreciably poorer without the Penguins. In the same series as "The Warden" and "Silas Marner," Hawthorne's "Scarlet Letter" and Goldsmith's "Vicar of Wakefield" are either out or coming shortly.

Other current or forthcoming Penguins and Pelicans which are especially worth looking out for are Jack London's remarkable political prophecy, "The Iron Heel," James Burnham's "Managerial Revolution," and Somerset Maugham's novel, founded on the life of the French painter, Gauguin, "The Moon and Sixpence."

The Editions Penguin, in French, are a new departure and very nicely got up for two and sixpence. Anyone who reads French reasonably well—and Anatole France's French is simpler than most—will enjoy that disillusioning story of revolution, "Les Dieux Ont Soif."

Professor Vermeil's essays were first published just before the Battle of France, and are a study of the threat to religion presented by the modern totalitarian State.

[Fee: £8.0.0; 25.10.44]

1. The paragraph referring to *The Small House at Allington* was almost certainly part of the preceding paragraph in Orwell's typescript. See *2463. n. 2* for the breaking-up of Orwell's contributions into short paragraphs by the *Manchester Evening News*
2. Harding played the 'cello.

2573. 'As I Please,' 47

Tribune, 3 November 1944

Penguin Books have now started publishing books in French, very nicely got up, at half-a-crown each. Among those to appear shortly is the latest instalment of André Gide's Journal, which covers a year of the German occupation. As I glanced through an old favourite, Anatole France's *Les Dieux Ont Soif* (it is a novel about the Reign of Terror during the French Revolution), the thought occurred to me: what a remarkable anthology one could make of pieces of writing describing executions! There must be hundreds of them scattered through literature, and—for a reason I think I can guess—they must be far better written on average than battle pieces.

Among the examples I remember at the moment are Thackeray's description of the hanging of Courvoisier, the crucifixion of the gladiators in *Salambo*,° the final scene of *A Tale of Two Cities*, a piece from a letter or diary of Byron's, describing a guillotining, and the beheading of two Scottish noblemen after the 1745 rebellion, described by, I think, Horace Walpole. There is a very fine chapter describing a guillotining in Arnold Bennett's *Old Wives' Tale*, and a horrible one in one of Zola's novels (the one about the Sacré Cœur). Then there is Jack London's short story, *The Chinago*, Plato's account of the death of Socrates—but one could extend the list indefinitely. There must also be a great number of specimens in verse, for instance the old hanging ballads, to which Kipling's *Danny Deever* probably owes something.

The thing that I think very striking is that no one, or no one I can remember, ever writes of an execution *with approval*. The dominant note is always horror. Society, apparently, cannot get along without capital punishment—for there are some people whom it is simply not safe to leave alive—and yet there is no one, when the pinch comes, who feels it right to kill another human being in cold blood. I watched a man hanged once. There was no question that everybody concerned knew this to be a dreadful, unnatural action. I believe it is always the same—the whole jail, warders and prisoners alike, is upset when there is an execution. It is probably the fact that capital punishment is accepted as necessary, and yet instinctively felt to be wrong, that gives so many descriptions of executions their tragic atmosphere. They are mostly written by people who have actually watched an execution and feel it to be a terrible and only partly comprehensible experience which they want to record; whereas battle literature is largely written by people who have never heard a gun go off and think of a battle as a sort of football match in which nobody gets hurt.

Perhaps it was a bit previous to say that no one writes of an execution with approval, when one thinks of the way our newspapers have been smacking their chops over the bumping-off of wretched quislings in France and elsewhere. I recall, in one paper, a whole series of photos showing the execution of Caruso, the ex-chief of the Rome police. You saw the huge, fat body being straddled across a chair with his back to the firing squad, then the cloud of smoke issuing from the rifle barrels and the body slumping sideways. The editor who saw fit to publish this thought it a pleasant titbit, I suppose, but then he had not had to watch the actual deed. I think I can imagine the feelings of the man who took the photographs, and of the firing squad.

To the lovers of useless knowledge (and I know there are a lot of them, from the number of letters I always get when I raise any question of this kind) I present a curious little problem arising out of the recent Pelican, *Shakespeare's England*. A writer named Fynes Morrison,[1] touring England in 1607, describes melons as growing freely. Andrew Marvell, in a very well-known poem[2] written about fifty years later, also refers to melons. Both references make it appear that the melons grew in the open, and indeed they must have done so if they grew at all. The hotbed was a recent invention in 1600, and glass-houses, if they existed, must have been a very great rarity. I imagine it would be quite impossible to grow a melon in the open in England nowadays. They are hard enough to grow under glass, whence their price. Fynes Morrison also speaks of grapes growing in large enough quantities to make wine. Is it possible that our climate has changed radically in the last three hundred years?[3] Or was the so-called melon actually a pumpkin?

As from November 10th, *Tribune* intends to replan its book reviews. The present policy of trying to give every book a review of about a column is felt to be unsatisfactory, because with the small space at our disposal we cannot keep up to date, and the more important books frequently do not get the detailed treatment they deserve. The best solution seems to be to make some reviews shorter and others longer.

Daniel George's novel reviews will not be affected, but for the rest we intend to have about nine very short notices—a sort of guide to the current books—and one very long one, probably of about 1,500 words. This will allow us to cover rather more books than at present and keep more nearly up to date, but it will have the added advantage that serious books can be seriously treated. In every week there is at least *one* book that deserves a full-length review, even if its importance is only indirect.

From years of experience as a book reviewer I should say that the rock-bottom minimum in which you can both summarise and criticise a book is

800 words. But a book review is seldom of much value *as a piece of writing* if it is under 1,000 words. The generally higher standard of criticism in monthly and quarterly magazines is partly due to the fact that the reviewers are less pinched for space. In the old days of the *Edinburgh* and the *Quarterly*, a hundred years ago, a reviewer often had fifteen pages to play with!

If this policy does not work out well we shall scrap it, but we shall give it several months' trial. Our aim is to produce leading reviews which thoroughly criticise the chosen book and at the same time are worth-while articles in themselves. Apart from people who already write fairly frequently for *Tribune*, we have collected a first-rate team of reviewers, including Herbert Read, Stephen Spender, Franz Borkenau, Hugh Kingsmill, Michael Roberts, Mulk Raj Anand, Arturo Barea, Arthur Koestler and several others.[4]

1. Fynes Moryson (1566–1630), *An Itinerary containing his Ten Yeares Travel through the Twelve Dominions of Germany, Bohmerland, Sweitzerland, Netherland, Denmarke, Poland, Italy, Turky, France, England, Scotland and Ireland* (1617).
2. 'The Garden'; 'Stumbling on melons, as I pass, / Insnar'd with flow'rs, I fall on grass.'
3. The climate has changed. Temperatures in the middle ages in England were 0.7°C to 1.0°C warmer than the twentieth-century average. See H. H. Lamb, *Climate History and the Modern World* (1982), 170–71; a map shows the distribution of vineyards in medieval England. Vineyards have, of course, been successfully developed in England in recent years.
4. Although Rayner Heppenstall was not included in this list, Orwell had written to him asking him to be one of this team; see *2563* and *2563, n. 1*. Among others Orwell asked was Osbert Sitwell. Orwell's letter has not been traced, but a reply from Sitwell, dated 29 November 1944, says he would like to write a long review for *Tribune* although not in the near future. He said he would look out for something appropriate and would telephone when he came to London (he was at Renishaw Hall, near Sheffield). Nothing by Sitwell was published in *Tribune* under Orwell's aegis, however.

2574. To Tom Driberg

4 November 1944   Typewritten

27B Canonbury Square
Islington
London N 1

Dear Mr Driberg,
Many thanks for the information. I won't trouble you for the loan of your copies, as I would like to get hold of some copies of the paper myself for my collection.

Yours sincerely
[Signed] Geo. Orwell
George Orwell

1. Driberg replied to Orwell's letter of 30 October on 2 November. The periodical was *Counterblast*, of which three issues had been published. The editor was Desmond Stewart. Driberg had thought it undesirable to advertise his name in his column 'as a few of the sillier "intellectual" undergraduates' seemed to be under his influence. Stewart was 'a protégé of the

extremely undesirable Robert Sencourt (R.C., Fascist).' Desmond Stirling Stewart (1924–1981), a classical scholar who lived from 1948 in the Near East, became a contributor in the fifties to the monthly *The European: A Journal of Opposition* (1953–59). This was edited by Diana Mosley and was sympathetic to neo-Fascist ideas. See Philip Rees, *Fascism in Britain* (1979), 204.

2575. Review of *Singapore Goes Off the Air* by Giles Playfair *Britain and Malaya* by Sir Richard Winstedt

Manchester Evening News, 8 November 1944

The rapid loss of Malaya in the early months of 1942 is universally admitted to be a blot on British history, but the lessons that it teaches have not been well learned, nor was the Malayan campaign adequately reported at the time. The more light that can be cast upon it from all angles the better, especially as the causes of the disaster were political and social, rather than strictly military.

Mr. Giles Playfair, who had been sent out from Britain to help organise the Malaya Broadcasting Corporation, arrived in Singapore on December 8, 1941, the day after Pearl Harbour. His job, therefore, for the next two months, was to make daily announcements over the air of the latest Japanese advance, and to improvise programmes which might keep up the morale of the civilian population and counteract Japanese propaganda.

The orders of the M.B.C. staff [1] were to keep Singapore on the air as long as possible, and then to blow up the transmitters and get out while the going was good. In the end they got out three or four days before the island capitulated, and most of them ultimately reached India or Australia, after weeks of dodging submarines in crowded ships where there was hardly any drinking water and only the bare deck to sleep on.

Mr. Playfair was a stranger to the Far East, he did not feel himself to be part of Singapore society, and he says frankly that he disliked the stupid, lazy, frivolous life that many or most of the Europeans led there.

He has plenty of tales to tell of official incompetence and of the refusal of civilians to take the war seriously, and he saw from the start that the propaganda side of the war was being hopelessly mishandled.

No effort had been made beforehand to prepare the Asiatic population for war, or even to protect them—there was not a single underground air-raid shelter on Singapore Island—and it was small wonder that the dock coolies deserted in droves as soon as a Japanese aeroplane appeared, while the population up country looked on passively at the Japanese advance.

Even when Singapore was all but invested, Mr. Playfair notes, the colour bar was as obtrusive as ever. And he records certain incidents which are quite unforgivable. For instance, the important town of Penang was allowed to fall into Japanese hands in so undamaged a state that the Japanese were broadcasting from the radio station within two days.

All the same, Mr. Playfair does not think that the accepted picture of what happened in Malaya is a truthful one, and he writes with some warmth of the journalists, mostly Americans, who circulated sensationally anti-British stories at the time. What he says needed saying, and helps to put the story of the Singapore diasaster in its proper perspective.

An impression prevails that the whole debacle was the fault of complacent "blimps" and permanently drunk rubber-planters, and that it would somehow have been different if the Malayan Government had armed the people, abolished colour distinctions, and issued patriotic slogans.

This is a distorted picture. To begin with, the purely military disaster was inevitable. With Britain fighting for its life in Europe, and Indo-China in the hands of the Japanese, the Malay Peninsula was strategically untenable, and Singapore itself was quite incapable of standing a siege.

It was not a fortress, but merely a naval base, like Plymouth, and it had a million inhabitants and a water supply only sufficient for a few days. Had the commander[2] not surrendered when he did hundreds of thousands of innocent Asiatics would have died of thirst.

Nor was it practicable at short notice to stimulate large-scale popular resistance against the invaders. The population of Malaya is extremely mixed (actually the Malays are in a minority, the Chinese being an equally large minority), and had been completely demilitarised by many years of British rule. The great fault of this kind of "paternal" government is that it robs its subjects of any sense of patriotism or responsibility. When London was bombed, London "took it." When Singapore suffered what by our standards would be very small air raids, the heterogeneous population of Chinese, Indians, Malays, and Arabs simply concluded that the Japanese were dangerous people whom it was better not to oppose. The same thing happened in Burma.

These disasters demonstrated that subject peoples, even when they are not grossly exploited, are simply a liability from a military point of view. But the situation in Malaya could only have been righted if certain reforms had been set in hand decades earlier, and, as Mr. Playfair insists, it is unfair to put the main blame on the people on the spot. The culprits are the British public, who are vaguely anti-Imperialist but take no interest in the concrete problems of their colonial possessions. And if some of the British in Malaya behaved badly in the moment of collapse, others, as Mr. Playfair demonstrates, showed devotion and intelligence.

Though it is lightly written (it is mostly in diary form) and does not pretend to much local knowledge, this book is a useful addition to the literature of the Malayan campaign.

Sir Richard Winstedt's[3] little book is one of a series dealing with the various countries of the British Commonwealth. It probably presents a somewhat too rosy picture of British dealings with Malaya, but it gives valuable background information and a short history of the country from the eighteenth century onwards. It has excellent photographs. Sir Richard Winstedt was for many years an official in Malaya and has been partly responsible for the Malay broadcasts from London.

Other forthcoming books in this series which are likely to be informative and readable are "Britain and West Africa," by Joyce Cary (the author of "The Case for African Freedom"), and "Britain and Burma," by G. E. Harvey.

[Fee: £8.0.0; 6.11.44]

1. One of those from whom Orwell might have obtained direct information of orders given to the Malaya Broadcasting Corporation was Eric Robertson (1915–1987), who worked for the Corporation in 1941–42 and was responsible for evacuation arrangements. He then ran the Far Eastern Service of All-India Radio to 1945. He met Orwell at the BBC in London. In 1970 he was appointed Controller of the BBC Overseas Service (verbal communication).
2. General Arthur Ernest Percival (1887–1968), in command of British forces in Malaya from April 1941. He surrendered to the Japanese in Singapore on 15 February 1942.
3. Orwell knew Winstedt at the BBC; see *1669, n. 1*. A copy of Winstedt's 'little book' was among the pamphlets Orwell collected, now in the British Library.

2576. Books and the People[1]: *The Vicar of Wakefield* by Oliver Goldsmith

Tribune, 10 November 1944

When Mark Twain said of *The Vicar of Wakefield*, "Nothing could be funnier than its pathos, and nothing could be sadder than its humour," he was probably not exaggerating his own feelings very greatly. To a man of Mark Twain's generation it was natural that the elegance of the eighteenth century should seem frigid and ridiculous, just as it was natural that Dr. Johnson should see nothing to admire in the Robin Hood ballads. *The Vicar of Wakefield*, now reprinted by Penguin Books in the "English Classics" series, is esssentially a period piece, and its charm is about equalled by its absurdity. It is impossible to be moved by its story, which has none of the psychological realism that can be found in some eighteenth-century novels—for instance, *Amelia*. Its characters are sticks and its plot is somewhat less probable than those of the serial stories in *Peg's Paper*. But it remains extremely readable, and it has never been quite out of print in the 177 years since its first appearance. Like a Japanese woodcut, it is something perfectly executed after its own fashion, and at this date there is a historical interest in the remoteness of the standards of conduct which it is trying to uphold.

The Vicar of Wakefield is intended as a "moral tale," a sermon in fiction form. Its theme is the familiar one, preached without much success by hundreds of writers from Horace to Thackeray, of the vanity of worldly ambitions and the pleasures of the simple life. Its hero, Dr. Primrose (he tells his own story in the first person), is a clergyman in what used to be called "easy circumstances," who temporarily loses his fortune and has to remove to another parish, where he supports himself by farming his own land. Here a whole series of disasters fall upon the family, traceable in every case to their having ambitions "above their station" and trying to associate with the nobility instead of with the neighbouring farmers. The eldest daughter is seduced by a heartless rascal, the farmhouse is burnt to the ground, the eldest son is arrested for manslaughter, Primrose himself is thrown into a debtors' prison, and various other calamities happen. In the end, of course, everything is put right in an outrageously improbable way, one detail after another clicking into place like the teeth of a zip fastener. Primrose's fortune is restored, the seemingly seduced daughter turns out to be an "honest woman" after all, the suitor of the second daughter, who has been posing as a poor man in order to try her affections, is discovered to be a wealthy nobleman, and so on and so forth. Virtue is rewarded and vice punished with relentless thoroughness. But the confusion in Goldsmith's mind between simple goodness and financial prudence gives the book, at this date, a strange moral atmosphere.

The main incidents are the various marriages, and the cold-blooded eighteenth-century attitude towards marriage is indicated on the first page when Dr. Primrose remarks (Goldsmith probably does not intend this ironically): "I had scarcely taken orders a year, before I began to think seriously of matrimony, and choose my wife, as she did her wedding gown, not for a fine glossy surface, but such qualities as would wear well." But quite apart from this notion of choosing a wife as one might choose a length of cloth, there is the fact that getting married is inextricably mixed up with the idea of making a good financial bargain. A thumping dowry or a secure settlement is the first consideration, and the most passionate love match is promptly called off if the expected cash is not forthcoming. But together with this mercenary outlook there goes a superstitious regard for the sanctity of marriage which makes the most dramatic episode in the book ridiculous and even slightly disgusting.

Olivia is seduced by a Mr. Thornhill, a wealthy young squire who has dazzled the Primrose family with his fashionable clothes and London manners. He is represented as a complete scoundrel, the "betrayer," as it was called, of innumerable women, and with every possible vice, even including physical cowardice. To entrap Olivia he uses the favourite eighteenth-century device of a false marriage. A marriage licence is forged, somebody impersonates a priest, and the girl can then be "ruined" under the delusion that she is married. Today it seems almost incredible that anyone should go to such lengths, but stratagems like this are inevitable in a society where technical chastity is highly valued and a woman has in effect no profession except marriage. In such a society there is an endless struggle between the sexes—a struggle which from the woman's point of view resembles an egg-and-spoon race, and from the man's a game of ninepins. Having been deceived in this manner, Olivia is now finished for life. She herself is made to express the current outlook by singing the justly famous lyric which Goldsmith throws into the tale:—

> When lovely woman stoops to folly,
> And finds too late that men betray,
> What charm can soothe her melancholy?
> What art can wash her guilt away?

> The only act her guilt to cover,
> To hide her shame from every eye,
> To give repentance to her lover,
> And wring his bosom, is—to die.[2]

Olivia indeed ought to die, and does actually begin to die—of sheer grief, after the manner of novel-heroines. But here comes the *dénouement*, the great stroke of fortune that puts everything right. It turns out that Olivia was *not* seduced; she was legally married! Mr. Thornhill has been in the habit of "marrying" women with a false priest and a false licence, but on this occasion a confederate of his, for purposes of his own, has deceived him by bringing a genuine licence and a real priest in holy orders. So the marriage was valid after all! And at this glorious news "a burst of pleasure seemed to fill the whole apartment. . . . Happiness was expanded upon every face, and even Olivia's cheeks seemed flushed with pleasure. To be thus restored to reputation and fortune at once was a rapture sufficient to stop the progress of decay and restore former health and vivacity."

When Olivia was believed to have "lost her virtue" she had lost all reason for living, but when it is discovered that she is tied for life to a worthless scoundrel all is well. Goldsmith does not make the ending quite so ridiculous as he might, for it is explained that Olivia continues to live apart from her husband. But she has the all-important wedding ring, and a comfortable settlement into the bargain. Thornhill's rich uncle punishes him by depriving him of his fortune, and bestowing part of it on Olivia. We are never, indeed, allowed quite to forget the connection between cash and virtue. Olivia sees herself "restored to reputation *and fortune at once*," while Thornhill sees "a gulf of infamy *and want*" opening before him.

Except for a scene or two in the debtors' prison and a few minor adventures at horse fairs and on muddy country roads, there is no realistic detail in *The Vicar of Wakefield*. The dialogue is quite exceptionally improbable. But the main theme—the hollowness of fashionable life and the superiority of country pleasures and family affection—is not so false as the absurd incidents which are meant to illustrate it make it appear. In inveighing against social ambition, against absentee landlords, against fine clothes, gambling, duelling, cosmetics and urban raffishness generally, Goldsmith is attacking a real tendency of his time, which Swift and Fielding had also denounced, after their own fashion.

A phenomenon he is very much aware of is the growth of a new monied class with no sense of responsibility. Thanks to the expansion of foreign trade, wealth accumulated in the capital and the aristocracy were ceasing to be rustics. England was becoming more and more of an oligarchy, and the life of the countryside was broken up by the enclosure of the common lands and the magnetic pull of London. The peasants were proletarianised, the petty gentry were corrupted. Goldsmith himself described the process in the often-quoted lines from *The Deserted Village*:—

> Ill fares the land, to hastening ills a prey,
> Where wealth accumulates and men decay;

Princes and lords may nourish or may fade,
A breath can make them as a breath has made;
But a bold peasantry, their country's pride,
When once destroyed, can never be supplied.

Thornhill stands for the new kind of rich man, the Whig aristocrat; the Primroses, who make their own gooseberry wine and even in the days of their wealth have hardly been ten miles from home, stand for the old type of yeoman farmer or small landlord.

In praising country life, Goldsmith was probably praising something that he did not know much about. His descriptions of country scenes have an unreal, idyllic atmosphere, and the Primroses are not shown as doing much work on their farm. More often they are sitting under some shady tree, reciting ballads, and listening to the blackbirds—pastimes that a practical farmer would seldom have time for. Nor do we hear much of Dr. Primrose's ministrations as a clergyman: indeed, he only seems to remember at intervals that he is in orders. But the general moral of the book is clear enough, and thrust rather irrelevantly into one chapter there is a long political discourse against oligarchy and the accumulation of capital. Goldsmith's conclusion—no doubt it was a common Tory theory at the time—is that the only defence against oligarchy is a strong monarchy. Dr. Primrose's son George, returning from travels in Europe, is made to come to the same conclusion: "I found that monarchy was the best government for the poor to live in, and commonwealths for the rich." Dictatorship is defended on the same grounds in our own day, and it is an instance of the way in which the same political ideas come up again and again in slightly different forms that George continues: "I found that riches in general were in every country another name for freedom; and that no man is so fond of liberty himself as not to be desirous of subjecting the will of some individuals in society to his own."

But though there is some serious social criticism buried under its artificialities, it is not there that the enduring charm of *The Vicar of Wakefield* lies. The charm is in its manner—in the story, which for all its absurdity is beautifully put together, in the simple and yet elegant language, in the poems that are thrown in here and there, and in certain minor incidents, such as the well-known story of Moses and the green spectacles. Most people who read at all have read this book once, and it repays a second reading. It is one of those books which you can enjoy in one way as a child and in another as an adult, and which do not seem any the worse because you are frequently inclined to laugh in the wrong places.

1. This was the first in the series of longer reviews called Books and the People announced by Orwell in 'As I Please,' 47, 3 November 1944; see *2573*. Orwell did not write an instalment of 'As I Please' for this issue of *Tribune*. At the end of this 3 November essay, he stated that next week's Books and the People review would be by Stephen Spender.
2. In line 5, 'act' should be 'art'. This could be a typographic error or Orwell may be quoting from memory. As Orwell had recently compared Eliot's earlier and later poetic styles (2259), he may have been attracted to the song by Eliot's parody of it in 'The Waste Land': 'When lovely woman stoops to folly . . . She smoothes her hair with automatic hand, / And puts a record on the gramophone' (253, 255–6).

2577. Review of *Gerard Manley Hopkins* by W. H. Gardner

The Observer, 12 November 1944

It is a hundred years since the birth of Gerard Manley Hopkins, and also since the birth of his friend Robert Bridges, who outlived him by forty years and edited the "Poems" that appeared in 1918. It is at least possible that if it had not been for Bridges we should never have heard Hopkins's name, and the current notion—shared intermittently by Mr. Gardner—that Bridges behaved throughout the whole affair like an ignorant philistine seems quite unjustified. His admiration for Hopkins was qualified, but he had had the acuteness to see as early as the 'seventies that Hopkins had first-rate talents, and by holding up the publication of the "Poems" till 1918 he probably did his reputation a great service. For by that time public taste, educated by Pound, Eliot, the renewed vogue of Donne, and also by certain poems of Bridges's own, was ready for Hopkins. Mr. Gardner fills a whole chapter with extracts from reviews and criticisms, and the striking thing about them, with very few exceptions, is how respectful they are. Mr. Gardner appears to feel that Hopkins has been underpraised, but one has only to think of the streams of abuse that greeted Joyce and Lawrence to realise that Hopkins, ignored during his lifetime, has not done so badly after death.

Mr. Gardner, writing as a disciple rather than a critic, is apt to be on the defensive when he speaks either of Hopkins's vocabulary or his religious beliefs. Underlying this is a question always present when Hopkins is discussed, though not often brought out into the open: Did the fact that Hopkins was a Jesuit priest damage him as a poet?

Mr. Gardner evidently thinks that it did not, and almost certainly he is right. The most severe discipline, if it does not entail actual dishonesty, is not necessarily damaging to a poet, and in Hopkins's case his life as a priest *was* his subject matter. Art arises out of suffering, and it is clear that Hopkins was unhappy, and not merely because he was of poor health, neglected as a poet and condemned to unsympathetic work in dreary places. He was also unhappy because although his faith was secure, to live up to it was not easy. He was in the position of a soldier fighting in a war which he believes to be just but which he does not pretend to enjoy. Intellectually and emotionally he was full of anomalies. He was intensely an Englishman, preferring England to other countries, and yet a Catholic convert, a devout Christian, and yet full of an almost pantheistic love of Nature which made him feel a certain kinship with Whitman. One may guess that he could embrace poverty and chastity a good deal more easily than obedience, and that he was never able to efface his own individuality so completely as he would have wished.

There is no reason to suppose that he would have been a better poet if he had been an unbeliever. Probably he would have been a less original poet, giving less evidence of strain, and less tortured in his language.

Everyone has felt that there is some connection between Hopkins's religious struggles and his strange diction, and it is hard not to feel that over and above the endless search for exact meanings, there is also at work an unconscious desire to be unusual. He was completely subordinated in one world, that of the Church, and he may have wanted to compensate himself by being a rebel in another, that of poetry. Needless to say, Mr. Gardner will not hear of this interpretation. He comes near to claiming that Hopkins's language is entirely free from affectation, and adds that Hopkins always strove "to put *meaning* before mere suggestion and sound." It is true, of course, that one gets used to Hopkins's diction (for instance, his trick of dropping relative pronouns), and that much that seems arbitrary is justified if one looks more closely. But it is also true that one cannot read far in his work without coming upon some word that appears to have been pushed in either because it is strange or because the sound of some nearby word has called it up. And similar tendencies—inversion of words and phrases, for instance—appear in his prose.

Mr. Gardner is right in proclaiming Hopkins a great poet, but not in asking readers—as in effect he does—to lay aside their critical faculties. In no single instance does he admit that an adverse criticism of Hopkins is justified, and he sometimes hints that such criticisms are not honest, either. One ought to be able to say of Hopkins, as one can of any other poet, that some of his work is good and some bad. One ought to be able to say that "Felix Randal" is probably the best short poem in the English language, and at the same time that one objects to a phrase like "very-violet-sweet" and agrees with Bridges that to rhyme "communion" with "boon he on" is "hideous." Mr. Gardner's attitude is "Take it or leave it." This is a book that anyone interested in Hopkins ought to read, but the second volume which Mr. Gardner promises will be more valuable if he remembers that criticism and hagiography are different things.

[Fee: £10.0.0; 10.11.44]

2578. Review of *The English Spirit (Essays in History and Literature)* by A. L. Rowse; *Brendan and Beverley* by Cassius (Michael Foot)

Manchester Evening News, 16 November 1944

There is an old music-hall song with the refrain:
Give yourself a pat on the back,
Pat on the back, pat on the back;
and anyone who has ever heard it will be liable to find it coming back into his head when he reads "The English Spirit." For though this book is a collection of essays and broadcasts written at various times during the past 10 years, and not in all cases connected with the war, as an exhibition of own-trumpet-blowing it would be hard to beat.

It is true that Mr. Rowse has an excuse. He is a Cornishman, and he chooses to regard this as different from being an Englishman—he is therefore free, he explains, to say things on behalf of the English that they could hardly say for themselves. Why should we not be reasonably and instructedly proud of the extraordinary record and achievement of this country? Why should we be expected to apologise for it, as if it were something to be half ashamed about? I say reasonably proud meaning "not without reason."

Granted that there is nothing sillier or more offensive than an ignorant and uninformed chauvinism, which does not know why or what we have to admire in the past—on the other hand, the habit of depreciation, of being afraid to recognise what there is to be proud of, is no less deleterious.

If anything, more so. . . . Besides, this habit of depreciation is liable to be taken by foreigners *au pied de la lettre*. It is stupid of them, and also bad for them. Really obtuse foreigners, like the Germans, are apt to get some nasty shocks when they believe what their own propaganda told them for a second time in a generation—that we are a decadent people.

One might allow that there is some truth in this, and that the contempt for England which has been fashionable among English intellectuals for the past 20 years is ill-founded, and still be made uneasy by Mr. Rowse's way of going to work.

For, to begin with, it is not the ordinary people of England that he is most concerned to praise. "This may be the century of the common man," he says, "It certainly is of the common cliché—but I prefer to look for the uncommon man, the man of genius or ability." And in fact he does bestow most of his praise on people already famous, especially the Elizabethan adventurers so dear to the compilers of school text books.

But in his comments on the English character in general it would be difficult to find an uncomplimentary remark. We are, it seems, gentle, kindly, fair-minded, imaginative, daring, stubborn, heroic, intelligent—and, of course, insufficiently conscious of our own merits. It is all rather reminiscent of those fortune-tellers who tell you that "your worst fault is generosity," and it would be very gratifying if it came from a foreigner—but it would have to be someone rather more foreign than a Cornishman.

In reprinting these essays Mr. Rowse probably had his eye on America. It is notorious that there are strong currents of anti-British feeling in the United States, some of them traceable to ignorance of English history and out-of-date notions about the English social system, and clearly they need to be counteracted.

But it is doubtful whether this book will have that effect. There is too much insistence on British achievement, too much praise of "great" but morally dubious men like Cromwell and the Duke of Marlborough, too much military glory altogether, and almost no mention of the best trait of the English people, the fact that they don't value military glory and are more inclined to remember defeats than victories.

Perhaps the most useful essay in the book is the opening one on Winston Churchill. It is rather too adulatory in tone, and it insists more than is needed on Mr. Churchill's aristocratic ancestry, but it may remind some readers of one thing that we are liable to forget—that Mr. Churchill is not only a Statesman but also a writer, and quite a good one. It was well worth reminding the public of that very readable book, "My Early Life."

There is also an informative essay on Erasmus, who spent 10 years in

England about the beginning of the sixteenth century. But the general impression left by this book, and even the titles of the chapters ("The Spirit of Adventure—British Interpretation." "Drake's Way," "Seamen and Empire"), is that this is not how England ought to be praised.

Perhaps the remark that Bernard Shaw puts into the mouth of one of his characters, "Every true Englishman hates the English," is not such an exaggeration as it sounds.

Mr. Michael Foot's book (for the identity of "Cassius" has now been officially disclosed) is a very light squib, and perhaps less successful than "The Trial of Mussolini." It is concerned with a Mr. Taper and a Mr. Tadpole, these being very thinly disguised portraits of Mr. Brendan Bracken and Mr. Beverley Baxter.[1] Mr. Taper is the intelligent kind of Tory, and Mr. Tadpole is the stupid kind. They are engaged (the time is a little in the future) in thinking out a plan of campaign for the forthcoming General Election, which involves covering up the Tory record during the past 20 years.

Mr. Tadpole makes imbecile attempts to explain away Chamberlain's mistakes instead of quietly ignoring them—Mr. Taper is aware that the Tories are more likely to win if they can assume the colours of their adversaries. Mr. Foot makes a devastating exposure of the folly of our rulers from 1918 onwards, but is inclined to pull his punches when the Labour party is concerned.

The familiar charge that the appeasement policy was inevitable because Britain had been weakened by the pacifism of the Left has enough truth in it to merit more than a debating-society answer. To take simply one example, the Labour party voted against conscription as late as 1939, although it was at the same time demanding a firm stand against Hitler.

In Britain this step was intelligible, but all over Europe, including France and probably the U.S.S.R., it simply created the impression that Britain did not intend to fight. Even the idiotic "King and country" resolution of the Oxford Union in 1935, which in this country could be seen in its true perspective, brought encouragement to the Italian Fascists. The book ends with an imaginary election speech by Mr. Churchill, and another, entitled, "The other speech that could win," by an unnamed Labour leader, both of them exhibiting at its best Mr. Foot's talent for Corinthian oratory.

[Fee: £8.0.0; 14.11.44]

1. For Brendan Bracken; see 2490, n. 2; for Beverley Baxter, 2490, n. 3.

2579. 'As I Please,' 48

Tribune, 17 November 1944

Some weeks ago, in the course of some remarks on schools of journalism, I carelessly described the magazine the *Writer* as being "defunct." As a result I have received a severe letter from its proprietors, who enclose a copy of the November issue of the *Writer* and call on me to withdraw my statement.[1]

I withdraw it readily. The *Writer* is still alive and seems to be much the same as ever, though it has changed its format since I knew it. And I think this specimen copy is worth examining for the light it throws on schools of journalism and the whole business of extracting fees from struggling free-lance journalists.

The articles are of the usual type ("Plotting Technique (fifteenth instalment,") by William A. Bagley, etc.), but I am more interested in the advertisements, which take up more than a quarter of the space. The majority of them are from people who profess to be able to teach you how to make money out of writing. A surprising number undertake to supply you with ready-made plots. Here are a few specimens:

"Plotting without tears. Learn my way. The simplest method ever. Money returned if dissatisfied. 5/- post free."

"Inexhaustible plotting method for women's Press, 5/3d. Gives real mastery. Ten days' approval."

"PLOTS. Our plots are set out in sequence all ready for write-up, with lengths for each sequence. No remoulding necessary—just the requisite clothing of words. All types supplied."

"PLOTS: in vivid scenes. With striking opening lines for actual use in story. Specimen conversation, including authentic dialect. . . . Short-short, 5/-. Short story, 6/6d. Long-complete (with tense, breathless 'curtains') 8/6d. Radio plays, 10/6d. Serial, novel, novelette (chapter by chapter, appropriate prefix, prose or poetical quotations if desired), 15/6d.—1 gn."

There are many others. Somebody called Mr. Martin Walter claims to have reduced story-construction to an exact science and "eventually evolved the Plot Formula according to which his own stories and those of his students throughout the world are constructed. . . . Whether you aspire to write the 'literary' story or the popular story, or to produce stories for any existing market, remember that Mr. Walter's Formula *alone* tells you just what a 'plot' is and how to produce one." The Formula only costs you a guinea, it appears. Then there are the "Fleet Street journalists" who are prepared to revise your manuscripts for you at 2/6 per thousand words. Nor are the poets forgotten:

"GREETINGS.

"Are you poets neglecting the great post-war demand for sentiments?

"Do you specialise and do you know what is needed?

"Aida Reuben's famous Greeting Card Course is available to approved students willing to work hard. Her book 'Sentiment and Greeting Card Publishers,' published at 3/6d., may be obtained from," etc., etc.

I do not wish to say anything offensive, but to anyone who is inclined to respond to the sort of advertisement quoted above, I offer this consideration. If these people really know how to make money out of writing, why aren't they just doing it instead of peddling their secret at 5/- a time? Apart from any other consideration, they would be raising up hordes of competitors for themselves. This number of the *Writer* contains about 30 advertisements of this stamp, and the *Writer* itself, besides giving advice in its articles, also runs its own Literary Bureau in which manuscripts are "criticised by acknowledged experts" at so much a thousand words. If each of these various teachers had even ten successful pupils a week, they would between them be letting loose on to the market some fifteen thousand successful writers per annum!

Also, isn't it rather curious that the "Fleet Street journalists," "established authors" and "well-known novelists" who either run these courses or write the testimonials for them are not named—or, when named, are seldom or never people whose published work you have seen anywhere? If Bernard Shaw or J. B. Priestley offered to teach you how to make money out of writing, you might feel that there was something in it. But who would buy a bottle of hair restorer from a bald man?

If the *Writer* wants some more free publicity it shall have it, but I dare say this will do to go on with.

One favourite way of falsifying history nowadays is to alter dates.[2] Maurice Thorez,[3] the French Communist, has just been amnestied by the French Government (he was under sentence for deserting from the army). Apropos of this, one London newspaper remarks that Thorez "will now be able to return from Moscow, where he has been living in exile for the last six years."

On the contrary, he has been in Moscow for at most five years, as the editor of this newspaper is well aware. Thorez, who for several years past has been proclaiming his anxiety to defend France against the Germans, was called up at the outbreak of war in 1939, and failed to make an appearance. Some time later he turned up in Moscow.

But why the alteration of date? In order to make it appear that Thorez deserted, if he did desert, a year *before* the war and not after the fighting had started. This is merely one act in the general effort to whitewash the behaviour of the French and other Communists during the period of the Russo-German pact. I could name other similar falsifications in recent years. Sometimes you can give an event a quite different colour by switching its date only a few weeks. But it doesn't much matter so long as we all keep our eyes open and see to it that the lies do not creep out of the newspapers and into the history books.[4]

A correspondent who lacks the collecting instinct has sent a copy of *Principles or Prejudices*, a sixpenny pamphlet by Kenneth Pickthorn, the Conservative M.P., with the advice (underlined in red ink): "Burn when read."

I wouldn't think of burning it. It has gone straight into my archives. But I agree that it is a disgusting piece of work, and that this whole series of pamphlets (the *Signpost Booklets*, by such authors as G. M. Young, Douglas Woodruff and Captain L. D. Gammans) is a bad symptom. Mr. Pickthorn is one of the more intelligent of the younger Tory M.P.s ("younger" in political circles means under sixty), and in this pamphlet he is trying to present Toryism in a homely and democratic light while casting misleading little snacks[5] at the Left. Look at this, for instance, for a misrepresentation of the theory of Marxism:

"Not one of the persons who say that economic factors govern the world believes it about himself. If Karl Marx had been more economically than politically interested he could have done better for himself than by accepting the kindnesses of the capitalist Engels and occasionally selling articles to American newspapers."

Aimed at ignorant people, this is meant to imply that Marxism regards *individual* acquisitiveness as the motive force in history. Marx not only did not say this, he said almost the opposite of it. Much of the pamphlet is an attack on the notion of internationalism, and is backed up by such remarks as: "No British statesman should feel himself authorised to spend British blood for the promotion of something superior to British interests." Fortunately, Mr. Pickthorn writes too badly to have a very wide appeal, but some of the other pamphleteers in this series are cleverer. The Tory Party used always to be known as "the stupid party." But the publicists of this group have a fair selection of brains among them, and when Tories grow intelligent it is time to feel for your watch and count your small change.

Tribune on 8 December 1944 published three letters, the third a long one from the Director of the British Institute of Fiction-Writing Science Ltd.

I don't think George Orwell is quite fair to the "Writer" and the various schools of journalism. As a hobby it is no worse than stamp collecting, and it does help all sorts of people to become more articulate. Surely this is a good thing in a democracy. Admittedly, the kind of articles and fiction that can be most easily taught are not of any high intellectual or literary content, but life would be very dull if we were to be highbrow all the time. I enjoy a "blood"[6] as a relaxation from theology and economics. Orwell may say that the people catered for remain at the tripe level all the time. I don't think this is true. One must walk before one can run. To this day Billy Bunter remains my favourite character in fiction.

Austin Lee

You devote nearly two columns in *Tribune* to the activities of various schools of writing, etc., and your remarks should prevent a lot of ambitious young men wasting their money on these rackets. At the same time I have to point out that this "Somebody called Martin Walter" is responsible for the British Institute of Fiction Writing Science, Ltd., which organisation advertises regularly in *Tribune*.[7] This orgnisation does not want stories as advertised, but fees for its particular racket. What about seeing the advertising manager of *Tribune* and allowing him to see your illuminating remarks? Or does *Tribune* have to descend to the moral levels of the cheap capitalistic Press and be willing to accept advertising revenue from any source irrespective of its nature?

E. R. Ward

As your Mr. George Orwell has now added my name to his gallery of Aunt Sallies, I would consider it a contribution to the ideals of socialist justice if you were to allow me some space to hit back.

Your Mr. George Orwell states that I claim "to have reduced story-construction to an exact science." This statement is as false as his recent reference to the writer° as "defunct," and I would appreciate the publication of either evidence in its support or an admission that in this instance also Mr. George Orwell was "careless." Are my claims to have discovered a *qualitative* science to be ridiculed and distorted merely because fiction writing has not yet been recognised as a qualitative science by the Universities which now recognise Psychic Science, Psychological Science and Political Science? Since your Mr. George Orwell ridicules my Plot Formula and my scientific analysis of the meaning of "plot," will he kindly offer a more scientific analysis himself and will he also point to a more impressive list of published fiction which he and his students constructed according to his analysis?

Your Mr. George Orwell refers to "the business of extracting fees from struggling free-lance journalists." The description is ludicrous. The vast majority of struggling free-lance journalists who part with their money in exchange for literary instruction are absolutely satisfied. In my twelve years' experience as a tutor my dissatisfied students have numbered under 3 per cent., and in these cases the dissatisfaction has always been due to an unwillingness to carry out or complete the instruction. Furthermore, in a considerable number of cases the fees are paid not by "struggling free-lance journalists" but by otherwise professionally engaged or retired individuals who willingly pay the fees for something which to them is a spare-time relaxation. My students in this category include a University professor and an Army surgeon. And since your Mr. George Orwell thinks fit to doubt the genuineness of testimonials, I must add that, at least in my case, originals of testimonials are available for inspection by appointment, and that I have never solicited a testimonial in my life.

Referring to literary tutors in general, your Mr. George Orwell asks: "If these people really know how to make money out of writing, why aren't they just doing it instead of peddling their secret at 5s. a time." The answer is as simple as the question is naive. Most of these people *are* making money out of writing—and they are making additional money by peddling their secret; the rest have *made* money out of writing and now make money by teaching because it is less arduous. Your Mr. George Orwell might just as well ask: "Why do pianoforte teachers give lessons in pianoforte if there is money to be made by playing the piano?" Still dealing with this point, your Mr. George Orwell writes: "If Bernard Shaw or J. B. Priestley offered to teach you how to make money out of writing you might feel that there was something in it. Must Arthur Rubinstein or Charlie Kunz offer to teach us how to make money out of piano-playing before we can feel there is something in it? In any case, Sir Max Pemberton[8] offers to teach; his school advertises regularly in your columns. "Who," asks your Mr. George Orwell, "would buy a bottle of hair restorer from a bald man?" WHO, I ask your Mr. George Orwell, is offering to teach writing yet cannot point to his own published work?

And, finally, Sir, here are two points with which you yourself are directly concerned: (1) My refutation of your Mr. George Orwell's recent suggestion that all schools of writing are spreading the capitalist idea was recently sent to your advertisement manager in the form of one of my printed course booklets in which I advocate Socialism and I recommend the student to read John Strachey's *The Theory and Practice of Socialism*; and I would like to know whether you think it would be fair to publish this fact in your columns? (2) My claims in connection with my Plot Formula have been published in full column advertisements in *Tribune*, and I would like to know whether you allow your advertisers to offer propositions to your readers which you do not believe to be genuine.

Martin Walter,
Director, British Institute of
Fiction-Writing Science, Ltd.

Orwell responded to Martin Walter in 'As I Please,' 51, 8 December 1944; see *2590*. Finally, on 19 January 1945, *Tribune* published this letter from a satisfied customer.

Having read George Orwell's article on page 10 of your number of November 17, I feel that it is only fair to write and tell you that, from my personal knowledge, the Greeting Card Course sent out by Miss Aida Reubens is both genuine and constructive. I have read this Course, and I know that quite a number of her pupils have actually sold a good many verses while still receiving tuition. I am well aware that many of these so-called "Courses" are quite useless and merely a means of extracting money from a credulous public, but I do not consider that this special Course comes under this category in any way.

I am myself a contributor of poems to *The Sunday Times, Country Life*, etc., and had one included in *Best Poems of 1943*, so you will understand that I am not writing this letter from any personal motive. Miss Aida Reubens is genuinely interested in helping struggling poets, and she gives a good deal of time to this object, which could be much more profitably used in her own work, of which she sells a very great deal.

B. R. Gibbs

1. 'As I Please,' 43, 6 October 1944; see *2560*.
2. See Gleb Struve's letter of 19 November 1944 (*2583*), in response to Orwell's statement.
3. Maurice Thorez (1900–1964), Secretary-General of the French Communist Party. Orwell states that Thorez 'failed to make an appearance'; William Steinhoff says, 'but once in the army he had almost immediately deserted and fled to the Soviet Union' (*George Orwell and the Origins of 1984*, 114). In 1939–40, Germany and the Soviet Union were allied and not at war one with the other. *France Today and the People's Front* by Maurice Thorez was the first book published by the Left Book Club (May 1936).
4. This second section of 'As I Please,' 48, from 'One favourite way of falsifying history . . .' to '. . . into the history books,' was reprinted under an item headed 'Communists Whitewashed' in the regular feature on the Press ('Through the Press') in *War Commentary—for Anarchism*, 25 November 1944.

5. Perhaps 'smacks' or 'snooks' is intended. The original copy is perfectly clear.
6. A "blood" is a sensational story, a 'penny-dreadful.'
7. See *2560, n. 1* for another writing school attacked by Orwell which also advertised in *Tribune.*
8. Sir Max Pemberton (1863–1950) edited *Chums*, 1892–93, *Cassell's Magazine*, 1896–1906, was author of many novels. He was a director of Northcliffe newspapers, and wrote a memoir of Lord Northcliffe. He founded the London School of Journalism in 1920, the first of what were to be many correspondence courses for would-be authors and journalists. Robert Graves and Alan Hodge thought that, though few people earned large incomes as a result of pursuing such courses, 'these schools of journalism were not a "racket", for they did teach their pupils certain journalistic formalities which had to be observed if they were to get anything published at all' (*The Long Week-End: A Social History of Great Britain 1918–1939* (1940), 61–62; U.S.: 51–52).

2580. Review of *Last Essays* by J. A. Spender; *Palestine, Land of Promise* by Walter Clay Lowdermilk; *Selected Writing* by Reginald Moore

Manchester Evening News, 23 November 1944

J. A. Spender, the famous Liberal journalist, editor for many years of the "Westminster Gazette" (which was swallowed in 1928 by the "Daily News"), was born in 1863 and died when the present war was well under way.[1] He knew Lloyd George and Lord Grey, he had often talked with Gladstone, he had met Browning and Matthew Arnold, he had seen Disraeli, and at Oxford he had studied under Ruskin.

Inevitably his memories are the most interesting thing about him, but the publishers are justified in claiming on the dust jacket that these essays are "just as applicable to our times as when they first appeared."

Spender stood for the very best traditions of old-style English journalism—traditions that included not only a most vigilant regard for truthfulness and freedom of expression but also a respect for the intellect, which is not too common to-day.[2]

There is a little anecdote in the book which unconsciously illustrates this. In the eighties Spender was editing a very obscure provincial newspaper, and Matthew Arnold had been engaged to deliver a lecture to the local literary and philosophical society.

Arnold called on Spender and asked him not to publish a report of the lecture, as if it were unprinted he could sell it elsewhere. Spender assured him that this was useless, since all the other local papers would be certain to report it; and it emerges that his own report was to take up five columns.

One can hardly imagine a lecture by Matthew Arnold, or anyone resembling him, being "news" to that extent to-day!

When he writes of liberty, and especially the liberty of the Press, Spender makes one realise what an advantage it was to have formed one's dominant ideas in the nineteenth century. Few modern people are able to be so unafraid of the consequences of liberty.

In 1937, when appeasement was in fashion, we find him boldly speaking out against the European dictatorships, and in 1940, when Britain's situation was desperate, we find him still insisting that it pays to tell the truth and that honest criticism must not be silenced.

Nor was he frightened of taking the unpopular side. One of his last pieces of writing is a defence of Chamberlain. No doubt Chamberlain's policy was wrong and Spender was mistaken in defending it, but still at that date (November, 1940) it took courage to plunge into print, voluntarily, on such a subject.

This is only a slight book and some of the essays in it were hardly worth reprinting, but it would be worth reading merely for the reminiscences of Gladstone, Grey, Botha, Haig and others. And there are some excellent remarks in it here and there. For instance:

> "The saviours of their country are in fact, for the most part, disagreeable and dangerous people. As history shows, it is almost as great a misfortune for a country to be 'saved' as to be ruined outright.
> "When a country has been saved, the saviour should, like the poet in Plato's republic, be crowned with garlands and conducted to the frontier."

An amusing item is a letter to Spender's nephew, Mr. Stephen Spender, expressing his views (unfavourable) on contemporary poetry. But even there Spender keeps his head and is willing to admit—remembering the reception that some of Browning's poems had from his contemporaries—that he may be wrong.

Dr. Lowdermilk's book is a well-documented account of the achievement of the Zionist settlers in Palestine, with some impressive photographs of dense forests and populous cities in places which were desert only 20 years ago.

The author is an American expert on soil conservation. He produces much evidence to show that the desiccation of Palestine in modern times (it was a flourishing province under the Romans) is not due to any change of climate but to the inefficient agricultural methods of the Arabs and to their all-devouring herds of goats.

He favours the setting up of a Jordan Valley authority, similar to the Tennessee Valley authority, and considers that by this means the soil of Palestine could be made to support another four million human beings. This would solve the "Jewish Question" once and for all.

Though not a Jew himself, Dr. Lowdermilk is a warm supporter of Zionism. His book deserves to be read, but with the proviso that applies to all Zionist and pro-Zionist literature—that there is also an Arab viewpoint, and, owing to the fact that the Arabs have little footing in the Press outside their own country, it seldom gets a hearing.

The collection of stories and poems in "Selected Writing" consists mostly of hitherto unpublished material, and is above the average level of present-day anthologies.

Specially deserving of mention are a short story of Army life by Alun Lewis, who was recently killed in Burma; and another by Fred Urquhart, who has a remarkable gift for constructing neat stories with convincing dialogue.

There is an amusing trifle by Maclaren-Ross, a fragment of Alex Comfort's recently published novel, "The Power House," and a good Welsh story by Rhys Davies.

The poems selected by J. Tambimuttu[3] and prefaced by some cryptic remarks suggesting clique warfare, include contributions from George Barker, Ruthven Todd, Julian Symons, and Kathleen Raine.

[Fee: £8.0.0; 21.11.44]

1. J. A. Spender died in 1942.
2. The hyphenation of 'to-day' here and three paragraphs later is a clear indication of the effect of sub-editing on Orwell's text. He always wrote and typed 'today.' It is highly likely that the punctuation of Orwell's contributions, especially to the *Manchester Evening News*, has been made to conform to sub-editors' style.
3. M. J. Tambimuttu (see *867, n. 1*) gave several talks under Orwell's aegis at the BBC in 1941 and 1942.

2581. 'As I Please,' 49

Tribune, 24 November 1944

There have been innumerable complaints lately about the rudeness of shopkeepers. People say, I think with truth, that shopkeepers appear to take a sadistic pleasure in telling you that they don't stock the thing you ask for. To go in search of some really rare object, such as a comb or a tin of boot polish, is a miserable experience. It means trailing from shop to shop and getting a series of curt or actually hostile negatives. But even the routine business of buying the rations and the bread is made as difficult as possible for busy people. How is a woman to do her household shopping if she is working till six every day while most of the shops shut at five? She can only do it by fighting round crowded counters during her lunch hour. But it is the snubs that they get when they ask for some article which is in short supply that people dread most. Many shopkeepers seem to regard the customer as a kind of mendicant and to feel that they are conferring a favour on him by selling him anything. And there are other justified grievances—for instance, the shameless overcharging on uncontrolled goods such as secondhand furniture, and the irritating trick, now very common, of displaying in the window goods which are not on sale.

But before blaming the shopkeeper for all this, there are several things one ought to remember. To begin with, irritability and bad manners are on the increase everywhere. You have only to observe the behaviour of normally longsuffering people like 'bus conductors to realise this. It is a neurosis produced by the war. But, in addition, many small independent shopkeepers (in my experience you are treated far more politely in big shops) are people with a well-founded grievance against society. Some of them are in effect the ill-paid employees of wholesale firms, others are being slowly crushed by the competition of the chain stores, and they are often treated with the greatest inconsiderateness by the local authorities. Sometimes a rehousing scheme will rob a shopkeeper of half his customers at one swoop. In war time this may happen even more drastically owing to bombing and the call-up. And war has other special irritations for the shopkeeper. Rationing puts a great deal of extra work on to grocers, butchers, etc., and it is very exasperating to be asked all day long for articles which you have not got.

But after all, the main fact is that at normal times both the shop assistant and the independent shopkeeper are downtrodden. They live to the tune of "the customer is always right." In peace time, in capitalist society, everyone is trying to sell goods which there is never enough money to buy, whereas in war time money is plentiful and goods scarce. Matches, razor blades, torch batteries, alarm clocks and teats for babies' feeding bottles are precious rarities, and the man who possesses them is a powerful being, to be approached cap in hand. I don't think one can blame the shopkeeper for getting a bit of his own back, when the situation is temporarily reversed. But I do agree that the behaviour of some of them is disgusting, and that when one is treated with more than normal haughtiness it is a duty to the rest of the public not to go to that shop again.

Examining recently a copy of *Old Moore's Almanac*, I was reminded of the fun I used to extract in my boyhood from answering advertisements. Increase your height, earn five pounds a week in your spare time, drink habit conquered in three days, electric belts, bust developers and cures for obesity, insomnia, bunions, backache, red noses, stammering, blushing, piles, bad legs, flat feet and baldness—all the old favourites were there, or nearly all. Some of these advertisements have remained totally unchanged for at least thirty years.

You cannot, I imagine, get much benefit from any of these nostrums, but you can have a lot of fun by answering the advertisements and then, when you have drawn them out and made them waste a lot of stamps in sending successive wads of testimonials, suddenly leaving them cold. Many years ago I answered an advertisement from Winifred Grace Hartland (the advertisement used to carry a photograph of her—a radiant woman with a sylphlike figure), who undertook to cure obesity. In replying to my letter she assumed that I was a woman—this surprised me at the time, though I realise now that the dupes of these advertisements are almost all female. She urged me to come and see her at once. "Do come," she wrote, "before ordering your summer frocks, as after taking my course your figure will have altered out of recognition." She was particularly insistent that I should make a personal visit, and gave an address somewhere in London Docks. This went on for a long time, during which the fee gradually sank from two guineas to half a crown, and then I brought the matter to an end by writing to say that I had been cured of my obesity by a rival agency.

Years later I came across a copy of the cautionary list which *Truth* used to issue from time to time in order to warn the public against swindlers. It revealed that there was no such person as Winifred Grace Hartland, this swindle being run by two American crooks named Harry Sweet and Dave Little. It is curious that they should have been so anxious for a personal visit, and indeed I have since wondered whether Harry Sweet and Dave Little were actually engaged in shipping consignments of fat women to the harems of Istanbul.

Everyone has a list of books which he is "always meaning to read," and now and again one gets round to reading one of them. One that I recently crossed off my list was George Bourne's *Memoirs of a Surrey Labourer*.[1] I was slightly disappointed with it, because, though it is a true story, Bettesworth, the man it is about, was not quite an ordinary labourer. He had been a farm worker, but had become a jobbing gardener, and his relation with George Bourne was that of servant and master. Nevertheless there is some remarkable detail in it, and it gives a true picture of the cruel, sordid end with which a lifetime of heavy work on the land is often rewarded. The book was written more than thirty years ago, but things have not changed fundamentally. Immediately before the war, in my own village in Hertfordshire, two old men were ending their days in much the same bare misery as George Bourne describes.

Another book I recently read, or rather re-read, was *The Follies and Frauds of Spiritualism*, issued about twenty years ago by the Rationalist Press Association. This is probably not an easy book to get hold of, but I can equally recommend Mr. Bechhofer Roberts's book on the same subject. An interesting fact that these and similar books bring out is the number of scientists who have been taken in by spiritualism. The list includes Sir William Crookes, Wallace the biologist, Lombroso, Flammarion the astronomer (he afterwards changed his mind, however), Sir Oliver Lodge,[2] and a whole string of German and Italian professors. These people are not perhaps, the topnotchers of the scientific world, but you do not find, for instance, poets in comparable numbers falling a prey to the mediums. Elizabeth Barrett Browning is supposed to have been taken in by the famous medium Home, but Browning himself saw through him at a glance and wrote a scarifying poem about him (*Sludge the Medium*).[3] Significantly, the people who are *never* converted to spiritualism are conjurors.

1. George Bourne (pseudonym of George Sturt, 1890–1927) worked for a time as a schoolteacher, but at his father's death took over his wheelwright's business. *Memoirs of a Surrey Labourer* was published in 1907. His *Change in the Village* (1912) and, especially, *The Wheelwright's Shop* (1923) have been particularly admired. Sturt and the world he described influenced some literary critics in the 1930s, particularly the *Scrutiny* school, who envisaged an 'organic community' in contradistinction to the world of mass production and technology.
2. Sir William Crookes (1832–1919), chemist and physicist who discovered thalium and invented the Crookes Tube; Alfred Russel Wallace (1823–1913), botanist and biologist, author of many scientific and travel books and of *Miracles and Modern Spiritualism* (1876); Cesare Lombroso (1835–1909), Italian criminologist; Camille Flammarion (1842–1925), French astronomer; Sir Oliver Lodge (1851–1940), physicist who took a special interest in wireless telegraphy, psychic research, and the reconciliation of religion and science. In the original, the 'n' is omitted from Flammarion.
3. Daniel Dunglas Home (1833–1886), a popular American medium who recognised that he was the model for Sludge. See *Robert Browning: The Poems*, edited by John Pettigrew and Thomas J. Collins (1981), Vol. 1, 1163.

2582. Review of *A Critical History of English Poetry* by
Herbert J. C. Grierson and J. C. Smith

The Observer, 26 November 1944

A book of 521 pages, which starts with "Beowulf" and ends with Mr. Henry
Treece, necessarily lays the emphasis on history rather than on criticism. This
book, which deals at varying lengths with something over 300 English poets,
is primarily a work of reference, and as such it will be extremely useful in
these days when libraries are scattered and minor classics often unprocurable.

The authors trace the development of English poetry from the Dark Ages
onwards, following more or less the usual methods of classification. A few
major poets get a chapter to themselves, and Irish and Scottish poetry are
given their due share of attention. Poetic drama is adequately dealt with, and
even hymns are not despised. But in so inclusive a book it seems a pity that
there is almost no mention of comic verse, which till recently often contrived
to be a species of poetry, and a species in which the races of the British Isles
were pre-eminent. There is no reference to Barham, Thackeray, or Lewis
Carroll, for instance, and Calverley only just makes the grade. Mr. Belloc is
dismissed with the remark that "some of his sonnets, epigrams, and
'cautionary' rhymes are not yet forgotten," which is, to put it mildly, an
understatement. Nor is there any mention of the English nursery rhymes—a
pity, not only because some of them are true poems, but because the authors
could have done a public service by pointing out the disgraceful fact that no
full collection of nursery rhymes has ever been printed.

The purpose for which the average reader consults a book of this kind is to
be told something about the lesser-known poets (the fifteenth-century ones,
for instance), or about such works as "The Faerie Queene," which he knows
he ought to admire but feels disinclined to read. Necessarily he has to take a
good deal on trust. But there is one way in which the critical judgments in
such a book can be tested—that is, by seeing what it says about contemporary
poetry, on which no established body of opinion yet exists. It is astonishing
how badly many anthologies and works of academic criticism emerge from
this test. The "Oxford Book of English Verse" is an example. It is a good
selection up to the point at which the compiler had to begin using his own
judgment, after which it deteriorates noticeably.

Professor Grierson and Dr. Smith, however, have kept well in touch with
recent developments, and perhaps even give contemporary verse more space
than it deserves. There is, indeed, much in their judgment that one might
quarrel with. They confess to a preference for the Georgians (we are told of
Mr. Ralph Hodgson, for instance, that "almost all he has written is
memorable"), they only mention Hopkins very shortly, and though they
give Mr. Eliot a page or two they do not mention the Sweeney poems, and
make only a slighting reference to "Prufrock." Pound is excluded from
mention on what appear to be political grounds, and Joyce is not spoken of as
a verse-writer, although he wrote the only successful villanelle in English.[1]
But still, the authors do not share the delusion, only too common with the
possessors of great learning, that literature stopped about forty years ago.

They are willing to take seriously not merely Auden and MacNeice but even Dylan Thomas and the Apocalyptics. The ordinary reader who is not a scholar can therefore accept what they tell him about (say) Henryson or Traherne or Shenstone with some confidence.

The book's greatest weakness—perhaps, however, it could not have been avoided without making the book much longer—is that it says only the minimum about the social background of literature. Changes of form, subject-matter, and language are recorded, but only very briefly explained. After the English language has settled into more or less its modern shape—at about the beginning of the sixteenth century, say—the striking thing about English poetry is its diversity and the ebb and flow of certain moods. In one age almost anyone seems capable of writing a passable lyric poem, while in another, perhaps less than a hundred years later, the lyric seems almost to have vanished. Throughout the greater part of the eighteenth century the heroic couplet is almost the only mode, Shakespeare is only doubtfully admired, and Pope's rewriting of Chaucer is looked upon as an improvement; then, quite suddenly, the classical style of writing seems stilted and even ridiculous, and poetry is governed for more than a hundred years by the wildest romanticism.

Professor Grierson and Dr. Smith do make some attempt to relate such changes as these to major historical events, but on the whole they treat the history of poetry as the history of individuals or of "schools" centring on individuals. This was, perhaps, unavoidable if they were to mention so many poets as they contrive to do, but frequently as one reads one finds oneself wishing for more background information—more explanation of *why* the English were once the most musical people in Europe and then fell from that position, or *why* one age should ignore Nature, another worship it, and another find it slightly horrifying. However, the authors no doubt narrowed their field intentionally, and what they set out to do they have done successfully. It is an informative book, and anyone who buys it is likely to keep it.

[Fee: £10.0.0; 24.11.44]

1. See Orwell's letter to Ralph C. Elsley, 5 December 1944, *2588*.

2583. To Gleb Struve

28 November 1944   Typewritten

In 'As I Please,' 48, 17 November 1944 (see *2579*), Orwell referred to falsifying history by altering dates, a technique he would satirise in *Nineteen Eighty-Four*. On 19 November, Gleb Struve[1] wrote to him giving further examples of this as practised by Soviet Communists. He was prompted, he wrote, to draw Orwell's attention to

a curious official Soviet publication called "Reference Calendar for 1944" which contains two chronological tables entitled "Principal dates in the history of the USSR" and "Principal dates in modern history". If you look up the year 1939 in the former you will find that there were no events of note between "the 18th Congress of the Communist Party" (March 10–21) and "the crossing by the Red Army of the Soviet frontier for the defence of the lives and property of the peoples of western Ukraine and western Belorussia" (Sept. 17th). No mention of the Soviet German Pact of August 1939. Nor is it mentioned in the other table where events of international importance are listed. Here you have: "The seizure of Tirana (Albania's capital) by Italy. The suppression of Albania's independence" (April 1939) and "Germany's attack on Poland. The outbreak of war in Europe" (Sept. 1, 1939). There is, of course, no tampering with dates here, but the Soviet-German pact is simply struck out of history: the omission serves a propaganda purpose, though events of lesser national and international importance are mentioned.

In the domestic chronological table there is also the following remarkable entry: "1936, June 18. — The villainous murder of M. Gorky by the Trotskyist-Zinovievist-Bukharinist bandits."

Should you wish to use this information in print, I would ask you to withhold my name.

Orwell replied:

Tribune

Dear Mr. Struve,
Many thanks for the information. I'll no doubt have an opportunity to make use of it some time, and, as you ask, I won't mention your name.[2]

Yours sincerely,
[Signed] Geo. Orwell
George Orwell

1. For Gleb Struve, see *2421, n. 1.*
2. See Orwell's letter to Frank Barber, 15 December 1944, *2591.*

2584. Review of *Noblesse Oblige—Another Letter to Another Son* by James Agate; *Perspective for Poetry* by Jack Lindsay

Manchester Evening News, 30 November 1944

Some months ago Sir Osbert Sitwell wrote a little book entitled "A Letter To My Son,"[1] which was in effect a plea for the independence, or even the irresponsibility, of the artist. The son (an imaginary son, thought of as an artist or writer) was counselled to regard himself as an Ishmael, and preserve his intellectual integrity at no matter what cost.

Now Mr. James Agate[2] has written a vigorous, not to say violent, reply, in which he asserts that the artist is not to be treated as a special kind of being, but has the same obligations as any other citizen.

Much of what Mr. Agate says is justified. It is quite true that the artist cannot exist in a vacuum and that he has an interest in defending our own relatively free society against conquest from without. The plea that writers and artists ought to be exempted from military service has not much to recommend it.

All the same, Sir Osbert Sitwell's main point is only partly met, and the tone of Mr. Agate's reply will antagonise many people who might be disposed to agree with him.

In a healthy society everyone would be an artist of sorts. In our own society the artist is an exceptional person, and he has to practise cunning—not, indeed, to keep alive, but to keep his soul his own.

Instead of seeing this as a temporary and evil phenomenon, Mr. Agate chooses to regard it as a law of nature. The average person, he says, is totally unmoved by art or literature, and he implies that this will always be so. "Let me say," he says, "that I have little or no belief in the power of education.

"So far as I can see, it leads the child out of the darkness of healthy ignorance into the much denser night of soul-destroying commonness," and he implies all the way through that he sympathises, or partly sympathises, with the average man's contempt for the arts. There are the usual jeers against "highbrows," the people who compose "an unintelligible poem" or paint "a picture of three sardines swimming in a top-hat," while golf, cricket, and other pastimes are declared to have "moved the ordinary man more than all the poets put together."

What Mr. Agate does not see is that it is exactly this attitude, common enough in the general public and encouraged by people like himself, that makes artists and intellectuals irresponsible. If you treat people as pariahs, they behave like pariahs.

Some of the younger English writers and artists have behaved in an unworthy way in the present war, and a species of individualism, usually calling itself anarchism, is probably on the upgrade. But the solution is not to congratulate the ordinary man on his bad taste. The solution, ultimately, is through the education which Mr. Agate disbelieves in. Sir Osbert Sitwell's pamphlet deserves a better answer.

Mr Jack Lindsay is a different proposition. He is dealing with almost exactly the same subject—the position of the poet in present-day society—but his short pamphlet contrives also to be a compressed history of the literary movement from the last war onwards, with some backward glances at earlier periods.

It must be one of the ablest pieces of Marxist literary criticism that have been written for some years past. It is not easy reading, partly because the need to squeeze his material into 25 pages causes Mr. Lindsay to write in a sort of shorthand, but it is well worth the effort it entails.

Mr. Lindsay's thesis is that poetry can only truly flourish in a classless society. In the primitive past there was no conflict between the individual and the group. There was a collective consciousness of the whole tribe, and the poet, who was also a priest, merely expressed in a heightened form what was

477

felt by everybody else. He was an exceptional being, but he was not isolated in the same sense as the modern intellectual.

With the appearance of class distinctions and class conflict, the communal basis of poetry disappeared, and with it the freedom of the poet, who was now necessarily at odds with his environment.

His position will only be fully restored when the classless society is established, but even in our own age he can be relatively free so long as he recognises and accepts the necessary drift of history. He is most truly individual when he surrenders his individuality to the struggle for the classless society.

The various attempts and failures to do this are illustrated by the successive schools of poetry that have flourished in this country in the last 30 years—Housman and the Georgians, the war poets, Mr. Eliot and his followers, the Auden group, and finally Mr. Herbert Read and the young anarchist-pacifist poets who have appeared during the last few years.

In very broad terms there is little doubt that Mr. Lindsay's theory is correct, but one has to be on one's guard against his political loyalties.

He does not say but he implies that to throw oneself into the struggle for the classless society means joining the Communist party, or at least being in sympathy with it. There is, however, no strong reason for thinking that the various Communist parties of the world are likely or even anxious to bring a classless society into existence, and Mr. Lindsay's refusal to countenance any but his own version of Marxism leads him into a false assumption.

He claims that those who reject orthodox Communism do so because they fear discipline and wish to cling to an intellectual liberty which is, in fact, illusory.

No doubt that is the motive in some cases, but certainly not in all. On the whole, the best literary brains of our time have rejected Communism not because it entailed discipline but because it involved them in falsification.

A writer who joins the Communist party is involved, sometimes quite directly, in the sordid game of power politics, and there are various issues on which it is very difficult for him to write what he knows to be the truth. He can, of course, toe the line, but at a fearful intellectual price.

This accounts for the fact—and it ought not to be a fact if Mr. Lindsay's theory were quite watertight—that over a quarter of a century the whole Communist movement has produced so little worthwhile literature.

But that does not invalidate Mr. Lindsay's main theory. The poet is most free, least isolated from his fellows, when he is helping the historical process along—that much one can accept while disagreeing with Mr. Lindsay about the exact nature and tempo of the historical process.

This is a good pamphlet, and an effective counterblast against the frank declarations of irresponsibility that have been made by various young poets recently.

[Fee: £8.0.0; 28.11.44; it is not recorded by Orwell in his Payments Book whether he was paid for his rejoinder to Agate, published on 21 December 1944.]

James Agate replied in the *Manchester Evening News*, 21 December 1944; his reply was published in the same series as Orwell's reviews ('Life, People and Books') and under the heading 'Agate and Orwell.'

In his review of my book, "Noblesse Oblige—Another Letter to Another Son," Mr. George Orwell provides yet one more example of the tangled web woven for themselves by those who mistake feeling for thinking. Here is Mr. Orwell:

> "Mr. Agate implies all the way through that he sympathises, or partly sympathises, with the average man's contempt for the arts . . . while golf, cricket, and other pastimes are declared to have moved the ordinary man more than all the poets put together."

Consider here this passage from my book:

> "To define the flame of ecstasy is to go back to the first principles of all art. Shortly we may allege the passionate quest for beauty, the search for light that never was on sea or land, the expression of all that some mysterious madness has taught the artist to be supremely worth while setting down in word or paint or sound, the effort to perpetuate beyond the grave and in terms of his art that consciousness of the world about him which has been said to be civilised man's 'Marvel and treasure.'"

How can Mr. Orwell think it possible that a man who has written this can sympathise, or partly sympathise, with contempt for the arts? And is it not a fact that our football stadiums, cricket grounds, boxing rings, and racecourses draw more adherents than the Old Vic? [3]

Mr. Orwell pretends that I congratulate the ordinary man on his bad taste. This shows how completely he has misread my book. Here in simple words is the argument of *noblesse oblige*, which is a reply to Sir Osbert Sitwell's "A Letter to My Son."

It would be easier perhaps if I tabulate it:

(1) Sir Osbert says that a man should be prepared to fight and die for the flowers of his country's soil. I say that he should fight for his country's soil.

(2) Sir Osbert would have all artists exempt from war-service. I say that all artists should be conscripted, leaving it for other judgment to decide whether by continuing in their art they will serve their country better. Examples: William Walton, John Gielgud, Robert Helpmann, Tommy Trinder. [4]

(3) Sir Osbert maintains that art is more than life's most exquisite decoration, that it is life's "finest and most spiritual essence." I agree, but I also ask whom that finest essence affects and reaches? Obviously it is only those who are capable of appreciating art, say ten per cent of the community. And I contend that just as Shakespeare imparts ecstacy to those capable of understanding Shakespeare, so Alec James [5] imparted ecstacy to non-art-lovers. If actors are to be exempt, why not footballers?

(4) War, says Sir Osbert, may kill a budding Shakespeare. Yes, but it may also kill a budding Churchill, Lutyens, Eddington, Horder, Augustus

John. Wherefore, if artists are exempt, potentially great men in all kinds must be exempt. It is absurd to exempt a Malcolm Sargent and not a Malcolm Campbell.[6]

(5) Sir Osbert says that the best way of getting to understand another nation is to understand its works of art.

To which I reply that Englishmen should not let their love of Goethe, Heine, Bach, Beethoven, and Wagner blind them to the German mentality in the matter of war-making.

To conclude, I do not sympathise with the average man's contempt for the arts. I do not congratulate him on his lack of taste. The last page of my little book contains these words: "I realise that the taste of the Walworth Road is low, and I hold that 95 per cent of it cannot be improved. I may be wrong, but I am putting my case at its strongest. I maintain that it is the duty of the artist to fight for the Walworth Road, however low its taste, as manfully and resolutely as the Walworth Road fights for—heaven forgive me—its betters."

I cannot understand how a man of Mr. Orwell's intelligence can take this for sympathy with low taste, or congratulation on its possession.

I deplore the standard of taste in this country. I say that it is the duty of those whose standard is higher to fight for those less happily endowed.

If any reader of the above can find any words into which to put more plainly what I obviously mean, I promise to use them in my little book's next edition.

Orwell responded in the same issue of the *Manchester Evening News*:

It would take too long to answer Mr. Agate's objections one by one, but there are two points that I would like to take up:

1. *Contempt for the Artist*: Mr. Agate's little book is sown all the way through with the usual contemptuous asides about "Bloomsbury," and remarks such as "even intellectuals are thinking beings," quite obviously with the purpose of enlisting the highbrow-baiting section of the public on his side. In addition he condones or even approves the current lack of taste by stating that the pleasure that the spectators get out of cricket, horse-racing, etc., is *of the same nature* as the pleasure that can be derived from poetry or music.

"I say that cricket has moved the ordinary man to the top of his spiritual bent, and that all infinities are equal." This is repeated in various forms over and over again. It follows from this that a good cricketer is just as valuable a being as a good poet. The point Mr. Agate doesn't meet, however, is that poets are a lot *rarer* than cricketers, and that what they do has a value, or can have a value, that is not purely ephemeral.

Shakespeare has made life more worth living for ten generations of Englishmen, while W. G. Grace, even granting that his famous stroke which broke the clock in the Lord's pavilion was somehow the eqivalent of *Macbeth* or *King Lear*, is already a fading memory.

In the decay of the Byzantine Empire, who can doubt that Mr. Agate's then equivalent was pointing out that the mob got much more kick out of the chariot races than out of the verses of Homer? But Homer is still there, while the chariot-drivers are forgotten. And more than this, in looking back we can see the spectacles of the Roman arena for what they were—dope to keep the masses from thinking. Our own commercialised sport will have the same appearance when society regains its mental health.

Isn't there, therefore, some reason for thinking that poetry, music, and painting, in spite of the hordes of charlatans they admittedly attract, are more important to the human race than cricket, golf, or pugilism?

I fully agree with Mr. Agate—and I said so—that the artist as such has no right to claim exemption from National Service. But I notice that Mr. Agate, while vociferously opposing exemption for poets, is in favour of exempting popular entertainers. "Obviously," he says, "a wise Government will not put a bayonet into the hands of a William Walton, a Constant Lambert, a Clifford Curzon, a Noel Coward, a John Gielgud, or a Tommy Trinder."

In practice, of course, the Government does not put bayonets into the hands of people of that kind, but does put them into the hands of writers, painters, etc., if they are young enough. Several of our more promising younger writers have been killed already, and the war of 1914–18 caused a positive slaughter of poets. Looking back, I think it might have been better for the human race if the authorities had seen fit to exempt Wilfred Owen and conscript Horatio Bottomley.

2. *Contempt for the Common Man*: Although calling the common man, or ordinary man, to his aid on almost every page, Mr. Agate shows his contempt for him by asserting that he not only has not but can never be expected to have any feeling for the arts. "I realise that the taste of the Walworth Road is low, and I hold that 95 per cent of it cannot be improved." And he firmly declares his disbelief in the power of education. It follows that the ugliness and vulgarity of modern machine civilisation are unalterable, and that the artist, who caters for a tiny minority, is a mere excrescence on society, a producer of "pretty things."

Sir Osbert Sitwell, it is worth noticing, was less contemptuous of the ordinary man.

The working classes, he said, are less actively hostile to the arts than the comfortable middle classes. But the point Mr. Agate misses is that bad taste is *not* an ineradicable human characteristic. Shakespeare was a popular writer, the plays of Aristophanes were popular entertainments, and to this day there are primitive peoples among whom good taste is all but universal.

We in this country have bad taste, as we have bad teeth, because of complex but discoverable social causes. It is a thing to be fought against, and an important part of the fight devolves on the artist and the critic. The artist fights against it by preserving his integrity; the critic fights against it by educating the public. And flattery is not a form of education. To assume that the big public is inevitably composed of fools, and then to imply that there is something lovable and even meritorious in being a fool, is less useful and less admirable than retreating to an ivory tower with all the windows barred.

1. See 'As I Please,' 41, 8 September 1944, *2547*, for Orwell's discussion of Sitwell's book.
2. James Evershed Agate (1877–1947), a prominent dramatic critic and prolific writer noted for his forceful opinions, worked successively for the *Daily Dispatch*, *Manchester Guardian*, *Saturday Review*, *Sunday Times*, and the BBC. He published his autobiography in nine parts as *Ego*, *Ego 2*, and so on to *Ego 9* (1935–48). See James Laver, 'Critics Who Have Influenced Taste: 28, James Agate,' *The Times*, 14 November 1963.
3. It is, of course, a 'fact' that football stadiums, cricket grounds, boxing rings, and racecourses, *taken together*, draw more adherents than the Old Vic, but this is a misleading comparison. Statistics of attendances can be chosen from a vast range of sources, but Agate's claim can be put into perspective by a glance at one or two figures. The Society of West End Theatres reported that in 1990, despite the recession, the number of seats sold in West End of London theatres was 11,321,000; in the rest of Britain some 13,400,000 seats were sold, giving a total of 24,721,000 (*Daily Telegraph*, 19 December 1991). Soccer attracts about half a million spectators a week in the United Kingdom. In the 1990–91 season, the total number of those attending Football League matches was some 19,500,000; attendances at the various Cup and international matches would bring that to a total of 22,500,000. Soccer attracts far more spectators than any other sport, and the figure for theatres takes no account of other forms of live entertainment (never mind cinema attendances). Jeremy Paxman, in *Friends in High Places* (1991), quoted figures showing that in the mid-1980s some 39,000,000 people attended live arts, as compared to 48,000,000 who visited historic houses (34 and note 28). For various reasons (for example, the popularity of music halls), the position in 1944 would be little different for theatre versus soccer. Furthermore, in Britain, football is watched mainly by men, whereas theatre and the arts appeal equally to men and women. It is surprising that so prominent a drama critic as Agate should have helped perpetuate the myth that soccer is so much more popular than the theatre.
4. The thrust of Agate's examples is indicated by the inclusion of a popular comedian of the music hall (vaudeville), Tommy Trinder (1909–1989) among those representing 'high art': William Walton (1902–1983; Kt., 1951), composer; John Gielgud (1904–; Kt., 1953), actor; and Robert Helpmann (1909–1986; Kt., 1968), ballet dancer and actor. When, later, Orwell quotes from Agate's book, Helpmann is omitted; instead, Agate listed Clifford Curzon (1907–1982; Kt., 1971), concert pianist; and Constant Lambert (1905–1951), composer, conductor, and critic.
5. Alexander James (1901–1953), an outstanding soccer player for Scotland and, especially, Arsenal, 1929–37. He served in the Maritime Anti-Aircraft Regiment, 1939–45, but, since he had by then retired from football, he was not particularly well-chosen as one who deserved to be exempted from military service.
6. Malcolm Sargent (1895–1967; Kt., 1947), organist and orchestral conductor; Malcolm Campbell (1885–1948; Kt., 1931), racing-car driver and first person to exceed a speed of 300 mph in a car. Both men were over age for military service by 1939, so, as for Alec James, they were not, as individuals, good examples for exemption.

2585. 'Funny, But Not Vulgar'

1 December 1944; *Leader Magazine*, 28 July 1945[1]

The great age of English humorous writing—not witty and not satirical, but simply humorous—was the first three-quarters of the nineteenth century.

Within that period lie Dickens's enormous output of comic writings, Thackeray's brilliant burlesques and short stories, such as *The Fatal Boots* and *A Little Dinner at Timmins's*, Surtees's *Handley Cross*, Lewis Carroll's *Alice in Wonderland*, Douglas Jerrold's *Mrs. Caudle's Curtain Lectures*, and a considerable body of humorous verse by Thomas Barham, Thomas Hood, Edward Lear, Arthur Hugh Clough, Charles Stuart Calverley, and others. Two other comic masterpieces, F. Anstey's *Vice Versa* and the two Grossmiths' *Diary of a Nobody*, lie only just outside the period I have named. And, at any rate until 1860 or thereabouts, there was still such a thing as comic draughtsmanship, witness Cruikshank's illustrations to Dickens, Leech's illustrations to Surtees, and even Thackeray's illustrations of his own work.

I do not want to exaggerate by suggesting that, within our own century, England has produced no humorous writing of any value. There have been, for instance, Barry Pain, W. W. Jacobs, Stephen Leacock,[2] P. G. Wodehouse, H. G. Wells in his lighter moments, Evelyn Waugh, and—a satirist rather than a humorist—Hilaire Belloc. Still, we have not only produced no laugh-getter of anything like the stature of *Pickwick Papers*, but, what is probably more significant, there is not and has not been for decades past, any such thing as a first-rate humorous periodical. The usual charge against *Punch*, that it "isn't what it was," is perhaps unjustified at this moment, since *Punch* is somewhat funnier than it was ten years ago: but it is also very much *less* funny than it was ninety years ago.

And comic verse has lost all its vitality—there has been no English light verse of any value within this century, except Mr. Belloc's, and a poem or two by Chesterton—while a drawing that is funny in its own right, and not merely because of the joke it illustrates, is a great rarity.

All this is generally admitted. If you want a laugh you are likelier to go to a music-hall or a Disney film, or switch on Tommy Handley,[3] or buy a few of Donald McGill's postcards, than to resort to a book or a periodical. It is generally recognised, too, that American comic writers and illustrators are superior to our own. At present we have nobody to set against either James Thurber or Damon Runyan.

We do not know with certainty how laughter originated or what biological purpose it serves, but we do know, in broad terms, what causes laughter.

A thing is funny when—in some way that is not actually offensive or frightening—it upsets the established order. Every joke is a tiny revolution. If you had to define humour in a single phrase, you might define it as dignity sitting on a tintack. Whatever destroys dignity, and brings down the mighty from their seats, preferably with a bump, is funny. And the bigger the fall, the bigger the joke. It would be better fun to throw a custard pie at a bishop than at a curate. With this general principle in mind, one can, I think, begin to see what has been wrong with English comic writing during the present century.

Nearly all English humorists to-day are too genteel, too kind-hearted and too consciously lowbrow. P. G. Wodehouse's novels, or A. P. Herbert's verses, seem always to be aimed at prosperous stockbrokers whiling away an odd half hour in the lounge of some suburban golf course. They and all their kind are dominated by an anxiety not to stir up mud, either moral, religious, political or intellectual. It is no accident that most of the best comic writers of our time—Belloc, Chesterton, "Timothy Shy" and the recent "Beach-comber"—have been Catholic apologists; that is, people with a serious purpose and a noticeable willingness to hit below the belt. The silly-ass tradition in modern English humour, the avoidance of brutality and horror of

483

intelligence, is summed up in the phrase *funny without being vulgar*. 'Vulgar"
in this context usually means "obscene," and it can be admitted at once that
the best jokes are not necessarily dirty ones. Edward Lear and Lewis Carroll,
for instance, never made jokes of that description, and Dickens and
Thackeray very rarely.

On the whole, the early-Victorian writers avoided sex jokes, though a few,
for instance Surtees, Marryatt and Barham, retained traces of eighteenth-
century coarseness. But the point is that the modern emphasis on what is
called "clean fun" is really the symptom of a general unwillingness to touch
upon any serious or controversial subject. Obscenity is, after all, a kind of
subversiveness. Chaucer's "Miller's Tale" is a rebellion in the moral sphere,
as *Gulliver's Travels* is a rebellion in the political sphere. The truth is that you
cannot be memorably funny without *at some point* raising topics which the
rich, the powerful and the complacent would prefer to see left alone.

I named above some of the best comic writers of the nineteenth century,
but the case becomes much stronger if one draws in the English humorists of
earlier ages—for instance, Chaucer, Shakespeare, Swift and the picaresque
novelists, Smollett, Fielding and Sterne. It becomes stronger, again, if one
considers foreign writers, both ancient and modern: for example, Aristophanes, Voltaire, Rabelais, Boccaccio and Cervantes. All of these writers
are remarkable for their brutality and coarseness. People are tossed in
blankets, they fall through cucumber frames, they are hidden in washing
baskets, they rob, lie, swindle, and are caught out in every conceivable
humiliating situation. And all great humorous writers show a willingness to
attack the beliefs and the virtues on which society necessarily rests. Boccaccio
treats Hell and Purgatory as a ridiculous fable, Swift jeers at the very
conception of human dignity, Shakespeare makes Falstaff deliver a speech in
favour of cowardice in the middle of a battle. As for the sanctity of marriage,
it was the principal subject of humour in Christian society for the better part
of a thousand years.

All this is not to say that humour is, of its nature, immoral or anti-social. A
joke is at most a temporary rebellion against virtue, and its aim is not to
degrade the human being but to remind him that he is already degraded. A
willingness to make extremely obscene jokes can co-exist with very strict
moral standards, as in Shakespeare. Some comic writers, like Dickens, have a
direct political purpose, others, like Chaucer or Rabelais, accept the
corruption of society as something inevitable; but no comic writer of any
stature has ever suggested that society is *good*.

Humour is the debunking of humanity, and nothing is funny except in
relation to human beings. Animals, for instance, are only funny because they
are caricatures of ourselves. A lump of stone could not of itself be funny; but
it can become funny if it hits a human being in the eye, or if it is carved into
human likeness.

However, there are subtler methods of debunking than throwing custard
pies. There is also the humour of pure fantasy, which assaults man's notion of
himself as not only a dignified but a rational being. Lewis Carroll's humour
consists essentially in making fun of logic, and Edward Lear's in a sort of

poltergeist interference with common sense. When the Red Queen remarks, "*I've* seen hills compared with which you'd call that one a valley," she is in her way attacking the bases of society as violently as Swift or Voltaire. Comic verse, as in Lear's poem *The Courtship of the Yonghy-Bonghy-Bò*, often depends on building up a fantastic universe which is just similar enough to the real universe to rob it of its dignity. But more often it depends on anti-climax—that is, on starting out with high-flown language and then suddenly coming down with a bump. For instance, Calverley's lines:

Once, a happy child, I carolled
On green lawns the whole day through,
Not unpleasingly apparelled
In a tightish suit of blue,

in which the first two lines would give the impression that this is going to be a sentimental poem about the beauties of childhood. Or Mr. Belloc's various invocations to Africa in *The Modern Traveller*:

O Africa, mysterious land,
Surrounded by a lot of sand,
And full of grass and trees . . .
Far land of Ophir, mined for gold
By lordly Solomon of old,
Who, sailing northward to Perim,
Took all the gold away with him
And left a lot of holes, etc.[4]

Bret Harte's sequel to *Maud Muller*, with such couplets as —

But the very day that they were mated
Maud's brother Bob was intoxicated

plays essentially the same trick, and so in a different way do Voltaire's mock epic, *La Pucelle*, and many passages in Byron.

English light verse in the present century—witness the work of Owen Seaman, Harry Graham, A. P. Herbert, A. A. Milne and others—has mostly been poor stuff, lacking not only in fancifulness but in intellectuality. Its authors are too anxious not to be highbrows—even, though they are writing in verse, not to be poets. Early-Victorian light verse is generally haunted by the ghost of poetry; it is often extremely skilful as verse, and it is sometimes allusive and "difficult." When Barham wrote—

Your Callipyge's injured behind,
Bloudie Jack,
Your de Medici's injured before,
And your Anadyomene's injured in so many
Places, I think there's a score,
If not more,
Of her fingers and toes on the floor

he was performing a feat of sheer virtuosity which the most serious poet would respect. Or, to quote Calverley again, in his *Ode to Tobacco*:

Thou, who when fears attack,
Bidst them avaunt, and Black
Care, at the horseman's back
Perching, unseatest;
Sweet when the morn is grey,
Sweet when they've cleared away
Lunch, and at close of day
Possibly sweetest!

Calverley is not afraid, it will be seen, to put a tax on his reader's attention and to drag in a recondite Latin allusion.[5] He is not writing for lowbrows, and—particularly in his *Ode to Beer*—he can achieve magnificent anti-climaxes because he is willing to sail close to true poetry and to assume considerable knowledge in his readers.

It would seem that you *cannot* be funny without being vulgar—that is, vulgar by the standards of the people at whom English humorous writing in our own day seems mostly to be aimed. For it is not only sex that is "vulgar." So are death, childbirth and poverty, the other three subjects upon which the best music-hall humour turns. And respect for the intellect and strong political feeling, if not actually vulgar, are looked upon as being in doubtful taste. You cannot be really funny if your main aim is to flatter the comfortable classes: it means leaving out too much. To be funny, indeed, you have got to be serious. *Punch*, for at least forty years past, has given the impression of trying not so much to amuse as to reassure. Its implied message is that all is for the best and nothing will ever really change.

It was by no means with that creed that it started out.

A letter from Harry Fowler in response to this article was published in *Leader Magazine* on 11 August 1945. He said: 'Anybody dealing with humorous writing in our century ought to mention the late Neil Lyons.[6] Many of those who have read "Arthurs," "Sixpenny Pieces," *etc.* will urge that Neil Lyons deserves a place alongside, if not above, W. W. Jacobs.'

1. This essay was entered in Orwell's Payments Book at this date; the fee was £15.0.0. It was published in *Leader Magazine* under the general heading 'Personal Notes.' The article was illustrated with 'The Learned Fish' from Hilaire Belloc's *The Bad Child's Book of Beasts*, two cartoons by Thurber, and three from *Lilliput*, the last with the caption 'Most Modern Humour Depends On Misunderstanding And The Macabre.' Orwell probably did not select the illustrations. For the second (and only other) article by Orwell in this series, see 'Personal Notes on Scientifiction,' 21 July 1945, *2705*.
2. Stephen Leacock (1869–1944), although born in England, emigrated to Canada when he was seven and was educated and worked there. From 1908–36 he was head of the Department of Economics and Political Science at McGill University; he published on these subjects as well as writing many comic books, the first of which was *Literary Lapses* (1910).
3. Tommy Handley (1894–1949), music-hall comedian who, during the war, starred in a particularly popular radio half-hour comedy show, 'It's That Man Again' (ITMA); this was credited with doing much to raise morale.
4. Belloc's sister, Marie Belloc Lowndes, wrote to say how delighted she was by this reference;

she asked to meet Orwell. See Orwell's reply to her, 31 July 1945, *2711.* In this letter he says he quoted this passage (from 'a great favourite of mine in my boyhood') from memory.

5. Calverley refers to Horace, *Odes*, III, i.40: 'Post equitem sedet atra Cura' (Black Care sits on the horseman's pillion). The ode contrasts the risks and dangers of those who would exchange the peacefulness of the poet's secluded valley for wealth, which brings only cares with it. In his 'Ode to Beer' Calverley quotes a line in Latin: 'Dulce est desipere in loco' (in the proper place it is sweet to set aside one's learning) (*Odes*, IV, xii.28). Such references must have taxed the readers of *Leader Magazine*, and Orwell may have been indulging in a little leg-pulling. (Orwell scored 1,782 marks out of 2,000 for Latin in the examination for entry to the Indian Imperial Police in 1922—his best paper; see *63.*) In the first line, 'fears' is sometimes given as 'cares.'

6. A. Neil Lyons (b. 1880), despite Mr. Fowler's plea, has not survived in the memory as well as W. W. Jacobs. Among his books were *Hookey* (1902), *Arthur's* (1908), *Sixpenny Pieces* (1909), *Robert Blatchford* (1910), a biography of the campaigning socialist journalist and editor of *Clarion*, for which Lyons wrote, *Cottage Pie* (1911), *Kitchener Chaps* (1915), and *A London Lot* (1919).

2586. 'As I Please,' 50

Tribune, 1 December 1944

V2 (I am told that you can now mention it in print so long as you just call it V2 and don't describe it too minutely)[1] supplies another instance of the contrariness of human nature. People are complaining of the sudden unexpected wallop with which these things go off. "It wouldn't be so bad if you got a bit of warning," is the usual formula. There is even a tendency to talk nostalgically of the days of V1. The good old doodle-bug did at least give you time to get under the table, etc., etc. Whereas, in fact, when the doodle-bugs were actually dropping, the usual subject of complaint was the uncomfortable waiting period before they went off. Some people are never satisfied. Personally, I am no lover of V2, especially at this moment when the house still seems to be rocking from a recent explosion, but what most depresses me about these things is the way they set people talking about the next war. Every time one goes off I hear gloomy references to "next time," and the reflection: "I suppose they'll be able to shoot them across the Atlantic by that time." [2] But if you ask who will be fighting whom when this universally expected war breaks out, you get no clear answer. It is just war in the abstract—the notion that human beings could ever behave sanely having apparently faded out of many people's memories.

Maurice Baring, in his book on Russian literature, which was published in 1907 and must have been the means of introducing many people in this country to the great Russian novelists, remarks that English books were always popular in Russia. Among other favourites he mentions *The Diary of a Nobody* (which, by the way, is reprinted by the Everyman Library, if you can run across a copy).

I have always wondered what on earth *The Diary of a Nobody* could be like in a Russian translation, and indeed I have faintly suspected that the Russians may have enjoyed it because when translated it was just like Chekov. But in a way it would be a very good book to read if you wanted to get a picture of English life, even though it was written in the 'eighties and has an intensely strong smell of that period. Charles Pooter is a true Englishman both in native gentleness and his impenetrable stupidity. The interesting thing, however, is to follow this book up to its origins. What does it ultimately derive from? Almost certainly, I think, from *Don Quixote*, of which, indeed, it is a sort of modern anglicised version. Pooter is a high-minded, even adventurous man, constantly suffering disasters brought upon him by his own folly, and surrounded by a whole tribe of Sancho Panzas. But apart from the comparative mildness of the things that befall him, one can see in the endings of the two books the enormous difference between the age of Cervantes and our own.

In the end the Grossmiths have to take pity on poor Pooter. Everything, or nearly everything, comes right, and at the last there is a tinge of sentimentality which does not quite fit in with the rest of the book. The fact is that, in spite of the way we actually behave, we cannot any longer feel that the infliction of pain is merely funny. Nietzsche remarks somewhere that the pathos of *Don Quixote* may well be a modern discovery. Quite likely Cervantes didn't mean Don Quixote to seem pathetic—perhaps he just meant him to be funny and intended it as a screaming joke when the poor old man has half his teeth knocked out by a sling-stone. However this may be with Don Quixote, I am fairly certain that it is true of Falstaff. Except possibly for the final scene in *Henry V*, there is nothing to show that Shakespeare sees Falstaff as a pathetic as well as a comic figure.[3] He is just a punching-bag for fortune, a sort of Billy Bunter with a gift for language. The thing that seems saddest to us is Falstaff's helpless dependence on his odious patron, Prince Harry, whom Sir John Masefield aptly described as a "disgusting beefy brute." There is no sign, or, at any rate, no clear sign, that Shakespeare sees anything pathetic or degrading in such a relationship.

Say what you like, things *do* change. A few years ago I was walking across Hungerford Bridge with a lady aged about sixty or perhaps less. The tide was out, and as we looked down at the beds of filthy, almost liquid mud, she remarked:

"When I was a little girl we used to throw pennies to the mudlarks down there."

I was intrigued and asked what mudlarks were. She explained that in those days professional beggars, known as mudlarks, used to sit under the bridge waiting for people to throw them pennies. The pennies would bury themselves deep in the mud, and the mudlarks would plunge in head first and recover them. This was considered a most amusing spectacle.

Is there anyone who would degrade himself in that way nowadays? And how many people are there who would get a kick out of watching it?

Shortly before his assassination, Trotsky had completed a *Life* of Stalin. One may assume that it was not an altogether unbiased book, but obviously a biography of Stalin by Trotsky—or, for that matter, a biography of Trotsky by Stalin—would be a winner from a selling point of view. A very well-known American firm of publishers were to issue it. The book had been printed and—this is the point that I have been waiting to verify before mentioning this matter in my notes—the review copies had been sent out when the U.S.A. entered the war. The book was immediately withdrawn, and the reviewers were asked to co-operate in "avoiding any comment whatever regarding the biography and its postponement."

They have co-operated remarkably well. This affair has gone almost unmentioned in the American Press and, as far as I know, entirely unmentioned in the British Press, although the facts were well known and obviously worth a paragraph or two.

Since the American entry into the war made the U.S.A. and the U.S.S.R. allies, I think that to withdraw the book was an understandable if not particularly admirable deed. What is disgusting is the general willingness to suppress all mention of it. A little while back I attended a meeting of the P.E.N. Club, which was held to celebrate the tercentenary of *Areopagitica*, Milton's famous tract on the freedom of the Press. There were countless speeches emphasising the importance of preserving intellectual liberty, even in wartime. If I remember rightly, Milton's phrase about the special sin of "murdering" a book was printed on the P.E.N. leaflet for the occasion. But I heard no references to this particular murder, the facts of which were no doubt known to plenty of people there.

Here is another little brain-tickler. The following often-quoted passage comes from Act V of Shakespeare's tragedy, *Timon of Athens*:

> Come not to me again: but say to Athens
> Timon hath made his everlasting mansion
> Upon the beachèd verge of the salt flood:
> Who once a day with his embossed froth
> The turbulent surge shall cover.

This passage contains three errors. What are they?

On 22 December 1944, *Tribune* published this letter from J. T. Price on 'Mudlarking,' to which Orwell had referred:

The old lady's story about the mudlarks of Hungerford Bridge seems to have surprised your columnist, although the episode probably dates back fifty years. It may surprise Mr. Orwell even more to learn that up to quite recent years gangs of boys and youths could be seen any day of the week diving for coins at low tide in the ooze banks down at Portsmouth (or was it Southampton?).[4]

When I first saw this spectacle I was frankly revolted, and asked a nearby police constable on the quayside if nothing could be done to stop it. "Good gracious, no, sir!" he said. "This is where the local lads begin their apprenticeship before going to sea." They would completely disappear in a sea of grey slime, and come up a few moments later grasping the treasure in a state of indescribable filth. I believe more recently some London showmen attempted to commercialise this depraved form of entertainment by staging mud bath "all-in" wrestling.

P.S. The Tories will probably revive this latter sport in the near future.

1. See headnote to London Letter, *Partisan Review*, Winter 1944–45, *2553*.
2. Precisely, of course, what the development of the intercontinental ballistic missile demonstrated.
3. Reviewing a shortened version of *The Merry Wives of Windsor* in *Time and Tide* on 4 January 1941 (see *742*), Orwell wrote: 'Falstaff is fat, and it is well known that fat people have no finer feelings; he is also dishonest and cowardly, and "the cause of wit in others". But he is nevertheless a highly intelligent man, one of the very few among Shakespeare's characters who can be described as "intellectuals". It would be a wonderful thing if some actor would some day recognize this and act Falstaff with as much care as is usually given to Hamlet. Falstaff always speaks in prose, but it is highly poetical prose . . . the poetry of the Falstaff scenes never gets across, because it is the convention to treat them as very low farce. . . .' Orwell was reviewing Donald Wolfit as Falstaff. His performance, he wrote, 'had the usual faults, but much less markedly than usual.'
4. Mudlarking was practised at least until the end of 1939 by young boys diving off one of the bridges crossing the canal that runs through Regent's Park, London, near the London Zoo. It was also an entertainment offered to tourists by Maori boys in New Zealand, at least until the late 1960s.

2587. To Frank Barber

5 December 1944   Typewritten

Tribune

Dear Sir,

Apart from what I said in my column,[1] the only detail I know personally is that the American firm which was to publish Trotsky's book was Harper's. Also that two other books of similar tendency (one of them by an ex-Soviet diplomat named Barmine)[2] were withdrawn about the same time.

The people who might be able to tell you more about this are the editors of the "Partisan Review", 45 Astor Place, New York 3, N.Y., U.S.A. If writing to them you could mention me as they know me. It was in a back number of the Partisan Review that I came upon the fact that the review copies of the book *had* been sent out. I wanted to be sure of this before mentioning the matter.

Another "murdered" book is Chiang Kai-Shek's book written a year or two ago, in which I believe he criticises British imperialism very violently.[3]

Yours truly,
[Signed] Geo. Orwell
George Orwell

Barber, who was assistant editor of the *Leeds Weekly Citizen*, replied on 8 December.

Thank you for your letter and for the information regarding Trotsky's suppressed book. Since I wrote to you a friend has told me that he knows of the book, but he insists that it was a life on° Lenin, not Stalin. He is going to try to clear up this point, and as he has gone up to London for the Labour Party conference I am holding up my note for the Citizen until he returns.

A long time ago I heard that a book by Alexander° Barmine was to be published in America, but as I heard nothing more I took it that Barmine had either died or failed to find a publisher.

You may be interested in an experience of ours concerning Barmine. At the beginning of 1938 we published in the Citizen a proclamation by Barmine addressed to the League for the Rights of Man in Paris, in which he gave his record of service for Soviet Russia and expressed his horror at the Moscow trials and some other developments in Russia. Six months later we received a letter from a reader saying he had sent our story to Moscow and asked for explanation. He told us that he received no reply to his first letter, but when he wrote again he received a denial that Barmine ever existed! On this information our reader practically accused us of lying. However, we were able to discover that the Paris correspondent of the Daily Herald had interviewed Barmine and that the New York Times had published three articles by Barmine.

For Orwell's response, see 15 December 1944, *2591*.

1. 'As I Please,' 50, 1 December 1944, *2586*.
2. An editorial note in *Partisan Review*, March–April 1942, stated: "Three books, either critical or definitely hostile to the present régime in Russia, have been withdrawn from publication after having been publicly announced. Doubleday, Doran has cancelled the publication this spring of *One Who Survived*, the reminiscences of a former Soviet diplomat, Alexander° Barmine. Harper has withdrawn *My Year in the USSR*, by the former *NY Times* Moscow correspondent, G. E. R. Gedye, and also Trotsky's *Life of Stalin*. The latter book was actually sent out for review, only to be recalled a few days later (on December 12) by a note signed by President Cass Canfield which concludes, 'We hope you will co-operate with us in the matter of avoiding any comment whatever regarding the biography and its postponement'." Alexandre Barmine had been a member of the Arms Export Commission of the Supreme Soviet Defence Council when Marshal Tukhachevsky and other senior Soviet generals were executed on Stalin's orders on trumped-up charges in May 1937. His *One Who Survived* was published in New York by Putnam, in 1945, with an introduction by Max Eastman. He also published *Memoirs of a Soviet Diplomat* (London, 1938) and *A Russian View of the Moscow Trials* (New York, 1938); Gedye's book was never published.
3. Generalissimo Chiang Kai-shek (1887–1975) was a prolific speaker and writer and, from as early as a long statement issued in 1926, expressed himself strongly on imperialist interference in China. The book Orwell refers to has not been identified, and Orwell and Barber do not pursue it. Chiang's 1926 declaration— which begins 'The imperialists, seeing the opportunity to control our financial arteries, are making desperate efforts to enrich themselves and to lengthen the duration of their hold'—takes six pages of the authorised biography by Hollington K. Tong, *Chiang Kai-Shek°, Soldier and Statesman*, which (though printed in Shanghai) was published in London in 1938 (I, 127–33). Its tone is exemplified by its statement 'The only aim of the National Revolution is to crush all that pertains to imperialism and militarism and at the same time to establish an independent and free nation' (I, 127–28), reiterated in paragraph six of Chiang Kai-shek's programme, which demands the end of all 'unequal treaties' giving foreign nations extraterritorial rights in China. This book, with this clear statement of Chiang Kai-shek's aim to end the rights of the British, Americans, and other foreigners in China, was available from 26 November 1938 in, among other places, the London Library. By the time Orwell wrote, the unequal treaties imposed by Britain and the United States on China had been formally abrogated, both nations disclaiming their treaty

rights on 11 January 1943, except that Britain retained its claim to the Kowloon territory of Hong Kong. On 11 January, the Chinese government sent the British government a Note in which it recorded its right to reopen the question of Kowloon at some future date—although it would not be Chiang Kai-shek who would be in power to do that (*Chiang Kai-Shek: His Life and Times*, Keiji Furuya, abridged English edition by Chun-Ming Chan, New York, 1981, 734–36).

2588. To Ralph C. Elsley

5 December 1944   Typewritten

Tribune

Dear Mr. Elsley,[1]
The vilanelle° I referred to is in "Portrait of the Artist"—the poem beginning "Are you not weary of ardent ways?" It is a true vilanelle and a very good one. They are very hard to do in English because of the lack of rhymes. There is one of John Davidson, but it is not much good.

Yours truly,
[Signed] Geo. Orwell
George Orwell

1. Ralph Elsley, writing to Bernard Crick, 7 November 1983, enclosed a copy of this letter to him and explained that he had written to Orwell to find out about the villanelle mentioned in *The Observer*, 26 November 1944; see *2582*.

2589. Review of *Bridge into the Future: Letters of Max Plowman*

Manchester Evening News, 7 December 1944

One cannot read straight through a book of letters, especially so long a book as this, and for the average reader the main interest of this book will lie round about the years 1918 and 1935–41.

Purely personal things apart, there were two great preoccupations in Max Plowman's life[1]—Blake's poems (which he helped to edit) and pacifism. And it is in the years when war was looming up over the horizon or was actually raging that these letters have their deepest interest.

Even those who disapproved most strongly of Max Plowman's pacifism were never angered by it, and they often made the rather curious comment that you could forgive him for being a pacifist because he was not a temperamental one. This was true enough, and these letters bring it out strongly.

He was by nature a rather pugnacious man, of strong physique and simple tastes, a lover of cricket and gardening, and in a sense not an intellectual. His pacifism was not bound up with any definite political programme, and indeed his political judgment was far from sound.

Towards the end of this book we find him assuming that Munich has saved the peace, and apparently believing, even as late as August, 1939, that war would be averted.

What he did possess, however, was an immovable sense of right and wrong, and a power of acting upon his convictions. He believed profoundly that—in his own words—"doing and being are more important than thinking," and he was much more concerned with promoting the cause of peace by concrete actions than by arguments.

The earliest letters in this book show him as a man of nearly thirty, young for his age and naively pleased by the small amount of praise that his first book of poems had won for him. He came of a comfortable middle-class family (his parents were Plymouth Brethren, but this strain in his upbringing does not seem to have left much mark on him), and he followed a business career until he was in his late twenties.

At just about the time when he had begun to find his intellectual feet the war intervened, and in 1916 and 1917 he gathered the material for "A Subaltern on the Somme," one of the best of the English war books, though not one of the best known.

Early in 1918 he was wounded and invalided home, and it was only after this, when he was in a place of safety, that he came to the conclusion that the killing of human beings can lead to no good result.

He did not reach this conclusion quickly—indeed in his earlier war letters he makes out a clearer case against pacifism than he was afterwards to make out in favour of it—but as soon as he had reached it he acted on it. He wrote to the adjutant of his regiment, stating that he had changed his mind about the war and resigning his commission.

One has got to cast one's mind back to 1918 to appreciate the courage of this action. It was not merely that war hysteria had reached heights never approached in the present war, and the treatment of conscientious objectors was far more ruthless—a little earlier than this, indeed, the authorities were accused of silencing one poet by threatening to certify him as a lunatic.[2]

There was also the fact that at that date the unthinking "King and Country" type of patriotism was far more taken for granted than it is now.

Max Plowman had to fight against his upbringing, perhaps even against his feelings. But he did not hesitate when his mind was made up, and though in the event he was not sent to prison, he fully expected to be so when he wrote the fateful letter.

From about 1930 onwards Max Plowman was associated with the "Adelphi," a magazine which never attained a large circulation but was remarkably enterprising both in encouraging young writers and letting its contributors say what they chose.

A few years later he met Dick Sheppard and Brigadier-General Crozier and by their joint efforts the Peace Pledge Union was founded. Max Plowman was its secretary for some years.

If one tries without evasion to answer the question "What are you going to do about Hitler?" it is difficult not to feel that the Peace Pledge Union is based on a mistaken world-view and that some of its activities have been mischievous. But somehow one cannot feel that any blame attaches to Max Plowman himself.

It is not only that his activities were always entirely unselfish, but that they were eminently practical. His deeds were better than his opinions.

Thus, when the Spanish Civil War broke out, Max Plowman and his group did not support the Spanish Republic very strongly, but on the other hand they took in 50 refugee Basque children and cared for them for a number of years.

Max Plowman approved of the Munich settlement, but in a letter to the "Manchester Guardian" he suggests that the British Government should follow it up by paying compensation to all the Czech refugees from the Sudetenland. And his answer to the problem of the German Jews was to advocate unlimited Jewish immigration into Britain—a plan which was never put into operation, of course, but which might have averted the death or suffering of millions of people.

The later letters in the book are concerned mostly with the Adelphi centre at Langham, in Essex. Having started out as a socialist summer school, this had developed early in the war into an agricultural colony for conscientious objectors.

Both Max Plowman and his friend, Middleton Murry, believed that colonies of this kind could play rather the same part as was played by the Christian monasteries in the Dark Ages—that is, they could be centres of peace in a warring world, and could gradually extend their influence to the rest of society.

This idea is probably a mistaken one. It does not take account of the fact that modern tyrannies are much more thorough than anything that existed in the Dark Ages, and that in a world where such oases were really necessary, they would not be allowed to survive.

But Max Plowman's favourite saying was "Pacifism is friendship in action," and he could hardly think of pacifism except in terms of mutual help and manual work done in common.

He did not write easily, and after 30 years largely given up to writing he did not leave many books behind. But he was a good correspondent and, curiously enough, his letters are much more vivid and witty than most of his published works.

Those who knew and loved him, even when they thought him wrong-headed, will be glad that so large a number of his letters have been recovered and put on record.

[Fee: £8.0.0; 6.12.44]

1. Max Plowman (1883–1941), journalist and author, worked on *The Adelphi* with John Middleton Murry, 1929–41, who was joint editor with Sir Richard Rees, 1930–32 (see 95). He was Warden of The Adelphi Centre, 1938–41; an ardent supporter of the Peace Pledge Union from its foundation, 1934, and General Secretary, 1937–38. In addition to the books Orwell mentions, Plowman wrote *The Faith Called Pacifism*. He encouraged Orwell at the beginning of his writing career. Many of Orwell's first reviews were published in *The Adelphi* from 1930 to 1941, as were 'The Spike' (April 1931), 'A Hanging' (August 1931), and several of Orwell's poems. Plowman and his wife, Dorothy, remained friends of Orwell's.

2. Siegfried Sassoon.

2590. 'As I Please,' 51

Tribune, 8 December 1944

For years past I have been an industrious collector of pamphlets,[1] and a fairly steady reader of political literature of all kinds. The thing that strikes me more and more—and it strikes a lot of other people, too—is the extraordinary viciousness and dishonesty of political controversy in our time. I don't mean merely that controversies are acrimonious. They ought to be that when they are on serious subjects. I mean that almost nobody seems to feel that an opponent deserves a fair hearing or that the objective truth matters so long as you can score a neat debating point. When I look through my collection of pamphlets—Conservative, Communist, Catholic, Trotskyist, Pacifist, Anarchist or what-have-you—it seems to me that almost all of them have the same mental atmosphere, though the points of emphasis vary. Nobody is searching for the truth, everybody is putting forward a "case" with complete disregard for fairness or accuracy, and the most plainly obvious facts can be ignored by those who don't want to see them. The same propaganda tricks are to be found almost everywhere. It would take many pages of this paper merely to classify them, but here I draw attention to one very widespread controversial habit—disregard of an opponent's motives. The key-word here is "objectively."

We are told that it is only people's objective actions that matter, and their subjective feelings are of no importance. Thus, pacifists, by obstructing the war effort, are "objectively" aiding the Nazis: and therefore the fact that they may be personally hostile to Fascism is irrelevant. I have been guilty of saying this myself more than once. The same argument is applied to Trotskyists. Trotskyists are often credited, at any rate by Communists, with being active and conscious agents of Hitler; but when you point out the many and obvious reasons why this is unlikely to be true, the "objectively" line of talk is brought forward again. To criticise the Soviet Union helps Hitler: therefore "Trotskyism is Fascism," And when this has been established, the accusation of conscious treachery is usually repeated.

This is not only dishonest; it also carries a severe penalty with it. If you disregard people's motives, it becomes much harder to foresee their actions. For there are occasions when even the most misguided person can see the results of what he is doing. Here is a crude but quite possible illustration. A pacifist is working in some job which gives him access to important military information, and is approached by a German secret agent. In those circumstances his subjective feelings *do* make a difference. If he is subjectively pro-Nazi he will sell his country, and if he isn't, he won't. And situations essentially similar though less dramatic are constantly arising.

In my opinion a few pacifists are inwardly pro-Nazi, and extremist Left-wing parties will inevitably contain Fascist spies. The important thing is to discover *which* individuals are honest and which are not, and the usual blanket accusation merely makes this more difficult. The atmosphere of hatred in which controversy is conducted blinds people to considerations of this kind. To admit that an opponent might be both honest and intelligent is felt to be intolerable. It is more immediately satisfying to shout that he is a fool or a scoundrel, or both, than to find out what he is really like. It is this habit of mind, among other things, that has made political prediction in our time so remarkably unsuccessful.

The following leaflet (printed) was passed to an acquaintance of mine in a pub:

"LONG LIVE THE IRISH!

"The first American soldier to kill a Jap was Mike Murphy.

"The first American pilot to sink a Jap battleship was Colin Kelly.

"The first American family to lose five sons in one action and have a naval vessel named after them were the Sullivans.

"The first American to shoot a Jap plane was Dutch O'Hara.

"The first coastguardsman to spot a German spy was John Conlan.

"The first American soldier to be decorated by the President was Pat Powers.

"The first American admiral to be killed leading his ship into battle was Dan Callahan.

"The first American son-of-a-bitch to get four new tyres from the Ration Board was Abie Goldstein."

The origin of this thing might just possibly be Irish, but it is much likelier to be American. There is nothing to indicate where it was printed, but it probably comes from the printing-shop of some American organisation in this country.[2] If any further manifestos of the same kind turn up, I shall be interested to hear of them.

This number of *Tribune* includes a long letter from Mr. Martin Walter, Controller of the British Institute of Fiction-writing Science, Ltd., in which he complains that I have traduced him.[3] He says (a) that he did not claim to have reduced fiction-writing to an exact science, (b) that numbers of successful writers *have* been produced by his teaching methods, and (c) he asks whether *Tribune* accepts advertisements that it believes to be fraudulent.

With regard to (a). "It is claimed by this Institute that these problems (of fiction-writing) have been solved by Martin Walter, who, convinced of the truth of the hypothesis that *every art is a science at heart*, analysed over 5,000 stories and eventually evolved the Plot Formula according to which all his own stories and those of his students throughout the world are constructed." "I had established that the nature of the 'plot' is strictly scientific." Statements of this type are scattered throughout Mr. Walter's booklets and advertisements. If this is not a claim to have reduced fiction-writing to an exact science, what the devil is it?

With regard to (b). Who are these successful writers whom Mr. Walter has launched upon the world? Let us hear their names, and the names of their published works, and then we shall know where we are.

With regard to (c). A periodical ought not to accept advertisements which have the appearance of being fraudulent, but it cannot sift everything beforehand. What is to be done, for instance, about publishers' advertisements, in which it is invariably claimed that every single book named is of the highest possible value? What is most important in this connection is that a periodical should not let its editorial columns be influenced by its advertisements. *Tribune* has been very careful not to do that—it has not done it in the case of Mr. Walter himself, for instance.

It may interest Mr. Walter to know that I should never have referred to him, if he had not accompanied the advertisement he inserted some time ago with some free copies of his booklets (including the Plot Formula), and the suggestion that I might like to mention them in my column. It was this that drew my attention to him. Now I have given him his mention, and he does not seem to like it.

Answer to last week's problem. The three errors are:

(a) The "who" should be "whom."

(b) Timon was buried below the high-tide mark. The sea would cover him twice a day, not once, as there are always two high tides within the twenty-four hours.

(c) It wouldn't cover him at all, as there is no perceptible tide in the Mediterranean.

1. Orwell's collection of pamphlets is in the British Library; see *2385, n. 1* and *3733*.
2. A copy of this leaflet survives in the British Library and a photocopy is in the Orwell Archive, University College London.
3. Martin Walter's letter is printed after 'As I Please,' 48, 17 November 1944; see *2579*. For Walter's quotation from 'As I Please,' 6, 7 January 1944, see *2401, n. 2*.

2591. To Frank Barber

15 December 1944   Typewritten

27B Canonbury Square
Islington
London N 1

Dear Mr. Barber,

Many thanks for your letter of 8th December. I am pretty sure it *was* a life of Stalin, not Lenin. I had heard of this from other sources, but on looking up again the copy of the "Partisan Review" which is my authority for the recall of the review copies, I find it definitely referred to as a "Life of Stalin." This number of PR mentions 3 books as having been withdrawn in this way, the Stalin book, Barmine's book, which was entitled "One who survived", and "My Year in the USSR," by G. E. R. Gedye, who used to be Moscow correspondent for the New York Times. I suppose the British Trotskyists could give further confirmation, but I have no contacts with them.

I was very interested in your note about Barmine. In my small way I have been fighting for years against the systematic faking of history which now goes on. I think you will be interested in article° which a friend of mine will publish shortly in "World Review",[1] dealing with some of the lies which have been used against Mihailovich.[2] A Russian acquaintance (I can't give his name[3]) writes to give me some details of the official Soviet publication "Reference Calendar for 1944." This consists of chronological tables of important events, and the Russo-German pact of 1939 is not mentioned in it! My attention was first drawn to this deliberate falsification of history by my experiences in the Spanish civil war. One can't make too much noise about it while the man in the street identifies the cause of Socialism with the USSR, but I believe one can make a perceptible difference by seeing that the true facts get into print, even if it is only in some obscure place.

A person who could probably give you some interesting information along these lines is the veteran (ex) Communist Ruth Fischer,[4] who is in America. She can be found care of "Politics," 45 Astor Place, New York 3, N.Y., U.S.A.

Yours sincerely
[Signed] Geo. Orwell
George Orwell

1. "The Truth about Mihailovich" by R. V. Elson, *World Review*, January 1945.
2. Draža Mihailović (1893?–1946) Yugoslav patriot and military leader of the nationalist guerrilla (Chetnik) forces in Jugoslavia, formed in 1941, when the Germans invaded the country. He later became involved in a struggle for control of the guerrilla movement and was executed by the Tito government. See *1579, n. 2*.
3. Gleb Struve; see *2583*.
4. Ruth Fischer (1895–1961), former General Secretary of the German Communist Party 1923–26; she was expelled as a Trotskyist. A refugee from Hitler's Germany, she lived in France and the United States and wrote on political subjects. Her *Stalin and German Communism* was published in 1948. See *3603* for her correspondence with Orwell.

2592. 'Oysters and Brown Stout'

Tribune, 22 December 1944[1]

G. K. Chesterton said once that every novelist writes one book whose title seems to be a summing-up of his attitude to life. He instanced, for Dickens, *Great Expectations*, and for Scott, *Tales of a Grandfather*.

What title would one choose as especially representative of Thackeray? The obvious one is *Vanity Fair*, but I believe that if one looked more closely one would choose either *Christmas Books*, *Burlesques*, or *A Book of Snobs*—at any rate, one would choose the title of one of the collections of scraps which Thackeray had previously contributed to *Punch* and other magazines. Not only was he by nature a burlesque writer, but he was primarily a journalist, a writer of fragments, and his most characteristic work is not fully separable from the illustrations. Some of the best of these are by Cruikshank, but Thackeray was also a brilliant comic draughtsman himself, and in some of his very short sketches the picture and the letterpress belong organically together. All that is best in his full-length novels seems to have grown out of his contributions to *Punch*, and even *Vanity Fair* has a fragmentary quality that makes it possible to begin reading in it at almost any place, without looking back to see what has happened earlier.

At this date some of his major works—for instance, *Esmond* or *The Virginians*—are barely readable, and only once, in a rather short book, *A Shabby Genteel Story*, did he write what we should now regard as a serious novel. Thackeray's two main themes are snobbishness and extravagance, but he is at his best when he handles them in the comic vein, because—unlike Dickens, for instance—he has very little social insight and not even a very clear moral code. *Vanity Fair*, it is true, is a valuable social document as well as being an extremely readable and amusing book. It records, with remarkable fidelity so far as physical detail goes, the ghastly social competition of the early nineteenth century, when an aristocracy which could no longer pay its way was still the arbiter of fashion and of behaviour. In *Vanity Fair*, and indeed throughout Thackeray's writings, it is almost exceptional to find anyone living inside his income.

To live in a house which is too big for you, to engage servants whom you cannot pay, to ruin yourself by giving pretentious dinner parties with hired footmen, to bilk your tradesmen, to overdraw your banking account, to live permanently in the clutches of moneylenders—this is almost the norm of human behaviour. It is taken for granted that anyone who is not halfway to being a saint will ape the aristocracy if possible. The desire for expensive clothes, gilded carriages and hordes of liveried servants is assumed to be a natural instinct, like the desire for food and drink. And the people Thackeray is best able to describe are those who are living the fashionable life upon no income whatever—people like Becky Sharp and Rawdon Crawley in *Vanity Fair*, or the innumerable seedy adventurers, Major Loder, Captain Rook, Captain Costigan, Mr. Deuceace, whose life is an endless to-and-fro between the card-table and the sponging-house.

So far as it goes, Thackeray's picture of society is probably true. The types he depicts, the mortgage-ridden aristocrats, the brandy-drinking army officers, the elderly bucks with their stays and their dyed whiskers, the matchmaking mothers, the vulgar City magnates, did exist. But he is observing chiefly externals. In spite of endless musings on the French Revolution, a subject that fascinated him, he does not see that the structure of society is altering: he sees the nation-wide phenomenon of snobbery and extravagance, without seeing its deeper causes. Moreover, unlike Dickens, he does not see that the social struggle is three-sided: his sympathies hardly extend to the working class, whom he is conscious of chiefly as servants. Nor is he ever certain where he himself stands. He cannot make up his mind whether the raffish upper class or the money-grubbing middle class is more objectionable. Not having any definite social, political or, probably, religious convictions, he can hardly imagine any virtues except simplicity, courage and, in the case of women, "purity." (Thackeray's "good" women, incidentally, are completely intolerable.) The implied moral of both *Vanity Fair* and *Pendennis* is the rather empty one: "Don't be selfish, don't be worldly, don't live outside your income." And *A Shabby Genteel Story* says the same thing in a more delicate way.

But Thackeray's narrow intellectual range is actually an advantage to him when he abandons the attempt to portray real human beings. A thing that is very striking is the vitality of his *minor* writings, even of things that he himself must have thought of as purely ephemeral. If you dip almost anywhere in his collected works—even in his book reviews, for instance—you come upon the characteristic flavour. Partly it is the atmosphere of surfeit which belongs to the early nineteenth century, an atmosphere compounded of oysters, brown stout, brandy and water, turtle soup, roast sirloin, haunch of venison, Madeira and cigar smoke, which Thackeray is well able to convey because he has a good grip on physical detail and is extremely interested in food.

He writes about food perhaps more often even than Dickens, and more accurately. His account of his dinners in Paris—not expensive dinners, either—in *Memorials of Gormandising* is fascinating reading. *The Ballad of the Bouillabaisse* is one of the best poems of that kind in English. But the characteristic flavour of Thackeray is the flavour of burlesque, of a world where no one is good and nothing is serious. It pervades all the best passages in his novels, and it reaches its perfection in short sketches and stories like *Dr. Birch and his Young Friends*, *The Rose and the Ring*, *The Fatal Boots* and *A Little Dinner at Timmins's*.

The Rose and the Ring is a sort of charade, similar in spirit to the *Ingoldsby Legends*; *A Little Dinner at Timmins's* is a relatively naturalistic story, and *The Fatal Boots* is about midway between the two. But in all these and similar pieces Thackeray has got away from the difficulty that besets most novelists and has never been solved by any characteristically English novelist—the difficulty of combining characters who are meant to be real and exist "in the round" with mere figures of fun.

English writers from Chaucer onwards have found it very difficult to resist burlesque, but as soon as burlesque enters the reality of the story suffers. Fielding, Dickens, Trollope, Wells, even Joyce, have all stumbled over this problem. Thackeray, in the best of his short pieces, solves it by making *all* his characters into caricatures. There is no question of the hero of *The Fatal Boots* existing "in the round." He is as flat as an ikon. In *A Little Dinner at Timmins's*—one of the best comic short stories ever written, though it is seldom reprinted—Thackeray is really doing the same thing as he did in *Vanity Fair*, but without the complicating factor of having to simulate real life and introduce disinterested motives. It is a simple little story, exquisitely told and rising gradually to a sort of crescendo which stops at exactly the right moment. A lawyer who has received an unusually large fee decides to celebrate it by giving a dinner party. He is at once led into much greater expense than he can afford, and there follows a series of disasters which leave him heavily in debt, with his friends alienated and his mother-in-law permanently installed in his home. From start to finish no one has had anything from the dinner party except misery. And when, at the end, Thackeray remarks, "Why, in fact, did the Timminses give that party at all?" one feels that the folly of social ambition has been more conclusively demonstrated than it is by *Vanity Fair*. This is the kind of thing that Thackeray could do perfectly, and it is the recurrence of farcical incidents like this, rather than their central story, that makes the longer novels worth reading.

1. In place of 'As I Please.'

2593. Review of *An Interlude in Spain* by Charles d'Ydewalle, translated by Eric Sutton

The Observer, 24 December 1944

Unwilling witnesses are generally accounted the most reliable, and Mr. Charles d'Ydewalle is at least partly an unwilling witness against Franco's Spain. He is a Belgian journalist (evidently a devout Catholic), and during the Spanish civil war he was a warm partisan of General Franco, in whose territory he appears to have spent some months. When his own country was subjugated by the Germans and he set out on the roundabout journey to England, he was quite confident that Nationalist Spain, whose "crusade" he had supported as best he could, would offer no obstacle. It was therefore with some surprise that he found himself arrested and flung into jail almost as soon as he had set foot on Spanish soil.

This was towards the end of 1941. He was not released until eight months later, and at no time did he discover what offence, if any, he was charged with. Presumably he had been arrested because his flight to England indicated Allied sympathies. He was incarcerated first of all in the Model Prison in Barcelona, which had been built to hold 700 prisoners and at this time was holding 8,000. Later he was placed in a concentration camp among refugees of many different nationalities. Here the conditions were comparatively sympathetic; it was possible to buy small luxuries; one could choose one's hut mates, and there was international rivalry in the matter of digging tunnels under the barbed wire. It was the Model Prison that opened or partially opened Mr. d'Ydewalle's eyes to the nature of the regime.

At the end of 1941, nearly three years after the ending of the civil war, people were still being shot, in this prison alone, at the rate of five or six a week. In addition there was torture, presumably for the purpose of extracting confessions, and on occasion the torturer "went too far." Political prisoners and ordinary criminals were more or less mixed up together, but the majority of the prisoners were left-overs from the civil war, usually serving sentences of thirty years. In many cases, Mr. d'Ydewalle noted, this would take them to the ripe age of ninety-five or so. The shootings were carried out with the maximum of cruelty. No one knew, until the actual morning of execution, whether he was to be shot or not.

Early every morning there would be a trampling of boots and a clanking of bayonets along the corridor, and suddenly this door or that would be thrown open and a name called out. Later in the day the dead man's mattress would be seen lying outside the cell door. Sometimes a man was reprieved and then shot a day or two later for some different offence. But there were no shootings on Sundays or holidays. The display of religiosity with which the life of the prison was conducted stuck in Mr. d'Ydewalle's gizzard almost more than the cruelty.

Mr. d'Ydewalle spent only a day or two in Spain as a free man, but in the concentration camp he noted that the wretched Spanish soldiers who guarded them were glad to beg scraps of food from the better-off internees. He does not record things like this with any satisfaction, and is reluctant to draw their full moral. To the end, indeed, he seems to have remained convinced that in the civil war Franco was in the right, and that it was only afterwards that things went wrong. In prison he sometimes comforted himself with the thought that the wretched victims round about him had been doing the same thing to Nationalist sympathisers only a few years before. He reiterates his belief in "red atrocities," and shows more than a trace of anti-Semitism.

The main impression that the book conveys is one of bewilderment. Why had he been locked up? How could the "glorious crusade" have led to this kind of thing? He even expresses astonishment that a regime calling itself Catholic could lend its support to Hitler and Mussolini: which does seem to be carrying simplicity rather far, since General Franco can hardly be accused of having concealed his political affiliations.

Naturally it is not easy for someone who in good faith supported the Nationalist cause at the time of the civil war to admit that the horrors of the Model Prison were implicit in the Nationalist regime from the beginning. But Mr. d'Ydewalle also had the handicap of coming from a comparatively orderly and well-governed country and therefore not having any preliminary understanding of totalitarianism.

The essential fact about a totalitarian regime is that it has no laws. People are not punished for specific offences, but because they are considered to be politically or intellectually undesirable. What they have done or not done is irrelevant. It took Mr. d'Ydewalle some time to get used to this idea, and, as he observed, there were other Western European prisoners who had difficulty in grasping it as well. When he had been several months in jail some British soldiers, escaped from France, came to join him. He told them about the shootings. At the beginning they flatly disbelieved him, and only gradually, as mattress after mattress appeared outside this cell or that, came to realise that what he said was true: whereupon they commented, not inaptly, "Well, give me England every time."

This book is a useful footnote to history. The author's simplicity of outlook is an advantage to him as a narrator. But, if one may make a guess, the next variant of General Franco who appears will not have Mr. d'Ydewalle's support.

[Fee: £10.0.0; 22.12.44]

2593A. To Daniel George, 28 December 1944: see Vol. xx, Appendix 15

2594. Review of *Lovely Is the Lee* by Robert Gibbings;
The Cup of Astonishment by Vera T. Mirsky

Manchester Evening News, 28 December 1944

It is difficult to be sure how much of Mr. Gibbings's book to believe. Not that anything in his description of the climate, the flora and fauna, the wayside inns, and the casual conversations of western Ireland rings false—but is the belief in fairies (generally called, with propitiatory intention, "the good people") really so general as he seems to imply?

". . . Castle Hackett is the home of all the fairies in Mayo, as everyone knows. There was a field there that no man had ever ploughed. It was the field of the Battle of Athenry, and in that battle there was 10,000 killed.

" 'I don't give a damn what was fought there,' said the man. 'One field is the same as another,' he said. But his horses were very nervous when he put them to the plough. Well, he started away to turn the sod, and he hadn't gone two furrows when a small little woman comes up to him. 'What do you mean by destroying my houseen?' said she. But, sure, he only laughed at her. And he went on with his work, and he finished the furrow he was on, and he was half-way back on the next when the plough fell out of his hands with the pain that struck him.

"He lay there on the ground and he couldn't move so much as one toe inside his boot until the neighbours came out and carried him in. With that he got the pneumonia that near killed him. His two horses were dead inside a week. His wife died, and his children were ever ailing, his crops went bad, and the plough is lying to this day half-way down the furrow, and no man will touch it."

Anecdotes of this kind occur every few pages. It is interesting to notice that though "the good people" are usually identifiable as fairies, they sometimes appear to be confused with ghosts. There are also many references to talking animals, seals which can change into human shape at will, and dreams which reveal the whereabouts of buried treasure.

There are also stories of mysterious horses which come out of the sea and can be caught and made to work, provided that a special kind of halter, made of straw, is used. A charming fancy, but it is hard to believe that the Irish peasants, wringing a livelihood from a stony soil, are much governed by superstitions of this kind.

However, Mr. Gibbings's book is not exclusively concerned with fairies. It is the story of a visit to the valley of the Lee, in his native County Cork, with some excursions to the islands off the west coast.

"Cork," says Mr. Gibbings, "is the loveliest city in the world. Anybody who doesn't agree with me either was not born there or is prejudiced."

And all allowance for the tenderness that anyone feels towards the countryside in which he spent his boyhood, it does appear that life in western Ireland has a peculiar leisurely charm, not easily found elsewhere in the modern world.

The smell of cows and peat smoke seems to hang about everything, and though nearly everyone works no one is in a hurry—the bus waits patiently at the roadside while an intending passenger does her hair—and fishing and shooting are more important than money.

The people's speech has an almost poetic vividness. "That evening I asked a man if he could tell me the way to the college. 'Know the way to the college?' he said. 'If I was to take off me two boots and put them on the pavement before me, they'd find their own way there.'"

Or here are two market women discussing matrimonial affairs—"But when I says to him, 'How would she look under a cow?' sure, that finished him. He never threw a thought to her since . . . But there's Mary Ryan is getting married, and him without as much as you'd jink on a tombstone, and that small you could blow him off the palm of your hand."

On another occasion a peer, with a double-barrelled title, is seen crossing the Market Place. "'Isn't that Lord Clare and Galway?' said one farmer to another. 'It is,' said the other, 'and both of them's drunk.'"

Ireland is exceptionally rich in Bronze Age and Stone Age relics, and this book contains much curious information about megaliths and about the lake dwellings, similar to those of Switzerland, which are to be found in Lough Carra and elsewhere. It also contains a good deal of information about birds, about sea fishing, illicit whisky, place names, donkeys (which it seems were almost unknown in Ireland until the 19th century), fresh-water pearls and other out-of-the-way subjects.

There is an interesting digression on St. Brandon's Isle, the imaginary island far out in the Atlantic, in whose existence the world continued to believe until not much more than a century ago. The text is illustrated with numerous black and white drawings done by the author. This is an attractive book for the odd half-hour, and remarkable for containing no direct mention of the war.

It is a far cry from the lonely lakes and mountains of Ireland to the concentration camps of Continental Europe. The publishers of "The Cup of Astonishment" are mistaken in describing it as a "most unusual book," since essentially the same story has been told a number of times, but it deserves to be retold from time to time lest it be forgotten.

The author, a White Russian, was living in France at the outbreak of war, and was of doubtful political background—doubtful, that is to say, in the sense that she was known to be anti-Fascist.

As a result, like countless other anti-Fascists, she was promptly arrested and imprisoned without trial by the Daladier Government as soon as the war against Fascism began. The Russo-German pact and the resulting anti-war activities by the French Communists made it possible for the French authorities to claim that all "Reds" were traitors, but this was, of course, merely a pretext for crushing their political enemies.

The camp in which the author was confined contained 600 women, and it was impossible to find a single pro-Nazi among them. The pro-Nazis were at large, while those who had been fighting against Hitler since 1933 were in gaol, or at any rate under deep suspicion.

The author was released in 1940 and managed to get out of France soon after the German invasion of the U.S.S.R. There are tiresome passages in her book, resulting from a too-perfect political orthodoxy, but the description of the physical details of life in the camp, with its boredom, its unbearable overcrowding, and the deterioration of character in enforced idleness, is a valuable addition to prison literature.[1]

1. Orwell's Payments Book shows, with great regularity, the completion of reviews for the *Manchester Evening News* and *The Observer* a day or two before their appearance in print. It is possible to be fairly certain that these pairs of dates correspond because of the gaps between the submission of some items and because of the way the distinction between reviews and articles is recorded. It would have been expected that there would be an entry about 26 December for this review. The last date anything is recorded as submitted to the *Manchester Evening News* is 6 December 1944. Entries are shown at the beginning of 1945 for 3, 10, 17, 24, and 31 January and 7 Feburary; for all these dates except 17 January, a review appears a day or two later. Whether an entry was missed about 26 December 1944, or that for 17 January 1945 is intended to make good an omitted entry for this review, or whether a review was submitted on 17 January but not printed is unclear, although in the last case it would be unlikely that Orwell would have been paid the £8.0.0 recorded. It is most probable that the entry for 17 January is an afterthought for one that should have been made for 26 December.

2595. 'As I Please,' 52

Tribune, 29 December 1944

I am indebted to an article by Mr. Dwight Macdonald in the September number of *Politics*, the New York monthly, for some extracts from a book entitled *Kill—or Get Killed: a Manual of Hand-to-Hand Fighting* by Major Rex Applegate.

This book, a semi-official American publication, not only gives extensive information about knifing, strangling, and the various horrors that come under the heading of "unarmed combat," but describes the battle schools in which soldiers are trained for house-to-house fighting. Here are some sample directions:

". . . Before entering the tunnel, the coach exposes dummy A and the student uses the knife on it. While the student is proceeding from target No. 1 to target No. 4, the 'Gestapo Torture Scene' or the 'Italian Cursing' sequence is played over the loudspeaker . . . Target No. 9 is in darkness, and as the student enters this compartment the 'Jap Rape' sequence is used . . . While the coach is reloading the student's pistol, the 'Get that American son-of-a-bitch' sequence is used. As the coach and student pass through the curtain into the next compartment, they are confronted by a dummy which has a knife stuck in its back, and represents a dead body. This dummy is illuminated by a green light and is not to be fired at by the student, although practically all of them do."

Mr. Macdonald comments: "There is one rather interesting problem in operating the course. Although the writer never states so directly, it would seem there is danger that the student's inhibitions will be broken down so thoroughly that he will shoot or stab the coach who accompanies him . . . The coach is advised to keep himself in a position to grab the student's gun arm 'at any instant'; after the three dummies along the course have been stabbed, 'the knife is taken away from the student to prevent accident'; and finally: 'There is no place on the course where total darkness prevails while instructor is near student.'"

I believe the similar battle courses in the British army have now been discontinued or toned down, but it is worth remembering that *something like* this is inevitable if one wants military efficiency. No ideology, no consciousness of having "something to fight for," is fully a substitute for it. This deliberate brutalising of millions of human beings is part of the price of society in its present form. The Japanese, incidentally, have been experts at this kind of thing for hundreds of years. In the old days the sons of aristocrats used to be taken at a very early age to witness executions, and if any boy showed the slightest sign of nausea he was promptly made to swallow large quantities of rice stained the colour of blood.[1]

The English common people are not great lovers of military glory, and I have pointed out elsewhere that when a battle poem wins really wide popularity, it usually deals with a disaster and not a victory. But the other day, when I repeated this in some connection, there came into my head the once popular song—it might be popular again if one of the gramophone companies would bother to record it—"Admiral Benbow." This rather jingoistic ballad seems to contradict my theory, but I believe it may have owed some of its popularity to the fact that it had a class war angle which was understood at the time.

Admiral Benbow, when going into action against the French, was suddenly deserted by his subordinate captains and left to fight against heavy odds. As the ballad puts it:

"Said Kirby unto Wade, 'We will run, we will run,'
Said Kirby unto Wade, 'We will run;
For I value no disgrace
Nor the losing of my place,
But the enemy I won't face,
Nor his guns, nor his guns.'"

So Benbow was left to fight single-handed and, though victorious, he himself was killed. There is a gory but possibly authentic description of his death:

"Brave Benbow lost his legs, by chain shot, by chain shot,
Brave Benbow lost his legs, by chain shot:
Brave Benbow lost his legs
And all on his stumps he begs,
'Fight on, my English lads,
'Tis our lot, 'tis our lot.'

The surgeon dressed his wounds, Benbow cries, Benbow cries,
The surgeon dressed his wounds, Benbow cries;
'Let a cradle now in haste
On the quarter-deck be placed,
That the enemy I may face
Till I die, till I die.' "

The point is that Benbow was an ordinary seaman who had risen from the ranks. He had started off as a cabin boy. And his captains are supposed to have fled from the action because they did not want to see so plebeian a commander win a victory. I wonder whether it was this tradition that made Benbow into a popular hero and caused his name to be commemorated not only in the ballad but on the signs of innumerable public-houses?

I believe no recording of this song exists, but—as I discovered when I was broadcasting and wanted to use similar pieces as five-minute fill-ups—it is only one of a long list of old popular songs and folk songs which have not been recorded. Until recently, at any rate, I believe there was not even a record of "Tom Bowling" or of "Greensleeves," i.e., the words as well as the music. Others that I failed to get hold of were "A cottage well thatched with Straw," "Green grow the rushes, O," "Blow away the morning dew," and "Come lasses and lads." Other well-known songs are recorded in mutilated versions, and usually sung by professional singers with such a stale perfunctoriness that you seem to smell the whisky and cigarette smoke coming off the record. The collection of recorded carols is also very poor. You can't, I believe, get hold of "Minstrels and Maids," "Like silver lamps in a distant shrine," or "Dives and Lazarus," or other old favourites. On the other hand, if you want a record of "Roll out the barrel," "Boomps-a-daisy," etc., you would find quite a number of different renderings to choose from.[2]

A correspondent in *Tribune* of December 15 expressed his "horror and disgust" at hearing that Indian troops had been used against the Greeks, and compared this to the action of Franco in using Moorish troops against the Spanish Republic.[3]

It seems to me important that this ancient red herring should not be dragged across the trail. To begin with, the Indian troops are not strictly comparable to Franco's Moors. The reactionary Moorish chieftains, bearing rather the same relationship to Franco as the Indian Princes do to the British Conservative Party, sent their men to Spain with the conscious aim of crushing democracy. The Indian troops are mercenaries, serving the British from family tradition or for the sake of a job, though latterly a proportion of them have probably begun to think of themselves as an *Indian* army, nucleus of the armed forces of a future independent India. It is not likely that their presence in Athens had any political significance. Probably it was merely that they happened to be the nearest troops available.

But in addition, it is of the highest importance that Socialists should have no truck with colour prejudice. On a number of occasions—the Ruhr occupation of 1923 and the Spanish civil war, for instance—the cry "using coloured troops" has been raised, as though it were somehow worse to be shot up by Indians or Negroes than by Europeans. Our crime in Greece is to have interfered in Greek internal affairs at all: the colour of the troops who carry out the orders is irrelevant. In the case of the Ruhr occupation, it was perhaps justifiable to protest against the use of Senegalese troops, because the Germans probably felt this as an added humiliation, and the French may have used black troops for that very reason. But such feelings are not universal in Europe, and I doubt whether there is anywhere any prejudice against Indian troops, who are conspicuously well-behaved.

Our correspondent might have made the point that in an affair of this kind it is particularly mean to make use of politically ignorant colonial troops who don't understand in what a dirty job they are being mixed up. But at least don't let us insult the Indians by suggesting that their presence in Athens is somehow more offensive than that of the British.

In this issue, *Tribune* printed a letter from Mrs. O. Grant questioning the value of book reviews. Orwell takes this up, reproducing almost all of her letter, in 'Books and the People: A New Year Message,' *Tribune*, 5 January 1945; see *2598*.

1. For Orwell's Home Guard lecture on street fighting, see *731*.
2. The songs mentioned by Orwell are not listed in the 1944 *Catalogue of Recorded Music*, a combined, wartime catalogue which included Columbia, Decca, HMV, Parlophone, Regal-Zonophone, and Odeon records. This may have been a result in part of reduced production and stocks owing to the war. 'Tom Bowling,' for example, had been finely recorded by Walter Widdop in 1930. The catalogue listed two versions of 'Boomps-a-daisy' but, curiously, none of 'Roll out the barrel.'
3. The letter to which Orwell refers was from E. A. Hope:
   Printable words fail me when I try to express the horror and disgust I felt on hearing the B.B.C. broadcast that Indian troops have been used against the Greek forces of democracy.
   I well remember the loathing with which the democratic forces in this country learned that General Franco was using Moorish troops against the Spanish Republicans. We now learn that the British Government—in which the Labour Party participates—is exactly paralleling their action.
   Parties of the extreme Left—I.L.P., Trotskyist, etc.—have consistently proclaimed that a Tory dominated British Government plus capitalist America would be incapable of carrying out a progressive policy in Europe and now we begin to see that there was perhaps more than a grain of truth in their assertions.
   There can be no further shilly-shallying: If the Government do not immediately reverse their policy towards the resistance movements in Greece, Belgium, etc., every Socialist, every Democrat, every Trade Unionist in the country should demand the immediate withdrawal of the Labour Party from the Government and a General Election forthwith.
   I am not, I may add, a member of the Communist Party or even a Communist sympathiser, merely a rank and file Labour Party member.

2596. Review of *Flower of Evil: A Life of Charles Baudelaire* by Edwin Morgan

The Observer, 31 December 1944

The general outline of Baudelaire's life, his debts, his drug-taking, his Negro mistress, his almost infantile attachment to his mother and hatred of his blimpish stepfather, is well known. Except for his brief visit to Mauritius he never travelled further than Belgium, and in a physical sense his life was not adventurous. The two main factors in it were the morass of debts from which he never escaped, and his dependence, both financial and emotional, on his mother. To the last he continued writing to her, discussing all his projects, sending copies of his poems, boasting of future successes, and never once, apparently, arousing in her a flicker of interest in his work or any other reaction than a desire that he should "try to be like other people." He died in her arms, a worn-out, white-haired old paralytic, at the age of forty-six.

It is impossible to feel that even with the best of luck Baudelaire's life could have been in the ordinary sense successful. He wrote his own history in the famous line

Ses ailes de géant l'empêchent de marcher,[1]

and if he had been capable even for a moment of respectability or common sense we should probably never have heard his name. He is the poet of squalor, of perversity, of self-disgust, and of ennui, which Mr. Morgan inadequately translates as "boredom." (There is no exact English equivalent of this word in the sense in which Baudelaire uses it. Perhaps *taedium vitae* would be a correct translation.) and it hardly seems worth re-telling his story unless one is willing to recognise the considerable element of moral revolt which his work contains.

Unfortunately, Mr. Morgan's book is an attempt to build Baudelaire up into a good Catholic—or, at any rate, a "true" Catholic. The grounds for this are Baudelaire's alleged return to the Church during his last year of life, and the claim that Baudelaire's writings are essentially Christian, even when, as is often the case, he chooses to turn the Christian ethical code upside down. This claim has been made—and refuted—before. Even the concrete evidence by which Mr. Morgan seeks to prove Baudelaire's orthodoxy, is very unsatisfactory.

The ultimate conversion seems to rest on the testimony of only two or three people. Did Baudelaire ever make any definite submission to the Church, and if so, was he sane when he made it? He lost the power of speech about a year before his death and does not seem ever to have regained it completely. This is only a short book and does not claim to be an exhaustive biography: still, it calls itself a "life", and what is one to think of a "life" of Baudelaire which never once mentions that Baudelaire was syphilitic? Possibly Mr. Morgan does not believe that this was so—for it has been disputed—but he should at least have mentioned it and produced some other reason for Baudelaire's death as a paralytic at forty-six. This is not merely a piece of scandal: it is a point upon which any biographer of Baudelaire must make up his mind. For the nature of the disease has a bearing not only on the poet's mental condition during his last year but on his whole attitude to life.

Mr. Morgan's implied claim throughout the book is that in writing of vice, folly, and their after-effects, Baudelaire is displaying a Christian understanding of the vanity of human happiness. He claims Baudelaire, in effect, as a Christian pessimist, and traces his known dislike of liberalism, democracy, and the idea of progress to other-worldliness. But how can anyone who is suffering from such a disease as Baudelaire's be a disinterested witness on the question of whether earthly happiness is possible? Nor is it easy, on the evidence of Baudelaire's writings, to feel that he was a Catholic in any other than a cultural or, as one might say, anthropological sense. He sometimes toyed with Satanism, but Satanism is not, as it is often declared to be, the mirror image of Christian belief.

This book gives the impression of having been written as propaganda rather than as either biography or criticism. The literal translations which accompany the many quotations from *Les Fleurs du Mal* show remarkable insensitivity. They are everywhere inadequate and in places doubtfully correct, and once or twice Mr. Morgan simply omits a phrase without indicating that anything has been left out. He does, however, give due praise to Miss Enid Starkie's biography; and if that book is brought to the attention of a few new readers, his efforts will not have been wasted.

[Fee: £10.0.0; 29.12.44]

1. The poet's 'giant wings prevent his walking' (from 'L'Albatros').

INDEX

Volume XVI

This is an index of names of people, places, and institutions, and of titles of books, periodicals, broadcasts, and articles; it is not (with a very few exceptions) a topical index. However, topics discussed in his column 'As I Please', and the London Letters to *Partisan Review*, are listed alphabetically under these titles in the Cumulative Index in Volume XX. This index lists titles of books and articles in the text, headnotes and afternotes; incidental references to people and places are unindexed. In general, references to England and Britain are not indexed nor are the names of authors and books significant to an author being reviewed but not necessarily to Orwell. Inhabitants of countries are indexed under their countries (e.g., 'Germans' under 'Germany'). Numbered footnotes are indexed more selectively; for example, books listed by an author who is the subject of a footnote are not themselves indexed unless significant to Orwell. Payments entered by Orwell in his Payments Book (given at the end of reviews and articles to which they refer) are not individually indexed because they will all be found in the reproduction of the Payments Book in Volume XVII (see item 2831).

Orwell's book titles are printed in CAPITALS; his poems, essays, articles, broadcasts, etc., are printed in upper and lower case roman within single quotation marks. Book titles by authors other than Orwell are in italic; if Orwell reviewed the book (in this volume), this is noted by 'Rev:' followed by the pagination and a semi-colon; other references follow. Both books and authors are individually listed unless a reference is insignificant. If Orwell does not give an author's name, when known this is added in parentheses after the title. Articles and broadcasts by authors other than Orwell are placed within double quotation marks. Page references are in roman except for those to numbered footnotes, which are in italic. The order of roman and italic is related to the order of references on the page. Editorial notes are printed in roman upper and lower without quotation marks. If an editorial note follows a title it is abbreviated to 'ed. note:' and the pagination follows. First and last page numbers are given of articles and these are placed before general references and followed by a semi-colon; specific pages are given for each book reviewed in a group. The initial page number is given for letters. Punctuation is placed outside quotation marks to help separate information.

Letters by Orwell, and those written on his behalf, are given under the addressee's name and the first letter is preceded by 'L:', which stands for letters, memoranda, letter-cards, and postcards; telegrams are distinguished by 'T:' to draw attention to their urgency. If secretaries sign letters on Orwell's behalf, they are not indexed. Letters from someone to Orwell follow the name of the sender and are indicated by 'L. to O:'. References to letters are given before other references, which are marked off by a semi-colon. Letters in response to Orwell's are indicated by (L) after the respondent's name and/or the page number; if they are summarised this is shown by 'sy'. Letters to *Tribune*, *Manchester Evening News*, or *The Observer* arising from Orwell's contributions to these serials are indexed immediately after the item to which they refer; the name of the correspondent (and first page of the letter) follow the indication 'corr:'. These letters are also indexed under the names of the correspondents and indicated by '(corr.)'. References to Orwell, except in correspondence

Index

following his contributions to these three serials, are listed under 'Orwell, refs to:'.

Items are listed alphabetically by the word or words up to the first comma or bracket, except that Mc and M' are regarded as Mac and precede words starting with 'M'. St and Sainte are regarded as Saint.

Three cautions. First, some names are known only by a surname and it cannot be certain that surnames with the same initials, refer to the same person. If there is doubt, both names are indexed. Secondly, the use of quotation marks in the index differs from that in the text in order to make Orwell's work listed here readily apparent. Thirdly, a few titles and names have been corrected silently and dates of those who have died in 1997 (after the page-proofs of the text were completed) are noted in the index.   P.D.; S. D.

A.B.C.A. (Army Bureau of Current Affairs), 311
Abyssinia, 80, 82, 146, 205, 245, 284, 417
Acland, Sir Richard, 65, 70, 157, 311
Action Stories, 351
Acts, The Book of, 377
Adam and Eve, Rev: 432–4; 287, [288], 333, *333*, 441–2
Adelphi, 288, 295, 320
Adelphi Centre, Langham, 494
"Admiral Benbow", 506–7
Adventures of Sherlock Holmes, The, 25, 59, 60, 349, 353, 384
Aesop, 305
Afghanistan, 285
Agag, King, *155*
Agate, James, *Noblesse Oblige – Another Letter to Another Son*, Rev: 476–7; corr: J. Agate 479;
   Orwell 480; *482*
"Agate and Orwell", 479–82
Age d'Or, L' (film), 237, *237*
Air-raids and bombing (1916), 327; (1939–45), 46, 47, 88–9, 158, 171, 193–4, 195–6, *197*, 201, 284–7, 321, 403–4;
   Tube shelters, 318
Aitken, James, ed., *English Diaries of the Nineteenth Century*, Rev: 308–10
Albania, 476
Albany, Piccadilly, *356*
"Albatros, L' ", 509, *510*
Albert, Prince, 308
Albertine rose, 78, *79*
Alcibiades, 27–8
Alcott, Louisa M., *Little Women*, 87
Alexander, Gen. Sir Harold, *21*
Alexander, Horace, *India since Cripps*, Rev: 255
Alexander, Miss B. H., 261, 274
Alexandria, 247, 414
"Alfred J. Prufrock": see "Love Song of J. Alfred Prufrock, The"

Alice in Wonderland, 482
Alington, Dr Cyril, 440, *445*
Allegory of Love, The, 443
Allen, C. K., *Democracy and the Individual*, Rev: 71
Allenby in Egypt, Rev: 53–4; *98*
Allied Military Government (AMG), 65, *70*
All the Year Round, 383
Allwood, J. B. (corr) 115 (sy)
Amalgamated Press, 105
Amateur Cracksman, The (Raffles) (E. W. Hornung), 25
Amelia, 408, 456
American Civil War, 6, 7, 8, 205
American Notes, 96
American Problem, The, Rev: 406–7
AMG: see Allied Military Government
Amiens, Peace of, 47, *47*
Analytical Enquiry into the Principles of Taste, An, 92, *94*
Anand, Mulk Raj, 135
Anderson, Evelyn, 3
Anderson, Mrs (Wallington), 324, *326*
Anderson, Sir John, *76*
Anglo-American Relations, 220–1, 230
Angus, Ian, *199, 266*
ANIMAL FARM, 3, *18, 23*, 59, 79, 99, 127, 134, 141, *142*, 155, 156, *156*, 175, 182, 229, 251, *251, 266, 277*, 282, 283, 292, 335, 358
Anna Karenina, 137
Anstey, F., *Vice Versa*, 483
Anti-Semitism: see Jews
Aplin, C. A. (corr) 369
Aplin, John (corr) 372
Applegate, Maj. Rex, *Kill – or Get Killed*, 505
Appleton, G., *Buddhism in Burma*, Rev: 416
Aragon, Louis, 114
'Are Books Too Dear?', ed. note: 241, 242–4; end note: 244
Areopagitica, 489

"Are you not weary of ardent ways", 492
Aristophanes, 481
Armies and the Art of Revolution, Rev: 51–2
Armstrong, John, 368, 374
Army Bureau of Current Affairs: see ABCA
Arnold, Matthew, 469
Arrival and Departure, Rev: 19–20; 393, 397, 398–9, 400
Art and Scientific Thought, Rev: 280–2
'Arthur Koestler', ed. note: 391–2; 392–402
"Ash Wednesday", 421, *422*
'As I Please', ed. note: 3–4; 14, 38; Topics listed in Cumulative Index, Vol. XX;
  1: 12–14; corr: Richard McLaughlin 14; Harold T. Bers 15; "Unity" 16; W. T. Grose 16; G. H. Thomson, 17;
  2: 23–4;
  3: 25–8; corr: D. N. Pritt 28; Orwell 28;
  4: 34–6; corr: Conrad Voss-Bark 36;
  5: 45–7;
  6: 55–8;
  7: 60–1; corr: James Burnham 62; Orwell 63;
  8: 76–8; corr: Eileen E. Purber 78;
  9: 80–2; corr: Douglas Goldring 82; Paul Potts *83*;
  10: 88–90; corr: H. Jacobs *91*;
  11: 91–3; corr: A. Perlmutt 94; H. Pollins 94 (sy); Peter Lambda 94 (sy); Sydney Horler 94 (sy);
  12: 100–2;
  13: 103–5; corr: Robert A. Lewis 105; Orwell 105;
  14: 111–3; corr: Mary Murphy 114 (sy); J. H. Symons 114 (sy), Charles Davey 114 (sy); E. L. T. Mesens, Roland Penrose, Jacques B. Brunius, and Patrick Waldberg 114; J. B. Allwood 115 (sy);
  15: 117–20; corr: J. A. Turnbull *119*;
  16: 124–6;
  17: 131–3; corr: Richard Pugh 133 (sy); J. P. N. 133;
  18: 137–41;
  19: 145–7; corr: Frank Preston 147, *166*; R. J. Walden 148;
  20: 151–2; corr: Statistician 153; G. W. Gower 154; Orwell 154; A. M. Currie 155; Orwell 155 (and see 171);
  21: 164–6;
  22: 171–4;
  23: 175–7;
  24: 182–5; corr: J. F. Horrabin 185; Orwell 186;
  25: 193–5; corr: Vera Brittain 195; Orwell 196;

26: 230–2;
27: 244–7; corr: D. R. Brewley 247–8;
28: 251–3;
29: 258–60; corr: S. H. Hassall 260;
30: 261–3; corr: George Richards 263 (sy); H. McCormack 264; Anthony Silvestre 264; Alan Leavett 264;
31: 272–4; response from Tom Driberg *274*;
32: 275–7; corr: G. A. Weller *277*;
33: 284–6; corr: A. Clark Smith 284 (sy); Gerald Brenan 284 (sy); Vera Brittain 286 (sy) (and see 284);
34: 292–5;
35: 304–6; corr: Walter Tyrer 306;
36: 317–9; corr: Michael Sorensen *319*;
37: 328–30; corr: Duke of Bedford 330 (sy); C. Jack 331 (sy); Reg Reynolds 331;
38: 336–8; corr: Betty Lilly *338* (sy); Dorothy V. Carter *338* (sy);
39: 343–5;
40: [Warsaw Uprising] 362–76: ed. note: 362; "Who Deserted Warsaw" 362 (sy); "What's Happening": "Stalin's Promise" 362–3; "Moscow's Appeal to Warsaw" 363;
  'As I Please, 40': 363–6; corr: G. Barraclough 364;
  "What's Happening": "Soviets and Warsaw" 366; "Polish Home Army" 366–7;
  Corr: Lucjan Blit 367; John Armstrong 368; C. A. Aplin 369; Douglas Goldring 370, *376*; Kingsley Martin *371*, *376*; John Aplin 372; Arthur Koestler 374; Julian Symons 374, *376*; Bryan Matheson 375;
  end note: 375;
41: 385–7; corr: Frank Smith 387; "Young Writer" 388; P. Philips Price 389; W. R. Hutton and Miles Carpenter 390; D. M. C. Granville 390;
42: 402–5;
43: 423–6; L. to Orwell from Ada Dodd *426*;
44: 427–9; corr: "Writer" *430*;
45: 434–6;
46: 439–42; corr: Sylvia Barrett 442; William Empson 443; Francophil 444;
47: 451–3;
48: 463–6; corr: Austin Lee 466; E. R. Ward 466; Martin Walter 467; B. R. Gibbs 468;
49: 471–3;
50: 487–9; corr: J. J. Price 489;
51: 495–7;

Index

52: 505–8; corr: Mrs O. Grant 508 (sy)
Assignment in Utopia, *385*
Astor, David, *292, 380*
Athenaeum, 60
Atkins, John, 3
Atlas of Post-War Problems, 93, 94
Atlas of War Geography = Atlas of Post-War Problems, 93, 94
Auden, W. H., 475, 478
Australia, 303
Autobiography (Anthony Trollope), 92–3, 449
A.V.G. (American Volunteer Group), 417, *418*

"Baa, Baa, Black Sheep", *383*
Back to Sanity, *17*
Bacon, Francis, 40
Baedeker air raids, 46, *47*
Baker, Denys Val, *116*
"Ballad of the Bouillabaisse, The", *500*
"Ballad upon a Wedding", 121
Balogh, Thomas, 180
Ba Maw, 360
Baptism of Fire (film), 284
Barbara [Cooper?], 324
Barber, Frank, L: 490. 497; L. to Orwell 490
Barcelona, 284, 501
Barchester Towers, 450
Barham, Richard (= Thomas Ingoldsby), *The Ingoldsby Legends*, 90, 485, *500*; *482, 484, 485*
Baring, Maurice, 487
Barmine, Alexandre, *One Who Survived*, *491, 497*; *490, 491*
Barnes, G. R., 268
Barnhill, Jura, *380*
Barraclough, G. (corr) 364; 367, 368
Barrès, Philippe, *Charles de Gaulle*, 178 (and see 177–9)
Barrett, Sylvia, *Beyond the Wilderness*, 442; (corr) 442, 444
Barrie, James, *Der Tag* (play), *140; Peter Pan* (play), 238; *239*
Bartlett, Vernon, 366
Barzun, Jacques, *Romanticism and the Modern Ego*, Rev: 296–7; *280, 280*
Basic English, 31, 32, 81–2, 108, 218, 338
Basic English versus the Artificial Languages, 81
Bastille, The, 5
Baudelaire, Charles, Rev: of *Life*, 509–10; "L'Albatros", *509, 510; Les Fleurs du Mal*, 510
Baxter, Beverley, 259, *260, 463*
BBC, 3, 17, 22, 25, 66, 68, 76–7, 79, *83*, 108, 146, 148, *148*, 164–5, *181*, 188, 219, 220, 225, 245, 258, 268, 279, 291, 300,

314, 315, 343, *385, 386*, 388, 389, 414, 428, *436*, 438, 442, 444; 'Voice 6', 38
BBC Indian Section, 76–7, 108, 232
BBC Monitoring Service, 81
BBC Written Archive, *436*
"Beachcomber" (= J. B. Morton), 37, 262–4, *265*, 483
Beardsley, Aubrey, 238
Beaverbrook, Lord, 55, 262, 264, 272
Bêche-de-mer, 218, *228*
Bedford, Duke of (corr) 330 (sy); 330, *332*
Before the Storm: Recollections of I. M. Maisky, *228*
Beggar My Neighbour, *23*, 38
Behind the Spanish Mask, Rev: 9
Belgian Congo, 342
Belgium, 411
Belloc, Hilaire, "The Modern Traveller", 121, *485*; 92, 180, 276, 443, 483, 485
'Benefit of Clergy', 233–41
Bennett, Arnold, *The Old Wives' Tale*, 451; 86
Benson, R. H., *440, 445*
Benzie, Miss I. D., 268
Berdyaev, Nicholas, 35, 37
Beresford, John Davys, L. to Orwell: 115 (sy); *A Candidate for Truth*, 115
Berlin, 36, 286, 287, 334
Bernal, J. D., 180, *181*
Bernanos, Georges, 170
Bernhardi, Friedrich von, *Deutschland und der nächste Krieg*, *140; The New Bernhardi: "World Power and Downfall"* *140; 139, 140*
Bers, Harold T. (corr) *15*
Best Poems of 1943, *468*
Bevan, Aneurin, 3, 4, *103*, 150
Beveridge, Sir William, 35, 37, 263, *265*, 441
Beveridge Report, 210, 249, *265*
Bevin Boys, 192, *192*
Beyond Personality, Rev: 437–9; *439*
Beyond the Wilderness, 442
Bibliotheca Classica, 29
Biliad, or, How to Criticize: A Satire, The, 94
Bismark, Otto von, 184–5
Blackshirts, 211
Blair, Eileen, L. to Lydia Jackson: ed. note: 323; 324; *325, 326*, 418, *419*
Blair, Richard Horatio, *288*, 295, 323, 325, 420, *420*, 434
Blake, William, 29, 107, 111, 204, 238, 310, 339, *340*, 492
Blit, Lucjan, (corr) 367; 370
Blok, Aleksandr, 99
"Blow away the morning dew", 507
Blum, Léon, 178
Blunden, Edmund, *Cricket Country*, Rev:

161–3; "Report on Experience" ("I have been young"), 162
Bo'ddin O'Cowls, A, 230
Boer War, 36, 60, 206, 349
Boileau, Nicolas, 297
Bokhari, Zulfaqar Ali, L: 291; L. to Orwell: 291
Bombing Restriction Committee, 193
Bondfield, Margaret, 270, *272*
Booklovers' Corner, 3, *379*
Book of Snobs, A, 498
Books and the People: series title, 456, *459*
"Boomps-a-daisy", 507, *508*
Bor: see Komorowski, Gen. Tadeusz
Borkenau, Franz, 180, 392, *400*
Bose, A. N., *83*
Bose, Ras Behari, 36
Bose, Subhas Chandra, 159
Bottomley, Horatio, 481
Boule de Suif, 246
Bourne, George, *Memoirs of a Surrey Labourer*, 473; *473*
Bowra, Maurice, 113
Boy's Own Paper, 60
Bracken, Brendan, 259, *260*, 463
Brailsford, Noel, 3
"Brains Trust, The", 258, *260*, 263, 314
Branch Street, Rev: 334–5; 318
Brave New World, 38, 40
"Bread and Butter for the Teacher", 179
Brenan, Gerald (corr) 284 (sy)
Brendan and Beverley, Rev: 463
Brest-Litovsk, Treaty of, 139, *140*
Breughel (Brueghel), Pieter, "The Land of the Sluggard", 41
Brewley, D. R. (corr) 247–8 ("Effects of Propaganda")
Bridge into the Future: Letters of Max Plowman, Rev: 492–4; *494*
Bridges, Robert, "London Snow", 38; *39*, 460
Briffault, Robert Stephen, *Reasons for Anger*, 17; 15
Briggs, Greta, "London under Bombardment", *121*
Bristol Writers' Association, 390
Britain and Burma, 456
Britain and Malaya, Rev: 455–6
Britain and West Africa, 456
Britain in Pictures, 59, *59*, 127, 142, 199
Britain in Pictures: A History and a Bibliography (Michael Carney) 200
British Ally, 290
British Council, The, 199, 237, 280, 290, 381
British Empire, 222, 285, 331
British Institute of Fiction-Writing Science Ltd., *58*, 466, 496; and see Walter, Martin

British Museum (Reading Room), 273, 332, 344, 349
British Union of Fascists, *17*
British Union Quarterly, 80, 194
Brittain, Vera, *Seed of Chaos*, 193, 195; (corr) 195; *196*, 284, 286
Brockway, Fenner, *83*
Brogan, D. W., *The American Problem*, Rev: 406–7; *The English People*, 406
Bronowski, Jacob, *A Man Without a Mask* [Blake], 107
Browder, Earl Russell, 370, *375–6*
Brown, Ford Madox, *310*
Brown, Ivor, L: *304*; L. to T. Jones, xx, App. 15
Brown Phoenix, 232
Browning, Elizabeth Barrett, 473
Browning, Robert, "Mr Sludge, 'The Medium' ", 473; *470*
Brumwell, J. R. M. (ed.), *This Changing World*, Rev: 179–80
Brunius, Jacques B., (corr) 114
Bryant, Arthur, 280, *280*, 290
Buchman, Frank, *439*
Buddhism in Burma, Rev: 416
Bukharin, Nikolai, 396, 397
Bunyan, John, *The Pilgrim's Progress*, 437, 439, 442; *440*
Burke, Thomas Henry, 189
Burlesques (Thackeray), 498
Burma, 143–4, 175, 253–5, 343–4, 358–62, *362*, 416–8, 434–6
Burma, Rev: 417
Burma Background, Rev: 416
'Burma': Interview by G. B. Pittock-Buss, 358–62
Burma Pamphlets, Rev: 416–7
Burma Setting, Rev: 416
Burma Surgeon, Rev: 253–5
BURMESE DAYS, 24, 175, *175*, 265, 359
Burnham, James, *The Machiavellians*, Rev: 72–4; 62, 63; *The Managerial Revolution*, 60–1, 62–3, 63–4, *64*, 74, 450; *64*, 132, 150, 294
Burns, Oates and Washbourne, 155–6
Burroughs, Edgar Rice, 113
Burton, Jean, and Jan Fortune, *Elisabet Ney*, Rev: 97–8
Butler, Samuel, *Erewhon*, 155; "Musical Banks", 153, 155; *Note-books*, 292–3; *The Way of All Flesh*, 293
Byrne, Gerald, *265*
Byrne, Mrs Gerry (= Amy Charlesworth), L: *265*, 445, *446*(L); *265*, 324
Byron, Lord, *94*, 168, 275, 310, 451, 485

Cabell, James Branch, 238–9
Cairo, 414

Index

Call of the Wild, The, 274
Calverley, Charles Stuart, "Ode to Beer",
486, *487*; "Ode to Tobacco", 486, *487*;
"On a Distant Prospect of Making a
Fortune", 90, *91*, 485; 482
Calvinism, 206–7
*Campaign of Sedan: The Downfall of the Second
Empire, The* (1887), 184
Campbell, Malcolm, 480, *482*
Campbell, Roy, 280, *280*, 290
Canada, 304
Candidate for Truth, A, 115
Canfield, Cass, *491*
'Can Socialists be Happy?', ed. note: 37–8;
38–43; corr; J. Cryer 43; Ian Freed 44
Cape: see Jonathan Cape (publishers)
Capone, Al, 206, 353, 355
Caporetto, Battle of, 317
Carlyle, Thomas, 107, 205, 293, 297, 354
Carmen, 246, 383
Carpenter, Miles (corr) 390
Carr, Prof. E. H., 159, *161*
Carroll, Lewis, *Alice in Wonderland,* 482;
"The Walrus and the Carpenter", 90; 484
Carter, Dorothy V., (corr) *338*
Carthage, 35, 36, 37
Caruso, Pietro, 452
Cary, Joyce, *Britain and West Africa,* 456; *The
Case for African Freedom,* 456
Casablanca Conference, 21
Case for African Freedom, The, 456
"Cassius" (= Michael Foot), *Brendan and
Beverley,* Rev: 463
Catalonia, 289
Catholic Herald, 369, 373
Cauchemar en URSS, 396, *401*
Cavell, Nurse Edith, 138, *139*
Cavendish, Lord Frederick, 189
Céline, Louis-Ferdinand, 81
C.E.M.A. (Council for the Encouragement
of Music and the Arts), 388, 389, 390, *391*,
428
Cervantes, Miguel de, *Don Quixote,* 488; 408
Chamberlain, Houston, 273
Chamberlain, Neville, 87, 300, 463, 470
Chamber's Papers for the People, 383
Chang Hsien Ch'Ung, 143–4
Chaplin, Charles, 168, 205
Chappelle, Bonnier de la, *22*
Charles de Gaulle, 178 (and see 177–9)
Charles, Dr Enid, 154
'Charles Dickens', 37, 59, 135, 156, 251
Charlesworth, Amy: see Byrne, Mrs Gerry
Chartres Cathedral, 281
Chase, James Hadley, 'Raffles and Miss
Blandish', ed. note: 345–6; 346–58; *He
Won't Need It Now,* 351;

No Orchids for Miss Blandish, 79, 298, 345,
346, 347, 348, 349–56, *356*; 79
Chaucer, Geoffrey, "The Miller's Tale",
484; 475
Cheddar Pink (flower), 166, *166*
Chekhov, Anton, 487
Chelmsford, Lord, *362*
Chennault, Gen. Claire Lee, *418*
Chesterton, A. K., 36
Chesterton, Cecil, 443
Chesterton G. K., 36, 92, 104, 153, 155,
171, 204, 263, 264, 442, 443, 483, 498
Chiang Kai-shek, 253, 490, *491*
Chien Andalou, Le (film), 236
'Children Who Cannot be Billeted, The',
335
China, 205, 285, 287, 288, 321, 321–3, 361
"Chinago, The", 451
Choose Your Future, 28
Chorley, K. C., *Armies and the Art of
Revolution,* Rev: 51–2
Christmas Books, 498
Christmas Carol, A, 37, 39
Christy & Moore, 127; and see Moore,
Leonard
Chronological Tables . . . from the Creation,
47, *47*
Church, Richard, *The Porch and the
Stronghold,* Rev: 326–8, *328*
Churchill, R. C., 58
Churchill, Winston, *My Early Life,* 462; 21,
55, 69, 157, 172, 215, 272, 287, 312, 315,
321, 334, 374, 403, 411, 462, 463
Church of England, 204–5
Church Times, 81, 155
Citrine, Sir Walter, 56
Civil War (English), 376
Clemens, Mrs., 7
Clemens, Samuel Langhorne: see Twain,
Mark
CLERGYMAN'S DAUGHTER, A, *228*,
232
Clifton College, *163*
Clough, Arthur Hugh, "How pleasant it is
to have money", 90; 482
Coal output (British and German), 158, *161*
Cobbett, William, 309
Colchester, Lord, 309
Collected Poems & Verses (de la Mare), 107,
107
Collected Poems of W. H. Davies, Rev: 29–31;
38
Collins (publishers), 199
Collis, Maurice, *She Was a Queen,* Rev:
143–4
Colquhoun, Ethel, L. to Orwell: 128 (sy);
"The Signalman", 128

"Come lasses and lads", 507
Comfort, Alex, L: 9; *The Power House*, 471; 25, *116–7*, 295, 419; as Obadiah Hornbooke, 306, *307*
Coming of Age in Samoa, Rev: 144–5
COMING UP FOR AIR, 232, 251, *251*
Comintern, *299*
Common Wealth (Party), 65, *70*, 132, 154, 157, 300, *312*, 412
Common Wealth (journal), 151, 153
Communist Parties: British: 211, 300, 302, 394, 478, *508*
Polish: 372
Spanish: 290
USA: *376*
Condor Legion, 284
Connecticut Yankee in King Arthur's Court, A, 7
Conrad, Joseph, *Heart of Darkness*, 383; *Youth*, 246
Conservative Party, 65, 67, 209–10, 259, 300, 301, 507
Controversy, 3, 155
Cooper, Lettice, 324, *325*
Corinthians, I, 340, *342*
Cork, 503
Cornhill Magazine, 60, 113
Correspondence with Antonia White, 169–71
"Cottage well thatched with straw, A", 507
Council for the International Recognition of Indian Independence, *82–3*
Counterblast, 453–4
Country Life, 468
"Courtship of the Yonghy-Bonghy-Bò, The", 485
Coward, Noel, 481
Crabbe, George, *The Village*, 130; 129–30, *130*
Craig, Edward Gordon, 171
Craig, Mrs Edwin, *232*
Crainquebille, 262
Creasey, John, 354
Crécy, Battle of, 404, *404*
Crick, Bernard, 3, 4, *131*, *143*, 191–2, *266*, *292*, 323, *379*, *426*, *492*
Cricket Country, Rev: 161–3
Cripps, Sir Stafford, 3, 65, 66, 255, 343, 412, 441, *445*
Cripps Mission, 187, 255, 361, *455*
Criterion, 34, 246
CRITICAL ESSAYS, *18*, 59, *59*, 233, 345, 391
Critical History of English Poetry, A, Rev: 474–5
Cromwell, Oliver, 167, 168, 377, 462
Cromwell, Thomas, 74

Crookes, Sir William, 473, *473*
Crozier, Brig-Gen., 493
Cruikshank, George, 90, 498
Cryer, J. (corr) 43
Cup of Astonishment, The, Rev: 504–5
Currie, A. M. (corr) 155
Curzon, Clifford, 481, *482*
Czechoslovakia, *376*, 494

Daily Express, 27, 35, 216, 262, 264
Daily Graphic, 148
Daily Herald, 139, 148, 491
Daily Mail, 130, 253
Daily Mirror, 145–6, 148
Daily Sketch, 145, *148*, 369, 373
Daily Telegraph, 253, 331, 332, 369, 373
Daily Worker, 124, 125, 132, 192, 208, 215, *228*, 276, 363, 366, 371
Daladier, Édouard, 397, 504
Dali, Salvador, 'Benefit of Clergy: Some Notes on Salvador Dali', ed. note: 233; 233–41; "Le Jeu Lugubre", 235; "Mannequin Rotting in a Taxicab", 236, 237, 240; *The Secret Life of Salvador Dali*, 233–41, *234*; *117*, *119*, 127, 233
Dame aux Camélias, La (Dumas *fils*), 323
"Danny Deever", 451
Dark, Sidney, 152, *155*
Darkness at Noon, 19, 256, 328, 368, 374, 393, 395–7
Darlan, Adml. Jean-François, 21, *21*, 27, 178
Darlington, C. D., 180, *181*
Darwin, Charles, 6, 239
Davey, Charles (corr) 114 (sy)
David Copperfield, 408
Davidson, John, 492
Davies, Dr Martin, *94*
Davies, Rhys, 471
Davies, W. H., *Collected Poems*, Rev: 29–31; 38; "The Two Children", 29–30
"Dead, The", 109, 110, 246, 383
"Debate Continues, The", *70*
Defoe, Daniel, *Robinson Crusoe*, 172, 275
de Gaulle, Gen. Charles, 21, 55, 177–9, 190
de la Mare, Walter, *Collected Poems & Verses*, 107, *107*; 281
Democracy and the Individual, Rev: 71
Dempsey, Jack, 355
"Der Tag", 139, *140*
Der Tag (play), *140*
Descartes, René, 264
de Selincourt, Basil, 30
Deserted Village, The, 458–9
Deutsch, André, *156*
Deutschland und der nächste Krieg, *140*
De Valera, Eamon, 190

Index

Devil and the Jews, The, Rev: 84–5
Dewey, Thomas, 24, *24*
Dial Press, 127, *127*, 135, 141, 142, 174, 175, 182, 232, 291, 358, 419
Diary of a Nobody, 483, 487–8
Dickens, Charles, 'Charles Dickens', 37, 59, 135, 156;
  Martin Chuzzlewit, Rev: 95–6;
  American Notes, 96; *A Christmas Carol*, 37, 39; *David Copperfield*, 408; *Great Expectations*, 348, 498; *Hard Times*, 104; *Pickwick Papers*, 39, 95, 118, 162, 408, 483; *A Tale of Two Cities*, 451; *Dickens and Daughter* (Gladys Storey), 117;
  14, 18, 39, 42, 117, 118, 251, 482, 484
Dickens and Daughter (Gladys Storey), 117
DICKENS, DALI AND OTHERS, 345, 391; US title of *Critical Essays* (which see)
Dickson, George (corr) 150
Dieux ont Soif, Les, 262, 451
Diggers, 376, 377
Dint, 115
Disraeli, Benjamin, 272
Disraeli and the New Age, Rev: 71
"Dives and Lazarus", 507
Dodd, Ada, *426*
Domba Asi Avon (We Burmans League), 360
Donne, John, "Satyr 3", *124*; 176
Don Quixote, 488
Doodle-bug: see V-1
Doriot, Jacques, 398
Dostoievsky, Feodor, *Notes [Letters] from Underground*, 384, *384*
Dover, Cedric, *Brown Phoenix*, 232; *Half-Caste*, 323; *Hell in the Sunshine*, 232; *24*, 116, *116*, 232
Downing Literary Society, 58
Doyle, Conan, *The Adventures of Sherlock Holmes*, 25, 59, 60, 349, 353, 384
Dragon Beards versus the Blue Prints, The, Rev: 321–3
"Drake's Drum", 121
"Dr Birch and his Young Friends", 500
Dream, The, 39
Dreiser, Theodore, 26, 180
Dreyfus, Capt. Alfred, 6, 92, 262
Driberg, Tom, L: 448, 453, *453*(L); *274*, *448*
Drucker, Peter, 132
Drummond, J. C., 181, *181*
"Drums of the Fore and Aft", 383
Dubliners, 109, 110, 118
Duff Cooper, Alfred, 312
Duncan, Isadora, 98, *98*
Dundas, Lawrence, *Behind the Spanish Mask*, Rev: 9
Dunkirk, 202, 312, 413

Dunsany, Lord, 239
Duranty, Walter, *I Write As I Please*, 3
Dürer, Albrecht, 238
Dutt, Palme, *Why This War?*, 28

Eagle and the Dove, The, 113
Economist, 364
Economist, 1843–1943, The, 85, *85*
Eden, Anthony, 157
Edge of the Abyss, The, Rev: 105–7
Edinburgh Review, 246, 453
Éditions Penguin, 450–1
Education Act (1871), 215
Edward VIII, King, 69, 145
"Effects of Propaganda", 247–8
Egypt, 27, 53–4
18B Regulations, 68, *70*
'Eight Years of War: Spanish Memories, The', 288–90
Eisenhower, Gen. Dwight D., 160
El Alamein, 247
"Elegy Written in a Country Churchyard", 44, 45, 202
Elementary Russian Grammar, 340, 437
Eliot, George, *Silas Marner*, Rev: 450; 113
Eliot, T. S., L: 10, *10*(L), 269, 282, 379, *380*(L), 418, *418*(L);
  Four Quartets, Rev: 420–3; *420*, 422–3, *430–1*;
  "Ash Wednesday", 421, *422*; "The Journey of the Magi", 38; "The Love Song of J. Alfred Prufrock", 420, 421, 422, 474; "The Responsibility of the Man of Letters in the Cultural Restoration of Europe", 388; "Sweeney Agonistes", 313, 316, 420, 422, 474; "The Waste Land", 422, *459*;
  30, 39, 60, 118, *131*, 155, *156*, 226, 237, 265, 280, 290, 296, 313, 381, *382*, 474, 478
Elisabet Ney, Rev: 97–8
Elizabeth I, Queen, 167
Elsley, Ralph C., L: 492
Elson, R. V., "The Truth about Mihailovich⁰", *498*
Elton, Lord, *It Occurs to Me*, 3; 236, 237, 259
Eluard, Paul, 114
Emmett, E. V. H., 310–11, *316*
Empire, Rev: 186–7
Empson, William (corr) 443, *445*
Encyclopaedia Britannica, 88
Ends and Means, 37
Enemy of the People, An, 450
"England at First Glance", 200–4
England, My England, 246, 383
'English Class System, The', 213–7
English Diaries of the Nineteenth Century, Rev: 308–10

'English Language, The', 217–21
ENGLISH PEOPLE, THE, ed. note: 199–200; 200–28; *57, 79*; Rev. by Charles Humana, *228* (extracts);
Sections: 'England at First Glance', 200–4; 'The Moral Outlook of the English People', 204–9; 'The Political Outlook of the English People', 209–13; 'The English Class System', 213–7; 'The English Language', 217–21; 'The Future of the English People', 221–8
English People, The (D. W. Brogan), 406, *407*
English Spirit, The, Rev: 461–3
Enriquez, Major, 343
ENSA (Entertainments National Service Association), 388, 389, *391*
Epictetus, 305
E. R. (corr) 34
Erasmus, 462–3
Ervine, St. John, *Parnell*, Rev: 188–90; *186*
Esmond, 499
Esperanto, 108
Etching of a Tormented Age, 321
'Ethics of the Detective Story, from Raffles to Miss Blandish', ed. note: 345–6; *335*; see 'Raffles and Miss Blandish'
Eton College, 102
Europe, 222
Europe (maps of), 93, *95*
Evening Standard, *34*, 146, 276, 337, 364
Everyman's Library, 273
Eyre & Spottiswoode, *127*, 130, 155

Faber & Faber, 131, *131, 156*, 269, 282, 292
Faith, Reason and Civilisation, Rev: 122–3; *10* 175, 298, 313
Fallas, Carl, 19
Farewell to Berlin = Goodbye to Berlin, 382, *384*
"Fatal Boots, The", 482, 500
Faulkner, William, *Sanctuary*, 350, 354, *357, 381, 382*
"Felix Randal", 461
Femina Vie-Heureuse Prize (1938), 326
Fen, Elisaveta, *319*; see Jackson, Lydia
Fenian Movement, 189
Fergar, Feyyaz, *Gestes à la Mer*, 115; *114*
Fielden, Lionel, *Beggar My Neighbour*, 23, 38
Fielding, Henry, *Amelia*, 408, 456; *Joseph Andrews*, 410; *Tom Jones*, 275, 408
53 bus, *46 47*
Finland, 436
Finnegans Wake, 109, 110, 111, 119
Fischer, Louis, *Empire*, Rev: 186–7
Fischer, Ruth, 498, *498*
Fisher, James, 181, *181*

Fitter, R. S. R., L: 85, 99, 380; *85, 380*
Flammarion, Camille, 473, *473*
Flaubert, Gustave, *Salammbô*, 305, 394, 451; *394*
Fleg, Edmond, *Why I am a Jew*, Rev: 84
Fletcher, Robin and Margaret, *380*
Fleurs du Mal, Les, 510
Flight to Arras (Antoine de Saint-Exupéry), 328
Florrie, 324, *325*
Flower of Evil: A Life of Charles Baudelaire, Rev: 509–10
Flying Tigers, *418*
Focus, 391
Follies and Frauds of Spiritualism, The, 473
Fontaine, 58, 59, 444
Fontamara, 393
Foot, Michael, 241; corr: James C. Smith 241; *The Trial of Mussolini* 463; *463*; and see "Cassius"
Ford, Ford Madox, *310*
Ford, Henry, 353
Foreign Legion (French), 202, 349
For Sinners Only (A. J. Russell), 437, *439*
Forster, E. M., *A Passage to India*, 428; 60, 232
Fort Hertz, 417
Fortune, Jan and Jean Burton, *Elisabet Ney*, Rev: 97–8
'42 to '44: A Contemporary Memoir, Rev: 197–9; *199*, 241, 242; and see 181, *181*
For Whom the Bell Tolls (Ernest Hemingway), 256, 328
Four Quartets, Rev: 420–3; *430–1*
Fourth International, 195
Fowler, Harry (corr) 486, *487*
Fowler's (Ludgate Circus), 316
"Fox, The", 383
France, 60, 118, 184, 285, 289, 452, 465, 502, 505, 508
France, Anatole, *Les Dieux ont Soif*, Rev: 451; 262; *Crainquebille*, 262; *La Pierre Blanche*, 262; *La Rôtisserie de la Reine Pédauque*, 262; 6, 238, 261, *262*
Franco, Gen. Francisco, 8, 9, 23, 88, 174, 190, 192, 193, 205, 245, *280*, 289, 290, 300, 381, 501, 502, 507, *508*
Francophil (corr) 444
Franco-Prussian War, 205
Freed, Ian (corr) 45
Freeman, John, 37
Freiman, Dr I., *437*
French Revolution, 52, 104, 297, 451
Freud, Sigmund, 356
Friends in High Places, 482
From One Generation to Another, Rev: 269–72
Froude, Hurrell, 308

Index

"Fryolet, A", [153], 155
Fuad, King, 53, 54
Fuller, Maj-Gen. J. F. C., *Back to Sanity* 17; 17, 193
Fuller, Roy, L: 116; "Fletcher", 116, *116–7*; *116*
'Funny, But Not Vulgar', 482–6; corr: Harry Fowler, 486 (sy); 38
'Future of the English People, The', 221–8

Gala (wife of Salvador Dali), 234
Gallacher, William, 67, *70*
Gandhi, Mahatma, 55, 72, 190, 253, 332, 376, 377, 429, 447
'Gandhi in Mayfair', 59, 287
Gang of Ten, A, 85, *85*
"Garden, The", *453*
Gardner, W. H., *Gerard Manley Hopkins*, Rev: 460–1
Gascoyne, David E., *Poems 1937–1942*, 114, 115
Gauguin, Paul, 450
Gaumont-British News (film), 310–11
Gedye, G. E. R., *My Year in the USSR*, 491, 497
G for Genevieve (Fl. Lt. Herbert), 402, *402*, 427
Geneva (play), 284
"Gentleman Rankers", 348
Gentleman's Magazine, The, 60
George, Daniel, L: 426; 19, *266*, *426–7*, 452; L. xx, App. 15
George Allen & Unwin, 331, 334
George V, King, 68, 69, 145, 212, 213
George VI, King, *21*, 70, 160, 337
Gerard Manley Hopkins, Rev: 460–1
Germany, 36, 43, 46–7, 60, 61–4, 74, 125, 150, 151, 153, 158, 161, 168, 172–3, 184 (Prussia), 191, 193, 206, 209, 272, 273, 284–7, 289, 302, 317, 319, 320, 321, 329, 331, 333, *338*, 348, 349, 363, 411, 413, 429, 431, 462, 465, 476, 494, 505, 508; see Huns
Gestapo, 42, 118, 173, 194, 355, 396
Gestes à la Mer, 115
Giant in the Age of Steel: The Story of General de Gaulle, A, Rev: 177–9
Gibbings, Robert, *Lovely is the Lee*, Rev: 503–4
Gibbs, B. R., 468
Gide, André, *Retour de l'URSS*, 96; 451
Gielgud, John, 479, 481, *482*
Gilded Age, The, 7
Gill, Eric, *In a Strange Land: Last Essays*, Rev: 278–9
Giraud, Gen. Henri, *21*
G. K.'s Weekly, 155
Gladiators, The, 305, 393, 394–5
Gladstone, William Ewart, 87, 188, 189

Glinto Darcy, *Lady – Don't Turn Over*, 345, 346, *357*
Gobineau, Joseph Arthur, Comte de, 273
"God Save the King", 46, 47
Goebbels, Josef, 213, 253, 268, *280*, 374
Goering, Hermann, 287
Golden Star, 304
Goldring, Douglas (corr) 82, *83*; (corr) 370; 374
Goldsmith, Oliver, *The Vicar of Wakefield*, Rev: 456–9; *450*; *The Deserted Village*, 458–9;
    "When lovely woman stoops to folly", 457–8, *459*
Gollancz, Victor, L: 127, 134; L. to Orwell, 134 (sy), 135 (sy); L. to Jonathan Cape, *266* (sy); L. to Leonard Moore, *142* (sy), 251 (sy);
    Transl.: *Why I am a Jew*, 83;
    3, 59, 126, 130, 135, 142, *143*, 155, 156, *156*, 182, 250, 251, *251*, 265, 266, 269, 335, *358*
Good, Alan P., *70*, 157
Goodbye to Berlin (as *Farewell to Berlin*), 382, *384*
Goodhart, A. L., *What Acts of War are Justifiable*, 195–6, *196–7*
Gordon, Gen. Charles George (Chinese Gordon), 417
Gorki, Maxim, 476
Gosse, Sir Edmund, 176, *177*
Gower, G. W. (corr) 154
GPO, 103, 105
GPU: see NKVD
Grace, W. G., 480
Graham, Harry, *Ruthless Rhymes for Heartless Homes*, 239
'Grandeur et décadence du roman policier anglais', 25, 442
Grant, Mrs O. (corr) 508 (sy)
Granville, D. M. C. (corr) 390
Gray, Thomas, "Elegy Written in a Country Churchyard", 44, *45*, 202; "Ode on a Distant Prospect of Eton College", *91*
Great Expectations, 348, 498
Great War, 1914–18, 330
Greece, 205, 507, 508, *508*
"Green grow the rushes, O", 507
Green Mansions: A Romance of the Tropical Forest, 129
"Greensleeves", 507
Greenwich Hospital, 46
Greenwich Observatory, 46
Greenwich Park, 46
"Greeting Card Course", 464, 468
Grenfell, Joyce, *197*, *275*, *319*
Greville, Fulke, 309

"Grey Sleepers, The", 316
Grierson, Herbert J. C. and J. C. Smith, *A Critical History of English Poetry*, Rev: 474–5
Grose, W. T. (corr) 16
Grossmith, George and Weedon, *Diary of a Nobody*, 483, 487–8
Grotius, Hugo, 195, *197*
Groves, Reg (corr) 378–9, *379*
Gulliver's Travels, 38, 40, 275, 282, 484

Habberton, John, *Helen's Babies*, 87
Habeas Corpus, 184, *186*, 201, 441
Haile Selassie: see Selassie, Emperor Haile
Haiti, 329
Haldane, J. B. S., 181, *181*
Haldane, Lord, 387
Half-Caste, 232
Hallam, Henry, *94*
Hamblett, Charles, L: 181; 111, 113–4, *181*, 199, 241
Hamilton, Leonard (ed.) *Selections from the Works of Gerrard Winstanley*, Rev: 376–8; corr: Reg Groves, 378–9
Hamlet, 110
Hampson, John, 346
Handley Cross (R. S. Surtees), 90, 482
Handley, Tommy, 483
Hansard, 68, 259
Harcourt, Brace, *251*
Hard Times, 104
Harper's (publishers), 490, *491*
Harriet Martineau (J. C. Nevill), 85, *85*, 99
Harris, Air Marshal Arthur 'Bomber', 196, *197*, *284*
Harris, Frank, *My Life and Loves*, 234
Harrow School, 102
Harte, Bret, "Maud Muller", a sequel, 485; 5
Hartland, Winifred Grace, 472
Harvey, G. E., *Britain and Burma*, 456
Hassell, S. H. (corr) 260
Hatry, Clarence, 135, *136*
Hawthorne, Nathaniel, *The Scarlet Letter*, 450
Hay, Ian, 410, *410*
Hayek, F. A., *The Road to Serfdom*, Rev: 149; (corr) George Dickson 150
Heard, Gerald, 43, *45*
Heart of Darkness, 383
Helen's Babies (John Habberton), 87
Hell in the Sunshine, 232
Helpmann, Robert, 479, *482*
Hemingway, Ernest, *For Whom the Bell Tolls*, 256, 328
Hemingway, Kenneth, *Wings Over Burma*, Rev: 417
Henriques, Basil, 173, *174*

Henry, O., 25
Henry IV, Pt 1, 121
Henry V, 488
Heppenstall, Rayner, L: 107, 280, 290, 295, 316, 419, 430; L. to Orwell, *420*; 229, 230, 420 430–1, 453
Herbert, A. P., 258, 483
Herodotus, 246
"Her Soviet Lover", 305
Hertfordshire Express, 260
Hertfordshire Mercury, 260
Hess, Rudolf, 295, *296*
Hessenstein, Alfred, *A Giant in the Age of Steel: The Story of General de Gaulle*, Rev: 177–9
He Won't Need It Now, 351, 352
Heydrich, Reinhard, *376*
Hibaw, King of Burma, 144
Hill, Christopher, 378
Himmler, Heinrich, 45
Hinks, C. A., 229, *229*
Hitchin Mercury (= *Hertfordshire Mercury*?), 259, 260
Hitler, Adolf, *Mein Kampf*, 91; 27, 28, 45, 55, 69, 107, 119, 138, 139, 146, 151, 153, 159, 168, 173, 190, 191, 195, 196, 198, 205, 212, 226, 262, 263, 267, 272, 284, 287, 290, 314, 341, 354, 399, 451, 463, 493, 495, 502, 504
Hitler et le Christianisme, Rev: 451
Hoare, Sir Samuel, 171–2
Ho Chi Minh, 299
Hodgson, Ralph, 474
Hogarth, William, 90
Hogben, Lancelot, *Interglossa*, Rev: 31–3; (corr) F R 33; 81–2
Holden, Inez, *199*, 266, 277, 283, 419
Holland, 436
Hollis & Carter, *127*, 130
Holy Bible, The: Acts, 377; *1 Corinthians*, 340, *342*; *1 Samuel*, 155
HOMAGE TO CATALONIA, *126*, 232, 379
Home, Daniel Dunglas, *473*
Home Companion and Family Journal, 103–4, 105
Home Guard, 60, 132, *174*, 216, 302, *303*, 318, 328, 411, 416, 431–2, *432*, *508*; and see LDV
'Home Guard Lessons for the Future', 431–2
Homer, *The Odyssey*, 109; 481
Home Rule, Irish, 188–90
Hong Kong, 491
Honours List, 55–6, 226
Hood, Robin, 354
Hood, Thomas, 90, *482*
Hooper, George, *The Campaign of Sedan:*

Index

The Downfall of the Second Empire (1887), 184

Hope, E. A., L. to *Tribune*, 508

Hopkins, Gerard Manley, *Gerard Manley Hopkins*, Rev: 460–1; "Felix Randal", 461; 59, 121, 176, 261

Hopkins, Ldg. A/C. C., L: 255

Horace, *Odes*, 487

Horizon, 22, 23, 59, 60, 295, 345, 346, 381, 405

Horler, Sydney (corr) 94; *95*

Hornbooke, Obadiah: see Comfort, Alex

Hornung, E. W., *The Amateur Cracksman*, 25; *Raffles*, 25, *25*, 59, 79, 347, *347–9*, *349*, 352, 353, 356; 346–9, *347*, *349*, 352, 353, 356

Horrabin, J. F., *Atlas of Post-War Problems* (as *Atlas of War Geography*), 93, *94*; (corr) 185; "The War of the Three Oceans", 185

Horton, Mrs, 324, 325, *325*

House of Commons, 66–8

House of Lords, 66, 68

Housman, A. E., 296, 478

Howells, W. D., *My Mark Twain*, 7

'How Long is a Short Story', 382–5

"How pleasant it is to have money", 90

'How the Poor Die', 75

Hsiao Ch'ien, *The Dragon Beards versus the Blue Prints*, Rev: 321–3; *Etching of a Tormented Age*, 321; Translation of *Ulysses* 323; *323*

Huckleberry Finn, 5, 7, 86–7

Hudson, W. H., *Green Mansions: A Romance of the Tropical Forest*, 129; *129*

Hughes, Terence McMahon, *The Biliard; or, How to Criticize: A Satire*, 92, 94

"Hullo, Sweetheart", 103, 105

Hulme, T. E., 34

Humana, Charles, Rev. of *The English People*, 228 (extracts)

Humphry Clinker, The Expedition of, 408

Hungerford Bridge, 488, 489, *490*

Huns, 317

Hutchinson & Co (publishers), 126, 130, 135, 174, 233

Hutton, W. L., L. to *Tribune*, 430–1 (sy)

Hutton, W. R. (corr) 390

Huxley, Aldous, *Brave New World*, 38, 40; *Ends and Means*, 37; *34*, 35, 36, 37, 410

Huxley, Julian, *On Living in a Revolution*, Rev: 181

Ibsen, Henrik, *An Enemy of the People*, 450; 323

Ido, Sistema, 108, *109*

ILP (Independent Labour Party), 70, 132, 299, 374, *508*

In a Strange Land: Last Essays, Rev: 278–9

India, 23, 24, 65, 76, 77, 79, 151, 153, 154, 186–7, 253, 285, 288, 301, 321, 361, *362*, 429, 446–8, *448*, 507, *508*

Indian National Congress, 24, 65, 429, 447

India Since Cripps, Rev: 255

Indo-China, 359, 455

Ingoldsby Legends, The (Richard Barham), 90, 485, 500

Innocents at Home, The, 5, 86, 87

Inprecor, 125, *126*

INSIDE THE WHALE, 18, *18*

Interglossa, 81

Interglossa, Rev: 31–3; (corr) E. R. 33

Interlude in Spain, An, Rev: 501–2

Invincibles, The, 189

Ireland, 188–90, 206, 304

Irish Civil War, 51, 206

Iron Heel, The, 273–4, 450

Irving, Sir Henry, 31, *31*

Isherwood, Christopher, *Goodbye to Berlin* (as *Farewell to Berlin*), 382

Island of Dr Moreau, The, 199

Italy, 65, 158, 247–8, 284, 289, 317

It Occurs to Me, 3

I Write As I Please, 3

Izvestia, 373

Jack, C (corr) 331 (sy)

Jacket, The, 274

Jackson, Lydia (= Elisaveta Fen, *319*), L: 108, 141, 167, 228, 250, 268, 340, 402, 427, 437;

L. from Eileen Blair, ed. note: 323; *324*; "A Soviet Patriot: A Sketch of Serghei Dikovsky", *141*, *167*; "A Tender Bolshevik: A Sketch of A. G. Malyshkin", *250*; *108*, *167*

Jack the Dwarf Killer, 355

Jack the Giant Killer, 354

Jacobs, H. (corr) *91*

Jacobs, Ivor, 58

Jacobs, W. W., *483*, 486

James, Alec, 479, *482*

James, Henry, 246

James, Selwyn, *South of the Congo*, Rev: 340–2

James Joyce, Rev: 109–11; *117*, 118–9

Japan, 23, 26, 47, 61, 62, 151, 153, 154, 205, 285, 287, 288, 301, 320, 321, 341, 343, 359–61, 416, *418*, 454–5, 506

Jefferies, Richard, 129

Jefferson, Thomas, *375*

Jerrold, Douglas, *Mrs Caudle's Curtain Lectures*, 482

Jesus Christ, 105, 111

"Jeu Lugubre, Le", 235

Jews (and anti-semitism), 81, 83–5, 91–2, 93–4, 116, *116*, 191, 193–4, *280*, 386, 494, 502
"Jews in the Polish Army", 194
Jinnah, Mohamed Ali, 446
Joad, C. E. M., 148, 258, *260*, 263, *445*
Joan of Arc, 5, 86, 111, 262
'John Freeman', pseudonym of George Orwell: see ed. note: 37–8
Johnson, Martin, *Art and Scientific Thought*, Rev: 280–2
Johnson Samuel, 204, 281, 282, 296, 456
Jonathan Cape (publishers), L. to Victor Gollancz, *266* (sy); L. to Leonard Moore, *266* (sy);
131, *131*, 135, 155, 156, 182, 229, 251, *251*, 265, 269, 292
Jones, T., L. from I. Brown, xx, App. 15
Jordan, Philip, *Jordan's Tunis Diary*, Rev: 20–1; 26, 35–6; *29*
Jordan's Tunis Diary, Rev: 20–1; 26, 35–6
Joseph Andrews, 410
"Journey of the Magi, The", 38
Jouve, Pierre-Jean, 114
Joyce, James, *James Joyce*, Rev: 109–11; 117, 118–9; *119*, 237, 474;
"Are you not weary of ardent ways", 492; *Dubliners*, 109, 110, 118; "The Dead", 109, 110, 246, 383; *Finnegans Wake*, 109, 110, 111, 119; *A Portrait of the Artist as a Young Man*, 38, 41, 109, 110, 290, *291*, 492; *Stephen Hero 291*; *Ulysses*, 109, 110, 111, 119, *323*, 421
J. P. N. (corr) 133
June Purge, 376
Jura, *166*, *380*
"Just Meat", 274

Kachins, 254, 417
Karens, 254
Katha, 417, *418*
Kay, 325
KEEP THE ASPIDISTRA FLYING, *228*, 232, 251, *251*
Kemal Pasha, Mustapha (Kemal Atatürk), 151, 154
Kennedy, G. A. Studdert (Woodbine Willie), *Rough Rhymes of a Padre*, 176, 177
Kensington Gardens Dog Cemetery, 202
Kharkov, 45, 47, 66, 386, *391*
Kiev, *376*
Kill – or Get Killed, 505
Kimche, Jon, 3, 4, 38
King Lear, 237
Kingsmill, Hugh, The Poisoned Crown, Rev: 167–8
Kipling, Rudyard, "Baa, Baa, Black Sheep", 383; "Danny Deever", 451; "Drums of

the Fore and Aft", 383; "Gentleman Rankers", 348; 59, 107, 145, 176, 273
Knox, Ronald, 112, 114, 440, 442, *445*
Koestler, Arthur, L: see XX, 314, 315; (corr) 374; 180, 233, 251, *253*, 368;
'Arthur Koestler', ed. note: 391–2; 392–402;
Arrival and Departure, Rev: 19–20; 393, 397, 398–9, 400;
Darkness at Noon, 19, 256, 328, 368, 393, 395–7; *The Gladiators*, 305, 393, 394–5; "Literary Idolatry", 114, 115; *The Scum of the Earth*, 393, 397–8, *400*; *Spanish Testament*, 19, 393;
Kolarz, Walter, *Stalin and Eternal Russia*, 427
Komorowski, Gen. Tadeusz (Bor), 362, 363
Koniev, Gen. Ivan Stepanovich, *376*
Kowloon, *492*
Kublai Khan, 143, 144, 281
Kunz, Charlie, 467

Labour Monthly, 124, 219
Labour Party, 3, 4, 24, 28, 65, 67, 157, 209–10, 224, 300, 388, 508
Lady – Don't Turn Over (Darcy Glinto), 345, 346, *357*, 381
Lake Windermere, *338*
Lambda, Peter (corr) 94 (sy)
Lambert, Constant, 481, *482*
Lancet, The, 219
"Land of the Sluggard" (painting), 41
Lane, Homer, 334
Lane, John, 242, 251
Lardner, Ring, 384
Larwood, Harold, 346, 348
Laski, Harold, *Faith, Reason and Civilisation*, Rev: 122–3; 19, 175, 298, 313;
Reflections on the Revolution of Our Time, 122; 3, *299*, 314, 393, 400
Last Essays (J. A. Spender), Rev: 469–70
Laval, Pierre, 381
Lawrence, Col. T. E., 53, 417
Lawrence, D. H., *England, My England*, 246, 383; "The Fox", 383; "The Piano" (poem), 176; 41, 118, 176, 203, 237, 355
LDV (Local Defence Volunteers), 172, *174*; see Home Guard
Leacock, Stephen, 483, *486*
League of Nations, 35, 263
League for the Rights of Man, 491
Lear, Edward, "The Courtship of the Yonghy-Bonghy-Bò", 485; *482*, 484
Leavis, F. R., L. to Orwell, 58 (sy)
Lee, Austin (corr) 466
Leech, John, 90
Left, 155, 199
Left Book Club, 392, 394

Index

Left Forum, 155
Lehmann, John, L. to Orwell, 75 (sy)
Lehmann, Rosamund, 419
Lemprière, John, *Classical Dictionary*, 27, 29
Lenin, Vladimir Ilyich, 37, 39, 118, 123, 211, 274, 397, 491, 497
Leon, Derrick, *Tolstoy: His Life and Work*, Rev: 136–7; as *Life of Tolstoy*, 117
Leonardo da Vinci, 280, 281, 282
Letter to My Son, A, 385, 388, 427, 476, 479
Levellers, 377
Levin, Harry, *James Joyce*, Rev: 109–11; 117, 118–9
Lewis, Alun, 470
Lewis, C. S., *Beyond Personality*, Rev: 437–9; 439, 439–41, 442–4, 445; *The Allegory of Love*, 443; *The Pilgrim's Regress*, 443; *The Problem of Pain*, 443; *The Screwtape Letters*, 437, 439, 442
Lewis, Kid, 203
Lewis, Robert A. (corr) 105
Lewis, Sinclair, 256
Lewis, D. B. Wyndham ("Timothy Shy"), 194, 203, 262–4, 265
Liberal Party, 301
Liddell Hart, B. H., 51, 375
Lidice, 168, 374, 376
Life, 221
Life and Letters, 99
Life of Stalin, 488, 491, 497
Life of Tolstoy (= *Tolstoy: His Life and Work*), 117; and see 136–7
Life on the Mississippi, 5–7, 86, 87
Life, People and Books: ed. note: 18
"Like silver lamps in a distant shrine", 507
Lilly, Betty (corr) 338
Lincoln, Abraham, 7, 167–8, 355
Lindsay, Jack, *Perspective for Poetry*, Rev: 477–8
LION AND THE UNICORN, THE, Rev. by Dwight Macdonald, 405 (sy); 191, 228, 405
"Literary Idolatry", 114
"Little Apocalypse of Obadiah Hornbooke, The", 306, 307
Little, Dave, 472
"Little Dinner at Timmins's, A", 482, 500
Little Magazine, 120
"Little of what you fancy does you good, A", 208
Little Reviews Anthology, 116, 116
Little Women (Louisa M. Alcott), 87
Lloyd George, David, 87, 314, 315
Lloyd, Marie, 208
Lockhart, Leonora, 108, 109
Lodge, Sir Oliver, 473, 473
Lombroso, Cesare, 473, 473

London, 287, 334, 335
London, Jack, *The Call of the Wild*, 274; "The Chinago", 451; *The Iron Heel*, 273–4, 450; *The Jacket*, 274; "Just Meat", 274; *Love of Life and Other Stories*, 38, 274, 383; *The People of the Abyss*, 274; "A Piece of Steak", 274; *The Road*, 274; *White Fang*, 274; *When God Laughs* 274, 273–4
'London Letter': Topics Listed in Cumulative Index, Vol. XX;
  15 January 1944, 64–70;
  17 April 1944, 156–61;
  24 July 1944, 300–03;
  October(?) 1944, ed. note: 411; 411–6
London Library, 273
London School of Journalism, 426, 469
"London Snow" (poem), 38
"London under Bombardment" (poem), 121
"Long Live the Irish!", 496
Lonsdale, Lord, 338
'Looking Back on the Spanish War', 25
"Lord Arthur Savile's Crime", 383
Lord's Cricket Ground, 46, 47
Lorimer, E. O., *What the German Needs*, 329, 331
Lough Carra, 504
Louis XIV, King, 297
Louis XV, King, 319
Love and Mr Lewisham, 199
Lovely is the Lee, 503–4
Love of Life and Other Stories, 38, 274, 383
"Love Song of J. Alfred Prufrock, The", 420, 421, 422, 474
Lowdermilk, Walter Clay, *Palestine, Land of Promise*, Rev: 470
Lowndes, Marie Belloc, L. to Orwell, 486 (sy)
Lublin Committee/Government, 371; and see Polish (National) Committee of Liberation (Moscow)
Lucky Star, 304
Ludwig of Bavaria, King, 98
Lunn, Arnold, *Spanish Rehearsal*, 195
Lupin, Arsène (hero of Maurice Leblanc's crime novels), as *Arsène Lupin*, 347, 349
Luther, Martin, 84
Lwow, 367
Lynch, William, L. to *Tribune*, 192 (sy), 192
Lyons, Eugene, *Assignment in Utopia*, 385
Lyons, Messrs J. & L., 216
Lyons, Neil, 486, 487

McCormack, H. (corr) 263 (reference)
Macdonald, Dwight, L: 25, 79, 102, 298, 381; L. to Orwell, 24 (sy), 79 (reference); Rev. of *The Lion and the Unicorn*, 405–6 (sy);
  "Russomania in England", 299;

22, *124*, 259, 345, 346, 379, *382, 405*, 505
MacDonald, Ramsay, 54, 87
McGill, Donald, 483
McGrath, Sergeant, 11
Machiavelli, Niccolò, 205, 356
Machiavellians, The, Rev: 72–4; 62, 63
Mackenzie, Compton, *Mr. Roosevelt*, Rev: 33
Maclaren-Ross, Julian, 382, 471
McLaughlin, Richard (corr) 14
Macmillan, Harold, 21
Macmurray, John, 180, *181*
MacNeice, Louis, 475
Macready, William Charles, 308
Madrid, 289, 370
Maginot Line, 27
Magna Carta, 203
Main Street, 256
Maisky, Ivan M., *Before the Storm: Recollections*, 228; *228–9*
Maison de Madame Tellier, La, 246, 384
Majorca, 9
Malaga, 393
Malaya, 454–6
Malaya Broadcasting Corporation, 454, *456*
Mallock, W. H., *New Republic*, 439, 440; 438, *439*
Malraux, André, 392
Malvern Torch, 152
Malyshkin, A. G., 250, *250*
Mamun, Caliph al, 281
Ma Mya Sein, *Burma*, Rev: 417
Managerial Revolution, The, 60–1, 62–3, 63–4, *64*, 74, 450
Man and Superman, 279
Manchester Evening News, 18, 19, *34, 38*, *123–4, 179*, 241, 298, 299, *451*, 505
Manchester Guardian, 298, *299*, 310, 346, 494
Mandalay, 359
Mandel, Georges, 178
Mann, Erika, *A Gang of Ten* 85, *85*
"Mannequin Rotting in a Taxicab" (picture), 236, 237, 240
Mannheim, Karl, 180
Mansfield, Katharine, 384
"Man that Corrupted Hadleyburg, The", 383
Mark Rutherford's Deliverance, 13–14
'Mark Twain – The Licensed Jester', 5–8; and see Twain, Mark
Marlborough, Duke of, 462
Marryat, Frederick, 410, 484
Martin Chuzzlewit, Rev: 95–6
Martin, Kingsley, (corr) 371; 148, 375
Martindale, Hilda, *From One Generation to Another*, Rev: 269–71; *271*
Martineau, Harriet, 85, *85*, 99

Marvell, Andrew, 452; "The Garden", *453*
Marx, Karl, 35, 104–5, 363, 415, 466
Ma Saw, 143–4
Masefield, Sir John, 488
Mass Observation, *The Journey Home*, 250; 3, 83, 248–50, 301, 311–12, 337
Matheson, Bryan (corr) 375
Matrimonial Post, 230–1
Matrimonial Times, 246
"Maud Muller", a sequel, 485
Maugham, Robin, *The 1946 MS*, 13; *17*
Maugham, Somerset, *The Moon and Sixpence*, 450; *Rain*, 383
Maupassant, Guy de, *Boule de Suif*, 246; *La Maison de Madame Tellier*, 246, 384; 245–6
Maxton, James, 66, *70*
Mayakovsky, Vladimir, 113
Mayo, Katherine, *Mother India*, 446, *448*
MCC, 348, *357*
Mead, Margaret, *Coming of Age in Samoa*, Rev: 144–5
Medus, Betty, 261
Mein Kampf, 91
Mellor, William, 3
Memoirs of a Surrey Labourer, 473
"Memorials of Gormandising", 500
'Memories of the Blitz' (poem), 75–6; 38
Mendelson, Saul, *299*
Men Like Gods, 39
Meredith, George, 293
Mérimée, Prosper, *Carmen*, 246, 383
Merrick, Leonard, *The Position of Peggy Harper*, 344, *345*; *The Worldlings*, 344
Merry Wives of Windsor, The, 490
Merton, Arthur, 331
Mesens, E. L. T. (corr) 114
Michels, Robert, 73, 74
MI5, *17*, 132, *134*
Mihailovič, Draja, 498, *498*
Mikes, George, *156*
Miller, Henry, *237*
"Miller's Tale, The", 484
Milton, John, *Milton: Man and Thinker*, Rev: 338–40; *340*; *Areopagitica*, 489; *Paradise Lost*, 339; *Paradise Regained*, 339; 309
Milton: Man and Thinker, Rev: 338–40; *340*
Ministry of Food, 142, 310, 323, *326*, 446
Ministry of Information: see MOI
"Minstrels and Maids", 507
Mirror of the Past, The, Rev: 149–50
Mirsky, Vera T., *The Cup of Astonishment*, Rev: 504–5
Miss Callaghan Comes to Grief, 345, 352, *357*
"Miss Winchelsea's Heart", 383
Mission to Moscow (film), 159, *161*

"Modern Traveller, The", 121, 485
MOI (Ministry of Information), 237, 266, 268, 269, 277, 300, 386, 388, 389, 428
Molotov, Vyacheslav, 125
Moltke, Helmuth von, 140
'Monarchy, The', 68–70
Montagu, Edwin Samuel, 362
Montagu-Chelmsford Report, 359, 362
Montgomery, Edwin, 98
Montgomery, Gen. Bernard, 160
Moon and Sixpence, The, 450
Moore, Leonard, L: 17, 59, 126, 130, 135, 141, T: 141, L. 142, 155, 182, 229, 232, 250, 265, 291, 335, 358, 419;
   L. from Gollancz, 142 (sy), 251 (sy); L. from Jonathan Cape, 266 (sy); L. to Secker & Warburg, 358 (sy);
   58, 134, 199, 283; and see Christy & Moore
Moore, Reginald (ed.) Selected Writing, Rev: 470–1
'Moral Outlook of the English People, The', 204–9
Moral Re-Armament, 439
Morawski, Edward Osubka- (Premier, Lublin Government), 371
Morgan, Edwin, Flower of Evil: A Life of Charles Baudelaire, Rev: 509–10
Morocco, 93, 311
Morris, William, News from Nowhere, 38, 39, 40; 279
Mortimer, Raymond, 113
Morton, J. B. ("Beachcomber"), 262–4, 265
Moryson, Fynes, 452, 453
Mosca, Gaetano, 73, 74
Moscow, 290, 299, 363, 367, 393, 465, 491
"Moscow's Appeal to Warsaw", 363
Moslem League, 448
Mosley, Sir Oswald, 27, 28, 65, 69, 80, 194, 211, 249, 441
Mother India, 446, 448
Mr Roosevelt, Rev: 33
"Mr Sludge, 'The Medium' ", 473, 473
Mrs Caudle's Curtain Lectures, 482
Mrs Warren's Profession, 323
Mumford, Lewis, 180
Munich Agreement, 493, 494
Murphy, Mary (corr) 114 (sy)
Murphy, Robert Daniel, 21, 21
Murry, Middleton, L: 288, 295, 320, 332; L. to Orwell, 287 (sy), 319, 332 (extracts), 333 (sy);
   L. to Dr Alfred Salter, 287 (extract); 60, 494;
   Adam and Eve, Rev: 432–4; 287, 333, 441–2

"Musical Banks", 153, 155
Mussolini, Benito (Il Duce), 55, 74, 80, 82, 145, 312, 354, 443, 502
Mussolini, Bruno, 284
My Early Life, 462
Myitkyina, 417
My Mark Twain, 7
My Year in the USSR, 491, 497

Namkham, 254
Napoleon I, Emperor, 167, 168, 239–40, 272, 296, 297, 309
National Anthem, 46, 47
National Theatre, 226
National Trust, 336
Nazi-Soviet Pact: see Russo-German Pact
Négrin, Dr Juan, 289
Negro: His Future in America, The, 23–4
Neill, A. S., 334
Nelson, Margaret Fletcher, 380
Neumann, Robert, 126, 135
Never Again Society, 317
Nevill, J. C., Harriet Martineau, 85, 85, 99
New Bernhardi: "World Power or Downfall", The, 140
Newbolt, Sir Henry, "Drake's Drum", 121; "Vitaï Lampada", 121, 163
New Leader, 124, 260
New Order (Hitler's), 89
New Republic (journal), 23
New Republic, The, 439, 440
New Road, 25, 298, 302
News & Book Trade Review, 244
News Chronicle, 20, 29, 66, 176, 262, 329, 331, 332, 363, 365, 366, 393
News from Nowhere, 38, 39, 40
Newsom, J. H., "Bread and Butter for the Teacher", 179
New Statesman and Nation, 37, 355, 371, 375
New Yorker, 102, 351
New York Times, 3, 491, 491, 497
Ney, Elisabet, 97–8
Nichols, Beverley, Verdict on India, Rev: 446–8; 448
Nicolson, Harold, Public Faces, Rev: 450; 259
Nicolson & Watson, 126, 131, 135, 142, 155, 156
Nietzsche, Friedrich, 387, 488
NINETEEN EIGHTY-FOUR, 99, 191, 228, 384, 475
NKVD (GPU), 123, 355, 396, 397
Noailles, Vicomte de, 235
Noblesse Oblige – Another Letter to Another Son, Rev: 476–7; corr: J. Agate, 479; Orwell 480
Noncomfortist Church, 204–5

No Orchids for Miss Blandish, 79, 127, 298, 345, 346, 347, 348, 349–56, *356*, 381, *382*
North Africa, 20–1, 93, 311
Northcliffe, Lord, 128, 130, 146, 165, 353
Nostradamus (Michel de Nostradame), 415
Note-books (Samuel Butler), 292–3
Notes [Letters] from Underground, 384, *384*
Now, 75, 302
Noyes, Alfred, *The Edge of the Abyss*, Rev: 105–7; 176, 226, 236, 237, 259
Nuffield, Lord, 56, 355

Observer, The, 19, 85, 344, 379, *439*, 505
O'Casey, Sean, *79*
Odes (Horace), *487*
"Ode to Beer", 486, *487*
"Ode to Tobacco", 486, *487*
Odyssey, The, 109
Off the Record, Rev: 87
Of New Things (Rerum Novarum), *171*
Ogden, C. K., L: 108
Old Moore's Almanac, 46–7, *47*, 472
Old Vic Theatre, 479, *482*
Old Wives' Tale, The, 451
"On a Beautiful Young Nymph Going to Bed", 174
"On a Distant Prospect of Eton College", *91*
One Who Survived, *491*, 497
On Living in a Revolution, Rev: 181
Oracle, 304
Orator, The, 353
Orley Farm, 449
Orwell, references to, *156*, 169, 244, 247, 251, 263, *266*, 268, 283, 286, 325, 358–62, *419*
Orwell at *Tribune*, ed. note: 3–4
Orwell's Flat Bombed, ed. note: 283
O'Shaughnessy, Gwen, 324, 325
O'Shea, Capt. and Mrs., 188–90
Osservatore Romano, 364
Ossewa Brandwag (South African Fascist Party), 342
Othello, 308
Other Men's Flowers, Rev: 120–1
"Outlook for Young Writers", 388–9
Owen, Wilfred, 481
Oxford and Asquith, Countess of, *Off the Record*, Rev: 87
Oxford Group Movement, *439*
Oxford Movement, 308
Oxford Union, 463
'Oysters and Brown Stout', 498–501

Padmore, George, "The Story of Viet Nam", *299*; 299, *299*
Pain, Barry, 483
Paine, Tom, 56

Pakistan, 446, 448
Palestine, 417, *418*, 470
Palestine, Land of Promise, Rev: 470
Pamphlet Collection, Orwell's, 13, *17*
Paneth, Marie, *Branch Street*, Rev:334–5; 318
Papers for the People, 60
Paradise Lost, 339
Paradise Regained, 339
Pareto, Vilfredo, 73, 74, *74*
Paris, 402–3, 411
Paris Commune, 363
Parker, Dorothy, 384
'Parliament', 66–8
Parnell, Charles Stewart, 188–90
Parnell, Rev: 188–90
Partisan Review, 22, 24, 25, 135, *142*, 160, 182, 291, 379, 416, *418*, 490, 491, 497
Passage to India, A, 428
Paw Tun, 360
Paxman, Jeremy, *Friends in High Places*, *482*
Payments Book, Orwell's, 4; for details, see XVII, 463–80
Payne-Knight, Richard, 92, *94*; *An Analytical Enquiry into the Principles of Taste*, 92, *94*
Peace, Charles, 347, *356*
Peace News, 171, 332, 333, 433
Peace Pledge Union, 274, 279, *287*, 317, *319*, 493
Pearl Harbo(u)r, 26, 454
Pearn, V. R., *Burma Background*, Rev: 416
Pearse, Andrew, 391
Peel, J. H. B., *426*
Peers, E. Allison, *Spain in Eclipse, 1937–43*, 8, *9*
Peg's Paper, 304, 456
Pelagius, 440, *445*
Pelican Books, 308, 310
Pemberton, Max, 467, *469*
P.E.N. Club, 489
Pendennis, 499
Penguin Books, 174–5, 216, 232, 242–3, 246, 251, 260, 450, 451, 456; and see Lane, John
Penguin New Writing, 346
Penrose, Roland (corr) 114
People of the Abyss, The, 274
People's Convention, 27, 28–9
Percival, Gen. Arthur Ernest, *456*
Peregrine Pickle, 275, 408, 409
Perlmutt, A., 4; (corr) 94 (sy)
Personal Recollections of Joan of Arc, 5, 86
Perspective for Poetry, Rev: 477–8
Persuasion, 310, 444
Pétain, Henri-Philippe, 20, 34, 35, 37, 322
Peter Pan (J. M. Barrie), 238
Phillips, William, *127*
"Piano, The" (poem), 176

Index

Piccadilly, 348, *357*
Pickthorn, Kenneth, *Principles or Prejudices*, 465–6
Pickwick Papers, The, 39, 95, 118, 162, 408, 483
Picture Post, 55, 216
"Piece of Steak, A", 274
Pierre Blanche, La, 262
Pilgrim's Progress, The, 437, 439, 442
Pilgrim's Regress, The, 443
Pitter, Ruth, *231, 260*
Pittock-Buss, G. B., Interview with Orwell on Burma, 358–62
Plato, 293, 390, 451, 470
"Plattner Story, The", 383
Playfair, Giles, *Singapore Goes Off the Air*, Rev: 454–5
Plebs, 124
"Plot Formula", 464, 468, 496
Plowman, Max, *Letters*, Rev: 492–4; *333, 494*; *A Subaltern on the Somme*, 493
Poe, Edgar Allan, "The Purloined Letter", 383; *246*
"Poems from France", 115
Poems 1937–1942 (David Gascoyne), 114, 115
Poetry, London, 142, 302
Poetry, Scotland, 107, *107, 291*
Poisoned Crown, The, Rev: 167–8
Poland, 150, 194, 320, 333, 362–75, 476; and see Polish and Warsaw
Polish First Army, 375
Polish Folk-Lore Stories, 268, *268*
Polish Government-in-Exile (London), 362–75 passim
"Polish Home Army", 366–7; 362–75 passim
Polish (National) Committee of Liberation (Moscow; Lublin Government), 364, 365, 367, 371, 374
Polish Short Stories, 108, *167, 340*
Polite and Ingenious Conversations, 219
'Political Outlook of the English People, The', 209–13
'Political Theories and European Literature' (broadcast), 188, 261, 269; Contract, 274
Politics, 25, 79, 102, 124, *259*–60, 298, *299*, 345, 379, 381, 505
Pollins, H. (corr) 94 (sy)
Pope, Alexander, 296, 475
Popeye, 354
Popular Front, 394
"Population Statistics", 153–4 (re Orwell at 151)
Porch, The, Rev: 326–8, *328*
Portrait of the Artist as a Young Man, A, 38, 41, 109, 110, 290, *291*, 492
Position of Peggy Harper, The, 344, *345*
Postgate, Raymond, 3

Potts, Paul (corr) *83*, *292*; *304*
Pound, Ezra, 80, 81, 82, *83*, 107, 180
Power House, The, 471
Powisle, 368, *375*
Powys, John Cowper, 115
Practical Criticism, 175–6
Press Censor, L. to Orwell, 411 (sy), *416*
Preston, Frank (corr) 147; *166*
Price, J. J. (corr) 489
Price, R. Philips (corr) 387; *427*–8
Priestley, J. B., *315*, 465, 467
Principles or Prejudices, 465–6
Pritchett, V. S., "Sense of Humour", 382
Pritt, D. N. (corr) 28; 29, 300; *Choose Your Future*, 28
Problem of Pain, The, 443
'Propaganda and Demotic Speech', 310–6
Protocols of the Elders of Zion, 89, *90*, 91
Proust, Marcel, 237
Ptolemy (Claudius Ptolomaeus), 281
Public Faces, Rev: 450
Publishing in Peace & War, 244, 436
Pucelle, La, 38, 41, 485
Pucheu, Pierre, 137–8, *141*
Pugh, Richard (corr) 133 (sy); 134
Punch, 90, 91, 102, 216, 498, 499
Purber, Eileen E. (corr) 78
"Purloined Letter, The", 383
Pygmalion, 275

Quarterly Review, 60, 246, 453
Quiller-Couch, Sir Arthur, 444, *445*
Quinn, John, *119*
Quisling, Vidkun, 80, 194

Rabelais, François, 41, 273
Race Relations Act (1965), 85
Rackham, Arthur, 239
Raffles (The Amateur Cracksman), 25, *25*, 59, 79, *347*, 347–9, *349*, 352, 353, 356
'Raffles and Miss Blandish', ed. note: 345–6; 346–58; *25, 79, 335*, 381, *382*; as 'Ethics of the Detective Story from Raffles to Miss Blandish', *Horizon, Politics*; see 345–6
Rahv, Philip, L: 22, 174
Rain, 383
Raine, Kathleen, 180, 444
Rajan, Balachandra, 391
Rakovsky, Christian, 397
Raleigh, Sir Walter, 88, *90*
Rank, J. Arthur, 388, 389, *391*, 428
Rationing of Clothes, 89, *90*, 101
Rauschning, Hermann, 132, *134*
Rawson, O., 3
Read, Herbert, 155, *156*, 180, *181*, 478
Red Army, 27, 52, 66, 159, *299*, 333, 362, 369, 476

Redbrick University, *9*
Red Cross, 145
Reed, Douglas, 36, *37*, 258
Rees, Sir Richard, *288*
Reflections on the Revolution of Our Time, 122
Reign of Terror (France), 451
Reith, Sir John, 148
"Report on Experience" ("I have been young"), 162
Rerum Novarum, *171*
Reshaping Man's Heritage, Rev: 181
"Responsibility of the Man of Letters in the Cultural Restoration of Europe, The", 388
Rest Centres, *404*
Retour de l'URSS, 96
Reuben, Aida, "Greeting Card Course", *464*, 468
Reykjavik, 436
Reynaud, Paul, 178
Reynold's News, 274
Reynolds, Reg (corr) 331; *329, 331*
Richards, George (corr) 263 (sy)
Richards, I. A., *Practical Criticism*, 175–6
Rifle Clubs, 60
Ripon Cathedral, 449
Road, The, 274
Road to Serfdom, The, Rev: 149; corr: George Dickson, 150
ROAD TO WIGAN PIER, THE, 11, 157, 335, *405*
Robert Cain, Rev: 255–7
Roberts, Carl Eric Bechhofer, 473
Roberts, Michael (= W. E. Roberts), *T. E. Hulme*, 34
Robertson, Eric, 456
"Robin Hood" (ballads), 456
Robinson Crusoe, 172, 275
Robinson, Henry Crabbe, 309–10
Rochelle, Pierre-Eugène Drieu La, 261
Roderick Random, 408, 409, 410
Rokossovsky, Marshal Konstantin, 363, *376*
Rola-Zymierski, Gen. Michal (Lublin Government), 371
"Roll out the Barrel", 507, *508*
Rolo, Charles J., *Wingate's Raiders*, Rev: 417–8
Roman Catholic Church, 111–12, 113–4, 132, 169–71, *171*, 211, 245, 262–4, 339, 502, 509
Romanticism and the Modern Ego, Rev: 296–7; *280*
Rommel, Gen. Erwin, 21, 414
Roosevelt, Franklin Delano, *Mr. Roosevelt*, Rev: 33; *43*; 73
Rose and the Ring, The, 500
Rosebay Willowherb, 345; and see Willowherb

Rôtisserie de la Reine Pédauque, La, 262
Rouge et le Noir, Le (Stendhal), 348
Roughing It, 5, 6, 86, 87
Rough Rhymes of a Padre, 176
Rousseau, Jean-Jacques, 296
Routh, Dennis, "The Twentieth Century Revolutions", *64*
Routledge & Kegan Paul, *156*
Rowse, A. L., *The English Spirit*, Rev: 461–3
Royal Literary Fund, L: 232
Rubinstein, Artur, 467
'Rudyard Kipling', 59
Runyon, Damon, 384
Russell, A. J., *For Sinners Only*, 437, *439*
Russell, Earl, 145
Russell, William, *Robert Cain*, Rev: 255–7; *257*
Russia: see USSR
Russian Civil War, 334
Russian Revolution, 52, 318, 400
Russo-Finnish War, 205
Russo-German Pact, 27, 63, 354, 405, 414, 465, 476, 498, 504
Russo-German War, 62, 63–4, 295, 319, 320
"Russomania in England", *299*
Rutherford, Mark, 13–14; *Mark Rutherford's Deliverance*, 13
Ruthless Rhymes for Heartless Homes, 239

Sackville-West, Victoria, *Seducers in Ecuador*, Rev: 450; *The Eagle and the Dove*, 113
St Augustine, 439
St Brandon's Isle, 504
Saint Exupéry, Antoine de, *328*
St Joseph of Copertino, 111, 113
St Paul's Cathedral, 101
St Teresa, 111
Salammbô, 305, 394, 451
Salazar, Antonio de Oliveira, 190
Salmesius, Claudius, 340
Salt, Signalman, 11
Salter, Dr Alfred, L. from John Middleton Murry, 287 (extract); *287*
Salvemini, Gaetano, 392, *400*
Samuel, First Book of, 155
Samuel, Viscount, *An Unknown Land*, 38, 40
Sanctuary, 350, 354, *357*, 381, *382*
Sandys, Duncan, 404, *404*
Sanjurjo Sacanell, Gen. José, 9, *9*
Santayana, George, 170
Sargent, Malcolm, 480, *482*
Saturday Book, 1944, The, 233
"Satyr 3" (Donne), *124*
Saurat, Denis, *Milton: Man and Thinker*, Rev: 338–40, *340*
Saw, U, 359
Sayers, Dorothy L., 381

Index

Scarlet Letter, The, 450
Schell (astrologer), 322
Schimanski, Stefan, 420
Schucking, L. L., The Sociology of Literary
    Taste, Rev: 266–8
Scotland, 206, 225, 290; and see Scottish
    Nationalists
Scotland Yard, 353
Scott, Sir Walter, Tales of a Grandfather, 498;
    310
Scottish Nationalists, 225, 275, 280
Screwtape Letters, The, 437, 439, 442
Scrutiny, 58
Scum of the Earth, The, 393, 397–8, 400
Seagrave, Gordon S., Burma Surgeon, Rev:
    253–5
Seal, P. B., 83
Secker & Warburg, 59, 251
Second Front, 64, 66, 157, 158, 229, 414
Secrets, 304
Seducers in Ecuador, Rev: 450
Seeds of Chaos, 193, 195
Selassie, Emperor Haile, 245
Selected Writing, Rev: 470–1
Selections from the Works of Gerrard Winstanley,
    Rev: 376–8; corr: Reg Groves, 378–9
Sencourt, Robert, 454
Senegal, 508
Senhouse, Roger, 345, 391
"Sense of Humour", 382
Serge, Victor, 299, 392
Service, Mr, 375
Shabby Genteel Story, A (= Philip), 499
Shaftesbury, Lord, 308, 309
Shakespeare, William, Hamlet, 110; Henry IV
    Pt 1, 121; Henry V, 488; King Lear, 237;
    The Merry Wives of Windsor, 490; Othello,
    308; Timon of Athens, 267, 489, 497; 203,
    204, 213, 266, 386, 475, 479, 484
Shakespeare's England, Life in (John Dover
    Wilson), 452
Shaw, George Bernard, Geneva, 284; Man and
    Superman, 279; Mrs Warren's Profession,
    323; Pygmalion, 275; 46, 79, 180, 261,
    323, 354, 400, 429 463, 465, 467
Shelden, Michael, 292
Sheldon, Miss, 282, 283
Shelley, Mary, 308
Sheppard, Rev. 'Dick', 493
She Was a Queen, Rev: 143–4
Shore, Emily, 308, 309
Short Story Competition, Tribune's, 57, 57,
    153, 176–7, 177, 245–6
"Shy, Timothy" (D. B. Wyndham Lewis),
    262–4, 265, 483
Siam, 359
"Signalman, The" (poem), 128

Signpost Booklets, 465
Silas Marner, Rev: 450
Silence de la mer, Le (Vercors), 114
Silone, Ignazio, Fontamara, 393; 392
Silver Jubilee (1935), 68–9, 212
Simpson, Mrs Wallis, 276
Singapore, 454–5
Singapore Goes Off the Air, Rev: 454–5
Sir Launcelot Greaves, 408
Sitwell, Sir Osbert, L. to Orwell, 453 (sy);
    A Letter to My Son, 385, 388, 427, 476,
    479; 30, 46, 385, 386, 388, 391, 476,
    477, 481
"Slip Under the Microscope, A", 383
Small House at Allington, The, 449, 451
Smith, A. Clark (corr) 284 (sy)
Smith, C. A., 3, 152, 155
Smith, Frank (corr) 387
Smith, James C., L. to Manchester Evening
    News, 241
Smith, J. C. and Herbert J. C. Grierson, A
    Critical History of English Poetry, Rev:
    474–5
Smith, Stevie (= Florence Margaret Smith),
    "Poems from France", 115; 114, 115,
    115
Smollett, Tobias, 'Tobias Smollett:
    Scotland's Best Novelist', 408–10;
    The Expedition of Humphry Clinker, 408;
    Peregrine Pickle, 275, 408, 409; Roderick
    Random, 408, 409, 410; Sir Launcelot
    Greaves, 408
Society of West End Theatres, 482
Sociology of Literary Taste, The, Rev: 266–8
Socrates, 451
Sorel, Agnes, 41
Sorel, Georges, 34, 35, 37, 73
Sosnokowski, Gen. Kasimierz (C-in-C,
    London), 364, 372
South Africa, 340–2
South America, 52
Southern Asiatic Federation, 361
South of the Congo, Rev: 340–2
Souvarine, Boris, Cauchemar en URSS, 396,
    401
"Soviet Patriot: A Sketch of Serghei
    Dikovsky, A", 141, 167
"Soviets and Warsaw", 366
Spain, 8–9, 23, 288–90, 290, 300, 393, 402,
    403, 501–2, 507
Spain in Eclipse, 1937–43, Rev: 8
Spanish Armada, 263
Spanish Civil War, 8–9, 24, 25, 25, 52, 88,
    93, 174, 205, 235, 245, 253, 280, 284,
    288–90, 290, 298, 370, 393, 494, 501–2,
    507, 508
Spanish Government, 8, 9, 289, 290

Spanish Rehearsal, 195
Spanish Testament, 19, 393, 394
Spartacus, 305–6, 394–5
Spate, O. H. K., *Burma Setting*, Rev: 416
Spectator, The, 22
Spender, J. A., *Last Essays*, Rev: 469–70
Spender, Stephen, "Surrealism", 115; 114, 115, 470
Squire, Sir John, 30
Stack, Sir Lee, 54
Stalin, Josef, *Life of Stalin* (= *Stalin: An Appraisal of the Man and his Influence*), 489–90, 490, 491, 497; 69, 118, 123, 126, 134, 159, 174, 190, 191, 192, 194, 195, 253, 266, 298, 299, 300, 320, 333, 353, 354, 355, 363–4, 365, 367, 374, 381, 397, 405, 415, 427, 491, 497
Stalin and Eternal Russia, 427
Stalingrad, 414
"Stalin's Promise" (Warsaw Uprising), 362–3
Stapledon, Sir R. George, *Disraeli and the New Age*, Rev: 71–2
Star, 386, 387
Starkie, Enid, 510
Statistician (corr) 153–4
Stephen Hero 291
Sterne, Laurence, *Tristram Shandy 385*
Stevenson, Robert Louis, 293
Stewart, Desmond Stirling, *453, 454*
Stilwell, Gen. Joseph ("Vinegar Joe"), 254
Stirling W. F., L: 188, 261
Stoke Poges Dog Cemetery, 202
Stores, The (Wallington), 79, 324, *325*
Storey, Gladys, *Dickens and Daughter*, 117
"Story of Viet Nam, The", 299
Strachan, W. J., L: 164, 316; "The Grey Sleepers" (poem), 316; *164*
Strachey, John, *The Theory and Practice of Socialism*, 468; 35
Strachey, Lytton, 261
Strand, The, 60, 383
Strauss, George, 3
Streicher, Julius, 55
Strong, L. A. G., *426*
Stronghold, The, Rev: 326–8, *328*
Struve, Gleb (died 1985), L: 99, 476; ed. note: 475; L. to Orwell, 475; *Twenty-five Years of Soviet Russian Literature*, 99; *99*
Sturt, George: see Bourne, George
Subaltern on the Somme, A, 493
Suckling, Sir John, "Ballad upon a Wedding", 121; "Why so pale and wan, fond lover?", 121
Sudan, 53, 54

Suez Canal, 54
Summerson, John, 180
Sunday Times, 468
Surtees, Robert Smith, *Handley Cross*, 90, 482; 90, 410, 484
'Survey of "Civvy Street" ', 248–50
Sutton, Eric, 501
"Sweeney Agonistes", 313, *316*, 420, 422, 474
Sweet, Harry, 472
Swift, Jonathan, *Gulliver's Travels*, 38, 40, 275, 282, 445, 484; "On a Beautiful Young Nymph Going to Bed", 174; *Polite and Ingenious Conversations*, 219; *Tale of a Tub*, 280; 40, 43, 59, 445
Switzerland, 52
Sylvestre, Anthony (corr) 264
Symons, J. G. (corr) 114 (sy); (corr) 374; 19, 411
Synopsis, 244

Tablet, 81
Tale of a Tub, 280
Tale of Two Cities, A, 451
Tales of a Grandfather, 498
TALKING TO INDIA, *23*, 232
Tambimuttu, Meary J., 471
T. E. Hulme, 34
"Tender Bolshevik: A Sketch of A. G. Malyshkin, A", *250*
Terry, Ellen, 171
Tertullian, 41
Thackeray, William Makepeace, 'Oysters and Brown Stout', 498–501; "The Ballad of Bouillabaisse", 500; *A Book of Snobs*, 498; *Burlesques*, 498; *Christmas Books*, 498; "Dr Birch and his Young Friends", 500; *Esmond*, 499; "The Fatal Boots", 482, 500; "A Little Dinner at Timmins's", 482, 500, "Memorials of Gormandising", 500; *Pendennis*, 499; *The Rose and the Ring*, 500; *A Shabby Genteel Story* (= *Philip*), 499; *Vanity Fair*, 498, 499, 500; *The Virginians*, 499; 60, 90, 451, 484
Thakin Movement (Burma), 343, 360
Theory and Practice of Socialism, The, 468
Thibaw, King of Burma, 143
This Changing World, Rev: 179–80
Thomas, Dylan, 475
Thomas, Hugh, *The Spanish Civil War*, 9
Thomas, Sir William Beach, *The Way of a Countryman*, Rev: 128–30; (corr) R. V. Walton *130* (sy); *130*, 344, 387
Thomson, G. H., 17
Thorez, Maurice, 465, *468*
Thornton, D. M., 3

Index

Three Clerks, The, 449
Tibetans, 429
Time, 221
Time and Tide, 93, *94*
Time Machine, The, 199
Times, The, 68, 118, 132, 157, 189, 236, 370
Timon of Athens, 267, 489, 497
Tirana, 476
'Tobias Smollett: Scotland's Best Novelist',
   408–10
Tojo, Hideki, 55
Tolstoy, Leo, *Tolstoy: His Life and Work,*
   Rev: 136–7; as *Life of Tolstoy,* 117;
   Anna Karenina, 137; *War and Peace,* 117,
   118, 137; 117–8
"Tom Bowling", 507, *508*
Tom Jones (Henry Fielding), 275, 408
Tom Sawyer, 5, 86–7
Tong, Hollington K., *Chiang Kai-Shek°,*
   Soldier and Statesman, 491
Trachtenberg, Joshua, *The Devil and the*
   Jews, Rev: 84–5
Transformation, 419, 420
Treece, Henry, L: 10, 18; "Duet for the
   Times" (poem), 18, *18*; *420*
Treitschke, Heinrich Gotthard von, 139, *139*
Trevelyan, G. M., 444
Trial of Mussolini, The, 463
Tribune, ed. note: 3; 9, 10, 14, 17, 22, 25, 37,
   38, 42, 58, 82, 102, 114–5, 128, 159,
   192, 194, 287, 298, 333, 358, 364, 371,
   373, *426,* 444, 452, 466, 468
Tribune Short Story Competition, 57, *57,*
   176–7, *177,* 245–6
Trinder, Tommy, 479, 481, *482*
Tristram Shandy, 385
Trollope, Anthony, *The Warden,* Rev: 449–
   50; 60, *94,* 113, 355, 428;
   Autobiography, 92–3, 449; *Barchester*
   Towers, 450; *Orley Farm,* 449; *The Small*
   House at Allington, 449, *451*; *The Three*
   Clerks, 449
Trotsky, Leon, *Life of Stalin* (= *Stalin: An*
   Appraisal of the Man and His Influence),
   488–9, 490, *491;* 497;
   64, 66, 118, 194, 195, 397
Truck Acts, 270, *272*
Truscot, Bruce (= E. Allison Peers),
   Redbrick University, 9
Truth, 472
"Truth about Mihailovich°, The", *498*
Tukhachevsky, Gen. Mikhail, *491*
Tunis, 20–1, 35–6
Turkey, 53, 54, 151, 154
Turnbull, J. A. (corr) *119* (sy)
Turner, W. J., 199, *439, 442*

Twain, Mark, 'Mark Twain – The Licensed
   Jester', 5–8; 353, 456;
   Tom Sawyer and Huckleberry Finn, Rev:
   86–7;
   A Connecticut Yankee in King Arthur's Court,
   7; *The Gilded Age,* 7; *Huckleberry Finn,* 5,
   7, 86, 87; *The Innocents at Home,* 5, 86, 87;
   Life on the Mississippi, 5–7, 86, 87; "The
   Man that Corrupted Hadleyburgh",
   383; *Personal Recollections of Joan of Arc,*
   5, 86; *Roughing It,* 5, 6, 86, 87; *Tom*
   Sawyer, 5, 86, 87; "What is Man?", 6
"Two Children, The", 29–30
Tyrer, Walter (corr) 306

Ukraine, 320
Ulysses, 109, 110, 111, 119, *120,* 421; Chinese
   translation, *323*
Umpleby, A. S., *A Bo'ddin O'Cowls,* 229,
   229, 230
Uncelestial City, The, 277
Uncle Tom's Cabin (Harriet Beecher Stowe),
   323, 393
'Unexpected Effects of Propaganda', *161*
Union of Polish Patriots (Moscow), 363
"Unity" (corr) 16
Universal Rights of Man (H. G. Wells), 197,
   198
Unknown Land, An, 38, 40 (as *An Unknown*
   Country)
Unwin, Stanley, L: 419; L. to Orwell, 244
   (sy); *Publishing in Peace & War,* 244, *419,*
   436
Urquhart, Fred, 470–1
Urquhart, Thomas, 273
USA, 12–13, 15–17, 25–7, 61–4, 80, 123,
   142, 156, 159, 167–8, 174, 175, 191, 206,
   210, 220–1, 222, 224, 225, 230, 252, 320,
   328–9, 350, 381, 406–7, 412, 415, 489
Ussher, James (Archbishop of Armagh), 47
USSR, 27, 28, 29, 52, 61–4, 74, 122–3, 150,
   151, 153–4, 159–60, 174, 183, 186, 191,
   205, 210, 211, 212, 222, 226, *229,* 245,
   283, 287, 289, 290, 298, *299,* 300, 301,
   302, 305, 319, 320, 321, 331, 332, 354,
   362–76 *passim,* 381, *382,* 389, 405, 411,
   413, 415, 429, 463, 476, 489, 491, 495,
   505

Vaidya, Suresh, 80, *82–3*
Vanity Fair, 498, 499, 500
Vansittart, Lord, 174, *175,* 302
Vatican, 369
Vatutin, Gen. Nikolai F., 370, *376*
Vercors (= Jean Bruller), *Le Silence de la mer,*
   114
Verdict on India, Rev: 446–8, *448*

Vermeil, Edmond, *Hitler et le Christianisme*, Rev: 451
Versailles, Treaty of, 139, *140*, 302
Vicar of Wakefield, The, Rev: 456–9; *450*
Vice Versa, 483
Vichy, 21, 375
Victoria, Queen, 68, 212, 220, 308, 349
Vienna, 334
Viet Nam, *299*
Village, The, *130*
Villon, François, 385
Vilna, 367
Virginians, The, 499
Vistula, River, 368, *375*
"Vitaï Lampada", 121, *163*
Voigt, F. A., 132, 167
Voltaire, François, *La Pucelle*, 38, 41, 485; 6, 7, 297
V–1, 70, *70*, [272], 277, 287, 300, 403–4, *404*, 411, *416*, 487
V–2, *70*, 411, *416*, 487
Voss-Bark, Conrad (corr) 36

Waddington, C. H., 180, *181*
Wafd Party, 53, 54
Waldberg, Patrick (corr) 114
Walden, R. J. (corr) 148
Wales, 206, 225
Walker, Roy, *332*
Wallace, Alfred Russel, 473, *473*
Wallace, Edgar, *The Orator*, 353; 25, 353–4
Wallington, 79, 324, *325*
Walpole Horace, 451
"Walrus and the Carpenter, The", 90
Walter, Martin, (corr) 467; "Plot Formula", 464, 468, 496; 57, 464, 466, 490–7, and see British Institute of Fiction-Writing Science Ltd.
Walton, Izaak, *The Compleat Angler*, 129
Walton, R. V. (corr) *130* (sy)
Walton, William, 479, 481, *482*
Wang Ching-wei, 159, 253
Wang Jen Chiu, 322
War and Peace, 117, 118, 137
Warburg, Fredric, L. from Leonard Moore, *358* (sy); 59, 107, 126, 292, 335, 358, 380, 382, 419
War Commentary – for Anarchism (journal), 161
Ward, Barbara, 170
Ward, E. R. (corr) 466
Warden, The, Rev: 449–50
War in the Air, The, 198
Warsaw, 362–75 *passim*
Warsaw City Council, 366
Warsaw Ghetto, 94, 284, 368
Warsaw Home Army, 362–75 *passim*

Warsaw Uprising, 362–76
War-time Diary, 27
"Waste Land, The", 422
Waugh, Evelyn, 410, 483
Wavell, Field-Marshal Viscount, *Allenby in Egypt*, Rev: 53–5; *Other Men's Flowers*, Rev: 120–1; *122*, 247, 311, 417
Way of a Countryman, The, Rev: 128–30; (corr) R. V. Walton *130* (sy)
Way of All Flesh, The, 293
'W. B. Yeats', 59
We, 99
Webster's Dictionary, 273
We Burmans League, 360
Wedgwood, C. V., *131*, *155*, *156*, *266*
Weekly Review, The, 36, 155
Weimar Republic, 151, 153
Weller, G. A., 277
Wells, H. G., *'42 to '44: A Contemporary Memoir. . .*, Rev: 197–9, *199*; 241, 242; and see *181*, *181*; *Anticipations*, 39; *The Dream*, 39; *The Island of Dr Moreau*, 199; *Love and Mr Lewisham*, 199; *Men Like Gods*, 39; "Miss Winchelsea's Heart", 383; *A Modern Utopia*, 38, 39; *The Plattner Story*, 383; "A Slip Under the Microscope", 383; *The Time Machine*, 199; *The War in the Air*, 198; 59, 69, 180, 181, 186, 383, 442, 483
'Wells, Hitler and the World State', 59
Westminster Gazette, 148, 469
Westrope's Bookshop (Booklovers' Corner), 3, *379*
Weygand, Gen. Maxime, 178
What Acts of War are Justifiable, 195–6, *196–7*
What Happened in Burma, 343, 345
'What is Fascism?' ('As I Please', 17), 131–3
"What is Man?", 6
"What's Happening", 362–3, 366–7
What the German Needs, 329, 331
When God Laughs, 274
"When lovely woman stoops to folly", 457–8, *459*
Where the Rainbow Ends (Clifford Mills and John Ramsay), 239
White, Antonia, L. to Orwell, ed. note: 169; 169–71 (extracts); *171*, 444
White, Hale: see Rutherford, Mark
White Fang, 274
Whiteway Community, *434*
Whitman Press, *292*
Whitman, Walt, 5, 6, 460
"Who Deserted Warsaw?", 362
Who's Who, 259
Why I Am a Jew, Rev: 84
"Why so pale and wan, fond lover?", 121
Why This War?, 28

Index

Widdop, Walter, *508*
Wigan, *356*, 376
Wigan Pier, 11, *11*
Wilde, Oscar, "Lord Arthur Savile's Crime", 383
Wilhelm II, Kaiser, 138
Wilkinson, Ellen, 3
Willmett, Noel, L: 190
Willowherb, 344, 380, 387, *391*
Wills, Colin, 11
Wilson, Sir Arnold, 259, *260*
Wimpffen, Emmanuel Félix de, 184, 185
Wingate, Gen. Orde Charles, 417–8, *418*, 434
Wingate's Raiders, Rev: 417–8; *436*
Wings Over Burma, Rev: 417
Winn, Godfrey, 78
Winstanley, Gerrard, 376–9
Winstedt, Sir Richard, *Britain and Malaya*, Rev: 455–6; *456*
Winterton, Lord, 276
Witts, L. J., 181
Wodehouse, P. G., 483
Wola, 368, *375*
Wolfe, Humbert, *The Uncelestial City*, 277
Woodbine Willie: see Kennedy, G. A. Studdert
Woodlock, Father, 112, 114
Woolworth's, 78
Wordsworth, Dorothy, 308, 309
Wordsworth, Mary, 309
Wordsworth, William, 204, 297, 309, 310

Worker's Challenge (German radio station), 245
"World Goes By, The" (broadcast), 268
Worldlings, The, 344
World Review, 498, *498*
Writer, 424, *426*, 463–5, 466, 467
Writer's and Artist's Yearbook, 424

Yalta Conference, *229*
Yang Kwang-hsien, 322
Yank Mags, 352, *352*
d'Ydewalle, Charles, *An Interlude in Spain*, Rev: 501–2
Yeats, W. B., 59, 420
Young, G. M., 108, *109*, 258
"Young Writer" (corr) 388, 389
Your M. P. (Anonymous; published by Gracchus), 259
"Your Questions Answered": 'Wigan Pier' (broadcast), 11, *11*
Youth, 246

"Z" (Rocket) Batteries, *174*, 432
Zaghlul, Saad, 54
Zamyatin, Yevgeny, *We*, 99, *99*
Zeppelin air raids, 327
Zilliacus, Konni, *The Mirror of the Past*, Rev:149–50
Zingari, I, 347, *356*
Zinoviev Letter, 369
Zola, Émile, 262, 451
Zoliborz, 368, *375*